COMMENTARY

ON THE

EPISTLE TO THE ROMANS

COMMENTARY

ON THE

EPISTLE TO THE ROMANS

BY

CHARLES HODGE, D.D.,

WM. B. EERDMANS PUBLISHING COMPANY
GRAND RAPIDS   MICHIGAN

This is a reproduction of the
Revised Edition of this work
published in 1886.

ISBN 0-8028-8136-X

Set up and printed, January 1947

Reprinted, May 1993

PHOTOLITHOPRINTED BY EERDMANS PRINTING COMPANY
GRAND RAPIDS, MICHIGAN, UNITED STATES OF AMERICA

PREFACE.

THE author of this Commentary is more widely known as a writer in the departments of controversial and systematic theology than as an expositor of Scripture. Nevertheless, his whole life was primarily devoted to the critical and systematic study of the Bible, and his entire theological method and system is eminently biblical. He became a teacher of the Original Languages of Scripture in Princeton Theological Seminary in 1820, and the professor of Oriental and Biblical Literature in 1822. He spent two years in Germany, from 1826 to 1828, with Tholuck and Hengstenberg and Gesenius, in pursuing exclusively biblical studies. For twenty years his time was wholly occupied with the study of the languages, literature, historical genesis, criticism, and interpretation of the Bible, especially of the New Testament. He continued to lecture on the Pauline Epistles to successive classes for fifty-six years, — from 1822 to 1878.

It was not until 1840 that, much to his own regret, he was transferred to the department of Didactic Theology. And hence the result was inevitable that his theology should bear the mark of his own personal history and habit, and that it should be distinguished from that of the majority of his eminent contemporaries, alike of the New England and of the German schools, as being a simple induction from the teachings of Scripture, instead of being adjusted to, if not founded upon, some of the prevalent philosophical schemes of the day. It is the mode in this day of violent reactions to exaggerate one-sidedly partial truths. Especially is it asserted with unconscientious indiscrimination that systematic theologians of the past as a class have ignored the human and historical genesis of the several writings which compose the Bible; and that, evolving their systems by a speculative process from narrow premises, they have sought to support them by disconnected and irrelevant citation of separate texts. Yet even Archdeacon Farrar, in his recent "Bampton Lectures," acknowledges that Calvin, the father of Protestant systematic theology, "was one of the greatest interpreters of Scripture who ever lived." Yet Calvin published his Institutes first, and his Commentaries afterwards. The order in which Dr. Hodge was providentially led to conduct his studies was more natural and more certain to result in a system in all its elements and proportions inspired and controlled by the word of God. All candid students of the theology of the past generation must acknowledge that Dr. Hodge has anticipated and preserved in his system much of the results of the deservedly vaunted discipline of Biblical Theology, having, as a matter of actual history, as well as of intention, so immediately drawn his material from a continuous study of the sacred text.

His "Commentary on Romans" was first published in 1835. An abridged edition appeared in 1836. The former was translated and published in France in 1841, and the latter republished in England in 1838. The whole work was rewritten and enriched with his mature studies in 1864. It is this last and most perfect edition which is now offered to the public. It should continue to be used by all students of the author's "Systematic Theology," presenting as it does, in continuous exposition of the most systematic of the doctrinal Epistles, the biblical ground and verification of the "system" which he elsewhere so clearly states and defends.

A. A. HODGE.

PRINCETON, N. J., August, 1886.

INTRODUCTION

THE APOSTLE PAUL.

WHEN Paul and the other Apostles were called to enter upon their important duties, the world was in a deplorable and yet most interesting state. Both Heathenism and Judaism were in the last stages of decay. The polytheism of the Greeks and Romans had been carried to such an extent as to shock the common sense of mankind, and to lead the more intelligent among them openly to reject and ridicule it. This scepticism had already extended itself to the mass of the people, and become almost universal. As the transition from infidelity to superstition is certain, and generally immediate, all classes of the people were disposed to confide in dreams, enchantments, and other miserable substitutes for religion. The two reigning systems of philosophy, the Stoic and Platonic, were alike insufficient to satisfy the agitated minds of men. The former sternly repressed the best natural feelings of the soul, inculcating nothing but a blind resignation to the unalterable course of things, and promising nothing beyond an unconscious existence hereafter. The latter regarded all religions as but different forms of expressing the same general truths, and represented the whole mythological system as an allegory, as incomprehensible to the common people, as the pages of a book to those who cannot read. This system promised more than it could accomplish. It excited feelings which it could not satisfy, and thus contributed to produce that general ferment which existed at this period. Among the Jews, generally, the state of things was hardly much better. They had, indeed, the form of true religion, but were in a great measure destitute of its spirit. The Pharisees were contented with the form ; the Sadducees were sceptics ; the Essenes were enthusiasts and mystics. Such being the state of the world, men were led to feel the need of some surer guide than either reason or tradition, and some better foundation of confidence than either heathen philosophers or Jewish sects could afford. Hence, when the glorious gospel was revealed, thousands of hearts, in all parts of the world, were prepared, by the grace of God, to exclaim, This is all our desire and all our salvation !

The history of the apostle Paul shows that he was prepared to act in such a state of society. In the first place, he was born, and probably educated in part, at Tarsus, the capital of Cilicia ; a city almost on a level with Athens and Alexandria, for its literary zeal and advantages. In one respect, it is said by ancient writers to have been superior to either of them. In the other cities mentioned, the majority of students were strangers, but in Tarsus they were the inhabitants themselves.* That Paul passed the early

* Strabo, Lib. 14, chap. 5.

part of his life here is probable, because the trade which he was taught, in accordance with the custom of the Jews, was one peculiarly common in Cilicia. From the hair of the goats, with which that province abounded, a rough cloth was made, which was much used in the manufacture of tents. The knowledge which the apostle manifests of the Greek authors, 1 Cor. xv. 33, Titus i. 12, would also lead us to suppose that he had received at least part of his education in a Grecian city. Many of his characteristics, as a writer, lead to the same conclusion. He pursues, far more than any other of the sacred writers of purely Jewish education, the logical method in presenting truth. There is almost always a regular concatenation in his discourses, evincing the spontaneous exercise of a disciplined mind, even when not carrying out a previous plan. His epistles, therefore, are far more logical than ordinary letters, without the formality of regular dissertations. Another characteristic of his manner is, that in discussing any question, he always presents the ultimate principle on which the decision depends. These and similar characteristics of this apostle are commonly, and probably with justice, ascribed partly to his turn of mind, and partly to his early education. We learn from the Scriptures themselves, that the Holy Spirit, in employing men as his instruments in conveying truth, did not change their mental habits ; he did not make Jews write like Greeks, or force all into the same mould. Each retained his own peculiarities of style and manner, and, therefore, whatever is peculiar to each, is to be referred, not to his inspiration, but to his original character and culture. While the circumstances just referred to, render it probable that the apostle's habits of mind were in some measure influenced by his birth and early education in Tarsus, there are others (such as the general character of his style) which show that his residence there could not have been long, and that his education was not thoroughly Grecian. We learn from himself, that he was principally educated at Jerusalem, being brought up, as he says, at the feet of Gamaliel. (Acts xxii. 3).

This is the second circumstance in the providential preparation of the apostle for his work, which is worthy of notice. As Luther was educated in a Roman Catholic seminary, and thoroughly instructed in the scholastic theology of which he was to be the great opposer, so the apostle Paul was initiated into all the doctrines and modes of reasoning of the Jews, with whom his principal controversy was to be carried on. The early adversaries of the gospel were all Jews. Even in the heathen cities they were so numerous, that it was through them and their proselytes that the church in such places was founded. We find, therefore, that in almost all his epistles, the apostle contends with Jewish errorists, the corrupters of the gospel by means of Jewish doctrines. Paul, the most extensively useful of all the apostles, was thus a thoroughly educated man; a man educated with a special view to the work which he was called to perform. We find, therefore, in this, as in most similar cases, that God effects his purposes by those instruments which he has, in the ordinary course of his providence, specially fitted for their accomplishment.

In the third place, Paul was converted without the intervention of human instrumentality, and was taught the gospel by immediate revelation. "I certify you, brethren," he says to the Galatians, "that the gospel which was preached of me, is not after man. For I neither received it of man, neither was I taught it, but by the revelation of Jesus Christ." These circumstances are important, as he was thus placed completely on a level with the other apostles. He had seen the Lord Jesus, and could therefore be one of the witnesses of his resurrection ; he was able to claim the authority of an original inspired teacher and messenger of God. It is obvious that he laid great stress upon this point, from the frequency with which he refers to it. He was thus furnished not only with the advantages of his early education, but with the authority and power of an apostle of Jesus Christ.

His natural character was ardent, energetic, uncompromising, and severe. How his extravagance and violence were subdued by the grace of God, is abundantly evident from the moderation, mildness, tenderness, and conciliation manifested in all his epistles. Absorbed in the one object of glorifying Christ, he was ready to submit to anything, and to yield any thing necessary for this purpose. He no longer insisted that others should think and act just as he did. So that they obeyed Christ, he was satisfied ; and he willingly conformed to their prejudices, and tolerated their errors, so far as the cause of truth and righteousness allowed. By his early education, by his miraculous conversion and inspiration, by his natural disposition, and by the abundant grace of God, was this apostle fitted for his work, and sustained under his multipled and arduous labours.

ORIGIN AND CONDITION OF THE CHURCH AT ROME.

One of the providential circumstances which most effectually contributed to the early propagation of Christianity, was the dispersion of the Jews among surrounding nations. They were widely scattered through the East, Egypt, Syria, Asia Minor, Greece, and Italy, especially at Rome. As they were permitted, throughout the wide extent of the Roman Empire, to worship God according to the traditions of their fathers, synagogues were everywhere established in the midst of the heathen. The apostles, being Jews, had thus always a ready access to the people. The synagogues furnished a convenient place for regular assemblies, without attracting the attention or exciting the suspicion of the civil authorities. In these assemblies they were sure of meeting not only Jews, but the heathen also, and precisely the class of heathen best prepared for the reception of the gospel. The infinite superiority of the pure theism of the Old Testament Scriptures to any form of religion known to the ancients, could not fail to attract and convince multitudes among the pagans, wherever the Jewish worship was established. Such persons became either proselytes or "devout," that is, worshippers of the true God. Being free from the inveterate national and religious prejudices of the Jews, and at the same time convinced of the falsehood of polytheism, they were the most susceptible of all the early hearers of the gospel. It was by converts from among this class of persons, that the churches in all the heathen cities were in a great measure founded. There is abundant evidence that the Jews were very numerous at Rome, and that the class of proselytes or devout persons among the Romans was also very large. Philo says (Legatio in Caium, p. 1041, ed. Frankf.) that Augustus had assigned the Jews a large district beyond the Tiber for their residence. He accounts for their being so numerous, from the fact that the captives carried thither by Pompey were liberated by their masters, who found it inconvenient to have servants who adhered so strictly to a religion which forbade constant and familiar intercourse with the heathen. Dion Cassius (Lib. 60, c. 6) mentions that the Jews were so numerous at Rome, that Claudius was at first afraid to banish them, but contented himself with forbidding their assembling together. That he afterwards, on account of the tumult which they occasioned, did banish them from the city, is mentioned by Suetonius (Vita Claudii, c. 25), and by Luke, Acts xviii. 2. That the Jews, on the death of Claudius, returned to Rome, is evident from the fact that Suetonius and Dion Cassius speak of their being very numerous under the following reigns : and also from the contents of this epistle, especially the salutations (chap. xvi.) addressed to Jewish Christians.

That the establishment of the Jewish worship at Rome had produced considerable effect on the Romans, is clear from the statements of the heathen writers themselves. Ovid speaks of the synagogues as places of fashionable resort; Juvenal(Satire 14) ridicules his countrymen for becoming Jews ;* and Tacitus (Hist. Lib. 5, ch. 5†) refers to the presents sent by Roman proselytes to Jerusalem. The way was thus prepared for the early reception and rapid extension of Christianity in the imperial city. When the gospel was first introduced there, or by whom the introduction was effected, is unknown. Such was the constant intercourse between Rome and the provinces, that it is not surprising that some of the numerous converts to Christianity made in Judea, Asia Minor, and Greece, should at an early period find their way to the capital. It is not impossible that many, who had enjoyed the personal ministry of Christ, and believed in his doctrines, might have removed or returned to Rome, and been the first to teach the gospel in that city. Still less improbable is it, that among the multitudes present at Jerusalem at the day of Pentecost, among whom were " strangers of Rome, Jews and proselytes," there were some who carried back the knowledge of the gospel. That the introduction of Christianity occurred at an early period, may be inferred not only from the probabilities just referred to, but from other circumstances. When Paul wrote this epistle, the faith of the Romans was spoken of throughout the world, which would seem to imply that the church had already been long established. Aquila and Priscilla, who left Rome on account of the decree of Claudius banishing the Jews, were probably Christians before their departure ; nothing at least is said of their having been converted by the apostle. He found them at Corinth, and being of the same trade, he abode with them, and on his departure took them with him into Syria.

The tradition of some of the ancient Fathers, that Peter was the founder of the church at Rome, is inconsistent wiih the statements given in the Acts of the Apostles. Irenæus (Hæres. III. 1) says, that " Matthew wrote his gospel, while Peter and Paul were in Rome preaching the gospel and founding the church there." And Eusebius (Chron. ad ann. 2 Claudii) says, " Peter having founded the church at Antioch, departed for Rome, preaching the gospel." Both these statements are incorrect. Peter did not found the church at Antioch, nor did he and Paul preach together at Rome. That Peter was not at Rome prior to Paul's visit, appears from the entire silence of this epistle on the subject ; and from no mention

---

* Quidam sortiti metuentem sabbata patrem,
　Nil præter nubes et cœli numen adorant :
　Nec distare putant humana carne suillam,
　Qua pater abstinuit, mox et præputia ponunt.
　Romanas autem soliti contemnere leges,
　Judaicum ediscunt, et servant, ac metuunt jus,
　Tradidit arcano quodcunque volumine Moses, &c.

† Pessimus quisque, spretis religionibus patriis, tributa et stipes illuc congerebant, unde auctæ Judæorum res.

being made of the fact in any of the letters written from Rome by Paul during his imprisonment. The tradition that Peter ever was at Rome, rests on very uncertain authority. It is first mentioned by Dionysius of Corinth, in the latter half of the second century, and from that time it seems to have been generally received. This account is in itself improbable, as Peter's field of labour was in the East, about Babylon ; and as the statement of Dionysius is full of inaccuracies. He makes Peter and Paul the founders of the church at Corinth, and makes the same assertion regarding the church at Rome, neither of which is true. He also says that Paul and Peter suffered martyrdom at the same time at Rome, which, from the silence of Paul respecting Peter, during his last imprisonment, is in the highest degree improbable.* History, therefore, has left us ignorant of the time when this church was founded, and the persons by whom the work was effected.

The condition of the congregation may be inferred from the circumstances already mentioned, and from the drift of the apostle's letter. As the Jews and proselytes were very numerous at Rome, the early converts, as might be expected, were from both these classes. The latter, however, seem greatly to have predominated, because we find no such evidence of a tendency to Judaism, as is supposed in the Epistle to the Galatians. Paul no where seems to apprehend that the church at Rome would apostatize, as the Galatian Christians had already done. And in chapters xiv. and xv. his exhortations imply that the Gentile party were more in danger of oppressing the Jewish, than the reverse. Paul, therefore, writes to them as Gentiles (chap. i. 13,) and claims, in virtue of his office as apostle to the Gentiles, the right to address them with all freedom and authority (xv. 16.) The congregation, however, was not composed exclusively of this class ; many converts, originally Jews, were included in their numbers, and those belonging to the other class were more or less under the influence of Jewish opinions. The apostle, therefore, in this, as in all his other epistles addressed to congregations similarly situated, refutes those doctrines of the Jews which were inconsistent with the gospel, and answers those objections which they and those under their influence were accustomed to urge against it. These different elements of the early churches were almost always in conflict, both as to points of doctrine and discipline. The Jews insisted, to a greater or less extent, on their peculiar privileges and customs ; and the Gentiles disregarded, and at times despised the scruples and prejudices of their weaker brethren. The opinions of the Jews particularly controverted in this epistle are : 1. That connection with Abraham by natural descent, and by the bond of circumcision, together with the observance of the law, is sufficient to secure the favour of God. 2. That the blessings of the Messiah's reign were to be confined to Jews and those who would consent to become proselytes. 3. That subjection to heathen magistrates was inconsistent with the dignity of the people of God, and with their duty to the Messiah as King.

There are clear indications in other parts of Scripture, as well as in their own writings, that the Jews placed their chief dependence upon the covenant of God with Abraham, and the peculiar rites and ordinances connected with it. The Baptist, when speaking to the Jews, tells them, "Say not, We have Abraham to our father ; for I say unto you, that God is able of

---

* See Eichhorn's Einleitung, Vol. III. p. 203, and Neander's Geschichte der Pflanzung, &c. p. 456.

these stones to raise up children unto Abraham," (Luke iii. 8). It is clearly implied in this passage, that the Jews supposed that to have Abraham as their father was sufficient to secure the favour of God. The Rabbins taught that God had promised Abraham, that his descendants, though wicked, should be saved on account of his merit. Justin Martyr mentions this as the ground of confidence of the Jews in his day. "Your Rabbins," he says, "deceive themselves and us, in supposing that the kingdom of heaven is prepared for all those who are the natural seed of Abraham, even though they be sinners and unbelievers." (*Dialogue with Trypho.*) They were accustomed to say, "Great is the virtue of circumcision ; no circumcised person enters hell." And one of their standing maxims was, "All Israel hath part in eternal life."*

The second leading error of the Jews was a natural result of the one just referred to. If salvation was secured by connection with Abraham, then none who were not united to their great ancestor could be saved. There is no opinion of the Jews more conspicuous in the sacred writings, than that they were greatly superior to the Gentiles ; that the theocracy and all its blessings belonged to them ; and that others could attain even an inferior station in the kingdom of the Messiah only by becoming Jews. The indisposition of the Jews to submit to heathen magistrates, arose partly from their high ideas of their own dignity, and their contempt for other nations ; partly from their erroneous opinions of the nature of the Messiah's kingdom ; and partly, no doubt, from the peculiar hardships and oppressions to which they were exposed. The prevalence of this indisposition among them is proved by its being a matter of discussion whether it was even lawful to pay tribute to Cæsar ; by their assertion that, as Abraham's seed, they were never in bondage to any man ; and by their constant tumults and rebellions, which led first to their banishment from Rome, and finally to the utter destruction of their city. The circumstances of the church at Rome, composed of both Jewish and Gentile converts ; surrounded by Jews who still insisted on the necessity of circumcision, of legal obedience, and of connection with the family of Abraham, in order to salvation ; and disposed on many points to differ among themselves, sufficiently account for the character of this epistle.

Time and Place of its Composition.

There are no sufficient data for fixing accurately and certainly the chronology of the life and writings of the apostle Paul. It is, therefore, in most cases, only by a comparison of various circumstances, that an approximation to the date of the principal events of his life can be made. With regard to this epistle, it is plain, from its contents, that it was written just as Paul was about to set out on his last journey to Jerusalem. In the fifteenth chapter he says, that the Christians of Macedonia and Achaia had made a collection for the poor saints in Jerusalem, and that he was on the eve of his departure for that city (ver. 25.) This same journey is mentioned in Acts xv., and occurred most probably in the spring (see Acts xx. 16) of the year 58 or 59. This date best suits the account of his long imprisonment, first at Cesarea, and then at Rome, of four years, and his

---

* See Raymundi Martini Pugio Fidei, P. III. Disc. 3, c. 16. Pococke's Miscellanea, p. 172, 227. Witsii Miscellanea, P. II. p. 553. Michaelis' Introduction to the New Testament, Vol. III. p. 93.

probable liberation in 62 or 63. His subsequent labours and second imprisonment would fill up the intervening period of two or three years, to the date of his martyrdom, towards the close of the reign of Nero. That this epistle was written from Corinth, appears from the special recommendation of Phebe, a deaconess of the neighbouring church, who was probably the bearer of the letter (chap. xvi. 1); from the salutations of Erastus and Gaius, both residents of Corinth, to the Romans (chap xvi. 23); compare 2 Tim. iv. 20, and 1 Cor. i. 14 ; and from the account given in Acts xx. 2, 3. of Paul's journey through Macedonia into Greece, before his departure for Jerusalem, for the purpose of carrying the contributions of the churches for the poor in that city.

AUTHENTICITY OF THE EPISTLE.

That this epistle was written by the apostle Paul, admits of no reasonable doubt. 1. It, in the first place, purports to be his. It bears his signature, and speaks throughout in his name. 2. It has uniformly been recognised as his. From the apostolic age to the present time, it has been referred to, and quoted by a regular series of authors, and recognised as of divine authority in all the churches. It would be requisite, in order to disprove its authenticity, to account satisfactorily for these facts, on the supposition of the epistle being spurious. The passages in the early writers, in which this epistle is alluded to or cited, are very numerous, and may be seen in Lardner's *Credibility,* Vol. II. 3. The internal evidence is no less decisive in its favour. (*a*) In the first place, it is evidently the production of a Jew, familiar with the Hebrew text and the Septuagint version of the Old Testament, because the language and style are such as no one, not thus circumstanced, could adopt ; and because the whole letter evinces such an intimate acquaintance with Jewish opinions and prejudices. (*b*) It agrees perfectly in style and manner with the other epistles of this apostle. (*c*) It is, in the truth and importance of its doctrines, and in the elevation and purity of its sentiments, immeasurably superior to any uninspired production of the age in which it appeared. A comparison of the genuine apostolic writings with the spurious productions of the first and second centuries, affords one of the strongest collateral evidences of the authenticity and inspiration of the former. (*d*) The incidental or undesigned coincidences, as to matters of fact, between this epistle and other parts of the New Testament, are such as to afford the clearest evidence of its having proceeded from the pen of the apostle. Compare Rom. xv. 25—31 with Acts xx. 2, 3, xxiv. 17, 1 Cor. xvi. 1—4, 2 Cor. viii. 1—4, ix. 2 ; Rom. xvi. 21—23 with Acts xx. 4 ; Rom. xvi. 3, et seqq. with Acts xviii. 2, 18—26, 1 Cor. xvi. 19, &c. (see Paley's Horæ Paulinæ). 4. Besides these positive proofs, there is the important negative consideration, that there are no grounds for questioning its authenticity. There are no discrepancies between this and other sacred writings ; no counter testimony among the early Fathers ; no historical or critical difficulties which must be solved before it can be recognised as the work of Paul. There is, therefore, no book in the Bible, and there is no ancient book in the world, of which the authenticity is more certain than that of this epistle.

ANALYSIS OF THE EPISTLE.

The epistle consists of three parts. The first, which includes the first eight chapters, is occupied in the discussion of the doctrine of justification and its consequences. The second, embracing chs. ix.—xi., treats of the calling of the Gentiles, the rejection and future conversion of the Jews. The third consists of practical exhortations and salutations to the Christians at Rome.

THE FIRST PART the apostle commences by saluting the Roman Christians, commending them for their faith, and expressing his desire to see them, and his readiness to preach the gospel at Rome. This readiness was founded on the conviction that the gospel revealed the only method by which men can be saved, viz., by faith in Jesus Christ, and this method is equally applicable to all mankind, Gentiles as well as Jews, chap. i. 1—17. Paul thus introduces the two leading topics of the epistle.

In order to establish his doctrine respecting justification, he first proves that the Gentiles cannot be justified by their own works, chap. i. 18—39; and then establishes the same position in reference to the Jews, chs. ii. iii. 1—20. Having thus shown that the method of justification by works is unavailable for sinners, he unfolds that method which is taught in the gospel, chap. iii. 21—31. The truth and excellence of this method he confirms in chs. iv. and v. The obvious objection to the doctrine of gratuitous acceptance, that it must lead to the indulgence of sin, is answered, and the true design and operation of the law are exhibited in chs. vi. and vii.; and the complete security of all who confide in Christ is beautifully unfolded in chap. viii.

In arguing against the Gentiles, Paul assumes the principle that God will punish sin, chap. i. 18, and then proves that they are justly chargeable both with impiety and immorality, because, though they possessed a competent knowledge of God, they did not worship him, but turned unto idols, and gave themselves up to all kinds of iniquity, chap. i. 19—32.

He commences his argument with the Jews by expanding the general principle of the divine justice, and especially insisting on God's impartiality by showing that he will judge all men, Jews and Gentiles, according to their works, and according to the light they severally enjoyed, chap. ii. 1—16. He shows that the Jews, when tried by these rules, are as justly and certainly exposed to condemnation as the Gentiles, chap. ii. 17—29.

The peculiar privileges of the Jews afford no ground of hope that they will escape being judged on the same principles with other men, and when thus judged, they are found to be guilty before God. All men, therefore, are, as the Scriptures abundantly teach, under condemnation, and consequently cannot be justified by their own works, chap. iii. 1—20.

The gospel proposes the only method by which God will justify men— a method which is entirely gratuitous; the condition of which is faith; which is founded on the redemption of Christ; which reconciles the justice and mercy of God; humbles man; lays the foundation for an universal religion, and establishes the law, chap. iii. 21—31.

The truth of this doctrine is evinced from the example of Abraham, the testimony of David, the nature of the covenant made with Abraham and his seed, and from the nature of the law. He proposes the conduct of Abraham as an example and encouragement to Christians, chap. iv. 1-25.

Justification by faith in Christ secures peace with God, present joy, and the assurance of eternal life, chap. v. 1—11. The method, therefore, by which God proposes to save sinners, is analogous to that by which they were first brought under condemnation. As on account of the offence of one, sentence has passed on all men to condemnation ; so on account of the righteousness of one, all are justified, chap. v. 12—21.

The doctrine of the gratuitous justification of sinners cannot lead to the indulgence of sin, because such is the nature of union with Christ, and such the object for which he died, that all who receive the benefits of his death, experience the sanctifying influence of his life, chap. vi. 1—11. Besides, the objection in question is founded on a misapprehension of the effect and design of the law, and of the nature of sanctification. Deliverance from the bondage of the law and from a legal spirit is essential to holiness. When the Christian is delivered from this bondage, he becomes the servant of God, and is brought under an influence which effectually secures his obedience, chap. vi. 12—23.

As, therefore, a woman, in order to be married to a second husband, must first be freed from her former one, so the Christian, in order to be united to Christ, and to bring forth fruit unto God, must first be freed from the law, chap. vii. 1—6.

This necessity of deliverance from the law, does not arise from the fact that the law is evil, but from the nature of the case. The law is but the authoritative declaration of duty ; which cannot alter the state of the sinner's heart. Its real operation is to produce the conviction of sin (vers. 7—13), and, in the renewed mind, to excite approbation and complacency in the excellence which it exhibits, but it cannot effectually secure the destruction of sin. This can only be done by the grace of God in Jesus Christ, chap. vii. 7—25.

Those who are in Christ, therefore, are perfectly safe. They are freed from the law ; they have the indwelling of the life-giving Spirit : they are the children of God ; they are chosen, called, and justified according to the divine purpose ; and they are the objects of the unchanging love of God, chap. viii. 1—39.

THE SECOND PART of the epistle relates to the persons to whom the blessings of Christ's kingdom may properly be offered, and the purposes of God respecting the Jews. In entering upon this subject, the apostle, after assuring his kindred of his affection, establishes the position that God has not bound himself to regard as his children all the natural descendants of Abraham, but is at perfect liberty to choose whom he will to be heirs of his kingdom. The right of God to have mercy on whom he will have mercy, he proves from the declarations of Scripture, and from the dispensations of his providence. He shows that this doctrine of the divine sovereignty is not inconsistent with the divine character or man's responsibility, because God simply chooses from among the undeserving whom he will as the objects of his mercy, and leaves others to the just recompense of their sins, chap. ix. 1—24.

God accordingly predicted of old, that he would call the Gentiles and reject the Jews. The rejection of the Jews was on account of their unbelief, chs. ix. 25—33, x. 1—5. The two methods of justification are then contrasted for the purpose of showing that the legal method is impracticable, but that the method proposed in the gospel is simple and easy, and adapted to all men. It should, therefore, agreeably to the revealed purpose of God, be preached to all men, chap. x. 6—21.

The rejection of the Jews is not total ; many of that generation were brought into the church, who were of the election of grace, chap. xi. 1—10. Neither is this rejection final. There is to be a future and general conversion of the Jews to Christ, and thus all Israel shall be saved, chap. xi. 11—36.

The THIRD or practical part of the epistle, consists of directions, first, as to the general duties of Christians in their various relations to God, chap. xii.; secondly, as to their political or civil duties, chap. xiii.; and thirdly, as to their ecclesiastical duties, or those duties which they owe to each other as members of the church, chs. xiv. xv. 1—13.

The epistle concludes with some account of Paul's labours and purposes, chap. xv. 14—33, and with the usual salutations, chap. xvi.

THE

EPISTLE TO THE ROMANS

CHAPTER I

CONTENTS.

ROMANS I. 1—17.

ANALYSIS.

THIS section consists of two parts. The first from vers. 1 to 7 inclusive, is a salutatory address; the second, from vers. 8 to 17, is the introduction to the epistle. Paul commences by announcing himself as a divinely commissioned teacher, set apart to the preaching of the gospel, ver. 1. Of this gospel, he says, 1. That it was promised, and of course partially exhibited in the Old Testament, ver. 2. 2. That its great subject was Jesus Christ, ver. 3. Of Christ he says, that he was, as to his human nature, the Son of David; but as to his divine nature, the Son of God, vers. 3, 4. From this Divine Person he had received his office as an apostle. The object of this office was to bring men to believe the gospel; and it contemplated all nations as the field of its labour, ver. 5. Of course the Romans were included, ver. 6. To the Roman Christians, therefore, he wishes grace and peace, ver. 7. Thus far the salutation.

Having shown in what character, and by what right he addressed them, the apostle introduces the subject of his letter by expressing to them his respect and affection. He thanks God, not only that they believed, but that their faith was universally known and talked of, ver. 8. As an evidence of his concern for them, he mentions, 1. That he prayed for them constantly, ver. 9. 2. That he longed to see them, vers. 10, 11. 3. That this wish to see them arose from a desire to do them good, and to reap some fruit of his ministry among them, as well as among other Gentiles, vers. 12, 13. Because he was under obligation to preach to all men, wise and unwise, he was therefore ready to preach even at Rome, vers. 14, 15. This readiness to preach arose from the high estimate he entertained of the gospel. And his reverence for the gospel was founded not on its excellent system of morals merely, but on its efficacy in saving all who believe, whether Jews or Gentiles, ver. 16. This efficacy of the gospel arises from its teaching the true method of justification, that is, the method of justification by faith, ver. 17. It will be perceived how naturally and skilfully the apostle introduces the two great subjects of the epistle—the method of salvation, and the persons to whom it may properly be offered.

COMMENTARY.

VERSE 1. *Paul, a servant of Jesus Christ, called an apostle.* Agreeably to the ancient mode of epistolary address, the apostle begins with the declaration of his name and office. It was his office which gave him the right to address the believers at Rome, and elsewhere, with that tone of authority which pervades all his epistles. Speaking as the messenger of Christ, he spake as he spake, as one having authority, and not as an ordinary teacher.

The original name of the apostle was Saul, שָׁאוּל demanded. He is first called Paul in Acts xiii. 9. As this change of his name is mentioned in the paragraph which contains the account of the conversion of Sergius Paulus, the proconsul of Cyprus, some have supposed that the name was assumed in compliment to that distinguished convert. This supposition does not seem to accord with the apostle's character, and is, on other grounds, less probable than either of the two following. First, as it was not unusual, among the Jews, to change the name of a person in consequence of some remarkable event, as in the case of Abraham and Jacob, Gen. xvii. 5; xxxii. 28; or when he was advanced to some new office or dignity, Gen. xli. 45; Dan. i. 6, 7; so that a new name is sometimes equivalent to a new dignity, Rev. ii. 17, it may be supposed that the apostle received the name of Paul, when called to the office of an apostle. This supposition is favoured by the consideration that he received the name soon after he entered upon the public exercise of his apostleship, and by the fact that Simon was called Cephas when called to be an apostle, John i. 42; Matt. x. 2, and that James and John were called Boanerges, Mark iii. 17. Hence Theophylact says that it was in order that even in this matter, he should not be behind the very chief of the apostles, that Saul was called Paul. Second, as it was very common for those Jews who had much intercourse with the heathen to bear two names, one Jewish and the other Greek or Roman, which names were sometimes entirely distinct, as Hillel and Pollio, sometimes nearly related as Silas and Silvanus, it is very probable that this was the case with the apostle. He was called Saul among the Jews, and Paul among the Gentiles; and as he was the Apostle of the Gentiles, the latter name became his common designation. As this change was, however, made or announced at an epoch in the apostle's history, Acts xiii. 9, the two explanations may be united. "The only supposition," says Dr. J. A. Alexander, in his comment on Acts xiii. 9, "which is free from all these difficulties, and affords a satisfactory solution of the facts in question, is, that this was the time fixed by Divine authority for Paul's manifestation as Apostle of the Gentiles, and that this manifestation was made more conspicuous by its coincidence with his triumph over a representative of unbelieving and apostate Judaism, and the conversion of an official representative of Rome, whose name was identical with his own apostolic title."

In calling himself *a servant* (bondsman) *of Jesus Christ*, he may have
intended either to declare himself the dependent and worshipper of Christ,
as all Christians are *servants* (slaves) *of Christ*, Eph. vi.
6 ; or to express
his official relation to the church as the minister of Christ. This is the
more probable· explanation, because, in the Old Testament עֶבֶד יְהוָֹה is a
common official designation of any one employed in the immediate service
of God, Joshua i. 1, xxiv. 29, Jer. xxix. 19, Isaiah xlii.
1 ; and because
in the New Testament we find the same usage, not only in the beginning
of several of the epistles, as " Paul and Timothy, the servants of Jesus
Christ," Phil. i. 1, " James, the servant of God and of Jesus Christ,"
James i. 1, " Peter, a servant and apostle of Jesus Christ," 2 Peter i. 1 ;
but also in other cases where the word δοῦλος is interchanged with
διάκονος *minister.*   Comp. Col. i. 7, iv. 7, 12.   It is, therefore, a general
official designation of which in the present case, *apostle* is the specific explanation.   " Apostolatus ministerii est species."   *Calvin.*   It has also
been properly remarked, that as the expression, servant of Christ, implies
implicit obedience and subjection, it supposes the Divine authority of the
Redeemer.   That is, we find the apostle denying that he was the servant
of men, rejecting all human authority as it regards matters of faith and
duty, and yet professing the most absolute subjection of conscience and
reason to the authority of Jesus Christ.

χλητὸς ἀπόστολος, *called an apostle.*   Paul was not only a servant of
Christ, but by Divine appointment an apostle. This idea is included in
the word χλητός which means not only *called*, but *chosen, appointed ;* and
the κλῆσις, or vocation, as well of believers to grace and salvation, as of the
apostles to their office is uniformly ascribed to God or Christ ; see Gal. i.
1 ; 1 Cor. i. 1 ; Tit. i. 1 ; Gal. i. 15.   As the immediate call of Christ was
one of the essential requisites of an apostle, Paul means to assert in the
use of the word κλητός that he was neither self-appointed nor chosen by
men to that sacred office.

The word ἀπόστολος occurs in its original sense of *messenger* in several
cases in the New Testament.   John xiii. 16, οὐχ ἔστι ἀπόστολος μείζων τοῦ
πέμψαντος αὐτόν.   Phil. ii. 25, Ἐπαφρόδιτον . . . ὑμῶν δὲ ἀπόστολον.
Comp. iv. 18.   In 2 Cor. viii. 23, Paul speaking of the brethren who
were with him, calls them ἀπόστολοι ἐκκλησιῶν ; τουτέστιν says Chrysostom,
ὑπὸ ἐκκλησιῶν πεμφθέντες.   Theophylact adds, καὶ χειροτονηθέντες.   Our
translators, therefore, are doubtless correct in rendering this phrase,
messengers of the churches.   As a strict official designation, the word
apostle is confined to those men selected and commissioned by Christ himself to deliver in his name the message of salvation. It appears from
Luke vi. 13, that the Saviour himself gave them this title. " And when
it was day, he called his disciples, and of them he chose twelve, whom
also he named apostles." If it be asked why this name was chosen, it is
perhaps enough to say, that it was peculiarly appropriate. It is given to
those who were sent by Christ to perform a particular service, who were
therefore properly called messengers. There is no necessity to resort for
an explanation of the term, to the fact that the word שָׁלִיחַ *messenger,* was
applied sometimes to the teachers and ministers of the synagogue, sometimes to plenipotentiaries sent by the Sanhedrim to execute some ecclesiastical commission.

The apostles, then, were the immediate messengers of Christ, appointed
to bear testimony to what they had seen and heard. " Ye also shall bear

witness," said Christ, speaking to the twelve, " because ye have been with me from the beginning." John xv. 27. This was their peculiar office ; hence when Judas fell, one, said Peter, who has companioned with us all the time that the Lord Jesus went in and out among us, must be ordained to be a witness with us of his resurrection. Acts i. 21. To be an apostle, therefore, it was necessary to have seen Christ after his resurrection, 1 Cor. ix. 1, and to have a knowledge of his life and doctrines derived immediately from himself. Without this no man could be a witness, he would only report what he had heard from others, he could bear no independent testimony to what he himself had seen and heard. Christ, therefore, says to his disciples, after his resurrection, " Ye shall be my witnesses," Acts i. 8, and the apostles accordingly constantly presented themselves in this character. Acts ii. 32, iii. 15, xiii. 31. " We are witnesses," said Peter, speaking of himself and fellow-apostles, " of all things which he did, both in the land of Judea, and in Jerusalem." Acts x. 39. When Paul was called to be an apostle, the Saviour said to him, " I have appeared unto thee for this purpose, to make thee a minister and a witness both of these things which thou hast seen, and of those things in the which I will appear unto thee." Acts xxvi. 16. We accordingly find, that whenever Paul was called upon to defend his apostleship, he strenuously asserted that he was appointed not of men nor by man, but by Jesus Christ ; and as to his doctrines, that he neither received them of man, neither was he taught them, but by revelation of Jesus Christ. Gal. i. 12.

As the testimony which the Apostles were to bear related to all that Jesus had taught them, it was by preaching the gospel that they discharged their duty as witnesses. Hence Paul says, " Christ sent me not to baptize but to preach the gospel." 1 Cor. i. 17. To the elders of Ephesus he said, " I count not my life dear unto me, so that I might finish my course with joy, and the ministry which I have received of the Lord Jesus, to testify the gospel of the grace of God." Acts xx. 24.

To give authority to this testimony the apostles were inspired, and as religious teachers infallible. John xiv. 26, xvi. 13. They had the power of working miracles, in confirmation of their mission. Matt. x. 8, and the Acts of the Apostles *passim*. This power they could communicate to others by the laying on of their hands. Acts ix. 15, 17, 18, xix. 6. This is what is meant by giving the Holy Ghost, for the apostles never claimed the power of communicating the sanctifying influences of the Spirit. Nor was the power of giving the Spirit, in the sense above-mentioned, peculiar to them, for we read that Ananias, a disciple, was sent to Paul that he might receive the Holy Ghost. Acts ix. 17. The apostles seem also to have had the gift of " discerning spirits," 1 Cor. xii. 10, and of remitting sins. John xx. 23. They ordained presbyters over the congregations gathered by their ministry, Acts xiv. 23, &c. ; and exercised a general jurisdiction over the churches. 1 Cor. v. 3—5, 2 Cor. x. 6, 8, 11, 1 Tim. i. 20. The apostles, therefore, were the immediate messengers of Jesus Christ, sent to declare his gospel, endued with the Holy Spirit, rendering them infallible as teachers, and investing them with miraculous powers, and clothed with peculiar prerogatives in the organization and government of the Church.

It is in explanation of his apostolic office, and in the further assertion of his divine commission that Paul adds, ἀφωρισμένος εἰς εὐαγγέλιον Θεοῦ, *separated unto the gospel of God.* Ἀφορίζειν is *to limit off, to separate, to select from among others.* It is so used in Levit. xx. 24, 26, "I am the

Lord your God, which have separated you from other people." In the same sense, in Gal. i. 15, "when it pleased God, who separated me from my mother's womb ;" that is, who singled me out, or chose me. It is obvious, therefore, that the apostle here refers to his appointment by God to his office. In Acts xiii. 2, it is said, " Separate (ἀφορίσατε) unto me Barnabas and Saul," where a separation not to the ministry, much less to the apostleship, but to a special mission is referred to. Paul's designation to office was neither of man, nor by man. Gal. i. 1. The words εἰς εὐαγγέλιον, *unto the gospel,* express the object to which he was devoted when thus separated from the mass of his brethren ; it was to preach the gospel. The divine origin of the gospel is asserted in calling it *the gospel of God.* It is the glad annunciation which God makes to men of the pardon of sin, of restoration to his favour, of the renovation of their nature, of the resurrection of the body, and of eternal life.

VERSE 2. *Which he promised afore.* That is, the gospel which Paul was sent to preach, was the same system of grace and truth, which from the beginning had been predicted and partially unfolded in the writings of the Old Testament. The reason why the Apostle here adverts to that fact probably was, that one of the strongest proofs of the divine origin of the gospel is found in the prophecies of the Old Testament. The advent, the character, the work, the kingdom of the Messiah, are there predicted, and it was therefore out of the Scriptures that the apostles reasoned, to convince the people that Jesus is the Christ ; and to this connection between the two dispensations they constantly refer, in proof of their doctrines. See ch. iii. 21; iv. 3; ix. 27, 33 ; x. 11. 20. Comp. Luke xxiv. 44; John xii. 16 ; Acts x. 43.

By his prophets in the Holy Scriptures. As in Scripture the term προφήτης, Heb. נָבִיא, is applied to any one who spake by inspiration as the ambassador of God and the interpreter of his will ; προφητῶν here includes all the Old Testament writers, whether prophets in the strict sense of the term, or teachers, or historians. Meyer indeed insists that the line of the prophets begins with Samuel, according to Acts iii. 24—"all the prophets from Samuel, and those who follow after," and therefore that the earlier writers of the Old Testament are not here included. But Moses was a prophet, and what is here expressed by the words "his prophets," is explained by the phrase "the law and the prophets," in ch. iii. 21.

By the *Holy Scriptures* must of course be understood, those writings which the Jews regarded as holy, because they treated of holy things, and because they were given by the inspiration of the Holy Ghost.

VERSE 3. *Concerning his Son.* These words are either to be connected with εὐαγγέλιον, *the gospel concerning his Son ;* or with προεπηγγείλατο, *which he promised concerning his Son.* The sense in either case is much the same. As most commentators and editors regard the second verse as a parenthesis, they of course adopt the former construction ; but as there is no necessity for assuming any parenthesis, the natural grammatical connection is with προεπηγγείλατο. The personal object of the ancient promises is the Son of God.

It is a well known scriptural usage, that the designations employed in reference to our Lord are sometimes applied to him as a historical person, God and man, and sometimes exclusively to one or the other of the two natures, the divine and human, which enter into the constitution of the *theanthropos.* Thus the term Son designates the Logos in all those passages in which he is spoken of as the Creator of all things ; at other times it designates the incarnate Logos ; as when it is said, "the Son shall make you free." Sometimes the same term is used in the same passage in reference first to the incarnate Word, and then to the Word as the second person of the Trinity. Thus in Heb. i. 2, it is said, " Hath spoken unto us by his Son, (the historical person, Jesus Christ,) by whom (the eternal Word) he made the worlds." So here "concerning his Son," means the Son of God as clothed in our nature, the Word made flesh ; but in the next clause, "declared to be the Son of God," the word Son designates the divine nature of Christ. In all cases, however, it is a designation implying participation of the divine nature. Christ is called the Son of God because he is consubstantial with the Father, and therefore equal to him in power and glory. The term expresses the relation of the second to the first person in the Trinity, as it exists from eternity. It is therefore, as applied to Christ, not a term of office, nor expressive of any relation assumed in time. He was and is the Eternal Son. This is proved from John i. 1—14 where the term υἱός is interchanged with λόγος. It was the Son, therefore, who in the beginning was with God, who was God, who created all things, in whom was life, who is the light of men, who is in the bosom of the Father. In John v. 17—31, Christ calls himself the Son of God, in a sense which made him equal to the Father, having the same power, the same authority, and a right to the same honour. In John x. 29—42, Christ declares God to be his Father in such a sense as to make himself God, one with the Father ; and he vindicates his claim to this participation of the divine nature by appealing to his works. In Col. i. 13—17, he is said as Son to be the image of the invisible God, the exact exemplar, and of course the revealer of the Divine nature ; the Creator of all things that are in heaven and that are in earth, visible and invisible. In Heb. i. 4—6, the title *Son* is adduced as proof that he is superior to the angels, and entitled to their worship. He is therefore called God's proper Son, ἴδιος, Rom. viii. 32, (comp. πατέρα ἴδιον ἔλεγεν τὸν θεόν, John v. 18) ; his own Son, ἑαυτοῦ, Rom. viii. 3 ; *his only begotten Son*, μονογενής, John i. 14, 18 ; iii. 16, 18 ; 1 John iv. 9. Hence giving, sending, not sparing this Son, is said to be the highest conceivable evidence of the love of God, John iii. 16 ; Rom. viii. 32 ; 1 John iv. 9. The historical sense of the terms λόγος, εἰκών, υἱός, πρωτότοκος, as learned from the Scriptures and the *usus loquendi* of the apostolic age, shows that they must, in their application to Christ, be understood of his Divine nature.

Who was made of the seed of David. As γίνομαι, from the assumed theme γένω, to beget, signifies *to begin to be, to come into existence,* it is often used in reference to descent or birth, γενόμενον ἐκ γυναικός, Gal. iv. 4 ; ἧς ἐγενήθητε τέκνα, 1 Pet. iii. 6. "Made of the seed of David," is therefore equivalent to " born of the seed of David." That the Messiah was to be of the family of David, was predicted in the Old Testament, and affirmed in the New. Isa. xi. 1 ; Jer. xxiii. 5 ; Matt. xxii. 45 ; John vii. 42 ; Acts xiii. 23.

The limitation κατὰ σάρκα, *according to the flesh,* obviously implies the superhuman character of Jesus Christ. Were he a mere man, it had been enough to say that he was of the seed of David ; but as he is more than man, it was necessary to limit his descent from David to his human nature. That the word σάρξ here means *human nature* is obvious both from the scriptural usage of the word, and from the nature of the case. See John i. 14 ; Rom. ix. 5 ; 1 Tim. iii. 16 ; 1 John iv. 2, 3. It is not the flesh or body, as opposed to the soul, but the human, as opposed to the divine nature, that is intended. Neither does σάρξ here mean the purely material element with its organic life, the σῶμα and ψυχή, to the exclusion of the πνεῦμα, or rational principle, according to the Apollinarian doctrine, but the entire humanity of Christ, including "a true body and a reasonable soul." This is the sense of the word in all the parallel passages in which the incarnation is the subject. As when it is said, "The Word was made flesh," John i. 14 ; or, "God was manifested in the flesh," 1 Tim. iii. 16. These are explained by saying, "He was found in fashion as a man," Philip. ii. 8. The word therefore includes everything which constitutes the nature which a child derives from its progenitors.

Verse 4. *Declared to be the Son of God.* The word ὁρίζειν means, 1. To limit, or bound, and, in reference to ideas, to define. 2. To determine. Luke xxii. 22; Acts ii. 23 ; Heb. iv. 7. 3. To appoint, or constitute. Acts x. 42. ὁ ὡρισμένος ὑπὸ τοῦ Θεοῦ κριτὴς ζώντων καὶ νεκρῶν. Acts xvii. 31. This last sense is given by some few commentators to ὁρισθέντος in this passage. The apostle would then say that Christ was appointed, or constituted the Son of God, by or after his resurrection. But this is inconsistent with what he elsewhere teaches, viz., that Christ was the Son of God before the foundation of the world, Col. i. 15. As shown above, Son of God is not a title of office, but of nature, and therefore Christ cannot be said to have been constituted the Son of God. This interpretation also would involve the latter part of the verse in great difficulties. Hence even those commentators who most strenuously insist on adhering to the signification of words, are constrained, *ex necessitate loci*, to understand ὁρισθέντος here declaratively, or in reference to the knowledge of men. That is, when Christ is said to be constituted the Son of God, we are not to understand that he became or was made Son, but was, in the view of men, thus determined.*

The vulgate reads, *qui praedestinatus est*, which version is followed by most of the Roman Catholic interpreters, and by Grotius. This rendering is probably founded on the reading προορισθέντος, which, although old, has little evidence in its favour. Neither is the sense thus expressed suited to the context. Christ was not predestinated to be the Son of God. He was such from eternity.

With power; τουτέστι, says Theophylact, ἀπὸ τῆς δυνάμεως τῶν σημείων ὧν ἐποίει ; Theodoret also understands these words to refer to the miracles which Jesus, by the power of the Holy Ghost, wrought in confirmation of his claim to be the Son of God. The former of these commentators takes ἐν δυνάμει, κατὰ πνεῦμα, ἐξ ἀναστάσεως, as indicating three distinct sources of proof of the Sonship of Christ. He was proved by his miraculous power, by the Holy Spirit either as given to him, or as by him given to his people (the latter is Theophylact's view), and by his resurrection, to be the Son of God. But the change of the prepositions, and especially the antithetical structure of the sentence, by which κατὰ πνεῦμα is obviously opposed to κατὰ σάρκα, are decisive objections to this interpretation. Others propose to connect ἐν δυνάμει with υἱοῦ, *Son in power*, for powerful Son ; a more common and more natural construction is to connect them with ὁρισθέντος, proved, or declared with power, for powerfully, effectually

---

* Es bleibt daher, says De Wette, nichts übrig, als den Gedanken des *Bestimmen* modalisch, d. h. in Beziehung, auf die menschliche Erkenntniss, zu nehmen. Much to the same purpose Fritzsche says, Fuerit enim Christus, ut fuit, ante mundum Dei filius, hoc certe apparet, eum *inter mortales* iis demum rebus talem a Deo constitutum esse, sine quibus eum esse Dei filium homines cognoscere non potuissent, velut reditu ex inferis.

proved to be the Son of God. He was declared with emphasis to be the Son of God, *ita ut ejus rei plenissima et certissima sit fides.* Winzer. *According to the Spirit of holiness.* As just remarked, these words are in antithesis with κατὰ σάρκα ; as to the flesh he was the Son of David, as to the Spirit the Son of God. As σάρξ means his human nature, πνεῦμα can hardly mean anything else than the higher or divine nature of Christ. The word πνεῦμα may be taken in this sense in 1 Tim. iii. 16, ἐδικαιώϑη ἐν πνεύματι, *justified by the Spirit*, i. e., he was shown to be just, his claims were all sustained by the manifestations of his divine nature, *i.e.,* of his divine power and authority. Heb. ix. 14, ὅς διὰ πνεύματος αἰωνίου, *who with an eternal Spirit* offered himself unto God. 1 Pet. iii. 18 is a more doubtful passage. The genitive ἀγιωσύνης is a qualification of πνεῦμα, Spirit of holiness ; the Spirit whose characteristic is holiness. This expression seems to be here used, to prevent ambiguity, as Holy Spirit is appropriated as the designation of the third person of the Trinity. As the word holy often means *august, venerandus,* so ἀγιωσύνη expresses that attribute of a person which renders him worthy of reverence ; πνεῦμα ἀγιωσύνης is, therefore, *Spiritus summe venerandus,* the ϑεότης, divine nature, or Godhead, which dwelt in Jesus Christ ; the Logos, who in the beginning was with God, and was God, and who became flesh and dwelt among us. That πνεῦμα does not here mean the spiritual state of exaltation of Christ, is plain ; first, because the word is never so used elsewhere; and, secondly, because it is inconsistent with the antithesis to κατὰ σάρκα. Those who understand the phrase "Spirit of holiness" to refer to the Holy Spirit, either, as before remarked, suppose that the apostle refers to the evidence given by the Spirit to the Sonship of Christ, hence Calvin renders κατὰ πνεῦμα *per Spiritum* ; or they consider him as appealing to the testimony of the Spirit as given in the Scriptures. ‘Christ was declared to be the Son of God, agreeably to the Spirit.’ To both these views, however, the same objection lies, that it destroys the antithesis.

ἐξ ἀναστάσεως νεκρῶν, is rendered by Erasmus, Luther, and others, *after* the resurrection from the dead. It was not until Christ had risen that the evidence of his Sonship was complete, or the fulness of its import known even to the apostles. But it is better suited to the context, and more agreeable to the Scripture, to consider the resurrection itself, as the evidence of his Sonship. It was by the resurrection that he was proved to be the Son of God. "God," says the apostle, "will judge the world in righteousness by that man whom he hath ordained, whereof he hath given assurance unto all, in that he hath raised him from the dead." Acts xvii. 31. The apostle Peter also says, that "God hath begotten us to a lively hope by the resurrection of Jesus Christ from the dead." 1 Pet. i. 3. Comp. iii. 21; Acts xiii. 35; xxvi. 23; 1 Cor. xv. 20. In these and many other passages the resurrection of Christ is represented as the great conclusive evidence of the truth of all that Christ taught, and of the validity of all his claims. If it be asked how the resurrection of Christ is a proof of his being the Son of God, it may be answered, first, because he rose by his own power. He had power to lay down his life, and he had power to take it again. John x. 18. This is not inconsistent with the fact taught in so many other passages, that he was raised by the power of the Father, because what the Father does the Son does likewise ; creation, and all other external works, are ascribed indifferently to the Father, Son, and Spirit. But in the second place, as Christ had openly declared himself to be the Son of God, his rising from the dead was the seal of God to the truth of that declaration. Had he continued under the power of death, God would thereby have disallowed his claim to be his Son; but as he raised him from the dead, he publicly acknowledged him; saying, Thou art my Son, this day have I declared thee such. "If Christ be not risen, then is our preaching vain," says the apostle, "and your faith is also vain. But now is Christ risen, and become the first fruits of them that slept."

Jesus Christ our Lord. These words are in apposition with τοῦ υἱοῦ αὐτοῦ of the third verse; "his Son, Jesus Christ our Lord." All the names of Christ are precious to his people. He is called Jesus, *Saviour*, because he saves his people from their sins. Matt. i. 21. The name Christ, *i.e.*, Messiah, Anointed, connects him with all the predictions and promises of the Old Testament. He is the anointed prophet, priest, and king, to whom all believing eyes had been so long directed, and on whom all hopes centred. He is κύριος ἡμῶν our Lord. This word indeed is often used as a mere term of respect, equivalent to Sir, but as it is employed by the LXX. as the common substitute of Jehovah, or rather as the translation of אֲדֹנָי, in the sense of supreme Lord and possessor, so it is in the New Testament applied in the same sense to Christ. He is our supreme Lord and possessor. We belong to him, and his authority over us is absolute, extending to the heart and conscience as well as to the outward conduct; and to him every knee shall bow and every tongue confess that he is Lord, to the glory of God the Father. He, then, who in this exalted sense is our Lord, is, as to his human nature, the Son of David, and, as to his Divine nature, the Son of God.

VERSE 5. *Through whom we have received grace and apostleship.* As it was of the utmost importance that Paul's authority as an apostle should be acknowledged in the Church, he here repeats the assertion that he received his office immediately from Jesus Christ, whose exalted character as the Son of God and our supreme Lord he had just declared. Though δι οὗ properly means *through* whom, by whose instrumentality, the preposition must here be taken in a more general sense as indicating the source *from* whom. Comp. Gal. i. 1, διὰ θεοῦ πατρός. Rom. xi. 36; 1 Cor. i. 9. The words χάριν καὶ ἀποσολήν may either be taken together and rendered the favour of the apostleship, or each word may be taken separately. Then χάρις refers to the kindness of God manifested to the apostle in his conversion and vocation. 'Through whom we received *grace*, favour in general, and specially, the apostleship.'

Unto the obedience of faith. These words express the object of the apostleship; πίστεως is either the genitive of apposition, "obedience which consists in faith;" or it is the genitive of the source, "obedience which flows from faith;" or it is the genitive of the object, "obedience to faith;" *i.e.*, to the gospel. In favour of the last interpretation reference may be made to 2 Cor. x. 5. ἡ ὑπακοὴ τοῦ Χριστοῦ; 1 Pet. i. 22, ἡ ὑπακοὴ τῆς ἀληθείας, *obedience to the truth.* See Gal. i. 23; Acts vi. 7; Jude 3 for examples of the use of πίστις in this objective sense. The subjective sense, however, of the word πίστις in the New Testament is so predominant that it is safest to retain it in this passage. The obedience of faith is that obedience which consists in faith, or of which faith is the controlling principle. The design of the apostleship was to bring all nations so to believe in Christ the Son of God that they should be entirely devoted to his service. The sense is the same if πίστις be taken objectively, understood, however, not of the gospel, but of the inward principle of faith to which the nations were to be obedient. *Among all nations.* The apostles were not diocesans restricted in jurisdiction to a particular territory. Their commission was general. It was to all nations. If these words are connected with *we received*, they express directly the extent of the apostle's mission, ' We have received a mission among all nations.' If, as is much more natural, on account of their position, they are connected with the immediately preceding words, they express the same idea indirectly ; his office was to promote obedience to the faith among all nations. *For his name.* That is for the sake of (ὑπέρ) his name or glory. These words are most naturally connected with the whole preceding verse, and express the final end of the apostleship, viz., the honour of Christ. It was to promote the knowledge and glory of Christ that Paul had received his office and laboured to make the nations obedient to the gospel.

VERSE 6. *Among whom are ye also.* The apostle thus justifies his addressing the Church at Rome in his official character. If the commission which he had received extended to all nations, he was not transcending its limits in writing as an apostle to any church, though it had not been founded by his instrumentality, nor enjoyed his personal ministry. *Called of Jesus Christ.* This may mean, Those whom Christ has called. But as the κλῆσις, or vocation of believers, is generally in the New Testament referred to God, the meaning probably is, The called who belong to Christ. Qui Dei beneficio estis Jesu Christi. *Beza.* The word κλητός is never in the epistles applied to one who is merely invited by the external call of the gospel. Οἱ κλητοί, *the called*, means the effectually called ; those who are so called by God as to be made obedient to the call. Hence the κλητοί are opposed to those who receive and disregard the outward call. Christ, though an offence to the Jews and Greeks, is declared to be (τοῖς κλητοῖς) *to the called* the wisdom and power of God. 1 Cor. i. 24. Hence, too, κλητοί and ἐκλεκτοί are of nearly the same import ; κατὰ πρόθεσιν κλητοί, Rom. viii. 28 ; comp. Rom. ix. 11 ; 1 Cor. i. 26, 27. We accordingly find κλητοί used as a familiar designation of believers, as in Rev. xvii. 14, οἱ μετ' αὐτοῦ κλητοὶ καὶ ἐκλεκτοὶ καὶ πιστοί. See Jude i. 1. Comp. Rom. viii. 30; ix. 24 ; 1 Cor. i. 9 ; vii. 17, et seq., Gal. i. 15 ; Eph. iv. 1 ; Col. iii. 15 ; 1 Thess. ii. 12 ; v. 24 ; 2 Tim. i. 9. In these and in many other passages, the verb καλέω expresses the inward efficacious call of the Holy Spirit.

Theophylact remarks that the word κλητοί is applied to Christians, since they are drawn by grace, and do not come of themselves. God, as it were, anticipates them. The same remark may be made of most of the other terms by which believers are designated. They all more or less distinctly bring into view the idea of the agency of God in making them to differ from others. They are called ἐκλεκτοί θεοῦ. Rom. viii. 33; Col. iii. 12; 1 Tim. i. 1 ; or more fully ἐκλεκτοί κατὰ πρόγνωσιν θεοῦ, 1. Pet. i. 2 ; ἡγιασμένοι, *sanctified*, which includes the idea of separation, 1 Cor. i. 2 ; Jude. i. 1 ; προορισθέντες κατὰ πρόθεσιν τοῦ θεοῦ, Eph. i. 11 ; σωζόμενοι, 1 Cor. i. 18 ; 2 Cor. ii. 15 ; τεταγμένοι εἰς ζωὴν αἰώνιον, Acts xiii. 48.

VERSE 7. *To all who are in Rome.* These words are, in sense, connected with the first verse, " Paul, the servant of Jesus Christ, to all who are in Rome." *Beloved of God.* This is the great distinction and blessedness of believers, they are the beloved of God. They are not so called simply because, as was the case with the ancient Israelites, they are selected from the rest of the world, and made the recipients of peculiar external favours ; but because they are the objects of that great love wherewith he hath loved those whom, when they were dead in sins, he hath quickened together with Christ, Eph. ii. 4, 5. They are the elect of God, holy and beloved, Col. iii. 12 ; they are brethren beloved of the Lord, 2 Thess. ii. 13. *Called to be saints.* The former of these words stands in the same relation to the latter that κλητός does to ἀπόστολος in ver. 1., *called to be an apostle, called to be saints.* It is one of those designations peculiar to the true people of God, and expresses at once their vocation, and that to which they are called, viz. holiness. The word ἅγιος, in accordance with the meaning of קָדוֹשׁ in the Old Testament, signifies *clean, pure* morally, *consecrated,* and especially as applied to God, *holy, worthy of reverence.* The people of Israel, their land, their temple, &c., are called holy, as separated and devoted to God. The term ἅγιοι as applied to the people of God under the new dispensation, includes this idea. They are *saints,* because they are a community separated from the world and consecrated to God. But agreeably to the nature of the Christian dispensation, this separation is not merely external ; believers are assumed to be really separated from sin, that is, clean, pure. Again, as the impurity of sin is, according to Scripture, twofold, its pollution, and guilt or just liability to punishment, so the words, καθαίρειν, καθαρίζειν, ἁγιάζειν, which all mean *to cleanse,* are used both to express the cleansing from guilt by expiation, and from pollution by the Holy Spirit. Sometimes the one and sometimes the other, and often both of these ideas are expressed by the words. See John xv. 2 ; Heb. x. 2, for the use of καθαίρω ; Acts xv. 9; Eph. v. 26; Tit. ii. 14; Heb. ix. 14, 22; 1 John i. 7 ; for the use of καθαρίζω ; John xvii. 19 ; Acts xxvi. 16; 1 Tim. iv. 5; Heb. ii. 11 ; x. 10, 14, 29 ; for the use of ἁγιάζω. Hence Christians are called ἅγιοι, ἡγιασμένοι, not only as those who are consecrated to God, but also as those who are cleansed both by expiation, and by the renewing of the Holy Ghost.

"Novam hîc periodum incipio," says Beza, "adscripto puncto post ἁγίοις." In this punctuation he is followed by Knapp, Lachmann, Fritzsche, and many others. The sense then is, "Paul, an apostle—to the saints in Rome." And then follows the salutation, "Grace and peace to you." That the words χάρις καὶ εἰρήνη are in the nominative, and the introduction of ὑμῖν show that a new sentence is here begun.

Grace be to you, and peace. Χάρις is kindness, and especially undeserved kindness, and therefore it is so often used to express the unmerited goodness of God in the salvation of sinners. Very frequently it is used metonymically for the effect of kindness, that is, for a gift or favour. Anything, therefore, bestowed on the undeserving may be called χάρις. In this sensePaul calls his apostleship χάρις, Rom. xii. 3 ; Eph. iii. 2, 8; and all the blessings conferred on sinners through Jesus Christ, are graces, or gifts. It is in this sense repentance, faith, love, and hope are graces. And especially the influence of the Holy Spirit in the heart, in connection with the gift of the Son, the greatest of God's free gifts to men, is with peculiar propriety called χάρις, or grace. Such is its meaning in 1 Cor. xv. 10 ; 2 Cor. viii. 1 ; Rom. xii. 6 ; Gal. i. 15, and in many other passages. In the text, it is to be taken in the comprehensive sense in which it is used in the apostolic benediction, for the favour and love of God and Christ. The word εἰρήνη, which is so often united with χάρις in the formulas of salutation, is used in the wide sense of the Hebrew word שָׁלוֹם, well-being, prosperity, every kind of good. Grace and peace therefore include everything that we can desire or need, the favour of God, and all the blessings that favour secures. " Nihil prius optandum," says Calvin, " quam ut Deum propitium habeamus ; quod designatur per gratiam. Deinde ut ab eo prosperitas et successus omnium rerum fluat, qui significatur Pacis vocabulo." *From God our Father, and the Lord Jesus Christ.* This association of the Father and Christ as equally the object of prayer, and the source of spiritual blessings, is a conclusive proof that Paul regarded Christ as truly God. God is called our Father, not merely as the author of our existence, and the source of every blessing, but especially as reconciled towards us through Jesus Christ. The term expresses the peculiar relation in which he stands to those who are his sons, who have the spirit of adoption, and are the heirs or recipients of the heavenly inheritance. Jesus Christ is our Lord, as our supreme Ruler, under whose care and protection we are placed, and through whose ministration all good is actually bestowed.

VERSE 8. From this verse to the end of the 17th, we have the general introduction to the epistle. It has the usual characteristics of the introductory portions of the apostle's letters. It is commendatory. It breathes the spirit of love towards his brethren, and of gratitude and devotion towards God ; and it introduces the reader in the most natural and appropriate manner to the great doctrines which he means to exhibit. *First, I thank my God.* The words πρῶτον μέν imply an enumeration, which however is not carried out. Comp, 1 Cor. xi. 18 ; 2 Cor. xii. 12, and other cases in which the apostle begins a construction which he does not continue. *My God,* that is, the God to whom I belong, whom I serve, and who stands to me in the relation of God, as father, friend, and source of all good. "I will be to them a God, and they shall be to me a people," is the most comprehensive of all promises. *Through Jesus Christ,* are not to be connected with the immediately preceding words, 'My God, through Jesus Christ ;' but with εὐχαριστῶ, 'I thank God, through Jesus Christ.' This form of expression supposes the mediation of Christ, by whom alone we have access to the Father, and for whose sake alone either our prayers or praises are accepted. See Rom. vii. 25 ; Eph. v. 20, " Giving thanks always for all things unto God and the Father, in the name of our Lord Jesus Christ." And Col. iii. 17, " Whatsoever ye do in word or deed, do all in the name of the Lord Jesus, giving thanks to God and the Father by him." Heb. xiii. 15, " By him therefore let us offer the sacrifice of praise to God." All this is in accordance with the command of Christ, John xiv. 13, and xvi. 23, 24, " Hitherto have ye asked nothing in my name : ask, and ye shall receive." Such then being the clear doctrine of the Bible, that in all our approaches to God in prayer or praise, we must come in the name of Christ, that is, in him, referring to him as the ground of our acceptance, there is no need of the various forced interpretations of the words in the text, which have been given by those who are unwilling to admit the idea of such mediation on the part of Christ. *For you all.* Several manuscripts have περί instead of ὑπέρ, which is probably a correction. The sense is the same. The special ground of the apostle's thankfulness is expressed in the following clause : *That your faith is spoken of throughout the whole world.* Their faith was of such a character as to excite general attention and remark. Not only the fact that the Romans believed, but that their faith was of such a character as to be everywhere spoken of, was recognized by the apostle as cause of gratitude to God. God therefore is the giver of faith.

VERSE 9. In confirmation of his declaration of gratitude for their conversion, and for the eminence of their faith, Paul appeals to his constant remembrance of them in his prayers. *For God is my witness.* This reverent appeal to God as the searcher of hearts, is not uncommon in the apostle's writings. 2 Cor. i. 23 ; Gal. i. 20 ; Philip. i. 8. It is an act of worship, a devout recognition of God's omnipresence and omniscience. *Whom I serve.* The word λατρεύω is in the New Testament always used of religious service, either as rendered to God or to creatures—' Who worship and serve the creature more than the Creator,' chap. i. 25. This service may consist either in worship, or in the performance of external duties of a religious nature. The service of which Paul here speaks is characterized in the following clause ; *in my spirit.* This is opposed at once to an insincere, and to a mere external service. *In the gospel of his Son.* That is, it was a service rendered in preaching the gospel. The priests served, ἐλάτρευσαν, when performing the duties of their office ; and Paul served in performing the duties of an apostle. *The gospel of his Son,* may mean either the gospel concerning his Son, or which his Son himself taught. The former, perhaps, is more in accordance with the use of this and similar phrases, as, 'gospel of the kingdom,' 'gospel of the grace of God,' &c. *That I constantly make mention of you.* It is plain, from the occurrence of the word δεόμενος in the next verse, and from the use of this expression in other places, Philip. i. 3 ; 1 Thess. i. 2, that Paul here refers to his remembering the Roman Christians in his prayers, and not to his bearing them in his mind, or talking about them. The particle ὡς may be connected with ἀδιαλείπτως, *how uninterruptedly ;* or with the clause, ' God is my witness *that,*' &c. Comp. Acts x. 28 ; 1 Thess. ii. 10.

VERSE 10. I make mention of you, *always in my prayers praying (εἴ πως) if possibly, if it may be,* expressing the submission to the will of God with which the apostle urged his request. ἤδη ποτέ, *now at last,* as though he had long looked forward with desire to what there was now a prospect of his seeing accomplished. *I may be so happy, by the will of God, to come to you.* Εὐοδοῦν is, to lead in the right way, to prosper one's journey, Gen. xxiv. 48, and figuratively, to prosper, 1 Cor. xvi. 2 ; 3 John 2. In the passive voice, it is, to be prospered, successful, favoured. In the present case, as Paul had neither commenced his journey, nor formed any immediate purpose to undertake it, see chap. xv. 25—29, his prayer was not that his journey might be prosperous, but that he might be permitted to undertake it ; that his circumstances should be so favourably ordered that he might be able to execute his long cherished purpose of visiting Rome. Knowing, however, that all things are ordered of God, and feeling that his own wishes should be subordinated to the Divine will, he adds, *by the will of God ;* which is equivalent to, If it be the will of God. ' Praying continually, that, if it be the will of God, I may be prospered to come unto you.'

VERSE 11. Why the apostle was anxious to visit Rome, he states in this verse. He desired to see them, not merely for his own gratification, but that he might confer some spiritual gift upon them, which would tend to strengthen their faith. *For I long to see you, that I may impart (μεταδῶ share with you) some spiritual gift.* By *spiritual* gift is not to be understood a gift pertaining to the soul in distinction from the body, but one derived from the Spirit. The gifts of which the Holy Spirit is the author, include not only those miraculous endowments of which such frequent mention is made in the Epistle to the Corinthians, and the ordinary gifts of teaching, exhortation, and prophesying, 1 Cor. xii., but also those graces which are the fruits of the Spirit. The extraordinary gifts were communicated by the imposition of the apostles' hands, Acts viii. 17; xix. 6, and therefore abounded in churches founded by the apostles, 1 Cor. i. 7; Gal. iii. 5. As the church at Rome was not of this number, it has been supposed that Paul was desirous of conferring on the Roman Christians some of those miraculous powers by which the gospel was in other places attended and confirmed. The following verses, however, are in favour of giving the phrase here a wider signification. Any increase of knowledge, of grace, or of power, was a χάρισμα πνευματικόν in the sense here intended. *In order that ye may be strengthened.* This includes not only an increase of confidence in their belief of the gospel, but an increase of strength in their religious feelings, and in their purpose and power of obedience. Comp. 1 Thess. iii. 2 ; I sent Timothy—" to establish you, and to comfort you concerning your faith." And 2 Thess. ii. 17, " Now our Lord Jesus Christ comfort your hearts, and stablish you in every good word and work." And the apostle prays that the Ephesians might be strengthened as to the inner man.

VERSE 12. *That is, that I may be comforted among you.* This is obviously intended to be an explanation or correction of what precedes. He had desired to see them, in order that he might do them good ; but this was not his whole object, he hoped to receive benefit himself. As to the grammatical construction, the infinite συμπαρακληθῆναι may depend on στηριχθῆναι. The sense would then be, ' That you may be strengthened, that I may be comforted.' Or the one infinitive is coördinate with the other ; then both depend on the ἵνα μεταδῶ of ver. 10, 'That I may impart some spiritual gift to you, in order that you may be strengthened ; that is, that I may be comforted together with you.' This seems the most natural construction ; yet as Paul expected to be refreshed by their faith, and not by his giving them spiritual gifts, the sense seems to require that συμπαρακληθῆναι should depend on the first words of ver. 10, ' I desire to see you, that I may impart (ἵνα μεταδῶ) some spiritual gift to you; that is, that I may be comforted (συμπαρακληθῆναι),' &c. It is not a valid objection to this interpretation, that it supposes a change of the construction from the subjunctive to the infinitive. A similar change occurs (probably) in ch. ix. 22, 23 ; and much greater irregularities are not unfrequent in the New Testament.

The word παρακαλέω is used in such various senses, that it is not easy to determine what precise meaning should be attached to it here. It signifies *to call near, to invite,* Acts xxviii. 20, *to call upon,* and more generally to address, either for instruction, admonition, exhortation, confirmation, or consolation. Our translators and the majority of commentators choose the last mentioned sense, and render συμπαρακληθῆναι (ἐμέ) *that I may be comforted.* This is probably too narrow. The word expresses all that excitement and strengthening of faith and pious feeling, as well as consolation, which is wont to flow from the communion of saints. This appears from the context, and especially from the following clause, διὰ τῆς ἐν ἀλλήλοις πίστεως, ὑμῶν τε καὶ ἐμοῦ, *through our mutual faith, as well yours as mine.* The faith of the Romans would not only comfort, but strengthen the apostle ; and his faith could not fail to produce a like effect on them. Ὑμῶν τε καὶ ἐμοῦ are the explanation of the preceding ἐν ἀλλήλοις, and should therefore be in the dative. Fritzsche refers to Luke i. 55, for a similar case of variation in the construction.

VERSE 13. *I would not have you ignorant, brethren ;* a mode of expression which the apostle often adopts, when he would assure his readers of anything, or call their attention to it particularly. *That oftentimes I purposed to come unto you.* In chap. xv. 23, he states that he had cherished this purpose for many years. *And was hindered until now.* Our version renders καί adversatively *but.* This is objected to as unnecessary, especially as καί often introduces a parenthesis ; and such is this clause, because the following ἵνα must depend on προεθέμην of the preceding clause. As in the fifteenth chapter the apostle says, that having no more place in the countries around Greece, he was ready to visit Rome, it is probable that the hindering to which he here refers, was the incessant calls for apostolic labour, which left no time at his command. As, however, his course seems to have been under the guidance of a special providence, Acts xvi. 6, 7, 9, it may be that the Spirit who had forbidden his preaching in Asia, had hitherto forbidden his visiting Rome. *That I may have some fruit among you, as among other gentiles.* Καρπὸν ἔχειν is *to have profit,* or *advantage.* See chap. vi. 21, 22. The profit, however, which Paul desired, was the fruit of his ministry, the conversion or edification of those to whom he preached.

VERSE 14. *Both to Greeks and barbarians, to the wise and to the unwise, I am debtor.* That is, I am under obligation (to preach) to all classes of men. His commission was a general one, confined to no one nation, and to no particular class. Greeks and barbarians, mean all nations ; wise and unwise, mean all classes. Βάρβαρος means properly a foreigner, one of another language, 1 Cor. xiv. 11. Greeks and barbarians, therefore, is equivalent to Greeks and not Greeks, all nations. As the Greeks however, excelled other nations in civilization, the word came to signify *rude, uncultivated;* though even by later writers it is often used in its original sense, and not as a term of reproach. The apostle distinguishes men first as nations, Greeks and not Greeks, and secondly as to culture, wise and unwise. The Romans, whose city was called "an epitome of the world," belonged exclusively neither to the one class nor to the other. Some were wise and some unwise, some Greeks and some barbarians.

VERSE 15. *And so,* or *hence.* That is, since I am bound to all men, Greeks and barbarians, I am ready to preach to you who are at Rome. The clause, τὸ κατ᾽ ἐμὲ πρόθυμον, admits of different interpretations. According to the English version, τὸ κατ᾽ ἐμέ must be taken together ; πρόθυμον is taken as a substantive, and made the nominative to ἐστί. Hence, as much as is in me, (or, as far as I am concerned), there is a readiness, *i. e.* I am ready. Thus Calvin, "Itaque, quantum in me est, paratus sum." This gives a good sense, and is specially suited to the context, as it renders prominent Paul's dependence and submission. He did not direct his own steps. As far as he was concerned, he was willing to preach in Rome ; but whether he should do so or not, rested not with him, but with God. A second explanation makes τὸ κατ᾽ ἐμέ the subject of the sentence, and πρόθυμον the predicate. 'What is in me is ready.' Thus Beza, "Quicquid in me situm est, id promptum est." Or, as Beza also proposes, τὸ κατ᾽ ἐμέ may be taken as a periphrase for ἐγώ, and the clause be translated, "Promptus sum ego." But it is denied that such a periphrase for the personal pronoun ever occurs ; τὰ ὑμέτερα for ὑμεῖς, and τὰ ἐμά for ἐγώ, to which Beza refers, are not parallel. The third explanation, refers τό to πρόθυμον, and makes κατ᾽ ἐμέ equal to ἐμοῦ, 'My readiness, or desire is." Comp. Eph. i. 15, τὴν καθ᾽ ὑμᾶς πίστιν, *your faith;* Acts xvii. 28. τῶν καθ᾽

ὑμᾶς ποιητῶν, xviii. 15, νόμου τοῦ καθ' ὑμᾶς. *To preach the gospel.* The verb εὐαγγελίσασθαι is commonly followed by some word or phrase expressing the subject of the message—kingdom of God, gospel, word of God, Christ. In writing to Christians, who knew what the glad tidings were, the apostles often, as in the present case, use the word absolutely so that the word by itself means, to preach the gospel, &c. See chap. xv. 20 ; Acts xiv. 7 ; Gal. iv. 13.

VERSE 16. *For I am not ashamed of the Gospel of Christ.** This he assigns as the reason why he was ready to preach even at Rome. To the wise of this world the gospel was foolishness, 1 Cor. i. 23, yet Paul was not ashamed of it, but was ready among the wise and unwise to preach Christ and him crucified. The reason of this regard for the gospel is stated in the following clause : *For it is the power of God unto salvation.* By δύναμις Θεοῦ, some understand *great power*, in accordance with an assumed Hebrew idiom, agreeably to which 'mountains of God' mean great mountains, 'wind of God' great wind, 'zeal of God' great zeal, &c. But the existence of such an idiom in the Hebrew is very doubtful, and its application to this passage is unnatural and unnecessary. Others make Θεοῦ a mere qualifying genitive, 'power of God,' meaning 'divinely powerful.' Beza's explanation is, "Organon Dei vere potens et efficax." The gospel is then declared to be that through which God exercises his power. Most commonly Θεοῦ is taken as the genitive of the Author, and power of God is made to mean power derived from God. There are two things then asserted of the gospel, first that it is powerful, and secondly that it is from God. Comp. 1 Cor. i. 18, 24. The main idea, however, is that expressed by Beza, The gospel is that in which God works, which he renders efficacious—εἰς σωτηρίαν, *unto salvation.* That is, it is efficacious to save. The nature of the salvation here intended is to be learned from the nature of the gospel. It is deliverance from sin and its punishment, and admission into eternal life and blessedness. This is what no means of man's devising, no efforts of human wisdom or human power could effect for any human being. The gospel effects it παντὶ τῷ πιστεύοντι, *for every one that believes.* Emphasis must be laid on both the members of this clause. The gospel is thus efficacious to *every one*, without distinction between Jew and gentile, Greek or barbarian, wise or unwise ; and it is efficacious to every one that *believes*, not to every one who is circumcised, or baptized, or who obeys the law, but to every one who believes, that is, who receives and confides in Jesus Christ as he is offered in the gospel. We have here the two great doctrines set forth in this epistle. First, salvation is by faith ; and secondly, it is universally applicable, to the Greek as well as to the Jew. The faith of which the apostle here speaks includes a firm persuasion of the truth, and a reliance or trust on the object of faith. Sometimes the one, sometimes the other of these ideas is expressed by the word, and very often both are united. The meaning of the term is not to be determined so much by philosophical analysis as by scriptural usage. For the question is not what is the abstract nature of the act of believing, philosophically considered, but what act or state of mind is expressed by the words πιστεύειν and πίστις in the various constructions in which they occur. It is rare indeed that the state of mind

---

* The words τοῦ Χριστοῦ are omitted in the MSS. A. B. C. D. E. G. 17. 67. in many of the versions and Fathers, and are rejected by Mill, Bengel, Griesbach, Lachmann, Tischendorf, and others. They are found in the Complutensian text, and are defended by Wetstein and Matthæi.

expressed by any word is so simple as not to admit of being resolved into various elements. The exercise expressed by the world *love*, for example, includes the perception of agreeable qualities in its object, a judgment of the mind as to their nature, a delight in them, and a desire for their enjoyment. And these differ specifically in their nature, according to the nature of the thing loved. It is not to any one of these elements of the complex affection that the word *love* is applied, but to the state of mind as a whole. So also with the word *faith*, the exercise which it expresses includes a perception of its object and its qualities, that is, it includes knowledge ; secondly, an assent of the mind to the truth of the thing believed, and very often a reliance or trust on the object of faith. Assent is therefore but one of the elements of saving faith, that is, it is but one of the constituents of that state of mind which, in a multitude of cases, is in the Bible expressed by the word. And as the great object of interest to Christians is not a philosophical definition of a word, but a knowledge of the sense in which it is used in the word of God, we must recur to the usage of the Scriptures themselves to determine what that faith is which is connected with salvation.

There is no doubt that πιστεύειν is often used to express mere assent. It means—to receive as true, to be persuaded of the truth of any thing. Hence πίστις is persuasion of the truth. When πιστεύειν has this simple meaning, it is commonly followed by the accusative, as in 1 Cor. xi. 18; John xi. 26; or by the dative, Mark xvi. 13, οὐδὲ ἐκείνοις ἐπίστευσαν, John v. 46 ; or by ὅτι, Mark xi. 23, Rom. x. 9. Yet in these cases the word often expresses confidence or trust, as well as assent ; πιστεύειν Θεῷ is in many connections, to confide in God ; as Acts xxvii. 25, πιστεύω γὰρ τῷ Θεῷ ὅτι οὕτως ἔσται.

When πιστεύειν is followed by ἐπί with an accusative, as in Rom. iv. 5, πιστεύοντι ἐπὶ τὸν δικαιοῦντα, or by ἐπί with a dative, as Rom. ix. 33, ὁ πιστεύων ἐπ᾽ αὐτῷ, 1 Tim. i. 16, it commonly means *to trust, to believe upon, to confide in.* It has the same sense when followed by εἰς, as in John xiv. i., πιστεύετε εἰς τὸν Θεόν, καὶ εἰς ἐμὲ πιστεύετε, xvi. 9, Rom. x. 14; Gal. ii. 16, and often elsewhere. The construction with ἐν is less common ; see, however, Mark i. 15, μετανοεῖτε, καὶ πιστεύετε ἐν τῷ εὐαγγελίῳ; comp. Gal. v. 10, πέποιθα ἐν Κυρίῳ, 2 Thess. iii. 4.

The substantive πίστις also in various constructions signifies reliance, or trust ; thus when followed by εἰς, as in Acts xx. 21, πίστιν τὴν εἰς τὸν Κύριον ἡμῶν, xxiv. 24; xxvi. 18 ; by ἐπί, with the accusative, Heb. vi. 1 ; by πρός, as 1 Thess. i. 8, πίστις ὑμῶν ἡ πρὸς τὸν Θεόν; by ἐν Rom. iii. 25, διὰ τῆς πίστεως ἐν τῷ αὐτοῦ αἵματι, comp. Gal. iii. 26; 1 Tim. iii. 13, πίστει τῇ ἐν Χριστῷ, 2 Tim. iii. 15 ; or by the genitive, as in Rom. iii, 22, 26, Gal. ii. 16, iii. 22, and often. That faith, therefore, which is connected with salvation, includes knowledge, that is, a perception of the truth and its qualities ; assent, or the persuasion of the truth of the object of faith ; and trust, or reliance. The exercise, or state of mind expressed by the word *faith*, as used in the Scriptures, is not mere assent, or mere trust, it is the intelligent perception, reception, and reliance on the truth, as revealed in the gospel.

To the Jew first, and also to the Greek. To render πρῶτον (*first*), here *especially*, would make the apostle teach that the gospel was peculiarly adapted to the Jews, or specially designed for them. But he frequently asserts that this is not the case, chap. iii. 9, 22, 29; x. 12. Πρῶτον, therefore, must have reference to time, 'To the Jew in the first instance, and then to the Greek.' Salvation, as our Saviour said to the woman of Samaria, is of the Jews. Of them the Messiah came, to them the gospel was first preached, and by them preached to the Gentiles. The apostle often, as in the present instance, says Jews and Greeks, for Jews and Gentiles, because the Greeks were the Gentiles with whom, at that period, the Jews were most familiar.

VERSE 17. The reason why the gospel has the efficacy ascribed to it in the preceding verse, is not because of its pure morality, or because it reveals and confirms a future state of retribution, but because *the righteousness of God* is therein revealed. As this is one of those expressions which are employed to convey ideas peculiar to the gospel, its meaning is to be learned not merely from the signification of the words, but from parallel passages, and from the explanations given in the gospel itself of the whole subject to which it relates. That δικαιοσύνη cannot here be understood of a divine attribute, such as rectitude, justice, goodness,· or veracity, is obvious, because it is a δικαιοσύνη ἐκ πίστεως, *a righteousness which is by faith, i.e.*, attained by faith, of which the apostle speaks. Besides, it is elsewhere said to be without law, Rom. iii. 21, to be a gift, v. 17, not to be our own, x. 3, to be from God, Philip.· iii. 9. These and similar forms of expression are inconsistent with the assumption that the apostle is speaking of a divine attribute. The righteousness of God, therefore, must mean either the righteousness of which God is the author, or which he approves. Luther, Calvin, and many others, prefer the latter. "Die Gerechtigkeit die vor Gott gilt," is Luther's version. Calvin says, "Justitiam Dei accipio, quæ apud Dei tribunal approbatur." Beza, Reiche, De Wette, Rückert, and others, prefer the former. These ideas are not incompatible. This righteousness is at once a δικαιοσύνη ἡ ἐκ Θεοῦ, Philip. iii. 9; and a δικαιοσύνη παρὰ τῷ Θεῷ, Rom. ii. 13; iii. 20; Gal. iii. 11. The gospel reveals a righteousness, which God gives, and which he approves ; it is a righteousness, "qua quisquis donatus est, sistitur coram Deo, sanctus, inculpatus, et nullius labis possit postulari." *Beza.*

This interpretation is confirmed by all that the Scriptures teach respecting the manner of our justification before God. The Bible represents God in the character of a moral governor or judge. Man is placed under a law which is the rule of his duty, and the standard by which he is to be judged. This law may be variously revealed, but it is ever substantially the same, having the same precepts, the same sanction, and the same promises. Those who comply with the demands of this law are δίκαιοι, *righteous ;* those who break the law are ἄδικοι, *unrighteous ;* to pronounce one righteous is δικαιοῦν, *to justify ;* the righteousness itself, or integrity which the law demands is δικαιοσύνη. Those who are righteous, or who have the righteousness which the law requires, or who are justified,· have a title to the favour of God.

Now, nothing is more clearly taught in the Scriptures than that no man in himself is righteous in the sight of God. "There is none righteous, no not one ; for all have sinned and come short of the glory of God." It is no less clearly taught that no man can make himself righteous ; that is, he cannot attain the righteousness which the law demands, and which is necessary to his acceptance with God. The reason is, that the law demands perfect obedience, which no one has rendered, or can render. It is hence plain that by the works of the law no flesh can be justified before God. Rom. iii. 20; Gal. ii. 16 ; δικαιοσύνη is not ἐκ νόμου, Gal. iii. 21, or διὰ νόμου, ii. 21, or ἐξ ἔργων, ii. 16. Men are not justified ἰδίᾳ δικαιοσύνῃ by their own righteousness. Rom. x. 3. And yet righteousness is absolutely necessary to our justification and salvation. Such a righteousness the gospel reveals ; a righteousness which is χωρὶς νόμου, *without the law ;* which is not of works ; a δικαιοσύνη πίστεως or ἐκ πίστεως, *which is by faith ;* a righteousness which is not our own, Philip. iii. 9 ; which is the gift of God, Rom. v. 17 ; which is ἐκ Θεοῦ *from God ;* which is imputed χωρὶς ἔργων without works. Christ is our righteousness, 1 Cor. i. 30, or we are righteous before God in him. 2 Cor. v. 21.

From this contrast between a righteousness which is our own, which is of works, and that which is not our own, which is of God, from God, the gift of God, it is plain that the δικαιοσύνη Θεοῦ of which the apostle here speaks, is that δικαιοσύνη by which we are made δίκαιοι παρὰ τῷ Θεῷ ; it is a righteousness which he gives and which he approves. This is the interpretation which is given substantially by all the modern commentators of note, as Tholuck, Reiche, Fritzsche, Rückert, Koellner, De Wette, &c., however much they may differ as to other points. "Alle Erklärungen," says De Wette, "welche das Moment der Zurechnung übersehen, und das thun besonders die katholischen, auch die des Grotius, sind falsch." That is, "All interpretations which overlook the idea of imputation, as is done in the explanations given by the Romanists, and also in that of Grotius, are false."

The nature of this righteousness, it is one great design of this epistle, and of the whole gospel to unfold. This, therefore, is not the place to enter fully into the examination of that point ; it will present itself at every step of our progress. It is sufficient here to specify the three general views of the nature of that righteousness by which men are justified before God. The first may be called the Pelagian, according to which the apostle teaches that righteousness cannot be attained by obedience to the ritual law of the Jews, but consists in works morally good. The second view is that of the Romanists, who teach that the works meant to be excluded from our justification are legal works ; works done without grace and before regeneration ; but the righteousness which makes us just before God, is that inherent righteousness, or spiritual excellence which is obtained by the aid of divine grace. The third view, which is the common doctrine of Protestant churches is, that the righteousness for which we are justified is neither anything done by us nor wrought in us, but something done for us and imputed to us. It is the work of Christ, what he did and suffered to satisfy the demands of the law. Hence not merely external or ceremonial works are excluded as the ground of justification ; but works of righteousness, all works of whatever kind or degree of excellence. Hence this righteousness is not our own. It is nothing that we have either wrought ourselves, or that inheres in us. Hence Christ is said to be our righteousness ; and we are said to be justified by his blood, his death, his obedience ; we are righteous in him, and are justified by him or in his name, or for his sake. The righteousness of God, therefore, which the gospel reveals, and by which we are constituted righteous, is the perfect righteousness of Christ which completely meets and answers all the demands of that law to which all men are subject, and which all have broken.

This righteousness is said in the text to be *of faith.* It is obvious that the words ἐκ πίστεως are not to be connected with ἀποκαλύπτεται. They must be connected either directly or indirectly with δικαιοσύνη. It is either δικαιοσύνη ἐκ πίστεως ἀποκαλύπτεται, *righteousness by faith is revealed ;*

or διχαιοσύνη ἀποχαλύπτεται ἐχ πίστεως οὖσα, *righteousness is revealed, being of faith,* i.e., which is by faith. Not an excellence of which faith is the germinating principle, or which consists in faith, because this is inconsistent with all those representations which show that this righteousness is not subjective.

The meaning of the words εἰς πίστιν in the formula ἐχ πίστεως εἰς πίστιν, *from faith to faith,* is very doubtful. They must be explained in a manner consistent with their connection with διχαιοσύνη. It is a righteousness which is of faith to faith. Now it cannot be said that our justification depends on our believing first the Old Testament, and then the New, which is the interpretation of Theodoret—δεῖ γὰρ πιστεῦσαι τοῖς προφήταις, χαὶ δι᾽ ἐχείνων εἰς τὴν τοῦ εὐαγγελίου πίστιν ποδηγηθῆναι ; nor does it seem to suit this connection to make the phrase in question express a progress from a weak or imperfect faith to that which is more perfect. This however is a very generally received interpretation. Calvin says, " Quum initio gustamus evangelium, laetam quidem et exporrectam nobis cernimus Dei frontem, sed eminus ; quo magis augescit pietatis eruditio, velut propiore accessu clarius ac magis familiariter Dei gratiam perspicimus." The sense is however perfectly clear and good, if the phrase is explained to mean, faith alone. As " death unto death" and " life unto life" are intensive, so " faith unto faith" may mean, entirely of faith. Our justification is by faith alone : works form no part of that righteousness in which we can stand before the tribunal of God. " Dicit," says Bengel, " fidem meram ; namque justitia ex fide subsistit in fide, sine operibus. . . . . Fides, inquit Paulus, manet fides ; fides est prora et puppis, apud Judæos et Gentiles, etiam apud Paulum, usque ad ipsam ejus consummationem." Most of the modern commentators regard εἰς in the words εἰς πίστιν, as indicating the terminus. Righteousness is from faith and unto faith, comes to it. This makes πίστιν here virtually equivalent to πιστεύοντας, as in chap. iii. 22, the διχαιοσύνη Θεοῦ is said to be εἰς πάντας τοὺς πιστεύοντας. Righteousness then is by faith and unto faith, *i.e.* is granted unto or bestowed upon believers.

This doctrine of the apostle, that the righteousness which is unto life is to be obtained by faith, he confirms by a reference to Hab. ii. 4, where it is said, ὁ δὲ δίχαιος ἐχ πίστεως, ζήσεται, *he that is righteous by faith, shall live ;* or, *the righteous shall live by faith.* The connection of ἐχ πίστεως with δίχαιος is certainly best suited to the apostle's object, which is to show that righteousness is by faith ; but in either construction the sense is substantially the same. Salvation is by faith. In the Hebrew also, either construction is allowable, as the words are " The righteous in his faith shall live." The Masoretic accentuation however connects, as Paul does, the first two words together, ' The righteous in his faith shall live.' *Shall live,* shall attain that life which Christ gives, which is spiritual, blessed, and everlasting ; comp. chap. v. 17 ; viii. 13 ; x. 3. This passage is cited in confirmation of the apostle's own doctrine, and is peculiarly pertinent as it shows that under the old dispensation as well as under the new, the favour of God was to be secured by faith.

DOCTRINE.

1. The apostolic office, except as to what was peculiar and extraordinary, being essentially the same with the ministerial office in general, Paul teaches, 1. That ministers are the servants of Christ, deriving their authority from him, and not from the people; 2. That their

calling is to preach the gospel, to which all other avocations must be made subordinate ; 3. That the object of their appointment is to bring men to the obedience of faith ; 4. That their field is all nations ; 5. That the design of all is to honour Christ ; it is for his name, vers. 1—5.

2. The gospel is contained in its rudiments in the Old Testament. It is the soul of the old dispensation, ver. 2.

3. Christ is the Alpha and Omega of the Gospel. In stating the substance of the gospel, Paul says, ' It concerns Jesus Christ,' ver. 3.

4. Christ is at once God and man ; the son of David and the son of God, vers. 3, 4.

5. Christ is called the Son of God in reference to his Divine nature, and on account of the relation in which, as God, he stands to the Father. The name, therefore, is expressive of his Divine character, vers. 3, 4.

6. He is the proper object of prayer, and the source of spiritual blessings, ver. 7.

7. He is the Mediator through whom our prayers and thanksgiving must be presented to God, ver. 8.

8. God is the source of all spiritual good ; is to be worshipped in spirit, and agreeably to the gospel ; and his providence is to be recognised in reference to the most ordinary affairs of life, vers. 8—10.

9. Ministers are not a class of men exalted above the people, and independent of them for spiritual benefits, but are bound to seek, as well as to impart good, in all their intercourse with those to whom they are sent, vers. 11, 12.

10. Ministers are bound to preach the gospel to all men, rich as well as poor, wise as well as unwise ; for it is equally adapted to the wants of all, vers. 14, 15.

11. The salvation of men, including the pardon of their sins and the moral renovation of their hearts, can be effected by the gospel alone. The wisdom of men, during four thousand years previous to the advent of Christ, failed to discover any adequate means for the attainment of either of these objects ; and those who, since the advent, have neglected the gospel, have been equally unsuccessful, ver. 16, &c.

12. The power of the gospel lies not in its pure theism, or perfect moral code, but in the Cross, in the doctrine of justification by faith in a crucified Redeemer, ver. 17, &c.

REMARKS.

1. Ministers should remember that they are "separated unto the gospel," and that any occupation which, by its demands upon their attention, or from its influence on their character or feelings, interferes with their devotion to this object, is for them wrong, ver. 1.

2. If Jesus Christ is the great subject of the gospel, it is evident that we cannot have right views of the one, without having correct opinions respecting the other. What think ye of Christ ? cannot be a minor question. To be Christians, we must recognise him as the Messiah, or Son of David ; and as Divine, or the Son of God; we must be able to pray to him, to look for blessings from him, and recognise him as the Mediator between God and man, vers. 1—8.

3. Christians should remember that they are *saints;* that is, persons separated from the world and consecrated to God. They therefore cannot serve themselves or the world, without a dereliction of their character.

They are saints, because called and made such of God. To all such, grace and peace are secured by the mediation of Christ, and the promise of God, ver. 7.

4. In presenting truth, everything consistent with fidelity should be done to conciliate the confidence and kind feelings of those to whom it is addressed ; and everything avoided, which tends to excite prejudice against the speaker or his message. Who more faithful than Paul ? Yet who more anxious to avoid offence ? Who more solicitous to present the truth, not in its most irritating form, but in the manner best adapted to gain for it access to the unruffled minds of his readers ? vers. 8—14.

5. As all virtues, according to the Christian system, are graces (gifts), they afford matter for thanksgiving, but never for self-complacency, ver. 8.

6. The intercourse of Christians should be desired, and made to result in edification, by their mutual faith, ver. 12.

7. He who rejects the doctrine of justification by faith, rejects the gospel. His whole method of salvation, and system of religion, must be different from those of the apostles, ver. 17.

8. Whether we be wise or unwise, moral or immoral, in the sight of men, orthodox or heterodox in our opinions, unless we are believers, unless we cordially receive " the righteousness which is of God," as the ground of acceptance, we have no part or lot in the salvation of the gospel, ver. 17.

ROMANS I. 18—32.

ANALYSIS.

The apostle having stated that the only righteousness available in the sight of God is that which is obtained by faith, proceeds to prove that such is the case. This proof required that he should, in the first instance, demonstrate that the righteousness which is of the law, or of works, was insufficient for the justification of a sinner. This he does, first in reference to the Gentiles, chap. i. 18—32 ; and then in relation to the Jews, chap. ii., iii. 1—20. The residue of this chapter then is designed to prove that the Gentiles are justly exposed to condemnation. The apostle thus argues: God is just; his displeasure against sin (which is its punishment) is clearly revealed, ver. 18. This principle is assumed by the apostle, as the foundation of his whole argument. If this be granted, it follows that all who are chargeable with either impiety or immorality are exposed to the wrath of God, and cannot claim his favour on the ground of their own character or conduct. That the Gentiles are justly chargeable with both impiety and immorality, he thus proves. They have ever enjoyed such a revelation of the divine character as to render them inexcusable, vers. 19, 20. Notwithstanding this opportunity of knowing God, they neither worshipped nor served him, but gave themselves up to all forms of idolatry. This is the height of impiety, vers. 21—23. In consequence of this desertion of God, he gave them up to the evil of their own hearts, so that they sank into all manner of debasing crimes. The evidences of this corruption of morals were so painfully obvious, that Paul merely appeals to the knowledge which all his readers possessed of the fact, vers. 24—31. These various crimes they do not commit ignorantly ; they are aware of their ill-desert ; and yet they not only commit them themselves, but encourage others in the same course, ver. 32.

The inference from the established sinfulness of the Gentile world, Paul does not draw until he has substantiated the same charge against the Jews. He then says, since all are sinners before God, no flesh can be justified by the works of the law, chap. iii. 20.

COMMENTARY.

VERSE 18. Ἀποκαλύπτεται γὰρ ὀργὴ Θεοῦ ἀπ᾽ οὐρανοῦ. *For the wrath of God is revealed from heaven.* The apostle's object is to prove the doctrine of the preceding verse, viz., that righteousness is by faith. To do this it was necessary to show that men in themselves are exposed to condemnation, or are destitute of any righteousness which can satisfy the demands of God. His argument is, God is just ; he is determined to punish sin, and as all men are sinners, all are exposed to punishment. Hence this verse is connected by γάρ to the preceding one. Men must be justified by faith, *for* the wrath of God is revealed, &c.

The wrath of God is his punitive justice, his determination to punish sin. The passion which is called anger or wrath, and which is always mixed more or less with malignity in the human breast, is of course infinitely removed from what the word imports when used in reference to God. Yet as anger in man leads to the infliction of evil on its object, the word is, agreeably to a principle which pervades the Scriptures, applied to the calm and undeviating purpose of the Divine mind, which secures the connection between sin and misery, with the same general uniformity that any other law in the physical or moral government of God operates.

Is revealed. Ἀποκαλύπτω is properly to *uncover,* to bring to light, and hence to make known, whether by direct communication, or in some other way. A thing is said to be revealed, when it becomes known from its effects. It is thus that the thoughts of the heart, the arm of the Lord, and wrath of God are said to be "revealed." It is not necessary therefore to infer from the use of this word, that the apostle meant to intimate that the purpose of God to punish sin was made known by any special revelation. That purpose is manifested in various ways ; by the actual punishment of sin, by the inherent tendency of moral evil to produçe misery, by the voice of conscience. Nor do the words "from heaven" imply any extraordinary mode of communication. They are added because God dwells in heaven, whence all exhibitions of his character and purposes are said to proceed. It is however implied in the whole form of expression, that this revelation is clear and certain. Men know the righteous judgment of God ; they know that those who commit sin are worthy of death. As this is an ultimate truth, existing in every man's consciousness, it is properly assumed, and made the basis of the apostle's argument.

This displeasure of God is revealed *against all ungodliness and unrighteousness of men ;* that is, against all impiety towards God (ἀσέβεια), and injustice towards men (ἀδικία). This distinction is kept up in the following part of the chapter, in which the apostle proves first the impiety, and then the gross immorality of the heathen. *Who hold the truth in unrighteousness.* The word ἀλήθεια is used in the Scriptures in a more comprehensive sense than our word *truth.* It often means what is right, as well as what is true ; and is therefore often used in antithesis to ἀδικία, *unrighteousness,* as in Rom. ii. 8 ; see Gal. iii. 1 ; v. 7. It is used especially of moral and

religious truth ; see John iii. 21 ; viii. 32 ; 2 Cor. iv. 2 ; 2 Thess. ii. 12.
It is therefore equivalent to true religion, that is, what is true and right, in
reference to God and duty.   As κατέχειν sometimes means to have in the
sense of possessing, as in 1 Cor. vii. 30, this clause may be rendered, ' Who
have the truth, together with unrighteousness ;' *i.e.*, although they possess
the truth, are unrighteous.   Comp. James ii. 1, μὴ ἐν προσωπολημψίαις ἔχετε
τὴν πίστιν.   The sentiment is then the same as in ver. 21, where the
heathen are said to know God, and yet to act wickedly.   But as κατέχειν
also means to detain, to repress or hinder, 2 Thess. ii. 6, 7, the passage
may be translated, Who hinder or oppose the truth.   The great majority
of commentators are in favour of this latter interpretation.   The words ἐν
ἀδικίᾳ may either express the means of this opposition, and be rendered,
through unrighteousness ; or they may be taken adverbially, Who unjustly,
or wickedly oppose the truth.   The former is to be preferred.

VERSE 19.   That this opposition is wicked, because inexcusable on the
plea of ignorance, is proved in this and the following verses.   They
wickedly oppose the truth, because the knowledge of God is manifest
among them.   Agreeably to this explanation, this verse is connected with
the immediately preceding clause.   It may however refer to the general
sentiment of ver. 18.   God will punish the impiety and unrighteousness of
men, because he has made himself known to them.   The former method
is to be preferred as more in accordance with the apostle's manner and
more consistent with the context, inasmuch as he goes on to prove that the
impiety of the heathen is inexcusable.   *Since that which may be known of
God, is manifest in them.*   This version is not in accordance with the
meaning of γνωστόν, which always in the Bible means, what is known, not
what may be known.   Besides, the English version seems to imply too
much ; for the apostle does not mean to say that everything that may be
known concerning God was revealed to the heathen, but simply that they
had such a knowledge of him as rendered their impiety inexcusable.   We
find γνωστός used in the sense of γνωτός, *known*, Acts i. 19 ; ii. 14 ; xv. 18 ;
γνωστὰ ἀπ' αἰῶνός ἐστι τῷ Θεῷ πάντα τὰ ἔργα αὐτοῦ ; and often elsewhere.
Hence τὸ γνωστόν is = γνῶσις, as in Gen. ii. 9, γνωστὸν τοῦ καλοῦ καὶ τοῦ
πονηροῦ.   The knowledge of God does not mean simply a knowledge that
there is a God, but, as appears from what follows, a knowledge of his
nature and attributes, his eternal power and Godhead, ver. 20, and his
justice, ver. 32.   Φανερόν ἐστιν ἐν αὐτοῖς, may be rendered, either is manifest
among them, or *in* them.   If the former translation be adopted, it is not
to be understood as declaring that certain men, the Pythagoreans, Pla-
tonists, and Stoics, as Grotius says, had this knowledge ; but that it was
a common revelation, accessible, manifest to all.   *In them*, however, here
more properly means, in their minds.   " In ipsorum animis," says Beza,
"quia haec Dei notitia recondita est in intimis mentis penetralibus, ut, velint
nolint idololatriae, quoties sese adhibent in consilium, toties a seipsis redar-
guantur."   It is not of a mere external revelation of which the apostle is
speaking, but of that evidence of the being and perfections of God which
every man has in the constitution of his own nature, and in virtue of which
he is competent to apprehend the manifestations of God in his works.   *For
God hath revealed to them*, viz. the knowledge of himself.   This knowledge is a revelation ; it is the manifestation of God in his works, and in
the constitution of our nature.   " Quod dicit," says Calvin, " Deum mani-
festasse, sensus est, ideo conditum esse hominem, ut spectator sit fabriæ
mundi ; ideo datos ei oculos, ut intuitu tam pulchræ imaginis, ad auctorem

ipsum feratur." God therefore has never left himself without a witness. His existence and perfections have ever been so manifested that his rational creatures are bound to acknowledge and worship him as the true and only God. VERSE 20. This verse is a confirmation and amplification of the preceding, inasmuch as it proves that God does manifest himself to men, shows how this manifestation is made, and draws the inference that men are, in virtue of this revelation, inexcusable for their impiety. The argument is, God has manifested the knowledge of himself to men, for the invisible things of him, that is, his eternal power and Godhead, are, since the creation, clearly seen, being understood by his works ; they are therefore without excuse. *The invisible things of him.* By the invisible things of God Theodoret says we are to understand creation, providence, and the divine judgments ; Theophylact understands them to refer to his goodness, wisdom, power, and majesty. Between these interpretations the moderns are divided. The great majority prefer the latter, which is obviously the better suited to the context, because the works of God are expressed afterwards by ποιήματα, and because the invisible things are those which are manifested by his works, and are explained by the terms "power and Godhead." The subsequent clause, ἡ τε ἀΐδιος αὐτοῦ δύναμις καὶ θειότης, is in apposition with and an explanation of the former one. The particle τέ followed by καί, serves then, as Tholuck remarks, to the partition of ἀόρατα into the two ideas δύναμις and θειότης, and not to annex a distinct idea, as though the meaning were, 'and also his power and Godhead.' The power of God is more immediately manifested in his works ; but not his power alone, but his divine excellence in general, which is expressed by θειότης, from θεῖος. Θεότης, from Θεός, on the other hand, expresses the being, rather than the excellence of God. The latter is Godhead; the former, divinity, a collective term for all the divine perfections.

This divine revelation has been made ἀπὸ κτίσεως κόσμου, *from the creation of the world,* not *by* the creation; for κτίσις here is the act of creation, and not the thing created ; and the means by which the revelation is made, is expressed immediately by the words τοῖς ποιήμασι, which would then be redundant. The ποιήματα τοῦ Θεοῦ, in this connection, are the things made by God, rather than the things done by him. The apostle says the ἀόρατα καθορᾶται, *the unseen things are seen,* because they are perceived by the mind ; νοούμενα being understood by means of the things made. *So that they are inexcusable.* These words are, by Griesbach, Knapp, and others, made to depend on the last clause of ver. 19 ; and then the interpretation of Beza and the elder Calvinists would be the most natural. God has revealed the knowledge of himself to men, *in order that* they might be without excuse. But this, to say the least, is unnecessary. The connection with καθορᾶται is perfectly natural. 'The perfections of God, being understood by his works, are seen, *so that* men are without excuse.' Paul does not here teach that it is the design of God, in revealing himself to men, to render their opposition inexcusable, but rather, since this revelation has been made, they have in fact no apology for their ignorance and neglect of God. Though the revelation of God in his works is sufficient to render men inexcusable, it does not follow that it is sufficient to lead men, blinded by sin, to a saving knowledge of himself. As Paul says of the law, that it was weak through the flesh, that is, insufficient on account of our corruption, so it may be said of the light of nature, that, although sufficient in itself as a revelation, it is not sufficient, considering the indisposition and inattention of men to divine things. " Sit haec distinctio," says Calvin, "demonstratio Dei, qua gloriam suam in creaturis perspicuam facit, esse, quantum ad lucem suam, satis evidentem ; quantum ad nostram cæcitatem, non adeo sufficere. Cæterum non ita cæci sumus, ut ignorantiam possimus prætexere, quin perversitatis arguamur."

VERSE 21. *Since knowing God.* The most natural and obvious connection of this verse is with the last clause of the preceding, ' Men are without excuse, since, although they knew God, they worshipped him not as God.' This connection, moreover, is in accordance with the apostle's manner, who often establishes a proposition, which is itself an inference, by a new process of argument. Thus in the present instance, in vers. 19, 20, he proved that the heathen had a knowledge of God which rendered them inexcusable, and then the fact that they were without excuse, is proved by showing that they did not act in accordance with the truth. Rückert, however, who is followed by Tholuck, considering that the apostle's object is to show that the heathen wickedly oppose the truth, as stated in ver. 18 ; and that this proof consists of two parts—first, the heathen had the knowledge of the truth, vers. 19, 20 ; and secondly, that they did not act according to it, vers. 21—23; assumes that the connection is rather with the last clause of ver. 18, and that something is implied here which is not expressed, and that the logical reference of διότι is to this omitted thought. 'The heathen are without excuse, *and wickedly oppose the truth,* since, although they knew God, they glorified him not as God.' This sense is good enough, but it is a forced and unnatural interpretation.

The apostle having shewn in ver. 19, that the knowledge of God was revealed to men, has no hesitation in saying that the heathen knew God ; which does not mean merely that they had the opportunity of knowing him, but that in the constitution of their own nature, and in the works of creation, they actually possessed an intelligible revelation of the Divine existence and perfections. This revelation was indeed generally so neglected, that men knew not what it taught. Still they had the knowledge, in the same sense that those who have the Bible are said to have the knowledge of the will of God, however much they may neglect and disregard it. In both cases there is knowledge presented, and a revelation made, and in both ignorance is without excuse. As there is no apology for the impiety of the heathen to be found in any unavoidable ignorance, their idolatry was the fruit of depravity. The apostle therefore says, that although they knew God, *they glorified* him not *as God,* *neither were thankful* to him. Δοξάζειν is to ascribe honour to any one, to praise, and also to honour, to make glorious, or cause that others should honour any one. Men are said to glorify God either when they ascribe glory to him, or when they so act as to lead others to honour him. In the present case, the former idea is expressed by the word. They did not reverence and worship God as their God ; neither did they refer to him the blessings which they daily received at his hands.

Instead of thus rendering unto God the homage and gratitude which are his due, *they became vain in their imaginations.* *Vain* (ἐματαιώθησαν) that is, according to constant scriptural usage, became both foolish and wicked. *Vain* conversation is corrupt conversation, 1 Pet. i. 18 ; and *vanity* is wickedness, Eph. iv. 17. These words are all frequently used in reference to idolatry, as idols are in the Bible often called μάταια *vanities.* In *their imaginations,* διαλογισμοῖς properly *thoughts ;* but usually, in the New Testament, with the implication of evil; evil thoughts or machinations. Here the word also has a bad sense. The thoughts of the heathen concerning God were perverted and corrupt thoughts. The whole clause therefore means, that the heathen, in refusing to recognize the true God, entertained foolish and wicked thoughts of the Divine Being ; that is, they sank into the folly and sin of idolatry. *And their foolish heart was darkened;* they lost the light of divine knowledge ; ἀσύνετος, destitute of σύνεσις understanding, insight into the nature of divine things. The consequence of this want of divine knowledge was darkness. The word καρδία, *heart*, stands for the whole soul. Hence men are said to understand with the heart, Matt. xiii. 15 ; to believe with the heart, Rom. x. 10 ; the heart is said to be enlightened with knowledge, 2 Cor. iv. 6 ; and the eyes of the heart are said to be opened, Eph. i. 8. The word διανοία *mind*, is used with the same latitude, not only for the intellect, but also for the seat of the affections, as in Eph. ii. 3, we read of the desires of the mind. It is not merely intellectual darkness or ignorance which the apostle describes in this verse, but the whole moral state. We find throughout the Scriptures the idea of foolishness and sin, of wisdom and piety, intimately connected. In the language of the Bible, a fool is an impious man ; the wise are the pious, those who fear God ; foolishness is sin ; understanding is religion. The folly and darkness of which the apostle here speaks are therefore expressive of want of divine knowledge, which is both the effect and cause of moral depravity.

VERSE 22. *Professing themselves to be wise,* Φάσκοντες εἶναι σοφοί, (for σοφούς, by attraction). *Saying* in the sense of pretending to be. The more they boasted of their wisdom, the more conspicuous became their folly. What greater folly can there be, than to worship beasts rather than God ? To this the apostle refers in the next verse.

VERSE 23. They became fools, *and exchanged the glory of the incorruptible God for the likeness of the image of corruptible man.* Herein consisted their amazing folly, that they, as rational beings, should worship the creature in preference to the Creator. The common construction of the verb ἀλλάσσειν in Greek when it means to exchange, is either τί τινος, or τί ἀντί τινος; but the apostle imitates the Hebrew construction, הֵמִיר בְּ, which by the LXX. is rendered ἀλλάσσειν ἐν, as in Ps. cvi. 20. The sense is not that they change one thing into another, but that they exchanged one thing for another. *The glory,* a collective term for all the divine perfections. They exchanged the substance for the image, the substantial or real divine glories for the *likeness of an image of corruptible man,* i.e., an image like to corruptible man. The contrast is not merely between God and man, or between the incorruptible, imperishable, eternal God, and frail man, but between this incorruptible God and the image of a man. It was not, however, in the worship of the images of men only that the degradation of the heathen was manifested, for they paid religious homage to birds, beasts, and reptiles. In such idolatry the idol or animal was, with regard to the majority, the ultimate object of worship. Some professed to regard the visible image as a mere symbol of the real object of their adoration ; while others believed that the gods in some way filled these idols, and operated through them ; and others again, that the universal principle of being was reverenced under these manifestations. The Scriptures take no account of these destinctions. All who bowed down to stocks and stones are denounced as worshipping gods which their own hands had made ; and idolatry is made to include not merely the worship of false gods, but the worship of the true God by images. The universal prevalence of idolatry

among the heathens, notwithstanding the revelation which God had
made of himself in his works, is the evidence which Paul adduces to
prove that they are ungodly, and consequently exposed to that wrath which
is revealed against all ungodliness. In the following verses, to the end of
the chapter, he shows that they are unrighteous ; that as the consequence
of their departure from God, they sank into the grossest vices.

VERSE 24. *Wherefore also he gave them, in their lusts, unto uncleanness.*
The most natural construction of this passage is to connect εἰς ἀκαθαρσίαν
with παρέδωκεν, *he gave up unto uncleanness.* We have the same construction
in vers. 26, 28, and frequently elsewhere. To construct παρέδωκεν with ἐν
ταῖς ἐπιθυμίαις, as Beza and others do, gives indeed a good sense, *He gave
them up to their desires unto uncleanness*, *i.e.*, so that they became unclean,
but is opposed to the constant usage of the New Testament, inasmuch as
παραδίδωμι never occurs in construction with ἐν. If the former construction be adopted, ἐν ταῖς ἐπιθυμιαις may be rendered as in our version,
through their lusts ; or better *in* their lusts ; ἐν expressing their condition, or circumstances ; *them in their lusts*, *i.e.*, being in them,
immersed in them. *To dishonour*, τοῦ ἀτιμάζεσθαι. This infinitive with
τοῦ may depend on the preceding noun ; 'the uncleanness of dishonouring,'
&c., "quæ cernebatur in," &c. *Winer*, § 45. 4. *b*. But as the infinitive with
the genitive article is so frequently used to express design, or simple
sequence, it is better to make it depend on the whole preceding clause,
' He gave them up to uncleanness, to dishonour,' *i.e.*, either in order that
they might dishonour, or *so that* they dishonoured, &c ; ἀτιμάζεσθαι may
be taken either as middle, *so that they dishonoured their bodies ;* or as
passive, *so that their bodies were dishonoured*. The former best suits the
context. 'Εἰ ἑαυτοῖς is either equivalent to ἐν ἀλλήλοις, *reciprocally*, they
dishonoured one another, as to their bodies ; or *in themselves*, dishonouring
their bodies in themselves ; "significantius exprimit," says Calvin," quàm
profundas et ineluibiles ignominiæ notas corporibus suis inusserint."

This abandonment of the heathen to the dominion of sin is represented
as a punitive infliction. They forsook God, διὸ καί, *wherefore also* he gave
them up to uncleanness. This is explained as a simple permission on the
part of God. But it removes no real difficulty. If God permits those
who forsake him to sink into vice, he does it intelligently and inten-
tionally. The language of the apostle, as well as the analogy of Scripture,
demands more than this. It is at least a judicial abandonment. It is as
a punishment for their apostasy that God gives men up to the power of
sin. Tradidit Deus ut justus judex. He withdraws from the wicked the
restraints of his providence and grace, and gives them over to the dominion
of sin. God is presented in the Bible as the absolute moral and physical
ruler of the world. He governs all things according to the counsel of his
own will and the nature of his creatures. What happens as consequences
does not come by chance, but as designed ; and the sequence is secured by
his control. "It is beyond question," says Tholuck, "that, according to
the doctrine of the Old and New Testaments, sin is the punishment of sin." So
the Rabbins teach, "The reward of a good deed is a good deed, and of an evil
deed, an evil deed." This is also the teaching of all experience. We see
that sin follows sin as an avenger. De Wette truly says, "Diese Ansicht
ist nicht bloss jüdisch, sondern allgemein wahr vom absoluten Standpunkte
der Religion aus." "This is no mere Jewish doctrine, but it is universally
true from the absolute stand-point of religion." God is not a mere idle
spectator of the order of events ; he is at once the moral governor and

efficient controller of all things. "Man is not 'a virtue-machine,'" says Meyer, "when God rewards virtue with virtue ; neither is he 'a sin-machine,' when God punishes sin with sin." Men are as free in sinning as they are in obeying ; and what in one passage and from one point of view, is properly presented as the work of God, in another passage and from another point of view, is no less properly presented as the work of man. What is here said to be God's work, in Eph. iv. 19 is declared to be the sinner's own work. VERSE 25. Who change (οἵτινες). The pronoun has a causal sense, *being such as those who,* i. e., *because they exchanged the truth of God for a lie.* The construction is the same as in ver. 23, μετήλλαξαν ἐν, *they exchanged for,* not *they changed into.* *The truth of God,* either a peri-phrase for the true God, or the truth concerning God, i. e., right concep-tions of God. *For a lie,* that is, either a false god, or falsehood, i. e., false views of God. The former is the better explanation. The glory of God is God himself as glorious, and the truth of God, in this connection, is God himself as true ; that is, the true God. In the Old Testament, as in Jer. xiii. 25 ; xvi. 19, the gods of the heathen are spoken of as lies. Anything which is not what it pretends to be, or what it is supposed to be, is in the Scriptures called a lie. The proof of this apostasy is, that *they worshipped* (ἐσεβάσθησαν) *and served* (ἐλάτρευσαν). These words are often synonymous, both being used to express inward reverence and out-ward worship ; although the former properly expresses the feeling, and the latter the outward service. *The creature* (κτίσει), not the creation, but any particular created thing. This noun belongs, in sense, to both the preceding verbs, although the first by itself would require the accusative. *More than the Creator,* παρὰ τὸν κτίσαντα, i. e., *beyond,* in the sense of more than, or in the sense of passing by, neglecting ; "præterito Creatore," as Beza translates. The latter suits best. *Who is blessed for ever. Amen.* Who, notwithstanding the neglect of the heathen, is the ever-blessed God. This is the natural tribute of reverence toward the God whom men dishonoured by their idolatry. The word εὐλογητός is by Harless, Eph. i. 3, and by Meyer, made to mean *praised,* as the Hebrew בָּרוּךְ, to which it so constantly answers ; not, therefore, worthy of praise, but who is in fact the object of praise to all holy beings. Bretschneider (Lexicon), Tholuck, and others, render it "celebrandus, venerandus.' *Amen* is properly a Hebrew adjective, signifying true or faithful. At the beginning of a sentence it is often used adverbially, *verily, assuredly ;* at the end of a sentence it is used to express assent, *it is true, so let it be.* Paul says Amen to the declaration that God is the ever-blessed.

VERSE 26. *For this cause,* &c. That is, because they worshipped the creature rather than the Creator, God gave them up to corrupt affections. Πάθη ἀτιμίας, *shameful lusts,* passions which are degrading, and the indulgence of which covers men with ignominy. This verse is therefore an amplification of the idea expressed in ver. 24. The reasons why Paul refers in the first instance to the sins of uncleanness, in illustration and proof of the degradation of the heathen, probably were, that those sins are always intimately connected with idolatry, forming at times even a part of the service rendered to the false gods ; that in turning from God and things spiritual, men naturally sink into the sensual ; that the sins in question are peculiarly degrading ; and that they were the most notorious, prevalent, and openly acknowledged of all the crimes of the heathen

world. This corruption of morals was confined to no one class or sex.
The description given by profane writers of the moral corruption of the
ante-Christian ages, is in all respects as revolting as that presented by the
apostle. Of this the citations of Wetstein and Grotius furnish abundant
proof. Paul first refers to the degradation of females among the heathen,
because they are always the last to be affected in the decay of morals, and
their corruption is therefore proof that all virtue is lost.

VERSE 27.. The apostle for the third time repeats the idea that the
moral degradation of the heathen was a punishment of their apostacy from
God. *Receiving*, he says, *in themselves the meet recompence of their error.*
It is obvious from the whole context that πλάνη here refers to the sin of
forsaking the true God ; and it is no less obvious that the recompense or
punishment of this apostasy was the moral degradation which he had just
described.

The heathen themselves did not fail to see the intimate connection
between impiety and vice. *Silius*, iv. 794. " Heu primæ scelerum causæ
mortalibus ægris naturam nescire Deûm." *Cicero* De natura Deorum, 12.
" Haud scio, an, pietate adversus Deos sublatâ, fides etiam et societas, et
una excellentissima virtus justitia tollatur." See WETSTEIN. Those
therefore who would merge religion into morality, or who suppose that
morality can be sustained without religion, are more ignorant than the
heathen. They not only shut their eyes to all the teachings both of philosophy and of history, but array against themselves the wrath of God,
who has revealed his purpose to abandon to the most degrading lusts
those who apostatize from him.

VERSE 28. *And as they did not think it worth while to retain God in
their knowledge, he gave them up to a reprobate mind.* Another repetition of the sentiment is expressed in vers. 24, 26, that God abandons
those who abandon him. *And as*, καὶ καθώς. The cases are parallel ; *as*
they deserted God, so God abandoned them ; comp. John xvii. 2. *They
did not like*, οὐκ ἐδοκίμασαν ; the verb means to try or put to the test, to
examine, to approve, and, *dignum habere*, to regard as worthy, 1 Cor.
xvi. 3 ; 1 Thess. ii. 4, and when followed by an infinitive, to *think it
worth while*. The heathen did not think it worth the trouble to retain
the knowledge of God. They considered religion as useless, and supposed
they could live without God. The phrase ἔχειν ἐν ἐπιγνώσει is stronger
than simply *to know ;* both because ἐπίγνωσις, *full knowledge*, is stronger
than γνῶσις, and because ἔχειν ἐν ἐπιγνώσει is stronger than ἐπιγιγνώσκειν.
The text therefore means *to retain in accurate or practical knowledge.* It
was the practical recognition of the only true God, whose eternal power
and Godhead are revealed in his works, that men were unwilling constantly to make. *God gave them up to a reprobate mind.* Beza, Bengel,
and others, give ἀδόκιμος here the sense of *judicii expers*, incapable of
judgment or discernment. But this is contrary to usage, and contrary to
the etymology of the word. Δόκιμος, from δέχομαι, means *receivable*,
worthy of being received ; and ἀδόκιμος, *worthy of rejection*, reprobate.
To do things not becoming ; that is, to do things not becoming the nature
and duties of man. Of the things meant, the following verses contain a
long and painful catalogue. Ποιεῖν is the exegetical infinitive, *to do*, that
is, *so that they did*. It expresses the consequence of the dereliction just
spoken of, and the natural fruit of a reprobate mind.

VERSES 29–31. *Being filled with all unrighteousness, fornication,
wickedness*, &c. The accusative πεπληρωμένους is connected with αὐτοὺς of

the preceding verse. *He gave them up, filled with all unrighteousness;* or it depends on the preceding infinitive ποιεῖν, *so that they, filled with all unrighteousness, should commit,* &c.   It is not so connected with παρέδωκεν, as to imply that God gave them up after they were thus corrupt, but it is so connected with ποιεῖν as to express the consequence of God's abandoning them to do the things which are not convenient. The crimes here mentioned were not of rare occurrence. The heathen were filled with them. They not only abounded, but in many cases were palliated and even justified. Dark as the picture here drawn is, it is not so dark as that presented by the most distinguished Greek and Latin authors, of their own countrymen. Commentators have collected a fearful array of passages from the ancient writers, which more than sustain the account given by the apostle. We select a single passage from Senca de Ira, II. 8 : "Omnia sceleribus ac vitiis plena sunt ; plus committitur quàm quod possit coercitione sanari. Certatur ingenti quodam nequitiæ certamine ; major quotidie peccandi cupiditas, minor verecundia est. Expulso melioris aequiorisque respectu, quocunque visum est, libido se impingit ; nec furtiva jam scelera sunt, præter oculos eunt. Adeoque in publicum missa nequitia est, et in omnium pectoribus evaluit, ut innocentia non rara, sed nulla sit. Numquid enim singuli aut pauci rupere legem ? undique, velut signo dato, ad fas nefasque miscendum coorti sunt." What Paul says of the ancient heathen world, is found to be true in all its essential features of men of all generations. Wherever men have existed, there have they shown themselves to be sinners, ungodly and unrighteous, and therefore justly exposed to the wrath of God. Of the vices with which the heathen were filled, πορνεία stands first as the most prominent ; πονηρία, *malice,* the disposition to inflict evil ; πλεονεξία, *rapacity,* the desire to have more than is our due ; κακία, *malignity,* malice in exercise ; φθόνος and φόνος, *envy* and *murder,* united either from similarity in sound or because the former tends to the latter ; ἔρις, δόλος, *contention* and *fraud,* nearly related evils. The primary meaning of δόλος is a bait, food exposed to entrap an animal ; then the disposition to deceive, or an act of deception ; κακοήθεια (κακός and ἦθος), *malevolence,* the disposition to make the worst of everything ; ψιθυριστής, a *whisperer,* clandestine slanderer ; κατάλαλος, a *detractor,* one who speaks against others ; θεοστυγής, *hateful to God,* or *hating God.* Usage is in favour of the passive sense, the connection of the active. All wicked men, and not any one particular class, are the objects of the divine displeasure. To meet this difficulty, Meyer proposes to make this word a mere qualification of the preceding, *God-abhorred detractors.* This, however, is out of keeping with the whole passage. The great majority of commentators adopt the active sense. Then follow three designations, expressive of the different forms of pride, ὑβρισταί, *the insolent ;* ὑπερήφανοι, *the self-conceited ;* ἀλαζόνες, *boasters :* ἐφευρεταὶ κακῶν, *inventors of crimes ;* γονεῦσιν ἀπειθεῖς, *disobedient to parents.* That such should be included in this fearful list, shows the light in which filial disobedience is regarded by the sacred writers. In ver. 31, all the words begin with the ἀ privative, ἀσυνέτους, *without* (σύνεσις) insight into moral or religious things, *i. q.,* blinded, besotted, so as to think evil good, and good evil ; ἀσυνθέτους, *perfidious ;* ἀστόργους, those in whom the natural affection for parents or children is suppressed ; ἀσπόνδους, *implacable ;* ἀνελεήμονας, *without pity.*

VERSE 32.   *Who well knowing the righteous judgment of God;* that is, *although they well know,* &c.   They were (οἵτινες) *such as who.* The heathen whose acts had been just described, are declared to be, *Men who, although they knew the righteous judgment,* &c., (δικαίωμα) *decree,* a declaration of what is right and just; and δικαίωμα τοῦ Θεοῦ is the declaration of God as to what is right and just. The import of this declaration is contained in the clause, *that they who do* (πράσσουσι, *commit*) *such things are worthy of death.* By *death* here, as often elsewhere, is meant punishment, in the general meaning of that word. It expresses the penalty of the law, and includes all evil inflicted for the satisfaction of justice. Paul therefore teaches that the heathen knew they deserved punishment for their crimes, or in other words, that they were justly exposed to the wrath of God, which was revealed against all ungodliness and unrighteousness of men. The source of this knowledge he explains in the following chapter, ver. 14. It was a knowledge written on their hearts, or included in the constitution of their nature; it was implied in their being moral agents. As he had before shown that the impiety of the heathen was without excuse, inasmuch as they had a knowledge of the true God, so here he shows that their immorality was inexcusable, since their sins were not committed in ignorance of their nature or desert. This passage also shows that the judicial abandonment of God does not destroy the free agency or responsibility of men. They are given up to work iniquity, and yet know that they deserve death for what they do. The stream which carries them away is not without, but within. It is their own corrupt nature. It is themselves. Notwithstanding this knowledge of the ill-desert of the crimes above enumerated, *they not only commit them, but approve of those who do* (or practise) *them.* This is the lowest point of degradation. To sin, even in the heat of passion, is evil; but to delight in the sins of others, shows that men are of set purpose and fixed preference, wicked. Such is the apostle's argument to prove that the heathen are all under sin, that they are justly chargeable with ungodliness and unrighteousness, and consequently exposed to the wrath of God.

DOCTRINE.

1. The punitive justice of God is an essential attribute of his nature. This attribute renders the punishment of sin necessary, and is the foundation of the need of a vicarious atonement in order to the pardon of sinners. This doctrine the apostle assumes as a first principle, and makes it the basis of his whole exposition of the doctrine of justification, ver. 18.

2. That sin is a proper object of punishment, and that, under the righteous government of God, it will be punished, are moral axioms, which have "a self-evidencing light," whenever proposed to the moral sense of men, vers. 18, 32.

3. God has never left himself without a witness among his rational creatures. Both in reference to his own nature and to the rule of duty, he has, in his works and in the human heart, given sufficient light to render the impiety and immorality of men inexcusable, vers. 19, 20, 32.

4. Natural religion is not a sufficient guide to salvation. What individual or what nation has it ever led to right views of God or of his law? The experience of the whole world, under all the variety of circumstances in which men have existed, proves its insufficiency; and, consequently, the necessity of a special divine revelation, vers. 21—23.

5. The heathen, who have only the revelation of God in his works and in their own hearts, aided by the obscure traditionary knowledge which has

come down to them, need the gospel. In point of fact, the light which they enjoy does not lead them to God and holiness, vers. 21—23.

6. Error (on moral and religious subjects) has its root in depravity. Men are ignorant of God and duty, because they do not like to retain him in their knowledge, vers. 21, 28.

7. God often punishes one sin by abandoning the sinner to the commission of others. Paul repeats this idea three times, vers. 24, 26, 28. This judicial abandonment is consistent with the holiness of God and the free agency of man. God does not impel or entice to evil. He ceases to restrain. He says of the sinner, Let him alone, vers. 24—28.

8. Religion is the only true foundation, and the only effectual safeguard for morality. Those who abandon God, he abandons. Irreligion and immorality, therefore, have ever been found inseparably connected, vers. 24—28.

9. It evinces, in general, greater depravity to encourage others in the commission of crimes, and to rejoice in their commission, than to commit them one's self, ver. 32.

10. The most reprobate sinner carries about with him a knowledge of his just exposure to the wrath of God. Conscience can never be entirely extirpated, ver. 32.

REMARKS.

1. It lies in the very nature of sin, that it should be inexcusable, and worthy of punishment. Instead, therefore, of palliating its enormity, we should endeavour to escape from its penalty, vers. 18, 32.

2. As the works of God reveal his eternal power and Godhead, we should accustom ourselves to see in them the manifestations of his perfections, vers. 18—21.

3. The human intellect is as erring as the human heart. We can no more find truth than holiness, when estranged from God ; even as we lose both light and heat, when we depart from the sun. Those, in every age, have sunk deepest into folly, who have relied most on their own understandings. "In thy light only, O God, can we see light," ver. 21, &c.

4. If the sins of the heathen, committed under the feeble light of nature, be inexcusable, how great must be the aggravation of those committed under the light of the Scriptures, ver. 20.

5. As the light of nature is insufficient to lead the heathen to God and holiness, it is one of the most obvious and urgent of our duties to send them the light of the Bible, vers. 20—23.

6. Men should remember that their security from open and gross sins is not in themselves, but in God ; and they should regard as the worst of punishments, his withdrawing from them his Holy Spirit, vers. 24—28.

7. Sins of uncleanness are peculiarly debasing and demoralizing. To be preserved from them is mentioned in Scripture as a mark of the divine favour, Eccl. vii. 26 ; Prov. xxii. 14 ; to be abandoned to them, as a mark of reprobation.

8. To take pleasure in those who do good, makes us better ; as to delight in those who do evil, is the surest way to become even more degraded than they are themselves, ver. 32.

CHAPTER II.

CONTENTS.

THE OBJECT OF THIS CHAPTER IS TO ESTABLISH THE SAME CHARGES AGAINST THE JEWS, WHICH HAD JUST BEEN PROVED AGAINST THE GENTILES ; TO SHOW THAT THEY ALSO WERE EXPOSED TO THE WRATH OF GOD. IT CONSISTS OF THREE PARTS. THE FIRST CONTAINS AN EXHIBITION OF THOSE SIMPLE PRINCIPLES OF JUSTICE UPON WHICH ALL MEN ARE TO BE JUDGED, VERS. 1—16. THE SECOND IS AN APPLICATION OF THESE PRINCIPLES TO THE CASE OF THE JEWS, VERS. 17—24. THE THIRD IS AN EXHIBITION OF THE TRUE NATURE AND DESIGN OF CIRCUMCISION, INTENDED TO SHOW THAT THE JEWS COULD NOT EXPECT EXEMPTION ON THE GROUND OF THAT RITE, VERS. 25—39.

ROMANS II. 1—16.

ANALYSIS.

That men so impious and immoral, as those described in the preceding chapter, deserved the divine displeasure, and could never, by their own works, secure the favour of God, the Jew was prepared readily to admit. But might there not be a set of men, who, in virtue of some promise on the part of God, or of the performance of some special duties, could claim exemption from the execution of God's purpose to punish all sin ? To determine this point, it was necessary to consider a little more fully the justice of God, in order to see whether it admitted of impunity to sinners on the ground supposed. This first section of the chapter, therefore, is employed in expanding the principle of ver. 18 of the first chapter. It contains a development of those principles of justice which commend themselves at once to every man's conscience. The first is, that he who condemns in others what he does himself, does thereby condemn himself, ver. 1. The second, that God's judgments are according to the truth or real state of the case, ver. 2. The third, that the special goodness of God, manifested towards any individual or people, forms no ground of exemption from merited punishment ; but being designed to lead them to repentance, when misimproved aggravates their condemnation, vers. 3—5. The fourth, that the ground of judgment is the works, not the external relations or professions of men : God will punish the wicked and reward the good, whether Jew or Gentile, without the least respect of persons, vers. 6—11. The fifth, that the standard of judgment is the light which men have severally enjoyed. Those having a written law shall be judged by it, and those who have only the law written on their hearts, (and that the heathen have such a law is proved by the operations of conscience, vers. 13—15,) shall be judged by that law, ver. 12. These are the principles according to which all men are to be judged in the last day, by Jesus Christ, ver. 16.

COMMENTARY.

Verse 1. In order to appreciate the force of the apostle's reasoning in this and the following verses, it should be remembered that the principal

ground on which the Jews expected acceptance with God, was the covenant
which he had made with their father Abraham, in which he promised to
be a God to him and to his seed after him. They understood this promise
to secure salvation for all who retained their connection with Abraham, by
the observance of the law and the rite of circumcision. They expected,
therefore, to be regarded and treated not so much as individuals, each being
dealt with according to his personal character, but as a community to whom
salvation was secured by the promise made to Abraham. Paul begins his
argument at a distance ; he states his principles in such general terms,
that they could not fail to secure the assent of the Jew, before he was
aware of their application to himself. That the Jews are addressed in this
chapter is evident from the whole strain of the argument, and from the
express application of the reasoning to the case of the Jews, from ver. 17
onward. This view of the passage is now generally adopted, though many
of the earlier commentators supposed either that no particular class of persons is here addressed, or that the apostle has in view the better portion
of the heathen, or at least those who did not seem to approve of the crimes
mentioned in the preceding chapter, but rather condemned them.

The connection between this chapter and what precedes, as indicated by
the particle δὶὸ, *wherefore*, is somewhat doubtful. Some suppose the
inference to be drawn from the doctrine taught from ver. 18 of the preceding chapter. God is just, and determined to punish all unrighteousness
and ungodliness of men ; wherefore they are without excuse who commit
the sins which they condemn in others. In this case, however, the conclusion is not exactly in the form suited to the premises. It is not so
much the inexcusableness of sinners as the exposure to punishment, that
follows from the justice of God. Most commentators, therefore, consider
the inference as drawn from the last verse of the preceding chapter. It is
there said that all men know that those who sin are worthy of death ;
and the inference is, that they who commit sin are without excuse, however censorious their self-conceit may render them towards others. *Every
one who judges.* Though from what follows it is plain that the Jews are
here intended, yet for the reasons above stated the proposition is made
general. Κρίνων, *judging;* but by implication, condemning. *For wherein
thou judgest another, thou condemnest thyself.* 'Wherein (ἐν ᾧ,) either *in
the thing which,* or *thereby, i.e.,* in the same judgment, or *whilst.* See
Mark ii. 19 ; John v. 7. The reason of this assertion is given in the following clause, *for thou that judgest doest the same things.* It is the thing
done which is the ground of condemnation ; and therefore he who condemns the act, condemns the agent, whether the agent be himself or some
one else, whether he be a Jew or a Gentile.

VERSE 2. *But we know.* That is, however perverse and partial may be
the judgment you pass on yourself, we know, &c. *We* does not refer to
the Jews, as peculiarly instructed, but to all men. Every one knows.
The proposition contained in this verse is : *The judgment of God is against
those who do such things.* That is, however they may excuse themselves,
God will judge them. The words κατὰ ἀλήθειαν, therefore, do not form
the predicate of the sentence, as though the sense were, The judgment of
God is according to truth. The meaning rather is, the judgment of God,
which is according to truth, is against those, &c. There are two things
therefore asserted, the certainty of this divine judgment, and its being
according to truth, *i.e.,* without error, without respect of persons. It is
not founded upon mere appearances or professions, but upon the real truth

of the case. Comp. Prov. xxix. 14, ἐν ἀληθείᾳ κρίνων πτωχούς, and John viii. 16, ἡ κρίσις ἡ ἐμὴ ἀληθής ἐστιν. This verse, then, contains the second general principle of justice, according to which all men, whether Jews or Gentiles, are to be judged. The whole hope of the Jews was founded on the assumption that the judgment of God regarding them would be guided by some other rule than truth. He was not to judge them according to their real merits, but according to their national and ecclesiastical relations, just as men now hope to be saved because they belong to the true Church.

VERSE 3.   *But thinkest thou this, O man, that judgest,* &c. The truth that God's judgment is just, and will fall on those who themselves commit the sins which they condemn in others, is so plain, that the apostle exclaims at the folly of those who seem to deny it. The emphasis lies on the word *thou,* in the middle of the verse. Dost thou think that *thou,* a Jew, and because a Jew, shalt escape the righteous judgment of God? *Shalt escape,* ἐκφεύξῃ. "Every one," says Bengel, "who is arraigned, φεύγει, *tries to escape;* he who is acquitted, ἐκφεύγει, *escapes.*" In ver. 1, the apostle had shown that the man who did what he condemned in others, condemned himself. "If then," as Theophylact says, "he cannot escape his own judgment, how can he escape the judgment of God? If forced to condemn ourselves, how much more will the infinitely Holy condemn us?" The ground on which this false and absurd expectation rested is mentioned in the following verse :

VERSE 4.   *Or despisest thou the riches of his goodness, and forbearance, and long-suffering?* That is, admitting the general principle, that those who do what they condemn in others are themselves exposed to condemnation, do you expect exemption on the ground of the peculiar goodness of God? That this was the expectation of the Jews is plain from the apostle's argument here and in the following chapter, and from chap. ix. and xi. Comp. also Matt. iii. 9, "Think not to say, We have Abraham to our father," and John viii. 33. *Despisest.* To despise, καταφρονεῖν, is to form a low estimate of. They despise the goodness of God, who form such a wrong estimate of it, as to suppose that it gives them a license to sin ; who imagine that he will not punish, either because he long forbears, or because his goodness towards us is so great that we shall escape, though others perish. The words χρηστότης, ἀνοχή, and μακροθυμία, express the Divine goodness under different aspects. The first means kindness in general, as expressed in giving favours ; the second, patience ; the third, forbearance, slowness in the infliction of punishment. The reason why the Jews, as referred to by the apostle, and men in general, thus abuse the goodness of God, is expressed by the clause, *not knowing that the goodness of God leadeth thee to repentance.* Ἀγνοῶν, not knowing, not understanding; and here, not comprehending the true nature and design of. Men abuse the goodness of God, because they do not rightly apprehend that instead of indicating a purpose not to punish, it is designed to lead them to forsake their sins. The goodness of God leads us to repentance, because it shows us our duty towards a Being who is so kind, and because it gives us ground to hope for acceptance.   "The word ἄγει, *leads,*" says Dr. Wordsworth, Canon of Westminster, in his elegant and scholarly work on the Greek Testament, "intimates not only the will of God, but the will of man. God leads, but man *may* refuse to be led : 'Deus ducit volentem duci,' as Bengel says, 'Ducit suaviter non cogit.'" Very true ; but who gives the will to be led? Is there no preventing grace? Does not God work in us to *will,* as well as to do. Surely there is such a thing as being made willing without being forced. There is a middle ground between moral suasion and coercion. God supersedes the necessity of forcing, by making us willing in the day of his power. The apostle, however, is not here speaking of gracious influence, but of the moral tendencies of providential dispensations. VERSE 5. The goodness of God, so far from being a ground of reasonable expectation that we shall ultimately escape punishment, becomes, when abused, an aggravation of our guilt. This principle the apostle here applies to the Jews, who, through their abuse of the peculiar mercy of God, were treasuring up wrath for themselves. Κατὰ δὲ τὴν σκληρότητά σου, *after thy hardness*, i.e., as might be expected from thy hardness; agreeably to its nature and degree—καὶ ἀμετανόητον καρδίαν, *heart incapable of repentance.* "'Αμετανόητος, vim activam habet, *animus, qui resipicere non potest, poenitere nescius.* Enervat hunc locum Grotius quum explicat, *animus, qui poenitentiam non agit.*" *Fritzsche.* To treasure up is to lay up little by little, and thus accumulate a store of anything, whether good or evil. The abusers of God's goodness accumulate a store of wrath for themselves. 'Εν ἡμέρᾳ ὀργῆς is commonly rendered *unto* the day of wrath; but this unnecessarily gives ἐν the force of εἰς. It is better, with De Wette, Meyer, and others, to connect ἐν with ὀργὴν, 'wrath *at* or *on* the day of wrath.' They treasure up for themselves wrath at that day when wrath shall be manifested. That day is further described as the day ἀποκαλύψεως δικαιοκρισίας τοῦ Θεοῦ, *of the revelation of the righteous judgment of God.* Some manuscripts insert καί between ἀποκαλύψεως and δικαιοκρισίας; which reading is preferred by Bengel, Wetstein, Mill, and Knapp. The sense then is, *the day of revelation, and of the righteous judgment of God.* The day of revelation, *viz.*, of Christ, whose second coming is always associated in Scripture with the final judgment; and therefore the day of revelation may well express the day of judgment. But as the phrase, "day of revelation" nowhere else occurs in this sense, and as the oldest manuscripts are in favour of the common text, it should be allowed to stand.

VERSE 6. *Who will render to every man according to his works.* This is the fourth important principle which the apostle teaches us regulates the judgment of God. He will judge men neither according to their professions nor their relations, but according to their works. The question at his bar will be, not whether a man is a Jew or a Gentile, whether he belongs to the chosen people or to the heathen world, but whether he has obeyed the law. This principle is amplified and applied in what follows, in vers. 7—11. The question has been asked, how the declaration that God will render to every man, whether Jew or Gentile, according to his works—to the good, eternal life, to the wicked, indignation and wrath—is to be reconciled with the apostle's doctrine, that no man is justified by works, that righteousness and life are not by works, but by faith, and through grace. In answering this question, two things are to be borne in mind. The first is, that notwithstanding the doctrine of gratuitous justification, and in perfect consistency with it, the apostle still teaches that the retributions of eternity are according to our works. The good only are saved, and the wicked only are condemned. "For we must all appear before the judgment-seat of Christ, that every one may receive the things done in his body, whether good or bad," 2 Cor. v. 10 ; Eph. vi. 8. "Reproborum," says Calvin, "malitiam justa ultione si puniet Dominus, rependet illis quod meriti sunt. Rursum quia sanctificat, quos olim statuit glorificare, in illis quoque bona opera coronabit, sed non pro merito." With this accord the words of Bernard : "Bona opera sunt via regni, non causa regnandi." The wicked will be punished on account of their works, and according to their works ; the righteous will be rewarded, not on account of, but according to their works. Good works are to them the evidence of their belonging to that class to whom, for Christ's sake, eternal life is graciously awarded ; and they are, in some sense and to some extent, the measure of that reward. But it is more pertinent to remark, in the second place, that the apostle is not here teaching the method of justification, but is laying down those general principles of justice, according to which, irrespective of the gospel, all men are to be judged. He is expounding the law, not the gospel. And as the law not only says that death is the wages of sin, but also that those who keep its precepts shall live by them, so the apostle says, that God will punish the wicked and reward the righteous. This is perfectly consistent with what he afterwards teaches, that there are none righteous ; that there are none who so obey the law as to be entitled to the life which it promises ; and that for such the gospel provides a plan of justification without works, a plan for saving those whom the law condemns. He is here combating the false hopes of the Jews, who, though trusting to the law, were, by the principles of the law, exposed to condemnation. This he does to drive them from this false dependence, and to show them that neither Jew nor Gentile can be justified before the bar of that God, who, while he promises eternal life to the obedient, has revealed his purpose to punish the disobedient. All, therefore, that this passage teaches is that, irrespective of the gospel, to those who either never heard of it, or who, having heard, reject it, the principle of judgment will be law.

Verses 7, 8. The principle laid down in ver. 6, is here amplified. God will render eternal life to the good, indignation and wrath to the wicked, without distinction of persons ; to the Jews no less than to the Gentiles. Though the sense of these verses is plain, there is great difference of opinion as to the grammatical construction. The explanation adopted by our translators is perhaps the most natural, and is the one which is most generally followed. To the verb ἀποδώσει of ver. 6, belong the two accusatives ζωὴν αἰώνιον, and θυμὸν καὶ ὀργήν ; and the two datives, τοῖς μὲν—ζητοῦσι and τοῖς δὲ ἐξ ἐριθείας. The accusatives δόξαν καὶ τιμὴν καὶ ἀφθαρσίαν then of course depend on ζητοῦσι, and καθ' ὑπομονὴν ἔργου ἀγαθοῦ is an adverbial qualification. The passage then reads : " To those who through perseverance in good works, seek glory, honour, and immortality, eternal life ; but to those who are contentious, indignation and wrath." Another construction, adopted by Bengel, Fritzsche, and others, supposes that τοῖς μὲν καθ' ὑπομονὴν ἔργου ἀγαθοῦ (scil. οὖσι) are to be taken together ; *to those who are according to perseverance, i.e., to those who persevere ;* (comp. οἱ κατὰ σάρκα = οἱ σαρκικοί, and οἱ κατὰ Πνεῦμα = οἱ πνευματικοί). The following clause, δόξαν—ζητοῦσι, is then in apposition with the preceding : " To those who persevere in good works, seeking glory, honour and immortality,' he will render eternal life." This view of the passage is recommended by the correspondence thus established between the τοῖς μὲν καθ' ὑπομονήν of ver. 7, and the τοῖς δὲ ἐξ ἐριθείας of ver. 8. It is opposed, however, by the following considerations : 1. The interpretation of the phrase οἱ καθ' ὑπομονὴν ἔργου ἀγαθοῦ is hardly borne out by a reference to the phrases of οἱ κατὰ σάρκα and οἱ κατὰ Πνεῦμα. 2. The second clause of ver 7, if a mere amplification of the first clause, should be introduced by καὶ, as in ver. 8 : Τοῖς δὲ ἐξ ἐριθείας, καὶ ἀπειθοῦσι. Luther, after Oecumenius, translates thus : *Welcher geben wird* Preis und Ehre und unvergängliches Wesen denen, die mit Geduld in guten Werken trachten nacn dem ewigen Leben :" Who will give glory, honour, and immortality to those who, in patient continuance in well-doing, seek eternal life." According to this view, the accusatives δόξαν, τιμὴν, ἀφθαρσίαν, depend upon ἀποδώσει, and ζωὴν αἰώνιον on ζητοῦσι. But this the position of the words will hardly bear. Luther's fluent and forcible version is effected by an entire transposition of the clauses. The construction therefore first mentioned is on the whole to be preferred. In the English version of the words καθ᾽ ὑπομονήν, κατά is rendered *through*. So also Grotius, De Wette, and others. See 1 Cor. xii. 8 ; Eph. iii. 3, 7. Others translate it by the Latin preposition *secundum*, according to, or in virtue of. Ὑπομονή is rendered *patience* by the Vulgate, and Luther ; *patiens expectatio*, by Beza ; constancy, or patient continuance in our version. In illustration of the combination ὑπομονὴν ἔργου ἀγαθοῦ comp. ὑπομονὴ τῆς ἐλπίδος, 1 Thess. i. 3. The sing. ἔργου is used collectively for ἔργων, as in Gal. vi. 4 ; 1 Thess. i. 3 ; and elsewhere. What is immediately afterwards expressed by *eternal life*, is here expressed by the three words, glory, honour, and immortality. The manifested excellence or splendour of the future condition of the saints is expressed by δόξα ; the honour due such excellence by τιμή ; and the endless nature of their blessedness by ἀφθαρσία.

VERSE 8. *To those who are of contention,* that is, *the contentious.* Comp. οἱ ἐκ πίστεως, *believers ;* οἱ ἐκ περιτομῆς, *the circumcised ;* οἱ ἐκ ἀκροβυστίας, *the uncircumcised ;* οἱ ἐκ νόμου, *those who belong to the law, legalists.* Instead of the ordinary derivation of ἐριθεία from ἔρις, Ruckert traces it to ἔριθος, *a hireling,* which derivation is sustained by Tholuck, " Beiträge zur Spracherklärung des Neuen Testaments," p. 25, and Fritzsche, Excursus to his Commentary on the second chapter of this epistle, and is now generally adopted. The signification of the word, as determined by its etymology and its classical usage is, *work for hire, selfishness, ambition, party spirit, malice.* In the New Testament it is used several times in the same sense as in Philip. i, 16, οἱ μὲν ἐξ ἐριθείας, *some of rivalry,* or malice ; the antithetical expression is οἱ δὲ ἐξ ἀγάπης. In Philip. ii. 3, it is connected with κενοδοξία, *vain glory.* In James iii. 14, 16, it is connected with ζῆλος, *envy.* In 2 Cor. xii. 20, it is distinguished from ἔρις. These passages show that the scriptural usage of the word agrees with the classical. Still in the present case it seems to have a somewhat wider meaning. It is not envy, or rivalry, but malicious opposition to God and his requirements that is here expressed. This is plain from the explanatory causes that follow. The disposition expressed by ἐριθεία is manifested in disobeying the truth, and obeying unrighteousness. Bretschneider therefore explains οἱ ἐξ ἐριθείας to mean *qui malitia ducti Deo,* i.e. *rei divinæ, adversantur:* "those who through malice oppose themselves to God." The same interpretation is given by Reiche and De Wette, as well as by the older commentators. *Who obey not the truth.* Ἀπειθέω is *to refuse belief,* to disbelieve, as well as to disobey. This clause therefore means, *who refuse assent and obedience to the truth.* Ἀλήθεια is divine truth ; what is true and right as to faith and practice. See i. 18. "Saepe," says Bengel, "haec duo (ἀλήθεια and ἀδικία) inter se opponuntur: veritas continet justitiam, et injustitia connotat mendacium." *Who yield themselves to,* or *follow unrighteousness, indignation, and wrath,* (shall be rendered). The words θυμὸς καὶ ὀργή should regularly be in the accusative, as depending on ἀποδώσει of ver. 6 ; but as they are in the nominative, ἔσται or ἀποδώσεται must be supplied. There may be, as some suppose, force in the change of construction and omission of the verb. God gives eternal life ; indignation and wrath come as earned by man, so to speak, *Deo nolente.* God wills all men to be saved. Comp. Rom. vi. 23. Both words are used for the sake of intensity. As to their specific difference, both ancient and modern philologists differ. The majority make Ͽυμός express the momentary impulse of anger, ὀργή the permanent feeling. Others make ὀργή to include the desire of vengeance, and therein to differ from Ͽυμός. The former distinction is more in accordance with the primary meaning of the words ; as Ͽυμός means the mind as the seat of the emotions, and hence is used for any strong passion, and ὀργή means disposition, habit of mind.

Verse 9. *Tribulation and anguish;* Ͽλῖψις, (from Ͽλίβω, *to press,*) means *pressure, affliction;* στενοχωρία, *straitness of place, anguish.* They are often associated ; see chap. viii. 35 ; 2 Cor. vi. 4. The latter is the stronger of the two terms, as may be inferred from its always following the other, and especially from 2 Cor. iv. 8, Ͽλιβόμενοι, 'αλλ' οὐ στενοχω-ρούμενοι, *troubled, but not distressed. Every soul of man,* that is, every man. Comp. Acts ii. 43 ; Romans xiii. 1, and the Hebrew כָּל־נֶפֶשׁ אָדָם. Rückert, Meyer, and others, give ψυχή its full force, *upon every soul that belongs to a man,* to express the idea that the soul and not the body is to suffer the penalty. But in xiii. 1, ψυχή evidently stands for the whole person : ' let every soul,' means let every person ; and such is a common scriptural meaning of the word, " if a soul sin," " if a soul lie," "if the priest buy a soul with his money," &c. *Of the Jew first, and also of the Greek.* It becomes now apparent that the apostle, in laying down these general principles of justice, had the Jews specially in view. God, he says, will render to every man according to his works, to the good, eternal life ; to the evil, tribulation and anguish. And lest the *every man* should fail to arrest attention, he adds expressly, that the Jew as well as the Greek is to be thus judged. The word πρῶτον may express either order or preëminence. If the former, the sense is what is expressed by Calvin, " Haec universalis est divini judicii lex, quæ a Judæis incipiet, et comprehendet totum orbem." The judgment shall begin with the Jews, and extend to the Gentiles. If the latter, the sense is, The Jew shall not only be punished as certainly as others, but more severely, because he has been more highly favoured. " The Jew first," is equivalent then to the Jew especially. The same remark applies to the following verse. If the Jew is faithful, he shall be specially rewarded. What is true of all men, is specially true of those to whom God has revealed himself in a peculiar manner.

Verse 10. *But glory, honour and peace, to every one doing good ; to the Jew first, and also to the Greek.* This verse completes the statement of the principle of law announced in ver. 6. The law, while it threatens death to the transgressor, promises life to the obedient ; and it matters not in either case, whether it is a Jew or Gentile who receives its award. Glory, honour and peace are descriptive terms for eternal life. It is a life glorious in itself, an object of reverence or regard to others, and a source of unspeakable blessedness or peace.

Verse 11. *For there is no respect of persons with God.* He is righteous and impartial, looking not at the person, but the conduct of those whom he judges. This is the ground of the assurance that he will judge Jews and Gentiles according to their works. The words προσωπροληψία, προσωπολήπτης, προσωπολημπτέω, are all peculiar to the New Testament, and all owe their origin to the phrase πρόσωπον λαμβάνειν, which is used in the sense of the Hebrew phrase, פָּנִים נָשָׂא, to lift up, or accept the face of any one, that is, to be favourable to him. This is sometimes used in a good sense, as Gen. xxxii. 20, "Peradventure he will accept of me," literally, *lift up my face*. Gen. xix. 21 ; Job xlii. 8. Most frequently in a bad sense, for partiality. Hence judges are forbidden to accept the face of any one, Lev. xix. 15 ; Deut. x. 17. In the New Testament, all the expressions above mentioned are used in the sense of unjust partiality. All προσωπολήψία, *respect of persons*, is denied to God, and forbidden to men. See Eph. vi. 9 ; Col. iii. 25 ; James ii. 1.

VERSE 12. In the preceding verse it was stated that God is just and impartial in all his judgments. This is confirmed not only by the previous assertion, that he will judge every man according to his works, but also by the exhibition of that important principle contained in this verse. Men are to be judged by the light they have severally enjoyed. The ground of judgment is their works ; the rule of judgment is their knowledge. *For as many as sinned without law.* That is, God is impartial, *for* he will judge men according to the light which they have enjoyed. Our Lord teaches the same doctrine when he says, "The servant which knew his lord's will, . . . shall be beaten with many stripes ; but he that knew not, and did commit things worthy of stripes, shall be beaten with few stripes." Luke xii. 47, 48. By *law*, is here meant a written or supernaturally revealed law. In 1 Cor. ix. 21, the heathen are called ἄνομοι, *without law*, as distinguished from the Jews, who were ὑπὸ νόμον *under law*. Νόμος, as used by the apostle, means *the rule of duty*, the will of God revealed for our obedience ; commonly, however, with special reference to the revelation made in the Scriptures. Ἀνόμως is equivalent to χωρὶς νόμου, *without law*, and is not to be taken in its moral sense, *without restraint*, *i. e.* recklessly. Ἀνόμως καὶ ἀπολοῦνται, *shall also perish without law*, that is, their punishment shall be assigned without reference to the written law. Καί before ἀπολοῦνται, says Rückert and Tholuck, indicates the relation between the cause and effect, or premise and conclusion ; or as Fritzsche says, " necessitatem indicat, quâ τὸ ἀνόμως ἀπόλλυσθαι ex τῷ ἀνόμως ἁμαρτάνειν consequatur." Neither of these explanations seems to express the true force of the particle ; it rather serves to indicate that as the sinning is ἀνόμως, so also is the punishment. Ἀπόλλυμι is to *destroy*, to put to death, spoken of physical death, and also of eternal death, Matt. x. 28 ; Luke iv. 34 ; and in the passive form, Luke xiii. 3, 5 ; John iii. 15, 16 ; 1 Cor. viii. 11. The word is strong in its own import ; and as explained by other passages, it here teaches that those who sin without a written revelation—although they are to be judged fairly, and are to be treated far less severely than those who have enjoyed the light of revelation—are still to perish. " Vide igitur, quale patrocinium suscipiant, qui præposterâ misericordiâ gentes evangelii lumine privatas ignorantiæ prætextu Dei judicio eximere tentant." *Calvin.*

VERSE 13. *For not the hearers of the law.* This verse is connected with the last clause of the preceding, and assigns the reason why the Jews shall be judged or punished according to the law ; the mere possession or knowledge of the law would not avail, *for* it is not the hearers, but the doers of the law that are just before God. The expression *hearers* instead of *readers*, is explained by the fact that the law was read in the presence of the people, and by hearing rather than by reading, their knowledge of it was obtained. Comp. Matt. v. 21 ; John xii. 34 ; Gal. iv. 21 ; James i. 22. *To be just before God*, and to be justified, are the same thing. They are both forensic expressions, and indicate the state rather than the character of those to whom they refer. Those are just in the sight of God, or are justified, who have done what the law requires, and are regarded and treated accordingly ; that is, are declared to be free from condemnation, and entitled to the favour of God. In obvious allusion to the opinion, that being a Jew was enough to secure admission to heaven, the apostle says, It is not the hearers but *the doers of the law* that are justified. He is not speaking of the method of justification available for sinners, as revealed in the gospel, but of the principles of justice which will be applied to all who look to the law for justification. If men rely on works, they must have works ; they must be doers of the law ; they must satisfy its demands, if they are to be justified by it. For God is just and impartial ; he will, as a judge administering the law, judge every man, not according to his privileges, but according to his works and the knowledge of duty which he has possessed. On these principles, it is his very design to show that no flesh living can be justified.

VERSE 14. *For whenever the Gentiles, not having the law.* In the preceding verse the apostle had said, That not the hearers but the doers of the law are justified before God ; and then adds, *For* whenever the Gentiles, not having the law, do by nature the things of the law, they are a law unto themselves. But the fact that the Gentiles are a law unto themselves, has nothing to do, either as an illustration or confirmation, with the general proposition contained in ver. 13. Those who insist on establishing such a connection, suppose that ver. 14 refers to the last clause of ver. 13, and is designed to prove either that with regard to the Gentiles as well as Jews, *doing* is the thing required ; or that there are doers of the law who may be justified, among the heathen. ʻThe doers of the law,ʼ says the apostle, ʻshall be justified ; but the heathen do the law, therefore they shall be justified.ʼ This, however, is not the conclusion at which the apostle is aiming. He is not teaching the method of justification, or arguing to prove that the Gentiles as well as the Jews may be doers of the law, and thus be justified in the sight of God. He is expounding the law ; he is showing the principles by which God will judge the world, Gentiles as well as Jews. Those who are without the written law, he will judge without any reference to that law ; and those who are under the law, he will judge by that law. This general proposition he confirms first by saying, in ver. 13, that the mere possession of the law is not enough ; and secondly by saying, in ver. 14, that the Gentiles have a law by which they may be judged. The logical connection of ver. 14, therefore, is not with ver. 13, but with ver. 12. Thus Calvin, who says, " Probationem prioris membri (ver. 12) nunc repetit. Probat enim frustra obtendi a gentibus ignorantiam, quum factis suis declarent, nonnullam se habere justitiæ regulam. Nulla enim gens unquam sic ab humanitate abhorruit, ut non se intra leges aliquas contineret." *When, whenever, as often as,* which may be the sense of the particle in this case, ʻWhenever, or as often as the heathen do so or so.ʼ Or it may have the sense of *while, because :* ʻBecause, or since the heathen do so or so.ʼ Comp. 1 Cor. xv. 27. As ἔθνη is without the article, many would render it *heathen*, that is, *some heathen.* But in the first place, it is evident from the context that this is not what the apostle means to say. His object is to show that the heathen world have a rule of duty written on their hearts ; a fact which is not proved by some heathen obeying the law, but which is proved by the moral conduct of all men. Men generally, not some men, but all men, show by their acts that they have a knowledge of right and wrong. And secondly, this word has, without the article, in virtue of its frequent occurrence, a definite sense. Comp. iii. 29 ; ix. 24, and especially ver. 30 : ἔθνη . . . . . κατέλαβε δικαιοσύνην; *the* heathen attained righteousness. *Do by nature the things of the law.* There are two misinterpretations of the phrase, τὰ τοῦ νόμου ποιεῖν. The one is, that it means to fulfil the law; the other, to do the office of the law, *i.e.*, to command and forbid. The former is unnecessary, and is in direct opposition to the express and repeated declaration of the apostle, that none, whether Jew or Gentile, has ever fulfilled the law. To do the things of the law, is indeed to do what the law prescribes (comp. x. 5; Gal. iii. 12); but whether complete or partial obedience is intended, depends upon the context. The man who pays his debts, honours his parents, is kind to the poor, does the things of the law ; for these are things which the law prescribes. And this is all the argument the apostle requires, or his known doctrine allows us to understand by the phrase, in the present instance. This being the case, there is no need of resorting to the second interpretation mentioned above, which was proposed by Beza, and adopted by Wetstein, Flatt, and others. Though ποιεῖν τὰ τοῦ νόμου might mean to do what the law does, prescribe what is good and forbid what is evil, it certainly has not that sense elsewhere in Paul's writings, see x. 5 ; Gal. iii. 12; and is especially out of place here, in immediate connection with the phrase ποιηταί τοῦ νόμου, in the sense of *doers of the law.* The heathen do φύσει, *by nature,* the things of the law. The φύσις of anything is the peculiarity of its being, that in virtue of which it is what it is ; it is that which belongs to its original constitution, and is opposed to what is taught, acquired, or made. The word is sometimes used for a disposition or sentiment arising out of our nature, as opposed to mere arbitrary rules, as in 1 Cor. xi. 14. In the present case, the opposition is to νόμος. It is *by nature,* not by an external law, that the Gentiles are led to perform moral acts. Comp. Gal. iv. 8 ; Eph. ii. 3. The proper connection of φύσει with τὰ τοῦ νόμου ποιῇ, *they do by nature the things of the law,* is retained in our version, and by the great majority of commentators. Bengel, Rückert, and a few others, connect it with μὴ νόμον ἔχοντα, *not having the law by nature ;* but this is saying very little to the purpose of the apostle. His object is to show that φύσις supplies to the Gentiles the place of νόμος. *These not having the law, are a law unto themselves.* Νόμον, without the article, may be rendered either, *a law,* "not having a law," by implication, a written, external law ; or *the law, i.e.,* the Jewish law, since that word is often used without the article for the law of the Jews; that is, the law of God, as revealed in the Scriptures. The Gentiles, then, are a law unto themselves; they have in their own nature a rule of duty ; a knowledge of what is right, and a sense of obligation. As the absence of all moral acts among the lower animals shows that they have no sense of right and wrong, that they are not under a moral law, so the performance of such acts by the Gentiles, shows that they have a law written on their hearts.

VERSE 15. *Who show the work of the law written on their hearts.* Here, as in i. 25, and often elsewhere, the relative has a causal force : ' They are a law unto themselves, *because* they show the work of the law,' &c. Wolf, Tholuck, and others make ἔργον τοῦ νόμου a periphrase for the law itself ; Grotius, the effect of the law, that is, a knowledge of right and wrong ; most modern commentators make τὸ ἔργον equivalent to τὰ ἔργα. The same works which the Jews have prescribed in their law, the Gentiles show to be written on their hearts. It is by doing the things of the law, that the Gentiles show they have this inward rule of duty ; *their conscience also bearing witness.* Grotius, Koppe, and Tholuck, take συμμαρτυρεῖν in the sense of the simple verb. Comp. Jer. xi. 7, in the LXX., Rom. ix. 1 ; viii. 16. 'Their conscience bearing witness,' that is, to the fact that there is a law written on their hearts. But as συμμαρτυρεῖν is properly *una testari*, and as the context presents no reason for departing from the common meaning of the word, the great majority of commentators give the σύν its proper force. That with which conscience joins its testimony is the *honestas vitæ*, the moral acts of the heathen ; and the fact to which this joint testimony is borne, is that they are a law unto themselves. The apostle appeals not only to their external conduct, but to the inward operations of their moral nature. Συνείδησις is the *conscientia consequens*, the inward judge, whose acts are described in the following clause : *Their thoughts alternately accusing or even excusing.* Our version takes μεταξύ as an adverb, and makes ἀλλήλων the object of the following participles, 'And in the meanwhile, their thoughts accusing, or else excusing one another.' Köllner defends this interpretation, and declares that μεταξύ, *between*, cannot mean *vicissim*. It is used, he asserts, only of time, *between* two portions of time, *i.e.*, *during ;* or of space, *between* two places, persons, or things. It is not, however, so much the signification of the word μεταξύ, as the sense of the phrase μεταξύ ἀλλήλων, that is expressed by the translation, *vicissim*, sive *alternante sententiâ*. 'Between one another,' implies reciprocal or alternate action ; comp. Matt. xviii. 15. The order of the words is obviously opposed to the separation of ἀλλήλων from μεταξύ, and to making the former the object of the following participles ; which are rather to be taken absolutely. Their thoughts alternately accusing and excusing, viz., their conduct. The inward monitor acquits or condemns, as the case demands. Bengel remarks on the ἢ καί, *or even*, that καί is concessive, and shows "cogitationes longe plus habere quod accusent, quàm quod defendant."

VERSE 16. The greatest difficulty in relation to this verse is to determine its connection with the preceding context. In the common copies of our Bible, vers. 13, 14, 15, are marked as a parenthesis, and ver. 16 is placed in connection with ver. 12 : 'The heathen shall be judged without the law, and the Jews by the law, in the day when God shall judge the secrets of men.' Thus the passage is arranged by Griesbach and Knapp ; a mode of connection adopted also by Beza, Grotius, Reiche, and others. The objections to this explanation are, first, the distance at which this verse stands from ver. 12 ; and secondly, that the intervening verses have not the nature of a parenthesis, but are intimately connected with the idea contained in ver. 12. Calvin, Bengel, Rückert, Fritzsche, De Wette, Meyer, Tholuck, &c., connect this verse with ver. 15. The difficulty then is, that the verb and participles of ver. 15 are in the present tense, whereas κρινεῖ of this verse is future : 'Their thoughts accusing or excusing in the day when God shall judge the secrets of men.' To meet this difficulty, Calvin proposes to give ἐν ἡμέρᾳ the force of εἰς ἡμέραν, in the sense of *until*, or *in reference to the day*. Tholuck modifies this by making ἐν include εἰς, 'until on that day.' Not only does conscience now exercise its office, but will do so especially on the day of judgment. Rückert, De Wette, and others, suppose that the apostle thought only of the present when he wrote ἐνδείκνυνται, but extends the reference to the future, in the latter part of the verse. That is, the present participles express what will be present on the day of judgment : ' The heathen show the work of the law written on their hearts, and their conscience also bearing witness,' &c., on the day of judgment. But the main objection to this connection is, that the sense thus expressed is not suited to the apostle's object. He designs to prove that the Gentiles are a law to themselves. This is proved by the present operation of conscience, which approves or condemns their conduct. But it seems forced to bring that proof from what conscience will do on the day of judgment. It seems best therefore to refer this verse back to ver. 12. God, it is said, will judge *the secrets of men ;* the things which have escaped the knowledge of others ; those hidden deeds of the heart and life, which are the surest criterion of character. The searching character of this judgment ; its justice, as not guided by mere external appearance ; and its contrast with mere human judgments, are all intimated by this expression. The clause, *according to my gospel,* is not to be connected with κρινεῖ, as though the gospel was to be the rule of this divine judgment ; for this would contradict the apostle's doctrine, that men are to be judged by the light they possess. It refers to the fact of a final judgment, which is declared to be in accordance with the gospel, or a part of that message which Paul was commissioned to deliver. *By Jesus Christ* is to be connected with κρινεῖ. God will judge the world through Jesus Christ, agreeably to our Saviour's own declaration, "The Father judgeth no man, but hath committed all judgment unto the Son." Sometimes this judgment is referred directly to the Messiah, as in 1 Cor. iv. 5 ; 2 Cor. v. 10 ; 2 Tim. iv. 1 ; sometimes indirectly, as though he were but the representative of God, as in Acts xvii. 31. These representations, how-ever, are perfectly consistent. The preposition διά in such cases only expresses the idea that the power or authority which belongs to the God-head is specially exercised through the Son. Thus sometimes it is said, God created all things *through* the Son, Heb. i. 2 ; and sometimes that the Son himself is the Creator, Col. i. 16.

Such then are the principles on which Paul assures us that all men are to be judged. They commend themselves irresistibly to every man's con-science as soon as they are announced, and yet every false hope of heaven is founded on their denial or neglect. It may be proper to repeat them, that it may be seen how obviously the hopes of the Jews, to which Paul, from ver. 17 onward, applies them, are at variance with these moral axioms. 1. He who condemns in others what he does himself, *ipso facto* condemns himself. 2. God's judgments are according to the real character of men. 3. The goodness of God, being designed to lead us to repentance, is no proof that he will not punish sin. The perversion of that goodness will increase our guilt, and aggravate our condemnation. 4. God will judge every man according to his works, not according to his professions, his ecclesiastical connections or relations. 5. Men shall be judged by the knowledge of duty which they severally possess. God is therefore perfectly impartial. These are the principles on which men are to be tried, in the last day, by Jesus Christ ; and those who expect to be dealt with on any other plan, will be dreadfully disappointed.

DOCTRINE.

1. The leading doctrine of this section is, that God is just. His judg-ments are infinitely removed above all those disturbing causes of ignorance and partiality, by which the decisions of men are perverted, vers. 1, 16.

2. The refuge which men are always disposed to seek in their supposed advantages of ecclesiastical connection, as belonging to the true Church, &c., is a vain refuge. God deals with men according to their real character, vers. 2, 3.

3. The goodness of God has both the design and tendency to lead men to repentance. If it fails, the fault must be their own, ver. 4.

4. It is a great abuse of the divine goodness and forbearance to derive encouragement from them to continue in sin. Such conduct will certainly aggravate our condemnation, vers. 3—5.

5. None but the truly good, no matter what the professions, connections or expectations of others may be, will be saved ; and none but the truly wicked, whether Gentile or Jew, Christian or heathen, will be lost, vers. 6—10.

6. The goodness which the Scriptures approve consists, in a great degree, in the pursuit of heavenly things : it is a seeking after glory, honour and immortality, by a persevering continuance in well-doing. It is the pursuit of the true end of our being, by the proper means, ver. 7.

7. The responsibility of men being very different in this world, their rewards and punishment will, in all probability, be very different in the next. Those who knew not their Lord's will, shall be beaten with few stripes. And those who are faithful in the use of ten talents, shall be made rulers over ten cities, vers. 9, 10.

8. The heathen are not to be judged by a revelation of which they never heard. But as they enjoy a revelation of the divine character in the works of creation, chap. i. 19, 20, and of the rule of duty in their own hearts, vers. 14, 15, they are inexcusable. They can no more abide the test by which they are to be tried, than we can stand the application of the severer rule by which we are to be judged. Both classes, therefore, need a Saviour, ver. 12.

9. The moral sense is an original part of our constitution, and not the result of education, ver. 14.

10. Jesus Christ, who is to sit in judgment upon the secrets of all men, must be possessed of infinite knowledge, and therefore be divine, ver. 16.

REMARKS.

1. The deceitfulness of the human heart is strikingly exhibited in the different judgments which men pass upon themselves and others ; condemning in others what they excuse in themselves. And it not unfrequently happens that the most censorious are the most criminal, vers. 1, 3.

2. How does the goodness of God affect us ? If it does not lead us to repentance, it will harden our hearts, and aggravate our condemnation, vers. 4, 5.

3. Genuine repentance is produced by discoveries of God's mercy, legal repentance by fear of his justice, ver. 4.

4. Any doctrine which tends to produce security in sin, must be false. The proper effect of the enjoyment of peculiar advantages is to increase our sense of responsibility, and our gratitude to God, and not to make us suppose that we are his special favourites. God is no respecter of persons, vers. 3—10.

5. How vain the hopes of future blessedness, indulged by the immoral,

founded upon the expectation either that God will not deal with them according to their works, or that the secrets of their hearts will not be discovered! vers. 6—10, 16.

6. If God is a just God, his wrath is not to be escaped by evasions, but in the way of his own appointment. If we have no righteousness of our own, we must seek that of the Saviour, vers. 1—16.

7. He who died for the sins of men is to sit in judgment upon sinners. This is a just ground of fear to those who reject his offered mercy, and of confidence to those who trust in his righteousness, ver. 16.

ROMANS II. 17—29.

ANALYSIS.

This section consists properly of two parts. The first, vers. 17—24, contains an application of the principles laid down in the former section, to the case of the Jews. The second, vers. 25—29, is an exhibition of the nature and design of circumcision. The principal grounds of dependence on the part of the Jews were, 1. Their covenant relation to God. 2. Their superior advantages as to divine knowledge. 3. Their circumcision. Now if it is true that God will judge every man, Jew or Gentile, according to his works, and by the law which he has enjoyed, what will it avail any to say, We are Jews, we have the law, ver. 17 ; we have superior knowledge, ver. 18 ; we can act as guides and instructors to others? ver. 19. This may all be very true ; but are you less a thief, merely because you condemn stealing? less an adulterer, because you condemn adultery? or less a blasphemer, because you abhor sacrilege? vers. 21, 22. This superior knowledge, instead of extenuating, only aggravates your guilt. While boasting of your advantages, you by your sins bring a reproach on God, vers. 23, 24. According to the first principles of justice, therefore, your condemnation will be no less certain, and far more severe than that of the Gentiles. As to circumcision, to which the Jews attached so much importance, the apostle shows that it could avail nothing, except on condition of obedience to the law or covenant to which it belonged, ver. 25. If the law be broken, circumcision is worthless, ver. 25, latter clause. On the other hand, if the law is obeyed, the want of circumcision will not prevent a blessing, ver. 26. More than this, if those less favourably situated than the Jews are found obedient, they will rise up in judgment against the disobedient, though favoured people of God, ver. 27. All this proves that an external rite can, in itself, have no saving power ; because God is a Spirit, and requires and regards spiritual obedience alone. This principle is stated, first negatively, he is not a Jew who is such in profession merely, ver. 28 ; and then affirmatively, he is a Jew who is one inwardly, ver. 29.

COMMENTARY.

VERSE 17. Instead of *ἰδέ, behold,* which is in the common text, most of the ancient manuscripts, many of the versions, and of the Fathers, read *εἰ δέ, but if;* which reading is adopted by Bengel, Griesbach, Knapp, and Lachmann, and is followed by almost all the recent commentators. We have then the protasis of a sentence of which the apodosis does not follow: 'But if thou art called a Jew, and hast the law, *thou shouldst act accord-*

ing to it;' comp. 2 Pet. ii. 4. Or the answering clause may be found in ver. 21, ' If thou art called a Jew,' &c., ' teachest thou then (ουν) not thyself?' *Winer,* § 63, I. 1. *Art called,* ἐπονομάζῃ, *called after,* or *in addition to;* a sense insisted on here by Theodoret, who says, " ουκ εἶπεν ὀνομάζῃ, ἀλλ' ἐπονομάζῃ." Bengel, Köllner, Meyer, and others, take the same view of the meaning of the word : ' Besides your proper name, you call yourself a Jew.' But as the compound word is used for the simple one in Gen. iv. 17, 25, 26, and elsewhere, and as Jew was then the common name of the people, it is better rendered, *thou art called.* Ἰουδαῖος, *a Jew,* a descendant of Judah, in the New Testament applied to all the Israelites, as inhabitants of Judea. It was considered a title of honour, not only on account of its etymology, יְהוּדָה, meaning *praised,* Gen. xlix. 8, but because it designated the people of God. Comp. vers. 28, 29, and Rev. ii. 9 : " I know the blasphemy of those who say they are Jews, and are not." To be a Jew in this sense was to be one of the covenant people of God, a member of the theocracy, or of the true Church. As this was the principal ground of the false confidence of the Jews, the apostle mentions it before all others. It was not enough that they were the children of Abraham ; if they sinned, they were exposed to the displeasure of that God who will render to every man according to his works, to the Jew first, and also to the Gentile. *And restest on the law.* That is, Thou placest thy confidence upon the law. In the Septuagint, the word occurs in Micah iii. 11, a passage illustrative of the one before us, " The heads thereof judge for reward, and the priests thereof teach for hire, and the prophets thereof divine for money : yet will they lean upon the Lord and say, Is not the Lord among us ? none evil can come upon us." *The law* here means the whole Mosaic system, the civil and religious polity of the Jews. This they relied upon ; the fact that they were within the Church, were partakers of its sacraments and rites ; that they had a divinely appointed priesthood, continued in unbroken succession from Aaron, and invested with the power to make atonement for sin, was the ground on which they rested their hope of acceptance with God. Within that pale they considered all safe ; out of it there was no salvation. Such was the false confidence of the Jews ; such has been and is the false confidence of thousands of Christians. *And makest thy boast of God.* See *Winer,* § 13. 2, on the form of the word καυχᾶσαι. To boast, or glory in any person or thing, is to rejoice in him or it as a source of honour, happiness, or profit to ourselves. We are forbidden thus to glory in ourselves, or any creature, as the ground of our confidence and source of our blessedness. "Let no man glory in men ; but he that glories, let him glory in the Lord." This glorying in God may be right or wrong, according to the reasons of it. If it proceeds from a sense of our own emptiness, and from right apprehensions of the excellence of God, and from faith in his promises, then it is that glorying which is so often commanded. But if it arises from false notions of our relation to him, as his peculiar favourites, then it is vain and wicked. The Jews regarded themselves in such a sense the people of God, as to be secure of his favour, let their personal character be what it might. They boasted that he was their God, that they monopolized his favour, all other nations being his enemies.

VERSE 18. *And knowest the will,* &c., of God. Superior knowledge was another of the peculiar distinctions of the Jews. The particulars to which the apostle refers in this, as well as in the preceding and succeeding

verses, constituted real and great privileges, by which the Jews were distinguished from all other people.   To be the people of God, to have the
law, to know the divine will, were indeed great advantages ; but these advantages only increased the obligations of those who enjoyed them.   They
did not of themselves constitute any ground of confidence of acceptance
with God; much less did the mere possession of these distinguishing
favours give exemption from those principles of just retribution, according
to which God will judge the world.   The apostle, however, grants the
Jews all they claimed: he grants that they were the people of God; that
they had the law, knew the divine will, &c., and then shows that they
were, nevertheless, exposed to condemnation.   If real advantages, such as
distinguished the Jews above all other nations, were of no avail to their justification or acceptance before God, what is to be said or thought of those
who place their confidence in fictitious advantages, in mere imaginary
superiority to their fellow men or fellow Christians; as belonging to the
true Church, having the true succession, the real sacraments, when in fact
in these respects they are even less favoured than those whom they look
upon as outside the Church and the covenant ?   *And approvest the things
that are more excellent.*   Δοκιμάζειν is *to try, to examine*, as in 1 Cor. iii.
13; and then, *to regard as tried*, *i.e.*, *to approve*, as in 1 Cor. xvi. 3.
Διαφέρειν means *to differ*, as in Gal. ii. 6; and also, *to excel*, as in Matt. x.
31. See also Matt. vi. 26; Luke xii. 7, &c.   This is the most common
meaning of the word in the New Testament.   We have then the choice
of the two interpretations, *Thou approvest the things that are more excellent*, or, *Thou dost distinguish the things that are different.*   Our version
gives the former, both here and in Philip. i. 10, where the same words
occur.   The latter is adopted by Theodoret, who explains διαφέροντα by
ἐναντία ἀλλήλοις, δικαιοσύνην καὶ ἀδικίαν ; and Theophylact, τί δεῖ πρᾶξαι καὶ
τί μὴ δεῖ πρᾶξαι.   The same view is taken by most of the recent commentators.   It is suitable to the context, in as much as the apostle is here
speaking of the peculiar advantages of the Jews, one of which was their
superior knowledge, and their ability to do what others could not, that is,
decide what was and what was not consistent with the will of God.   On
the other hand, however, to approve of what is right, to discern it to be
right, is a higher attainment than merely to discriminate between good and
evil.   And as the apostle is here conceding to the Jews everything they
could claim, it is better to give his words their highest sense.   He
admits that theoretically they were right in their judgments.   It was not
their moral judgments, but their moral conduct that was in fault.   *Being
instructed*, κατηχούμενος, (orally instructed, as the word literally means,)
out of the law, *i.e.*, the Scriptures, as νόμος often means.   The word or law
of God was a light to their feet, to which they could, at all times, refer to
guide their steps.

VERSES 19, 20.   *And art confident that thou thyself art a guide of the
blind.*   The apostle, in these verses, states the effect which the peculiar
advantages of the Jews produced upon them.   They considered themselves
to be greatly superior to all other nations; capable of instructing them;
and of being the guides and light of the world.   This idea is presented in
different lights, in what follows—*a light of them which are in darkness, an
instructor of the foolish, a teacher of babes.*   They looked upon themselves
as qualified to act as the instructors of others, ἔχοντα, *having*, *i.e.*, because
they had the form, &c.   *Having the form of knowledge and of truth in
the law.*   Μόρφωσις occurs in the New Testament only here and in 2 Tim.

iii. 5. In the latter passage it is opposed to the reality (δύναμις,) and means mere appearance. This, however, cannot be its meaning here; for the clause in which it occurs, assigns the reason which the Jews felt themselves to have, and which they had in fact, for their superior knowledge. They supposed themselves to be able to guide others because they had the form of knowledge in the law. It, therefore, here means, *forma quæ rem exprimat*, as Grotius expresses it. The form of knowledge, is knowledge as represented or expressed in the law. In other words, the exhibition of knowledge and truth in the law is given in a form which expresses their true nature. The words γνῶσις and ἀλήθεια do not essentially differ. The former, says De Wette, is truth as known; the latter, truth in itself.

Verses 21, 22. *Thou therefore that teachest another.* We have here the virtual apodosis of ver. 17. 'If thou, although a Jew, and related to God as one of his peculiar people, and well instructed out of the law, violate the law, and do the things thou condemnest in others, how canst thou escape the judgment of that God who will render to every man *according to* his works?' It is evident the apostle means to assert that the Jews were guilty of the crimes here specified; and it matters little whether the several classes be read interrogatively or affirmatively. The former, as the more forcible is generally preferred. To set ourselves up as instructors, and yet not to apply our principles to ourselves, is not only an inconsistency, but offensive arrogance and hypocrisy. To steal and to commit adultery are great sins, but for those who preach against them and condemn them in others, to commit them, is to quadruple their guilt. The Jews, therefore, who committed the sins which they so loudly condemned in the heathen, were more guilty in the sight of God than the heathen themselves. While flattering themselves that they were secure from the divine wrath, in the enclosure of the theocracy, they were the special objects of God's displeasure; so that publicans and harlots were nearer to the kingdom of God than they. *Thou that abhorrest idols, dost thou rob temples?* That the Jews, subsequently to the captivity, did abhor idols, is a well known fact; that they robbed the temples of idols is not known. Besides, robbing the temples of idols was not sacrilege; for in the mind of the Jew there was no sacredness in those temples. It was to him robbery, and nothing more; probably something less. The objurgatory character of these several clauses requires that the thing here charged should be of the same nature with idolatry, not its opposite. The Jew taught that men should not steal, yet he stole himself; he said, Commit not adultery, yet he was guilty of that crime; he abhorred idols, yet was guilty of idolatry. It is something analogous to idolatry that is here charged, not the despoiling of heathen temples, which would be the natural expression of the abhorrence of idols. The essence of idolatry was profanation of God; of this the Jews were in a high degree guilty.

They had made his house a den of thieves. Instead, therefore, of taking the word ἱεροσυλεῖς literally, which the context forbids, it should be understood in a secondary sense. It expresses the sin of irreverence in its higher forms; either as manifested in withholding from God his due, which the prophet denounces as robbery—"Will a man rob God? yet ye have robbed me. But ye say, Wherein have we robbed thee? In tithes and offerings," Mal. iii. 8; or it may be taken in the still more general sense of profanation, the irreverent disregard of God and holy things. This is all the context requires: 'You profess great reverence for God, in eschewing idolatry; and yet, in other forms, you are guilty of the greatest irreverence.'

Verses 23, 24.   Another striking instance of the inconsistency between their principles and their conduct was, that while they made a boast of the law, they so disregarded its precepts as to lead the heathen to think and speak evil of that God who gave the law, of whose character they judged by the conduct of his people. This charge he expresses in the language of their own prophets; see Isa. lii. 5, and Ezek. xxxvi. 20, 23. In the former passage we find in the LXX. nearly the same words as those used by the apostle: "*δἰ ὑμᾶς διαπαντὸς τὸ ὄνομά μου βλασφημεῖται ἐν τοῖς ἔθνεσι.*" Both Isaiah and Ezekiel, indeed, refer to that blaspheming of God by the heathen, which arose from the misery of his people, whose God they were thus led to regard as unable to protect his worshippers. This, however, does not render the reference of the apostle less appropriate; for it is the mere fact that God's name was blasphemed among the Gentiles, on account of the Jews, that the apostle means to confirm by this reference to the Scriptures. And besides, as their sins were the cause of their captivity, their sins were the cause also of the evil speaking of God, of which their sufferings were the immediate occasion.

Verse 25.   The apostle, in vers. 1-16 of this chapter, had proved that God would judge both Jew and Gentile according to their works; in vers. 17-24, that the Jews, notwithstanding their peculiar privileges, were no less sinful than the Gentiles; the obvious conclusion therefore was, that they were no less liable to condemnation. It is with this conclusion implied, but not expressed, that this verse is connected by the particle *γάρ:* "You are exposed to condemnation, *for* circumcision, in which you trust, profits only on condition that you keep the law.' Comp. chap. iv. 2, and iv. 9, and other places in which *γάρ* refers to a thought omitted. Circumcision is not here to be taken for Judaism in general, of which that rite was the sign, but for the rite itself. It is obvious that the Jews regarded circumcision as in some way securing their salvation. That they did so regard it, may be proved not only from such passages of the New Testament where the sentiment is implied, but also by the direct assertion of their own writers. Such assertions have been gathered in abundance from their works by Eisenmenger, Schœttgen, and others. For example, the Rabbi Menachem, in his Commentary on the Books of Moses, fol. 43, col. 3, says, "Our Rabbins have said, that no circumcised man will see hell." In the Jalkut Rubeni, num. 1, it is taught, "Circumcision saves from hell." In the Medrasch Tillim, fol. 7, col. 2, it is said, "God swore to Abraham, that no one who was circumcised should be sent to hell." In the book Akedath Jizehak, fol. 54, col. 2, it is taught that "Abraham sits before the gate of hell, and does not allow that any circumcised Israelite should enter there."* The apostle considers circumcision under two different aspects. First, as a rite supposed to possess some inherent virtue or merit of its own; and secondly, as a sign and seal of God's covenan . In the former view, Paul here as well as elsewhere, says, "Circumcision is nothing, and uncircumcision is nothing," Gal. vi. 15 ; in the latter, it had its value. As a seal it was attached in the first place to the national covenant between God and the Jews. It was a sign of the existence of that covenant, and that the person to whom it was affixed was included within its pale. It was a pledge on the part of God that he would fulfil the promises of that covenant. If any Jew fulfilled his part of the national covenant, and in that sense kept the law, his circumcision profited him.

---

* Eisenmenger's Entdecktes Judenthum, Part II. 285.

It secured to him all the advantages of Judaism. But this rite was, in the second place, attached to the spiritual covenant formed with Abraham; that is, "it was a seal of the righteousness of faith;" it was designed as an assurance that Abraham was, in virtue of his faith, regarded as righteous in the sight of God. To all those Jews who had the faith of Abraham, and thus kept the covenant established with him, circumcision was in like manner profitable. It was the visible sign and pledge that all who believed should be justified. On the other hand, if either the national or spiritual covenant was broken, circumcision was of no avail. The fact that an Israelite was circumcised, did not save him from excision from the people, if he broke any of the fundamental laws of Moses; neither could circumcision save those who, being destitute of the faith of Abraham, appeared as sinners before the bar of God. Paul therefore teaches that circumcision had no inherent, magical efficacy; that it had no value beyond that of a sign and seal; that it secured the blessings of the covenant to those who kept the covenant; but to the transgressors of the law it was of no avail. This latter idea he expresses by saying, ἡ περιτομή σου ἀκροβυστία γέγονεν, *thy circumcision has become uncircumcision.* That is, it is of no use. It cannot prevent your being dealt with as a transgressor, or treated as though you had never been circumcised.

Verse 26. *Therefore, if the uncircumcision keep the righteousness of the law.* This verse is an inference (οὖν) from the preceding. It was there taught that everything depends upon obedience to the law. God will judge every man according to his works. If a Jew, though circumcised, break the law, he shall be condemned; and if a Gentile, though uncircumcised, keep the law, he shall be justified. The one proposition flows from the other; for if circumcision is in itself nothing, its presence cannot protect the guilty; its absence cannot invalidate the claims of the righteous. Δικαιώματα, *decrees, precepts,* what the law prescribes as right. The apostle does not mean to intimate that the Gentiles do in any case keep the righteousness of the law; contrary to his own explicit assertion, that there is none righteous, no not one. It is a mere hypothetical statement, designed to show that everything depends on obedience, and that circumcision cannot be the ground either of justification or condemnation. *Shall not his uncircumcision be counted for circumcision?* The phrase λογίζεσθαί τι εἰς τι, in accordance with the Hebrew לְ חָשַׁב, 1 Sam. i. 13; Isa. xxix. 17, often means to reckon or regard one thing as another. Uncircumcision shall be taken for circumcision.

Verse 27. Calvin makes this verse a part of the interrogation begun in ver. 26, a mode of pointing followed by Koppe, Lachmann, Fritzsche, and many others. 'Shall not uncircumcision be reckoned circumcision, and condemn you who break the law?' Our translators supply οὐχί before κρινεῖ, and make ver. 27 a distinct interrogation, 'and shall not the uncircumcision condemn you,' &c. Meyer takes ver. 27 categorically, and and καί in the sense of *even* or *moreover*, so that ver. 27 is virtually an answer to the preceding question. 'Shall not uncircumcision be taken for circumcision? (Yes, verily), it will even condemn you,' &c. In either way the idea is, that the obedient uncircumcised heathen would be better off, he would stand on higher ground, than the disobedient circumcised Jew. It is only putting the truth taught in this verse into different words to say, 'the unbaptized believer shall condemn the baptized unbeliever.' *The uncircumcision which is by nature,* ἡ ἐκ φύσεως ἀκροβυστία. The position of the article shows plainly that ἐκ φύσεως qualifies ἀκροβυστία, and is not to be connected with the following participle τελοῦσα. The sense is, "the uncircumcision which is natural," and not 'which by nature keeps the law.' *If it fulfil the law*, i. e., provided it is obedient, and therefore righteous. *Shall judge*, κρινεῖ, by implication, *shall condemn;* the judgment is by the context supposed to be a condemnatory one. Comp. Matt. xii. 41. *Thee who by the letter*, &c.; σὲ τὸν διὰ γράμματος, *thee with the letter*, i. e., the written law. In the present case it is not used in a disparaging sense, for the mere verbal meaning in opposition to the spirit. The context rather requires that γράμμα and περιτομή should be taken as expressing the real and substantial benefits of the Jews. Our version renders διά *by*, Beza also has *per*. He understands the apostle to mean that external circumcision being profaned only rendered the Jews so much the worse. But as διά with the genitive so often means *with*, as expressing the circumstances under which anything is done (as δἰ ὑπομονῆς *with patience*, διὰ προσκόμματος *with offence*), the meaning is, *Te, qui literas et circumcisionem habens, contra legem facis.* Notwithstanding they had the law and circumcision, they were transgressors of the law. Calvin makes *letter and circumcision* to mean literal circumcision; but this is unnecessary, and unsuited to the context; for when speaking of the advantages of the Jews, the law is of too much importance to allow of the word which expresses it being merged into a mere epithet.

VERSES 28, 29. *For not he who is externally a Jew, is a Jew*, &c. These verses assign the reason why the external rite of circumcision can avail so little. God looks upon the heart, and does not regard mere external circumstances. It is not, therefore, mere descent from Abraham, nor connection with the external theocracy or church, that can secure his favour; but the possession of those internal dispositions which external rites are intended to symbolize. Verse 28 contains the negative, ver. 29 the affirmative statement of this general truth. The word Ἰουδαῖος is to be supplied in the first member of the sentence, as the subject is ὁ ἐν τῷ φανερῷ Ἰουδαῖος, and the predicate Ἰουδαῖός ἐστιν. The same remark may be made with regard to the following clause, where the subject is ἡ ἐν τῷ φανερῷ, ἐν σαρκὶ περιτομή, and the predicate περιτομή ἐστιν. *External circumcision in the flesh is not circumcision.* Φανερός, *apparent, visible*, what falls under the observation of the senses, hence *external*. The word Jew is of course to be taken as the designation of the people of God. 'He is not one of the people of God who is such externally.' It is nothing external that constitutes or secures this peculiar relation to God. The affirmative statement is, ἀλλ' ὁ ἐν τῷ κρυπτῷ Ἰουδαῖος [Ἰουδαῖός ἐστιν], *but the Jew in secret is a Jew.* As in the preceding verse, part of the subject is borrowed from the predicate, so here and in the following clause the predicate is to be borrowed from the subject; that is, Ἰουδαῖός ἐστιν is to be supplied after the first clause, and περιτομή ἐστιν after the second clause of this verse, so that the whole reads thus: "But he who is inwardly a Jew *is really a Jew*; and the circumcision of the heart, in spirit and not in letter, *is circumcision*." This is the construction of the passage almost universally adopted. Κρυπτός *hidden*, and as opposed to φανερός, *inward;* hence ἐν τῷ κρυπτῷ, *inwardly, in heart.* Comp. 1 Pet. iii. 4. True circumcision is described as περιτομὴ καρδίας, ἐν πνεύματι, οὐ γράμματι. These latter words admit of different interpretations. The apostle contrasts πνεῦμα and γράμμα in Rom. vii. 6, and 2 Cor. iii. 6, much as he does here.

In chap. vii. 6, *oldness of the letter* may mean the condition and spirit of those who were under the law, now become old ; and *newness of the spirit* may mean that new condition and temper which the Holy Spirit gives. In 2 Cor. iii. 6, Paul says he was made a minister of the new covenant, οὐ γράμματος, ἀλλὰ πνεύματος, *not of the letter, but of the spirit, i.e.*, not of the law, but of the gospel ; not of a mere objective, legal covenant, but of that which derives its whole character from the Spirit, and therefore is *spirit*, or in the widest sense of the word, *spiritual*. Comp. also Gal. iii. 3. Guided by these passages, Rückert understands πνεῦμα here to mean the new principle of life imparted by the Holy Spirit, and ἐν to express instrumentality. Thus the sense is : The circumcision of the heart is not produced or effected by the law, but by this new divine principle of life. The same interpretation substantially is given by Köllner. It is not, however, strictly in accordance with the mode of representation adopted in the Scriptures, to speak of the circumcision of the heart, *i. e*, sanctification, as effected by anything implanted in us. Beza makes ἐν πνεύματι simply exegetical of καρδίας, and gives the sense thus : " Cujus vis est interior et in animo, sive qua circumcisi sunt affectus." Erasmus : " Quæ Spiritu constat, referens ad Spiritum Sanctum, cujus unius opus est ista circumcisio ἀχειροποίητος. Mihi vero videtur ἐν πνεύματι additum partim propter antithesin γράμματος, partim ut explicaret, quid vocaret circumcisionem cordis." According to this view, ἐν πνεύματι is *in heart*, and is tautological with the clause (circumcision of the heart) which it should explain. And besides, the opposition between πνεῦμα and γράμμα is thus destroyed. Others again take ἐν πνεύματι and ἐν γράμματι adverbially, " after a spiritual, not after a literal or external way ;" or adjectively, *spiritual*, not *literal*. The most common, and on the whole the preferable interpretation, refers πνεῦμα to the Holy Spirit, and gives ἐν the sense of *by*. The circumcision of the heart is then effected by the Spirit, and not by the letter, *i.e.*, in obedience to the prescriptions of the law. *Whose praise is not of men, but of God.* The relative ου is to be referred to Ἰουδαῖος. The true Jew, or child of God, is one whose excellence is internal, seen and acknowledged by God ; not in its nature external, securing the notice and approbation of men. If the relative οὗ be taken as neuter, then the idea is the same, but presented in another form : ' Of which (*i.e.*, of this spiritual Judaism) the praise is of God.' As, however, Ἰουδαῖος is the main subject in the context, the former explanation is the more natural. The spiritual import of circumcision was clearly taught in the Old Testament, as in Deut. xxx. 6 : " The Lord thy God will circumcise thine heart, and the heart of thy seed, to love the Lord thy God." See Deut. x. 16 ; Jer. iv. 4 : " Circumcise yourselves to the Lord, and take away the foreskins of your heart." The wicked are therefore called "the uncircumcised in heart," Jer. ix. 26 ; Ezek. xliv. 9 ; Acts vii. 51. Comp. Col. ii. 11 : " In whom also ye are circumcised with the circumcision made without hands." This is what he calls "the circumcision of Christ," or Christian circumcision, that which Christ secures and gives. As circumcision thus signifies inward purification, and was a seal of the righteousness of faith, it was, as to its import and design, identical with baptism. Hence what in Col. ii. 11, Paul expresses by saying, "Ye are circumcised," he expresses in ver. 12 by saying, "Ye are buried with him in baptism." What, therefore, he teaches of the worthlessness of external circumcision, without internal purity, and of the possibility of the external sign being received without the internal grace, is no less true of baptism. See 1 Cor. vii. 18, 19 ; Gal. vi. 15.

DOCTRINE.

1. Membership in the true Church, considered as a visible society, is no security that we shall obtain the favour of God. The Jews, before the advent, were members of the true and only Church, and yet Paul teaches that they were not on this account the more acceptable to God. Multitudes of Jewish converts were members of the apostolic Church, and yet, retaining their former doctrines and spirit, were in the gall of bitterness, ver. 17.

2. Mere knowledge cannot commend us to God. It neither sanctifies the heart, nor of itself renders men more useful. When made the ground of confidence, or the fuel of pride and arrogance, it is perverted and destructive, vers. 18—20.

3. Superior knowledge enhances the guilt of sin, and increases the certainty, necessity, and severity of punishment, without in itself increasing the power of resistance. It is, therefore, a great mistake to make knowledge our sole dependence in promoting the moral improvement of men, vers. 21, 22.

4. The sins of the professing people of God are peculiarly offensive to him, and injurious to our fellow-men, vers. 22—24.

5. Here, as in the former part of the chapter, the leading idea is, that God is just. He asks not whether a man is a Jew or a Gentile, a Greek or Barbarian, bond or free, but what is his character? Does he *do* good or evil? vers. 17—24.

6. According to the apostle, the true idea of a sacrament is not that it is a mystic rite, possessed of inherent efficacy, or conveying grace as a mere *opus operatum;* but that it is a seal and sign, designed to confirm our faith in the validity of the covenant to which it is attached; and, from its significant character, to present and illustrate some great spiritual truth, ver. 25.

7. All hopes are vain which are founded on a participation of the sacraments of the Church, even when they are of divine appointment, as circumcision, baptism, and the Lord's supper; much more when they are of human invention, as penance, and extreme unction, vers. 26, 27.

8. Religion and religious services, to be acceptable to God, must be of the heart. Mere external homage is of no account, vers. 28, 29.

REMARKS.

1. The sins and refuges of men are alike in all ages. The Jew expected salvation because he was a Jew, so does the Roman Catholic because he is a Roman Catholic, the Greek because he is a Greek, and so of others. Were it ever so certain that the Church to which we belong is the true, apostolic, universal Church, it remains no less certain that without holiness no man shall see God, ver. 17, &c.

2. The possession of superior knowledge should make us anxious, first, to go right ourselves, and then to guide others right. To preach against evils which we ourselves commit, while it aggravates our guilt, is little likely to do others much good, ver. 18, &c.

3. Christians should ever remember that they are the epistles of Jesus Christ, known and read of all men; that God is honoured by their holy

living, and that his name is blasphemed when they act wickedly, vers. 23, 24.

4. Whenever true religion declines, the disposition to lay undue stress on external rites is increased. The Jews, when they lost their spirituality, supposed that circumcision had power to save them. ' Great is the virtue of circumcision,' they cried ; ' no circumcised person enters hell.' The Christian Church, when it lost its spirituality, taught that water in baptism washed away sin. How large a part of nominal Christians rest all their hopes on the idea of the inherent efficacy of external rites ! ver. 25, &c.

5. While it is one dangerous extreme to make religion consist in the observance of external ceremonies, it is another to undervalue them, when of divine appointment. Paul does not say that circumcision was useless ; he asserts its value. So, likewise, the Christian sacraments, baptism and the Lord's supper, are of the utmost importance, and to neglect or reject them is a great sin, ver. 26, &c.

6. If the heart be right in the sight of God, it matters little what judgment men may form of us ; and, on the other hand, the approbation of men is a poor substitute for the favour of God, ver. 29.

CHAPTER III.

CONTENTS.

THIS CHAPTER MAY BE DIVIDED INTO THREE PARTS. THE FIRST CONTAINS A BRIEF STATEMENT AND REFUTATION OF THE JEWISH OBJECTIONS TO THE APOSTLE'S REASONING, VERS. 1—8. THE SECOND A CONFIRMATION OF HIS DOCTRINE FROM THE TESTIMONY OF SCRIPTURE ; AND A FORMAL DRAWING OUT AND DECLARATION OF HIS CONCLUSION, THAT BY THE WORKS OF THE LAW NO FLESH LIVING CAN BE JUSTIFIED BEFORE GOD, VERS. 9—20. THE THIRD, AN EXPOSITION OF THE GOSPEL METHOD OF JUSTIFICATION, VERS. 21—31.

ROMANS III. 1—8.

ANALYSIS.

THE first objection to Paul's reasoning here presented is, that according to his doctrine the Jew has no advantage over the Gentile, ver. 1. The apostle denies the correctness of this inference from what he had said, and admits that the Jews have great advantages over all other people, ver. 2. The second objection is, that God having promised to be the God of the Jews, their unfaithfulness, even if admitted, does not release him from his engagements, or make his promise of no effect, ver. 3. Paul, in answer, admits that the faithfulness of God must not be called in question, let what will happen, vers. 4, 5 ; but he shows that the principle on which the Jews expected exemption from punishment, viz. because their unrighteousness commended the righteousness of God, was false. This he proves by showing first, that if their principle was correct, God could not punish any one, Gentile or Jew, vers. 5—7 ; and secondly, that it would lead to this absurdity, that it is right to do evil that good may come, ver. 8.

COMMENTARY.

VERSE. 1. *What then is the advantage of the Jew ?* The conclusion at which the apostle had arrived at the end of the preceding chapter was, that the Jews, no less than the Gentiles, are to be judged according to their works, and by their knowledge of the divine will; and that being thus judged, they are exposed to condemnation, notwithstanding their circumcision and all their other advantages. The most obvious objection in the mind of a Jew to this conclusion must have been, that it was inconsistent with the acknowledged privileges and superiority of his nation. This objection the apostle here presents ; the answer follows in the next verse : Περισσός, *over and above, abundant ;* and in a comparative sense *better,* and substantively, as in the present instance,'*excellence, pre-eminence.* What is the pre-eminence or superiority of the Jew ? Comp. Eccles. vi. 11, τί περισσὸν τῷ ἀνθρώπῳ ; *what advantage has man ?* The second question in this verse, *what is the benefit of circumcision ?* is by some considered as a repetition of the first'; circumcision being taken as the mere sign of Judaism. ' What is the advantage of the Jew ? or what is the benefit of Judaism ?' But circumcision as a rite was so important in the estimation of the Jews, and is made so prominent by the apostle in the preceding context, that it is better to consider the second question as referring to the rite itself.

VERSE 2. *Much, in every way.* The answer to the objection implied in the preceding verse, is a denial of its correctness as an inference from the apostle's reasoning. It does not follow, because the Jews are to be judged according to their works, that there is no advantage in being the peculiar people of God, having a divine revelation, &c. Πρῶτον μὲν γάρ. These words are rendered by Beza, *primarium enim (illud est) ;* comp. Luke xix. 47 ; Acts xxv. 2. Calvin says, " πρῶτον significat præcipue vel præsertim, hoc sensu, Etsi unum istud esset, quod habent Dei oracula sibi commissa, satis valere debet ad eorum dignitatem." Our translators adopt the same view. But to both of the interpretations the particle γάρ furnishes an objection. The third and simplest view is, that the words in question mean *first,* in the first place, as in 1 Cor. xi. 18 ; γάρ is then *namely, for example.* That the enumeration is not carried on, is no serious objection to this explanation, as we have other examples of the same kind. See chap. i. 8. *Because they were entrusted with the oracles of God.* The subject of ἐπιστεύθησαν, viz. 'Ιουδαῖοι is implied by the connection ; τὰ λόγια is the accusative ; comp. Gal. ii. 7 ; πεπίστευμαι τὸ εὐαγγέλιον, 1 Cor. ix. 17 ; 1 Thess. ii. Some, as Theodoret, Beza, &c., understand by τὰ λόγια τοῦ Θεοῦ, the law ; others, as Grotius, Tholuck, &c., the Messianic promises ; others, as Calvin, Rosenmüller, De Wette, the whole Scriptures. In favour of this last is the usage of the phrase which in the Old Testament is used for the revelation of God in general, and in the New Testament, for any divine communication. Heb. v. 12 ; 1 Pet. iv. 11. The words therefore are general in their meaning, and there is nothing in the context to limit them ; for the apostle is speaking of the treasure committed to the safe custody of the Jews ; that deposit of divine knowledge by which they were distinguished from all other nations. Here, as in innumerable other places, the sacred writers of the New Testament use forms of expression which clearly imply that they regarded the sacred writings of the Jews as really the word of God.

Verse 3. Tί γάρ; *What then?* See Philip. i. 18—a formula used to introduce an explanation, confirmation, or vindication of a preceding assertion; or to start an objection for the purpose of answering it. In the present instance it is agreed that the apostle designs to vindicate what he had previously taught; but whether ver. 3 refers to ver. 2, or to the conclusion that the Jews were as much exposed to condemnation as the Gentiles, is not so plain. According to the former view, the design of this verse is to confirm what is said in ver. 2 : 'To the Jews were committed the promises of God, or oracles of God. This is a great advantage ; for if some of them disbelieve those promises, and reject the Messiah, God remains faithful, and will accomplish all his gracious purposes.' Thus substantially, Calvin, Beza, Tholuck, Fritzsche, Rückert, Meyer, and many others. According to the other view, the apostle here presents and answers another objection to his previous reasoning : 'What if we are unfaithful,' says the Jew, ' does that invalidate the faithfulness of God ? Has he not promised to be a God to Abraham and to his seed ? Has he not entered into a solemn covenant to grant his people all the benefits of the Messiah's kingdom ? This covenant is not suspended on our moral character. If we adhere to the covenant by being circumcised and observing the law, the fidelity of God is pledged for our salvation. We may therefore be as wicked as you would make us out to be ; that does not prove that we shall be treated as heathen.' For the latter view it may be urged, 1. That it is better suited to the context. It is plain that the whole of the first part of this chapter is an answer to the objections of the Jews to the apostle's doctrine that they were exposed to condemnation. This is clear as to the first verse, and to the fifth and those that follow it. It is, therefore, more consistent with the design of the passage, to make this verse an answer to the main objection of the Jews, than to consider it a mere confirmation of what is said in ver. 2. This consideration has the more force, since, on the other view of the passage, the principal ground of confidence of the Jews, *viz.*, their peculiar relation to God, is left unnoticed. Their great objection to Paul's applying his general principles of justice to their case was that their situation was peculiar : 'God has chosen us as his people in Abraham. If we retain our relation to him by circumcision and the observance of the law, we shall never be treated or condemned as the Gentiles.' Traces of this opinion abound in the New Testament, and it is openly avowed by the Jewish writers. "Think not," says the Baptist, "to say within yourselves, We have Abraham to our father," Matt. iii. 9. "We be Abraham's seed," John viii. 33. Comp. Rom. ii. 17; ix. 6, and other passages, in which Paul argues to prove that being the natural descendants of Abraham is not enough to secure the favour of God. That such was the doctrine of the Jews is shown by numerous passages from their writings. "If a Jew commit all manner of sins," says Abarbanel, "he is indeed of the number of sinning Israelites, and will be punished according to his sins ; but he has, notwithstanding, a portion in eternal life." The same sentiment is expressed in the book Torath Adam, fol. 100, in nearly the same words, and the reason assigned for it, "That all Israel has a portion in eternal life."* This is a favourite phrase with the Rabbins, and frequently occurs in their writings. Justin Martyr, as quoted by Grotius on chap.

* Eisenmenger's Ent. Judenthum, Part II. p. 293.

ii. 13, attributes this doctrine to the Jews of his day: "They suppose that to them universally, who are of the seed of Abraham, no matter how sinful and disobedient to God they may be, the eternal kingdom shall be given." This interpretation, therefore, makes the verse in question present the objection which the Jews would be most likely to urge. 2. A second consideration in its favour is, that it best satisfies the meaning of the words. The other view makes Paul say that the unfaithfulness of some of the Jews, some here and there, could not render the promise of no effect. It would be natural for the Jews thus to soften down the statement of the case. But Paul had not said that some of the Jews were unfaithful, but that they were all under condemnation; that as to this point there was no difference between them and the Gentiles, since all had sinned and come short of the glory of God. It cannot escape notice how completely the doctrine of the Jews has been transferred by ritualists to Christianity. They held that if a man was circumcised and remained within the Theocracy, he might be punished for his sins, but he would ultimately be saved. So ritualists hold that all who are baptized and remain within the pale of the true Church, though they may suffer for their sins here or hereafter (in purgatory) are certain to be finally saved.

If some did not believe? The word ἠπίστησαν may mean *disbelieved*, or *were unfaithful.* Tholuck, Fritzsche, Rückert (2d edition) Meyer, say the former, and explain the passage thus : ʿThe promises (τὰ λόγια) committed to the Jews are a great distinction; and though some of the Jews have not believed those promises, nor received the Messiah, still God is faithful.ʾ The great majority of commentators say the latter, and consider the apostle as stating the want of fidelity of the Jews to the trust committed to them, *i.e.*, to the covenant made with their fathers, as no reason for assuming a want of fidelity on the part of God. That ἀπιστεῖν may have the sense here assigned to it is plain from 2 Tim. ii. 13 : and from the sense of ἀπιστία in Heb. iii. 12, 19, and of ἄπιστος in Luke xii. 46; Rev. xxi. 8. To understand the passage as referring to want of faith in Christ, seems inconsistent with the whole context. The apostle has not come to the exposition of the gospel; he is still engaged in the preliminary discussion designed to show that the Jews and Gentiles are under sin, and exposed to condemnation; an exposure from which no peculiar privileges of the former, and no promise of God to their nation, could protect them.

Verse 4. *Let it not be;* the frequently recurring formula to express strong aversion or denial. The objection presented in the preceding verse is, that the apostle's doctrine as to the condemnation of the Jews is inconsistent with the faithfulness of God. Is the faith of God without effect? asks the objector. By no means, answers the apostle; that is no fair inference from my doctrine. There is no breach of the promises of God involved in the condemnation of wicked Jews. How the condemnation of the Jews is consistent with the promises of God, he shews in a subsequent part of his epistle, chaps. ix.—xi.; here he merely asserts the fact, and shows that the opposite assumption leads to an absurdity. *Let God be true, but every man a liar.* That is, the truth and fidelity of God must be acknowledged, whatever be the consequence. This is said to express the strongest aversion to the consequence charged on his doctrine. Γινέσθω has its proper sense, *fiat, let him become, i.e.*, be seen and acknowledged as true. This disposition to justify God under all circumstances, the apostle illustrates by the conduct and language of David, who acknowledged the justice of God even in his own condemnation, and said,

"Against thee only have I sinned; that thou mightest be justified in thy sayings, and overcome when thou art judged;" *i.e.*, that thy rectitude, under all circumstances, might be seen and acknowledged. In the Hebrew, the last verb of the verse is active, *when thou judgest;* in the Septuagint, a passive form is used, *when thou art judged.* This latter Paul follows, because the sentiment in either case is the same. God is seen and acknowledged to be just. The sacred writers of the New Testament often depart from the words of the Old Testament in their citations, being careful only to give the mind of the Spirit. "Scimus," says Calvin, "apostolos in recitandis Scripturæ verbis sæpe esse liberiores; quia satis habebant si ad rem apposite citarent; quare non tanta illis fuit verborum religio."

VERSE 5. *But if our unrighteousness commend the righteousness of God, what shall we then say ?* Ἀδικία is not to be taken in the restricted sense of *injustice,* nor as equivalent to ἀπιστία in the preceding verse, but in the comprehensive sense of *unrighteousness, wickedness.* It is the opposite of δικαιοσύνη, *rectitude, righteousness,* which includes all moral excellence. The righteousness of God is here, not his goodness, which the context does not require, and usage does not authorize, but rectitude, that attribute which is manifested in doing right. Συνίστημι in the New Testament, is *to place with* or *before* any one ; and hence either *to commend, to recommend,* Rom. xvi. 1 ; 2 Cor. iii. 1 ; v. 12 ; or *to set forth, to render conspicuous ;* see Rom. v. 8 ; 2 Cor. vi. 4. The latter is obviously the sense required in the present instance. That this verse is in answer to an objection is obvious ; but that objection is not derived from the language of ver. 4. Paul had said nothing there to give any colour to the suggestion, that he himself held that it would be unrighteous in God to punish the wicked. He had simply said, that the truth of God was to be admitted and acknowledged, though all men were liars. From this it could not be made an inference that we may do evil that good may come. It is not a false inference from ver. 4, but a new objection to his general conclusion that he is here answering : 'Not only is God's fidelity pledged to our salvation, but the very fact of our being unrighteous will render his righteousness the more conspicuous ; and consequently it would be unjust in him to punish us for what glorifies himself.' This is the thought ; the form in which it is presented is determined by the fact that the apostle does not introduce the person of the objector, but states the objection in his own person, in the form of a question. It is plain, however, that the point of the argument is that God cannot consistently punish those whose unrighteousness serves to display his own rectitude ; and this is supposed to be urged to show that the Jews, notwithstanding their sins, were not exposed to condemnation. If our unrighteousness commend the righteousness of God is the suggestion ; the inference, which the Jews were disposed to draw, and which Paul asks, whether they would venture to make, is that God is unjust who taketh vengeance : ὁ Θεὸς ὁ ἐπιφέρων τὴν ὀργήν, *God the taker of vengeance ;* he whose prerogative it is to inflict the punishment due to sin. That the apostle is not in this verse expressing his own sentiments, he intimates by saying, κατὰ ἄνθρωπον λέγω, *I speak as a man.* This formula, which is of frequent occurrence, means to speak as men are accustomed to speak ; and as men are in general wicked, to speak or act after the manner of men, is to speak or act wickedly. It depends, however, entirely on the context whether this idea is implied. When Paul asks, "Are ye not carnal, and walk as men?" 1 Cor. iii. 3,

the case is plain. But when in Gal. iii. 15, he says, " Brethren, I speak
as a man," he means merely to appeal to what is commonly acknowledged
as true among men. See also 1 Cor. ix. 8. When in Rom. vi. 19, he
says, ἀνθρώπινον λέγω, it is plain from the context that he means, in a
manner adapted to the comprehension of men. And in the present case,
where he is not expressing his own sentiments, κατὰ ἄνθρωπον λέγω is
designed to declare that he is not speaking in his character of an apostle
or Christian, but speaking as others speak, expressing their thoughts, not
his own.

Verse 6.   In answer to the question whether God is unjust in punishing those whose unrighteousness renders his own righteousness the more
conspicuous, he says, *By no means, since in that case how can God judge
the world?* There is here an answer to the question, and a proof of the
correctness of that answer.   There are three views which may be taken of
the nature of this proof. The first supposes κόσμος to mean the Gentiles as
distinguished from the Jews. The sense then is : If God cannot punish
sin under the circumstances supposed, he cannot even punish the heathen,
for their unrighteousness serves to commend his righteousness. This view
is clear and satisfactory as far as the argument is concerned, and is adopted
by Koppe, Reiche, Olshausen, &c. Besides the pertinency of the argument as thus explained, this interpretation is supported by the frequent
use of κόσμος to designate the world in distinction from the Theocracy, or
the Church. 1 Cor. vi. 2 ; xi. 32 ; Rom. xi. 12 ; John xii. 31 ; 1 John
iv. 17, &c. The principal objection to it arises from the difficulties in
which it involves the explanation of the following verse. The second
view of the passage supposes the argument to rest on the admitted fact
that God is the judge of all the earth ; if so, he must be just. It is
impossible that God should be unjust, if he is to judge the world ; but he
is to judge the world, therefore he is not unjust. " Sumit argumentum
ab ipsius Dei officio," says Calvin, " quo probet id esse impossibile ;
judicabit Deus hunc mundum, ergo injustus esse non potest." To the
same purpose Grotius says : " Nullo modo possumus Deum injustum
imaginari quem cum Abrahamo *judicem mundi* agnoscimus." This view
is given also by Tholuck, De Wette, Rückert, Köllner and Meyer. The
obvious objection to it is, that it makes the apostle assume the thing to be
proved. He says, ' God cannot be unjust, because he is the judge of the
world, and the judge of the world must be just.' But it is no more certain that the judge of the world must be just, than that God is just,
which is the point to be established. Rückert, in his characteristic
assumption of superiority to the apostle, admits that the argument is
" weak, very weak ;" but he not the less confidently ascribes it to the
apostle. The misapprehension of the argument in this verse arises out of
a misapprehension of the previous reasoning, and of the precise point of the
objection which is here answered. Paul is not guarding against any
false inference from his own reasoning ; he is not teaching that though
God is seen to be just when he speaks, and clear when he judges, we must
not hence infer that he is unjust in punishing the sin which commends
his own righteousness, which would be indeed " eine erbärmliche Einwen-
dung," (a pitiable subterfuge), as Reiche calls it ; but he is answering the
objections of the Jews to his doctrine, not their false inferences. To the
declaration that they were exposed to condemnation, the Jews pleaded the
promise of God, which their unfaithfulness could not render of no effect,
and the less so because their unrighteousness would serve to render the

righteousness of God the more conspicuous. Paul says on this principle God cannot judge the world. The ground assumed by the Jews might be assumed by all mankind, and if valid in the one case it must be in all. In this view the answer is complete and satisfactory ; it is a *reductio ad absurdum*. The correctness of this explanation is confirmed by what follows.

VERSES 7, 8. These verses are the amplification and confirmation of the answer given in the sixth to the objection of the Jews. These verses are designed to show that if the ground assumed by them was valid, not only may every sinner claim exemption, but it would follow that it is right to do evil that good may come. The connection by γάρ is therefore with the sixth verse : ' God could not judge the world, *for* any sinner may say, If the truth of God more abounds through my lie, to his glory, why am I yet judged as a sinner ?' *The truth of God.* As ἀλήθεια is not unfrequently opposed to ἀδικία, it may have here the sense of δικαιοσύνη, and designate the divine excellence ; then ψεῦσμα, in the following clause, must mean *falsehood* towards God, *wickedness :* ' If the excellence of God is rendered more conspicuous by my wickedness.' But as it was on the truth or veracity of God, his adherence to his promises, that the false confidence of the Jews was placed, it is probable that the apostle intended the words to be taken in their more limited sense. *Hath more abounded unto his glory.* Περισσεύειν, *to be abundant, rich,* or *great ;* and by implication, in a comparative sense, to be more abundant, or conspicuous, Matt. v. 20 ; 1 Cor. xv. 58. The latter is the sense here, ' If the truth of God has been made the more conspicuous ;' εἰς τὴν δόξαν αὐτοῦ, *so that he is glorified.* *Why am I also still judged as a sinner ?* κἀγώ, either *even I,* or *I also ;* I as well as others ; or even I, a Jew ; or, according to another view of the context, even I a Gentile : ἔτι, *yet, i.e.* notwithstanding my falsehood is the means of displaying the glory of God. According to the view now given, the use of the first person is sufficiently explained by saying, as has often been done, "suam personam ponit pro quâvis aliâ." *I*, therefore, stands for any one : ' Any one may say, Why am I also judged as a sinner?' Those however who understand κόσμος, in the preceding verse, to mean the Gentiles, suppose that the apostle here personates a heathen, who is made to ask, ' If the divine majesty is the more displayed by my idolatry, why am even I judged as a sinner ?' This interpretation gives a very good sense, because the Jews readily admitted that the Gentiles were exposed to condemnation, and therefore any principle which was shown to exculpate them, the Jews must acknowledge to be false. The objections to this view of the passage are the unnecessary limitation which it imposes on the word κόσμος, ver. 6, and the unusual, if not unauthorized sense, which it requires to be given to the words ἀλήθεια and ψεῦσμα, the latter not being elsewhere used for *idolatry*, and the former, in this connection at least, not admitting of the version, *truth concerning God, i.e., the true God.*

VERSE 8. Almost all the modern commentators are agreed in considering this verse as a continuation of the question commenced in the seventh, and in assuming an irregularity in the construction, arising from the introduction of the parenthetical clause in the middle of the verse : ' If your principle is correct, why am I judged as a sinner ; *and why not let us do evil, that good may come ?*' Having commenced the question, he interrupts himself to notice the slanderous imputation of this doctrine to himself—*as we are slandered, and as some affirm we say, that we should do evil that good may come.* Ποιήσωμεν, therefore, instead of being connected with the (τί) μή at the beginning of the verse is connected by ὅτι with the immediately preceding verb, See *Winer,* § 66. *Whose condemnation is just.* Paul thus expresses his abhorrence of the principle that we may do evil that good may come. Tholuck and others refer ω ν to the βλασφη-μοῦντες, to the slanderers of the apostle; but that clause is virtually paren-thetical, and it is not blaspheming the apostle, but teaching a doctrine subversive of all morality, that is here condemned. Calvin unites, in a measure, both views of the passage : "Duplici autem nomine damnabilis fuit eorum perversitas ; primum quibus venire haec impietas in mentem potuerit usque ad ipsum assensum, deinde qui traducendo evangelio calum-niam inde instruere ausi fuerint."

Such is the apostle's argument against the grounds of confidence on which the Jews rested their hope of exemption from condemnation. 'Our unfaithfulness serves to commend the faithfulness of God, therefore we ought not to be punished.' According to this reasoning, says Paul, the worse we are, the better: for the more wicked we are, the more conspicu-ous will be the mercy of God in our pardon; we may therefore do evil that good may come.' By reducing the reasoning of the Jews to a con-clusion shocking to the moral sense, he thereby refutes it. The apostle often thus recognizes the authority of the intuitive moral judgments of our nature, and thus teaches us that those truths which are believed on their own evidence, as soon as presented to the mind, should be regarded as fixed points in all reasonings ; and that to attempt to go beyond these intuitive judgments, is to unsettle the foundation of all faith and know-ledge, and to open the door to universal scepticism. Any doctrine, there-fore, which is immoral in its tendency, or which conflicts with the first principles of morals, must be false, no matter how plausible may be the arguments in its favour.

DOCTRINE.

1. The advantages of membership in the external Church, and of a participation of its ordinances, are very numerous and great, vers. 1, 2.

2. The great advantage of the Christian over the heathen world, and of the members of a visible ecclesiastical body over others not so situated, is the greater amount of divine truth presented to their understandings and hearts, ver. 2.

3. All the writings which the Jews, at the time of Christ and his apostles, regarded as inspired, are really the word of God, ver. 2.

4. No promise or covenant of God can ever be rightfully urged in favour of exemption from the punishment of sin, or of impunity to those who live in it. God is faithful to his promises, but he never promises to pardon the impenitently guilty, vers. 3, 4.

5. God will make the wrath of men to praise him. Their unrighteous-ness will commend his righteousness, without, on that account, making its condemnation less certain or less severe, vers. 5, 6.

6. Any doctrine inconsistent with the first principles of morals must be false, no matter how plausible the metaphysical argument in its favour. And that mode of reasoning is correct, which refutes such doctrines by showing their inconsistency with moral truth, ver. 8.

REMARKS.

1. We should feel the peculiar responsibilities which rest upon us as the inhabitants of a Christian country, as members of the Christian Church, and possessors of the word of God; as such, we enjoy advantages for which we shall have to render a strict account, vers. 1, 2.

2. It is a mark of genuine piety, to be disposed always to justify God, and to condemn ourselves. On the other hand, a disposition to self-justification and the extenuation of our sins, however secret, is an indication of the want of a proper sense of our own unworthiness and of the divine excellence, vers. 4, 5.

3. Beware of any refuge from the fear of future punishment, founded upon the hope that God will clear the guilty, or that he will not judge the world and take vengeance for our sins, vers. 6, 7.

4. There is no better evidence against the truth of any doctrine, than that its tendency is immoral. And there is no greater proof that a man is wicked, that his condemnation is just, than that he does evil that good may come. There is commonly, in such cases, not only the evil of the act committed, but that of hypocrisy and duplicity also, ver. 8.

5. Speculative and moral truths, which are believed on their own evidence as soon as they are presented to the mind, should be regarded as authoritative, and as fixed points in all reasonings. When men deny such first principles, or attempt to push beyond them to a deeper foundation of truth, there is no end to the obscurity, uncertainty, and absurdity of their speculations. What God forces us, from the very constitution of our nature, to believe, as, for example, the existence of the external world, our own personal identity, the difference between good and evil, &c., it is at once a violation of his will and of the dictates of reason to deny or to question. Paul assumed, as an ultimate fact, that it is wrong to do evil that good may come, ver. 8.

ROMANS III. 9—20.

ANALYSIS.

THE apostle having demonstrated that the Jews cannot expect exemption from condemnation, on the ground of their being the peculiar people of God, except on principles incompatible with the government of the world, and inconsistent with the plainest moral truths, draws, in ver. 9, the conclusion, that the Jew, as to the matter of justification before God, has no pre-eminence over the Gentile. He confirms his doctrine of the universal sinfulness of men by numerous quotations from the Scriptures. These passages speak of men in general as depraved, vers. 10—12 ; and then of the special manifestations of that depravity in sins of the tongue, vers. 13, 14 ; and in sins of violence, vers. 15—18. The inference from all his reasoning, from chap. i. 18, derived from consciousness, experience, and Scripture is, that " the whole world is guilty before God," ver 19 ; and that " no flesh can be justified by the deeds of the law," ver. 20.

COMMENTARY.

VERSE 9. *What then ? do we excel ?   What then ? i.e.*, what is the conclusion from the preceding discussion ? are we Jews better off than the Gentiles ? Wahl points the passage thus: Τί οὖν προεχόμεθα ; *What then do we,* or *can we pretend or present as an excuse ?* Then, however, as Rückert and others remark, the answer should be, οὐδέν, *nothing,* and not οὐ πάντως. The principal difficulty in this verse is to determine the meaning of προεχόμεθα. The most commonly received and the most satisfactory explanation assumes that the middle form has here the sense of the active. Προέχειν means *to hold before,* or intransitively and topically, *to have before* another, *to excel.* In the middle voice, the verb means *to hold before oneself,* as a shield, or figuratively, *to use as a pretext.* Though the middle does not elsewhere occur in the sense of the active, its use in the present instance in that sense, may be justified either by the remark, that the later writers often use the middle form where the earlier authors employ the active, (*Tholuck*) ; or by assuming the sense of the active to be here somewhat modified, since the apostle is speaking of a superiority which the Jews attributed to themselves, so that the strict sense is : " Licetne nobis tribuere majorem dignitatem ?" *Bretschneider.* The context suits the sense commonly attributed to the word. The whole discussion has brought the apostle to the conclusion, that the Jews as sinners have no advantage over the Gentiles, and this is the conclusion which he here confirms. If the middle force of the verb be retained, then the sense is, as given by Meyer : 'What then ? Have we protection or defence ?' That is, are we Jews and Gentiles, men as sinners, protected from the justice of God ? The answer is, By no means. But this does not so well suit the context or the form of the answer to the question presented. The verb προεχόμεθα should, as Rückert says, in that case have an accusative, designating the excuse or pretext : ' Have we *anything* for a pretext ?' And the answer would be, Nothing. The passive sense, *Are we excelled ?* adopted by Wetstein and others, is still less suited to the context. For whether the Gentiles or the Jews be supposed to ask the question, there is nothing to account for it, or to suggest it. Paul had given no reason to either to ask, Are we excelled ? He had not proved that the Gentiles were worse off than the Jews, or the Jews than the Gentiles, but that both were alike under condemnation. The question, therefore, Do we excel ? are we Jews better off than the Gentiles ? is the only one which the occasion calls for, or that the answer suits. This is the view given by Theophylact, who says, δείκνυσι μηδὲν αὐτοὺς ἔχειν περισσόν, ὅσον ἐκ τῶν οἰκείων πράξεων ; and which is adopted by Calvin, Beza, Grotius, and the modern commentators, Tholuck, Rückert (2d edition), Reiche, and De Wette.

Not at all, not in the least, (οὐ πάντως) the πάντως strengthening the negation. Grotius, Wetstein, and Köllner translate, *not altogether, not in all respects.* But the former version is shown by Winer, § 61, to be consistent with usage, and is much better suited to the context ; for it is the obvious design of the apostle to shew that, as to the point in hand, the Jews did *not at all* excel the Gentiles. This strong negation the following clause confirms. The Jews are not better off ; *for we have before charged both Jews and Gentiles with being under sin.* Αἰτιᾶσθαι is properly, *to accuse,* here as in other cases followed by an accusative and infinitive. Our version, *we have before proved,* though it may be justified by implication, is not in strict accordance with the meaning of the words. The same sense, however, is expressed by Erasmus, "ante causis redditis ostendimus," and is adopted by Reiche and others. There is force in the remark of Calvin : " Verbum Græcum αἰτιᾶσθαι proprie est judiciale : ideoque reddere placuit *constituimus.* Dicitur enim crimen in actione constituere accusator, quod testimoniis ac probationibus aliis convincere paratus. Citavit autem apostolus universum hominum genus ad Dei tribunal, ut totum sub unam damnationem includeret." To be *under sin* means to be under the power of sin, to be sinners, whether the idea of guilt, just exposure to condemnation, or of pollution, or both, be conveyed by the expression depends on the context. Comp. 1 Cor. xv. 17 ; Gal. iii. 10, 22 ; John xv. 22. Here both ideas are to be included. Paul had arraigned all men as sinners, as the transgressors of the law, and therefore exposed to condemnation.

Verses 10—18, contain the confirmation of the doctrine of the universal sinfulness of men by the testimony of the Scriptures. These passages are not found consecutively in any one place in the Old Testament. Verses 10—12 are from Psalms xiv. and liii.; ver. 13 is from Ps. v. 9 ; ver. 14 is from Ps. x. 7 ; vers. 15—17 are from Isa. lix. 7, 8 ; and ver. 18 is from Ps. xxxvi. 1. These passages, it will be observed, are of two different classes ; the one descriptive of the general character of men ; the other referring to particular sinful acts, on the principle " by their fruits ye shall know them." This method of reasoning is common and legitimate. The national character of a people may be proved by the prevalence of certain acts by which it is manifested. The prevalence of crime among men is a legitimate proof that the race is apostate, though every man is not a shedder of blood, or guilty of robbery or violence.

Verse 10. *There is none righteous, no not one.* Ps. xiv. 1, in the Hebrew is, "there is none doing good;" in the Septuagint it is ποιῶν χρηστότητα ; Paul has, οὐκ ἔστι δίκαιος, *there is none righteous.* The sense is the same. Paul probably uses δίκαιος, *righteous,* because the question which he is discussing is whether men are righteous, or can be justified on the ground of their own righteousness in the sight of God. This is a declaration of the universal sinfulness of men. The two ideas included in the negation of righteousness, want of piety and want of rectitude, are expressed in the following verses.

Verse 11. *There is none who understands, there is none who seeks after God.* In the Psalms it is said : " God looked down from heaven upon the sons of men, to see if there was one wise, seeking after God." Here again the apostle gives the thought, and not the precise words. Instead of " if there was one wise," he gives the idea in a negative form, " There is none who understands," οὐκ ἔστιν ὁ συνιῶν. The participle ὁ συνιῶν, *der verständige, the wise,* is stronger than the verb, who *understands;* as the former expresses a permanent characteristic, the latter properly only an act. The words συνίημι and σύνεσις are frequently used in the New Testament to express the right apprehension of divine truth. See Matt. xiii. 15 ; Acts vii. 25 ; Eph. iii. 4 ; v. 17 ; Col. i. 9 ; ii. 2. In this case, συνιῶν (συνίων, *Winer,* 14, § 3), answers to מַשְׂכִּיל, a word often used in a religious sense, as in the Scriptures, wisdom and religion are convertible terms. This right apprehension or spiritual discernment of divine things is always attended with right affections and right conduct—he that understands seeks after God—which latter expression includes all those exercises of desire, worship, and obedience, which are consequent on this spiritual discernment.

VERSE 12. *They are all gone out of the way.* Blinded by sin to the perfections and loveliness of God and truth, they have turned from the way which he has prescribed and which leads to himself, and have made choice of another way and of another portion. Here, as in the first chapter, the loss of the knowledge of God is represented as followed by spiritual blindness, and spiritual blindness by moral degradation. Men do not understand, *i.e.*, have no right apprehension of God ; then they turn away from him, then they become *altogether unprofitable, ἠχρειώθησαν, worthless, morally corrupt.* This depravity is universal, for *there is none that doeth good, no not one.* The words οὐκ ἕως ἑνός, *not so much as one,* are a Hebrewism for οὐδὲ εἷς. This passage is taken from the Septuagint translation of Psalm xiv. 3.

VERSES 13, 14. These verses relate to the sins of the tongue. The passages quoted are from Ps. v. 9 ; cxl. 3 ; and x. 7. *Their throat is an open sepulchre.* The point of comparison may be the offensive and pestiferous character of the exhalations of an open grave. This is forcible, and suited to the context. Or the idea is, that as the grave is rapacious and insatiable, so the wicked are disposed to do all the injury with their tongues which they can accomplish. In Jer. v. 16, it is said of the Chaldeans, "Their quiver is as an open sepulchre," *i. e.* destructive. But as in the following verses sins of violence are brought distinctly into view, the former explanation is to be preferred. What issues from the mouths of the wicked is offensive and pestiferous. *With their tongues they have used deceit.* The word ἐδολιοῦσαν is in the imperfect, for ἐδολιοῦν, implying continuous action. In the Hebrew it is, "They make smooth their tongue," *i.e.* they flatter. The LXX. and Vulgate give the version which the apostle adopts. *The poison of asps is under their lips.* This is the highest expression of malignity. The bite of the adder causes the severest pain, as well as produces death. To inflict suffering is a delight to the malignant. This is a revelation of a nature truly diabolical. *Their mouth is full of cursing and bitterness.* The Hebrew in Ps. x. 7, is, "His mouth is full of deceit and violence ;" the Septuagint, "His mouth is full of cursing, bitterness, and deceit." The Vulgate follows the LXX. ; Paul condenses the idea.

VERSES 15—17. These verses adduce the sins of violence common among men, in proof of the general depravity of the race. *Their feet are swift to shed blood.* That is, on the slightest provocation they commit murder. The life of their fellow-men is as nothing in their estimation, in comparison with the gratification of their pride or malice. The words are quoted from Isa. lix. 7 : "Their feet run to evil, and they make haste to shed innocent blood." Here the Septuagint agrees with the Hebrew, and Paul again condenses the sense. *Destruction and misery are in their ways.* Their path through life is marked not only with blood, but with the ruin and desolation which they spread around them. In Isaiah the passage runs, "Their thoughts are thoughts of iniquity ; wasting and destruction are in their paths." *The way of peace they have not known.* "The way of peace" is the way that leads to peace, or pacific ways. "They have not known," means they have not approved or frequented. The idea is to be taken in its most comprehensive form, as the apostle designs to prove, not from any specific form of violence, but from the general prevalence of sins of violence among men, that human nature is depraved. The tree which produces such fruit so abundantly must be evil.

VERSE 18. *There is no fear of God before their eyes.* This is taken from Psalm xxxvi. 1 : "The dictum of depravity concerning the wicked man in my heart is, There is no fear of God before his eyes." That is, his depravity proves or reveals to me that he does not fear God. See Alexander on the Psalms, who proposes this with other versions of the passage. However the previous part of the verse may be understood, the clause quoted by the apostle is plain. The course of wicked men, as previously described, is proof that they are destitute of the fear of God. And by "the fear of God" we may understand, according to Scripture usage, reverence for God, piety towards him ; or fear, in the more restricted sense, dread of his wrath. In either way, the reckless wickedness of men proves that they are destitute of all proper regard of God. They act as if there were no God, no Being to whom they are responsible for their conduct, and who has the purpose and power to punish them for their iniquity.

VERSE 19. *Now we know;* it is a thing plain in itself, and universally conceded, *that what things soever the law saith, it saith to them that are under the law.* The word νόμος means that which binds, that to which we are bound to be conformed. It is that which binds the reason, the conscience, the heart, and the life, whether it be revealed in the constitution of our nature, or in the decalogue, or in the law of Moses, or in the Scriptures. It is the word or revelation of the will of God, considered as the norm or rule to which men are to conform their faith and practice. It depends on the context, under what aspect this rule is in any particular case contemplated. It may be the rule as written on the heart, ii. 14, or the law of Moses, or the whole Scriptures, as John x. 34. In this passage it obviously means the whole Old Testament, for the quotations given above are taken from the Psalms and the Prophets. In every instance the principle applies, that what the law says it says to those who have the law. Those to whom any revelation of the divine will is made are bound to be conformed to it. What the law written in the heart says, it says to those who have that law ; and what the law as written in the Scripture says, it says to those who have the Scriptures. The declarations therefore contained in the Old Testament, which was the revelation of God's will made to the Jews, were the norm or rule to which they were obliged to conform their judgments and conduct. If the Old Testament declared that all men are under sin, that there is none righteous, no not one, the Jews could not deny the truth of this universal declaration in its application to themselves. These passages speak not of heathen as heathen, but of fallen men as such, and therefore are to be understood of all men, of the Jews as well as of the Gentiles. *That every mouth may be stopped.* The word is ἵνα, *in order that.* That is, the design of God in these general declarations was, that every mouth should be stopped ; that all men should be reduced to silence under the conviction that they had nothing to say against the charge of sin. This idea is expressed in another form in the following clause : *That the whole world* (πᾶς ὁ κόσμος), all mankind, Jews and Gentiles, *should become* (γένηται), in their own conviction, *guilty before God.* That is, that all men should be convinced of guilt. Guilt here, as always in theological language, means liability or exposure to punishment on account of sin. It is not to be confounded either with moral pollution or with mere demerit. It may exist where neither pollution nor personal demerit is to be found. And it may be removed where both remain. Christ is said to have borne the guilt of our sins, although immaculate and without personal demerit ; and justification removes the guilt (or just exposure to punishment) of the sinner, but it does not change his inward character. This is the proper meaning of ὑπόδικος (ἔνοχος δίκης), *guilty, satisfactionem alteri debens,* obnoxious to punishment. *Before God,* τῷ Θεῷ, in relation to God, as it is to him that satisfaction for sin is due. It is he whom we have offended, and under whose sentence we lie. There are three things involved in the consciousness of sin ; sense of moral turpitude, sense of demerit or of ill-desert, and the conviction that we ought to be punished. This last element is often most clearly revealed ; so that a criminal often voluntarily gives himself up to justice. It is this that is denominated guilt, the obligation to suffer punishment ; so that the guilty are not merely those who may be punished, but those whom justice (or moral rectitude) demands should be punished. It is this that stops the sinner's mouth ; and it is this which is met by satisfaction, so that although in the justified believer a sense of pollution and of ill-desert remains, there is no longer this dreadful conviction that God is bound to punish him. The conclusion to which the apostle's argument, from experience and Scripture, has thus far led is, that all men are guilty in the sight of God ; and if guilty, they cannot be justified on the ground of their personal character or conduct. To justify is to declare not guilty ; and therefore the guilty cannot, on the ground of character, be justified.

Verse 20. *Therefore by the deeds of the law shall no flesh be justified in his sight. Therefore.* The particle is διότι, which is equivalent to δἰ ὃ τι, *on account of which thing, wherefore.* In this sense it indicates a conclusion from preceding premises. This would suit this connection, as ver. 20 is a fair conclusion from what is said in ver. 19 : ' All the world is guilty before God, *wherefore,* hence it follows that, no one can be justified by works.' This is the conclusion which the apostle has had in view from the beginning of his argument. His whole design is to prove that men cannot be justified by their own righteousness, in order to prepare them to receive the righteousness of God. This view of the connection is assumed in our version by Beza, Turrettin, Rosenmüller, and others. But in the New Testament, διότι is almost uniformly, perhaps in every case, used in the sense of διὰ τοῦτο ὅτι, *on this account that,* or of the simple ὅτι *that.* The great majority of commentators therefore render it here, *because,* as in i. 19 ; viii. 7, &c. Verse 20 then assigns the reason of what is said in ver. 19 : ' Every mouth must be stopped, *because* no flesh can be justified by works.' This view is to be preferred, not because more suitable, but because more consistent with the common use of the particle in question. *No flesh.* When men are called *flesh,* in the Bible, there was originally a reference to their weakness and faults, as the flesh is earthly and perishable. But in many cases there is no such implication ; "no flesh" is simply equivalent to no man. The Greek is here πᾶσα σάρξ οὐ κ.τ.λ, *every flesh shall not ;* according to the familiar Hebraism, *no flesh shall.* The future is used not in reference to the day of final judgment, for the act of justification takes place in this life. It expresses the certainty of the thing affirmed : *No flesh shall ever be* (*i. e.* ever can be) *justified.* The apostle seems evidently to have had in his mind the passage in Psalm cxliii. 2 : "Enter not into judgment with thy servant; for in thy sight shall no man living be justified." Δικαιόω, *to justify,* is not simply to pardon. A condemned criminal, in whose favour the executive exercises his prerogative of mercy, is never said to be justified ; he is simply pardoned. Nor is it to pardon and to restore to favour. When a king pardons a rebellious subject, and restores him to his former standing, he does not justify him. Nor is it *to make just* inwardly. When a man accused of a crime is acquitted or declared just in the eye of the law, his moral character is not changed. *To justify* is a forensic term ; that is, it expresses the act of a judge. Justification is a judicial act. It is a declaration that the party arraigned is δίχαιος, *just ;* and δίχαιος, means *right,* conformed to the law. To justify, therefore, is to declare that the party implicated is *rectus in foro judicii ;* that δίχη, *justice,* does not condemn, but pronounces him just, or declares herself satisfied. This is the uniform meaning of the word, not only in Scripture, but also in ordinary life. We never confound justification with pardon, or with sanctification. It is always used in the sense antithetical to condemnation. To condemn is not merely to punish, but to declare the accused guilty or worthy of punishment ; and justification is not merely to remit that punishment, but to declare that punishment cannot be justly inflicted. Much less does *to condemn* mean to render wicked, and therefore neither does *to justify* mean to render good. When we justify God, we declare him to be just ; and when God justifies the sinner, he declares him to be just. In both cases the idea is, that there is no ground for condemnation ; or that the demands of justice are satisfied. Hence the terms and expressions used in Scripture, convertibly with the word to *justify,* all express the same idea. Thus, in ii. 13, it is said : " Not the hearers of the law are just before God (δίχαιοι παρὰ τῷ Θεῷ,) but the doers of the law shall be justified (δικαιωθήσονται.)" Here, to be just before God, (in his sight or estimation,) and to be justified, mean the same thing. It is clearly impossible that the apostle should mean that the doers of the law shall be pardoned. What should they be pardoned for ? Doing the law does not call for pardon : it is declared to be the ground of justification. Pardon and justification therefore are essentially distinct. The one is the remission of punishment, the other is a declaration that no ground for the infliction of punishment exists. Quite as evident is it that the apostle does not mean, in the passage referred to, to say that the doers of the law shall be made holy. To justify, therefore, cannot mean to make inherently just or good. In iv. 6, he speaks of the "blessedness of the man to whom the Lord imputeth righteousness without works." To impute righteousness is to justify. To impute is to ascribe to, to reckon to one's account. But when we pardon a man, we do not ascribe righteousness to him ; and therefore, again, justification is seen to be different from pardon. It is quite as clear, that to impute righteousness cannot mean to render holy ; and therefore to justify, which is to impute righteousness, cannot mean to make good. In viii. 1, the apostle says, "there is no condemnation to those who are in Christ Jesus." Not to condemn is neither to pardon nor to sanctify, but is to pronounce just. Nothing can be clearer as a question of exegesis, than that the word δικαιόω (to justify) expresses a judicial, as opposed to an executive, and also to an efficient act. This indeed is plain from the very form of the statement in this and other passages. It would be utterly unmeaning to say that " no flesh shall be pardoned by the works of the law," or that "no man shall be sanctified by the deeds of the law." In the fifth chapter of this epistle, Paul uses the phrase "sentence unto condemnation" (χρίμα εἰς χατάχριμα,) in antithesis to "sentence unto justification" (χρίμα εἰς δικαίωσιν.) Justification therefore is as much a sentence, χρίμα, a judgment, a declarative act, as condemnation. It need not be remarked that this is a point of vital importance. How can man be just with God, is the question which of all others most immediately concerns our eternal interests. The answer which Pelagians and Remonstrants give to this question is, that to justify is simply to pardon and to restore to divine favour. The Romanists say, that it is to render inwardly pure or good, so that God accepts as righteous only those who are inwardly conformed to the law, and because of that conformity. Protestants say, that to justify is to declare just; to pronounce, on the ground of the satisfaction of justice, that there is no ground of condemnation in the sinner ; or that he has a righteousness which meets the demands of the law. The Romish doctrine of subjective justification, against which the Protestants contended as for the life of the Church, has in our day been revived in different forms. The speculative and mystic theologians of Germany all repudiate the doctrine of objective justification ; they all teach in some way, that to justify is to make just ; to restore the ruined nature of man to its original state of purity or conformity to the law of God. They are all disposed to say, with Olshausen : " Von Gott kann nie etwas als gerecht anerkannt oder dafür erklärt werden, was es nicht ist;" i. e., *God can never acknowledge or declare that just, which is not so in itself.* This is said to prove that God cannot pronounce the sinner just, unless he is inherently righteous. If this is so, then no flesh living can be justified ; for no human being in this life, whether under the law or the Gospel, is inherently just, or inwardly conformed to the law of God. The conscience of the holiest man on earth condemns him, and God is greater than our hearts, and knoweth all things. If not righteous in our own eyes, how can we be righteous in the sight of omniscient and infinite holiness ? Agreeably to the principle just stated, Olshausen defines δικαιοσύνη, *conformity to law*, so that " not only the outward act, but the inward feeling and disposition answer to the divine law ;" and δικαιόω is said to express " die göttliche Thätigkeit des Hervorrufens der δικαιοσύνη, welches natürlich das Anerkennen derselben als solcher in sich schliesst." That is, to justify is to produce moral rectitude, and to acknowledge it as such. See *Olshausen's Commentary*, Rom. iii. 21. Justification therefore includes two things ; first, making a man inwardly just ; and secondly, acknowledging him to be so. No man therefore can be justified who is not inwardly conformed to the perfect law of God. This is a sentence of eternal condemnation on all mankind ; for there is none righteous, no not one ; neither by works nor by faith, neither by nature nor by grace. Blessed be God, this is not the doctrine of the Bible. God justifies the ungodly ; that is, he pronounces just those who, personally considered, are unjust. He imputes righteousness to those without works ; that is, to those who are in themselves unrighteous. In no instance in the Scriptures has δικαιόω the sense of producing δικαιοσύνη. We do not make God holy when we justify him ; the unrighteous judge does not make the wicked holy when he justifies him for a reward, Isa. v. 23. He surely is not an abomination to the Lord, who makes the unrighteous good, but he is declared to be such an abomination, who either justifies the wicked or condemns the just, Prov. xvii. 15. This doctrine is not less inconsistent with the faith of the Church than it is with the plain meaning of the Scriptures. The people of God of every denomination are led as by instinct to renounce all dependence upon anything done by them or wrought in them, and to cast themselves, for acceptance before God, on what Christ has done for them. Their trust is in him, and not on their own inward conformity to the law. No previous training, and no trammels of false doctrine can prevent those who are truly under the guidance of the

Spirit of God from thus renouncing their own inward righteousness, and trusting to the righteousness of the Son of God.

To justify, then, is not merely to pardon and restore to favour ; nor is it to make inwardly just or holy, but it is to declare or pronounce just ; that is, judicially to declare that the demands of justice are satisfied, or that there is no just ground for condemnation. The apostle here as everywhere teaches that no human being can be thus pronounced just on the ground of his personal character or conduct, because all have sinned and are guilty before God. This is here expressed by saying, that no flesh can be justified *by works of the law.* By works of the law are not meant works produced or called forth by the law as a mere objective rule of duty, as opposed to works produced by an inward principle of faith, but works which the law prescribes. It is not by obedience to the law, by doing the works which the law enjoins, that any man can be justified. As to the nature of the works which are thus expressly declared not to be the ground of justification, there are different opinions arising out of the different views taken of the plan of salvation revealed in the Scriptures. 1. The Pelagian doctrine, that the works intended are the ceremonial works prescribed by the Mosaic law. The doctrine assumed to be taught by the apostle, is, that men are not justified by external rites, such as circumcision and sacrifice, but by works morally good. 2. The Romish doctrine, that the works of the law are works performed under the stress of natural conscience. The Romish theory is, that works done before regeneration have only the merit of congruity ; but those done after regeneration, and therefore from a principle of grace, have the merit of condignity, and are the ground of acceptance with God. 3. The Remonstrant or Arminian doctrine is, that by the works of the law is to be understood the perfect legal obedience enjoined on Adam as the condition of eternal life. Under the gospel, such perfect obedience is not required, God for Christ's sake being willing to accept of imperfect obedience. Men therefore are not justified by the works of the law, but by the works of the gospel, which requires only a *fides obsequiosa.* 4. The modern doctrine already referred to is only a philosophical statement of the Romish theory. Olshausen, Neander, and the school to which they belong, teach that the law as an objective rule of duty cannot produce real inward conformity to the will of God, but only an outward obedience, and therefore there is need of a new inward principle which produces true holiness in heart and life. " Das Gesetz," says Olshausen, " konnte es nicht über eine äussere Legalität hinausbringen, durch die Wiedergeburt wird aber durch Gnade ein innerer Zustand, die δικαιοσύνη Θεοῦ, im Gläubigen geschaffen, der den höchsten Forderungen entspricht " (see his *Comment.* on i. 17). " The law can only effect an external legal obedience ; but by regeneration, an inward state, the δικαιοσύνη Θεοῦ, is produced by grace, which meets the highest demands." The works of the law, therefore, according to this view, the δικαιοσύνη τοῦ νόμου, or ἐκ νόμου, or δικαιοσύνη ἰδία, are those works or that righteousness which men by their own power, without the co-operation of divine grace, can effect ; (" der Mensch sie gleichsam mit seinen eignen nach dem Fall ihm gebliebenen sittlichen Kräften, ohne Wirkung der Gnade, zu Stande bringt.") Such works or such righteousness cannot justify ; but the inward righteousness produced by the grace of God, and therefore called the δικαιοσύνη Θεοῦ or ἐκ πίστεως, meets the demands of the law, is the true ground of justification. *Olshausen*, 3, 21. See also *Neander's Geschichte der Pflanzung*, pp. 503—510. The doctrine of the divines of the school of Schleiermacher, presented in formulas more or less mystic and transcendental is, that as we derive a corrupt nature from Adam, and on the ground of that nature are condemned, so we derive a holy nature from Christ, and on the ground of that nature are justified. 5. In opposition to all these views, which place the ground of justification, so far as it is a declarative act, in man's own inward character or state, Protestants with one heart and one voice teach that by the *works of the law*, which are excluded from the ground of justification, are meant not only ceremonial works, not merely the works of the unregenerate done without grace, not only the perfect obedience required by the law originally given to Adam, but works of all kinds, everything either done by us or wrought in us. In proof of this, it may be urged : 1. That the law of which the apostle speaks, is the law which binds all mankind. It is the law, the violation of which renders all men guilty before God, as stated in ver. 19. The whole of the preceding argument is designed to show that both Jews and Gentiles, viewed as to their personal character, are under sin and incapable of justification on the ground of their own character or conduct. 2. This law which thus binds all men, demands the highest kind of moral obedience. It is spiritual, extending not merely to the external act, but to the secret motives. It says, "thou shalt not covet ;" thus condemning all irregular or inordinate desires. It is holy, just, and good. It requires us to love God with all the heart, and our neighbour as ourselves. There can therefore be no form or kind of righteousness, whether natural or gracious, higher than that which the law demands, and which is comprehended in the works of the law. 3. The contrast or opposition is never between one kind of works and another. Paul does not teach that we cannot be justified by ceremonial works, but are justified by good works ; he does not exclude merely *opera ex solis naturæ viribus, i. e.* works of the unregenerate, and assert that works flowing from a principle of grace are the ground of justification ; he does not contrast imperfect obedience under the gospel with the perfect obedience required of Adam ; but the opposition is always between works in general, all works, and faith. 4. The works rejected as inadequate are called "works of righteousness," Titus iii. 5 ; that is, works of the highest order, for there is no designation of excellence of higher import than that. 5. The works intended are such as Abraham, the father of the faithful, whose obedience is held up as a model to all generations, performed. 6. Whenever the ground of our justification is affirmatively stated, it is declared to be the obedience, the death, the blood or work of Christ. 7. The objection to the apostle's doctrine, which he answers at length in chap. vi., supposes that good works of every kind are excluded from the ground of our justification. That objection is, that if works are not the ground of justification, then we may live in sin. There could be no room for such an objection, had the apostle taught that we are not justified by mere ceremonial or moral works, but by works of a higher order of merit. It was his rejecting all works, every kind and degree of personal excellence, and making something external to ourselves, something done for us as opposed to everything wrought in us, the ground of our acceptance with God, that called forth the objection in question. And this objection has been urged against Paul's doctrine from that day to this. 8. Appeal may safely be made on this subject to the testimony of the Church or the experience of the people of God of every age and nation. They with one accord, at least in their prayers and praises, renounce all dependence on their own inward excellence, and cast themselves on the work or merit of Christ. In reference to this cardinal doctrine, Calvin says : " Neque vero me latet, Augustinum secus exponere ; justitiam enim Dei esse putat regenerationis gratiam ; et hanc gratuitam esse fatetur, quia Dominus immerentes Spiritu suo nos renovat. Ab hac autem opera legis excludit, hoc est quibus homines a seipsis citra renovationem conantur Deum promereri. Mihi etiam plus satis notum est, quosdam novos speculatores hoc dogma superciliose proferre quasi hodie sibi revelatum. Sed apostolum omnia sine exceptione opera complecti, etiam quæ Dominus in suis efficit, ex contextu planum fiet. Nam certe regeneratus erat Abraham, et Spiritu Dei agebatur quo tempore justificatum fuisse operibus negat. Ergo a justificatione hominis non opera tantum moraliter bona (ut vulgo appellant) et quæ fiunt naturæ instinctu excludit, sed quæcunque etiam fideles habere possunt. Deinde si illa est justitiæ fidei definitio, Beati quorum remissæ sunt iniquitates, Ps. xxxii. 1 ; non disputatur de hoc vel illo genere operum; sed abolito operum merito sola peccatorum remissio justitiæ causa statuitur. Putant hæc duo optime convenire, fide justificari hominem per Christi gratiam ; et tamen operibus justificari, quæ ex regeneratione spirituali proveniant ; quia et gratuito nos Deus renovat, et ejus donum fide percipimus. At Paulus longe aliud principium sumit : nunquam scilicet tranquillas fore conscientias, donec in solam Dei misericordiam recumbant ; ideo alibi postquam docuit Deum fuisse in Christo, ut homines justificaret, modum simul exprimit, non imputando illis peccata."

For by the law is the knowledge of sin. No flesh can be justified by the law, *for* by the law we are convinced of sin. The law condemns by bringing sin clearly to our knowledge as deserving the wrath of God, which is revealed against all sin, and therefore it cannot justify. " Ex eadem scatebra," says Calvin, " non prodeunt vita. et mors." Ἐπίγνωσις *(full or accurate knowledge)* is stronger than the simple word γνῶσις *(knowledge.)* When the object of knowledge is something in our own consciousness, as in the case of sin, knowledge involves a recognition of the true nature of that object, and a corresponding experience. The knowledge of sin is therefore not a mere intellectual cognition, but an inward conviction, including both an intellectual apprehension and a due sense of its turpitude and guilt. This is the office of the law. It was not designed to give life, but so to convince of sin that men may be led to renounce their own righteousness and trust in the righteousness of Christ as the only and all-sufficient ground of their acceptance with God.

DOCTRINE.

1. However men may differ among themselves as to individual character, as to outward circumstances, religious or social, when they appear at the bar of God, all appear on the same level. All are sinners, and being sinners, are exposed to condemnation, ver. 9.

2. The general declarations of the Scriptures, descriptive of the character of men before the advent of Christ, are applicable to men in all ages of the world, because they describe human nature. They declare what fallen man is. As we recognise the descriptions of the human heart given by profane writers a thousand years ago, as suited to its present character, so the inspired description suits us as well as those for whom it was originally intended, vs. 10—18.

3. Piety and morality cannot be separated. If men do not understand, if they have no fear of God before their eyes, they become altogether unprofitable, there is none that doeth good, vs. 10—12.

4. The office of the law is neither to justify nor to sanctify. It convinces and condemns. All efforts to secure the favour of God, therefore, by legal obedience must be vain, ver. 20.

REMARKS.

1. As God regards the moral character in men, and as we are all sinners, no one has any reason to exalt himself over another. With our hands upon our mouth, and our mouth in the dust, we must all appear as guilty before God, ver. 9.

2. The Scriptures are the message of God to all to whom they come. They speak general truths, which are intended to apply to all to whom they are applicable. What they say of sinners, as such, they say of all sinners; what they promise to believers, they promise to all believers. They should, therefore, ever be read with a spirit of self-application, vers. 10—18.

3. To be prepared for the reception of the gospel, we must be convinced of sin, humbled under a sense of its turpitude, silenced under a conviction of its condemning power, and prostrated at the footstool of mercy, under a feeling that we cannot satisfy the demands of the law, that if ever saved, it must be by other merit and other power than our own, ver. 20.

ROMANS III. 21—31.

ANALYSIS.

Having proved that justification, on the ground of legal obedience or personal merit, is for all men impossible, Paul proceeds to unfold the method of salvation presented in the gospel. With regard to this method, he here teaches, 1. Its nature. 2. The ground on which the offer of justification is made. 3. Its object. 4. Its results.

I. As to its nature, he teaches, 1. That the righteousness which it proposes is not attainable by works, but by faith, vers. 21, 22. 2. That it is adapted to all men, Jews as well as Gentiles, since there is no difference as to their moral state, vers. 22, 23. 3. It is entirely gratuitous, ver. 24.

II. As to its ground, it is the redemption that is in Christ Jesus, or Jesus Christ as a propitiatory sacrifice, vers. 24, 25.

III. Its object is the display of the divine perfections, and the reconciliation of the justice of God with the exhibition of mercy to the sinner, ver. 26.

IV. Its results. 1. It humbles man by excluding all ground of boasting, vers. 27, 28. 2. It presents God in his true character as the God and father of all men, of the Gentile no less than of the Jew, vers. 29, 30. 3. It confirms the law, ver. 31.

COMMENTARY.

Verse 21. *But now the righteousness of God without the law is manifested,* &c. Having demonstrated that no flesh can be justified by the deeds of the law in the sight of God, the apostle proceeds to show how the sinner can be justified. With regard to this point, he teaches, in this verse, 1. That the righteousness which is acceptable to God is not a legal righteousness ; and, 2. That it had been taught already in the Old Testament. The words *but now* may be regarded as merely marking the transition from one paragraph to another, or as a designation of time, *now*, i. e. under the gospel dispensation. In favour of this view is the phrase, "to declare, *at this time*, his righteousness," in ver. 26 ; compare also i. 17. *Is manifested, i. e.* clearly made known, equivalent to the phrase *is revealed*, as used in i. 17. The words *righteousness of God*, are subjected here to the same diversity of interpretation that was noticed in the passage just cited, where they first occur. They may mean, 1. A divine attribute, the justice, mercy, or general rectitude of God. 2. That righteousness which is acceptable to God, which is such in his estimation. 3. God's method of justification ; compare i. 17. The last interpretation gives here a very good sense, and is one very commonly adopted. ' The method of justification by works being impossible, God has revealed another, already taught indeed, both in the law and prophets, a method which is not legal (without law), *i. e.* not on the condition of obedience to the law, but on the condition of faith, which is applicable to all men, and perfectly gratuitous,' vers. 21—24. But for the reason stated above, in the remarks on i. 17, the interpretation which best suits both the force of the words and Paul's usage is, 'The righteousness of which God is the author, which comes from him, which he gives, and which consequently is acceptable in his sight.' The word *righteousness* is employed to designate that excellence which the law demands, or which constitutes a man δίκαιος (*righteous*) in the sight of the law, and the genitive (τοῦ Θεοῦ) *of God*, indicates the source or author of that righteousness. As men therefore cannot attain such righteousness by the deeds of the law, God has revealed in the gospel another righteousness, which is not legal, but is attained or received by faith, and is offered to all men, whether Jews or Gentiles, as a free gift. The words χωρὶς νόμου, *without law*, may qualify the word righteousness. It is a righteousness without law, or with which the law has nothing to do. It is not a product of the law, and does not consist in our inward conformity to its precepts ; so that χωρὶς νόμου is equivalent to χωρὶς ἔργων νόμου, Gal. ii. 16. The connection however may be with the verb : ' Without the law (*i. e.* without the coöperation of the law) the righteousness of God *is revealed*.' But the whole context treats of justification without works, and therefore the interpretation which makes the apostle say that a righteousness without the works of the law is made known in the gospel, is more suited to the connection. The perfect πεφανέρωται has its appropriate force. The revelation has been made and still continues. This righteousness, which, so to speak, had long been buried under the types and indistinct utterances of the old dispensation, has now in the gospel been made (φανερά) clear and apparent. The apostle therefore adds, *being testified by the law and the prophets.* The word is μαρτυρουμένη, *being testified to ;* the present is used because the testimony of the Old Testament to the gospel was still continued. The Jews were accustomed to divide the Scriptures into two parts—*the Law* including the five books of Moses, and *the Prophets* including all the other books. The word *prophet* means one who speaks for God. All inspired men are prophets, and therefore the designation applies to the historical, as well as to the books which we are accustomed, in a more restricted sense of the word, to call prophetical. The Law and the Prophets therefore mean the Old Testament Scriptures. Matt. v. 17, vii. 12, Luke xvi. 31, Acts xiii. 15, &c. The words designated a well known volume, and had to the minds of the Jews as definite a meaning as the word *Bible* has with us. The constant recognition of that volume in the New Testament as of divine authority, relieves us of the necessity of proving separately the inspiration of its several books. In sanctioning the volume as the word of God, Christ and his apostles gave their sanction to the divine authority of all that the volume contains. That the Old Testament does teach the doctrine of "a righteousness without works," Paul proves in the next chapter, from the case of Abraham, and from the declarations of David.

VERSE 22. *Even the righteousness of God.* The repetition of the subject from the preceding verse ; δέ is therefore not adversative, but is properly rendered *even.* This righteousness, of which God is the author, and which is available before him, and which is now revealed, is more particularly described as a (δικαιοσύνη (οὖσα) διὰ πίστεως) righteousness which is of faith, *i.e.* by means of faith, not διὰ πίστιν, *on account of* faith. Faith is not the ground of our justification ; it is not the righteousness which makes us righteous before God, (it is not itself the δικαιοσύνη τοῦ Θεοῦ,) nor is it even represented as the inward principle whence that righteousness proceeds. It is indeed the principle of evangelical obedience, the source of holiness in heart and life ; but such obedience or holiness is not our justifying righteousness. Holiness is the consequence and not the cause of our justification, as the apostle proves at length in the subsequent parts of this epistle. This righteousness is *through* faith, as it is received and appropriated by faith. It is, moreover, not faith in general, not mere confidence in God, not simply a belief in the Scriptures as the word of God, much less a recognition of the truth of the spiritual and invisible, but it is *faith of Christ ;* that is, faith of which Christ is the object. A man may believe what else he may ; unless he receives and rests on Christ alone for salvation, receives him as the Son of God, who loved us and gave himself for us, he has not the faith of which the apostle here speaks as the indispensable condition of salvation. This important doctrine is not only clearly but frequently brought into view in the New Testament. What our Lord constantly demanded was not merely religious faith in general, but specifically faith in himself as the Son of God and Saviour of the world. It is only faith in Christ, not faith as such, which makes a man a Christian. "If ye believe not that I am he," saith our Lord, "ye shall die in your sins," John viii. 24. "As many as received him, to them gave he power to become the sons of God, even to them that believe on his name," John i. 12. "That whosoever believeth in him should not perish, but have eternal life," John iii. 15, 16. "Whosoever believeth on him, shall not be confounded," Rom. ix. 33. "How shall they call on him in whom they have not believed," x. 14. Such passages are almost innumerable. So when the object of saving faith is designated, it is said to be not truth in general, but Christ himself. See verse 25 (through faith in his blood), Gal. ii. 16, 20 ; iii. 24 ; Eph. iii. 12, &c. The act, therefore, which the sinner is required to perform, in order to be made a partaker of the righteousness of God, is to believe on Christ ; that is, to receive him as he is revealed in the gospel as the eternal Son of God, clothed in our nature, loving us and giving himself as a propitiation for our sins. As there is no verb in the text, of which δικαιοσύνη (*righteousness*) is the nominative, we must either borrow the verb πεφανέρωται from verse 21, "the righteousness of God is *manifested* unto all ;" or what better suits what follows, supply ἔρχεται, *comes* (or simply ἐστί, *is*) *unto all and upon all.* The words καὶ ἐπὶ πάντας (*and upon all*) are omitted in the MSS. A. c. 20. 31. 47. 66. 67 ; in the Coptic and Ethiopic versions ; and by several of the Fathers. Griesbach and Lachmann leave them out of the text ; most modern critical editions retain them, both on external and internal grounds. This righteousness is εἰς πάντας, extending unto all, καὶ ἐπὶ πάντας, and over all, as covering them or overflowing them. " Eine Gnadenfluth," says Olshausen, " die an alle herandringt und sogar über alle hinüberströmt." There is no distinction between Jew and Gentile recognized in this method of salvation. The question is not as to whether men are of this or that race, or of one or another rank in life, or in the Church visible or out of it. This righteousness is unto all who believe. Faith is all that is demanded. The reason why the same method of salvation is suited to all men is given in the following clause : *For there is no difference* among men as to their moral state or relation to God, or as to their need of salvation, or as to what is necessary to that end. What one man needs all require, and what is suited to one is suited to and sufficient for all. The characteristics, therefore, of the plan of salvation presented in this verse are : 1. That the righteousness of God which is revealed in the gospel is to be attained by faith, not by works, not by birth, not by any external rite, not by union with any visible Church, but simply and only by believing on Christ, receiving and resting upon him. 2. That this righteousness is suited to and sufficient for all men ; not only for all classes, but for all numerically ; so that no one can perish for the want of a right-eousness suitable and sufficient, clearly revealed and freely offered.

Verse 23. *For all have sinned.* This is the reason why there is no difference as to the condition of men. All are sinners. The apostle uses the aorist ἥμαρτον, *sinned*, and not the perfect, *have sinned.* Rückert says this is an inaccuracy ; Bengel explains it by assuming that the original act in paradise, and the sinful disposition, and also the acts of transgression flowing from it, are all denoted. Olshausen says that the reference is mainly to original sin ; for where there are no *peccata actualia*, there is still need of redemption. Dr. Wordsworth, Canon of Westminster, gives the same explanation : " All men sinned in Adam, all fell in him." Meyer says, " The sinning of each man is presented as an historical fact of the past." The idea that all men now stand in the posture of sinners before God might be expressed either by saying, All have sinned (and are sinners), or *all sinned.* The latter is the form adopted by the apostle. *And come short*, ὑστεροῦνται, in the present tense. The sinning is represented as past ; the present and abiding consequence of sin is the want of the *glory of God.* By δόξα τοῦ Θεοῦ is most naturally understood the approbation of God, the δόξα which comes from God ; comp. John xii. 43, " They loved the praise of men rather than the praise (δόξαν) of God." Calvin explains it as the glory *quæ coram Deo locum habet*, glory before God, *i.e.*, in his estimation, as he explains δικαιοσύνη Θεοῦ to be righteousness in his sight, what he regards as such. This is against the natural force of the genitive. Others understand δόξα in the sense of glorying, *non habent, unde coram Deo glorientur*, Estius ; so also Luther, Tholuck, (who refers to John v. 44, δόξαν παρὰ τοῦ Θεοῦ,) and others. This idea would be expressed by the word καύχησις, verse 27, or καύχημα, iv. 2 ; 1 Cor. v. 6 ; ix. 16, &c. Others again say that the *glory of God* here means that glory which God promises to the righteous, as in v. 2. So Beza, who says, " δόξα est meta ad quam contendimus, id est, vita æterna, quæ in gloriæ Dei participatione consistit." Rückert and Olshausen say it means the image of God :

"Men are sinners, and are destitute of the image of God." But this is not the sense of the words; "the glory of God" does not mean a glory like to that of God. The first interpretation, which is the simplest, is perfectly suited to the context. All men are sinners and under the disapprobation of God. In this respect there is no difference between them; and therefore all need a righteousness not their own, in order to their justification before God.

VERSE 24. *Being justified freely by his grace, through the redemption that is in Christ Jesus.* The apostle continues his exhibition of the method of salvation by using the participle "being justified," instead of the verb "we are justified," agreeably to a mode of construction not unusual in the Greek, though much more frequent in the Hebrew. Δικαιούμενοι therefore depends on ὑστεροῦνται, "all come short of the favour of God, being justified freely." That is, since justification is gratuitous, the subjects of it are in themselves unworthy; they do not merit God's favour. Justification is as to us δωρεάν, a matter of gift; on the part of God it is an act of grace; we are justified τῇ αὐτοῦ χάριτι by his grace. The act, so far as we are concerned, is altogether gratuitous. We have not the slightest degree of merit to offer as the ground of our acceptance. This is the third characteristic of the method of justification which is by the righteousness of God. Though it is so entirely gratuitous as regards the sinner, yet it is in a way perfectly consistent with the justice of God. It is through "the redemption that is in Christ Jesus," that is, of which he is the author.

The word ἀπολύτρωσις, *redemption*, has two senses in the New Testament. 1. It means properly 'a deliverance effected by the payment of a ransom.' This is its primary etymological meaning. 2. It means deliverance simply, without any reference to the mode of its accomplishment, whether by power or wisdom. Luke xxi. 28, "The day of redemption (*i. e.* of deliverance) draweth nigh;" Heb. ix. 15, and perhaps Rom. viii. 23; compare Isa. l. 2, "Is my hand shortened at all, that it cannot redeem?" &c. When applied to the work of Christ, as affecting our deliverance from the punishment of sin, it is always taken in its proper sense, *deliverance effected by the payment of a ransom.* This is evident, 1. Because in no case where it is thus used, is anything said of the precepts, doctrines, or power of Christ, as the means by which the deliverance is effected; but uniformly his sufferings are mentioned as the ground of deliverance. Eph. i. 7, "In whom we have redemption through his blood;" Heb. ix. 15, "By means of death, for the redemption of transgressions," Col. i. 14. 2. In this passage the nature of this redemption is explained by the following verse: it is not by truth, nor the exhibition of excellence, but through Christ 'as a propitiatory sacrifice, through faith in his blood.' 3. Equivalent expressions fix the meaning of the term beyond doubt. 1 Tim. ii. 6, "Who gave himself a ransom for all;" Matt. xx. 28, "The Son of man came to give his life as a ransom for many;" 1 Peter i. 18, "Ye were not redeemed with corruptible things, such as silver and gold, but with the precious blood of Christ," &c. Accordingly Christ is presented as a Redeemer, not in the character of a teacher or witness, but of a priest, a sacrifice, a propitiation, &c. That from which we are redeemed is the wrath of God; the price of our redemption is the blood of Christ. *That is in Christ Jesus.* This may mean *by* him, ἐν having its instrumental force, as in Acts xvii. 31, (ἐν ἀνδρὶ ᾧ,) *by the man.* As this use of the preposition with names of persons is infrequent, others retain its usual force, *in.* Compare Eph. i. 7, "In whom (ἐν ᾧ) we have redemption," &c.; and Col. i. 14. 'We are justified by means (διά) of the redemption which we have in virtue of union to Christ.'

VERSE 25. *Whom God hath set forth to be a propitiation through faith in his blood,* &c. This clause contains the ground of our deliverance from the curse of the law, and of our acceptance with God, and constitutes therefore the second step in the apostle's exhibition of the plan of salvation. He had already taught that justification was not by works, but by faith, and entirely gratuitous; he now comes to show how it is that this exercise of mercy to the sinner can be reconciled with the justice of God and the demands of his law. The word προέθετο, *hath set forth,* also signifies *to purpose, to determine,* Rom. i. 13; compare viii. 28. If this sense be adopted here, the meaning would be, 'whom God hath purposed or decreed *to be* a propitiation.' But the context refers to a fact rather than a purpose; and the words εἰς ἔνδειξιν (*for the manifestation*), as expressing the design of the manifestation of Christ, is decidedly in favour of the common interpretation. There are three interpretations of the word ἱλαστήριον (*propitiation*), which are worthy of attention. It was understood by many of the Fathers, and after them by Luther, Calvin, Grotius, Olshausen, and others, to mean the propitiatory, or mercy-seat, over the ark of the covenant, on which the high priest, on the great day of atonement, sprinkled the blood of the sacrifices. Here it was that God was propitiated, and manifested himself as reconciled to his people. The ground of this interpretation is, that the original word here used is employed in the Septuagint as the designation of the mercy-seat, Exod. xxv. 18—20; and often elsewhere. The meaning would then be, 'that God had set forth Jesus Christ as a mercy-seat, as the place in which, or the person in whom he was propitiated, and ready to forgive and accept the sinner.' But the objections to this interpretation are serious. 1. The use of the word by the Greek translators of the Old Testament, probably arose from a mistake of the proper meaning of the Hebrew term. The Hebrew word means properly *a cover;* but as the verb whence it comes means literally, *to cover,* and metaphorically, *to atone for, to propitiate,* the Greek translators incorrectly rendered the noun ἱλαστήριον, the Latin *propitiatorium,* and our translators, *the mercy-seat,* a sense which כַּפֹּרֶת never has. It is, therefore, in itself a wrong use of the Greek word. 2. This interpretation is not consistent with the analogy of Scripture. The sacred writers are not accustomed to compare the Saviour to the cover of the ark, nor to illustrate his work by such a reference. This passage, if thus interpreted, would stand alone in this respect. 3. According to this view, there is an obvious incongruity in the figure. It is common to speak of the blood of a sacrifice, but not of the blood of the mercy-seat. Besides, Paul in this very clause speaks of "*his* blood." See *Deylingii Observationes,* Part II., sect. 41, and *Krebs's New Testament,* illustrated from the writings of Josephus.

The second interpretation supposes that the word θῦμα (*sacrifice*) is to be supplied: 'Whom he has set forth as a propitiatory *sacrifice.*' 1. In favour of this interpretation is the etymology of the word. It is derived from ἱλάσκομαι, *to appease, to conciliate.* Hence ἱλαστήριος, as an adjective, is applied to anything designed to propitiate; as in the expressions "propitiatory monument," "propitiatory death." (*Josephus,* Ant. XVI. 7. 1 *Lib. de Macc.,* sect. 17. See *Krebs* on this verse.) 2. The use of analogous terms in reference to the sacrificial services under the old dispensation, as σωτήριον, *sacrificium pro salute*, Exod. xx. 24; xxviii. 29, for which we have in Exod. xxiv. 5, θυσία σωτηρίου; so χαριστήρια, *thank-offerings*, τὸ καθάρσιον, *the offering for purification.* In keeping with all these terms is the use of ἱλαστήριον (θῦμα) in the sense of propitiatory sacrifice. 3. The whole context favours this explanation, inasmuch as the apostle immediately speaks of the blood of this sacrifice, and as his design is to show how the gratuitous justification of men can be reconciled with the justice of God. It is only a modification of this interpretation, if ἱλαστήριον be taken substantively and rendered *propitiation*, as is done in the Vulgate and by Beza.

The third interpretation assumes that ἱλαστήριον is here used in the masculine gender, and means *propitiator*. This is the explanation given by Semler and Wahl; but this is contrary to the usage of the word and inconsistent with the context. The obvious meaning, therefore, of this important passage is, that God has publicly set forth the Lord Jesus Christ, in the sight of the intelligent universe, as a propitiatory sacrifice for the sins of men. It is the essential idea of such a sacrifice, that it is a satisfaction to justice. It terminates on God. Its primary design is not to produce any subjective change in the offerer, but to appease God. Such is the meaning of the word, from which we have no right to depart. Such also is the idea which it of necessity would convey to every Gentile and every Jewish reader, and therefore such was the idea which the apostle intended to express. For if we are not to understand the language of the Bible in its historical sense, that is, in the sense in which the sacred writers knew it would be understood by those to whom they wrote, it ceases to have any determinate meaning whatever, and may be explained according to the private opinion of every interpreter. But if such be the meaning of these words, then they conclusively teach that the ground of our justification is no subjective change in us, but the propitiatory sacrifice of Christ. Olshausen, who elsewhere plainly teaches the doctrine of subjective justification, in his comment on this verse, admits the common Church doctrine. He denies that the work of Christ terminates on the sinner. "Every sacrifice," he says, "proposed to expiate the guilt of man, and to appease the wrath of God, consequently the sacrifice of all sacrifices, in which alone all others have any truth, must accomplish that which they only symbolized." The doctrine of the Scotists, he adds, of *gratuita acceptatio*, refutes itself, because God can never take a thing for what it is not, and therefore cannot accept as a satisfaction what is no satisfaction. Grotius's view of an *acceptilatio*, which amounts to the same thing with the doctrine of Scotus, and resolves the atonement into a mere governmental display, (a popular theory reproduced as a novelty in the American Churches,) he also rejects. He says, "So there remains nothing but the acute theory of Anselm, properly understood, of a *satisfactio vicaria*, which completely agrees with the teachings of Scripture, and meets the demands of science." [*] According to Olshausen, therefore, ("die tiefste Erörterungen,") the profoundest disclosures of modern science have at last led back to the simple old doctrine of a real vicarious satisfaction to the justice of God, as the ground of the sinner's justification.

---

[*] So bleibt nur die richtig verstandene höchst scharfsinnige Anselmische Theorie (satisfactio vicaria) als diejenige übrig, die der Schriftlehre eben so sehr genügt, als dem Ansprücher der Wissenschaft.

Through faith. These words, διὰ πίστεως, may be connected with δικαιούμενοι as coördinate with διὰ ἀπολυτρώσεως : 'Being justified *through the redemption,* that is, being justified *through faith.*' But this breaks the connection between προέθετο and εἰς ἔνδειξιν. Meyer connects both διὰ πίστεως and ἐν τῷ αἵματι with προέθετο : 'God hath, by means of faith, by his blood, set forth Christ as a propitiation.' But the faith of man is not the means by which God set forth Christ. The most natural connection is with ἱλαστήριον, 'a propitiation through faith,' *i. e.* which is received or appropriated through faith. It is a more doubtful question how the words *in his blood* are to be connected. The most obvious construction is that adopted in our version, as well as in the Vulgate, and by Luther, Calvin, Olshausen, and many others, 'Through faith in his blood;' so that the blood of Christ, as a propitiatory sacrifice, is the ground of the confidence expressed in πίστις, "in Christi sanguine repositam habemus fiduciam." *Calvin.* To this it is objected, that the construction of πίστις with ἐν is altogether unauthorized. But there are so many cases in the New Testament in which this construction must be admitted, unless violence be resorted to, that this objection cannot be allowed much weight. See Gal. iii. 26 ; Eph. i. 15 ; Col. i. 4 ; 1 Tim. iii. 13 ; 2 Tim. iii. 15. Others connect both διὰ πίστεως and ἐν τῷ αἵματι as distinctly qualifying clauses with ἱλαστήριον ; the former, as De Wette says, expressing the means of the subjective appropriation, the other the means of the objective exhibition. That is, 'God has set forth Christ as a propitiation, which is available through faith, and he is a propitiation by his blood. Still another method is to connect ἐν τῷ αἵματι with ὅν : 'Whom God has set forth in his blood as a propitiation.' The construction first mentioned, and sanctioned by the translators of the English Bible, gives a perfectly good sense, and is most agreeable to the collocation of the words. *The blood* of Christ is an expression used in obvious reference to the sacrificial character of his death. It was not his death as a witness or as an example, but as a sacrifice, that expiates sin. And by *his blood,* is not to be understood simply his death, but his whole work for our redemption, especially all his expiatory sufferings from the beginning to the end of his life.

This whole passage, which Olshausen happily calls the "Acropolis of the Christian faith," is of special importance. It teaches that we are justified in a manner which is entirely of grace, without any merit of our own ; through, or by means of faith, and on the ground of the propitiatory sacrifice of Jesus Christ. It is evident from this statement, that Paul intended to exclude from all participation in the meritorious ground of our acceptance with God, not only those works performed in obedience to the law, and with a legal spirit, but those which flow from faith and a renewed heart. The part assigned to faith in the work of our reconciliation to God is that of an instrument ; it apprehends or appropriates the meritorious ground of our acceptance, the work or righteousness of Christ. It is not itself that ground, nor the means of attaining an inherent righteousness acceptable to God. This is obvious, 1. Because our justification would not then be gratuitous, or without works. Paul would then teach the very reverse of the doctrine which he has been labouring to establish, viz. that it is not on account of works of righteousness, *i. e.* works of the highest order of excellence, that we are accepted, since these works would then be the real ground of our acceptance. 2. Because we are said to be justified by faith, of which Christ is the object, by faith in his blood, by faith in him as a sacrifice. These expressions cannot possibly mean, that faith in Christ is, or produces, a state of mind which is acceptable to God.   Faith in a sacrifice is, by the very force of the terms, reliance on a sacrifice.   It would be to contradict the sentiment of the whole ancient and Jewish world, to make the design of a sacrifice the production of a state of mind acceptable to the Being worshipped, which moral state was to be the ground of acceptance.   There is no more pointed way of denying that we are justified on account of the state of our own hearts, or the character of our own acts, than by saying that we are justified by a propitiatory sacrifice.   This latter declaration places of necessity the ground of acceptance out of our-selves ; it is something done for us, not something experienced, or pro-duced in us, or performed by us.   There is no rule of interpretation more obvious and more important than that which requires us to understand the language of a writer in the sense in which he knew he would be understood by the persons to whom he wrote.   To explain, therefore, the language of the apostle in reference to the sacrifice of Christ, and the mode of our acceptance with God, otherwise, than in accordance with the universally prevalent opinions on the nature of sacrifices, is to substitute our philosophy of religion for the inspired teachings of the sacred writers.

To declare his righteousness for the remission of sins that are past, through the forbearance of God.   Having stated the nature and ground of the gospel method of justification, Paul comes, in this clause, to state its object : ' God has set forth Christ, as a propitiatory sacrifice, to declare his righteousness.'   It should be remembered that the object of the death of Christ, being very comprehensive, is variously presented in the word of God.   In other words, the death of Christ answers a great number of infinitely important ends in the government of God.   It displays " his manifold wisdom," Eph. iii. 10, 11 ; it was designed "to purify unto him-self a people zealous of good works," Titus ii. 14 ; to break down the dis-tinction between the Jews and Gentiles, Eph. ii. 15 ; to effect the recon-ciliation of both Jews and Gentiles unto God, Eph. ii. 16 ; "to deliver us from this present evil world," Gal. i. 4 ; to secure the forgiveness of sins, Eph. i. 7 ; to vindicate his ways to men, in so long passing by or remitting their sins, Rom. iii. 25 ; to reconcile the exercise of mercy with the requirements of justice, ver. 26, &c.   These ends are not inconsistent, but perfectly harmonious.   The end here specially mentioned is, *to declare his righteousness.*   These words here, as elsewhere, are variously explained.   1. They are understood of some one of the moral attributes of God, as his veracity, by Locke ; or his mercy, by Grotius, Koppe, and many of the moderns.   Both of these interpretations are forced, because they assign very unusual meanings to the word righteousness, and meanings little suited to the context.   2. Most commentators, who render the phrase 'righteousness, or justification of God,' in chap. i. 17, iii. 21, God's method of justification, adopt that sense here.   The meaning would then be, that ' God had set forth Christ as a propitiation, to exhibit his method of justification, both in reference to the sins committed under the old dispensation, and those committed under the new.'   But this is inconsistent with the meaning of δικαιοσύνη, which never has the sense of " method of justification," and is unsuited to the context.   3. The great majority of commentators under-stand the δικαιοσύνη Θεοῦ here spoken of to be the justice of God.   This is the proper meaning of the terms, and this the context demands.   Justice is the attribute with which the remission, or passing by, of sins without punishment, seemed to be in conflict, and which therefore required vindi-cation.   It was necessary that the justice of God should be publicly exhibited, because he forgave sin. Besides, the apostle himself explains what he means by δικαιοσύνη, when he adds that God set forth Christ as a propitiation, in order *that he might be just,* and yet justify the ungodly. The satisfaction of justice therefore was the immediate and specific end of the death of Christ. This was indeed a means to a higher end. Justice was satisfied, in order that men might be sanctified and saved ; and men are sanctified and saved, in order that might be known, in the ages to come, the exceeding riches of the grace of God.

For the remission of sins, διὰ τὴν πάρεσιν, κ.τ.λ. This admits of different explanations. 1. Some give διά with the accusative the same force as with the genitive ; *through* the forgiveness of sins. That is, the righteousness of God was manifested by means of remitting sins. This is contrary to the proper meaning of the words, and supposes that δικαιοσύνη means goodness. Beza, however, adopts this view, and renders the words, *per remissionem ;* so also Reiche, Koppe, and others. 2. It is taken to mean, *as to, as it regards.* This gives a good sense, ' To declare his righteousness, *as to,* or *as it regards* the remission of sins.' So Raphelius (*Observationes,* &c., p. 241,) who quotes Polybius, Lib. 5, ch. 24, p. 517, in support of this interpretation. This view is given by Professor Stuart. But the preposition in question very rarely if ever has this force. No such meaning is assigned to it by Wahl, Bretschneider, or Winer. 3. The common force of the preposition is retained, *on account of.* This clause would then assign the ground or reason of the exhibition of the righteousness of God. It became necessary that there should be this exhibition, because God had overlooked or pardoned sin from the beginning. This is the most natural and satisfactory interpretation of the passage. So the Vulgate, *propter remissionem,* and almost all the moderns.· 4. Others again make the preposition express the final cause or object, ' To declare his righteousness for the sake of the remission of sins,' *i.e.,* that sins might be remitted. So Calvin, who says, " Tantundem valet præpositio causalis, acsi dixisset, remissionis ergo, vel in hunc finem ut peccata deleret. Atque haec definitio vel exegesis rursus confirmat quod jam aliquoties monui, non justificari homines, quia re ipsa tales sint, sed imputatione." But this is a very questionable force of the preposition : See *Winer's Gram.,* § 49, *c.* The third interpretation, therefore, just mentioned, is to be preferred. The word πάρεσις, *remission,* more strictly means *pretermission, a passing by,* or *overlooking.* Paul repeatedly uses the proper term for *remission* (ἄφεσις), as in Eph. i. 7, Heb. ix. 22, &c. ; but the word here used occurs nowhere else in the New Testament. Many, therefore, consider the selection of this particular term as designed to express the idea, that sins committed before the advent of Christ might more properly be said to be overlooked, than actually pardoned, until the sacrifice of the Redeemer had been completed ; see *Wolf's Curæ.* Reference is made to Acts xvii. 30, where God is said to have overlooked the times of ignorance. But as the word used by the apostle is actually used to express the idea of *remission,* in Greek writers (see Elsner), the majority of commentators adopt that meaning here. The words πάρεσις and ἄφεσις express the same thing, but under different aspects. They differ only as *not punishing,* and *pardoning.* To say that God did not punish sins under the old dispensation, is only a different way of saying that he pardoned them. So "not to impute iniquity," is the negative statement of justification. This passage, however, is one of the few which the Romanists quote in support of their doctrine that there was no real pardon, justification, or salvation, before the advent of Christ. The ancient believers at death, according to their doctrine, did not pass into heaven, but into the *limbus patrum*, where they continued in a semi-conscious state until Christ's *descensus ad inferos* for their deliverance. The modern transcendental theologians of Germany, who approach Romanism in so many other points, agree with the Papists also here. Thus Olshausen says, " Under the Old Testament there was no real, but only a symbolical forgiveness of sins." Our Lord, however, speaks of Abraham as in heaven ; and the Psalms are filled with petitions and thanksgiving for God's pardoning mercy.

The words, *that are past*, seem distinctly to refer to the times before the advent of Christ. This is plain from their opposition to the expression, *at this time*, in the next verse, and from a comparison with the parallel passage in Heb. ix. 15, " He is the Mediator for the redemption of sins *that were* under the first testament." The words ἐν τῇ ἀνοχῇ, rendered *through the forbearance of God*, admit of different explanations. 1. They may be connected with the words just mentioned, and the meaning be, ' Sins that are past, or, which were committed during the forbearance of God ;' see Acts xvii. 30, where the times before the advent are described in much the same manner. 2. Or they may be taken, as by our translators, as giving the cause of the remission of these sins, 'They were remitted, or overlooked through the divine forbearance or mercy.' Forgiveness however is always referred to grace, not to forbearance. The former interpretation is also better suited to the context. The meaning of the whole verse therefore is, ' God has set forth Jesus Christ as a propitiatory sacrifice, to vindicate his righteousness or justice, on account of the remission of the sins committed under the former dispensation ;' and not under the former dispensation only, but also in the remission of sins at the present time, as the apostle immediately adds. The interpretation of the latter part of this verse, given above, according to which τὰ προγεγονότα ἁμαρτήματα, (*the sins before committed*,) mean the sins committed before the coming of Christ, is that which both the context and the analogy of Scripture demand. In the early Church, however, there were some who held that there is no forgiveness for post-baptismal sins—a doctrine recently reproduced in England by the Rev. Dr. Pusey. The advocates of this doctrine make this passage teach that Christ was set forth as a propitiation for the forgiveness of sins committed before baptism, that is, before conversion or the professed adoption of the gospel. Rückert and Reiche, among the recent German writers, give the same interpretation. This would alter the whole character of the gospel. There could be no salvation for any human being ; for all men sin hourly, after as well as before baptism or conversion. No man at any moment of his life is perfectly conformed to the law of God. Conscience always pronounces sentence against us. There could be no peace in believing, no imputation or possession of righteousness. We should not now be under grace, but under law, as completely as though Christ had never died.

VERSE 26. *To declare*, I say, *his righteousness*, &c. This clause is a resumption of what was said before, πρὸς ἔνδειξιν being coördinate with the foregoing εἰς ἔνδειξιν, both depending upon προέθετο : ' He set him forth εἰς and—πρός.' The two prepositions have the same sense, as both express the design or object for which anything is done : ' Christ was set forth as a sacrifice *for the manifestation* of the righteousness of God, on account of the remission of the sins of old—*for the manifestation* of his righteousness at this time.' There were two purposes to be answered ;

the vindication of the character of God in passing by former sins, and in passing them by now. The words ἐν τῷ νῦν καιρῷ, (*at this time,*) therefore stand opposed to ἐν τῇ ἀνοχῇ, (*during the forbearance.*) The death of Christ vindicated the justice of God in forgiving sin in all ages of the world, as those sins were by the righteous God, as Olshausen says, "punished in Christ."

That he might be just, &c., εἰς τὸ εἶναι αὐτὸν δίκαιον, *in order that,* as expressing the design, and not merely the result of the exhibition of Christ as a propitiatory sacrifice. This clause therefore expresses more definitely what is meant by εἰς ἔνδειξιν δικαιοσύνης. Christ was set forth as a sacrifice for the manifestation of the righteousness or justice of God, that is, that he might be just, although the justifier of the ungodly. The word *just* expresses the idea of uprightness generally, of being or doing what the nature of the case demands. But when spoken of the conduct of a judge, and in reference to his treatment of sin, it must mean more specifically that modification of general rectitude, which requires that sin should be treated according to its true nature, that the demands of law or justice should not be disregarded. A judge is unjust when he allows a criminal to be pronounced righteous, and treated accordingly. On the other hand he acts justly when he pronounces the offender guilty, and secures the infliction of the penalty which the law denounces. What the apostle means to say is, that there is no such disregard to the claims of justice in the justification of the sinner who believes in Christ. This is seen and acknowledged, when it is known that he is justified neither on account of his own acts or character, nor by a mere sovereign dispensing with the demands of the law, but on the ground of a complete satisfaction rendered by his substitute, *i. e.* on the ground of the obedience and death of Christ. The gratuitous nature of this justification is not at all affected by its proceeding on the ground of this perfect satisfaction. It is, to the sinner, still the most undeserved of all favours, to which he not only has not the shadow of a personal claim, but the very reverse of which he has most richly merited. It is thus that justice and mercy are harmoniously united in the sinner's justification. Justice is no less justice, although mercy has her perfect work ; and mercy is no less mercy, although justice is completely satisfied.

'Just *and* the justifier,' &c. In the simple language of the Old Testament, propositions and statements are frequently connected by the copulative conjunction whose logical relation would be more definitely expressed by various particles in other languages ; as Malachi ii. 14, "Against whom thou hast dealt treacherously, *and* she was thy companion," *i. e. although* she was thy companion. "They spake in my name, *and* (although) I sent them not ;" see *Gesenius's Lexicon.* In like manner the corresponding particle in the Greek Testament is used with scarcely less latitude. Matt. xii. 5, "The priests profane the Sabbath, *and* (and yet) are blameless ;" Rom. i. 13, "I purposed to come unto you, *and* (but) was let hitherto ;" Heb. iii. 9, "Proved me *and* (although *they*) saw my works ;" see *Whal's Lex.* and *Winer's Gram.*, § 53. So in the present instance it may be rendered, "That God might be just, *and yet,* or *although* the justifier," &c. *Him which believeth in Jesus,* literally, 'Him who is of the faith of Jesus ;' so Gal. iii. 7, "They which are of faith," for believers ; Gal. ii. 12, "They of the circumcision," *i. e.* the circumcised ; see Rom. ii. 8 ; iv. 12, &c. *Faith of Jesus,* faith of which Jesus is the object ; see ver. 22. Our version therefore expresses the sense accurately. He whom God is just in justifying, is the man who relies on Jesus as a propitiatory sacrifice. That justification is a forensic act, is of necessity implied in this passage. If to justify was to make subjectively just or righteous, what necessity was there for the sacrifice of Christ? Why should he die, in order that it might be just in God to render men holy? It were an act of mercy to make the vilest malefactor good; but to justify such a malefactor would be to trample justice under foot. The doctrine therefore of subjective justification perverts the whole gospel. It is worthy of remark, that the orthodox interpretation of the meaning of this whole paragraph is acknowledged to be correct, even by those who cannot themselves receive the doctrine which it teaches. Thus Köllner, one of the latest and most candid of the German commentators, says : " It is clear that the true sense of this passage entirely agrees with the doctrine of the Church concerning vicarious satisfaction, as unfolded in the Lutheran symbols. Nevertheless, although it is certain that Paul intended to teach the doctrine of vicarious satisfaction, not merely as a figure, (or in the way of accommodation,) but as a matter of full personal conviction; yet it is easy to see how he was necessarily led to adopt this view, from the current opinions of the age in which he lived." He proceeds to show that as the idea of vicarious punishment was incorporated in the Jewish theology, the guilt of the offender being laid upon the head of the victim offered in sacrifice, Paul was unavoidably led to conceive of the work of Christ under this form. As, however, this theory according to Köllner, arose out of a false view of the nature of God, and of his relation to the world, he cannot regard it as a divine revelation. He proceeds to unfold what he supposes to be the eternal truth contained under these Jewish ideas, (unter der Hülle der Zeitvorstellungen,) and presents very much the governmental view of the atonement introduced by Grotius, and reproduced in this country by the younger Edwards and his followers. " Did Paul," says Köllner, " merely teach that God made a symbolical exhibition of justice in the sufferings of Christ, we might acquiesce in his teaching, but he says more ; he constantly asserts that men are justified or constituted righteous through the blood of Christ, iii. 21 ; v. 19 ; Eph. i. 7 ; Col. i. 14." Such writers are at least free from the guilt of perverting the word of God. They allow the Bible to mean what it says, although they refuse to submit to its teaching. This is better than not only refusing to submit, but forcing the Scriptures to teach our own foregone conclusions. In Germany, the subjection of the Bible to philosophy has come to an end. In this country, it is still struggling for liberty. It is desirable that the separation should here, as there, be made complete, between those who bow to the authority of the word of God, and those who acknowledge some higher rule of faith. Then both parties can agree as to what the Bible really teaches.

Verse 27. *Where is boasting then? It is excluded. By what law? of works? Nay; but by the law of faith.* In this and the following verses the apostle presents the tendency and results of the glorious plan of salvation, which he had just unfolded. It excludes boasting, verse 27. It presents God in his true character, as the God and Father of the Gentiles as well as of the Jews, vers, 29, 30 ; and it establishes the law, ver. 31. The word καύχησις (*boasting*), is used to express the idea of self-gratulation with or without sufficient reason. In the former case, it is properly rendered *rejoicing*, as when Paul speaks of the Thessalonians being his " crown of rejoicing." In the latter, the word *boasting* is the correct version. The word properly means the act of *boasting* or *rejoicing ;* at times, by metonymy, the ground or reason of boasting, as in Rom. xv. 17. Either sense suits this passage. The article ἡ καύχησις, the boasting, may have its appropriate force. The reference, however, is not specially to ver. 1. of this chapter, *the* boasting of the Jews over the Gentiles, but *the* boasting of the sinner before God. The latter, however, includes the former. A plan of salvation which strips every man of merit, and places all sinners on the same level before God, of course cuts off all assumption of superiority of one class over another. Paul means to say that the result of the gospel plan of salvation is to prevent all self-approbation, self-gratulation, and exaltation on the part of the sinner. He is presented as despoiled of all merit, and as deserving the displeasure of God. He can attribute, in no degree, his deliverance from this displeasure to himself, and he cannot exalt himself either in the presence of God, or in comparison with his fellow-sinners. As sin is odious in the sight of God, it is essential, in any scheme of mercy, that the sinner should be made to feel this, and that nothing done by or for him should in any measure diminish his sense of personal ill-desert on account of his transgressions. This result obviously could not follow from any plan of justification that placed the ground of the sinner's acceptance in himself, or his peculiar advantages of birth or ecclesiastical connection ; but it is effectually secured by that plan of justification which not only places the ground of his acceptance entirely out of himself, but which also requires, as the very condition of that acceptance, an act involving a penitent acknowledgment of personal ill-desert, and exclusive dependence on the merit of another. In this connection, the phrases " by what law," " the law of works," and " the law of faith," are peculiar, as the word νόμος (*law*) is not used in its ordinary sense. The general idea, however, of *a rule of action* is retained. " By what rule ? By that which requires works ? Nay ; by that which requires faith." By the " law of faith," therefore, is obviously meant the gospel. Compare ix. 31.

Verse 28. *Therefore we conclude,* &c. The common text has οὖν, *therefore,* giving this verse the character of a conclusion from the preceding argument. The great majority, however, of the best manuscripts, the Vulgate and Coptic versions, and many of the Fathers, have γάρ, which almost all the modern editors adopt. This verse, then, is a confirmation of what is said before : " Boasting is excluded, λογιζόμεθα γάρ, *for we think, i e.,* are sure," &c. See ii. 3 ; viii. 18 ; 2 Cor. xi. 5, for a similar use of the word λογίζομαι. *That a man is justified by faith.* If by faith, it is not of works ; and if not of works, there can be no room for boasting, for boasting is the assertion of personal merit. From the nature of the case, if justification is by faith, it must be by faith alone. Luther's version, therefore, *allein durch den glauben,* is fully justified by the context. The Romanists, indeed, made a great outcry against that version as a gross perversion of Scripture, although Catholic translators before the time of Luther had given the same translation. So in the Nuremberg Bible, 1483, " Nur durch den glauben." And the Italian Bibles of Geneva, 1476, and of Venice, 1538, *per sola fede.* The Fathers also often use the expression, " man is justified by faith alone ;" so that Erasmus, *De Ratione Concionandi,* Lib. III., says, " Vox *sola,* tot clamoribus lapidata hoc sæculo in Luthero, reverenter in Patribus auditur." See Koppe and Tholuck on this verse.

Without works of the law. To be justified without works, is to be justified without anything in ourselves to merit justification. The works of the law must be the works of the moral law, because the proposition is general, embracing Gentiles as well as Jews. And as our Saviour teaches that the sum of the moral law is that we should love God with all the heart, mind, and strength, and our neighbour as ourselves, and as no higher form of excellence than supreme love to God is possible or conceivable, in excluding works of the law, the apostle excludes everything subjective. He places the ground of justification out of ourselves. Olshausen, on this verse, reverts to his Romish idea of subjective justification, and explains *works of the law* to mean works produced by the moral law, which he says spring only from ourselves, and are perishable, whereas "the works of faith are imperishable as the principle whence they spring." That is, we are not justified by works performed from a principle of natural conscience, but by those which are the fruits of a renewed nature. How utterly subversive this is of the gospel, has already been remarked. The works of the law are not works which the law produces, but works which the law demands, and the law demands all that the Spirit of God effects, even in the just made perfect. And therefore spiritual as well as legal works are excluded. The contrast is not between works produced by the law and works produced by faith, but between works and faith, between what is done by us (whether in a state of nature or a state of grace) and what Christ has done for us.

VERSES 29, 30. Is he *the God of the Jews only ?* is he *not also of the Gentiles ? Yes, of the Gentiles also ; seeing it is one God who shall justify, &c.* We have here the second result of the gospel method of justification ; it presents God as equally the God of the Gentiles and of the Jews. He is such, because ' it is one God who justifies the circumcision by faith, and the uncircumcision through faith.' He deals with both classes on precisely the same principles ; he pursues, with regard to both, the same plan, and offers salvation to both on exactly the same terms. There is, therefore, in this doctrine, the foundation laid for a universal religion, which may be preached to every creature under heaven ; which need not, as was the case with the Jewish system, be confined to any one sect or nation. This is the only doctrine which suits the character of God, and his relation to all his intelligent creatures upon earth. God is a universal, and not a national God ; and this is a method of salvation universally applicable. These sublime truths are so familiar to our minds that they have, in a measure, lost their power ; but as to the Jew, enthralled all his life in his narrow national and religious prejudices, they must have expanded his whole soul with unwonted emotions of wonder, gratitude, and joy. We Gentiles may now look up to heaven, and confidently say, "Thou art our Father, though Abraham be ignorant of us, and though Israel acknowledge us not."

Paul here, as in ver. 20, uses the future δικαιώσει, *will justify,* not for the present, nor in reference to the final judgment, but as expressing a permanent purpose. There is no distinction as to the meaning to be sought between ἐκ πίστεως (*by* faith) and διὰ πίστεως (*through* faith,) as Paul uses both forms indiscriminately; ἐκ, for example, in i. 17 ; iii. 20 ; iv. 16, &c., and διά in iii. 22, 25 ; Gal. ii. 16 ; and sometimes first the one, and then the other, in the same connection. There is no greater difference between the Greek prepositions, as here used, than between the English *by* and *through.*

VERSE 31. *Do we then make void the law through faith ? God forbid : yea, we establish the law.* This verse states the third result of this method of salvation; instead of invalidating, it establishes the law. As Paul uses the word *law* in so many senses, it is doubtful which one of them is here principally intended. In every sense, however, the declaration is true. If the law means the Old Testament generally, then it is true; for the gospel method of justification contradicts no one of its statements, is inconsistent with no one of its doctrines, and invalidates no one of its promises, but is harmonious with all, and confirmatory of the whole. If it means the Mosaic institutions specially, these were shadows of which Christ is the substance. That law is abolished, not by being pronounced spurious or invalid, but by having met its accomplishment, and answered its design in the gospel. What it taught and promised, the gospel also teaches and promises, only in clearer and fuller measure. If it means the moral law, which no doubt was prominently intended, still it is not invalidated, but established. No moral obligation is weakened, no penal sanction disregarded. The precepts are enforced by new and stronger motives, and the penalty is answered in Him who bore our sins in his own body on the tree. "Ubi vero ad Christum ventum est," says Calvin, "primum in eo invenitur exacta Legis justitia, quæ per imputationem etiam nostra fit. Deinde sanctificatio, qua formantur corda nostra ad Legis observationem, imperfectam quidem illam, sed ad scopum collimat." Instead of making ver. 31 the close of the third chapter, many commentators regard it as more properly the beginning of the fourth. The proposition that the gospel, instead of invalidating, establishes the law, they say is too important to be dismissed with a mere categorical assertion. This, however, is Paul's method. After showing that the law cannot save, that both justification and sanctification are by the gospel, he is wont to state in a sentence what is the true end of the law, or that the law and the gospel being both from God, but designed for different ends, are not in conflict. See above, ver. 20; Gal. iii. 19, 20. If this verse, however, be made the beginning of the exhibition contained in the following chapter, then by *law* must be understood the Old Testament, and the confirmation of the law by the gospel consists in the fact that the latter teaches the same doctrine as the former. 'Do we make void the law by teaching that justification is by faith? By no means: we establish the law; for the Old Testament itself teaches that Abraham and David were justified gratuitously by faith, and without works.' Although the sense is thus good, there does not appear to be any sufficient reason for departing from the common division of the chapters. The next chapter is not connected with this verse by γάρ, which the sense would demand, if the connection was what Meyer, De Wette, and others would make it: 'We establish the law when we teach faith, *for* Abraham was justified by faith.' The connecting particle is simply οὖν, *then*, and gives a very different sense. Besides it is a very subordinate object with the apostle to prove that the law and the gospel agree. His design is to teach the true method of justification. The cases of Abraham and David are referred to, to prove his doctrine on that point, and not merely the agreement between the old dispensation and the new.

DOCTRINE.

1. The evangelical doctrine of justification by faith is the doctrine of the Old, no less than of the New Testament, ver. 21.

2. Justification is pronouncing one to be just, and treating him accordingly, on the ground that the demands of the law have been satisfied concerning him, vers. 24—26.

3. The ground of justification is not our own merit, nor faith, nor evangelical obedience ; not the work of Christ in us, but his work for us, *i. e.* his obedience unto death, ver. 25.

4. An act may be perfectly gratuitous as regards its object, and at the same time proceed on the ground of a complete satisfaction to the demands of the law. Thus justification is gratuitous, not because those demands are unsatisfied, but because it is granted to those who have no personal ground of recommendation, vers. 24, 26.

5. God is the ultimate end of all his own acts. To declare his glory is the highest and best end which he can propose for himself or his creatures, ver. 25.

6. The atonement does not consist in a display to others of the divine justice. This is one of its designs and results; but it is such a display only by being a satisfaction to the justice of God. It is not a symbol or illustration, but a satisfaction, ver. 26.

7. All true doctrine tends to humble men, and to exalt God; and all true religion is characterized by humility and reverence, ver. 27.

8. God is a universal Father, and all men are brethren, vers. 29, 30.

9. The law of God is immutable. Its precepts are always binding, and its penalty must be inflicted either on the sinner or his substitute. When, however, it is said that the penalty of the law is inflicted on the Redeemer, as the sinner's substitute, or, in the language of Scripture, that "he was made a curse for us," it cannot be imagined that he suffered the same kind of evils (as remorse, &c.) which the sinner would have suffered. The law threatens no specific kind of evil as its penalty. The term *death,* in Scripture, designates any or all of the evils inflicted in punishment of sin. And the penalty, or curse of the law, (in the language of the Bible,) is any evil judicially inflicted in satisfaction of the demands of justice. To say, therefore, that Christ suffered to satisfy the law, to declare the righteousness of God, or that he might be just in justifying him that believes in Jesus, and to say that he bore the penalty of the law, are equivalent expressions, ver. 31.

REMARKS.

1. As the cardinal doctrine of the Bible is justification by faith, so the turning point in the soul's history, the saving act, is the reception of Jesus Christ as the propitiation for our sins, ver. 25.

2. All modes of preaching must be erroneous, which do not lead sinners to feel that the great thing to be done, and done first, is to receive the Lord Jesus Christ, and to turn unto God through him. And all religious experience must be defective, which does not embrace distinctly a sense of the justice of our condemnation, and a conviction of the sufficiency of the work of Christ, and an exclusive reliance upon it as such, ver. 25.

3. As God purposes his own glory as the end of all that he does, so ought we to have that glory as the constant and commanding object of pursuit, ver. 25.

4. The doctrine of atonement produces in us its proper effect, when it leads us to see and feel that God is just; that he is infinitely gracious; that we are deprived of all ground of boasting ; that the way of salvation, which is open for us, is open for all men ; and that the motives to all duty, instead of being weakened, are enforced and multiplied, vers. 25—31.

5. In the gospel all is harmonious : justice and mercy, as it regards God; freedom from the law, and the strongest obligations to obedience, as it regards men, vers. 25, 31.

CHAPTER IV.

CONTENTS.

THE OBJECT OF THIS CHAPTER IS TO CONFIRM THE DOCTRINE OF JUSTIFICATION BY FAITH. IT IS DIVIDED INTO TWO PARTS. THE FIRST, FROM VER. 1 TO 17 INCLUSIVE, CONTAINS THE ARGUMENTATIVE PORTION. THE SECOND, VER. 18 TO 25, IS AN ILLUSTRATION OF THE FAITH OF ABRAHAM.

ROMANS IV. 1—17.

ANALYSIS.

PAUL, from the 21st verse of the preceding chapter, had been setting forth the gospel method of salvation. That this is the true method he now proves, 1. From the fact that Abraham was justified by faith, vers. 1—5. That this was really the case he shows, first, because otherwise Abraham would have had ground of boasting, even in the sight of God, ver. 2 ; second, because the Scriptures expressly declare that he was justified by faith, ver. 8. Verses 4, 5, are designed to show that being justified by faith is tantamount with being justified gratuitously, and therefore all those passages which speak of the gratuitous forgiveness of sins may be fairly cited in favour of the doctrine of justification by faith. 2. On this principle he adduces Ps. xxxii. 1, 2, as his second argument ; for there David speaks not of rewarding the righteous as such, or for their righteousness, but of the free acceptance of the unworthy, vers. 6—8. 3. The third argument is designed to show that circumcision is not a necessary condition of justification, from the fact that Abraham was justified before he was circumcised, and therefore is the head and father of all believers, whether circumcised or not, vers. 9—12. 4. The fourth argument is from the nature of the covenant made with Abraham, in which the promise was made on the condition of faith, and not of legal obedience, vers. 13, 14. 5. And the fifth, from the nature of the law, vers. 15—17.

COMMENTARY.

VERSE 1. *What shall we then say that Abraham, our father as pertaining to the flesh, hath found ?* The connection of this verse with the preceding train of reasoning is obvious. Paul had taught that we are justified by faith ; as well in confirmation of this doctrine, as to anticipate an objection from the Jew, he refers to the case of Abraham : 'How was it then with Abraham ? How did he obtain justification ?' The point in dispute was, how justification is to be attained. Paul proposes to decide the question by reference to a case about which no one could doubt. All admitted that Abraham was justified. The only question was, How ? The particle οὖν, therefore, is not inferential, but simply indicates transition. What *then* shall we say about Abraham ? In the question, however, τί οὖν ἐροῦμεν, x.τ.λ. the τί belongs to εὑρηκέναι : 'What shall we say that Abraham hath found ?' *i. e.* attained. The words κατὰ σάρκα do not belong to πατέρα, 'our father according to the flesh,' but to the preceding infinitive, εὑρηκέναι, 'what hath he attained *through the flesh?*' Although the question is indefinite, the connection shows that Paul meant to ask whether Abraham secured justification before God, κατὰ σάρκα, *through the flesh.* The word *flesh* admits in this connection of different explanations. Calvin says it is equivalent to *naturaliter, ex seipso,* and Grotius much to the same effect, *propriis viribus,* 'through his own resources.' Not much different from this is the explanation of Meyer, Tholuck, and De Wette—*nach sein menschlicher Weise*—that is, after a purely human way; so that σάρξ stands opposed to the divine Πνεῦμα, (Holy Spirit) If this implies that Abraham was not justified by natural, but was justified by spiritual works, (works done after regeneration,) it contradicts the whole teaching of the apostle. This, however, though naturally suggested as the meaning of the passage as thus explained, is not the doctrine of either of the commentators just named. Paul gives his own interpretation of κατὰ σάρκα in the following verse : 'Did Abraham,' he asks, 'attain justification according to the flesh? No, for if he was justified by works, he hath whereof to boast.' It is plain that he uses the two expressions, *according to the flesh* and *by works,* as equivalent. This meaning of σάρξ is easily explained. Paul uses the word for what is external, as opposed to what is internal and spiritual, and thus for all external rites and ceremonial works, and then for works without limitation. See Gal. iii. 3 ; vi. 12 ; Philip. iii. 3, 4. In this last passage Paul includes, under *the flesh,* not only his Hebrew descent, his circumcision, his being a Pharisee, his blameless adherence to the Jewish law, but everything comprehended under his "own righteousness," as distinguished from "the righteousness which is of God (ἐπὶ πίστει) on the condition of faith." This is clearly its sense here. It includes everything meant by "works," and "works" includes all forms of personal righteousness. This same result is reached in another way. Κατὰ σάρκα may mean, as Meyer and others say, *after a human method, i.e.* after the manner of men ; and this may be understood to mean after the manner common among men, *i. e.* through works, or personal merit, which is the way that men adopt to secure favour with others. This is the explanation given by Köllner.

Verse 2. *For if Abraham were justified by works, he hath whereof to glory, but not before God.* The apostle's mode of reasoning is so concise as often to leave some of the steps of his argument to be supplied, which, however, are almost always sufficiently obvious from the context. As just remarked, a negative answer is to be supposed to the question in the first verse. Abraham did not attain the favour of God through the flesh. The force of *for* at the beginning of this verse, is then obvious, as introducing the reason for this answer. The passage itself is very concise, and the latter clause admits of different interpretations. 'If Abraham was justified by works, he might indeed assert his claim to the confidence and favour of his fellow-men, but he could not have any ground of boasting before God.' This view, however, introduces an idea entirely foreign from the passage, and makes the conclusion the very opposite of that to which the premises would lead. For if justified by works, he would have ground of boasting before God. The interpretation given by Calvin is altogether the most satisfactory and simple : " Epichirema est, id est imperfecta ratiocinatio, quæ in hanc formam colligi debet. Si Abraham operibus justificatus est, potest suo merito gloriari ; sed non habet unde glorietur apud Deum ; ergo non ex operibus justificatus est." 'If Abraham was justified by works he hath whereof to glory ; but he hath not whereof to glory before God, and therefore he was not justified by works;' the very conclusion which Paul intended to establish, and which he immediately confirms by the testimony of the Scriptures. The argument thus far is founded on the assumption that no man can appear thus confidently before God, and boast of having done all that was required of him. If the doctrine of justification by works involves, as Paul shows it does, this claim to perfect obedience, it must be false. And that Abraham was not thus justified, he proves from the sacred record.

VERSE 3. *For what saith the Scripture ? Abraham believed God, and it was counted unto him for righteousness.* The connection of this verse with the preceding is this : Paul had just said that Abraham had no ground of boasting with God ; *for*, what saith the Scripture ? Does it refer the ground of Abraham's justification to his works ? By no means. It declares he was justified by faith ; which Paul immediately shows is equivalent to saying that he was justified gratuitously. The passage quoted by the apostle is Gen. xv. 6, " Abraham believed God, and it was counted unto him (*i.e.*, imputed to him) for righteousness." This is an important passage, as the phrase "to impute faith for righteousness," occurs repeatedly in Paul's writings. 1. The primary meaning of the word λογίζομαι, here rendered *to count to*, or *impute*, is *to reason*, then *to reckon*, or *number ;* 2 Chron. v. 6, " Which could not be numbered for multitude ;" Mark xv. 28, " He was numbered with the transgressors ;" see Isa. liii. 12, &c. 2. It means *to esteem*, or *regard as something*, that is, to number as belonging to a certain class of things ; Gen. xxxi. 15, " Are we not counted of him strangers ?" Isa. xl. 17, &c. ; compare Job xix. 11, xxxiii. 10, in the Hebrew. 3. It is used in the more general sense of *purposing, devising, considering, thinking*, &c. 4. In strict connection with its primary meaning, it signifies *to impute, to set to one's account ;* that is, to number among the things belonging to a man, or chargeable upon him. It generally implies the accessory idea of ' treating one according to the nature of the thing imputed.' Thus, in the frequent phrase, *to impute sin*, as 2 Sam. xix. 19, " Let not my Lord impute iniquity unto me," *i. e.*, ' Let him not lay it to my charge, and treat me accordingly ;" compare 1 Sam. xxii. 15, in the Hebrew and Septuagint ; Ps. xxxii. 2, (Septuagint, xxxi.) " Blessed is the man to whom the Lord imputeth not iniquity," &c. And in the New Testament, 2 Cor. vi. 19, " Not imputing unto men their trespasses ;" 2 Tim. iv. 16, " *I pray God* that it may not be laid to their charge," &c. These and numerous similar passages render the Scriptural idea of imputation perfectly clear. It is laying anything to one's charge, and treating him accordingly. It produces no change in the individual to whom the imputation is made ; it simply alters his relation to the law. All those objections, therefore, to the doctrine expressed by this term, which are founded on the assumption that imputation alters the moral character of men ; that it implies an infusion of either sin or holiness, rest on a misconception of its nature. It is, so far as the mere force of the term is concerned, a matter of perfect indifference whether the thing imputed belonged antecedently to the person to whom the imputation is made or not. It is just as common and correct to speak of laying to a man's charge what does not belong to him, as what does. That a thing can seldom be *justly* imputed to a person to whom it does not personally belong, is a matter of course. But that the word itself implies that the thing imputed must belong to the person concerned, is a singular misconception. These remarks have, of course, reference only to the meaning of the word. Whether the Bible actually teaches that there is an imputation of either sin or righteousness, to any to whom it does not personally belong, is another question. That the Bible does speak both of imputing to a man what does not actually belong to him, and of not imputing what does, is evident from the following, among other passages, Levit. xvii. 3, 4 : " What man soever killeth an ox, and bringeth it not to the door of the tabernacle," &c., "blood shall be imputed to that man ;" that is, blood-guiltiness or murder, a crime of which he was not actually guilty, should be laid to his charge, and he should be put to death. " *Sanguis* hic est *cædes*, says Rosenmüller ; perinde Deo displicebit, ac si ille hominem occidisset, et mortis reus judicabitur." "Als Blutschuld soll es angerechnet werden diesem Manne." *Gesenius.* On the other hand, Levit. vii. 18, if any part of a sacrifice is eaten on the third day, the offering "shall not be imputed to him that made it." Paul, speaking to Philemon of the debt of Onesimus, says, "put that on my account," *i. e.*, impute it to me. The word used in this case is the same as that which occurs in Rom. v. 13, " Sin is not imputed where there is no law ;" and is in its root and usage precisely synonymous with the word employed in the passage before us, when the latter is used in reference to imputation. No less than twice also, in this very chapter, vers. 6 and 11, Paul speaks of 'imputing righteousness,' not to those to whom it personally belongs, certainly, but to the *ungodly*, ver. 5 ; to those who have no works, ver. 6.

Professor Storr, of Tübingen, De vario sensu vocis δίχαιος, &c., in *Nov. Test.*, in his *Opuscula*, Vol. I., p. 224, says, " Since innocence or probity (expressed by the word *righteousness*) does not belong to man himself, it must be ascribed or imputed to him. In this way the formula, 'righteousness which is of God,' Philip. iii. 9, and especially the plainer expressions, ' to impute faith for righteousness,' Rom. iv. 5, and ' to impute righteousness,' are to be understood." We readily admit, he says, that things which actually belong to a man may also be said to be imputed to him, as was the case with Phineas, &c., and then adds, "Nevertheless, as he is said not to impute an action really performed, Levit. vii.; 2 Sam. xix., &c., who does not so regard it as to decree the fruit and punishment of it ; so, on the other hand, those things can be imputed, Levit. xvii. 4, which are not, in fact, found in the man, but which are so far attributed to him, that he may be hence treated as though he had performed them. Thus righteousness may be said to be imputed, Rom. iv. 6, 11, when not his own innocence and probity, which God determines to reward, is ascribed to the believer, but when God so ascribes and imputes righteousness, of which we are destitute, that we are treated as innocent and just." On page 233, he says, "Verbum λογίζεσθαι monstrat gratiam, Rom. iv. 4, nam διχαιοσύνην nostram negat."

This idea of imputation is one of the most familiar in all the Bible, and is expressed in a multitude of cases where the term is not used. When Stephen prayed, Acts vii. 60, "Lord, lay not this sin to their charge," he expressed exactly the same idea that Paul did, when he said, 2 Tim. iv. 16, " *I pray God* it may not be laid to their charge," although the latter uses the word *impute* (λογισθείη,) and the former does not. So the expressions, " his sin shall be upon him," " he shall bear his iniquity," which occur so often, are perfectly synonymous with the formula, "his sin shall be imputed to him ;" and, of course, "to bear the sins of another," is equivalent to saying, " those sins are imputed." The objection, therefore, that the word *impute* does not occur in reference to the imputation of the sin or righteousness of one man to another, even if well founded, which is not the fact, is of no more force than the objections against the doctrines of the Trinity, vicarious atonement, perseverance of the saints, &c., founded on the fact that these *words* do not occur in the Bible. The material point surely is, Do the ideas occur ? The doctrine of the "imputation of righteousness" is not the doctrine of this or that school in theology. It is the possession of the Church. It was specially the glory and power of the Reformation. Those who differed most elsewhere, were perfectly agreed here. Lutherans and Reformed, alienated from each other by the sacramentarian controversy, were of one mind on this great doctrine. The testimony of the learned Rationalist, Bretschneider, if any testimony on so notorious a fact is necessary, may be here cited. Speaking with special reference to the Lutheran Church, he says, "The symbolical books, in the first place, contradict the scholastic representation of justification, followed by the Romish Church, that is, that it is an act of God, by which he communicates to men an inherent righteousness (*justitia habitualis, infusa*), *i.e.* renders them virtuous. They described it as a forensic or judicial act of God, that is, an act by which merely the moral *relation* of the man to God, not the man himself (at least not immediately,) is changed." "Hence, justification consists of three parts : 1. The imputation of the merit of Christ. 2. The remission of punishment. 3. The restoration of the favour and the blessedness forfeited by sin." "By the *imputatio justitiæ* (or *meriti*) *Christi*, the symbolical books understand that judgment of God, according to which he treats us as though we had not sinned, but had fulfilled the law, or as though the merit of Christ was ours ; see *Apol.*, Art. 9, p. 226, Merita propitiatoris—aliis donantur imputatione divina, ut per ea, tanquam propriis meritis justi reputemur, ut si quis amicus pro amico solvit aes alienum, debitor alieno merito tanquam proprio liberatur."— *Bretschneider's Entwickelung aller in der Dog. vorkommenden Begriffe*, pp. 631, 632, &c.

But to return to the phrase, 'Faith is imputed for righteousness.' It is very common to understand *faith* here, to include its object, *i.e.*, the righteousness of Christ ; so that it is not faith considered as an act, which is imputed, but faith considered as including the merit which it apprehends and appropriates. Thus *hope* is often used for the thing hoped for, as Rom. viii. 24, "Hope that is seen is not hope," &c. ; and *faith* for the things believed, Gal. i. 23, "He preacheth the faith," &c. In illustration of this idea, Gerhard, the leading authority in the Lutheran Church, during the seventeenth century, says, " Quemadmodum annulus, cui inclusa est gemma, dicitur valere aliquot coronatis, pretiosissima ita fides, quæ apprehendit Christi justitiam, dicitur nobis imputari ad justitiam, quippe cujus est organum apprehendens," Loci Tom. VII. 238. Although there are difficulties attending this interpretation, it cannot, with any consistency, be exclaimed against by those who make faith to include the whole work of the Spirit on the heart, and its fruits in the life ; as is done by the majority of those who reject this view of the passage. Besides this interpretation, there are three other explanations which deserve consideration. The first is that adopted by the Remonstrants, or Arminians. According to their view, δικαιοσύνη is to be taken in its ordinary sense of *righteousness*, that which constitutes a man righteous in the eye of the law. They understand the apostle, when he says, " Faith was imputed for righteousness," as teaching that faith was regarded or counted as complete obedience to the law. As men are unable to render that perfect obedience which the law given to Adam required, God, under the gospel, according to this view, is pleased to accept of faith (a *fides obsequiosa*, as it is called, *i.e.*, faith including evangelical obedience), instead of the righteousness which the law demands. Faith is thus made, not the instrument, but the ground of justification. It is imputed for righteousness in the sense of being regarded and treated as though it were complete obedience to the law. It must be admitted, that so far as this single form of statement is concerned, this interpretation is natural, and consistent with usage. Thus uncircumcision is said to be imputed for circumcision, that is, the former is regarded as though it were the latter. This, however, is not the only sense the words will naturally bear, and it is utterly inconsistent with what the Scriptures elsewhere teach. 1. It contradicts all those passages in which Paul and the other sacred writers deny that the ground of justification is anything in us, or done by us. These passages are too numerous to be cited ; see chap. iii. 20, where it is shown that the works which are excluded from the ground of justification are not ceremonial works merely, nor works performed with a legal spirit, but all works, without exception ; works of righteousness, Titus iii. 5, *i.e.*, all right or good works. But faith considered as an act, is as much a work as prayer, repentance, almsgiving, or anything of the kind. And it is as much an act of obedience to the law, as the performance of any other duty ; for the law requires us to do whatever is in itself right. 2. It contradicts all those passages in which the merit of Christ, in any form, is declared to be the ground of our acceptance. Thus in chap. iii. 25, it is Christ's propitiatory sacrifice; chap. v. 18, 19, it is his obedience or righteousness ; in many other places it is said to be his death, his cross, his blood. Faith must either be the ground of our acceptance, or the means or instrument of our becoming interested in the true meritorious ground, viz., the righteousness of Christ. It cannot stand in both relations to our justification. 3. It is inconsistent with the office ascribed to faith. We are said to be saved by, or through faith, but never on account of our faith, or on the ground of it. (It is always διὰ πίστεως, or ἐκ πίστεως, but never διὰ πίστιν.) The expressions, "through faith in his blood," iii. 25, "by faith in Jesus Christ," &c., admit of no other interpretation than 'by means of faith in the blood of Christ, or in Christ himself, as the ground of confidence.' The interpretation, therefore, under consideration is at variance with the very nature of faith, which necessarily includes the receiving and resting on Christ as the ground of acceptance with God ; and, of course, implies that faith itself is not that ground. 4. We accordingly never find Paul, nor any other of the sacred writers, referring his readers to their faith, or anything in themselves, as the ground of their confidence. Even in reference to those most advanced in holiness, he directs them to what Christ has done for them, not to anything wrought in them, as the ground of their acceptance. See a beautiful passage to this effect in *Neander's Gelegenheitschriften*, p. 23. After stating that the believer can never rest his justification on his own spiritual life, or works, he adds, " It would, indeed, fare badly with the Christian, if on such weak ground as this he had to build his justification, if he did not know that 'if he confesses his sins, and walks in the light, as he is in the light, the blood of Jesus Christ his Son cleanses from all sin.' Paul, therefore, refers even the redeemed, disturbed by the reproaches of conscience, amidst the conflicts and trials of life, not to the work of Christ *in themselves*, but to what the love of God in Christ has done *for them*, and which, even notwithstanding their own continued sinfulness, remains ever sure." 5. Paul, by interchanging the ambiguous phrase, 'faith is imputed for righteousness,' with the more definite expressions, 'justified through or by means of faith,' 'justified through faith in his blood,' fixes the sense in which the clause in question is to be understood. It must express the idea, that it was by means of faith that Abraham came to be treated as righteous, and not that faith was taken in lieu of perfect obedience. See this subject more fully discussed in *Owen on Justification*, chap. xviii.

According to the second view, the word *righteousness* is taken in a much more limited sense, and the phrase 'to impute faith for righteousness,' is understood to mean 'faith was regarded as right, it was approved.' This interpretation also is perfectly consistent with usage. Thus, Ps. cvi. 31, it is said of the zeal of Phineas, "It was counted unto him for righteousness." This of course does not mean that it was regarded as complete obedience to the law, and taken in its stead as the ground of justification. It means simply that his zeal was approved of. It was regarded, says Dr. Owen, "as a just and rewardable action." "Divinitus approbatum erat," says Tuckney, *Prælectiones*, p. 212, "tanquam justè factum." In like manner, Deut. xxiv. 13, it is said of returning a pledge, "It shall be righteousness unto thee before the Lord thy God." Agreeably to the analogy of these passages, the meaning of this clause may be, 'his faith was regarded as right;' it secured the approbation of God.' How it did this, must be learned from other passages. The third interpretation agrees with the first, in taking δικαιοσύνη in its proper sense (*righteousness*), but gives a different force to the preposition εἰς: 'Faith was imputed to him *unto righteousness*,' that is, in order to his being regarded and treated as righteous. In support of this view, reference is made to such frequently recurring expressions as εἰς σωτηρίαν (*unto salvation*), 'that they might be saved,' x. 1; εἰς μετάνοιαν (*unto repentance*), 'that they might repent,' Matt. iii. 11. In x. 10 of this epistle, the apostle says, 'With the heart man believeth unto righteousness' (εἰς δικαιοσύνην), *i.e.*, *in order to becoming righteous*, or *so as* to become righteous. Faith secures their being righteous. According to this view of the passage, all it teaches is, that faith and not works secured Abraham's justification before God. And this is the object which the apostle has in view. The precise relation in which faith stands to justification, whether it is the instrument or the ground, however clearly taught elsewhere, this particular expression leaves undetermined. It simply asserts that Abraham was justified as a believer, and not as a worker (ἐργαζόμενος), as Paul expresses it in the next verse.

The Rationalistic theologians of modern times agree with the Socinians in teaching that justification by faith, as distinguished from justification by works, is nothing more than the doctrine that moral character is determined more by the inward principle than by the outward act. By *faith*, in the case of Abraham, they understand confidence in God; a pious frame of mind, which is influenced by considerations drawn from the unseen and spiritual world, the region of truth and eternal principles, rather than by either mercenary feelings or outward objects. When, therefore, the Scriptures say, 'God imputed Abraham's faith for righteousness,' the meaning is, God accepted him for his inward piety, for the elevated principle by which his whole life was governed. If this is what Paul means, when he speaks of Abraham being justified by faith, it is what he means when he teaches that men are now justified by faith. Then the whole gospel sinks to the level of natural religion, and Christ is in no other sense a Saviour, than as by his doctrines and example he leads men to cultivate piety. It is perfectly obvious that Paul means to teach that sinners are now justified in the same way that Abraham was. He proves that we are justified by faith, because Abraham was justified by faith. If faith means inward piety in the one case, it must have the same meaning in the other. But as it is expressly said, over and over, in so many words, that men are now justified by faith in Christ, it follows of necessity that faith in Christ was the faith by which Abraham was justified. He believed the promise of redemption, which is the promise that we embrace when we receive and rest on Christ for salvation. Hence it is one principal object of the apostle's argument in the latter part of this chapter, and in the third chapter of his Epistle to the Galatians, to show that we are heirs of the promise made to Abraham, because we have the same faith that he had; the same, that is, both in its nature and object.

It is further to be remarked, that λογίζεσθαι εἰς δικαιοσύνην (to impute for righteousness), and δικαιοῦσθαι (to be justified), mean the same thing. Thus Calvin says, "Tantùm notemus, eos quibus justitia imputatur, justificari; quando haec duo a Paulo tanquam synonyma ponuntur." Yet, strange to say, Olshausen asserts that they are very different. To be justified (δικαιοῦσθαι) and to have righteousness imputed, he says, differ as the Romish and the Protestant doctrines of justification differ. The former means to be made subjectively righteous, the latter simply to be regarded as righteous. "Was Jemandem angerechnet wird, das hat er nicht, er wird aber angesehen und behandelt, als hätte er es." *What is imputed to a man, that he is not, but he is regarded and treated as though he had it.* Abraham therefore was not justified, because before the coming of Christ, any true righteousness (δικαιοσύνη Θεοῦ, as Olshausen says), was impossible; he was only regarded as righteous.* But as what is said of Abraham is said also of believers under the gospel, since to them as well as to him righteousness is said to be imputed, it follows that believers are not really justified in this life. This is the conclusion to which he is led by two principles. The first is, that the word δικαιόω means to make righteous inwardly (es bedeutet die göttliche Thätigkeit des Hervorrufens der δικαιοσύνη), and no man is perfectly holy in this life; the second is, that God cannot regard any one as being what he is not, and therefore he cannot regard the unrighteous as righteous. The former of these assumptions is utterly unfounded, as δικαιόω always means to declare just, and never to make just. The second principle, Olshausen, in his comment on this verse, modifies so far as to say that God can only regard as just those whom he purposes to render just; and as with God there are no distinctions of time, he regards as already possessed of right-

---

* The doctrine of the transcendentalists (so called) regarding the incarnation, the person of Christ, and his relation to the Church, necessarily leads to the assumption of a great distinction between the religion of the Old Testament and that of the New, and between the state and privileges of believers then and now. If our redemption consists in our being made partakers of the theanthropic nature of Christ, as there was no such nature before the manifestation of God in the flesh, there could be no real redemption, no deliverance from the guilt and power of sin, before that event. Hence Olshausen says there could be no δικαιοσύνη Θεοῦ really belonging to those who lived before the advent; and on page 171 he says, if we admit there was any regeneration at all under the Old Testament, it could only be symbolical; and on page 167 he says, before Christ, forgiveness of sin was not real, but only symbolical. In a foot note he adds, that under the theocracy there was the pardon of separate acts of transgression, but not the forgiveness of all sins, actual and original, which can only proceed from Christ. It follows also from this theory, that justification is a subjective change, a change wrought in the soul by the reception of a new nature from Christ. These conclusions the Romanists had reached long ago, by a different process. It is not wonderful, therefore, that so many of the transcendentalists of Germany, and of their abettors elsewhere, have passed over to the Church of Rome.

eousness those whom he has purposed to render so. (This would seem to imply external justification, or at least an imputation of righteousness from eternity to all whom God has purposed to save.) Without this modification, he says, the objection of Romanists to the Protestant doctrine would be unanswerable. There is a sense, however, in which the principle in question is perfectly sound. God must see things as they are, and pronounce them to be what they are. The Protestant doctrine does not suppose that God regards any person or thing as being other than he or it really is. When he pronounces the unjust to be just, the word is taken in different senses. He does not pronounce the unholy to be holy; he simply declares that the demands of justice have been satisfied in behalf of those who have no righteousness of their own. In sin there are the two elements of guilt and pollution—the one expressing its relation to the justice, the other its relation to the holiness of God; or, what amounts to the same thing, the one expressing its relation to the penalty, and the other its relation to the precept of the law. These two elements are separable. The moral character or inward state of a man who has suffered the penalty of a crime, and thus expiated his offence, may remain unchanged. His guilt, in the eye of human law, is removed, but his pollution remains. It would be unjust to inflict any further punishment on him for that offence. Justice is satisfied, but the man is unchanged. There may therefore be guilt where there is no moral pollution, as in the case of our blessed Lord, who bore our sins; and there may be freedom from guilt, where moral pollution remains, as in the case of every justified sinner. When, therefore, God justifies the ungodly, he does not regard him as being other than he really is. He only declares that justice is satisfied, and in that sense the man is just; he has a δικαιοσύνη which satisfies the demands of the law. His moral character is not the ground of that declaration, and is not affected by it. As to the distinction made by Olshausen between *imputing righteousness* and justifying, there is not the slightest ground for it. He himself makes them synonymous (p. 157). The two forms of expression are used synonymously in this very context. In ver. 3, it is said, 'faith is imputed for righteousness;' in ver. 5, 'God justifies the ungodly;' and in ver. 6, 'he imputes righteousness'—all in the same sense. Olshausen, although a representative man, exhibits his theology, in his commentary, in a very unsettled state. He not only retracts at times, in one volume, what he had said in another, but he modifies his doctrine from page to page. In his remarks on Romans iii. 21, he himself asserts the principle (as quoted above), that "by God nothing can ever be regarded or declared righteous, which is not righteous" (p. 145); but in his comment on this verse, he pronounces the principle, "das Gott nach seiner Wahrhaftigkeit nicht Jemanden für etwas ansehen kann, was er nicht ist—falsch und über den Heilsweg durchaus irreleitend" (p. 174). That is, he says that the principle "that God, in virtue of his veracity, cannot regard one as being what he is not —is false, and perverts the whole plan of salvation." On page 157 he says, "The passing over of the nature (Wesen) of Christ upon the sinner, is expressed by saying *righteousness is imputed to him;*" whereas, on pages 173—5, he labours to show that imputing righteousness is something very different from imparting righteousness. He prevailingly teaches the doctrine of subjective justification, to which his definition and system inevitably lead; but under the stress of some direct assertion of the apostle to the contrary, he for the time brings out the opposite doctrine. He exhibits similar fluctuations on many other points.

Verses 4, 5. *Now to him that worketh, is the reward not reckoned of grace, but of debt; but to him that worketh not,* &c. These verses are designed, in the first place, to vindicate the pertinency of the quotation from Scripture, made in ver. 3, by showing that the declaration 'faith was imputed for righteousness,' is a denial that works were the ground of Abraham's acceptance; and, secondly, that to justify by faith, is to justify gratuitously, and therefore all passages which speak of gratuitous acceptance are in favour of the doctrine of justification by faith.

Now to him that worketh, that is, either emphatically 'to him who does all that is required of him;' or 'to him who seeks to be accepted on account of his works.' The former explanation is the better. The words then state a general proposition, 'To him that is obedient, or who performs a stipulated work, the recompense is not regarded as a gratuity, but as a debt.' *The reward,* ὁ μισθός, the appropriate and merited compensation. *Is not imputed,* κατὰ χάριν, ἀλλὰ ὀφείλημα, not grace, but debt, which implies that a claim founded in justice is the ground and measure of remuneration. Paul's argument is founded on the principle, which is so often denied, as by Olshausen, (p. 172,) that man may have merit before God; or that God may stand in the relation of debtor to man. The apostle says expressly, that τῷ ἐργαζομένῳ, *to him that works,* the reward is a matter of debt. If Adam had remained faithful and rendered perfect obedience, the promised reward would have been due to him as a matter of justice; the withholding it would have been an act of injustice. When, therefore, the apostle speaks of Abraham as having a ground of boasting, if his works made him righteous, it is not to be understood simply of boasting before men. He would have had a ground of boasting in that case before God. The reward would have been to him a matter of debt.

But to him that worketh not, τῷ δὲ μὴ ἐργαζομένῳ. That is, to him who has no works to plead as the ground of reward; πιστεύοντι δὲ ἐπὶ κ.τ.λ., *but believeth upon,* i.e. putting his trust upon. The faith which justifies is not mere assent, it is an act of trust. The believer confides upon God for justification. He believes that God will justify him, although ungodly; for the object of the faith or confidence here expressed is ὁ δικαιῶν τὸν ἀσεβῆ, he who justifies the ungodly. Faith therefore is appropriating; it is an act of confidence in reference to our own acceptance with God. To him who thus believes, *faith is counted for righteousness, i. e.* it is imputed in order to his becoming righteous. It lies in the nature of the faith of which Paul speaks, that he who exercises it should feel and acknowledge that he is ungodly, and consequently undeserving of the favour of God. He, of course, in relying on the mercy of God, must acknowledge that his acceptance is a matter of grace, and not of debt. The meaning of the apostle is plainly this: 'To him that worketh, the reward is a matter of debt, but to him who worketh not, but believeth simply, the reward is a matter of grace.' Instead, however, of saying 'it is a matter of grace,' he uses, as an equivalent expression, "to him faith is counted for righteousness." That is, he is justified by faith. To be justified by faith, therefore, is to be justified gratuitously, and not by works. It is thus he proves that the passage cited in ver. 3, respecting Abraham, is pertinent to his purpose as an argument against justification by works. It at the same time shows that all passages which speak of gratuitous acceptance, may be cited in proof of his doctrine of justification by faith. The way is thus opened for his *second* argument, which is derived from the testimony of David.

It is to be remarked, that Paul speaks of God as justifying the *ungodly.* The word is in the singular, τὸν ἀσεβῆ, *the ungodly man,* not with any special reference to Abraham, as though he was the ungodly person whom God justified, but because the singular, ἐργαζομένῳ, (*to him that worketh,*) πιστεύοντι, (*to him that believeth,*) is used in the context, and because every man must believe for himself. God does not justify communities. If every man and all men are ungodly, it follows that they are regarded and treated as righteous, not on the ground of their personal character ; and it is further apparent that justification does not consist in making one inherently just or holy ; for it is as *ungodly* that those who believe are freely justified for Christ's sake. It never was, as shown above, the doctrine of the Reformation, or of the Lutheran and Reformed divines, that the imputation of righteousness affects the moral character of those concerned. It is true, whom God justifies he also sanctifies ; but justification is not sanctification, and the imputation of righteousness is not the infusion of righteousness. These are the first principles of the doctrine of the Reformers. " The fourth grand error of the Papists in the article of justification," says an old divine, " is concerning that which we call the form thereof. For they, denying and deriding the imputation of Christ's righteousness, (without which, notwithstanding, no man can be saved,) do hold that men are justified by infusion, and not by imputation of righteousness ; we, on the contrary, do hold, according to the Scriptures, that we are justified before God, only by the imputation of Christ's righteousness, and not by infusion. And our meaning, when we say that God imputeth Christ's righteousness unto us, is nothing else but this : that he graciously accepteth for us, and in our behalf, the righteousness of Christ, that is, both as to his obedience, which, in the days of his flesh, he performed for us ; and passive, that is, his sufferings, which he sustained for us, as if we had in our own persons both performed and suffered the same ourselves. Howbeit, we confess that the Lord doth infuse righteousness into the faithful ; yet not as he justifieth, but as he sanctifieth them," &c. *Bishop Downame on Justification,* p. 261. Tuckney, one of the leading members of the Westminster Assembly, and principal author of the Shorter Catechism, in his *Prælectiones,* p. 213, says, " Although God justifies the ungodly, Rom. iv. 5, *i. e.,* him who was antecedently ungodly, and who in a measure remains, as to his inherent character, *unjust* after justification, yet it has its proper ground in the satisfaction of Christ," &c. On page 220, he says, " The Papists understand by justification, the infusion of inherent righteousness, and thus confound justification with sanctification ; which, if it was the true nature and definition of justification, they might well deny that the imputation of Christ's righteousness is the cause or formal reason of this justification, *i.e.,* of sanctification. For we are not so foolish or blasphemous as to say, or even think, that the righteousness of Christ imputed to us renders us formally or inherently righteous, so that we should be formally or inherently righteous with the righteousness of Christ. Since the righteousness of Christ is proper to himself, and is as inseparable from him, and as incommunicable to others, as any other attribute of a thing, or its essence itself."

Verses 6—8. *Even as David also describeth the blessedness of the man to whom God imputeth righteousness without works.* Paul's first argument in favour of gratuitous justification was from the case of Abraham ; his second is from the testimony of David. The immediate connection of this verse is with ver. 5. At the conclusion of that verse, it was said, to him who had no works, faith is imputed, in order to his justification, *i.e.*, he is justified gratuitously, even as David speaks of the blessedness of him whom, although destitute of merit, God regards and treats as righteous. *Describeth the blessedness, i. e.*, pronounces blessed.   The words are λέγει τὸν μακαρισμόν, *utters the declaration of blessedness* concerning the man, &c. *To whom God imputeth righteousness without works*, that is, whom God regards and treats as righteous, although he is not in himself righteous. The meaning of this clause cannot be mistaken.   'To impute sin,' is to lay sin to the charge of any one, and to treat him accordingly, as is universally admitted; so 'to impute righteousness,' is to set righteousness to one's account, and to treat him accordingly.   This righteousness does not, of course, belong antecedently to those to whom it is imputed, for they are ungodly, and destitute of works.   Here then is an imputation to men of what does not belong to them, and to which they have in themselves no claim.   To impute righteousness is the apostle's definition of the term to *justify*.   It is not making men inherently righteous, or morally pure, but it is regarding and treating them as just.   This is done, not on the ground of personal character or works, but on the ground of the righteousness of Christ.   As this is dealing with men, not according to merit, but in a gracious manner, the passage cited from Ps. xxxii. 1, 2, is precisely in point: "Blessed are they whose iniquities are forgiven, and whose sins are covered.   Blessed is the man to whom the Lord will not impute sin." That is, blessed is the man who, although a sinner, is regarded and treated as righteous.   As the remission of sin is necessarily connected with restoration to God's favour, the apostle speaks of it as the whole of justification; not that the idea of remission exhausts the whole idea of justification, but it necessarily implies the rest.   In like manner, in Eph. i. 7, it is said, "in whom we have redemption . . . the forgiveness of sins;" which does not imply that forgiveness is the whole of redemption, that the gift of the Spirit, the glorification of the body, and eternal life, which are so constantly spoken of as fruits of Christ's work, as parts of the purchased inheritance, are to be excluded.

Here again the doctrine of a personal, inherent righteousness, which it is the special object of the apostle to exclude, is introduced by the modern mystical or transcendental theologians.   On the declaration that righteousness is imputed *without works*, Olshausen remarks: "No matter how abundant or pure works may be, the ground of blessedness is not in them, but in the principle whence they flow; that is, not in man, but in God." The whole doctrine of the apostle is made to be, that men are justified (made holy,) not by themselves, but by God; thus confounding, as Romanists do, justification with sanctification.   In Ps. xxxii. 1, 2, as quoted by Paul from the LXX., ἀφιέναι (*to remit*,) and ἐπικαλύπτειν (*to cover*,) are interchanged.   Olshausen says the former expresses the New Testament idea of forgiveness (die reale Hinwegschaffung der Sünde) *i. e.*, the real removal of sin; the latter, the Old Testament idea of non-imputation of sin—the sin remaining, but being overlooked.   This view of the nature of remission, and of the difference between the Old and the New Testament, is purely Romish.

Verse 9. *Cometh this blessedness upon the circumcision only, or upon the uncircumcision also?* &c.   The apostle's third argument, commencing with this verse and continuing to the 12th, has special reference to circumcision.   He had proved that Abraham was not justified on account of his works generally; he now proves that circumcision is neither the ground

nor condition of his acceptance. The proof of this point is brief and conclusive. It is admitted that Abraham was justified. The only question
is, was it before or after his circumcision? If before, it certainly was not
on account of it. As it was before, circumcision must have had some other
object.

'Cometh *this blessedness.*' There is nothing in the original to answer
to the word *cometh,* although some word of the kind must be supplied. The
most natural word to supply is λέγεται. David utters the declaration of
the blessedness "of the man whose sins are pardoned." Concerning whom
is this declaration uttered? The word rendered *blessedness* means, more
properly, 'declaration of blessedness.' 'This declaration of blessedness, is
it *upon, i.e.,* is it about (λέγεται), is it said concerning the circumcision
only?' The preposition (ἐπί) used by the apostle, often points out the
direction of an action, or the subject concerning which anything is said.
This question has not direct reference to the persons to whom the offers of
acceptance are applicable, as though it were equivalent to asking, 'Is this
blessedness confined to the Jews, or may it be extended to the Gentiles
also?' because this is not the subject now in hand. It is the ground or
condition of acceptance, and not the persons to whom the offer is to
be made, that is now under consideration. The question therefore is, in
substance, this: 'Does this declaration of blessedness relate to the circumcised, as such? Is circumcision necessary to justification?'—the blessing
of which Paul is speaking. The answer obviously implied to the preceding question is, 'It is not said concerning the circumcised, as such; *for*
we say that faith was imputed to Abraham for righteousness.' It was his
faith, not his circumcision, that was the condition of his justification. The
preceding verses are occupied with the testimony of David, which decided
nothing as to the point of circumcision. To determine whether this rite
was a necessary condition of acceptance, it was requisite to refer again to
the case of Abraham. To decide the point presented in the question at
the beginning of the verse, the apostle argues from the position already
established. It is conceded or proved that Abraham was justified by faith;
to determine whether circumcision is necessary, we have only to ask, Under
what circumstances was he thus justified, before or after circumcision?

Verse 10. *How was it then reckoned? when he was in circumcision
or uncircumcision? Not in circumcision, but in uncircumcision.* Of
course, his circumcision, which was long subsequent to his justification,
could not be either the ground or necessary condition of his acceptance
with God.

Verse 11. *And he received the sign of circumcision, the seal of the
righteousness of the faith which he had, being yet uncircumcised,* &c. As
Paul had shown that circumcision was not the condition of justification, it
became necessary to declare its true nature and design. *The sign of circumcision, i. e.* circumcision which was a sign, (genitive of apposition;) as
"the earnest of the Spirit," for 'the Spirit which is an earnest,' 2 Cor. i. 20.
The seal of the righteousness of faith, &c. The phrase, *righteousness of
faith,* is a concise expression for 'righteousness which is attained by faith,'
or, as it stands more fully in Philip. iii. 9, "the righteousness of God,
which is by faith." The word righteousness, in such connections, includes,
with the idea of excellence or obedience, that of consequent blessedness.
It is the 'state of acceptableness with God.' The circumcision of
Abraham was designed to confirm to him the fact, that he was regarded
and treated by God as righteous, through faith, which was the means of

his becoming interested in the promise of redemption. From this passage it is evident that circumcision was not merely the seal of the covenant between God and the Hebrews as a nation. Besides the promises made to Abraham of a numerous posterity, and of the possession of the land of Canaan, there was the far higher promise, that through his seed (*i. e.* Christ, Gal. iii. 16) all the nations of the earth should be blessed. This was the promise of redemption, as the apostle teaches us in Gal. iii. 13—18 : " Christ," he says, " has redeemed us from the curse of the law,—in order that the blessing of Abraham might come upon the Gentiles." The blessing promised to Abraham, in which the Gentiles participate through Jesus Christ, can be none other than redemption. As that blessing was promised to Abraham on the condition, not of works, but of faith, the apostle hence argues, that in our case also we are made partakers of that blessing by faith, and not by works. This was the covenant of which circumcision was the seal. All therefore who were circumcised, professed to embrace the covenant of grace. All the Jews were professors of the true religion, and constituted the visible Church, in which by divine appointment their children were included. This is the broad and enduring basis of infant church-membership.

Abraham, says the apostle, was thus assured of his justification by faith, (*εἰς τὸ εἶναι,*) *in order that* he might be the father ; or, *so that* he is the father, &c. The former explanation is to be preferred, not only because *εἰς* with the infinitive, commonly expresses design, but also because the whole context shows that the apostle intends to bring into view the purpose of God in the justification of Abraham. *The father of all them that believed though they be not circumcised, πάντων τῶν πιστευόντων δἰ ἀκροβυστίας, i. e.* ' of all believing, *with* uncircumcision.' That is, of all uncircumcised believers. The preposition, *διά,* here, as in ii. 27, and elsewhere, simply marks the attendant circumstances. The word *father* expresses community of nature or character, and is often applied to the head or founder of any school or class of men, whose character or course is determined by the relation to the person so designated : as Gen. iv. 20, 21 : " Jabal . . . was the father of such as dwell in tents ; " and, " Jubal . . . was the father of all such as handle the harp and organ." Hence teachers, priests, and kings are often called fathers. Believers are called the children of Abraham, because of this identity of religious nature or character, as he stands out in Scripture as *the* believer ; and because it was with him that the covenant of grace, embracing all the children of God, whether Jews or Gentiles, was reënacted ; and because they are his heirs, inheriting the blessings promised to him. As Abraham was the head and father of the theocratical people under the Old Testament, this relation was not disowned when the middle wall of partition was broken down, and the Gentiles introduced into the family of God. He still remained the father of the faithful, and we are " the sons of Abraham by faith," Gal. iii. 7. The Jews were accustomed to speak in the same way of Abraham : Michlol Jophi on Malachi ii. 15, by *the one* there mentioned, " Abraham is intended, for he was one alone, and the father of all who follow and imitate him in faith." Bechai, fol. 27, he is called " The root of faith, and father of all those who believe in one God." Jalkut Chadash, fol. 54, 4, " On this account Abraham was not circumcised until he was ninety-nine years old, lest he should shut the door on proselytes coming in." See *Schoettgen,* p. 508.

That righteousness might be imputed unto them also. The connection and design of these words are not very clear, and they are variously explained. They may be considered as explanatory of the former clause, and therefore connected with the first part of the verse. The sense would then be, 'Abraham was justified, being yet uncircumcised, that he might be the father of believers, although uncircumcised, that is, that righteousness might be imputed unto them also.' This clause is most commonly regarded as a parenthesis, designed to indicate the point of resemblance between Abraham and those of whom he is called the father : 'He is the father of uncircumcised believers, since they also are justified by faith, as he was.' The words εἰς τὸ λογισθῆναι are explanatory of εἰς τὸ εἶναι αὐτὸν πατέρα : ' He was justified in uncircumcision, *in order that he might be the father,* &c. ; that is, *in order that faith might be imputed to them also.*' From this it appears that " to impute faith for righteousness " and " to impute righteousness," are synonymous. To Abraham righteousness was imputed ; he had the (δικαιοσύνη τῆς πίστεως) righteousness of faith as truly and really as believers now have. Nothing can be more opposed to the whole tenor of apostolic teaching than the Romish and modern mystical doctrine, that the Old Testament believers were not fully justified ; that their sins were pretermitted, but not remitted ; that their regeneration was symbolical, but not real.

Verse 12. *And the father of circumcision to them who are not of the circumcision only,* &c. That the preceding clause is parenthetical is plain, because the grammatical construction in this verse is continued unbroken. *Father of circumcision, i. e.,* of the circumcised. *To them,* τοῖς. This change of construction from the genitive to the dative may be accounted for either by the fact, that in the Hebrew it may be said "father to" as well as " father of;" or by assuming that τοῖς is the dative of advantage, "*for* them." The meaning of this verse is somewhat doubtful. According to our version, which adheres closely to the Greek, the meaning is, ' Abraham is not the father of uncircumcised believers only, as stated in ver. 11, but he is the father of the circumcised also, provided they follow the example of his faith.' According to this view, as ver. 11 presents him as the father of the believing Gentiles, this presents him as the father of the believing Jews. The only grammatical objection to this interpretation is the repetition of the article τοῖς before στοιχοῦσι, which would seem to indicate that " those who follow the steps of his faith " were a different class from the circumcised. Hence some commentators interpret the passage thus : ' He is the father of the circumcision, and not of the circumcision only, but also of those who follow his faith, which he had being yet uncircumcised.' But this is inconsistent with the construction. 1. It overlooks the καί at the beginning of the verse, by which it is connected with ver. 11: 'He is the father of the uncircumcised, (ver. 11,) *and* father of the circumcised, (ver. 12.) 2. It requires a transposition of the words τοῖς οὐ, so as to read οὐ τοῖς. What Paul says is, 'To those who are not of the circumcision only.' This interpretation makes him say, 'Not to those only who are of the circumcision.' 3. It is very unnatural to make this verse repeat what had just been said in ver. 11. There Paul had said that Abraham was the father of Gentile believers ; why should he here say he was the father of the Jews, and also of the Gentiles ? The former interpretation, which is adopted by the great body of commentators, is therefore to be preferred.

Verse 13—16 contain two additional arguments in favour of the apostle's doctrine. The first, vers. 13, 14, is the same as that presented more at length in Gal. iii. 18, &c., and is founded on the nature of a covenant. The promise having been made to Abraham (and his seed), on the condition of faith, cannot now, consistently with fidelity, be made to depend on obedience to the law. The second argument, vers. 15, 16, is from the nature of the law itself.

VERSE 13. *For the promise, that he should be heir of the world, was not to Abraham, or to his seed, &c.* The word *for* does not connect this verse with the one immediately preceding, as a proof of the insufficiency of circumcision. It rather marks the introduction of a new argument in favour of the general proposition which the chapter is designed to establish. As Abraham was not justified for his circumcision, so neither was it on account of his obedience to the law. If, however, it be preferred to connect this verse with what immediately precedes, the argument is substantially the same. In the preceding verses Paul had said that Abraham is the father of believers ; in other words, that believers are his heirs, *for* the promise that he should inherit the world was made on the condition of faith. The promise here spoken of is, that Abraham and his seed should be the heirs of the world. The word *heir*, in Scripture, frequently means *secure possessor.* Heb. i. 2, vi. 17, xi. 7, &c. This use of the term probably arose from the fact, that among the Jews possession by inheritance was much more secure and permanent than that obtained by purchase. The promise was not to Abraham, *nor to his seed,* (ἢ τῷ σπέρματι αὐτοῦ,) *i. e.* neither to the one nor to the other. Both were included in the promise. And by *his seed,* is not here, as in Gal. iii. 16, meant Christ, but his spiritual children. This is evident from ver. 16, where the apostle speaks of πᾶν τὸ σπέρμα, *the whole seed.* The clause τὸ κληρονόμον αὐτὸν εἶναι is explanatory of ἡ ἐπαγγελία. It states the contents of the promise. The article τό, attached to the infinitive, renders it more prominent or emphatic. As no such promise as that mentioned in this verse is contained, in so many words, in the Old Testament, the apostle must have designed to express what he knew to be the purport of those actually given. The expression, however, has been variously explained. 1. Some understand *the world* to mean the land of Canaan merely. But in the first place, this is a very unusual, if not an entirely unexampled use of the word. And, in the second place, this explanation is inconsistent with the context ; for Paul has reference to a promise of which, as appears from ver. 16, believing Gentiles are to partake. 2. Others understand the apostle to refer to the promise that Abraham should be the father of many nations, Gen. xvii. 5, and that his posterity should be as numerous as the stars of heaven, Gen. xv. 5 ; promises which they limit to his natural descendants, who, being widely scattered, may be said, in a limited sense, to possess the world. But this interpretation is irreconcilable with ver. 16. 3. Besides the promises already referred to, it was also said, that in him all the nations of the earth shall be blessed, Gen. xii. 3. This, as Paul explains it, Gal. iii. 16, &c., had direct reference to the blessings of redemption through Jesus Christ, who was the seed of Abraham. And here too he speaks of blessings of which all believers partake. The possession of the world, therefore, here intended, must be understood in a manner consistent with these passages. The expression is frequently taken in a general sense, as indicating general prosperity and happiness. "To be heir of the world" would then mean, to be prosperous and happy, in the best sense of the words. Reference is made, in support of this interpretation, to such passages as Matt. v. 5, Ps. xxxvii. 11, "The meek shall inherit the earth ;"

Ps. xxv. 13, "His seed shall inherit the earth." The promise then, to be the heir of the world, is a general promise of blessedness. And as the happiness promised to believers, or the pious, as such, is of course the happiness consequent on religion, and is its reward, the promise in this sense may include all the blessings of redemption. So in Gal. iii. 14, Paul uses the expression "that the blessing of Abraham might come on the Gentiles," as equivalent to saying 'that all the blessings of the gospel might come upon them.' 4. Or the promises in question may have reference to the actual possession of the world by the spiritual seed of Abraham, and Christ their head. The declaration that Abraham should be the father of many nations, and that his seed should be as the stars of heaven for multitude, included far more than that his natural descendants should be very numerous. If they who are of faith 'are the seed of Abraham, and heirs of the promise,' Gal. iii. 9, 29, then will the promise, as stated by the apostle, have its literal accomplishment when the kingdoms of this world are given to the saints of the most high God (Dan. vii. 27,) and when the uttermost parts of the earth become the possession of Christ. In this sense, the promise includes the universal prevalence of the true religion, involving of course the advent of Christ, the establishment of his kingdom, and all its consequent blessings. The Jewish writers were accustomed to represent Abraham as the heir of the world. "Bemidbar, R. xiv., fol. 202, 'The garden is the world which God gave to Abraham, to whom it is said, Thou shalt be a blessing.' 'God gave to my father Abraham the possession of heaven and earth.' Midrasch Mischle, 19. Mechila, in Ex. xiv. 31, 'Abraham our father did not obtain the inheritance of this world, and the world to come, except through faith.'" *Wetstein.*

The promise to Abraham and his seed was not *through the law, but through the righteousness of faith.* That is, it was not on condition of obedience to the law, but on condition of his having that righteousness which is obtained by faith. *Through the law,* is therefore equivalent to *through the works of the law,* as appears from its opposition to the latter clause, 'righteousness of faith.' By *the law,* is to be understood the whole rule of duty, as in other passages of the same kind; see iii. 20. In this sense it of course includes the Mosaic law, which, to the Jews, was the most prominent portion of the revealed will of God, and by obedience to which especially they hoped for the mercy of God. The parallel passage, Gal. iii. 18, &c., where the law is said to have been given four hundred years after the covenant formed with Abraham, shows it was one part of the apostle's design to convince the Jews, that as Abraham was not justified by his circumcision, (ver. 11,) so also it was not in virtue of the Mosaic economy not yet established; and therefore the promise could not be made to depend on the condition of obedience to that dispensation. This idea, although included, is not to be urged to the exclusion of the more comprehensive meaning of the word *law,* which the usage of the apostle and the context show to be also intended. It was neither by obedience to the law generally, nor to the particular form of it, as it appeared in the Mosaic institutions, that the promise was to be secured.

Verse 14. *For if they which are of the law be heirs,* &c. The original condition being faith, if another be substituted the covenant is broken, the promise violated, and the condition made of none effect. "They who are of the law (*οἱ ἐκ νόμου,*) sometimes, as ver. 16, means the Jews, *i. e.* those who have the law; compare ver. 12, "Those of circumcision," &c. But here it means *legalists,* those who seek justification by the works of the law ; as 'those who are of faith ' are *believers,* those who seek justification by faith ; compare Gal. iii. 10, "As many as are of the works of the law are under the curse," *i. e.* as many as seek acceptance by their own works.

The apostle's meaning, therefore, obviously is, that if those who rely upon their own works are the heirs of the promise, and are accepted on the condition of obedience to the law, the whole covenant is broken, *faith is made void, and the promise made of none effect.* "Is made void" (κεκένωται,) is rendered useless; see 1 Cor. i. 17, "The cross of Christ is made useless," ix. 15, &c. ; compare 1 Cor. xv. 17, "Your faith is vain," not only without foundation but of no use. *The promise is made of none effect* (κατήργηται,) *i. e.* is invalidated ; see chap. iii. 3, 31. It is plain from the whole design and argument of the apostle, that by *law,* in this whole connection, he means not specifically the law of Moses, but the law of God, however revealed as a rule of duty for man. He has reference to the Gentiles as well as to the Jews. His purpose is not simply to convince his readers that obedience to the Mosaic law cannot save them, but that obedience in any form, works of any kind, are insufficient for a man's justification before God. So far, therefore, from the context requiring, as so many of the modern commentators assert, an exclusive reference in this connection to the law of Moses, it imperatively demands the reverse.

VERSE 15. *For the law worketh wrath,* &c.   That is, it causes men to be the subjects of wrath. It brings them under condemnation. So far from imparting life, it causes death. If, therefore, the inheritance is suspended on the condition of obedience to the law, it can never be attained ; for by the law no flesh living can be justified. The connection of this verse, therefore, may be with what immediately precedes. The promise fails if it be by the law, *for* the law worketh death. The truth here presented, however, although thus incidentally introduced, is none the less a new and substantive argument for the doctrine of justification by faith. It is the same argument as that urged in Gal. iii. 10, derived from the very nature of the law. If it works wrath, if all who are under the law are under the curse, if the law condemns, it cannot justify. As, however, there are two ways in which, according to the apostle, the law works wrath, so there are two views of the meaning of this passage. First, the law works wrath, because it says, "Cursed is every one who continueth not in all things written in the book of the law to do them," Gal. iii. 10. As the law, from its very nature, demands perfect obedience, and condemns all who are not perfect, it, by its very nature, is unsuited to give life to sinners. It can only condemn them. If there were no law, there would be no sin, and no condemnation. But as all are under the law, and all are sinners, all are under the curse. The other way in which the law works wrath is, that it excites and exasperates the evil passions of the heart ; not from any defect in the law itself, but from the nature of sin. This idea the apostle presents full in the seventh chapter ; where it is properly in place, as he is there treating of sanctification. Here where he is treating of justification, that idea would be inappropriate, and therefore the former interpretation is to be decidedly preferred. Calvin, Tholuck, and others, however, understand the apostle to reason thus : ' The law, instead of freeing men from sin, incidentally renders their transgressions more numerous, conspicuous, and inexcusable, and thus brings them more and more under condemnation.' "Nam quum Lex nihil quam ultionem generet, non potest affere gratiam. Bonis quidem ac integris viam vitæ monstraret ;

sed quatenus vitiosis ac corruptis præcipit, quid debeant, præstandi autem
vires non subministrat, reos apud Dei tribunal peragit. Quæ enim est
naturæ nostræ vitiositas, quo magis docemur, quid rectum sit ac justum, eo
apertius nostra iniquitas detegitur, maximeque contumacia; atque hoc
modo gravius Dei judicium accersitur." *For where there is no law, there
is no transgression.* The interpretation given to this clause depends upon
the view taken of the preceding one. It assigns the reason why the law
works wrath. If the law be understood to work wrath by exasperating
the evils of our corrupt nature, then the meaning of this confirmatory clause
must be, that the law makes sin more inexcusable. It exalts sin into
transgressions, ἁμαρτία into παράβασις. Thus again Calvin says, that the
reason why the law works wrath is, " quia cognitione justitiæ Dei per legem
perceptâ, eo gravius peccamus in Deum, quo minus excusationis nobis
superest—non loquitur apostolus," he adds, " de simplici justitiæ trans-
gressione, a quâ nemo eximitur ; sed transgressionem appellat, ubi animus
edoctus, quid Deo placeat quidve displiceat, fines voce Dei sibi definitos
sciens ac volens perrumpit. Atqui ut uno verbo dicam, transgressio hic
non simplex delictum, sed destinatam in violandâ justitiâ contumaciam
significat." But all this belongs to the inefficacy of the law to produce
holiness, and not to its impotency in the matter of justification, which is
the point here under consideration. The apostle's argument here is, that
the inheritance must be by faith, not by the law, for the law can only
condemn. It works wrath, for without it there would be no condemnation,
because there would be no transgression. Besides, Paul does not make
the distinction between *sin* and *transgression,* between ἁμαρτία and
παράβασις, which the former interpretation supposes. What is here said
of *transgression,* is, in v. 13, said of *sin.* Where there is no law, there
can be no sin, because the very idea of sin is the want of conformity to a
rule, to which conformity is due ; so that where there is no rule or standard, there can be no want of conformity. Such being the meaning of this
clause, it is plain that by *law,* the apostle does not intend the Mosaic law,
but law as the standard to which rational creatures are bound to be conformed. If men would only acquiesce in Paul's idea of law, they could
not fail to receive his doctrine concerning sin and justification. If the law
is holy, just, and good ; if it is spiritual, taking cognizance not only of
outward acts, but of feelings, not only of active feelings, but of the inherent states of the mind whence these (ἐπιθυμίαι) spring ; if it condemns all
want of conformity to its own inflexible standard of complete perfection,
then there must be an end to all hope of being justified by the law.

Verse 16. *Therefore it is of faith, that it might be by grace; to the
end that the promise might be sure to all the seed,* &c. This and the following verse contain the conclusion from the previous reasoning, and
especially from the two preceding arguments : ' The inheritance promised
to Abraham and his seed must be either of the law, or of faith. It cannot be of the law, for the law works wrath, *therefore* it is of faith.' The
expression in the original is simply διὰ τοῦτο ἐκ πίστεως, *therefore of faith.*
It matters little, so far as the sense is concerned, whether we supply the
words οἱ κληρονόμοι εἰσί (*therefore the heirs are of faith,*) from ver. 14,
or the word ἐπαγγελία (*the promise,*) from ver. 13, or with Luther,
δικαιοσύνη, out of the general context—*darum muss die Gerechtigkeit aus
dem Glauben kommen.* These are only different ways of saying the same
thing. The connection, as stated above, is in favour of the first explanation. The inheritance is of faith, (ἵνα κατὰ χάριν,) *in order that it might*

be a matter of grace. And it is of grace, (εἰς τὸ εἶναι βεβαίαν τὴν ἐπαγγελίαν,) *in order that the promise might be sure.* If salvation be in any form or to any degree dependent on the merit, the goodness, or the stability of man, it never can be sure, nay, it must be utterly unattainable. Unless we are saved by grace, we cannot be saved at all. To reject, therefore, a gratuitous salvation, is to reject the only method of salvation available for sinners. Salvation being of grace, suspended on the simple condition of faith, without regard to parentage, to national or ecclesiastical connection, it is available for all classes of men. And therefore the apostle says, ' The promise is sure (παντὶ τῷ σπέρματι) *to all the seed ;* i. e. to all the spiritual children of Abraham. He had already shown in vers. 11, 12, that Abraham was the father of believing Gentiles as well as of believing Jews. The word σπέρμα (*seed*) must therefore, in this connection, be understood of believers who, in a higher sense than mere natural descendants, are the children of Abraham. Both classes of his seed are included in the promise which is sure, (οὐ τῷ ἐκ τοῦ νόμου μόνον,) *not to that of the law only,* i. e. not only to that portion of the seed who are of the law, that is, believing Jews, but also (τῷ ἐκ πίστεως 'Αβραάμ) *to that |which is of the faith of Abraham.* These formulas are indefinite, and susceptible, taken by themselves, of different interpretations ; but the context renders all plain. Paul is speaking of the spiritual children of Abraham ; of those who are heirs of the inheritance promised to them. Of these there are two classes ; believing Jews and believing Gentiles. The former are distinguished as (ἐκ νόμου) of the law, the latter as of the faith of Abraham, because their connection with him is purely spiritual, whereas the Jewish believers were connected with him by a twofold tie—the one natural, the other spiritual. *Who is the father of us all,* i. e. of all believers. The highest privilege of New Testament saints is to be partakers of the inheritance promised to Abraham. They are not exalted above him, but united with him in the blessings which flow from union with Christ.

VERSE 17. *As it is written, I have made thee a father of many nations,* Gen. xvii. 5. This declaration, the apostle informs us, contains a great deal more than the assurance that the natural descendants of Abraham should be very numerous. Taken in connection with the promise, that " in him all the nations of the earth should be blessed," it refers to his spiritual as well as his natural seed, and finds its full accomplishment in the extension of the blessing promised to him, to those of all nations who are his children by faith. This clause is very properly marked as a parenthesis, as the preceding one, " who is the father of us all," must be connected immediately with the following words, *before him whom he believed,* even *God, who quickeneth the dead,* &c. The words κατέναντι ου ἐπίστευσεν Θεοῦ, admit of different explanations. They are commonly regarded as an example of the substantive being attracted to the case of the relative, instead of the relative to that of the substantive, Θεοῦ being in the genitive, because οὖ is. The clause may therefore be resolved thus : κατέναντι Θεοῦ ῷ ἐπίστευσεν, *before God whom he believed.* To this, however, it is objected, that this form of attraction with the dative is very unusual, and therefore Winer, § 24, 2, *b,* and others, adopt the simple explanation, κατέναντι Θεοῦ κατέναντι οὖ ἐπίστευσε, (*before God, before whom he believed.*) The sense in either case is the same. Abraham is the father of us all, (κατέναντι,) *before, in the sight* of that God in whom he believed. God looked upon him as such. He stood before his omniscient eye, surrounded by many nations of children.

It is not unusual for the apostle to attach to the name of God a descriptive periphrase, bringing into view some divine attribute or characteristic suited to the subject in hand. So here, when speaking of God's promising to Abraham, a childless old man, a posterity as numerous as the stars of heaven, it was most appropriate to refer to the omnipotence of God, to whom nothing is impossible. Abraham believed, what to all human appearance never could happen, because God, who made the promise, is he *who quickeneth the dead, and calleth those things which be not, as though they were.* To originate life is the prerogative of God. It requires almighty power, and is therefore in Scripture specified as one of God's peculiar works ; see Deut. xxxii. 39 ; 1 Sam. ii. 6 ; 2 Kings v. 7·; Ps. lxviii. 20. The being who can call the dead to life, must be able to fulfil to one, although as good as dead, the promise of a numerous posterity. The other clause in this passage, (καὶ καλοῦντος τὰ μὴ ὄντα ὡς ὄντα,) *and calling things that be not, as being,* is more doubtful. There are three interpretations of these words, founded on three different senses of the word (καλεῖν) *to call.* 1. *To call,* means to command, to control, to muster or dispose of. Thus the psalmist says, " The mighty God, *even* the Lord hath spoken, and called the earth, from the rising of the sun unto the going down thereof." Ps. l. 1. Isaiah, speaking of the stars, says, " Who . . . bringeth out their host by number : he calleth them all by name, by the greatness of his might," xl. 26 ; also Ps. cxlvii. 4 ; Isa. xlv. 3 ; xlviii. 13. This gives a sense perfectly suited to the context. God is described as controlling with equal ease things which are not, and those which are. The actual and the possible are equally subject to his command. All things are present to his view, and all are under his control. This interpretation also is suited to the peculiar form of expression, *who* calls (τὰ μὴ ὄντα ὡς ὄντα,) things not being, *as* being. It gives ὡς its appropriate force. 2. *To call,* however, is often used to express the creating energy of God. See Isa. xli. 4 ; xlviii. 13. Compare Ps. xxix. 3—9. Philo de Creat., τὰ μὴ ὄντα ἐκάλεσεν εἰς τὸ εἶναι. This also gives a good sense, as the omnipotence of God cannot be more forcibly expressed than by saying, ' He calls things not existing into existence.' But the difficulty is, that ὡς ὄντα is not equivalent with εἰς τὸ εἶναι, nor with ἐσόμενα, nor with εἰς τὸ εἶναι ὡς ὄντα, as Köllner and De Wette explain it. This indeed is not an impossible meaning, inasmuch as ὄντα, as Fritzsche says, may be the accusative of the effect, as in Philip. iii. 21, " He shall change our vile body (σύμμορφον) like unto his glorious body," *i.e.,* so as to be like ; see also 1 Thess. iii. 13. As, however, the former interpretation gives so good a sense, there is no need of resorting to these constrained explanations. 3. *To call,* is often used to express the effectual calling of men by the Holy Spirit. Hence some understand the apostle as here saying, ' God calls to be his children those who were not children.' But this is entirely foreign to the context. Paul is presenting the ground of Abraham's faith in God. He believed, because God was able to accomplish all things. Everything is obedient to his voice.

DOCTRINE.

1. If the greatest and best men of the old dispensation had to renounce entirely dependence upon their works, and to accept of the favour of God as a gratuity, justification by. works must, for all men, be impossible, vers. 2, 3.

2. No man can glory, that is, complacently rejoice in his own goodness

in the sight of God. And this every man of an enlightened conscience feels. The doctrine of justification by works, therefore, is inconsistent with the inward testimony of conscience, and can never give true peace of mind, ver. 2.

3. The two methods of justification cannot be united. They are as inconsistent as wages and a free gift. If of works, it is not of grace; and if of grace, it is not of works, vers. 4, 5.

4. As God justifies the ungodly, it cannot be on the ground of their own merit, but must be by the imputation of a righteousness which does not personally belong to them, and which they received by faith, vers. 5, 6, 11.

5. The blessings of the gospel, and the method of justification which it proposes, are suited to all men; and are not to be confined by sectarian limits, or bound down to ceremonial observances, vers. 9—11.

6. The sacraments and ceremonies of the Church, although in the highest degree useful when viewed in their proper light, become ruinous when perverted into grounds of confidence. What answers well as a sign, is a miserable substitute for the thing signified. Circumcision will not serve for righteousness, nor baptism for regeneration, ver. 10.

7. As Abraham is the father of all believers, all believers are brethren. There is neither Jew nor Gentile, bond nor free, among them as Christians, vers. 11, 12.

8. The seed of Abraham, or true believers, with Jesus Christ their head, are the heirs of the world. To them it will ultimately belong; even the uttermost parts of the earth shall be their possession, ver. 13.

9. To speak of justification by obedience to a law which we have broken, is a solecism. That which condemns cannot justify, ver. 15.

10. Nothing is sure for sinners that is not gratuitous. A promise suspended on obedience, they could never render sure. One entirely gratuitous needs only to be accepted to become ours, ver. 16.

11. It is the entire freeness of the gospel, and its requiring faith as the condition of acceptance, which renders it suited to all ages and nations, ver. 16.

12. The proper object of faith is the divine promise; or God considered as able and determined to accomplish his word, ver. 17.

REMARKS.

1. The renunciation of a legal self-righteous spirit is the first requisition of the gospel. This must be done, or the gospel cannot be accepted. ' He who works,' *i.e.* who trusts in his works, refuses to be saved by grace, vers. 1—5.

2. The more intimately we are acquainted with our own hearts and with the character of God, the more ready shall we be to renounce our own righteousness, and to trust in his mercy, vers. 2, 3.

3. Those only are truly happy and secure, who, under a sense of illdesert and helplessness, cast themselves upon the grace and promise of God, vers. 7, 8.

4. Nothing is more natural, and nothing has occurred more extensively in the Christian Church, than the perversion of the means of grace into grounds of dependence. Thus it was with circumcision, and thus it is with baptism and the Lord's supper; thus too with prayer, fasting, &c. This is the rock on which millions have been shipwrecked, vers. 9—12.

5. There is no hope for those who, forsaking the grace of God, take refuge in a law which worketh wrath, ver. 15.

6. All things are ours if we are Christ's; heirs of the life that now is, and of that which is to come, ver. 13.

7. As the God in whom believers trust is he to whom all things are known, and all things are subject, they should be strong in faith, giving glory to God, ver. 17.

ROMANS IV. 18—25.

ANALYSIS.

The object of this section is the illustration of the faith of Abraham, and the application of his case to our instruction. With regard to Abraham's faith, the apostle states, first, its object, viz. the divine promise, ver. 18. He then illustrates its strength, by a reference to the apparent impossibility of the thing promised, vers. 19, 20. The ground of Abraham's confidence was the power and veracity of God, ver. 21. The consequence was, that he was justified by his faith, ver. 22. Hence it is to be inferred that this is the true method of justification; for the record was made to teach us this truth. We are situated as Abraham was; we are called upon to believe in the Almighty God, who, by raising up Christ from the dead, has accepted him as the propitiation for our sins, vers. 23—25.

COMMENTARY.

VERSE 18. *Who against hope believed in hope.* Here ἐπ᾽ ἐλπίδι may be taken adverbially, *confidently:* 'Against all human hope or reasonable expectation, he confidently believed.' Or it may indicate the subjective ground of his faith: he believed, because he had a hope founded on the promise of God. He believed, *that he might become the father of many nations.* The Greek is, εἰς τὸ γενέσθαι αὐτὸν πατέρα, κ.τ.λ., that is, according to one explanation, the object of his faith was, that he should be the father of many nations. The idea thus expressed is correct. Abraham did believe that God would make him the father of many nations. But to this it is objected that πιστεύειν εἰς, with an infinitive used as a substantive, although grammatically correct, is a construction which never occurs. Had the apostle, therefore, intended to express the object of Abraham's faith, he would probably have used ὅτι, *he believed that he should be,* &c. Others make εἰς τὸ γενέσθαι express the result of his faith: 'He believed . . . . and hence he became,' &c. The consequence of his faith was, that the promise was fulfilled. Most recent commentators assume that εἰς with the infinitive here, as it commonly does, expresses design, or intention; not however the design of Abraham, but of God: 'He believed in order that, agreeably to the purpose of God, he might become the father of many nations.' This best agrees with what is said in ver. 11, and with the context. *According to that which was spoken, So shall thy seed be.* This is a reference to the promise which was the object of Abraham's faith. It is a quotation from Gen. xv. 5. The word *so* refers to the stars of heaven, mentioned in the passage as it stands in the Old Testament. The promise, therefore, particularly intended by the apostle is, that Abraham should be the father of many nations, or that his seed should be as numerous as the stars. It has already been seen, however, that the apostle understood this promise as including far more than that the natural descendants of Abraham should be very numerous; see vers. 13, 17. The expression in the text is a concise allusion to the various promises made to the ancient patriarch, which had reference to all nations being blessed through him. The promise of a numerous posterity, therefore, included the promise of Christ and his redemption. This is evident, 1. Because Paul had been speaking of a promise (ver. 16), in which believing Jews and Gentiles were alike interested; see Gal. iii. 14. 2. Because Paul asserts and argues that the seed promised to Abraham, and to which the promise related, was Jesus Christ, Gal. iii. 16. 3. So Abraham himself understood it, according to the declaration of our Saviour; John viii. 56, "Abraham rejoiced to see my day; and he saw it, and was glad." He looked forward under the greatest discouragements to the Redeemer as yet to come. We have the easier task to look back to the same Deliverer, who has died for our sins, and risen again for our justification, ver. 25.

VERSE 19. *And being not weak in faith, he considered not his own body, now dead,* &c. The 18th verse had stated it was contrary to all appearances that Abraham believed; this verse states the circumstances which rendered the accomplishment of the promise an apparent impossibility, viz. his own advanced age, and the age and barrenness of his wife. These circumstances he did not consider, that is, he did not allow them to have weight, he did not fix his mind on the difficulties of the case. Had he been weak in faith, and allowed himself to dwell on the obstacles to the fulfilment of the divine promise, he would have staggered. This does not imply that there was no inward conflict with doubt in Abraham's mind. It only says, that his faith triumphed over all difficulties. "The mind," says Calvin, "is never so enlightened that there are no remains of ignorance, nor the heart so established that there are no misgivings. With these evils of our nature," he adds, "faith maintains a perpetual conflict, in which conflict it is often sorely shaken and put to great stress; but still it conquers, so that believers may be said to be *in ipsa infirmitate firmissimi.*" Paul says Abraham was not weak, τῇ πίστει, *as to faith.*

VERSES 20, 21. *He staggered not at the promise of God;* οὐ διεκρίθη. The aorist passive is here used in a middle sense, *he was not in strife with himself,* i.e. he did not doubt; εἰς τὴν ἐπαγγελίαν, *in reference to the promise of God;* τῇ ἀπιστίᾳ, the dative has a causal force, *through* unbelief. Want of faith in God did not cause him to doubt the divine promise, ἀλλὰ, *but,* i.e. *on the contrary;* ἐνεδυναμώθη, not middle, *made himself strong,* but passive, *he was made strong;* τῇ πίστει, either *by,* or *as to* faith. *Giving glory to God;* that is, the strength was manifested in his giving glory to God. To give glory to God, is to take him to be what he really is, almighty and faithful. It is to show by our conduct that we give him credit, (so to speak,) that he will and can do what he says. Therefore the apostle adds, καὶ πληροφορηθείς, *and being fully persuaded;* that is, he gave glory to God by being fully persuaded that what he had promised he was able also to perform. "Quod addit," says Calvin, "*dedisse gloriam Deo,* in eo notandum est, non posse Deo plus honoris deferri quam dum fide obsignamus ejus veritatem; sicuti rursus nulla ei gravior contumelia inuri potest quam dum respuitur oblata ab ipso gratia, vel ejus verbo derogatur auctoritas. Quare hoc in ejus cultu præcipuum est caput, promissiones ejus obedienter amplecti : vera religio a fide incipit." It is therefore a very great error for men to suppose that to doubt is an evidence of humility. On the contrary, to doubt God's promise, or his love, is to dishonour him, because it is to question his word. Multitudes refuse to accept his grace, because they do not regard themselves as worthy, as though their worthiness were the ground on which that grace is offered. The thing to be believed is, that God accepts the unworthy; that for Christ's sake, he justifies the unjust. Many find it far harder to believe that God can love them, notwithstanding their sinfulness, than the hundred-years-old patriarch did to believe that he should be the father of many nations. Confidence in God's word, a full persuasion that he can do what seems to us impossible, is as necessary in the one case as in the other. The sinner honours God, in trusting his grace, as much as Abraham did in trusting his power.

Verse 22. *Therefore also it was imputed to him for righteousness.* That is, the faith of Abraham was imputed to him for righteousness. He was accepted as righteous on account of his faith ; not that faith itself was the ground, but the condition of his justification. He believed, and God accepted him as righteous ; just as now we believe, and are accepted as righteous, not on account of any merit in our faith, but simply on the ground of the righteousness of Christ, which is imputed to us when we believe ; that is, it is given to us, whenever we are willing to receive and rest upon it. "Nihil plus conferre fides nobis potest, quam a verbo acceperit. Quare non protinus justus erit, qui generali tantum confusaque notitia imbutus Deum veracem esse statuet, nisi in promissione gratiæ quiescat." Faith justifies by appropriating to ourselves the divine promise. But if that promise does not refer to our justification, faith cannot make us righteous. The object of justifying or saving faith, that is, of those acts of faith which secure our acceptance with God, is not the divine veracity in general, nor the divine authority of the Scriptures, but the specific promise of gratuitous acceptance through the mediation and merit of the Lord Jesus Christ.

Verses 23, 24. *Now, it was not written for his sake alone, that it was imputed to him.* The record concerning the faith and consequent justification of Abraham, was not made with the simple intention of giving a correct history of that patriarch. It had a much higher purpose. Abraham was a representative person. What was true of him, was true of all others who stood in the same relation to God. The method in which he was justified, is the method in which other sinners must be justified. That he was justified by faith, is recorded in the Scriptures to be a perpetual testimony as to the true method of justification before God. The apostle therefore adds, that it was δι ἡμᾶς, *on our account.* That is, on account of those *to whom it shall be imputed ;* οἷς μέλλει λογίζεσθαι *to whom it is appointed to be imputed ;* in case they should believe. As all men are sinners, the method in which one was certainly justified is the method by which others may secure the same blessing. If Abraham was justified by faith, we may be justified by faith. If the object of Abraham's faith was the promise of redemption, the same must be the object of our faith. He believed in God as quickening the dead, that is, as able to raise up from one as good as dead, the promised Redeemer. Therefore those to whom faith shall now be imputed for righteousness are described as *those who believe that God hath raised up Jesus from the dead.* By thus raising him from the dead, he declared him to be his Son, and the seed of Abraham, in whom all the nations of the earth were to be blessed. The object of the Christian's faith, therefore, is the same as the object of the faith of Abraham. Both believe the promise of redemption through the promised seed, which is Christ. When we are said to believe in God, who raised up Christ, it of course implies that we believe that Christ was thus raised up. As the resurrection of Christ was the great decisive evidence of the divinity of his mission, and the validity of all his claims, to believe that he rose from the dead, is to believe he was the Son of God, the propitiation for our sins, the Redeemer and the Lord of men ; that he was all he claimed to be, and had accomplished all he purposed to effect. Compare Rom. x. 9 ; Acts i. 22 ; iv. 33 ; 1 Cor. xv., and other passages, in which the resurrection of Christ is spoken of as the corner-stone of the gospel, as the great fact to be proved, and which, being proved, involves all the rest.

Verse 25. *Who was delivered for our offences, and raised again for our justification.* This verse is a comprehensive statement of the gospel. Christ was delivered *unto death* for our offences, *i.e.*, on account of them, and for their expiation ; see Isa. liii. 5, 6 ; Heb. ix. 28 ; 1 Peter ii. 21. This delivering of Christ is ascribed to God, Rom. viii. 32 ; Gal. i. 4, and elsewhere ; and to himself, Tit. ii. 14 ; Gal. ii. 20. It was by the divine purpose and counsel he suffered for the expiation of sin ; and he gave himself willingly to death. " He was led like a lamb to the slaughter, and as a sheep before her shearers is dumb, so he opened not his mouth." Christ is said to have been delivered unto death, διὰ τὰ παραπτώματα ἡμῶν, and to have been raised, διὰ τὴν δικαίωσιν ἡμῶν ; that is, he was delivered in order that our sins might be expiated, and he was raised in order that we might be justified. His death and his resurrection were alike necessary ; his death, as a satisfaction to divine justice. He bore our sins in his own body on the tree. That is, he bore the punishment of our sins. " Significat ergo Paulus," says Calvin, " satisfactionem pro peccatis nostris in cruce fuisse peractam. Nam ut Christus nos in gratiam Patris restitueret, reatum nostrum ab ipso aboleri oportuit ; quod fieri non poterat, nisi pœnam, cui solvendæ pares non eramus, nostro nomine lueret." His resurrection was no less necessary, first, as a proof that his death had been accepted as an expiation for our sins. Had he not risen, it would have been evident that he was not what he claimed to be. We should be yet in our sins, 1 Cor. xv. 17, and therefore still under condemnation. Our ransom, in that case, instead of being publicly accepted, had been rejected. And secondly, in order to secure the continued application of the merits of his sacrifice, he rose from the dead, and ascended on high, there to appear before God for us. He stands at the right hand of God, ever to make intercession for his people, thereby securing for them the benefits of his redemption. With a dead Saviour, a Saviour over whom death had triumphed and held captive, our justification had been for ever impossible. As it was necessary that the high priest, under the old economy, should not only slay the victim at the altar, but carry the blood into the most holy place, and sprinkle it upon the mercy-seat ; so it was necessary not only that our great High Priest should suffer in the outer court, but that he should pass into heaven, to present his righteousness before God for our justification. Both, therefore, as the evidence of the acceptance of his satisfaction on our behalf, and as a necessary step to secure the application of the merits of his sacrifice, the resurrection of Christ was absolutely essential, even for our justification. Its relation to inward spiritual life and eternal blessedness is not here brought into view ; for Paul is not here speaking of our sanctification. That δικαίωσις means justification, and not the act of making holy, need hardly be remarked. That follows of necessity, not only from the signification of the word, but from the whole scope of this part of the epistle. It is only by those who make justification identical with regeneration, that this is called into question. "Pervertunt autem," says Calovius, "sententiam Apostoli Papistæ, cum id eum velle contendunt, mortem Christi exemplar fuisse mortis peccatorum, resurrectionem autem exemplar renovationis et regenerationis internæ, per quam in novitate vitæ ambulamus, quia hic non agitur vel de morte peccatorum, vel de renovatione et novitate vitæ; de quibus, cap. vi., demum agere incipit Apostolus; sed de non imputatione vel remissione peccatorum, et imputatione justitiæ vel justificatione." Olshausen agrees substantially with the Romish interpretation of this passage, as he gives δικαίωσις an impossible sense, viz. (die den neuen Menschen schaffende Thätigkeit), *the regenerating activity* of God. It will be observed, that the theology of Olshausen, and of the mystical school to which he belongs, has far greater affinity for the Romish than for the Protestant system.

DOCTRINE.

1. Faith is an operative assent to the divine testimony, not the reception of truth as something which can be proved by our own arguments, verses 18, 20.

2. When faith is genuine it is founded on correct apprehensions of the divine character, and has a controlling influence over the heart and life, verses 20, 21.

3. The method of salvation has never been changed; Abraham was not only saved by faith, but the object of his faith was the same as the object of ours, verse 24, 17.

4. The resurrection of Christ, as an historical fact, established by the most satisfactory evidence (see 1 Cor. xv.), authenticates the whole gospel. As surely as Christ has risen, so surely shall believers be saved, ver. 25.

REMARKS.

1. The true way to have our faith strengthened is not to consider the difficulties in the way of the thing promised, but the character and resources of God, who has made the promise, ver. 19.

2. It is as possible for faith to be strong when the thing promised is most improbable, as when it is probable. Abraham's faith should serve as an example and admonition to us. He believed that a Saviour would be born from his family, when his having a son was an apparent impossibility. We are only called upon to believe that the Saviour has been born, has suffered, and risen again from the dead—facts established on the strongest historical, miraculous, and spiritual evidence, vers. 20, 24, 25.

3. Unbelief is a very great sin, as it implies a doubt of the veracity and power of God, verses 20, 21.

4. All that is written in the Scriptures is for our instruction. What is promised, commanded, or threatened (unless of a strictly personal naturer although addressed originally to individuals, belongs to them only as representatives of classes of men, and is designed for all of similar character, and in similar circumstances, ver. 23.

5. The two great truths of the gospel are, that Christ died as a sacrifice for our sins, and that he rose again for our justification. Whosoever, from the heart, believes these truths, shall be saved, ver. 25 ; Romans x. 9.

6. The denial of the propitiatory death of Christ, or of his resurrection from the dead, is a denial of the gospel. It is a refusing to be saved according to the method which God has appointed, ver. 25.

CHAPTER V.

CONTENTS.

FROM VERSE 1 TO 11, INCLUSIVE, THE APOSTLE DEDUCES SOME OF THE MORE OBVIOUS AND CONSOLATORY INFERENCES FROM THE DOCTRINE OF GRATUITOUS JUSTIFICATION. FROM THE 12TH VERSE TO THE END, HE ILLUSTRATES HIS GREAT PRINCIPLE OF THE IMPUTATION OF RIGHTEOUSNESS, OR THE REGARDING AND TREATING "THE MANY" AS RIGHTEOUS, ON ACCOUNT OF THE RIGHTEOUSNESS OF ONE MAN, CHRIST JESUS, BY A REFERENCE TO THE FALL OF ALL MEN IN ADAM.

ROMANS V. 1—11.

ANALYSIS.

THE first consequence of justification by faith is, that we have peace with God, ver. 1. The second, that we have not only a sense of his present favour, but assurance of future glory, ver. 2. The third, that our afflictions, instead of being inconsistent with the divine favour, are made directly conducive to the confirmation of our hope ; the Holy Spirit bearing witness to the fact that we are the objects of the love of God, verses 3—5. The fourth, the certainty of the final salvation of all believers. This is argued from the freeness and greatness of the divine love ; its freeness being manifested in its exercise towards the unworthy : and its greatness, in the gift of the Son of God, verses 6—10. Salvation is not merely a future though certain good, it is a present and abundant joy, verse 11.

COMMENTARY.

VERSE 1. *Therefore, being justified by faith, we have* peace with God;* that is, we are reconciled to God. We are no longer the objects of God's displeasure, his favour having been propitiated by the death of his Son, ver. 10. As a consequence of this reconciliation, we have conscious peace with God, that is, we have neither any longer the present upbraidings of

---

* Instead of ἔχομεν, *we have* peace, ἔχωμεν, *let us have*, is read in the MSS. A. C. D. 17, 18, 19, 22, 24, 34, 36, 37, 42, 44, 46, 55, 66, in the Syriac, Coptic, and Vulgate versions, and by several of the Fathers. The latter reading is adopted by Lachmann. But as the external authorities are nearly equally divided, and as the common reading gives a sense so much better suited to the context, it is retained by the majority of critical editors.

an unappeased conscience, nor the dread of divine vengeance. Both these ideas are included in the peace here spoken of. The latter, however, is altogether the more prominent. The phrase εἰρήνην ἔχομεν πρὸς τὸν Θεόν, *we have peace in regard to God*, properly means, God is at peace with us, his ὀργή (wrath) towards us is removed. It expresses, as Philippi says, "not a state of mind, but a relation to God."* It is that relation which arises from the expiation of sin, and consequently justification. We are no longer his enemies, in the objective sense of the term (see ver. 10), but are the objects of his favour. The whole context still treats of reconciliation and propitiation, of the removal of the wrath of God by the death of his Son, and not of inward sanctification. It is true that the immediate and certain effect of God's reconciliation to us is our reconciliation to him. If he is at peace with us, we have inward peace. Conscience is only the reflection of his countenance, the echo, often feeble and indistinct, often terribly clear and unmistakable, of his judgment ; and therefore subjective peace uniformly attends faith in the love of God, or assurance of our justification. Although, therefore, the primary idea of the apostle is, that God is at peace with us, it is nevertheless true that inward tranquillity of mind is the fruit of justification by faith. It is peculiarly an evangelical doctrine, that pious affections are the fruit of this reconciliation to God, and not the cause of it. Paul says this peace is the result of justification by faith. He who relies on his works for justification, can have no peace. He can neither remove the displeasure of God, nor quiet the apprehension of punishment. Peace is not the result of mere gratuitous forgiveness, but of justification, of a reconciliation founded upon atonement. The enlightened conscience is never satisfied until it sees that God can be just in justifying the ungodly ; that sin has been punished, the justice of God satisfied, his law honoured and vindicated. It is when he thus sees justice and mercy embracing each other, that the believer has that peace which passes all understanding ; that sweet quiet of the soul in which deep humility, in view of personal unworthiness, is mingled with the warmest gratitude to that Saviour by whose blood God's justice has been satisfied, and conscience appeased. Hence Paul says we have this peace *through our Lord Jesus Christ.* It is not through ourselves in any way, neither by our own merit, nor our own efforts. It is all of grace. It is all through Jesus Christ. And this the justified soul is ever anxious to acknowledge. " *Pacem habemus.* Singularis justitiæ fidei fructus. Nam siquis ab operibus conscientiæ securitatem petere velit, (quod in profanis et brutis hominibus cernitur,) frustra id tentabit. Aut enim contemptu vel oblivione Divini judicii sopitum est pectus, aut trepidatione ac formidine quoque plenum est, donec in Christum recubuerit. Ipse enim solus est pax nostra. Pax ergo conscientiæ serenitatem significat, quæ ex eo nascitur, quod Deum sibi reconciliatum sentit." *Calvin.*

VERSE 2. *By whom also we have access by faith into this grace,* &c. This verse admits of different interpretations. According to one view, it introduces a new and higher benefit than peace with God, as the consequence of our justification : ' We have not only peace, but access (to God), and joyful confidence of salvation.' Besides other objections to this interpretation, it overlooks the difference between ἔχομεν and ἐσχήκαμεν, rendering both, *we have :* ' We have peace, and we have access ;' whereas ἐσχή-

---

* Commentar über den Brief Pauli an die Römer von Friederich Adolph Philippi, Doktor un ord. Professor der Theologie zu Dorpat; since of Rostock.

καμεν is properly, *we have had.* This clause, therefore, instead of indicating an additional and higher blessing than the peace spoken of in ver. 1, expresses the ground of that peace : ' We have peace with God through Jesus Christ our Lord, through whom also we have had access into this grace.' So Meyer, Philippi, &c. ' We are indebted to Christ not only for peace, but also for access to this grace, (this state of justification,) which is the ground of our peace.' The word προσαγωγή means either *introduction* or *access.* In Eph. ii. 18 ; and iii. 12, it has the latter meaning, which may be retained here. In both the other places in which it occurs, it is used of access to God. Many commentators so understand it in this place, and therefore put a comma after ἐσχήκαμεν, and connect πίστει with εἰς τὴν χάριν ταύτην. The sense would then be, ' Through whom also we have had access to God, by faith on this grace.' The objections to this explanation are, that it supposes an omission in the text, and that the expression " faith on the grace," has no scriptural analogy. The obviously natural construction is to connect προσαγωγήν with εἰς τὴν χάριν ταύτην, as is done in our version, and by the great majority of commentators, and to take τῇ πίστει instrumentally, *by faith.* The grace to which we have access, or into which we have been introduced, is the state of justification. The fact, therefore, that we are justified, *we,* rather than others, is not due to anything in us. We did not open the way, or introduce ourselves into this state. We were brought into it by Christ. "Accessûs quidem nomine initium salutis a Christo esse docens, preparationes excludit, quibus stulti homines Dei misericordiam se antevertere putant ; acsi diceret, Christum nihil promeritis obviam venire manumque porrigere." *Calvin. In which we stand.* The antecedent of the relative (ᾗ) is not πίστει, but χάριν ; in which *grace* we stand ; that is, we are firmly and immovably established. So in John viii. 44, it is said of Satan, that *he stood not* (οὐχ ἔστηκεν) in the truth, did not remain steadfast therein. 1 Cor. xv. 1, " Wherein *ye stand,*" 2 Cor. i. 24. The state, therefore, into which the believer is introduced by Christ, is not a precarious one. He has not only firm ground on which to stand, but he has strength divinely imparted to enable him to keep his foothold. *And rejoice in hope of the glory of God.* The word καυχάομαι is one of Paul's favourite terms. It properly means *to talk of one's self, to praise one's self, to boast ;* then *to congratulate one's self, to speak of ourselves as glorious or blessed ;* and then *to felicitate ourselves in anything as a ground of confidence and source of honour and blessedness.* Men are commanded not to glory (καυχᾶσθαι) in themselves, or in men, or in the flesh, but in God alone. In this passage the word may be rendered, to rejoice, ' we rejoice in hope.' Still something more than mere joy is intended. It is a glorying, a self-felicitation and exultation, in view of the exaltation and blessedness which Christ has secured for us. *In hope of the glory of God.* The object or ground of the rejoicing or boasting expressed by this verb is indicated here by ἐπί ; commonly, in the New Testament, the matter of the boasting is indicated by ἐν, sometimes by ὑπέρ and περί. *The glory of God* may mean that glory which God gives, or that glory which he possesses. In either case, it refers to the exaltation and blessedness secured to the believer, who is to share in the glory of his divine Redeemer. " The glory which thou gavest me," said our Lord, " I have given them," John xvii. 22. There is a joyful confidence expressed in these words, an assurance of ultimate salvation, which is the appropriate effect of justification. We are authorized and bound to feel sure that, having through Jesus Christ been reconciled to God, we shall certainly be

saved. This is only a becoming confidence in the merit of his sacrifice, and
in the sincerity of God's love. This confidence is not founded on ourselves, neither on the preposterous idea that we deserve the favour of God,
nor the equally preposterous idea that we have in ourselves strength to
persevere in faith or obedience. Our confidence is solely on the merit of
Christ, and the gratuitous and infinite love of God. Although this assurance is the legitimate effect of reconciliation, and the want of it is evidence
of weakness, still in this, as in other respects, the actual state of the believer
generally falls far short of the ideal. He ever lives below his privileges,
and goes limping and halting, when he should mount up as with the wings
of the eagle. Still it is important for him to know that assurance is not
an unseemly presumption, but a privilege and duty. "Hic evertuntur,"
says Calvin, "pestilentissima duo sophistarum dogmata, alterum, quo jubent
Christianos esse contentos conjectura morali in percipienda erga se Dei
gratia, alterum, quo tradunt omnes esse incertos finalis perseverentiæ.
Atqui nisi et certa in præsens intelligentia, et in futurum constans ac minime
dubia sit persuasio, quis gloriari auderet ?"

Verses 3, 4. *And not only so, but we glory in tribulations also.* Not
only do we rejoice in this hope of future glory, but we glory in tribulations
also. Since our relation to God is changed, the relation of all things to us
is changed. Afflictions, which before were the expressions of God's displeasure, are now the benevolent and beneficent manifestations of his love.
And instead of being inconsistent with our filial relation to him, they
serve to prove that he regards and loves us as his children ; Rom. viii. 18;
Heb. xii. 6. Tribulations, therefore, although for the present not joyous,
but grievous, become to the believer matter of joy and thankfulness. The
words καυχώμεθα ἐν ταῖς θλίψεσιν do not mean that we glory in the midst
of afflictions, but on account of them. They are themselves the matter or
ground of the glorying. So the Jews are said to glory (ἐν) in the law, others
glory *in* men, the believer glories *in* the Lord ; so constantly. Afflictions
themselves are to the Christian a ground of glorying ; he feels them to be
an honour and a blessing. This is a sentiment often expressed in the word
of God. Our Lord says, "Blessed are they who mourn ;" " Blessed are
the persecuted ;" "Blessed are ye when men shall revile you." He calls
on his suffering disciples to rejoice and be exceeding glad when they are
afflicted. Matt. v. 4, 10—12. The apostles departed from the Jewish
council, "rejoicing that they were counted worthy to suffer shame for
Christ's name." Acts v. 41. Peter calls upon Christians to rejoice when
they are partakers of Christ's sufferings, and pronounces them happy when
they are reproached for his sake. 1 Pet. iv. 13, 14. And Paul says,
"Most gladly therefore will I glory in (on account of) my infirmities," (*i.e.*
my sufferings.) "I take pleasure," he says, "in infirmities, in reproaches,
in necessities, in persecutions, in distresses for Christ's sake." 2 Cor. xii. 9.
10. This is not irrational or fanatical. Christians do not glory in suffering, as
such, or for its own sake, but as the Bible teaches, 1. Because they consider it
an honour to suffer for Christ. 2. Because they rejoice in being the occasion
of manifesting his power in their support and deliverance ; and, 3. Because
suffering is made the means of their own sanctification and preparation for
usefulness here, and for heaven hereafter. The last of these reasons is that
to which the apostle refers in the context. We glory in afflictions, he says,
because *affliction worketh patience,* ὑπομονή, *constancy.* It calls into exercise that strength and firmness evinced in patient endurance of suffering,
and in perseverance in fidelity to truth **and** duty, under the severest trials.

And this constancy *worketh experience,* δοκιμή. This word means, 1. *Trial,* as in 2 Cor. viii. 2, "In a great trial of affliction," *i.e.* in affliction which is a trial, that which puts men to the test. 2. *Evidence* or *proof,* as in 2 Cor. xiii. 3, "Since ye seek a proof of Christ speaking in me." Compare 2 Cor. ii. 9 ; Philip. ii. 22. This would give a good sense here : ' Constancy produces evidence ' of the fidelity of God, or of our fidelity. 3. The word is used metonymically for the result of trial, *i.e. approbation,* or that which is proved worthy of approbation : ' δοκιμή est qualitas ejus, qui est δόκιμος.' *Bengel.* It is tried integrity, a state of mind which has stood the test. Compare James i. 12, " Blessed is the man that endureth temptation, (ὅς ὑπομένει πειρασμόν;) for when he is tried (ὅτι δόκιμος γενόμενος) he shall receive the crown of life." Ὑπομονή, the endurance of trial, therefore, makes a man δόκιμος ; in other words, it worketh δοκιμή. It produces a strong, *tested faith.* Hence the parallel expression, τὸ δοκίμιον ὑμῶν τῆς πίστεως, *the trying of your faith.* 1 Pet. i. 7. And this δοκιμή, *well tested faith,* or this endurance of trial produces hope ; tends to confirm and strengthen the hope of the glory of God, which we owe to our justification through Jesus Christ.

VERSE 5. *And hope maketh not ashamed,* (καταισχύνει.) Not to make ashamed, is not to put us to the shame of disappointment. The hope of the believer, says Calvin, " habet certissimum salutis exitum." It certainly eventuates in salvation. See ix. 33. The hope which true believers entertain, founded on the very nature of pious exercises, shall never disappoint them, Ps. xxii. 5. The ground of this assurance, however, is not the strength of our purpose, or confidence in our own goodness, but the love of God. The latter clause of the verse assigns the reason why the Christian's hope shall not be found delusive ; it is because *the love of God is shed abroad in our hearts, by the Holy Ghost given unto us.* 'The love of God ' is his love to us, and not ours to him, as appears from the following verses, in which the apostle illustrates the greatness and freeness of this love, by a reference to the unworthiness of its objects. *To shed abroad,* (ἐκκέχυται, it has been, and continues to be shed abroad,) is to communicate abundantly, and hence to evince clearly, Acts ii. 17, x. 45 ; Titus iii. 6. This manifestation of divine love is not any external revelation of it in the works of Providence, or even in redemption, but it is *in our hearts,* ἐν ταῖς καρδίαις ἡμῶν, diffused abroad within our hearts, where ἐν *in,* is not used for εἰς, *into.* "The love of God," says Philippi, " does not descend upon us as dew in drops, but as a stream which spreads itself abroad through the whole soul, filling it with the consciousness of his presence and favour. And this inward persuasion that we are the objects of the love of God, is not the mere result of the examination of evidence, nor is it a vain delusion, but it is produced by the Holy Ghost : " The Spirit itself beareth witness with our spirit, that we are the children of God," Rom. viii. 16 ; 2 Cor. i. 21, 22 ; Eph. i. 14. As, however, the Spirit never contradicts himself, he never bears witness that "the children of the devil" are the children of God ; that is, that the unholy, the disobedient, the proud or malicious, are the objects of the divine favour. Any reference, therefore, by the immoral, to the witness of the Spirit in their favour, must be vain and delusive.

VERSE 6. *For when we were yet without strength.* The connection of this verse, as indicated by γάρ, is with ver. 5. We are the object of God's love, *for* Christ died for us. The gift of Christ to die on our behalf, is everywhere in Scripture represented as the highest possible or conceivable proof of the love of God to sinners. John iii. 16 ; 1 John iii. 16 ; iv. 9, 10. The objection that the Church doctrine represents the death of Christ as exciting or procuring the love of an unloving God, is without the shadow of foundation. The Scriptures represent the love of God to sinners as independent of the work of Christ, and anterior to it. He so loved us as to give his only begotten Son to reconcile our salvation with his justice. In the Greek of this passage, ἔτι γὰρ Χριστὸς ὄντων ἡμῶν ἀσθενῶν, the ἔτι, yet, is out of its natural place ; it belongs to ὄντων ἀσθενῶν, (as in ver. 8, ἔτι ἁμαρτωλῶν,) and not to Χριστός. Such trajections of the particles are not unusual even in classical Greek. See Winer, § 61, 4 : ' Christ died for us, when we were yet weak.' This slight irregularity has given rise to considerable diversity of readings even in the older manuscripts. Some, instead of ἔτι at the beginning of the verse, have εἴγε or εἰς τί, and place ἔτι after ἀσθενῶν ; others have ἔτι both at the beginning and at the end of the clause. The great majority of editors and commentators retain the common reading, and refer the ἔτι to ὄντων, &c., as is done in our version. We being yet weak. The weakness here intended is spiritual weakness, destitution of strength for what is spiritually good, a weakness arising from, and consisting in sinfulness. The same idea, therefore, is expressed in ver. 8, by the words, ἔτι ἁμαρτωλῶν, when we were yet sinners. What, in Isa. liii. 4, is expressed by the LXX. in the words τὰς ἁμαρτίας ἡμῶν φέρει, he bears our sins, is, in Matt. viii. 17, expressed by saying, τὰς ἀσθενείας ἡμῶν ἔλαβε, he took our weaknesses. In due time, κατὰ καιρόν, are not to be connected with the preceding participial, ' we being weak according to (or considering) the time,' secundum rationem temporis, as Calvin and Luther, after Chrysostom and Theodoret, render it, but with the following verb, ἀπέθανε, he died κατὰ καιρόν. This may mean, at the appointed, or at the appropriate time. The former is more in accordance with the analogy of Scripture. Christ came at the time appointed by the Father. The same idea is expressed in Gal. iv. 4, by "the fulness of time ;" compare Eph. i. 10 ; 1 Tim. ii. 6 ; Titus i. 3 ; John v. 4. Of course the appointed was also the appropriate time. The question only concerns the form in which the idea is expressed. He died, ὑπὲρ ἀσεβῶν, for the ungodly. As the apostle had said, ' when we were weak,' it would have been natural for him to say, ' Christ died for us,' rather than that he died for the ungodly, had it not been his design to exalt the gratuitous nature of God's love. Christ died for us the ungodly ; and therein, as the apostle goes on to show, is the mysteriousness of the divine love revealed. That God should love the good, the righteous, the pure, the godly, is what we can understand ; but that the infinitely Holy should love the unholy. and give his Son for their redemption, is the wonder of all wonders. "Herein is love, not that we loved God, but that he loved us, and sent his Son to be a propitiation for our sins." 1 John iv. 10. As the love of a mother for her child, with which God condescends to compare his love towards us, is not founded on the attractive qualities of that child, but is often strongest when its object is the least worthy, so God loves us when sinners. The whole confidence of the apostle in the continuance of this love (and therefore in the final perseverance of the saints) is founded on its being thus gratuitous. If he loved us because we loved him, he would love us only so long as we love him, and on that condition ; and then our salvation would depend on the constancy of our treacherous hearts. But as God loved us as sinners, as Christ died for us as ungodly, our salvation depends, as the apostle argues, not on our loveliness, but on the constancy

of the love of God. This idea pervades this whole paragraph, and is
brought more distinctly into view in the following verses. Christ died *for*
the ungodly ; that is, in their place, and for their salvation. The idea of
substitution is not indeed necessarily involved in the force of the preposition ὑπέρ, which means *for, in behalf of,* while ἀντί means *in the place of.*
None the less certainly, however, is the doctrine here taught. To die *for*
a man, means to die for his benefit. And therefore, if this were all that
the Scriptures taught concerning the relation between Christ's death and
our salvation, it would remain undecided, whether he died *for* us as an
example, as a martyr, or as a substitute. But when it is said that he died
as a sacrifice, that he gave his life as a ransom, that he was a propitiation,
then the specific method in which Christ's death benefits us is determined.
It is therefore with ὑπέρ, as with our preposition *for ;* whether or not it
expresses the idea of substitution depends on the context, and the nature
of the subject. In such passages as this, and 2 Cor. v. 15, 20, 21 ; Gal.
iii. 13 ; Philemon 13, ὑπέρ involves in it the meaning of ἀντί.

VERSE 7. *For scarcely for a righteous man will one die, yet peradventure for a good man some would even dare to die.* The greatness and
freeness of the love of God is illustrated in this and the following verse,
by making still more prominent the unworthiness of its objects : 'It is
hardly to be expected that any one would die, in the place of a merely
righteous man, though for the good man, this self-denial might possibly
be exercised. But we, so far from being good, were not even righteous ;
we were sinners, ungodly, and enemies.' The difference between the words
righteous and *good,* as here used, is that which, in common usage, is made
between *just* and *kind.* The former is applied to a man who does all that
the law or justice can demand of him, the latter to him who is governed
by love. The just man commands respect ; the good man calls forth
affection. Respect being a cold and feeble principle, compared to love, the
sacrifices to which it leads are comparatively slight. This distinction between δίκαιος and ἀγαθός is illustrated by that which Cicero, *De Officiis,*
Lib. III. 15, makes between *justus* and *bonus :* " Si vir bonus is est qui
prodest quibus potest, nocet nemini, recte *justum* virum, *bonum* non facile
reperiemus." The interpretation given above is the one generally adopted ;
it suits the context, the signification of the words, and the structure of the
passage. The design of the apostle is to represent the death of Christ as
an unexampled manifestation of love. Among men, it was never heard of
that one died for a man simply just ; the most that human nature could
be expected to accomplish is, that one should die for his benefactor, or for
the good man—one so good as to be characterized and known as *the* good.
There is evidently a climax in the passage, as indicated by the opposition
between (μόλις and τάχα) *scarcely* and *possibly.* The passage, however,
has been differently interpreted. Luther takes both δικαίου and τοῦ
ἀγαθοῦ as neuters : "Scarcely for the right will any one die, possibly for
something good some one might dare to die." Calvin makes no distinction between the words : " Rarissimum sane inter homines exemplum
exstat, ut pro justo quis mori sustineat quanquam illud nonnunquam
accidere possit." Meyer takes δικαίου, as it is without the article, as masculine, but τοῦ ἀγαθοῦ as neuter, and renders the latter clause of the
verse interrogatively : " Hardly for a righteous man will one die, for who
can easily bring himself to die for what is good (τὸ ἀγαθόν, the good) ?"
The common interpretation is perfectly satisfactory, and to these, other
objections more or less decisive may be adduced. Instead of δικαίου, the

Syriac reads ἀδίκου, 'Scarcely for an *unrighteous* man will one die.' But this is not only unauthorized, but the sense is not so appropriate.

VERSE 8. *But God commendeth his love towards us, in that, while we were yet sinners, Christ died for us.* 'Commendeth,' συνίστησι, proves, or renders conspicuous; see iii. 5. What renders the love of God so peculiarly conspicuous, is his sending his Son to die, not for the good, nor even for the righteous, but for sinners, for those who were deserving of wrath instead of love. The word *sinners* expresses the idea of moral turpitude, and consequent exposure to the divine displeasure. It was *for,* or *in the place of* those who were at once corrupt, and the enemies of God, that Christ died.

VERSE 9. *Much more then, being now justified by his blood, we shall be saved from wrath through him.* This and the following verse draw the obvious inference, from the freeness and greatness of the love of God, as just exhibited, that believers shall be ultimately saved. It is an argument *a fortiori.* If the greater benefit has been bestowed, the less will not be withheld. If Christ has died for his enemies, he will surely save his friends. *Being justified.* To be justified is more than to be pardoned; it includes the idea of reconciliation or restoration to the favour of God, on the ground of a satisfaction to justice, and the participation of the consequent blessings. This idea is prominently presented in the following verse. ' We are justified *by his blood.*' This expression, as remarked above (chap. iv. 3), exhibits the true ground of our acceptance with God. It is not our works, nor our faith, nor our new obedience, nor the work of Christ in us, but what he has done for us; chap. iii. 25; Eph. ii. 13; Heb. ix. 12. Having by the death of Christ been brought into the relation of peace with God, being now regarded for his sake as righteous, *we shall be saved from wrath through him.* He will not leave his work unfinished; whom he justifies, them he also glorifies. The word *wrath,* of course, means the effects of wrath or punishment, those sufferings with which the divine displeasure visits sin; Matt. iii. 7; 1 Thess. i. 10; Rom. i. 18. Not only is our justification to be ascribed to Christ, but our salvation is *through* him. Salvation, in a general sense, includes justification; but when distinguished from it, as in this case, it means the consummation of that work of which justification is the commencement. It is a preservation from all the causes of destruction; a deliverance from the evils which surround us here, or threaten us hereafter; and an introduction into the blessedness of heaven. Christ thus saves us by his providence and Spirit, and by his constant intercession; chap. viii. 34; Heb. iv. 14, 15; vii. 25; Jude ver. 24; 1 John ii. 1. Olshausen here also introduces his idea of subjective justification, and says that the meaning of this passage is, " If God regenerates a man, we may hope that he will uphold and perfect him, and reduce his liability to apostasy to a minimum." According to this, to justify is to regenerate, and to save from wrath is to reduce our liability to apostasy to a minimum.

VERSE 10. *For if, when we were yet enemies, we were reconciled to God by the death of his Son,* &c. This verse contains nearly the same idea as ver. 9, presented in a different form. The word *enemies* is applied to men not only as descriptive of their moral character, but also of the relation in which they stand to God as the objects of his displeasure. There is not only a wicked opposition of the sinner to God, but a holy opposition of God to the sinner. The preceding verse presents the former of these ideas, and this verse the latter most prominently. There it is said, 'though *sinners,* we are justified;' and here, 'though *enemies,* we are reconciled.'

The word ἐχθροί has the same passive sense in xi. 28. And this is the principal difference between the two verses. *To be reconciled to God*, in such connections, does not mean to have our enmity to God removed, but his enmity to us taken out of the way, to have him rendered propitious, or his righteous justice satisfied. This is evident, 1. Because the reconciliation is ascribed to the death of Christ, or his blood, ver. 9. But, according to the constant representations of Scripture, the death of Christ is a sacrifice to satisfy divine justice, or to propitiate the favour of God, and not immediately a means of sanctification. The former is its direct object, the latter an incidental result. This is the very idea of a sacrifice. The most liberal commentators, that is, those least bound by any theological system, admit this to be the doctrine of Scripture, and of this particular passage. Thus Meyer: "Christi Tod tilgte nicht die Feindschaft der Menschen gegen Gott;" that is, "The death of Christ does not remove the enmity of men towards God, but as that which secures the favour of God, it removes his enmity towards men, whence the removal of our enmity towards him follows as a consequence." So also Rückert: "The reconciled here can only be God, whose wrath towards sinners is appeased by the death of his Son. On man's part nothing has happened; no internal change, no step towards God; all this follows as the consequence of the reconciliation here spoken of." De Wette also says, that "καταλλαγή must mean the removal of the wrath of God, and consequently the reconciliation is of God to man, which not only here, but in iii. 25; 2 Cor. v. 18, 19; Col. i. 21; Eph. ii. 16, is referred to the atoning death of Christ." 2. The object of the verse is to present us as enemies, or the objects of God's displeasure. 'If while we were the objects of the divine displeasure,' says the apostle, 'that displeasure has been removed, or God propitiated by the death of his Son, how much more shall we be saved,' &c. That is, if God has been reconciled to us, he will save us. 3. This is the proper meaning of the word, 2 Cor. v. 18, 19. See also Matt. v. 24, "First be reconciled to thy brother," *i.e.* go and appease his anger, or remove the ground of his displeasure; compare Heb. ii. 17, "He is a priest to make reconciliation (εἰς τὸ ἱλάσκεσθαι) for the sins of the people." It is the appropriate business of a priest to propitiate God, and not to reform men. See also 1 Sam. xxix. 4: "Wherewith should he reconcile himself (διαλλαγήσεται) to his master? should it not be with the heads of these men?" Eph. ii. 16, "That he might reconcile (ἀποκαταλλάξῃ) both unto God by the cross," not remove their enmity to God, but secure for them his favour and access to the Father, ver. 18. The verbs καταλλάσσω, διαλλάσσω, and ἀποκαταλλάσσω, are used interchangeably. The main idea, of course, as expressed by ἀλλάσσω, *to change*, is slightly modified by the force of the several prepositions with which it is combined—to change κατά *in relation to*, διά *between*, ἀπό *from*. The three verbs, however, are all used to express the idea of reconciliation, *i.e.* changing the relation of parties at enmity, so that they are at peace. Whether this reconciliation is effected by the propitiation of the justly offended party, or by a change of feeling in the offender, or both, depends on the connection. 4. The context obviously requires this sense here. "Being reconciled by the death of his Son," evidently corresponds to the phrase, "Being justified by his blood." The latter cannot mean that our feelings towards God are changed, but is admitted to express the idea that we are forgiven and restored to the divine favour. Such therefore must be the meaning of the former. Besides, it is the object of the apostle to illustrate the greatness and freeness of the love of God, from the unworthiness of its objects. While sinners, we are justified ; while enemies, we are reconciled. To make the passage mean, that when enemies we laid aside our enmity, and became the friends of God, would be to make it contradict the very assertion and design of the apostle. *We shall be saved by his life.* This rather unusual mode of expression was doubtless adopted for the sake of its correspondence to the words, *by his death*, in the preceding clause, and is a striking example of Paul's fondness for such antithetical constructions ; see chap. iv. 25 ; Gal. iii. 3 ; 2 Cor. iii. 6. The meaning is obvious : ' If while we were enemies, we were restored to the favour of God by the death of his Son, the fact that he lives will certainly secure our final salvation.' 1. His life is a pledge and security for the life of all his people ; see John xiv. 19, "Because I live, ye shall live also ;" Rom. viii. 11 ; 1 Cor. xv. 23. 2. He is able to save to the uttermost, "because he ever lives to make intercession for us," Heb. vii. 25, &c. 3. At his resurrection, all power in heaven and earth was committed to his hands, Matt. xxviii. 18 ; and this power he exercises for the salvation of his people ; Eph. i. 22, 'He is head over all things, for the benefit of his Church;' Rev. i. 18 ; Heb. ii. 10 ; 1 Cor. xv. 25, &c. ; see also the passages cited on the last clause of ver. 9. There is, therefore, most abundant ground for confidence for the final blessedness of believers, not only in the amazing love of God, by which, though sinners and enemies, they have been justified and reconciled by the death of his Son, but also in the consideration that this same Saviour that died for them still lives, and ever lives to sanctify, protect, and save them.

Verse 11. *Not only so, but we rejoice in God, through our Lord Jesus Christ ; οὐ μόνον δέ, ἀλλὰ καὶ καυχώμενοι ἐν τῷ Θεῷ.* There are three ways of explaining the participle καυχώνοι ; the one is to make it antithetical to καταλλαγέντς, ' not only reconciled, but exulting in God, shall we be saved.' But this is not only an unnatural form of expression, but in ver. 9, καταλλαγέντες is not a qualification of σωθησόμεθα. The meaning is not, ' We shall be saved reconciled,' but, ' Since we are reconciled we shall be saved.' Another interpretation supplies the verb from the preceding clause, ' Not only shall we be saved, but saved rejoicing in God.' The best sense is obtained by supplying ἐσμέν after the participle, as is assumed in the English version, and advocated by the majority of commentators : ' We shall not only be ultimately saved, but we now glory in God.' The benefits of redemption are not all future. It is not only deliverance from future wrath, but the joy and glory of the present favour and love of God, that we owe to Jesus Christ. Thus the Vulgate, which renders καυχώμενοι as a verb, (*sed et gloriamur,*) as does Luther, " Wir rühmen uns auch Gottes." We glory in God *through our Lord Jesus Christ.* That is, it is to him that we are indebted for this joy in God as our God and portion. *Through whom we have now received atonement.* This is the reason why we owe our present glorying in God to Christ ; it is because he has secured our reconciliation. The word rendered by our translators, *atonement*, is καταλλαγή, the derivative of καταλλάσσω, properly rendered in the context, as elsewhere, *to reconcile.* The proper rendering, therefore, of the noun would be *reconciliation :* ' Through whom we have received reconciliation, that is, have been reconciled.' This verse therefore brings us back to verse 2. There it is said, ' Having peace with God, we rejoice in hope of his glory ;' and here, ' Being reconciled, we glory or rejoice in God.' Salvation is begun on earth.

DOCTRINE.

1. Peace with God is the result of that system of religion which alone, by providing at once for the satisfaction of divine justice and the sanctification of the human heart, is suited to the character of God, and the nature of man. All history shows that no system other than the gospel has ever produced this peace, ver. 1.

2. All the peculiar blessings of redemption are inseparably connected with and grow out of each other. Those who are justified have peace with God, access to his presence, joy under the most adverse circumstances, assurance of God's love, and certainty of final salvation; see the whole section, and compare chap. viii. 30.

3. The Holy Ghost has intimate access to the human soul, controlling its exercises, exciting its emotions, and leading it into the knowledge of the truth, ver. 5.

4. The assurance of hope is founded on the consciousness of pious affections, and the witness of the Holy Spirit; and is a grace to which believers may and ought to attain, verses 4, 5.

5. The perseverance of the saints is to be attributed not to the strength of their love to God, nor to anything else in themselves, but solely to the free and infinite love of God in Christ Jesus. The praise is therefore no more due to them, than condemnation to a helpless infant for its mother's sleepless care. "Can a woman forget her sucking child," &c., verses 6—10.

6. Redemption is not by truth or moral influence, but by blood, verses 9, 10.

7. The primary object of the death of Christ was to render God propitious, to satisfy his justice, and not to influence human conduct, or display the divine character, for the sake of the moral effect of that exhibition. Among its infinitely diversified results, all of which were designed, some of the most important, no doubt, are the sanctification of men, the display of the divine perfections, the prevention of sin, the happiness of the universe, &c. But the object of a sacrifice, as such, is to propitiate, verses 9, 10; Heb. ii. 17.

8. All we have or hope for, we owe to Jesus Christ—peace, communion with God, joy, hope, eternal life; see the whole section, and the whole Bible.

REMARKS.

1. If we are the genuine children of God, we have peace of conscience, a sense of God's favour, and freedom of access to his throne. We endure afflictions with patience. Instead of making us distrustful of our heavenly Father, they afford us new proofs of his love, and strengthen our hope of his mercy. And we shall have, also, more or less of the assurance of God's love, by the indwelling of the Holy Spirit, verses 1—5.

2. None of these fruits of reconciliation with God can be obtained until the spirit of self-righteousness and self-dependence is removed. They are secured through faith, and by Christ Jesus, and not by our own works or merit, ver. 1, &c.

3. The hope of the hypocrite is like a spider's web; the hope of the believer is an anchor to his soul, sure and steadfast, ver. 5.

4. Assurance of the love of God never produces self-complacency or pride ; but always humility, self-abasement, wonder, gratitude, and praise. The believer sees that the mysterious fountain of this love is in the divine mind ; it is not in himself, who is ungodly and a sinner, verses 8—10.

5. As the love of God in the gift of his Son, and the love of Christ in dying for us, are the peculiar characteristics of the gospel, no one can be a true Christian on whom these truths do not exert a governing influence, verses 9, 10 ; compare 2 Cor. v. 14.

6. True religion is joyful, verses 2, 11.

ROMANS V. 12—21.

ANALYSIS.

I. *Scope of the passage.* The design of this section is the illustration of the doctrine of the justification of sinners on the ground of the righteousness of Christ, by a reference to the condemnation of men for the sin of Adam. That such is its design is evident, 1. From the context. Paul has been engaged from the beginning of the Epistle in inculcating one main idea, viz., that the ground of the sinner's acceptance with God is not in himself, but the merit of Christ. And in the preceding verses he had said, " we are justified by his blood," ver 9 ; by his death we are restored to the divine favour, ver. 10 ; and through him, *i.e.*, by one man, we have received reconciliation, that is, are pardoned and justified, ver. 11. As this idea of men's being regarded and treated, not according to their own merit, but the merit of another, is contrary to the common mode of thinking among men, and especially contrary to their self-righteous efforts to obtain the divine favour, the apostle illustrates and enforces it by an appeal to the great analogous fact in the history of the world. 2. From an inspection of verses 12, 18, 19, which contain the whole point and substance of the comparison. Verses 13—17 are virtually a parenthesis ; and verses 20, 21, contain two remarks, merely incidental to the discussion. Verses 12, 18, 19, must therefore contain the main idea of the passage. In the 12th, only one side of the comparison is stated ; but in verses 18, 19, it is resumed and carried out : ' As by the offence of one all are condemned, so by the righteousness of one all are justified.' This, almost in the words of the apostle, is the simple meaning of verses 18, 19, and makes the point of the comparison and scope of the passage perfectly clear. 3. The design of the passage must be that on which all its parts bear, the point towards which they all converge. The course of the argument, as will appear in the sequel, bears so uniformly and lucidly on the point just stated, that the attempt to make it bear on any other involves the whole passage in confusion. All that the apostle says tends to the illustration of his declaration, ' As we are condemned on account of what Adam did, we are justified on account of what Christ did.' The illustration of this point, therefore, must be the design and scope of the whole.

It is frequently and confidently said that the design of the passage is to exalt our views of the blessings procured by Christ, by showing that they are greater than the evils occasioned by the fall. But this is not only improbable, but impossible. 1. Because the *superabounding* of the grace of the gospel is not expressly stated until ver. 20. That is, not until the whole discussion is ended ; and it is introduced there merely incidentally, as involved in the apostle's answer to an objection to his argument, implied in the question, 'For what purpose did the law enter ?' Is it possible that the main design of a passage should be disclosed only in the reply to an incidental objection ? The pith and point of the discussion would be just what they are now, had no such objection been suggested or answered ; yet, if this view of the subject is correct, had the objection not been presented, the main design of the passage would have been unexpressed and undiscoverable. 2. The idea of the superiority of the blessings procured by Christ to the evils occasioned by Adam, although first expressly stated in ver. 20, is alluded to and implied in verses 16, 17. But these verses, it is admitted, belong to a parenthesis. It is conceded on all hands, that verses 13, 14, are designed to confirm the statement of ver. 12, and that verses 15—17, are subordinate to the last clause of ver. 14, and contain an illustration of its meaning. It is therefore not only admitted, but frequently and freely asserted, that verses 12, 18, 19, contain the point and substance of the whole passage, verses 13—17 being a parenthesis. Yet, in verses 12, 18, 19, the superabounding of the grace of Christ is not even hinted. Can the main design of a passage be contained in a parenthesis, and not in the passage itself ? The very nature of a parenthesis is, that it contains something which may be left out of a passage, and leave the sense entire. But can the main design and scope of an author be left out, and his meaning be left complete ! If not, it is impossible that an idea, contained only in a parenthesis should be the main design of the passage. The idea is in itself true and important, but the mistake consists in exalting a corollary into the scope and object of the whole discussion. The confusion and mistake in the exposition of a passage, consequent on an entire misapprehension of its design, may be readily imagined.

II. *The connection.* The design of the passage being the illustration of the doctrine of justification by the righteousness of Christ, previously established, the connection is natural and obvious : ' Wherefore, as by one man we have been brought under condemnation, so by one man we are brought into a state of justification and life.' The *wherefore* (διὰ τοῦτο) is consequently to be taken as illative, or marking an inference from the whole of the previous part of the epistle, and especially from the preceding verses. ' *Wherefore* we are justified by the righteousness of one man, even as we were brought into condemnation by the sin of one man.' It would seem that only a misapprehension of the design of the passage, or an unwillingness to admit it, could have led to the numerous forced and unauthorized explanations of these words. Some render them *moreover ;* others, *in respect to this,* &c.

III. *The course of the argument.* As the point to be illustrated is the justification of sinners on the ground of the righteousness of Christ, and the source of illustration is the fall of all men in Adam, the passage begins with a statement of this latter truth : ' As on account of one man, death has passed on all men ; so on account of one,' &c., ver. 12. Before carrying out the comparison, however, the apostle stops to establish his position, that all men are condemned on account of the sin of Adam. His proof is this : The infliction of a penalty implies the transgression of a law, since sin is not imputed where there is no law, ver. 13. All mankind are subject to death or penal evils ; therefore all men are regarded as transgressors of a law, ver. 13. This law or covenant, which brings death on all men, is not the law of Moses, because multitudes died before that was given, ver. 14. Nor is it the law of nature written upon the heart, since multitudes die who have never violated even that law, ver. 14. Therefore, as neither of these laws is sufficiently extensive to embrace *all* the subjects of the penalty, we must conclude that men are subject to death on account of Adam ; that is, it is for the offence of one that many die, vers. 13, 14. Adam is, therefore, a type of Christ. As to this important point, there is a striking analogy between the fall and redemption. We are condemned in Adam, and we are justified in Christ. But the cases are not completely parallel. In the first place, the former dispensation is much more mysterious than the latter ; for if by the offence of one many die, MUCH MORE by the righteousness of one shall many live, ver. 15. In the second place, the benefits of the one dispensation far exceed the evils of the other. For the condemnation was for one offence ; the justification is from many. Christ saves us from much more than the guilt of Adam's sin, ver. 16. In the third place, Christ not only saves us from death, that is, not only frees us from the evils consequent on our own and Adam's sin, but introduces us into a state of positive and eternal blessedness, ver. 17. Or this verse may be considered as an amplification of the sentiment of ver. 15.

Having thus limited and illustrated the analogy between Adam and Christ, the apostle resumes and carries the comparison fully out : ' THERE-FORE, as on account of one man all men are condemned ; so on account of one, all are justified,' ver. 18. 'For, as through the disobedience of one, many are regarded and treated as sinners ; so through the righteousness of one many are regarded and treated as righteous,' ver. 19. This then is the sense of the passage—men are condemned for the sin of one man, and justified for the righteousness of another. If men are thus justified by the obedience of Christ, for what purpose is the law ? 'It entered that sin might abound,' *i.e.* that men might see how much it abounded ; since by the law is the knowledge of sin. The law has its use, although men are not justified by their own obedience to it, ver. 20. As the law discloses, and even aggravates the dreadful triumphs of sin reigning, in union with death, over the human family, the gospel displays the far more effectual and extensive triumphs of grace through Jesus Christ our Lord, ver. 21.

According to this view of the passage it consists of five parts. The first, contained in ver. 12, presents the first member of the comparison between Christ and Adam. The second contains the proof of the position assumed in ver. 12, and embraces vers. 13, 14, which are therefore subordinate to ver. 12. *Adam, therefore, is a type of Christ.* The third, embracing vers. 15—17, is a commentary on this declaration, by which it is at once illustrated and limited. The fourth, in vers. 18, 19, resumes and carries out the comparison commenced in ver. 12. The fifth forms the conclusion of the chapter, and contains a statement of the design and effect of the law, and of the results of the gospel, suggested by the preceding comparison, vers. 20, 21.

COMMENTARY.

VERSE 12. *Wherefore, as by one man sin entered into the world, and death by sin,* &c. The force of διὰ τοῦτο, *wherefore,* has already been pointed out, when speaking of the connection of this passage with the preceding : ' It follows, from what has been said of the method of justification that *as* by one man all became sinners, *so* by one are all constituted righteous.' This passage, therefore, is the summation of all that has gone before

As (ὥσπερ), obviously indicates a comparison or parallel. There is however no corresponding clause beginning with *so*, to complete the sentence. Examples of similar incomplete comparisons may be found in Matt. xxv. 14, with ὥσπερ, and in 1 Tim. i. 3, with καθώς. It is however so obvious that the illustration begun in this verse is resumed, and fully stated in vers. 18, 19, that the vast majority of commentators agree that we must seek in those verses the clause which answers to this verse. The other explanations are unnecessary or unsatisfactory. 1. Some say that this verse is complete in itself, ' *As* by one man sin entered into the world, and death by sin, *so also* death passed on all men, because all sinned.' The two insuperable objections to this explanation are, first, that it does violence to the words. It makes the apostle say what he does not say. It makes καὶ οὕτως, *and so*, to mean the same with οὕτω καί, *so also*, which is impossible. And secondly, it is inconsistent with the whole design and argument of the passage. Instead of having a comparison between Christ and Adam, the comparison would be between Adam and other men : ' *As* he sinned and died, *so* they sinned and died.' 2. Others say, that we find in the last clause of ver. 14, in substance, although not in form, the apodosis of this clause : ' *As* by one man sin entered into the world, *so* Adam is the type of Christ.' But this is obviously inconsistent with the wording and connection of the clause in ver. 18. 3. De Wette proposes, after Cocceius, Elsner, and a few others, to make the ὥσπερ of this verse introduce not the first, but the second member of the comparison, the first being to be supplied in thought, or borrowed from what precedes : ' *We receive righteousness and life through Christ,* as by one man sin entered into the world ;' or, ' Wherefore Christ stands in a relation to mankind analogous to that of Adam, *as* by one man,' &c. But it is plain that no reader could imagine that Paul intended so essential a member of the comparison to be conjectured or framed from the preceding discussion. He does not leave his readers to supply one half of a sentence ; he himself completes it in ver. 18.

By one man sin entered into the world, δι ἑνὸς ἀνθρώπου, κ.τ.λ. These words clearly declare a causal relation between the one man, Adam, and the entrance of sin into the world. Benecke, who has revived the doctrine of the preëxistence of souls, supposes that Adam was the leader of the spirits who in the preëxistent state sinned, and were condemned to be born as men. Adam was therefore the cause of sin entering into the world, because he was the author of this ante-mundane apostasy. The Pelagian theory is, that Adam was the mere occasional cause of men becoming sinners. He was the first sinner, and others followed his example. Or, according to another form of the same general idea, his sin was the occasion of God's giving men up to sin. There was no real connection, either natural or judicial, between Adam's sin and the sinfulness of his posterity ; but God determined that if the first man sinned, all other men should. This was a divine constitution, without there being any causal connection between the two events. Others again say that Adam was the efficient cause of the sinfulness of his race. He deteriorated either physically or morally the nature which he transmitted to his posterity. He was therefore, in the same sense, the cause of the sinfulness of the race, that a father who impairs his constitution is the cause of the feebleness of his children. Others push this idea one step farther, and say that Adam was the race. He was not only *a* man, but man. The whole race was in him, so that his act was the act of humanity. It was as much and as truly ours as his.

Others say that the causal relation expressed by these words is that which exists between sin and punishment. It was the judicial cause or reason. All these views must come up at every step in the interpretation of this whole passage, for the explanation of each particular clause must be determined by the nature of the relation which is assumed to exist between Adam and his posterity. All that need be said here is, that the choice between these several explanations is not determined by the mere meaning of the words. All they assert is, that Adam was the cause of all men becoming sinners ; but whether he was the occasional, the efficient, or, so to speak, the judicial cause, can only be determined by the nature of the case, the analogy of Scripture, and the context. One thing is clear—Adam was the cause of sin in a sense analogous to that in which Christ is the cause of righteousness.

Sin entered into the world. It is hardly necessary to remark, that κόσμος does not here mean the universe. Sin existed before the fall of Adam. It can only mean the world of mankind. Sin *entered* the world ; it invaded the race. There is a personification here of sin, as afterwards of death. Both are represented as hostile and evil powers, which obtained dominion over man. By the words εἰσῆλθε εἰς τὸν κόσμον, much more is meant than that sin began to be in the world. It means that the world, κόσμος, mankind, became sinners ; because this clause is explained by saying, *all sinned.* The entrance of sin is made the ground of the universality of death, and therefore all were involved in the sin whose entrance is mentioned. The word ἁμαρτία means, 1. Actual sin (ἁμάρτημα), an individual act of disobedience or want of conformity to the law of God. In the plural form especially, ἁμαρτία means actual sin. Hence the expressions, "this sin," "respect of persons is sin," &c. 2. Sinful principle or disposition ; an immanent state of the mind, as in Rom. vii. 8, 9, 17, 23. 3. Both ideas are united, as when it is said, "the sting of death is sin," "an offering for sin." This comprehensive sense of the word is perhaps the most common. 4. It often means the guilt of sin as distinguished from sin itself, as when it is said, "he shall bear his sin," or, "the son shall not bear the sin of his father ;" or when Christ is said "to bear our sin," and, "to take away sin by the sacrifice of himself," &c. In this passage, when it is said "sin entered into the world," the meaning may be, actual sin commenced its course, men began to sin. Or the meaning is, depravity, corruption of nature invaded the world, men became corrupt. This is the interpretation given to the words by a large class of commentators, ancient and modern. So Calvin, "Istud peccare est corruptos esse et vitiatos. Illa enim naturalis pravitas, quam e matris utero afferimus, tametsi non ita cito fructus suos edit, peccatum est coram Deo, ejus ultionem meretur. Atque hoc est peccatum quod vocant originale." So also Olshausen, who says it means *habitus peccandi*, that inward principle of which individual sins are the expression or manifestation. Tholuck gives the same interpretation : a new, abiding, corrupting element, he says, was introduced into the organism of the world. De Wette's explanation amounts to the same thing : " Sünde als herrschende Macht (sin as a ruling power entered the world), partly as a principle or disposition, which, according to vii. 8, slumbers in every man's breast, and reveals itself in the general conduct of men, and partly as a sinful condition, such as Paul had described in th opening chapters of this epistle." Rückert, Köllner, Bretschneider, and most moderns, unite with the older expositors in this interpretation. Or ἁμαρτία may here have the third signification mentioned above, and " sin entered into the world," mean that men became guilty, *i.e.* exposed to condemnation. The objection to these several interpretations is, that each by itself is too limited. All three, taken collectively, are correct. " Sin entered into the world," means " men became sinners," or, as the apostle expresses it in ver. 19, " they were constituted sinners." This includes guilt, depravity, and actual transgression. " The sinfulness of that estate into which man fell (that is, the sin which Adam brought upon the world), consists in the guilt of Adam's first sin, the want of original righteousness, and the corruption of his whole nature, which is commonly called original sin ; together with all actual transgressions which proceed from it."

And death by sin ; that is, death entered the world, men became subject to death, διὰ τῆς ἁμαρτίας *by means of sin.* Sin was the cause of death ; not the mere occasional cause, not the efficient cause, but the ground or reason of its infliction. This passage, therefore, teaches that death is a penal evil, and not a consequence of the original constitution of man. Paul, in 1 Cor. xv. 40—50, appears to teach a contrary doctrine, for he there says that Adam's body, as formed from the earth, was earthy, and therefore corruptible. It was flesh and blood, which cannot inherit the kingdom of God. It must be changed, so that this corruptible put on incorruption, before we can be fitted for immortality. These representations, however, are not inconsistent. It is clear, from Gen. ii. 17 ; iii. 19, that had Adam never sinned, he would never have died ; but it does not follow that he would never have been changed. Paul says of believers, " we shall not all die, but we shall all be changed," 1 Cor. xv. 51. The penal character of death, therefore, which is so prominently presented in Scripture, or that death in the case of every moral creature is assumed to be evidence of sin, is perfectly consistent with what the apostle says of the σῶμα ψυχικόν (the natural body), and of its unsuitableness for an immortal existence. It is plain that θάνατος here includes the idea of natural death, as it does in the original threatening made to our first parents. In neither case, however, is this its whole meaning. This is admitted by a majority of the modern commentators—not only by such writers as Tholuck, Olshausen, and Philippi, but by others of a different class, as De Wette, Köllner, and Rückert. That the death here spoken of includes all penal evil, death spiritual and eternal, as well as the dissolution of the body, is evident, 1. From the consideration that it is said to be the consequence of sin. It must, therefore, mean that death which the Scriptures elsewhere speak of as the consequence and punishment of transgression. 2. Because this is the common and favourite term with the sacred writers, from first to last, for the penal consequences of sin. Gen. ii. 17, " In the day thou eatest thereof, thou shalt surely die," *i.e.* thou shalt become subject to the punishment due to sin ; Ezek. xviii. 4, " The soul that sinneth, it shall die ;" Rom. vi. 23, " The wages of sin is death ;" chap. viii. 13, " If ye live after the flesh, ye shall die." Such passages are altogether too numerous to be quoted, or even referred to ; see as further examples, Rom. i. 32 ; vii. 5 ; James i. 15 ; Rev. xx. 14, &c. 3. From the constant opposition between the terms *life* and *death*, throughout the Scriptures ; the former standing for the rewards of the righteous, the latter for the punishment of the wicked. Thus, in Gen. ii. 17, life was promised to our first parents as the reward of obedience ; and death threatened as the punishment of disobedience. See Deut. xxx. 15, " I have set before thee life and death ;" Jer. xxi. 8 ; Prov. xi. 19 ; Ps. xxxvi. 9 ; Matt. xxv. 46 : John iii. 15 ; 2 Cor. ii. 16, &c. 4. From the opposition in this passage between the life

which is by Christ, and the death which is by Adam, vers. 15, 17, 21,
'Sin reigns unto death, grace reigns through righteousness unto eternal
life.' As, however, natural death is a part, and the most obvious part of
the penal evils of sin, it no doubt was prominent in the apostle's mind, as
appears from vers. 13, 14. Death, therefore, in this passage, means the
evil, and any evil which is inflicted in punishment of sin.

And so death passed on all men. That is, as death is the necessary consequence of sin, death (διῆλθε) passed through, reached to all men, because
all sinned. Death is universal, because sin is universal. As Adam
brought sin on all men, he brought death on all. That this is the true
interpretation of this clause, or that καὶ οὕτως means *demzufolge, consequently, hence it happens,* is admitted by almost all modern commentators.
As already remarked, the interpretation which assumes that καὶ οὕτως is to
be rendered *so also,* is entirely inadmissible, 1. Because it is inconsistent
with their meaning. As it is impossible that *and so* should mean *so also,*
it is no less impossible that καὶ οὕτως should mean the same as οὕτω καί.
Compare verses 18, 19; 1 Cor. xi. 12; xii. 12; xv. 22. This interpretation, therefore, does violence to the language. 2. It is no less inconsistent with the context. It is not Paul's design to teach the inseparable
connection between sin and death, by saying, '*As* Adam sinned, and therefore died, so also all die, because all sin.' His purpose is to teach the connection between Adam's sin and the death of all men : 'It was *by one
man* that men became sinners, and hence all men die.' As all were involved in his sin, all are involved in his death. 3. The comparison
carried through this whole paragraph is not between Adam and his posterity, but between Adam and Christ; and therefore καὶ οὕτως cannot
possibly refer to the ὥσπερ at the beginning of the verse, as has been
already shown.

For that all have sinned, ἐφ' ᾧ πάντες ἥμαρτον. The words ἐφ' ᾧ are
rendered in the Vulgate, *in quo* (in whom), and are so understood by many
of the older interpreters, not only in the Romish Church, where the
Vulgate is of authority, but also by many Calvinists and Arminians. The
objections to this interpretation are, 1. It is not in accordance with the
meaning of the words as used elsewhere. It is inconsistent with the
proper force of ἐπί (*on, upon,*) which is not equivalent with ἐν (*in,*) and no
less inconsistent with the use of ἐφ' ᾧ in combination, which, in 2 Cor. v.
4, means, as here, *because ;* in Philip. iii. 12, *for which cause ;* and in
Philip. iv. 10, *for which.* In other places where it occurs, it means *on
which,* as a bed, Mark ii. 4; Luke v. 25; or as a place, Acts vii. 33. 2.
The proper meaning of the words is, ἐπὶ τούτῳ ὅτι, *on account of this,* or
that. 3. The structure of the sentence is opposed to this explanation.
The antecedent ἀνθρώπου is too far separated from the relative ᾧ; almost
the whole verse intervenes between them. 4. This interpretation is altogether unnecessary. The ordinary and natural force of the words expresses
a perfectly good sense : 'All men die, *because* all sinned.' So Calvin,
quandoquidem, Luther, *dieweil,* and all the moderns, except a few of the
Romanists. "Sin brought death, death has come on all, *because* sin came
on all; ἐφ' ᾧ must therefore necessarily be taken as a conjunction."
Philippi.

As to the important words πάντες ἥμαρτον, rendered in our version *all
have sinned,* we find that several interpretations already referred to as growing out of the different views of the nature of man and of the plan of salvation. First, on the assumption that all sin consists in the voluntary

transgression of known law, and on the further assumption that one man cannot, in any legitimate sense, be said to sin in another, a large class of commentators, from Pelagius down, say these words can only mean that all have sinned in their own persons. Death has passed on all men, because all have actually sinned personally. This interpretation, although consistent with the signification of the verb ἁμαρτάνω, is, by the almost unanimous judgment of the Church, utterly inadmissible. 1. It is inconsistent with the force of the tense. The aorist (ἥμαρτον) does not mean *do* sin, nor *have* sinned, nor are accustomed to sin. It is the simple historical tense, expressing momentary action in past time. All sinned, *i.e.*, sinned in Adam, sinned through or by one man. " Omnes peccârunt, peccante Adamo." This is the literal, simple force of the words. 2. It is also incompatible with the design of this verse, to make ἥμαρτον refer to the personal sins of men. As so often remarked, the design is to show that Adam's sin, not our own, is the cause of death. 3. Verses 13, 14, are intended to prove what is asserted in ver. 12 ; but they do not prove that all men personally sin, but the very reverse. 4. This interpretation destroys the analogy between Adam and Christ. It would make the apostle teach, that as all men die because they personally sin, so all men live because they are personally and inherently righteous. This is contrary not only to this whole passage, but to all Paul's teaching, and to the whole gospel. 5. This interpretation is not only thus inconsistent with the force of the tense in which the verb ἁμαρτάνω is here used, with the design of the verse, with the apostle's argument, and the analogy between Christ and Adam, but it makes the apostle assert what is not true. It is not true that all die because all personally sin ; death is more extensive than personal transgression. This is a fact of experience, and is asserted by the apostle in what follows. This interpretation, therefore, brings the sacred writer into conflict with the truth. Candid expositors admit this. They say Paul's argument is founded on a false assumption, and proves nothing. Even Meyer, one of the most dignified and able of the modern German commentators, who often defends the sacred writers from the aspersions of irreverent expositors, is obliged to admit that in this case Paul forgot himself, and teaches what is not true. " The question," he says, " how Paul could write ἐφ' ᾧ πάντες ἥμαρτον (*since all sinned,*) when children die, although they have not sinned, can only be answered by admitting that he did not think of this necessary exception. For, on the one hand, πάντες must have the same extent of meaning as the previous εἰς πάντας ἀνθρώπους, and on the other hand, the death of innocent children is proof positive that death is not in *all* men the consequence of individual sin ; and hence, moreover, the whole doctrine that death is by divine constitution due to sin, is overthrown." An interpretation which makes the apostle teach what is not true, needs no further refutation.

A second large class of commentators, as they make ἁμαρτία, in the former clause of the verse, to mean *corruption*, translate ἐφ' ᾧ πάντες ἥμαρτον, *because all are corrupt*. Adam having defiled his own nature by sin, that depraved nature was transmitted to all his posterity, and therefore all die because they are thus inherently corrupt. We have already seen that this is Calvin's interpretation of these words : " Nempe, inquit, quoniam omnes peccavimus. Porro istud peccare est corruptos esse et vitiatos." In this view several of the modern commentators concur. According to this interpretation, the doctrine of the apostle is, that the inherent, hereditary corruption of nature derived from Adam, is the ground or reason why all die. This is what is called mediate imputation ; or the doctrine that not the sin of Adam, but inherent depravity derived from him, is the ground of the condemnation of his race. Although Calvin gives this interpretation of the passage on which this theory is founded, it is not to be inferred that he was an advocate of that theory. He frequently and clearly discriminates between inherent depravity as a ground of condemnation and the sin of Adam as distinct, and says that we are exposed to death, not solely for the one, but also for the other. He lived in a day when the imputation of Adam's sin was made, by the theologians of the Romish Church, so prominent as to leave inherent depravity almost entirely out of view. The whole tendency of the Reformers, therefore, was to go to the opposite extreme. Every theology is a gradual growth. It cost the Church ages of controversy, before the doctrines of the Trinity and of the Person of Christ were wrought out and definitively settled. In like manner, the Theology of the Reformation was a growth. It was not the reproduction of the theology of any class of the schoolmen, nor of Augustin as a whole. It was the gathering up and systematizing of the teachings of the Scriptures, and of the faith of the Church as founded on Scripture. That this should be done without any admixture of foreign elements, or as perfectly at the first attempt, as in the course of successive subsequent efforts, would have been a miracle. That it was done as 'perfectly as it was, is due, under God, to the fact that the Reformers were men endowed with minds of the very highest order, and filled with the Spirit of Christ. Still it is only in obedience to an established law, that the theology of the Reformation appears in a purer form in the writers of the seventeenth, than in those of the sixteenth century. We need not then be surprised that inconsistencies appear in the writings of Luther and Calvin, which are not reproduced in those of Hutter or Turrettin.

In opposition to the interpretation which makes πάντες ἥμαρτον mean *all became corrupt*, it is obvious to object, 1. That it is contrary to the simple meaning of the words. In no case has ἁμαρτάνω the sense here assigned to it. 2. It supposes that the corresponding phrase, " sin entered into the world," means " men became depraved," which, as we have seen, is not the true or adequate meaning. 3. It is inconsistent with the apostle's argument. Verses 13, 14, are designed to prove, and do prove, that *all men* sinned in Adam ; but do not prove, and cannot be made to prove, that all men are inherently corrupt. 4. It vitiates the whole analogy between Christ and Adam, and therefore saps the very foundation of the gospel. That doctrine on which the hope of God's people, either implicitly or explicitly, has ever been founded is, that the righteousness of Christ as something out of themselves, something distinguished from any act or subjective state of theirs, is the ground of their justification. They know that there is nothing in them on which they dare for a moment rely, as the reason why God should accept and pardon them. It is therefore the essential part of the analogy between Christ and Adam, the very truth which the apostle designs to set forth, that the sin of Adam, as distinguished from any act of ours, and from inherent corruption as derived from him, is the ground of our condemnation. If this be denied, then the other great truth must be denied, and our own subjective righteousness be made the ground of our justification ; which is to subvert the gospel. 5. This interpretation is inconsistent with the true meaning of verses 15—19, and with the often repeated and explicit declaration of the apostle, that the sin of Adam was the ground of our condemnation. Although, therefore, it is true that our nature was corrupted in Adam, and has been transmitted to us in a depraved state, yet that hereditary corruption is not here represented as the ground of our condemnation, any more than the holiness which believers derive from Christ is the ground of their justification.

A third class of interpreters, especially those of the later mystical school, understand the apostle to assert that all men sinned actually in Adam ; that his act was not merely representatively or putatively their act, but theirs in the strict and proper sense of the term. He being not simply *a* man as one among many, but *the* man in whom humanity was concentrated as a generic life, his act as an act of that generic humanity was the act of all the individuals in whom human nature subsequently developed itself. But, 1. In the first place, the proposition " all men sinned actually in Adam," has no meaning. To say that " in Adam all die," conveys a distinct idea; but to say that " all actually expired in Adam," conveys no idea at all. It has no sense. Even on the extremest realistic assumption that humanity as such is an entity, the act of Adam was not the act of all men. His act may have vitiated his generic nature, not only for his own person, but for his posterity ; but this a very different thing from his act being their act. His sin was an intelligent act of self-determination ; but an act of rational self-determination is a personal act. Unless, therefore, all men as persons existed in Adam, it is impossible that they acted his act. To say that a man acted thousands of years before his personality began, does not rise even to the dignity of a contradiction ; it has no meaning at all. It is a monstrous evil to make the Bible contradict the common sense and common consciousness of men. This is to make God contradict himself. 2. It is hardly necessary to add, that this interpretation is inconsistent with the whole drift and design of the passage, and with the often repeated assertion of the apostle, that for the offence of one man (not of all men), the judgment came on all men to condemnation. If we all actually sinned in Adam, so that his act was strictly ours, then we all obeyed in Christ, and his righteousness and death were strictly our own acts; which again is not only unscriptural, but impossible.

The fourth class of interpreters, including commentators of every grade of orthodoxy, agree in saying that what is meant is, that all sinned in Adam as their head and representative. Such was the relation, natural and federal, between him and his posterity, that his act was putatively their act. That is, it was the judicial ground or reason why death passed on all men. In other words, they were regarded and treated as sinners on account of his sin. In support of this interpretation, it may be urged, 1. That it is the simple meaning of the words. It has already been remarked, that the aorist ἡμαρτον does not mean *are sinful*, or *have sinned*, but simply *sinned*. All sinned when Adam sinned. They sinned in him. But the only possible way in which all men can be said to have sinned in Adam, is putatively. His act, for some good and proper reason, was regarded as their act, just as the act of an agent is regarded as the act of his principal, or the act of a representative as that of his constituents. The act of the one legally binds the others. It is, in the eye of law and justice, their act. 2. This is sustained by the analogy of Scripture. Paul says, " in Adam all died." This cannot possibly be understood to mean that all men expired when Adam died. It can only mean that when Adam incurred the sentence of death for himself, he incurred it also for us. In like manner we are said to die in Christ ; we "were crucified with him," we "rose with him," we are now "sitting with him in heavenly places." All this obviously means, that as Christ was the head and representative of his people, all that he did in that character, they are regarded as having done. The rationalistic and the mystical interpretations of such passages are only different modes of philosophizing away the meaning of Scripture —the one having what is called "common sense," and the other pantheism as its basis. 3. The common interpretation of this passage may, in another form, be shown to be in accordance with scriptural usage. As remarked above, ἁμαρτία sometimes means *guilt*, and the phrase "sin entered into the world," may mean *men became guilty;* and ἁμαρτάνω at times means *to contract guilt;* or, as Wahl in his Lexicon defines its *peccati culpam sustineo;* equivalent to ἁμαρτωλὸς κατεστάθην. He refers to the use of חטא in Gen. xliv. 32, a passage which the LXX. renders ἡμαρτηκὼς ἔσομαι ; the Vulgate, *peccati reus ero;* Luther, "will ich die Schuld tragen ;" and the English, *I shall bear the blame.* So in Gen. xliii. 9, Judah says to his father, "If I bring him not back, I will bear the blame (literally, *I will sin*) all my days." In 1 Kings i. 21, Bathsheba says to David, (according to the Hebrew), "I and my son Solomon shall be sinners," where the LXX. translates, ἐσόμεθα ἐγὼ καὶ Σαλομὼν ὁ υἱός μου ἁμαρτωλοί, the sense of the passage being, as correctly expressed in our version, "I and my son Solomon shall be counted offenders." To sin, therefore, or to be a sinner may, in Scriptural language, mean *to be counted an offender*, that is, to be regarded and treated as such. When, therefore, the apostle says that *all men sinned* in Adam, it is in accordance not only with the nature of the case, but with scriptural usage, to understand him to mean that we are regarded and treated as sinners on his account. His sin was the reason why death came upon all men. Of course all that is meant by this is the universally recognised distinction between the signification and the sense of a word. Πάντες ἥμαρτον *signifies* "all sinned," and it can signify nothing else ; just as πάντες ἀπέθανον, 2 Cor. v. 15, *signifies* "all died." But when you ask in what *sense* all died in Christ, or all sinned in Adam, the question is to be answered from the nature of the case and the analogy of Scripture. We did not all literally and actually die in Christ, neither did we all actually sin in Adam. The death of Christ, however, was legally and effectively our death ; and the sin of Adam was legally and effectively our sin. 4. It is almost universally conceded that this 12th verse contains the first member of a comparison which, in vers. 18, 19, is resumed and carried out. But in those verses it is distinctly taught that 'judgment came on all men on account of the offence of one man.' This therefore is Paul's own interpretation of what he meant when he said "all sinned." They sinned in Adam. His sin was regarded as theirs. 5. This interpretation is demanded by the connection of this verse with those immediately following. Verses 13, 14, introduced by *for*, are confessedly designed to prove the assertion of ver. 12. If that assertion is, 'all men are regarded as sinners on account of Adam,' the meaning and pertinency of these verses are clear. But if ver. 12 asserts merely that all men are sinners, then vers. 13, 14 must be regarded as proving that men were sinners before the time of Moses—a point which no one denied, and no one doubted, and which is here entirely foreign to the apostle's object. Or if πάντες ἥμαρτον be made to mean *all became corrupt*, the objection still remains. The passage does not prove what it is designed to prove. Verses 13, 14, therefore, present insuperable difficulties, if we assign any other meaning than that just given to verse 12. 6. What verse 12 is thus made to assert, and verses 13, 14 to prove, is in verses 15—19, assumed as proved, and is employed in illustration of the great truth to be established : " For if through the offence of one many be dead," ver. 15. But where it is said, or where proved, that the many die for the offence of one, if not in ver. 12, and vs. 13, 14 ? So in all the other verses. This idea, therefore, must be contained in ver. 12, if any consistency is to be maintained between the several parts of the apostle's argument. 7. This interpretation is required by the whole scope of the passage, and drift of the argument. The scope of the passage, as shown above, is to illustrate the doctrine of justification on the ground of the righteousness of Christ, by a reference to the condemnation of men for the sin of Adam. The analogy is destroyed, the very point of the comparison fails, if anything in us be assumed as the ground of the infliction of the penal evils of which the apostle is here speaking. That we have corrupt natures, and are personally sinners, and therefore liable to other and further inflictions, is indeed true, but nothing to the point. In like manner it is true that we are sanctified by our union with Christ, and thus fitted for heaven ; but these ideas are out of place when speaking of justification. It is to illustrate that doctrine, or the idea of imputed righteousness, that this whole passage is devoted ; and, therefore, the idea of *imputed sin* must be contained in the other part of the comparison, unless the whole be a failure. Not only does the scope of the passage demand this view, but it is only thus that the argument of the apostle can be con sistently carried through. We die on account of Adam's sin, ver. 12 ; this is true, because on no other ground can the universality of *death* be accounted for, vers. 13, 14. But if we all die on Adam's account, how much more shall we live on account of Christ ! ver. 15. Adam indeed brings upon us the evil inflicted for the first great violation of the covenant, but Christ saves us from all our numberless sins, ver. 16. As, therefore, for the offence of one we are condemned, so for the righteousness of one we are justified, ver 18. As on account of the disobedience of one we are treated as sinners, so on account of the obedience of one we are treated as righteous, ver. 19. The inconsistency and confusion consequent upon attempting to carry either of the other interpretations through, must be obvious to any attentive reader of such attempts. 8. The doctrine which the verse explained teaches, is one of the plainest truths of the Scriptures and of experience. Is it not a revealed fact above all contradiction, and sustained by the whole history of the world, that the sin of Adam altered the relation in which our race stood to God ? Did not that sin of itself, and independently of anything in us, or done by us, bring evil on the world ? In other words, did we not fall when Adam fell ? The principle involved in this great transaction is explicitly and frequently asserted in the word of God, and runs through all the dispensations of his providence. He solemnly declares himself to be a God who " visits the iniquities of the fathers upon the children, and upon the children's children unto the third and fourth generation." And so he does. The curse of Canaan fell on his posterity ; the Egyptians perished for the sins of Pharaoh ; the Moabites and Amalekites were destroyed for the transgressions of their fathers ; the leprosy of Naaman was to cleave to Gehazi, and " to his seed for ever ;" the blood of all the prophets was exacted, says our Lord, of the men of his generation. We must become not only infidels but atheists, if we deny that God deals thus with men, not merely as individuals, but as communities and on the principle of imputation. The apostacy of our race in Adam, therefore, and the imputation of his sin to his posterity, although the most signal of the illustrations of this principle, is only one among thousands of a like kind. 9. The doctrine of the imputation of Adam's sin, or that on account of that sin all men are regarded and treated as sinners, was a common Jewish doctrine at the time of the apostle as well as at a later period. He employs the same mode of expression on the subject, which the Jews were accustomed to use. They could not have failed, therefore, to understand him as meaning to convey by these expressions the ideas usually connected with them. And such, therefore, if the apostle wished to be understood, must have been his intention ; see the Targum on Ruth iv. 22, " On account of the counsel given to Eve (and her eating the fruit,) all the inhabitants of the world were constituted guilty of death." R. Moses of Trana, Beth Elohim, fol. 105, *i. e.* " With the same sin with which Adam sinned, sinned the whole world." Many such passages are to be found in the pages of Wetstein, Schœttgen, Eisenmenger, Tholuck, and other collectors and commentators. Meyer therefore admits that such was undeniably the doctrine of the Jews. On this point, Knapp, in his Theological Lectures (German edition, page 29,) says, " In the Mosaic account of the fall, and in the Old Testament generally, the imputation of Adam's sin is not mentioned under the term *imputation*, although the doctrine is contained therein." " But in the writings of the Talmudists and Rabbins, and earlier in the Chaldee Paraphrases of the Old Testament, we find the following position asserted in express words, 'that the descendants of Adam would have been punished with death (of the body) on account of his sin, although they themselves had committed no sin.'" On the next page he remarks, " We find this doctrine most clearly in the New Testament, in Rom. v. 12, &c. The modern philosophers and theologians found here much which was inconsistent with their philosophical systems. Hence many explained and refined on the passage, until the idea of imputation was entirely excluded. They forgot, however, that Paul used the very words and expressions in common use on the subject at that time among the Jews, and that his immediate readers could not have understood him otherwise than as teaching this doctrine." And he immediately goes on to show, that unless we are determined to do violence to the words of the apostle, we must admit that he represents all men as subject to death on account of the sin of Adam. This is a theologian who did not himself admit the doctrine.

It may be well to remark, that this interpretation, so far from being the offspring of theological prejudice, or fondness for any special theory, is so obviously the true and simple meaning of the passage required by the context, that it has the sanction of theologians of every grade and class of doctrine. Calvinists, Arminians, Lutherans, and Rationalists, agree in its support. Thus Storr, one of the most accurate of philological interpreters, explains the last words of the verse in the manner stated above : " By one man all are subject to death, because all are regarded and treated as sinners, *i. e.* because all lie under the sentence of condemnation." The phrase, *all have sinned*, ver. 12, he says is equivalent to *all are constituted sinners*, ver. 19 ; which latter expression he renders, " sie werden als Sünder angesehen und behandelt," that is, they were regarded and treated as sinners ; see his Commentary on Hebrews, pp. 636, 640, &c. (Flatt renders *these words* in precisely the same manner.) The Rationalist, Ammon, also considers the apostle as teaching, that on account of the sin of Adam all men are subject to death ; see Excursus C. to Koppe's Commentary on the Epistle to the Romans. Zachariæ, in his *Biblische Theologie,* Vol. VI., p. 128, has an excellent exposition of this whole passage. The question of the imputation of Adam's sin, he says, is this, "whether God regarded the act of Adam as the act of all men, or, which is the same thing, whether he has subjected them all to punishment on account of this single act." This, he maintains, the apostle asserts and proves. On this verse he remarks : "The question is not here immediately about the propagation of a corrupted nature to all men, and of the personal sins committed by all men, but of universal guilt (*Strafwürdigkeit,* liability to punishment,) in the sight of God, which has come upon all men ; and which Paul, in the sequel, does not rest on the personal sins of men, but only on the offence of one man, Adam, ver. 16." Neither the corruption of nature, nor the actual sins of men, and their liability on account of them, is either questioned or denied, but the simple statement is, that on account of the sin of Adam, all men are treated as sinners. Zachariæ, it must be remembered, was not a Calvinist, but one of the modern and moderate theologians of Göttingen. Whitby, the great advocate of Arminianism, says on these words : "It is not true that death came upon all men, *for that,* or *because* all have sinned. [*He* contends for the rendering, *in whom.*] For the apostle directly here asserts the contrary, viz., that the death and the condemnation to it, which befell all men, was for the sin of Adam only ; for here it is expressly said, that *by the sin of one man many died;* that *the sentence was from one,* and *by one man sinning to condemnation ;* and that *by the sin of one, death reigned by one.* Therefore, the apostle doth expressly teach us that this death, this condemnation to it, came not upon us for the sin of all, but only for the sin of one, *i. e.,* of that one Adam, *in whom all men die,* 1 Cor. xv. 22." Dr. Wordsworth, Canon of Westminster, in his recent edition of the New Testament, says, in his comment on this verse : "Observe the *aorist* tense, ἥμαρτον, *they all sinned;* that is, at a particular time, And when was that? Doubtless at the fall. All men sinned in Adam's sin. All fell in his fall." Philippi says : "We must supply in thought to ἥμαρτον, ἐν 'Aδάμ, or more precisely, *Adamo peccante.* 'Non agitur de peccato singulorum,' says Bengel, 'omnes peccârunt, Adamo peccante.'" Such extracts might be indefinitely multiplied from the most varied sources. However these commentators may differ in other points, they almost all agree in the general idea, which is the sum of the whole passage, that the sin of Adam, and not their own individual actual transgressions, is the ground and reason of the subjection of all men to the penal evils here spoken of. With what plausibility can an interpretation, commanding the assent of men so various, be ascribed to theory or philosophy, or love of a particular theological system? May not its rejection with more probability be attributed, as is done by Knapp, to theological prejudice? Certain it is, at least, that the objections against it are almost exclusively of a philosophical or theological, rather than of an exegetical or philological character.

VERSES 13, 14. *For until the law. sin was in the world,* &c. These verses are connected by *for* with ver. 12, as introducing the proof of the declaration that death had passed on all men, on account of one man. The proof is this : the infliction of penal evils implies the violation of law ; the violation of the law of Moses will not account for the universality of death, because men died before that law was given. Neither is the violation of the law of nature sufficient to explain the fact that all men are subject to death, because even those die who have never broken that law. As, therefore, death supposes transgression, and neither the law of Moses nor the law of nature embraces all the victims of death, it follows that men are subject to penal evils on account of the sin of Adam. It is for the offence of one that many die.

In order to the proper understanding of the apostle's argument, it should be borne in mind that the term *death* stands for penal evil ; not for this or that particular form of it, but for any and every evil judicially inflicted for the support of law. Paul's reasoning does not rest upon the mere fact that all men, even infants, are subject to natural death ; for this might be accounted for by the violation of the law of Moses, or of the law of nature, or by their inherent native depravity. This covers the whole ground, and may account for the universality of natural death. But no one of these causes, nor all combined, can account for the infliction of all the penal evils to which men are subjected. The great fact in the apostle's mind was, that God regards and treats all men, from the first moment of their existence, as out of fellowship with himself, as having forfeited his favour. Instead of entering into communion with them the moment they begin to exist (as he did with Adam,) and forming them by his spirit in his own moral image, he regards them as out of his favour, and withholds the influences of the Spirit. Why is this ? Why does God thus deal with the human race ? The fact that he does thus deal with them is not denied by any except Pelagians. Why then is it ? Here is a form of death which the violation of the law of Moses, the transgression of the law of nature, the existence of innate depravity, separately or combined, are insufficient to account for. Its infliction is antecedent to them all ; and yet it is of all evils the essence and the sum. Men begin to exist out of communion with God. This is the fact which no sophistry can get out of the Bible or the history of the world. Paul tells us why it is. It is because we fell in Adam ; it is for the one offence of ONE MAN that all thus die. The covenant being formed with Adam, not only for himself, but also for his posterity (in other words, Adam having been placed on trial, not for himself only, but also for his race,) his act was, in virtue of this relation, regarded as our act ; God withdrew from us as he did from him ; in consequence of this withdrawing, we begin to exist in moral darkness, destitute of a disposition to delight in God, and prone to delight in ourselves and the world. The sin of Adam, therefore, ruined us ; it was the ground of the withdrawing of the divine favour from the whole race ; and the intervention of the Son of God in our salvation is an act of pure, sovereign, and wonderful grace.

Whatever obscurity, therefore, rests upon this passage, arises from taking the word *death* in the narrow sense in which it is commonly used among men. If taken in its scriptural sense, the whole argument is plain and conclusive. Let *penal evil* be substituted for the word *death*, and the argument will stand thus : ' All men are subject to penal evils on account of one man ; this is the position to be proved, ver. 12. That such is the case is evident, because the infliction of a penalty supposes the violation of law. But such evil was inflicted before the giving of the Mosaic law ; it comes on men before the transgression of the law of nature, or even the existence of inherent depravity ; it must therefore be for the offence of one man that judgment has come upon all men to condemnation.' The wide sense in which the sacred writers used the word *death*, accounts for the fact that the dissolution of the body (which is one form of the manifestation of the divine displeasure) is not only included in it, but is often the prominent idea.

Until the law. The *law* here mentioned is evidently the law of Moses. The word ἄχρι is properly rendered *until,* and not *during the continuance of,* a sense which the particle has in some passages. *Until the law* is immediately explained by the words *from Adam to Moses. Sin was in the world, i. e.* men were sinners, and were so regarded and treated. *Sin is not imputed,* that is, it is not laid to one's account, and punished. See iv. 8, "Blessed is the man to whom the Lord imputeth not iniquity;" and the familiar equivalent expressions. "His iniquity shall be upon him," Numb. xv. 31 ; and, "He shall bear his iniquity." The word (ἐλλογεῖται) here used, occurs nowhere else in any Greek writer, except in Philemon 18. The common word for impute is λογίζομαι. *When there is no law, μὴ ὄντος νόμου, there not being law.* Sin is correlative of law. If there is no law, there can be no sin, as Paul had already taught, iv. 15. But if there is no sin without law, there can be no imputation of sin. As, however, sin was imputed, as sin was in the world, as men were sinners, and were so regarded and treated before the law of Moses, it follows that there must be some more comprehensive law in relation to which men were sinners, and in virtue of which they were so regarded and treated. The principle here advanced, and on which the apostle's argument rests is, that the infliction of penal evil implies the violation of law. If men were sinners, and were treated as such before the law of Moses, it is certain that there is some other law, for the violation of which sin was imputed to them.

Instead of the interpretation just given, there are several other methods of explaining this verse, which should be noticed. Calvin, Luther, Beza, and not a few of the modern commentators, say that the clause, *sin is not imputed when there is no law,* means, men do not impute sin to themselves, *i. e.* do not regard themselves as sinners ; do not feel their guilt, when there is no law. To a certain extent, the sentiment thus expressed is true. Paul, in a subsequent chapter, vii. 8, says, "Without the law, sin was dead ;" that is, unknown and disregarded. It is true, that ignorance of the law renders the conscience torpid, and that by the clear revelation of the law it is brought to life ; so that by the law is the knowledge of sin. If, however, by *law,* is meant a written law, or a full and authenticated revelation of the will of God as a rule of duty, then it is only comparatively speaking true, that without law (*i. e.* such a law,) sin is unknown or disregarded. There is another law, as Paul teaches, ii. 14, 15, written on the heart, in virtue of which men feel themselves to be sinners, and know the righteous judgment of God, by which they are exposed to death ; see i. 32. The objections, however, to this interpretation are decisive : 1. In the first place, it is inconsistent with the meaning of the words here used. "To impute sin" never means to lay sin to heart. The imputation is always made from without, or by another, not by the sinner himself. Tholuck, therefore, calls this interpretation "a desperate shift." "Noch," he says, "ist eine gewalt same Hülfe zu erwähnen die Manche diesem Aussprüche des Apostels zu bringen gesucht haben. Sie haben dem ἐλλογεῖν eine andere Bedeutung beigelegt. Sie haben es in der Bedeutung *achten, Rücksicht nehmen* genommen." 2. This interpretation proceeds on a wrong assumption of the thing to be proved. It assumes that the apostle designs to prove that all men are in themselves sinners, and for their personal guilt or defilement, are exposed to death. But this, as has been shown, leaves out of view the main idea of ver. 12. It is true, that all men are sinners, either in the sense of actual transgressors, or of having a depraved nature, and consequently are exposed to death ; but the specific assertion of ver. 12 is, that it was BY ONE MAN death passed on all men. This, therefore, is the thing to be proved, and not that all men are person- ally sinners. Of course it is not denied that men are subject to death for their own sins ; but that is nothing to the point which the apostle has in hand. His design is to show that there is a form of death, or penal evil, to which men are subject, anterior to any personal transgression or inher- ent corruption. 3. This interpretation assumes that the apostle is answer- ing an objection which has no force, or refuting an opinion which no one entertained. It supposes that the Jews held that the Gentiles, before the law of Moses, were not sinners, whereas they regarded them as pre-emin- ently such. It makes the apostle reason thus : 'All men are sinners. No,' objects the Jew, ' before Moses there was no law, and therefore no sin. Yes,' replies Paul, ' they were sinners, although they were not aware of it.' But as no human being believed that men were not sinners before the giving of the Mosaic law, as Paul himself had proved at length that the whole world was guilty before God, as he had expressly taught that the Gentiles, although they had no written law, were a law unto them- selves, and that they stood self-condemned in the presence of God, it is unreasonable to suppose that the apostle would stop to refute an objection which has not force enough to be even a cavil. Paul had before laid down the principle (iv. 15,) that where there is no law, there is no trans- gression, which is only another form of saying, " sin is not imputed when there is no law." But as sin was imputed before the law of Moses, there must have been some other law, for the violation of which men were con- demned. It is that the apostle designs to prove, and not that men were personally sinners ; a fact, so far as the heathen were concerned, no Jew denied.

Another interpretation, which is adopted by a large number of com- mentators and theologians, supposes that the word *death* is to be understood of natural death alone. The reasoning of the apostle then is, ' As on account of the sin of one man, all men are condemned to die, so on account of the righteousness of one, all are made partakers of life,' ver. 12. The proof that all are subject to death on account of the sin of Adam, is given in vers. 13, 14 ; ' The infliction of the specific penalty of death, supposes the violation of a law to which that particular penalty was attached. This could not be the law of Moses, since those die who never violated that law ; and, in short, all men die, although they have never broken any express command attended by the sanction of death. The liability of all men, therefore, to this specific form of evil, is to be traced not to their own individual character or conduct, but to the sin of Adam.' Some of those who adopt this view of the passage, are consistent enough to carry it through, and make the *life* which is restored to all by Christ, as here spoken of, to be nothing more than the life of the body, *i.e.* the resurrec- tion from the dead.* It will be observed, that this interpretation is, as to its main principle, identical with that presented above as correct. That is, it assumes that ver. 12 teaches that God regarded the act of Adam as the act of the whole race, or in other words, that he subjected all men to punishment on account of his transgression. And it makes vers. 13, 14,

---

* See Whitby on this passage.

the proof that the subjection of all men to the penal evil here specially in view, to be, not the corruption of their nature, nor their own individual sins, but the sin of Adam. It is, however, founded on two assumptions; the one of which is erroneous, and the other gratuitous. In the first place, it assumes that the *death* here spoken of is mere natural death, which, as shown above, is contrary both to the scriptural use of the term and to the immediate context. And, secondly, it assumes that the violation of the law of nature could not be justly followed by the death of the body, because that particular form of evil was not threatened as the sanction of that law. But this assumption is gratuitous, and would be as well authorised if made in reference to any other punishment of such transgressions ; since no definite specific evil, as the expression of the divine displeasure, was made known to those who had no external revelation. Yet, as Paul says, Rom. i. 32, the wicked heathen knew they were worthy of death, *i.e.* of the effects of the divine displeasure. The particular manner of the exhibition of that displeasure is a matter of indifference. It need hardly be remarked that it is not involved either in this or the commonly received interpretation of this passage, that men, before the time of Moses, were not punishable for their own sins. While this is admitted and asserted by the apostle, he proves that they were punished for Adam's sin. No one feels that there is any inconsistency in asserting of the men of this generation, that although responsible to God for their personal transgressions, they are nevertheless born in a state of spiritual death, as a punishment of the sin of our great progenitor. The pains of child birth do not cease to be part of the penalty of the original transgression, although each suffering mother is burdened with the guilt of personal transgression.

As the effort to make these verses prove that all men are actual sinners fails of giving them any satisfactory sense, so the interpretation which assumes that they are designed to prove inherent, hereditary depravity, is no less untenable. If ἐφ' ᾧ πάντες ἥμαρτον, in ver. 12, means, ' Death has passed on all, *because all are tainted with the hereditary corruption derived from Adam,*' then the argument in verses 13, 14, must stand thus : ' All men are by nature corrupt, for as sin is not imputed when there is no law, the death of all men cannot be accounted for on the ground of their actual sins ; therefore, since those die who have never sinned, as Adam did, against a positive law, they must be subject to death for their innate depravity.' But, so far as this argument assumes that men, before the time of Moses, were not justly subject to death for their actual sins, it is contrary to truth, and to the express teaching of the apostle. Yet this is the form in which it is generally presented. And if it only means that actual sin will not account for the absolute universality of death, since those die who have never committed any actual transgression, the argument is still defective. Innate depravity being universal, may account for the universality of natural death ; but θάνατος includes much more than natural death. What is to account for spiritual death ? Why are men born dead in sin ? This is the very thing to be accounted for. The fact is not its own solution. Paul's argument is, that they are so born on account of Adam's sin. It is another objection to this interpretation, that it destroys he analogy between Christ and Adam, and therefore is inconsistent with the great design of the whole passage. Paul's object is to show, that as we are justified by the righteousness of Christ as something out of ourselves, so we are condemned for the sin of Adam as something out of ourselves.

To make him teach that we are condemned for our inherent depravity, to the exclusion of Adam's sin, necessitates his teaching that we are justified for our inherent goodness, which destroys all hope of heaven. There is no interpretation of this passage consistent with the meaning of the words, the nature of the argument, the design of the context, and the analogy of Scripture, but the one given above, as commonly received. Köllner complains that Paul's argument is very confused. This he accounts for by assuming that the apostle had two theories in his mind. The one, that men die for their own sins ; the other, that they die for the sin of Adam. His natural feelings led him to adopt the former, and he accordingly says, in verse 12, "Death passed on all men, because all have sinned." But as the Jewish doctrine of his age, that men were condemned for the sin of Adam, afforded such an admirable illustration of his doctrine of salvation through the merit of Christ, the apostle, says Köllner, could not help availing himself of it. Thus he has the two theories mixed up together, asserting sometimes the one, and sometimes the other. To those who reverence the Scriptures as the word of God, it is assuredly a strong argument in favour of the common interpretation of the passage, that it saves the sacred writer from such aspersions. It is better to admit the doctrine of imputation, than to make the apostle contradict himself.

VERSE 14. *Nevertheless death reigned from Adam to Moses.* That is, men were subject to death before the law of Moses was given, and consequently not on account of violating it. There must be some other ground, therefore, of their exposure to death. *Nevertheless* (αλλά), the clause thus introduced stands in opposition to the preceding clause, οὐκ ἐλλογεῖται. That is, ' *although* sin is not imputed when there is no law, *nevertheless* death reigned from Adam to Moses.' *Death reigned, i. e.*, had undisputed, rightful sway. Men were justly subject to his power, and therefore were sinners.

Even over them that had not sinned after the similitude of Adam's transgression. Instead of connecting ἐπὶ τῷ ὁμοιώματι, as is usually done with μὴ ἁμαρτήσαντας, Chrysostom connects them with ἐβασίλευσεν. The sense would then be, 'death reigned after the similitude of Adam's transgression, even over those who had not sinned.' That is, death reigned over those who had not personally sinned, just as it reigned over Adam. This interpretation is adopted by Bengel, who says, "Quod homines ante legem mortui sunt, id accidit eis *super similitudine transgressionis Adam, i. e.*, quia illorum eadem atque Adami transgredientis ratio fuit : mortui sunt, propter alium reatum, non propter eum, quem ipsi per se contraxere, id est, propter reatum ab Adamo contractum." Although the sense thus expressed is good, and suited to the context, the construction is evidently forced. It is much more natural to take the words as they stand. Death reigned over a class of persons who had not sinned as Adam had. The question is, What is the point of dissimilarity to which the apostle here refers ? Some say it is, that Adam violated a positive command to which the sanction of death was expressly added, and that those referred to did not. The principal objections to this interpretation are, 1. That it destroys the distinction between the two classes of persons here alluded to. It makes Paul, in effect, reason thus : ' Death reigned over those who had not violated any positive law, even over those who had not violated any positive law.' It is obvious that the first clause of the verse describes a general class, and the second clause, which is distinguished from the first by the word *even*, only a portion of that class. All men who died from

Adam to Moses, died without violating a positive command. The class, therefore, which is distinguished from them, must be contrasted with Adam on some other ground than that which is common to the whole. 2. This interpretation is inconsistent with the context, because it involves us in all the difficulties specified above, attending the sense which it requires us to put upon verses 13, 14, and their connection with ver. 12. We must suppose these verses designed to prove that all men are sinners, which, as just shown, is at variance with the context, with the obvious meaning of ver. 12, with the scope of the passage, and the drift of the argument. Or we must adopt the interpretation of those who confine the word *death* to the dissolution of the body, and make the apostle argue to show that this particular evil is to be referred not to the personal sins of men, but to the sin of Adam. Or we are driven to some other unsatisfactory view of the passage. In short, these verses, when the clause in question is thus explained, present insuperable difficulties.

Others understand the difference between Adam and those intended to be described in this clause, to be, that Adam sinned personally and actually, the others did not. In favour of this view it may be argued, 1. That the words evidently admit of this interpretation as naturally as of the other. Paul simply says, the persons referred to did not sin as Adam did. Whether he means that they did not sin at all ; that they were not sinners in the ordinary sense of that term ; or that they had not sinned against the same kind of law, depends on the context, and is not determined by the mere form of expression. 2. If ver. 12 teaches that men are subject to death on account of the sin of Adam, if this is the doctrine of the whole passage, and if, as is admitted, vers. 13, 14 are designed to prove the assertion of ver. 12, then is it necessary that the apostle should show that death comes on those who have no personal or actual sins to answer for. This he does : ' Death reigns not only over those who have never broken any positive law, but even over those who have never sinned as Adam did ; that is, who have never in their own persons violated any law, by which their exposure to death can be accounted for.' All the arguments, therefore, which go to establish the interpretation given above of ver. 12, or the correctness of the exhibition of the course of the apostle's argument, and the design of the whole passage, bear with all their force in support of the view here given of this clause. The opposite interpretation, as was attempted to be proved above, rests on a false exegesis of ver. 12, and a false view of the context. Almost all the objections to this interpretation, being founded on misapprehension, are answered by the mere statement of the case. The simple doctrine and argument of the apostle is, that THERE ARE PENAL EVILS WHICH COME UPON MEN ANTECEDENT TO ANY TRANSGRESSIONS OF THEIR OWN ; AND AS THE INFLICTION OF THESE EVILS IMPLIES A VIOLATION OF LAW, IT FOLLOWS THAT THEY ARE REGARDED AND TREATED AS SINNERS, ON THE GROUND OF THE DISOBEDIENCE OF ANOTHER. In other words, it was "by the offence of one man that judgment came on all men to condemnation." It is of course not implied in this statement or argument, that men are not now, or were not from Adam to Moses, punishable for their own sins, but simply that they are subject to penal evils, which cannot be accounted for on the ground of their personal transgressions, or their hereditary depravity. This statement, which contains the whole doctrine of imputation, is so obviously contained in the argument of the apostle, and stands out so conspicuously in the Bible, and is so fully established by the history of the world, that it is frequently and freely admitted by the great majority of commentators.

Who is a figure of him that was to come, τύπος τοῦ μέλλοντος. Πῶς τύπος; φησίν· ὅτι ὥσπερ ἐκεῖνος τοῖς ἐξ αὐτοῦ, καίτοιγε μὴ φαγοῦσιν ἀπὸ τοῦ ξύλου, γέγονεν αἴτιος θανάτου τοῦ διὰ τὴν βρῶσιν εἰσαχθέντος, οὕτω καὶ ὁ Χριστὸς τοῖς ἐξ αὐτοῦ, καίτοιγε οὐ δικαιοπραγήσασι, γέγονε πρόξενος δικαιοσύνης, ἥν διὰ τοῦ σταυροῦ πᾶσιν ἡμῖν ἐχαρίσατο· διὰ τοῦτο ἄνω καὶ κάτω τοῦ ἑνὸς ἔχεται, καὶ συνεχῶς τοῦτο εἰς μέσον φέρει.—*Chrysostom.* " How a type ? he says : because *as* he was the cause of the death introduced by eating (the forbidden fruit,) to all who are of him, although they did not eat of the tree ; *so* also Christ, to those who are of him, though they have not wrought righteousness, is become the procurer of the righteousness which, by means of the cross, he graciously gives to us all ; on this account he first and last makes *the one* so prominent, continually bringing it forward." This is an interesting passage coming from a source so different from the Augustinian school of theology. Every essential point of the common Calvinistic interpretation is fully stated. Adam is the cause of death coming on all, independently of any transgressions of their own ; as Christ is the author of justification without our own works. And *the many*, in the one clause, are all who are of Adam ; and *the many*, in the other, those who are of Christ.

The word rendered *figure*, τύπος, from τύπτω (*to strike*,) means *a print*, or *impression* made by a blow ; as in John xx. 25, τὸν τύπον τῶν ἥλων, *the print of the nails*. In a wider sense it means *a figure* or *form*, literally, as when spoken of an image, Acts vii. 43, or figuratively when used of a doctrine, Rom. vi. 17. More commonly in the Scriptures it means either a model after which anything is to be made, Heb. viii. 5, or an example to be followed, Philip. iii. 17, " as ye have us for an example," καθὼς ἔχετε τύπον ἡμᾶς. Besides these, so to speak secular meanings, it has the religious sense of *type*, a designed prefiguration or counterpart; either historically, as the passover was a *type* or significant commemoration of the passing over, by the destroying angel, of the habitations of the Hebrews in Egypt ; or prophetically, as the sacrifices of the Old Testament were types of the great sacrifice of the Lamb of God. A type, therefore, in the religious sense of the term, is not a mere historical parallel or incidental resemblance between persons or events, but a designed resemblance—the one being intended to prefigure or to commemorate the other. It is in this sense that Adam was the type of Christ. The resemblance between them was not casual. It was predetermined, and entered into the whole plan of God. As Adam was the head and representative of his race, whose destiny was suspended on his conduct, so Christ is the head and representative of his people. As the sin of the one was the ground of our condemnation, so the righteousness of the other is the ground of our justification. This relation between Adam and the Messiah was recognized by the Jews, who called their expected deliverer, הָאָדָם הָאַחֲרוֹן, *the last Adam*, as Paul also calls him in 1 Cor. xv. 45, ὁ ἔσχατος Αδάμ. Adam was the type, τοῦ μέλλοντος, either of the *Adam* who was to come, or simply *of the one to come*. The Old Testament system was preparatory and prophetic. The people under its influence were looking forward to the accomplishment of the promises made to their father. The Messianic period on which their hopes were fixed was called " the world or age to come," and the Messiah himself was ὁ ἐρχόμενος, ὁ μέλλων, *the one coming.**

* Philippi, Professor in the University at Rostock, one of the most recent as he is one of the best of the German commentators, says, in a note to this passage, " The Protestant

As Paul commenced this section with the design of instituting this comparison between Christ and Adam, and interrupted himself to prove, in vers. 13, 14, that Adam was really the representative of his race, or that all men are subject to death for his offence ; and having, at the close of verse 14, announced the fact of this resemblance by calling Adam a type of Christ, he again stops to limit and explain this declaration by pointing out the real nature of the analogy. This he does principally by showing, in vers. 15—17, the particulars in which the comparison does not hold. In verses 18, 19, which are a resumption of the sentiment of ver. 12, he states the grand point of their agreement.

VERSE 15. *But not as the offence, so also is the free gift.* The cases, although parallel, are not precisely alike. In the first place, it is far more consistent with our views of the character of God, that many should be benefited by the merit of one man, than that they should suffer for the sin of one. If the latter has happened, MUCH MORE may we expect the former to occur. The attentive reader of this passage will perceive constantly increasing evidence that the design of the apostle is not to show that the blessings procured by Christ are greater than the evils caused by Adam ; but to illustrate and confirm the prominent doctrine of the epistle, that we are justified on the ground of the righteousness of Christ. This is obvious from the sentiment of this verse, ' If we die for the sin of Adam, *much more* may we live through the righteousness of Christ.' *But not as the offence, &c.* Ἀλλ' οὐχ ὡς τὸ παράπτωμα, οὕτω καὶ τὸ χάρισμα, a singularly concise expression, which however the context renders sufficiently plain. Παράπτωμα from παραπίπτω (to fall,) means *fall,* and χάρισμα, *an act of grace* or *gracious gift,* which is explained by ἡ δωρεά in this verse, τὸ δώρημα in ver. 16, and ἡ δωρεὰ τῆς δικαιοσύνης (*the gift of righteousness,*) in ver. 17. The meaning therefore is, that the 'fall is not like the gracious restoration.' The reason why the one is not like the other, is stated in what follows, so that γάρ has its appropriate force : ' They are not alike, *for* if by the offence of one many be dead.' The dative παραπτώματι expresses the ground or reason. The offence of one was the ground or reason of the many dying ; and as death is a penalty, it must be the judicial ground of their death, which is the very thing asserted in ver. 12, and proved in vers. 13, 14. *Many be dead ;* the words are οἱ πολλοὶ ἀπέθανον, *the many died,* the aorist ἀπέθανον cannot mean *be dead.* By *the many* are intended all mankind, οἱ πολλοὶ and πάντες being interchanged throughout the context. They are called *the many* because they are many, and for the sake of the antithesis to *the one.* The many died for the offence of one ; the sentence of death passed on all for his offence. The same idea is presented in 1 Cor. xv. 22.

It is here, therefore, expressly asserted that the sin of Adam was the cause of all his posterity being subjected to death, that is, to penal evil. But it may still be asked whether it was the occasional or the immediate cause. That is, whether the apostle means to say that the sin of Adam was the occasion of all men being placed in such circumstances that they all sin, and thus incur death ; or that by being the cause of the corruption

Church had abundant scriptural authority as well as theological reasons for their doctrine of the *imputatio peccati Adamitici ad culpam et pœnam,* and its consequent *peccatum originale,* consisting in the *habitus peccandi,* and hence involving guilt. It is one of the merits of Julius Müller's work (die Christliche Lehre von der Sünde,) that he rejects the modern doctrine, that innate depravity or the corruption of nature in man, consequent on the fall of Adam, is simply an evil, so that only voluntary assent thereto is properly of the nature of sin."

of their nature, it is thus indirectly the cause of their condemnation ; or whether he is to be understood as saying that his sin is the direct judicial ground or reason for the infliction of penal evil. It has been frequently said that this is all theory, philosophy, system, &c. But any one may see that it is a mere exegetical question—what is the meaning of a given phrase? Does the dative here express the occasional cause, or the ground or reason of the result attributed to the offence of one man ? It is a mere question of fact ; the fact is all, and there is neither theory nor philosophy involved in the matter. If Paul says that the offence of one is the ground and reason of the many being subject to death, he says all that the advocates of the doctrine of imputation say. That this is the strict exegetical meaning of the passage appears from the following reasons : 1. That such *may* be the force and meaning of the words as they here stand, no one can pretend to doubt. That is, no one can deny that the dative case can express the ground or reason as well as the occasion of a thing. 2. This interpretation is not only possible, and in strict accordance with the meaning of the words, but it is demanded, in this connection, by the plainest rules of exposition ; because the sentiment expressed by these words is confessedly the same as that taught in those which follow ; and they, as will appear in the sequel, will not bear the opposite interpretation. 3. It is demanded by the whole design and drift of the passage. The very point of the comparison is, that as the righteousness of Christ, and not our own works, is the ground of our justification, so the sin of Adam, antecedently to any sins of our own, is the ground of the infliction of certain penal evils. If the latter be denied, the very point of the analogy between Christ and Adam is destroyed. 4. This interpretation is so plainly the correct and natural one, that it is, as shown above, freely admitted by the most strenuous opponents of the doctrine which it teaches.

Much more the grace of God, and the gift by grace, which is by one man, hath abounded unto many. Had Paul been studious of uniformity in the structure of his sentences, this clause would have been differently worded : 'If by the offence of one many die, much more by the free gift of one shall many live.' The meaning is the same. The force of the passage lies in the words *much more.* The idea is not that the grace is more abundant and efficacious than the offence and its consequences : this idea is expressed in ver. 20 ; but, 'if the one dispensation has occurred, much more may the other ; if we die for one, much more may we live by another.' The πολλῷ μᾶλλον does not express a higher degree of efficacy, but of evidence or certainty : 'If the one thing has happened, *much more* certainly may the other be relied upon.' The first clause of the verse may be thus interpreted, 'the grace of God, *even* the gift by grace ;' so that the latter phrase is explanatory of the former. If they are to be distinguished, the first refers to the cause, viz. the grace of God ; and the second to the result, viz. the gift by grace, *i. e.* the gracious or free gift, viz. the gift of righteousness, as explained in ver. 17. *Which is by one man, Jesus Christ* ; that is, which comes to us through Christ. This free gift is of course the opposite of what comes upon us for the sake of Adam. Guilt and condemnation come from him ; righteousness and consequent acceptance from Jesus Christ. What is here called the free gift is, in ver. 17, called the gift of righteousness. *Hath abounded unto many,* εἰς τοὺς πολλούς, *unto the many* ; that is, has been freely and abundantly bestowed on the many. Whether the many, in this clause, is co-extensive numerically with the many in the other, will be considered under ver. 18.

VERSE 16. *And not as it was by one that sinned,** so is the gift,* &c.
This clause, as it stands in the original, *and not as by one that sinned, the
gift,* is obviously elliptical. Some word corresponding to *gift* is to be
supplied in the first member; either *offence,* which is opposed to the *free gift*
in the preceding verse; or *judgment,* which occurs in the next clause. The
sense then is, 'The gift (of justification, see ver. 17) was not like the sentence
which came by one that sinned.' So Professor Stuart, who very appositely
renders and explains the whole verse thus: " Yea, the [sentence] by one who
sinned, is not like the free gift; for the sentence by reason of *one* [offence] was
unto condemnation [was a condemning sentence]; but the free gift [pardon]is
of *many* offences, unto justification, *i. e.* is a sentence of acquittal from
condemnation." The point of this verse is, that the sentence of condemnation which passed on all men† for the sake of Adam, was for *one* offence,
whereas we are justified by Christ from *many* offences. Christ does much
more than remove the guilt and evils consequent on the sin of Adam.
This is the second particular in which the work of Christ differs from that
of Adam.

For the judgment was by one to condemnation. By one, ἐξ ἑνός, either by
one *man,* or by one *offence.* As ἁμαρτήσαντος is the true reading in the
preceding clause, most modern commentators say that ἑνός, must be masculine, by one *man.* The antithesis, however, between ἑνός and πολλῶν is so
obvious, that it is more natural to supply παραπτώματος, from the next
clause, as in Hebrew parallelisms, an ellipsis in the first member must at
times be supplied from the second. An example of this kind Gesenius
finds in Isa. xlviii. 11. Here the very object of the apostle is to contrast
the one *offence* for which we suffer through Adam, with the many *offences*
from the guilt of which Christ delivers us. Luther, Beza, Olshausen,
Rothe, and others, take ἑνός as neuter, one *offence.* " A judgment to condemnation " is a Hebraic or Hellenistic idiom, for a condemnatory judgment, or sentence of condemnation.‡ The word κρίμα, rendered *judgment,*
properly means the decision or sentence of a judge, and is here to be taken
in its usual and obvious signification. It is then plainly stated that 'a
sentence of condemnation has passed on all men on account of the one sin
of Adam.' This is one of the clauses which can hardly be forced into the
meaning that the sin of Adam was the occasion merely of men being condemned, because it was the means of their being led into sin. Here again
we, have a mere exegetical question to decide; not a matter of theory or
deduction, but simply of exposition. What does the phrase 'a sentence
of condemnation by, or for one offence,' in this connection, mean? The
common answer to this question is, It means that the one offence was the
ground of the sentence. This answer, for the following reasons, appears
to be correct : 1. It is the simple and obvious meaning of the terms. To
say *a sentence is for an offence,* is, in ordinary language, to say that it is on

---

* Instead of ἁμαρτήσαντος, the MSS. D. E. F. G. 26, the Latin and Syriac versions read
ἁμαρτήματος. The common text is retained by most editors, even by Lachmann.

† The words *all men* are expressed in ver. 18, where this clause is repeated : "By the
offence of one, judgment came on all men to condemnation."

‡ See 1 Cor. xv. 45, 'The first Adam was made (εἰς ψυχὴν ζῶσαν) *to* a living soul.'
'The last Adam *to* a quickening spirit.' 'Or the preposition (εἰς) may express the grade
or point to which anything reaches, and εἰς κατάκριμα be equivalent *to* εἰς τὸ κατακρίνεσθαι,
a sentence unto condemnation; a decision which went to the extent of condemning. So,
in the next clause, εἰς δικαίωμα, *unto justification,* a sentence by which men are justified.—
See *Wahl,* p. 428.

account of the offence; and not that the offence is the cause of something else, which is the ground of the sentence. Who, uninfluenced by theological prejudice, would imagine that the apostle, when he says that condemnation for the offence of one man has passed on all men, means that the sin of Adam was the occasion of our sins, on account of which we are condemned? The preposition (ἐκ), here translated *by*, expresses properly the idea of the origin of one thing from another; and is, therefore, used to indicate almost any relation in which a cause may stand to an effect. The logical character of this relation depends, of course, on the nature of the subject spoken of. In the phrases "faith is by hearing" (ἐξ ἀκοῆς,) chap. x. 17; "*by this craft* (ἐκ ταύτης τῆς ἐργασίας) we have our wealth," Acts xix. 25; "our sufficiency is *of* God" (ἐκ τοῦ Θεοῦ,) 2 Cor. iii. 5; and a multitude of similar cases, the general idea of causation is expressed, but its precise character differs according to the nature of the subject. In the former of these examples the word indicates the instrumental, in the latter the efficient cause. But when it is said that "a man is not justified by works" (ἐξ ἔργων,) Gal. ii. 16; that the purpose of election "is not of works," Rom. ix. 11; that our salvation is not "by works of righteousness (ἐξ ἔργων τῶν ἐν δικαιοσύνῃ) which we have done," Tit. iii. 5; and in a hundred similar examples, the preposition expresses the ground or reason. We are not elected, or justified, or saved on account of our works. In like manner, when it is said we are condemned *by*, or *for* the offence of one, and that we are justified for the righteousness of another, the meaning obviously is, that it is *on account* of the offence we are condemned, and *on account* of the righteousness we are justified. If it is true, therefore, as is so often asserted, that the apostle here, and throughout this passage, states the fact merely that the offence of Adam has led to our condemnation, without explaining the *mode* in which it has produced this result, it must be because language cannot express the idea. The truth is, however, that when he says "the sentence was by one offence" (τὸ κρίμα ἐξ ἑνός,) he expresses the mode of condemnation just as clearly as he denies one *mode* of justification by saying it "is not by works;" and as he affirms another by saying it is "by the righteousness of Christ." 2. This interpretation is not only the simple and natural meaning of the words in themselves considered, but is rendered necessary by the context. We have, in this verse, the idea of pardon on the one hand, which supposes that of condemnation on the other. If the latter clause of the verse means, as is admitted, that we are pardoned for many offences, the former must mean that we are condemned for one. 3. The whole force of the contrast lies in this very idea. The antithesis in this verse is evidently between the *one offence* and the *many offences*. To make Paul say that the offence of Adam was the means of involving us in a multitude of crimes, from all of which Christ saves us, is to make the evil and the benefit exactly tantamount: 'Adam leads us into the offences from which Christ delivers us.' Here is no contrast and no superiority. Paul, however, evidently means to assert that the evil from which Christ saves us, is far greater than that which Adam has brought upon us. According to the simple and natural interpretation of the verse, this idea is retained: 'Adam brought the condemnation of *one* offence only; Christ saves us from that of *many*.' 4. Add to these considerations the obvious meaning of the corresponding clauses in the other verses, especially in ver. 19, and the design of the apostle in the whole passage, so often referred to, and it seems scarcely possible to resist the evidence in favour of this view of the passage. 5.

This interpretation is so clearly the correct one, that it is conceded by commentators and theologians of every shade of doctrine. "Justly indeed," says Koppe, "on account of one offence, many are subjected to punishment ; but by divine grace many are freed from the punishment of many offences." His own words are, "Jure quidem unius delicti causa pœnas subeunt multi ; ex gratia verò divina a multorum pœnis liberantur beanturque multi." Flatt says, "Κατάκριμα setzt als nicht nothwendig eigene Verschuldung voraus, so wie das gegentheil δικαίωμα nicht eigene δικαιοσύνη voraussetzt. Um einer einzigen Sünde willen wurden alle dazu verurtheilt, den θάνατος, (vers. 15, 17,) zu leiden." That is, 'Condemnation does not necessarily suppose personal transgression, any more than the opposite, justification, presupposes personal righteousness. On account of one single sin, all are condemned to suffer death.' So Storr : "Damnatio qua propter Adamum tenemur, unius peccati causa damnatio est." 'The condemnation which we suffer on account of Adam, is a condemnation on account of one sin.' Whitby expresses the meaning thus : "The judgment was by one *sin* to condemnation, we being all sentenced to death on account of Adam's sin."

The free gift is of many offences unto justification; that is, the free gift is justification. *The free gift,* τὸ δὲ χάρισμα, *the act of grace* is antithetical to κρίμα, *the judgment;* as the clauses κρίμα εἰς κατάκριμα and χάρισμα εἰς δικαίωμα (*sentence of condemnation* and *gratuitous justification*,) are opposed to each other. The word δικαίωμα is (i. 32) *righteous judgment;* here, as antithetical to κατάκριμα, *condemnation.* It means *justification,* which is a righteous judgment, or decision of a judge, pronouncing one to be just. This interpretation suits the signification of the word, and is to be preferred to making it mean *righteousness,* a sense which the word has in ver. 18, when opposed to *transgression,* and interchanged with *obedience.* This justification is ἐκ πολλῶν παραπτωμάτων, *from* many offences. The relation indicated by ἐκ, in the first clause, where it is said 'the sentence was ἐξ ἑνός, *for* one offence,' is slightly different from what it is in the second clause, where it is said justification is ἐκ πολλῶν παραπτωμάτων, *from* many offences. That is, sin stands in a different relation to condemnation from that which it sustains to justification ; both, however, may be expressed by the same preposition. Christ has done far more than remove the curse pronounced on us for the *one* sin of Adam ; he procures our justification from our own innumerable offences. This is the main idea presented in this verse.

Verse 17. *For if by one man's offence,* &c. The connection of this verse, as indicated by *for,* is with ver. 16 : 'We are justified by Christ not only from the guilt of Adam's first sin, but from our own innumerable transgressions ; *for* if death reigned over us for one offence, much more shall life reign through one who is none other and no less than Jesus Christ.' It is doubtful, however, whether this verse is a mere amplification of the idea of ver. 15, which, in import and structure, it so much resembles ; or whether the stress is to be laid on the last clause, *reigning in life;* so that the point of the difference between Adam and Christ, as here indicated, is, Christ not only delivers from death, but bestows eternal life ; or, finally, whether the emphasis is to be laid on the word *receive.* The idea would then be, 'If we are thus subject to death for an offence, in which we had no personal concern, how much more shall we be saved by a righteousness which we voluntarily embrace.' This appears to be Calvin's view, who says : "Ut miseria peccati hæreditate potiaris, satis est esse hominem, residet enim in carne et sanguine; ut Christi justitia fruaris, fidelem esse, necessarium est, quia fide acquiritur ejus consortium." The decision of these questions is not at all material to the general interpretation of the passage. Both of the ideas contained in the two latter views of the verse are probably to be included. *By one man's offence,* τῷ τοῦ ἑνὸς παραπτώματι, *by the offence of the one* (viz. Adam) *death reigned, i.e.,* triumphed over all men, *by one.* Here again the dative παραπτώματι has a causal force, and the assertion of the apostle is, that the offence of Adam was the cause of death coming on all men. His sin was not the cause of death by any physical efficiency; nor as the mere occasion of leading men to incur by their own act the penalty of death; nor by corrupting the nature of man, which corruption is the ground of the inflicted curse; but, as is asserted in the preceding verse, because his sin was the ground of the judicial condemnation, τὸ κρίμα εἰς κατάκριμα, which passed on all mankind. If that is so, *much more,* says the apostle, *shall they which receive;* ὁι λαμβάνοντες may be taken substantively, *the receivers;* or the present participle, *those receiving,* is used to express the condition on which the enjoyment of the blessing is suspended. *The abundance of grace,* the abounding grace, the grace which, in ver. 15, is said (ἐπερίσσευσε) *hath abounded* towards us. This grace is the unmerited love of God, which is the source of *the gift of righteousness,* δωρεὰ τῆς δικαιοσύνης, *i.e.,* righteousness is the gift offered and received. That righteousness here does not mean holiness, is evident from the constant use of the word by Paul in a different sense in this epistle; from the fact that it is pardon, justification, justifying righteousness, not sanctification, that Paul in the context represents as the blessing received from Christ; and because it is in this verse opposed to the reigning of death, or state of condemnation on account of the offence of Adam. Professor Stuart, therefore, in accordance with the great majority of commentators, very correctly states the sentiment of the verse thus: "For if all are in a state of condemnation by reason of the offence of one, much more shall those towards whom abundance of mercy and pardoning grace are shown, be redeemed from a state of condemnation, and advanced to a state of happiness." The general sentiment of the verse is thus correctly exhibited; but some of the more prominent terms do not appear to have their full force assigned to them. *They which receive the abundant grace,* expresses more than that this grace is manifested to them; all such do not reign in life. This phrase evidently implies the voluntary reception of the offered boon. *The gift of righteousness,* too, is something more than pardoning grace. It is that which is expressed in ver. 15, by the *free gift;* and in ver. 16, by the *free gift unto justification.* It is, therefore, the gift of justification; or what is but another method of stating the same idea, it is the righteousness of Christ by which we are justified, since the gift of justification includes the gift of Christ's righteousness. The meaning of the verse consequently is, 'If on account of the offence of one man we are condemned, much more shall those who receive the righteousness graciously offered to them in the gospel, not only be delivered from condemnation, but also reign in life by one, Jesus Christ;' that is, be gloriously exalted in the participation of that life of holiness and communion with God which is the end of our being.

By one, Jesus Christ. As it was by one man, antecedently to any concurrence of our own, that we were brought into a state of condemnation, so it is by one man, without any merit of our own, that we are delivered from this state. If the one event has happened, much more may we expect the other to occur. If we are thus involved in the condemnation of a sin in which we had no personal concern, much more shall we, who voluntarily receive the gift of righteousness, be not only saved from the consequences of the fall, but be made partakers of eternal life.

VERSE 18. *Therefore, as by the offence of one, judgment came on all men to condemnation; even so,* &c. The words ἄρα οὖν (*therefore*) are the inferential particles so often used in Paul's epistles, at the beginning of a sentence, contrary to the ordinary classical usage—vii. 3, 25 ; viii. 12 ; ix. 16, &c. They frequently serve to introduce a summation of what had previously been said. The inference from the whole discussion, from the beginning of the epistle to ver. 12 of this chapter, is introduced in that verse by διὰ τοῦτο, *wherefore.* It followed, from all the apostle had said of the method of justification through Jesus Christ, that there is a striking analogy between our fall in Adam and our restoration in Christ. The carrying out of this comparison was interrupted, in the first place, to prove, in vers. 13, 14, the position assumed in ver. 12, that all men are subject to death on account of the sin of Adam ; and, in the second place, to limit and explain the analogy asserted to exist between Christ and Adam, at the close of ver. 14. This is done in vers. 15—17. Having thus fortified and explained his meaning, the apostle now states the case in full. The word *therefore,* at the beginning of ver. 12, marks an inference from the whole doctrine of the epistle ; the corresponding words here are also strictly inferential. It had been proved that we are justified by the righteousness of one man, and it had also been proved that we are under condemnation for the offence of one. *Therefore,* as we are condemned, even so are we justified.

It will be remarked, from the manner in which they are printed, that the words *judgment came,* in the first clause of this verse, and the *free gift came,* in the second, have nothing to answer to them in the original. That they are correctly and necessarily supplied, is obvious from a reference to ver. 16, where these elliptical phrases occur in full. The construction in the clauses (κρίμα) εἰς κατάκριμα and (χάρισμα) εἰς δικαίωσιν ζωῆς, is the same as in ver. 16. Judgment unto condemnation is a sentence of condemnation, and the free gift unto justification is gratuitous justification. The sentence is said to be δι᾽ ἑνὸς παραπτώματος, *through the offence of one,* and the justification is δι᾽ ἑνὸς δικαιώματος, *through the righteousness of one.* In ver. 16, this word δικαίωμα is rendered *justification,* because it is there in antithesis to κατάκριμα, *condemnation;* it is here properly rendered *righteousness,* because it is in antithesis to παράπτωμα, *offence,* and because what is here expressed by δικαίωμα, is in ver. 19 expressed by ὑπακοή, *obedience.* This explanation is consistent with the signification of the word which means *a righteous thing,* whether it be an act, a judgment, or an ordinance. In Rev. xix. 8, τὰ δικαιώματα τῶν ἁγίων is correctly rendered *the righteousness* of the saints. Luther translates the word in the passage before us, *Gerechtigkeit,* agreeing with our translators. Calvin renders it *justificatio,* ' by the *justification* of one.' In this interpretation many of the modern commentators concur. The principal argument for this explanation of the word is, that it is used in that sense in ver. 16 ; but there, as just remarked, it is opposed to κατάκριμα, *condemnation,* while here it is opposed to παράπτωμα, *offence.* As the word may mean either *justification* or *righteousness,* that sense should be adopted which suits the immediate context. Many of the older theologians render it *satisfaction;* according to the Aristotelian definition, δικαίωμα τὸ ἐπανόρθωμα τοῦ ἀδικήματος. This gives a good sense : 'By the *satisfaction* of one, the free gift has come on all men unto justification of life.' But this, although in accordance with the strict classical use of the word, is not the sense in which it is used in the Bible, and it is not so suitable to the context.

Instead of rendering δι ἑνὸς παραπτώματος, *by the offence of one,* and δι ἑνὸς δικαιώματος, *by the righteousness of one,* a large class of commentators render them, 'by *one* offence,' and 'by *one* righteousness.' This does not materially alter the sense, and it is favoured by the absence of the article before ἑνός. In vers. 17, 19, it is τοῦ ἑνός, *the* one. In favour of the version in our English translation, however, it may be urged : 1. That ἑνός, throughout the whole context in vers. 12, 15, 17, 19, is masculine, except in ver. 16, where it is opposed to the neuter πολλῶν. The omission of the article is sufficiently accounted for from the fact that *the one* intended, viz. Adam, had been before distinctly designated. 2. The comparison is between Adam and Christ, rather than between the sin of the one and the righteousness of the other. 3. The expression, *one righteousness,* is awkward and unusual ; and if ἑνὸς δικαιώματος be rendered *one righteous act,* then it is inappropriate, inasmuch as we are not justified by one act of Christ, but by his whole life of obedience and suffering. 4. The natural opposition between *one* and all, requires ἑνός to be masculine : 'It was by the offence of *one* man that *all* men were condemned.'

That the apostle here again teaches that there is a causal relation between the sin of Adam and the condemnation of his race, cannot be denied. The only possible question is, What is the nature of that relation, as expressed by διά ? It was δι ἑνὸς παραπτώματος, '*by* the offence of one that judgment came upon all men.' Does this mean that the offence of one was simply the occasion of all being condemned, or that it was the ground or reason of their condemnation ? It is of course admitted that the proper force of διά with the genitive is, *by means of,* and with the accusative, *on account of.* As the genitive and not the accusative is here used, it might seem that the apostle designedly avoided saying that all were condemned (διὰ τὸ παράπτωμα τοῦ ἑνός) *on account of the offence of one.* But there is no necessity for departing from the ordinary force of the preposition with the genitive, in order to justify the interpretation given above. The relation of a means to an end, depends on the nature of that means. To say that condemnation is *through,* or by means of an offence, is to say that the offence is the rational or judicial means, *i.e.* the ground of the condemnation. No man doubts that when, in ver. 12, the apostle says, that death was (διὰ τῆς ἁμαρτίας) *by means of sin,* he means that it was on account of sin. This is not a solitary case. In chap. iii. 24, we are said to be justified (διὰ τῆς ἀπολυτρώσεως) *through the redemption* of Christ, *i.e.* by means of the redemption ; but the ransom paid by Christ, in being the means was the ground of our redemption. So in the familiar phrases, "through his blood," Eph. i. 7; Col. i. 20 ; "through his death," Rom. v. 10 ; Col. i. 22 ; "by his cross," Eph. ii. 16 ; "by the sacrifice of himself," Heb. ix. 26 ; "through the offering of the body of Jesus," and in many similar expressions the preposition retains its proper force with the genitive, as indicating the means, and yet the means, from the nature of the case, is the ground or reason. Thus also, in this immediate connection, we have the expressions, "*by* the righteousness of one" all are justified, and "*by* the obedience of one shall many be made righteous." We have, therefore, in this single passage, no less than three cases, vers. 12, 18, 19, in which this preposition with the genitive indicates such a means to an end, as the ground or reason on account of which something is given or performed. All this is surely sufficient to prove that it *may*, in the case before us, express the ground why the sentence of condemnation has passed on all men. That such, in this connection, must be its meaning, appears, 1. From the nature of the subject spoken of. To say that one man has been corrupted by another, may indeed express very generally, that one was the cause of the corruption of the other, without giving any information as to the mode in which the result was secured. But to say that a man was justified by means of a good action, or that he was condemned by means of a bad one; or plainer still, in Paul's own language, that a condemnatory sentence came upon him by means of that action ; according to all common rules of interpretation, naturally means that such action was the reason of the sentence. 2. From the antithesis. If the phrase, " by the righteousness of one all are justified," means, as is admitted, that this righteousness is the ground of our justification, the opposite clause, " by the offence of one all are condemned," must have a similar meaning. 3. The point of the comparison, as frequently remarked before, lies in this very idea. The fact that Adam's sin was the occasion of our sinning, and thus incurring the Divine displeasure, is no illustration of the fact that Christ's righteousness, and not our own merit, is the ground of our acceptance. There would be some plausibility in this interpretation, if it were the doctrine of the gospel that Christ's righteousness is the occasion of our becoming holy, and that on the ground of this personal holiness we are justified. But this not being the case, the interpretation in question cannot be adopted in consistency with the design of the apostle, or the common rules of exposition. 4. This clause is nearly identical with the corresponding one of ver. 16, " the judgment was by one (offence) to condemnation." But that clause, as shown above, is made, almost by common consent, to mean that the offence was the ground of the condemnatory sentence. Such, therefore, must be the meaning of the apostle in this verse ; compare also vers. 15, 17, 19.

The second question of importance respecting this verse is, whether the *all men* of the second clause is co-extensive with the *all men* of the first. Are the *all* who are justified for the righteousness of Christ, the *all* who are condemned for the sin of Adam ? In regard to this point, it may be remarked, in the first place, that no inference can be fairly drawn in favour of an affirmative answer to this question, from the mere universality of the expression. Nothing is more familiar to the readers of the Scriptures than that such universal terms are to be limited by the nature of the subject or the context. Thus John iii. 26, it is said of Christ, " all men come to him ;" John xii. 32, Christ says, " I, if I be lifted up, will draw all men unto me." Thus the expressions, " all the world should be taxed," " all Judea," " all Jerusalem," must, from the nature of the case, be limited. In a multitude of cases, the words *all, all things*, mean the *all* spoken of in the context, and not all, without exception ; see Eph. i. 10 ; Col. i. 20; 1 Cor. xv. 22, 51 ; 2 Cor. v. 14, &c. 2. This limitation is always implied when the Scriptures elsewhere speak of a necessary condition connected with the blessing to which all are said to attain. It is everywhere taught that faith is necessary to justification ; and, therefore, when it is said " all are justified," it must mean all believers. " By him," says the apostle, " *all that believe* are justified from all things," &c. Acts xiii. 39. 3. As if to prevent the possibility of mistake, Paul, in ver. 17, says it is those who " receive the gift of righteousness " that reign in life. 4. Even the *all men*, in the first clause, must be limited to those descended from

Adam "by ordinary generation." It is not absolutely all. The man Christ Jesus must be excepted. The plain meaning is, all connected with Adam, and all connected with Christ. 5. A reference to the similar passage in 1 Cor. xv. 22, confirms this interpretation, "As in Adam all die, so in Christ shall all be made alive;" that is, shall be made partakers of a glorious resurrection and of eternal life. Thus the original word ($\zeta\omega o\pi o\iota$-$\vartheta\eta\sigma o\nu\tau\alpha\iota$) and the context require the latter clause of that verse to be understood. The *all* there intended are immediately called "they that are Christ's," ver. 23, *i.e.* all connected with him, and not numerically the *all* that die in Adam. 6. This interpretation is necessary, because it is impossible, with any regard to scriptural usage or truth, to carry the opposite interpretation through. In this whole passage there are two classes of persons spoken of—those connected with Adam, and those connected with Christ. Of the former it is said "they die," ver. 15 ; "they are condemned," vs. 16, 18 ; "they are made sinners," ver. 19, by the offence of one man. Of the latter it is said, that to them "the grace of God and the gift by grace hath abounded," ver. 15 ; that "they are freely justified from many offences," vs. 16, 18 ; that "they shall reign in life through Christ Jesus," ver. 17; that "they are regarded and treated as righteous," ver. 19. If these things can be said of all men, of impenitent sinners and hardened reprobates, what remains to be said of the people of God? It is not possible so to eviscerate these declarations as to make them contain nothing more than that the chance of salvation is offered to all men. To say that a man is justified, is not to say that he has the opportunity of justifying himself ; and to say that a man shall reign in life, is not to say he may possibly be saved. Whoever announces to a congregation of sinners, that they are all justified, they are all constituted righteous, they all have the justification of life? The interpretation which requires all hese strong and plain declarations to be explained in a sense which they confessedly have nowhere else in the Bible, and which makes them mean hardly anything at all, is at variance with every sound principle of construction. If the *all* in the latter part of the verse is co-extensive with the *all* in the former, the passage of necessity teaches universal salvation ; for it is impossible that *to be justified, constituted righteous,* can mean simply that justification is offered to all men. The *all* who are justified are saved. If therefore the *all* means, all men, the apostle teaches that all men are saved. And this is the use to which many Universalists have put the passage. As, however, not only the Scriptures generally, but Paul himself, distinctly teach that all men are not to be saved, as in 2 Thes. i. 9, this interpretation cannot be admitted by any who acknowledge the inspiration of the Bible. It is moreover, an unnatural interpretation, even if the attention be limited to this one passage ; because, as death on account of Adam supposes union with Adam, so life on account of Christ supposes union with Christ. It is all who are in Adam who are condemned for his offence, and the all who are in Christ who are justified by his righteousness. The modern German commentators, even those who do not hesitate to differ from the apostle, admit this to be the meaning of the passage. Thus Meyer says, *Die* πάντες ἄνθρωποι in the first clause, are *die Gesammtheit der Adams-generation,* and in the second clause, *die Gesammtheit der Christus-generation.* Philippi says, "The limitation of the πάντες ἄνθρωποι is of necessity to be assumed. It can only mean *all who believe* . . . . The apostle views, on the one hand, the generation of those lost in Adam, and on the other, the generation of those saved in Christ."

VERSE 19. *For as by one man's disobedience many were made sinners, so by the obedience of one shall many be made righteous.* This verse presents the doctrine of the preceding one in a somewhat different form. As in the doctrine of justification, there are the two ideas of the ascription of righteousness, and treating as righteous ; and in the doctrine of the fall, the ascription of guilt (legal responsibility,) and the treating all men as guilty ; so either of these ideas is frequently presented more prominently than the other. In ver. 18, it is the latter, in each case, which is made most conspicuous, and in ver. 19, the former. In ver. 18, it is our being *treated* as sinners for the sin of Adam, and our being *treated* as righteous for the righteousness of Christ, that is most prominently presented. In ver. 19, on the contrary, it is our being *regarded* as sinners for the disobedience of Adam, and our being *regarded* as righteous for the obedience of Christ, that are rendered most conspicuous. Hence, Paul begins this verse with *for*: ' We are treated as sinners for the offence of Adam, *for* we are regarded as sinners on his account,' &c. Though the one idea seems thus to be the more prominent in ver. 18, and the other in ver. 19, yet it is only a greater degree of prominency to the one, and not the exclusion of the other, that is in either case intended.

By one man's disobedience. The disobedience here is evidently the first transgression of Adam, spoken of in ver. 16, as *the one offence.* The *obedience* of Christ here stands for all his work in satisfying the demands of the law ; his obedience unto and in death ; that by which the law was magnified and rendered honourable, as well as satisfied. From its opposition to the disobedience of Adam, his obedience, strictly speaking, rather than his sufferings, seems to be the prominent idea. " Paulus unterscheidet in dem Werke Christi diese beiden Momente, das Thun und das Leiden." *Neander.* ' Paul distinguishes, in the work of Christ, these two elements—doing and suffering.' *Geschichte der Pflanzung,* &c., p. 543. In the paragraph which follows this statement, Neander presents the old distinction between the active and passive obedience of Christ, very nearly in its usual form. On p. 546, he says, "Dies heilige Leben Christi will Gott als That der ganzen Menschheit betrachten." 'God regards the holy life of Christ as the act of all men.' The words *the many* in both clauses of this verse, are obviously equivalent to *the all* of the corresponding clauses of ver. 18, and are to be explained in the same manner.

The words ἁμαρτωλοὶ κατεστάθησαν οἱ πολλοί, rendered " the many were *made* sinners," properly mean, were set down in the rank or category of sinners. Καθίστημι never, in the New Testament, means *to make*, in the sense of effecting, or causing a person or thing, to be in its character or nature other than it was before. Καθιστάναι τινά ἁμαρτωλόν does not mean *to make one sinful*, but to set him down as such, to regard or appoint him to be of that class. Thus, when Christ is said to have been " constituted the Son of God," he was not made Son, but declared to be such : " Who constituted thee a ruler or judge ?" *i. e.* Who appointed thee to that office ? So, "Whom his lord made ruler." When, therefore, the apostle says, that the many were (κατεστάθησαν) constituted sinners by the disobedience of Adam, it cannot mean, that the many thereby were rendered sinful, but that his disobedience was the ground of their being placed in the category of sinners. It constituted a good and sufficient reason for so regarding and treating them.   The same remark applies, of course, to the other clause of this verse : δίκαιοι κατασταθήσονται οἱ πολλοί. This cannot mean, that by the obedience of one the many shall be made holy.   It can only mean, that the obedience of Christ was the ground on which the many are to be placed in the category of the righteous, *i. e.* shall be so regarded and treated.   It is not our personal righteousness which makes us righteous, but the imputation of the obedience of Christ. And the sense in which we are here declared to be sinners, is not that we are such personally, (which indeed is true,) but by the imputation of Adam's disobedience.

Of course the several interpretations above mentioned are applied to this verse.   1. That the sin of Adam was the mere occasion of other men becoming sinners ; whether this was by the force of example, or by an unfavourable change in their external circumstances, or in some other unexplained manner, being left undecided.   2. That in virtue of community, or numerical oneness of nature between Adam and his posterity, his act was strictly their act, and made them sinners as it made him a sinner. 3. That as the apostacy of Adam involved a corruption of nature, that corruption was transmitted to his descendants, by the general physical law of propagation.   4. That the sin of Adam was the judicial ground of the condemnation of his race.   They were by his sin constituted sinners in a legal or forensic sense ; as by the righteousness of Christ we are constituted legally righteous.

That this last is the true interpretation is plain, 1. Because it is in accordance with usage.   *To make clean, to make unclean, to make righteous, to make guilty*, are the constant expressions for regarding and treating as clean, unclean, righteous, or unrighteous.   2. The expression, *to make sin*, and *to make righteousness*, occurring in a corresponding sense, illustrate and confirm this interpretation.   Thus in 2 Cor. v. 21, Christ is said to be " made sin," *i. e.*, regarded and treated as a sinner, " that we might be made the righteousness of God in him," *i. e.*, that we might be regarded and treated as righteous in the sight of God, on his account.   3. The antithesis is here so plain as to be of itself decisive.   " To be made righteous" is, according to Professor Stuart, "to be justified, pardoned, regarded and treated as righteous."   With what show of consistency then can it be denied that " to be made sinners," in the opposite clause, means to be regarded and treated as sinners ?   If one part of the verse speaks of justification, the other must speak of condemnation.   4. As so often before remarked, the analogy between the case of Adam and Christ requires this interpretation.   If the first clause means either that the disobedience of Adam was the occasion of our committing sin, or that it was the cause of our becoming inherently corrupt, and on the ground of these sins, or of this corruption, being condemned ; then must the other clause mean that the obedience of Christ is the cause of our becoming holy, or performing good works, on the ground of which we are justified.   But this confessedly is not the meaning of the apostle.   If then the same words, in the same connection, and the same grammatical construction, have the same meaning, the interpretation given above must be correct.   5. The design of the apostle to illustrate the great doctrine of the gospel, that men, although in themselves ungodly, are regarded and treated as righteous for Christ's sake, demands this interpretation.   6. This view of the passage, so obviously required by the usage of the words and the context, is, as remarked above on ver. 16, adopted by commentators of every class, as to theological opinion. See the passages there quoted. " *The many* are here again *all*, who, from the opposition to the one, are in this place, as in ver. 15, denominated from their great number. These have without exception become sinners (ἁμαρτωλοὶ κατεστάθησαν), not in reference to their own inward corruption, of which Paul is not here speaking, but in reference to their guilt (Strafwürdigkeit) and actual punishment on account of Adam's sin."* Even Flatt, whose general view of the passage would lead to a different interpretation, gives, as a correct exhibition of the meaning of the apostle, " As on account of the disobedience of one the many are treated as sinners, so on account of the obedience of one shall the many be treated as righteous." Storr also renders the first clause, " They were regarded and treated as sinners;" this, he says, must be its meaning, from its opposition to the words " were constituted righteous," which obviously express the idea of justification, and also from the use of the word *condemnation* in the corresponding clause of ver. 18. These writers are referred to rather than Calvinistic commentators, to shew how entirely destitute of foundation is the reproach, that the interpretation given above is the result of theological prejudice.

The meaning then of the whole passage is this : BY ONE MAN sin entered into the world, or men were brought to stand in the relation of sinners to God ; death consequently passed on all, because for the offence of that one man they were all regarded and treated as sinners. That this is really the case is plain, because the execution of the penalty of a law cannot be more extensive than its violation ; and consequently, if all are subject to penal evils, all are regarded as sinners in the sight of God. This universality in the infliction of penal evil cannot be accounted for on the ground of the violation of the law of Moses, since men were subject to such evil before that law was given ; nor yet on account of the violation of the more general law written on the heart, since even they are subject to this evil, who have never personally sinned at all. We must conclude, therefore, that men are regarded and treated as sinners on account of the sin of Adam.

He is, therefore, a type of Christ. The cases, however, are not entirely analogous ; for if it is consistent with the Divine character, that we should suffer for what Adam did, how much more may we expect to be made happy for what Christ has done ! Besides, we are condemned for one sin only, on Adam's account ; whereas Christ saves us not only from the evils consequent on that transgression, but also from the punishment of our own innumerable offences. Now, if for the offence of one, death thus triumphs over all, how much more shall they who receive the grace of the gospel, not only be saved from evil, but reign in life through Christ Jesus !

Wherefore, as on account of one the condemnatory sentence has passed on all the descendants of Adam, so on account of the righteousness of one, gratuitous justification comes on all who receive the grace of Christ ; for as on account of the disobedience of one we are regarded as sinners, so on account of the obedience of the other we are regarded as righteous.

It may be proper to add a few remarks on the preceding interpretation of this whole section. 1. The first is, that the evidence of its correctness is cumulative, and is therefore not to be judged exclusively by what is said in favour of the view presented of any one of its parts. If it is *probable* that verse 12 asserts, that all men became subject to death on account of one man, this is rendered still plainer by the drift and force of vers. 13, 14 ; it is rendered almost certain by ver. 15, where it is asserted,

* Zachariæ Biblische Theologie, Vol. II., p. 388.

that for the offence of one the many die; by ver. 16, where it is said that for one offence all are condemned; by ver. 17, which affirms again, that the ground of death's reigning over all is to be found in this one offence; and it would appear to be raised almost beyond the reach of doubt by ver. 18, where the words of ver. 16 are repeated, and the analogy with the method of our justification is expressly asserted; and by ver. 19, in which this same idea is reiterated in a form which seems to set all efforts at misunderstanding or misinterpretarion at defiance.

2. The force of a remark previously made may now be more fully appreciated, viz., that the sentiment attributed to ver. 12, after having been proved in vers. 13, 14, is ever after assumed as the ground of illustrating the nature, and confirming the certainty of our justification. Thus, in ver. 16, FOR IF by the offence of one many be dead, &c.; and ver. 17, FOR IF by one man's offence, &c.; in ver. 18, THEREFORE AS by the offence of one all are condemned, *even so* by the righteousness of one all are justified; and, finally, in ver. 19, FOR AS by one man's disobedience, &c.

3. In connection with these remarks, it should be remembered that the interpretation given to the several clauses in this passage is the simple natural meaning of the words, as, with scarcely an exception, is admitted. The objections relied upon against it are almost exclusively of a theological rather than a philological or exegetical character. This interpretation, too, is perfectly consistent with itself, harmonious with the design of the apostle, and illustrative of the point which he proposed to explain. If all these separate sources of proof be properly considered and brought to bear, with their mutually sustaining force, on a candid mind, it can hardly fail to acknowledge that the commonly received view of this interesting portion of the word of God, is supported by an amount and force of evidence not easily overthrown or resisted.

4. This interpretation is old. It appears in the writings of the early Christian fathers; it has the sanction, in its essential features, of the great body of the Reformers; it has commanded the assent of men of all parties, and of every form of theological opinion. The modern Rationalist, certainly an impartial witness, who considers it a melancholy proof of the apostle's subjection to Jewish prejudices, unites with the devout and humble Christian in its adoption. An interpretation which has stood its ground so long and so firmly, and which has commended itself to minds so variously constituted, cannot be dismissed as a relic of a former age, or disparaged as the offspring of theological speculation.

5. Neither of the opposite interpretations can be consistently carried through. They are equally at variance with the design of the apostle, and the drift of his argument. They render the design and force of vers. 13, 14 either nugatory or unintelligible. They require the utmost violence to be done to the plainest rules of exposition; and the most unnatural interpretations to be given to the most perspicuous and important declarations of the apostle. Witness the assertion, that "receiving the abundance of grace and gift of righteousness," means to be brought under a dispensation of mercy; and that "to reign in life by one, Jesus Christ," is to be brought under a dispensation of life. Thus, too, "the free gift of justification of life has come upon all men," is made to mean that all are in a salvable state; and "all are constituted righteous," (*i. e.*, "justified, pardoned, regarded and treated as righteous,") is only to have the offer of pardon made to all. These are but a tithe of the exegetical difficulties attending the other interpretations of this passage, which make the reception of either the severest of all sacrifices to prejudice or authority.

Verse 20. *Moreover, the law entered that the offence might abound,*
&c. Paul having shown that our justification was effected without the
intervention of either the moral or Mosaic law, was naturally led to state
the design and effect of the renewed revelation of the one, and the super-
induction of the other. *The law* stands here for the whole of the Old
Testament economy, including the clear revelation of the moral law, and
all the institutions connected with the former dispensation. The main
design and result of this dispensation, considered as *law*, that is, apart from
the evangelical import of many of its parts, was ἵνα τὸ παράπτωμα πλεονάσῃ,
that the offence might abound. The offence τὸ παράπτωμα is in the context
used of the specific offence of Adam. But it is hard to see how the
entrance of the law made the offence of Adam to abound, unless the idea
is, that its dire effects were rendered more abundant. It is more probable
that the apostle uses the word in a collective sense ; compare Gal. iii. 19.
Agreeably to this view, the meaning of the clause is, that the great design
of the law (in reference to justification) is to produce the knowledge and
conviction of sin. Taking the word in its usual sense, the meaning is,
that the result of the introduction of the law was the increase of sin.
This result is to be attributed partly to the fact, that by enlarging
the knowledge of the rule of duty, responsibility was proportionably
increased, according to chap. iv. 15, and partly to the consideration
that the enmity of the heart is awakened by its operation, and transgressions actually multiplied, agreeably to chap. vii. 8. Both views of the
passage express an important truth, as the conviction of sin and its incidental increase are alike the result of the operation of the law. It seems,
however, more in accordance with the apostle's object, and with the
general, although not uniform force of the particle (ἵνα) rendered *that,* to
consider the clause as expressing the design, rather than the result simply
of the giving of the law. The word παρεισῆλθεν does not mean simply
entered, nor entered *between,* that is, came between Adam and Christ. This
is indeed historically true, but it is not the meaning of the word, and
therefore not the idea which the apostle intended to express. Nor does
the word mean here, as in Gal. ii. 4, entered *surreptitiously,* " crept in un-
awares," for this is not true. It rather means entered *thereto, i. e.,* as the
same idea is expressed in Gal. iii. 19, " it was added." It was superin-
duced on a plan already laid, and for·a subordinate, although necessary
purpose. It was not intended to give life, but to prepare men to receive
Christ as the only source of righteousness and salvation.

But where sin abounded, grace did much more abound. That is, great
as is the prevalence of sin, as seen and felt in the light of God's holy law,
yet over all this evil the grace of the gospel has abounded. The gospel or
the grace of God has proved itself much more efficacious in the production
of good, than sin in the production of evil. This idea is illustrated in the
following verse. The words οὗ and ἐκεῖ have a local force. *Where, i. e.,*
in the sphere in which sin abounded, *there,* in the same sphere, grace
superabounded ; ὑπερεπερίσσευειν is superlative, and not comparative, and
περισσεύειν is stronger than πλεονάζειν, as περισσόν is more than πλέον. The
fact, therefore, of the triumph of grace over sin, is expressed in the clearest
manner.

Verse 21. *That as sin hath reigned unto death,* &c. *That,* ἵνα, *in
order that,* as expressing the divine purpose. The design of God in permitting sin, and in allowing it to abound, was to bring good out of evil ;
to make it the occasion of the most wonderful display of his glory and

grace, so that the benefits of redemption should infinitely transcend the evils of the apostasy. *Sin reigned,* ἐν τῷ θανάτῳ, not *unto,* but *in death,* or *through* death. Death spiritual as well as temporal—evil in its widest sense, as the judicial consequence of sin, was the sphere in which the power or triumph of sin was manifested. *Even so might grace reign,* (ὥσπερ—οὕτω καί,) *as* the one has happened, *so also* the other. The one is in order to the other. Grace is the unmerited love of God and its consequences. *It reigns, i. e.,* it is abundantly and effectively displayed, *unto eternal life,* (εἰς ζωὴν αἰώνιον,) in securing as the result of its exercise, eternal life. This is done (διὰ δικαιοσύνης) *by means of righteousness,* and that righteousness is THROUGH JESUS CHRIST OUR LORD. As the triumph of sin over our race was through the offence of Adam, so the triumph of grace is through the righteousness of Christ. The construction of this passage, assumed in the above interpretation, is to be preferred to that which connects δικαιοσύνης εἰς ζωὴν αἰώνιον, 'righteousness *which is* unto eternal life,' because the antithesis is not between *death* and *righteousness,* but between *death* and *life:* 'Sin reigns in death, grace reigns unto life.' That the benefits of redemption shall far outweigh the evils of the fall, is here clearly asserted. This we can in a measure comprehend, because, 1. The number of the saved shall doubtless greatly exceed the number of the lost. Since the half of mankind die in infancy, and, according to the Protestant doctrine, are heirs of salvation; and since in the future state of the Church the knowledge of the Lord is to cover the earth, we have reason to believe that the lost shall bear to the saved no greater proportion than the inmates of a prison do to the mass of the community. 2. Because the eternal Son of God, by his incarnation and mediation, exalts his people to a far higher state of being than our race, if unfallen, could ever have attained. 3. Because the benefits of redemption are not to be confined to the human race. Christ is to be admired in his saints. It is through the Church that the manifold wisdom of God is to be revealed, throughout all ages, to principalities and powers. The redemption of man is to be the great source of knowledge and blessedness to the intelligent universe.

DOCTRINE.

I. The doctrine of imputation is clearly taught in this passage. This doctrine does not include the idea of a mysterious identity of Adam and his race; nor that of a transfer of the moral turpitude of his sin to his descendants. It does not teach that his offence was personally or properly the sin of all men, or that his act was, in any mysterious sense, the act of his posterity. Neither does it imply, in reference to the righteousness of Christ, that his righteousness becomes personally and inherently ours, or that his moral excellence is in any way transferred from him to believers. The sin of Adam, therefore, is no ground to us of remorse; and the righteousness of Christ is no ground of self-complacency in those to whom it is imputed. This doctrine merely teaches, that in virtue of the union, representative and natural, between Adam and his posterity, his sin is the ground of their condemnation, that is, of their subjection to penal evils; and that in virtue of the union between Christ and his people, his righteousness is the ground of their justification. This doctrine is taught almost in so many words in verses 12, 15—19. It is so clearly stated, so often repeated or assumed, and so formally proved, that very few commentators of any class fail to acknowledge, in one form or another, that it is the doctrine of the apostle.

It would be easy to prove that the statement of the doctrine just given is a correct exhibition of the form in which it was held by the great body of the Reformed Churches and divines. A few quotations from men of universally recognized authority, as competent witnesses on this subject, must suffice. Turrettin (*Theol. Elench. Quaest. IX.*, p. 678) says, "Imputation is either of something foreign to us, or of something properly our own. Sometimes that is imputed to us which is personally ours ; in which sense God imputes to sinners their transgressions. Sometimes that is imputed which is without us, and not performed by ourselves ; thus the righteousness of Christ is said to be imputed to us, and our sins are imputed to him, although he has neither sin in himself, nor we righteousness. Here we speak of the latter kind of imputation, not of the former, because we are treating of a sin committed by Adam, not by us." The ground of this imputation is the union between Adam and his posterity. This union is not a mysterious identity of person, but, 1. " Natural, as he is the father, and we are the children. 2. Political and forensic, as he was the representative head and chief of the whole human race. The foundation, therefore, of imputation is not only the natural connection which exists between us and Adam, since in that case all his sins might be imputed to us, but mainly the moral and federal, in virtue of which God entered into covenant with him as our head." Again, "We are constituted sinners in Adam in the same way in which we are constituted righteous in Christ." Again (Vol. II., p. 707), *to impute*, he says, "is a forensic term, which is not to be understood physically of the infusion of righteousness, but judicially and relatively." Imputation does not alter the moral character ; hence the same individual may, in different respects, be called both just and unjust : "For when reference is had to the inherent quality, he is called a sinner and ungodly ; but when the external and forensic relation to Christ is regarded, he is pronounced just in Christ." " When God justifies us on account of the righteousness of Christ, his judgment is still according to truth ; because he does not pronounce us just in ourselves subjectively, which would be false, but in another putatively and relatively." Tuckney (*Prælectiones*, p. 234), " We are counted righteous through Christ in the same manner that we are counted guilty through Adam. The latter is by imputation, therefore also the former." " We are not so foolish or blasphemous as to say, or even to think, that the imputed righteousness of Christ makes us formally and subjectively righteous ;" see further quotations from this writer on chap. iv. 5. Owen (in his work on *Justification*, p. 236,[*]) says, "Things which are not our own originally, inherently, may yet be imputed to us, *ex justitia*, by the rule of righteousness. And this may be done upon a double relation unto those whose they are, 1. Federal. 2. Natural. Things done by one may be imputed unto others, *propter relationem fœderalem*, because of a covenant relation between them. So the sin of Adam was imputed unto all his posterity. And the ground hereof is, that we stood in the same covenant with him who was our head and representative." On page 242,[†] he says, "This imputation (of Christ's righteousness) is not the transmission or transfusion of the righteousness of another into them which are to be justified, that they should become perfectly and inherently righteous thereby. For it is impossible that the righteousness of one should be transfused into another, to become his subjectively and inherently." Again, page 307,[‡] " As we

---

[*] Goold's edition of Owen's Works, vol. V., p. 169.   [†] Ibid., p. 173.   [‡] Ibid., p. 219.

are made guilty by Adam's actual sin, which is not inherent in us, but only imputed to us; so are we made righteous by the righteousness of Christ, which is not inherent in us, but only imputed to us." On page 468,* he says, " Nothing is intended by the imputation of sin unto any, but the rendering them justly obnoxious unto the punishment due unto that sin. As the not imputing of sin is the freeing of men from being subject or liable to punishment." It is one of his standing declarations, " To be *alienæ culpæ reus*, MAKES NO MAN A SINNER." Knapp (in his *Lectures on Theology*, sect. 76) says, in stating what the doctrine of imputation is, " God's imputing the sin of our first parents to their descendants, amounts to this : God punishes the descendants on account of the sin of their first parents." This he gives as a mere historical statement of the nature of the doctrine, and the form in which its advocates maintained it. Zachariæ (*Bib. Theologie*, Vol. II., p. 394) says, " If God allows the punishment which Adam incurred, to come on all his descendants, he imputes his sin to them all. And, in this sense, Paul maintains that the sin of Adam is imputed to all, because the punishment of the one offence of Adam has come upon all." And Bretschneider, as quoted above, on chap. iv. 3, when stating the doctrine of the Reformers, as presented in the various creeds published under their authority, says, that they regarded justification, which includes the idea of imputation, as a forensic or judicial act of God, by which the relation of man to God, and not the man himself, was changed. And imputation of righteousness they described as " that judgment of God, according to which he treats us as though we had not sinned, but had fulfilled the law, or as though the righteousness of Christ was ours." This view of justification they constantly maintained in opposition to the Papists, who regarded it as a moral change, consisting in what they called the infusion of righteousness.

Though this view of the nature of imputation, both of sin and righteousness, is so familiar, yet as almost all the objections to the doctrine are founded on the assumption that it proceeds on the ground of a mysterious identity between Adam and his race on the one hand, and Christ and his people on the other ; and that it implies the transfer of the moral character of the acts imputed, it seemed necessary to present some small portion of the evidence which might be adduced, to show that the view of the subject presented above is that which has always been held by the great body of the Reformed Churches. The objections urged against this doctrine at the present day, are precisely the same which were urged by the Roman Catholics against the Reformers ; and the answers which we are obliged to repeat, are the same which the Reformers and their successors gave to those with whom they had to contend.

It will be seen how large a portion of the objections are answered by the mere statement of the doctrine. 1. It is objected that this doctrine "contradicts the essential principles of moral consciousness. We never did, and never can feel guilty of another's act, which was done without any knowledge or concurrence of our own. We may just as well say we can appropriate to ourselves, and make our own, the righteousness of another, as his unrighteousness. But we can never, in either case, even force ourselves into a consciousness that any act is really our own, except one in which we have had a personal and voluntary concern. A transfer of moral turpitude is just as impossible as a transfer of souls ; nor does it lie within

---

* Goold's edition of Owen's Works, vol. V., p. 324.

the boundary of human effort, that we should repent of Adam's sin."
Prof. Stuart, p. 239. This idea is repeated very frequently in his commentary on this passage, and the *Excursus*, IV, V. "To say Adam's
disobedience was the occasion, or ground, or instrumental cause of all
men becoming sinners, and was thus an evil to them all, and to say that
his disobedience was *personally theirs*, is saying two very different things.
I see no way in which this last assertion can ever be made out by philo-
logy." Compare Mr. Barnes, p. 119. Professor Stuart further says, page
212, that if verse 12 speaks of the imputation of Adam's sin, it could not
be said men had *not* sinned after the likeness of Adam's transgression.
"So far from this must it be, that Adam's sin is their very sin, and the
ground why death reigns over them." Mr. Barnes says, page 119, "If
the doctrine of imputation be true, they not only *had* sinned after the
similitude of Adam's transgression, but had *sinned the very identical sin*.
It was precisely *like* him. It was the very thing itself." In like manner,
on page 96, he says, "But if the doctrine of the Scriptures was, that the
entire righteousness of Christ was set over to them, was really and truly
theirs, and was transferred to them in any sense, with what propriety
could the apostle say that God justified the ungodly?" &c. "They are
eminently pure, and have a claim not of grace, but of debt to the very
highest rewards of heaven." It will be at once perceived that these and
similar objections are all founded on a misapprehension of the doctrine in
question. They are all directed against the ideas of identity of person, and
transfer of moral character, neither of which is, as we have seen, included
in it; they are, moreover, not only inconsistent with the true nature of
the doctrine, but with the statements and arguments of these writers themselves. Thus Professor Stuart, page 239, says, "That 'the son shall not
die for the iniquity of the father,' is as true as that 'the father shall not
die for the iniquity of the son;' as God has most fully declared in Ezek.
xviii." According to this view of the subject, "for the son to die for the
iniquity of the father," is to have the sin of the father imputed to him, or
laid to his charge. The ideas of personal identity and transfer of moral
character are necessarily excluded from it, by its opponents themselves,
who thus virtually admit the irrelevancy of their previous objections.
The fact is, that imputation is never represented as affecting the moral
character, but merely the relation of men to God and his law. To impute
sin is to regard and treat as a sinner; and to impute righteousness is to
regard and treat as righteous.

2. It is said that this doctrine is nothing but a theory, an attempt to
explain what the apostle does not explain, a philosophical speculation, &c.
This again is a mistake. It is neither a theory nor a philosophical speculation, but the statement of a scriptural fact in scriptural language. Paul
says, For the offence of one man all men are condemned; and for the
righteousness of one all are regarded and treated as righteous. This is the
whole doctrine.

3. It is asserted that the word *impute* is never used in the Bible, in
reference to reckoning or charging upon a man any thing which is not
strictly and properly his own. But this has been shown to be incorrect;
see chap. iv. 3. It is used twice in chap. iv., of "imputing righteousness"
to those without works, to the ungodly, &c. But if the objection were
well founded, it would be destitute of any force; for if the word means so
to ascribe an action to a man as to treat him as the author of it, it would
be correct and scriptural to say that the sin or righteousness of one man

is imputed to another, when that sin or righteousness is made the ground of the condemnation or justification of any other than its personal authors.

4. It is denied that Adam was the representative of his posterity, because he is not so called in Scripture, and because a representative supposes the consent of those for whom he acts. But this a mistake. It is rare that a representative is appointed by the choice of all on whom his acts are binding. This is the case in no country in the world ; and nothing is more common than for a parent or court to appoint a guardian to act as the representative of a minor. If it is competent for a parent to make such an appointment, it is surely proper in God. It is a mere question of fact. If the Scriptures teach that Adam was on trial not for himself only, but also for his posterity ; if the race fell when he fell ; then do they teach that he was in fact and form their representative. That they do teach the fact supposed, can scarcely be denied ; it is asserted as often as it is stated that the sin of Adam was the ground of the condemnation of men.

5. It is said that the doctrine of imputation is inconsistent with the first principles of justice. This objection is only of force against the mis-taken view given above. It has no weight against the true doctrine. It is on all hands admitted that the sin of Adam involved the race in ruin. This is the whole difficulty. How is it to be reconciled with the divine character, that the fate of unborn millions should depend on an act over which they had not the slightest control, and in which they had no agency? This difficulty presses the opponents of the doctrine more heavily than its advocates. The former have no advantage over the latter ; not in the amount of evil inflicted, because they make the evil directly inflicted on account of Adam's sin much greater than the others do ; not in the pro-vision made for the redemption of the race from this evil, because both maintain that the work of Christ brings the offer of life to the whole race, while it infallibly secures the salvation of a multitude which no man can number. The opinion of those writers not only has no advantage over the common doctrine, but it is encumbered with difficulties peculiar to itself. It represents the race as being involved in ruin and condemnation, without having the slightest probation. According to one view, they "are born with a corrupt disposition, and with the loss of righteousness, and subjection to pain and wo," by a mere arbitrary appointment of God, and without a trial, either personally, or by a representative. According to another view, men are born without any such corrupt disposition, but in a state of indifference, and are placed on their probation at the very first moment of moral agency, and under a constitution which infallibly secures their becoming sinners. According to the realistic doctrine, revived by the modern speculative theologians of the school of Schleiermacher, humanity existed as a generic life in Adam. The acts of that life were therefore the acts of all the individuals to whom, in the development of the race, the life itself was communicated. All men consequently sinned in Adam, by an act of self-determination. They are punished, therefore, not for Adam's act, but for their own ; not simply for their innate depravity, nor for their personal acts only, but for the act which they committed thousands of years ago, when their nature, *i. e.* their intelligence and will, were determined to evil in the person of Adam. This is avowedly a philosophical doctrine. This doctrine assumes the objective reality of human nature as a generic life. It takes for granted that persons can act before they exist, or that actual sin can be committed by an impersonal nature, which is a contradiction in

terms, inasmuch as an intelligent, voluntary act is an act of a person. If *we* actually sinned in Adam, than *we* (as persons) were then in conscious being. This doctrine is directly opposed to Scripture, which expressly teaches that the sin of Adam, and not our personal sin, was the original ground of condemnation ; as the righteousness of Christ, and not our personal righteousness, is the ground of our justification. No less clearly does the Bible condemn the other doctrines just mentioned. Paul represents the evils which came on men on account of the offence of Adam, as a condemnation ; not as an arbitrary infliction, nor as a merely natural consequence. We are bound to acquiesce in the truth as taught in the Scriptures, and not to introduce explanations and theories of our own. The denial of this doctrine involves also the denial of the scriptural view of atonement and justification. It is essential to the scriptural form of these doctrines, that the idea of legal substitution should be retained. Christ bore our sins ; our iniquities were laid upon him, which, according to the true meaning of scriptural language, can only signify that he bore the punishment of those sins ; not the same evils, indeed either in kind or degree ; but still penal, because judicially inflicted for the support of law. It matters little whether a debt be paid in gold or copper, provided it is cancelled. And as a comparatively small quantity of the former is of equal value with a great deal of the latter, so the temporary sufferings of Christ are of more value for all the purposes of punishment, than the eternal sufferings of all mankind. It is then no objection to the scriptural doctrine of sacrifice and atonement, that Christ did not suffer the same kind or degree of evil, which those for whom he died must have endured in their own persons. This idea of legal substitution enters also into the scriptural view of justification. In justification, according to Paul's language, God imputes righteousness to the ungodly. This righteousness is not their own ; but they are regarded and treated as righteous on account of the obedience of Christ. That is, his righteousness is so laid to their account, or imputed to them, that they are regarded and treated as if it were their own ; or " as if they had kept the law." This is the great doctrine of the Reformation, Luther's *articulus stantis vel cadentis ecclesiæ.* The great question between the Papists and Protestants was, whether men are justified on account of inherent or imputed righteousness. For the latter, the Protestants contended as for their lives, and for the life of the Church. See the passages quoted above on chap. iv. 3, and the Confessions of that period.*

---

* Apol. art. 9. p. 226. Merita propitiatoris—aliis donantur *imputatione divina,* ut per ea, tanquam propriis meritis justi reputentur, ut si quis amicus pro amico solvit aes alienum, debitor alieno merito tanquam proprio liberatur.

F. Concordantiæ, art. 3, p. 687. Ad justificationem tria requiruntur: gratia Dei, meritum Christi et fides, quæ haec ipsa Dei beneficia amplectitur; qua ratione *nobis Christi justitia imputatur,* unde remissionem peccatorum, reconciliationem cum Deo, adoptionem in filios Dei et hæreditatem vitae aeternæ consequimur.

F. C. III., p. 684. Fides non propterea justificat, quod ipsa tam bonum opus, tamque præclara virtus sit, sed quia in promissione evangelii *meritum* Christi *apprehendit* et amplectitur, illud enim per fidem nobis applicari debet, si eo ipso merito justificari velimus.

F. C. III., p. 688. Christi *justitia nobis imputatur,* unde remissionem peccatorum consequimur.

Bretschneider, Dog., Vol. II., p. 254, says that, according to the creeds of the Reformation, justification " is that act of God in which he imputes to a man the merit of Christ, and no longer regards and treats him as a sinner, but as righteous." " It is an act in which neither man nor God changes, but the man is merely freed from guilt, and declared to be free from punishment, and hence the relation only between God and man is altered." This, he says, the symbolical books maintained, in opposition to the Romish Church, which makes justification a moral change.

6. As the term *death* is used for any and every evil judicially inflicted as the punishment of sin, the amount and nature of the evil not being expressed by the word, it is no part of the apostle's doctrine, that eternal misery is inflicted on any man for the sin of Adam, irrespective of inherent depravity or actual transgression. It is enough for all the purposes of his argument, that this sin was the ground of the loss of the divine favour, the withholding of divine influence, and the consequent corruption of our nature.   Turrettin *Theologia Elenct.*, vol. i., page 680 : " Pœna quam peccatum Adami in nos accersit, vel est *privativa*, vel *positiva*.   Quoad primam dicimus Adami peccatum nobis imputari immediate ad pœnam privativam, quia est causa privationis justitiæ originalis, et sic corruptionem antecedere debet saltem ordine naturæ : Sed quoad posteriorem potest dici imputari mediate quoad pœnam positivam, quia isti poenæ obnoxii non sumus, nisi postquam nati et corrupti sumus."

7. It is said that it is inconsistent with the omniscience and veracity of God, and consequently with his nature as God, that he should regard and treat as sinners those who are not sinners, or those as righteous who are in fact unrighteous.   God's judgments are according to truth, and therefore must be determined by the real, subjective character of those whom they concern.   This difficulty arises simply from the ambiguity of language. The words *sinner, just, unjust, righteous,* and *unrighteous,* in English, and the corresponding words in other languages, are familiarly and properly used in two distinct senses.   They sometimes express moral character, and sometimes legal relations.   A man may therefore be just and unjust, righteous and unrighteous at the same time.   A criminal who has satisfied the demands of justice, is just in the eye of the law ; he cannot be again or further punished for his offence, and is entitled to all his rights as a citizen, although morally unrighteous.   The sinner, and every sinner whom God accepts or pronounces righteous for the righteousness of Christ, feels himself to be in his own person most unrighteous.   God's judgment, in pornouncing him righteous, is none the less according to truth. He does not pronounce the sinner subjectively righteous, which he is not, but forensically righteous, which he is, because Christ has satisfied the demands of justice on his behalf.   In like manner, when our blessed Lord, although he knew no sin, is said to have been made sin, it only means that he assumed the responsibility of meeting the requirements of the law in our place ; so that his sufferings were not chastisements or calamities, but of the nature of punishment.   He was condemned for our sakes, as we are justified for his. It is no impeachment, therefore, of the omniscience or veracity of God, when he holds us as guilty on account of Adam's sin, as he does not pronounce us morally criminal for his offence, but simply declares that for the ends of justice we are involved in his condemnation.

8. Perhaps the most operative of all objections against the doctrine of imputation is founded on the assumption that moral character must be self-originated.   It is assumed that inherent, hereditary depravity in man cannot have the nature of sin and involve guilt, unless it is due to his own act.   This principle, however, is not only erroneous, but contrary to the plainest and most universally received doctrines of the Bible.   It is the intuitive judgment of men that moral qualities owe their character to their nature, and not to their origin.   A holy being is recognized as holy, whether his holiness be concreated, infused, or self-originated.   All Churches believe that Adam was created holy ; all Churches believe that holiness is the product of divine power in regeneration ; and all Churches,

that is, the Latin, Lutheran, and Reformed, acknowledge that innate depravity is truly sin, although anterior to any act of self-determination on our part to evil. It is not necessary, therefore, to assume that if men are born in sin, their sinfulness is to be referred to their personal act. It may, consistently with the common judgment of men, and with the faith of the Church universal, be a penal consequence of the sin of Adam.

II. Whatever evil the Scriptures represent as coming upon us on account of Adam, they regard as penal; they call it death, which is the general term by which any penal evil is expressed. It is not however the doctrine of the Scriptures, nor of the Reformed Churches, nor of our standards, that the corruption of nature of which they speak, is any depravation of the soul, or an essential attribute, or the infusion of any positive evil. "Original sin," as the Confessions of the Reformers maintain, " is not the substance of man, neither his soul nor body; nor is it anything infused into his nature by Satan, as poison is mixed with wine; it is not an essential attribute, but an accident,* *i. e.* something which does not exist of itself, an incidental quality," &c. *Bretschneider,* vol. ii., p. 30. These Confessions teach that original righteousness was lost, as a punishment of Adam's sin, *and by that defect,* the tendency to sin, or corrupt disposition, or corruption of nature is occasioned.† Though they speak of original sin as being, first, negative, *i. e.* the loss of righteousness; and secondly, positive, or corruption of nature; yet by the latter, they state, is to be understood, not the infusion of anything in itself sinful, but an actual tendency or disposition to evil, resulting from the loss of righteousness. This is clearly expressed in the quotation just made. It is therefore in perfect consistency with his own views, and with those of the Protestant creeds, that President Edwards teaches, in his book on Original Sin, " It is agreeable to the sentiments of the best divines, that all sin comes from a defective or privative cause," (p. 28;) and that he argues against the idea of any evil quality being infused, implanted, or wrought into our nature by any positive cause or influence whatever, either of God or the creature, &c. With equal consistency and propriety, he goes on to state that " the absence of positive good principles," and " the withholding of special divine influence," and " the leaving of the common principles of self-love, natural appetite, which were in man in innocence," are sufficient to account for all the corruption which appears among men. Goodwin, one of the strictest Puritanical divines, (vol. iii., p. 323,) has a distinct chapter to prove, "that there is no necessity of asserting original sin to be a positive quality in our souls, since the privation of righteousness is enough to infect the soul with all that is evil." Yet he, in common with the Reformers, represents original sin as having a positive as well as a negative side. This, however, results from the active nature of the soul. If there is no tendency to the love and service of God, there is, from this very defect, a tendency to self and sin. How large a portion of the objections to the doctrine of original sin is founded on the idea of its being an evil positively infused into our nature, " as poison is mixed with wine," may be inferred from the exclamation of Professor Stuart, in reference to the passage just quoted from President

---

* Accidens: quod non per se subsistit, sed in aliqua substantia est et ab ea discerni possit.

† F. Concor. I., p. 643: Etsi enim in Adamo et Heva natura initio pura, bona et sancta creata est; tamen per lapsum peccatum non eo modo ipsorum naturam invasit, ut Manichæi dixerunt—quin potius cum seductione Satanæ per lapsum, justo Dei judicio (in pœnam hominum) justitia concreata seu originalis amissa esset, *defectu illo,* privatione seu spoliatione et vulneratione, (quorum malorum Satan causa est) humana natura ita corrupta est, ut jam natura, una cum illo defectu et corruptione, &c.

Edwards. He says it is "a signal instance, indeed, of the triumph of the spontaneous feelings of our nature over the power of *system!*" It would seem from this, that he has no objection to the doctrine as thus stated. And yet this is the form in which, as we have just seen, it is presented in the creeds of the Reformers, and the works of the "best divines."

It will be at once perceived that all such questions as the following, proceed on an incorrect apprehension of the point at issue. It is often asked, if Adam's first sin is propagated to us, why not all his other sins, and the sins of all our ancestors? No one properly maintains that Adam's *first* sin, his act of eating the forbidden fruit, is propagated to any one. This is a sheer impossibility. We derive from Adam a nature destitute of any native tendency to the love and service of God ; and since the soul, from its nature, is filled as it were with susceptibilities, dispositions, or tendencies to certain modes of acting, or to objects out of itself, if destitute of the governing tendency or disposition to holiness and God, it has, of course, a tendency to self-gratification and sin. There is surely nothing incredible or inconceivable in the existence of a native tendency to delight in God, any more than in the existence of a tendency or disposition to delight in beauty, or social intercourse, or in our own offspring. Men have still an innate sense of right and wrong, a natural sense of justice, &c. Why then may not Adam have been created with an analogous tendency to delight in God? And if this disposition presupposes a state of friendship with his Maker, or if it is the result of special Divine influence, why may not that influence be withheld as the expression of God's displeasure for the apostacy and rebellion of man? This is perfectly analogous to the dealings of God in his providence, and agreeable to the declarations of his word. He abandons sinners to themselves as a punishment of their transgressions ; he withholds or withdraws blessings from children, in punishment, or as an expression of his displeasure, for the sins of their parents. There is, therefore, nothing in this doctrine at variance with the Divine character or conduct. On the contrary, it has in its support the whole tenor of his dealings with our race, from the beginning of the world. The objections, therefore, founded on the supposed absurdity of the propagation of sin, and especially of Adam's *first sin*, all rest on misapprehension of the doctrine in dispute.

Nor is the objection any better supported, that the doctrine of corruption of nature makes God, from whom that nature proceeds, the author of sin. Our nature is not corrupted by any positive act of God, or by the infusion, implanting, or inworking of any habit or principle of sin ; God merely withholds judicially those influences which produced in Adam a tendency or disposition to holiness; precisely as a monarch often, from the purest and wisest motives, withholds favours from the children of traitors or rebels, or bestows them upon the children of patriots and public benefactors. There is in every human being a tendency to act upon the same principle. We are all disposed to regard with less favour the children of the wicked than the children of the good. If this principle is recognized even in the ordinary dealings of Divine Providence, we need not wonder at its being acted upon in that great transaction which decided the fate of the world, as Adam was not on trial for himself alone, but also for his posterity.

As little weight is due to the objection, that the law of propagation does not secure the transmission of bodily defects, or mental and moral peculiarities of parents to their children. This objection supposes that the derivation of a corrupt nature from Adam is resolved into this general law ; whereas it is uniformly represented as a peculiar case, founded on the representative character of Adam, and not to be accounted for by this general law exclusively. It is constantly represented as resulting from the judicial withholding of the influences of the Holy Spirit from an apostate race. See the Confessions of the Reformers quoted above : *Defectus et concupiscentia sunt poenæ, Apologia I.*, p. 58. That the peculiarities, and especially that the piety of parents, are not transmitted by the law of propagation, from parents to children, does not therefore present a shadow of an objection to the common doctrine on this subject. The notorious fact, however, that the mental and moral peculiarities of parents are transmitted to their children, frequently and manifestly, though not with the uniformity of an established law, answers two important purposes. It shows that there is nothing absurd, or out of analogy with God's dealing with men, in the doctrine of hereditary depravity ; and also, that the doctrine is consistent with God's goodness and justice. For if, under the administration of the divine Being, analogous facts are daily occurring, it must be right and consistent with the perfections of God.

The most common and plausible objection to this doctrine is, that it is inconsistent with the nature of sin and holiness to suppose that either one or the other can be innate, or that a disposition or principle, which is not the result of choice, can possess a moral character. To this objection, President Edwards answers, " In the first place, I think it a contradiction to the nature of things, as judged of by the common-sense of mankind. It is agreeable to the sense of the minds of men in all ages, not only that the fruit or effect of a good choice is virtuous, but the good choice itself, from which that effect proceeds ; yea, and not only so, but the antecedent good disposition, temper, or affection of mind, from whence proceeds that good choice, is virtuous. This is the general notion, not that principles derive their goodness from actions, but that actions derive their goodness from the principles whence they proceed ; and so that the act of choosing that which is good is no farther virtuous than it proceeds from a good principle or virtuous disposition of mind, which supposes that a virtuous disposition of mind may be before a virtuous act of choice ; and that, therefore, it is not necessary that there should first be thought, reflection, and choice, before there can be any virtuous disposition. If the choice be first, before the existence of a good disposition of heart, what signifies that choice ? There can, according to our natural notions, be no virtue in a choice which proceeds from no virtuous principle, but from mere self-love, ambition, or some animal appetite." *Original Sin*, p. 140. It is certainly according to the intuitive judgment of men, that innate dispositions are amiable or unamiable, moral or immoral, according to their nature ; and that their character does not depend on the mode of their production. The parental instinct, pity, sympathy with the happiness and sorrows of others, though founded in innate principles of our nature, are universally regarded as amiable attributes of the soul ; and the opposite dispositions as the reverse. In like manner, the sense of justice, hatred of cruelty and oppression, though natural, are moral from their very nature. And the universal disposition to prefer ourselves to others, though the strongest of all the native tendencies of the mind, is no less universally recognized as evil.

The opposite opinion, which denies the possibility of moral dispositions prior to acts of choice, is irreconcilable with the nature of virtue, and involves us in all the difficulties of the doctrine, that *indifference* is necessary to the freedom of the will and the morality of actions. If Adam was created neither holy nor unholy, if it is not true that " God made man upright," but that he formed his own moral character, how is his choice of God as the portion of his soul to be accounted for ? Or what moral character could it have ? To say that the choice was made from the desire of happiness, or the impulse of self-love, affords no solution of the case ; because it does not account for the nature of the choice. It assigns no reason why God, in preference to any other object, was chosen. This desire could only prompt to a choice, but could not determine the object. If it be said that the choice was determined by the superior excellence of God as a source of happiness, this supposes that this excellence was, in the view of the mind, an object supremely desirable ; but the desire of moral excellence is, from the nature of the case, a moral or virtuous desire ; and if this determined the choice, moral character existed prior to this determination of the will, and neither consisted in it, nor resulted from it. On the other hand, if the choice was determined by no desire of the object as a moral good, it could have no moral character. How is it possible that the choice of an object which is made from no regard for its excellence, should have any moral character ? The choice, considered as an act of the mind, derives its character entirely from the motive by which it is determined. If the motive be desire for it as morally excellent, the choice is morally good, and is the evidence of an antecedent virtuous disposition f mind ; but if the motive be mere self-love, the choice is neither good nor bad. There is no way, on the theory in question, of accounting for this preference for God, but by assuming the self-determining power of the will, and supposing that the selection of one object, rather than another, is made prior to the rise of the desire for it as excellent, and consequently in a state of indifference.

This reasoning, though it applies to the origin of holiness, is not applicable to the origin of sin ; and, therefore, the objection that it supposes a sinful disposition to exist in Adam, prior to his first transgression, is not valid. Because an act of disobedience performed under the impulse of self-love, or of some animal appetite, is sinful, it does not follow that an act of obedience, performed under a similar impulse, and without any regard for God or moral excellence, is virtuous.

Of all the facts ascertained by the history of the world, it would seem to be among the plainest, that men are born destitute of a disposition to seek their chief good in God, and with a disposition to make self-gratification the great end of their being. Even reason, conscience, and natural affection, are less universal characteristics of our fallen race. For there are idiots and moral monsters often to be met with ; but for a child of Adam, uninfluenced by the special grace of God, to delight in his Maker, as the portion of his soul, from the first dawn of his moral being, is absolutely without example among all the thousands of millions of men who have inhabited our world. If experience can establish anything, it establishes the truth of the scriptural declaration, " that which is born of the flesh is flesh." It would seem no less plain, that this cannot be the original and *normal* state of man ; that human nature is not now what it was when it proceeded from the hand of God. Every thing else which God has made, answers the end of its being ; but human nature, since the fall, has uniformly worked badly : in no one instance has it spontaneously turned to God as its chief good. It cannot be believed that God thus made man ; that there has been no perversion of his faculties ; no loss of some original and guiding disposition or tendency of his mind. It cannot be credited that men are now what Adam was, when he first opened his eyes on the wonders of creation and the glories of God. Reason, Scripture, and experience, therefore, all concur in support of the common doctrine of the Christian world, that the race fell in Adam, lost their original rectitude, and became prone to evil as the sparks fly upward.

This doctrine has so strong a witness in the religious experience of Christians, that it is not wonderful that it has been almost universally received. Individual opponents and objectors have indeed appeared, from time to time ; but it is believed that no organized sect, bearing the Christian name, the Socinians excepted, have ever discarded it from the articles of their faith. It is so intimately connected with the doctrines of divine influence and redemption, that they have almost uniformly been held or rejected together. It has indeed often been said, because the term *original sin* was first used by Augustine, that the doctrine itself took its origin with him ; although perfectly synonymous expressions occur so constantly in the writings of the earlier Fathers. Equally destitute of foundation is the assertion, so often made, that Augustine was driven to his views on this subject by his controversy with Pelagius. He had arrived at all the conclusions on which he ultimately rested, at least ten years before any controversy on the subject.* He was led to these results by the study of the Scriptures, and by his own personal experience. His earlier views on the intimately related doctrines of depravity, ability, dependence, and grace, were all modified as he became more thoroughly acquainted with the word of God, and with his own heart. When he passed what Neander calls the crisis of his religious history, he saw clearly the depth of the evil which existed within him, and had corresponding views of the necessity and efficacy of the grace of God, by which alone this evil could be removed.

With regard to Pelagius, the case was just the reverse. His views of depravity being superficial, he had very high ideas of the ability of man, and very low conceptions of the operations of the Spirit of God. The latter, as the author just referred to strikingly remarks, was the representative and champion of " the general, moral, and religious consciousness of men ; " the other, of " the peculiar nature of Christian consciousness." A doctrine which enters so much into the experience of all Christians, and which has maintained its ground in all ages and sections of the Church, must have its deep foundations in the testimony of God, and the consciousness of men.

III. It is included in the doctrines already stated, that mankind have had a fair probation in Adam, their head and representative ; and that we are not to consider God as placing them on their probation, in the very first dawn of their intellectual and moral existence, and under circumstances (or " a divine constitution ") which secure the certainty of their sinning. Such a probation could hardly deserve the name.

IV. It is also included in the doctrine of this portion of Scripture, that mankind is an unit, in the sense in which an army, in distinction from a mob, is one ; or as a nation, a community, or a family, is one, in opposition to a mere fortuitous collection of individuals. Hence the frequent and extensive transfer of the responsibility and consequences of the acts of the heads of these communities to their several members, and from one member to others. This is a law which pervades the whole moral government and providential dispensations of God. We are not like the separ-

---

* Neander's Geschichte der Christlichen Religion und Kirche, ii., § 3.

ate grains of wheat in a measure, but links in a complicated chain. All influence the destiny of each, and each influences the destiny of all.

V. The design of the apostle being to illustrate the nature and to confirm the certainty of our justification, it is the leading doctrine of this passage, that our acceptance with God is founded neither on our faith nor our good works, but on the obedience or righteousness of Christ, which to us is a free gift. This is the fundamental doctrine of the gospel, verses 18, 19.

VI. The dreadful evil of sin is best seen in the fall of Adam, and in the cross of Christ. By the one offence of one man, what a waste of ruin has been spread over the whole world! How far beyond conception the misery that one act occasioned! There was no adequate remedy for this evil but the death of the Son of God, verses 12, 15, 16, &c.

VII. It is the prerogative of God to bring good out of evil, and to make the good triumph over the evil. From the fall has sprung redemption, and from redemption results which eternity alone can disclose, verses 20, 21.

REMARKS.

1. Every man should bow down before God, under the humiliating consciousness that he is a member of an apostate race; the son of a rebellious parent; born estranged from God, and exposed to his displeasure, verses 12, 15, 16, &c.

2. Every man should thankfully embrace the means provided for his restoration to the Divine favour, viz., "the abundance of grace and gift of righteousness," ver. 17.

3. Those that perish, perish not because the sin of Adam has brought them under condemnation; nor because no adequate provision has been made for their recovery; but because they will not receive the offered mercy, ver. 17.

4. For those who refuse the proffered righteousness of Christ, and insist on trusting to their own righteousness, the evil of sin and God's determination to punish it, show there can be no reasonable hope; while, for those who humbly receive this gift, there can be no rational ground of fear, ver. 15.

5. If, without personal participation in the sin of Adam, all men are subject to death, may we not hope that, without personal acceptance of the righteousness of Christ, all who die in infancy are saved?

6. We should never yield to temptation on the ground that the sin to which we are solicited appears to be a trifle (merely eating a forbidden fruit), or that it is but for ONCE. Remember that ONE offence of one man. How often has a man, or a family, been ruined for ever by ONE sin! ver. 12.

7. Our dependence on Jesus Christ is entire, and our obligations to him are infinite. It is through his righteousness, without the shadow of merit on our own part, that we are justified. He alone was adequate to restore the ruins of the fall. From those ruins he has built up a living temple, a habitation of God through the Spirit.

8. We must experience the operation of the law, in producing the knowledge and conviction of sin, in order to be prepared for the appreciation and reception of the work of Christ. The Church and the world

were prepared, by the legal dispensation of the Old Testament, for the gracious dispensation of the New, ver. 20.

9. We should open our hearts to the large prospects of purity and blessedness presented in the gospel; the victory of grace over sin and death, which is to be consummated in the triumph of true religion, and in the eternal salvation of those multitudes out of every tribe and kindred, which no man can number, ver. 21.

CHAPTER VI.

CONTENTS.

AS THE GOSPEL REVEALS THE ONLY EFFECTUAL METHOD OF JUSTIFICATION, SO ALSO IT ALONE CAN SECURE THE SANCTIFICATION OF MEN. TO EXHIBIT THIS TRUTH IS THE OBJECT OF THIS AND THE FOLLOWING CHAPTER. THE SIXTH IS PARTLY ARGUMENTATIVE, AND PARTLY EXHORTATORY. IN VERS. 1—11, THE APOSTLE SHOWS HOW UNFOUNDED IS THE OBJECTION, THAT GRATUITOUS JUSTIFICATION LEADS TO THE INDULGENCE OF SIN. IN VERS. 12—23, HE EXHORTS CHRISTIANS TO LIVE AGREEABLY TO THE NATURE AND DESIGN OF THE GOSPEL; AND PRESENTS VARIOUS CONSIDERATIONS ADAPTED TO SECURE THEIR OBEDIENCE TO THIS EXHORTATION.

ROMANS VI. 1—11.

ANALYSIS.

THE most common, the most plausible, and yet the most unfounded objection to the doctrine of justification by faith, is, that it allows men to live in sin that grace may abound. This objection arises from ignorance of the doctrine in question, and of the nature and means of sanctification. It is so preposterous in the eyes of an enlightened believer, that Paul deals with it rather by exclamations at its absurdity, than with logical arguments. The main idea of this section is, that such is the nature of the believer's union with Christ, that his living in sin is not merely an inconsistency, but a contradiction in terms, as much so as to speak of a live dead man, or a good bad one. Union with Christ, being the only source of holiness, cannot be the source of sin. In ver. 1, the apostle presents the objection. In ver. 2, he declares it to be unfounded, and exclaims at its absurdity. In vers. 3, 4, he exhibits the true nature and design of Christianity, as adapted and intended to produce newness of life. In vers. 5—7, he shows that such is the nature of union with Christ, that it is impossible for any one to share the benefits of his death, without being conformed to his life. Such being the case, he shows, verses 8—11, that as Christ's death on account of sin was for once, never to be repeated, and his life, a life devoted to God; so our separation from sin is final, and our life a life consecrated to God.

COMMENTARY.

VERSE 1. *What shall we say then ?* What inference is to be drawn from the doctrine of the gratuitous acceptance of sinners, or justification without works, by faith in the righteousness of Christ ?

Shall we continue in sin, that grace may abound ? i.e., be more conspicuously displayed. The form in which the objection to the apostle's doctrine is here presented, is evidently borrowed from the close of the preceding chapter. Paul had there spoken of the grace of the gospel being the more conspicuous and abundant, in proportion to the evils which it removes. It is no fair inference from the fact that God has brought so much good out of the fall and sinfulness of men, that they may continue in sin. Neither can it be inferred from the fact that he accepts of sinners on the ground of the merit of Christ, instead of their own, (which is one way in which grace abounds,) that they may sin without restraint.

VERSE 2. *God forbid, μὴ γένοιτο let it not be.* Paul's usual mode of expressing denial and abhorrence. Such an inference is not to be thought of. *How shall we, that are dead to sin, live any longer therein ?* The relative οἵτινες is as usual causative, and it stands first, for the sake of emphasis; ἀπεθάνομεν does not mean *are dead,* nor *have died,* but *died.* It refers to a specific act in our past history : 'Since we died to sin, how can we still live in it ?' The act which in its nature was a dying to sin, was our accepting of Christ as our Saviour. That act involves in it not only a separation from sin, but a deadness to it. No man can apply to Christ to be delivered from sin, in order that he may live in it. Deliverance from sin, as offered by Christ, and as accepted by the believer, is not mere deliverance from its penalty, but from its power. We turn from sin to God when we receive Christ as a Saviour. It is, therefore, as the apostle argues, a contradiction in terms, to say that gratuitous justification is a license to sin, as much as to say that death is life, or that dying to a thing is living in it. Instead of giving τῇ ἁμαρτίᾳ the usual force of the dative, *to,* or *as it respects,* sin, Storr, Flatt, and many other commentators, say it should be understood as in v. 15 ; xi. 20, *on account of.* How shall we, who in Christ, *died on account of sin, i.e.,* who suffered icariously its penalty, inasmuch as we were crucified in him, live any longer therein ?'

In favour of this interpretation, it is urged, 1. That this phrase must express the same idea with the subsequent clauses, *buried with him,* ver. 4 ; *associated in his death,* ver. 5 ; *dead with Christ,* ver. 8. 2. That it must have this meaning in ver. 10, where it is said of Christ, *he died unto sin, i.e.,* on account of sin. 3. The other interpretation, 'How shall we, who have renounced sin, live any longer therein ?' it is said, is not suited to the apostle's object ; because it does not give any adequate answer to the objection presented in ver. 1. In order to answer that objection, it was necessary to show not merely that the believer had renounced sin, but that the doctrine of gratuitous justification effectually secures this renunciation. According to the second interpretation, this answer is plain and conclusive : 'How shall we, who have died on account of sin, live any longer therein ? If we are regarded and treated by God, in virtue of our union with Christ, and if we regard ourselves, as having suffered and died with him on account of sin, we cannot but look npon it as hateful, and deserving of punishment.'

The objections to this interpretation, however, are serious. 1. It is not consistent with the common and familiar import of the expression, *to be dead to anything*, which occurs frequently in the New Testament ; as Gal. ii. 19, "dead to the law ;" 1 Pet. ii. 24, "dead to sins ;" Rom. vii. 4 ; Col. ii. 20 ; Gal. vi. 14, &c. In all cases the meaning is, *to be free from.* Sin has lost its power over the believer, as sensible objects are not able to affect the dead.   2. The opposite phrase, *to live therein*, requires this interpretation.   3. The object of the apostle does not require that a formal, argumentative answer should be supposed to commence in this verse.   He simply denies the justice of the inference from his doctrine, stated in ver. 1, and asks how it is possible it should be correct. How can a Christian, which is but another name for a holy man, live any longer in sin ?

VERSE 3. *Know ye not, that so many of us as were baptized into Jesus Christ, were baptized into his death ?*   In this and the following verse, we have something more in the form of argument in answer to the objection in question. The apostle reminds his readers, that the very design of Christianity was to deliver men from sin ; that every one who embraced it, embraced it for that object ; and, therefore, it was a contradiction in terms to suppose that any should come to Christ to be delivered from sin, in order that they might live in it. And, besides this, it is clearly intimated that such is not only the design of the gospel, and the object for which it is embraced by all who cordially receive it, but also that the result or necessary effect of union with Christ is a participation in the benefits of his death. *Or know ye not,* ἢ ἀγνοεῖτε, *or are you ignorant ?* If any doubt what is said in ver. 2, he must be ignorant of the nature and design of baptism, and of the relation to Christ which it involves. Βαπτίζειν εἰς always means *to baptize in reference to.* When it is said that the Hebrews were baptized *unto* Moses, 1 Cor. x. 2 ; or when the apostle asks the Corinthians, ' Were ye baptized unto the name of Paul ?' 1 Cor. i. 13 ; or when we are said to be baptized unto Christ, the meaning is, they were baptized *in reference to* Moses, Paul, or Christ; *i. e.*, to be brought into union with them, as their disciples, or worshippers, as the case may be. In like manner, in the expression *baptized into his death*, the preposition expresses the design and the result. The meaning therefore is, ' we were baptized in order that we should die with him,' *i.e.*, that we should be united to him in his death, and be partakers of its benefits. Thus, "baptism unto repentance," Matt. iii. 11, is baptism in order to repentance ; "baptism unto the remission of sins," Mark i. 4, that remission of sins may be obtained ; "baptized unto one body," 1 Cor. xii. 13, *i. e.*, that we might become one body, &c. Paul does not design to teach that the sacrament of baptism, from any inherent virtue in the rite, or from any supernatural power in him who administers it, or from any uniformly attending Divine influence, always secures the regeneration of the soul. This is contrary both to Scripture and experience. No fact is more obvious than that thousands of the baptized are unregenerate. It cannot be, therefore, that the apostle intends to say, that all who are baptized are thereby savingly united to Christ. It is not of the efficacy of baptism as an external rite, that he assumes his readers are well informed : it is of the import and design of that sacrament, and the nature of the union with Christ, of which baptism is the sign and the seal. It is the constant usage of Scripture to address professors as believers, to predicate of them as professors what is true of them only as believers. This is also the usage of common life. We address a company of professing Christians as true Christians; we call them brethren in Christ; we speak of them as beloved of the Lord, partakers of the heavenly calling, and heirs of eternal life. Baptism was the appointed mode of professing faith in Christ, of avowing allegiance to him as the Son of God, and acquiescence in his gospel. Those, therefore, who were baptized, are assumed to believe what they professed, and to be what they declared themselves to be. They are consequently addressed as believers, as having embraced the gospel, as having put on Christ, and as being, in virtue of their baptism as an act of faith, the children of God. When a man was baptized unto Christ, he was baptized unto his death; he professed to regard himself as being united to Christ, as dying when he died, as bearing in him the penalty of sin, in order that he might be reconciled to God, and live unto holiness. How could a man who was sincere in receiving baptism, such being its design and import, live in sin? The thing is impossible. The act of faith implied and expressed in baptism, is receiving Christ as our sanctification as well as our righteousness. "Extra controversiam est," says Calvin, "induere nos Christum in baptismo; et hac lege nos baptizari, ut unum cum ipso simus." Baptism, therefore, as an act of faith, as the formal reception of Christ as our Saviour, brings us into intimate union with him: "For as many as have been baptized unto Christ, have put on Christ." Gal. iii. 27. And this baptism has special reference to the death of Christ; *we are baptized unto his death*. That is, we are united to him in death. His death becomes ours; ours as an expiation for sin, as the means of reconciliation with God, and consequently as the means of our sanctification. Although justification is the primary object of the death of Christ, yet justification is in order to sanctification. He died that he might purify unto himself a peculiar people, zealous of good works. If such is the intimate connection between justification and sanctification in the purpose of God in giving his Son to die for us, there must be a like intimate connection between them in the experience of the believer. The very act of faith by which we receive Christ as the propitiation for sin, is spiritually a death to sin. It is in its very nature a renunciation of every thing which it was the design of Christ's death to destroy. Every believer, therefore, is a saint. He renounces sin in accepting Christ.

VERSE 4. *Therefore we are buried with him by baptism into death.* This is an inference from ver. 3, to confirm the proposition in ver 2, viz. that those dead in sin cannot live therein. *Therefore*, says the apostle, such being the nature of our union with Christ, expressed in baptism, it follows, that those who are baptised are buried with Christ; they are as effectually shut out from the kingdom of Satan, as those who are in the grave are shut out from the world. The words διὰ τοῦ βαπτίσματος εἰς τὸν θάνατον go together; *by baptism unto death, i. e.* by a baptism which has reference to Christ's death, and by which we are associated with him therein. *We are buried with him, i. e.* we are cut off from the world in and with him. If the words *unto death* are connected with *we were buried*, the sense would be, *we were buried unto death, i. e*, we were buried so as to come into the power of death. But this is an incongruous idea, and an unexampled form of expression. As in ver. 3 the apostle had said εἰς τὸν θάνατον αὐτοῦ ἐβαπτίσθημεν. there is no reason to doubt that he here designs to speak of *baptism unto death.* Compare Col. ii. 12, "buried with him in baptism." The same idea is expressed in ver. 8, by saying, "we are dead with him," and in ver. 5, "we are planted with him in the likeness of his death." It is not necessary to assume that there is any reference here to the immersion of the body in baptism, as though it were a burial. No such allusion can be supposed in the next verse, where we are said *to be planted* with him. The reference is not to the mode of baptism, but to its effect. Our baptism unites us to Christ, so that we died with him, and rose with him. As he died to sin, so do we ; as he rose to righteousness and glory, so do we. The same doctrine concerning baptism, and of the nature of union with Christ, therein expressed, is taught in Gal. iii. 27, and Col. ii. 12.

That like as Christ was raised up from the dead by the glory of the Father, even so we also should walk in newness of life. We die with Christ, in order that we should live with him. We share in his death, that we may be partakers of his life. Justification is in order to sanctification. The two are inseparable. There can be no participation in Christ's life without a participation in his death, and we cannot enjoy the benefits of his death unless we are partakers of the power of his life. We must be reconciled to God in order to be holy, and we cannot be reconciled without thereby becoming holy. Antinomianism, or the doctrine that the benefits of the atonement can be enjoyed without experiencing the renewing of the Holy Ghost, is therefore contrary to the very nature and design of redemption. As Christ died and rose again literally, so his people die and rise spiritually. As Christ's resurrection was the certain consequence of his death, so is a holy life the certain consequence of our dying with Christ. There is not only an analogy between Christ's literal death and resurrection, and the spiritual death and resurrection of the believer, but there is a causal relation between the two. The death and resurrection of Christ render certain the justification and sanctification of his people. Paul says Christ rose, διὰ τῆς δόξης τοῦ Πατρός, *by the glory of the Father.* Δόξα, *glory*, is the excellence of God, the sum of all his perfections, or any one perfection specially manifested. The exhibition, therefore, of God's holiness, or of his mercy, or of his power, is equally an exhibition of his glory. Here the reference is to his omnipotence, which was gloriously displayed in the resurrection of Christ. In 1 Cor. vi. 14, and 2 Cor. xiii. 4, it is said Christ was raised, ἐκ δυνάμεως Θεοῦ, *by the power of God.* In Col. i. 11, the apostle refers the sanctification of believers to the κράτος τῆς δόξης Θεοῦ, *to the power of his glory.* It is according to the analogy of Scripture, that the same event is attributed at one time to the efficiency of the Father, and at another to that of the Son. Christ rose from the dead by his own power. He had power to lay down his life, and he had power to take it again. This is perfectly consistent with the apostle's declaration, that he was raised by the power of God. The three persons of the Trinity are one God. The efficiency of the Father is also the efficiency of the Son. What the Father does, the Son also does. *That we should walk in newness of life,* ἐν καινότητι ζωῆς. The idea of purity is associated with that of newness in the word of God—a *new* heart, a *new* creature, the *new* man. Newness of life is a life that is new, compared with what is natural and original ; and it is a holy life, springing from a new source. It is not we that live, but Christ that liveth in us; and therefore our life is, in its manifestations, analogous to his. His people are like him.

Verse 5. *For if we have been planted together in the likeness of his death, we shall be also in the likeness of his resurrection.* This is a confirmation of what precedes. We shall walk in newness of life, if we are partakers of Christ's death, *for* community of death involves community of life. The general meaning of the verse is plain, although there is doubt as to the force of some of the words, and as to the construction. First, as to the words. Calvin and many others render σύμφυτος *insitus, inserted, engrafted*, as though it were derived from φυτεύω. It is, however, from φύω, which means both *to bear* and *to grow*. Hence σύμφυτος sometimes means *born with*, in the sense of innate ; sometimes it expresses community of origin, or nature, in the sense of cognate, congenial ; and sometimes it is used in reference to things born or produced at the same time. From the other meaning of the word φύω, come the senses *growing with, overgrown with*, &c. In all cases there is the idea of intimate union, and that is the idea which the word is here intended to express. As to the construction, so far as the first clause of the verse is concerned, we may connect σύμφυτοι with ὁμοιώματι, *we have grown together in death*, *i. e. been united in a like death ;* or we may supply the words τῷ Χριστῷ, we have been united *with Christ, as to*, or *by*, similarity of death. The former as it requires nothing to be supplied, is to be preferred. In the second clause, the word ὁομιώτατι may be supplied, as in our version : we shall be (united) *in the likeness* of *his* resurrection. But as σύμφυτος may be construed with the genitive as well as the dative, many commentators unite σύμφυτοι τῆς ἀναστάσεως ἐσόμεθα, *we shall partake of the resurrection*. The sense is the same ; if united in death, we shall be united in life ; if we die with him, we shall live with him. The future ἐσόμεθα does not here express obligation, nor futurity. The reference is not to what is to happen hereafter, but to the certainty of sequence, or causal connection. If the one thing happens, the other shall certainly follow. The doctrine of this passage is not simply that the believer dies and rises, *as* Christ died and rose ; that there is an analogy between his death and theirs ; but, as before remarked, the main idea is, the necessary connection between the death and resurrection of Christ and the death and resurrection of his people. Such is the union between them and him, that his death and resurrection render theirs a matter of necessity. The life or death of a tree necessitates the life or death of the branches. Says Calvin, "Insitio, non tantum exempli conformitatem designat, sed arcanam conjunctionem per quam cum ipso coaluimus, ita ut nos Spiritu suo vegetans ejus virtutem in nos transfundat. Ergo ut surculus communem habet vitæ et mortis conditionem cum arbore in quam insertus est ; ita vitæ Christi non minus quam et mortis participes nos esse consentaneum est." That the resurrection here spoken of is a spiritual rising from the dead, seems plain, both from what precedes and from what follows. The whole discussion relates to sanctification, to the necessary connection between the death of Christ as an atonement for sin, and the holiness of his people. Those who are cleansed from the guilt of sin, are cleansed also from its pollution. Although this is obvious, yet all reference to the future resurrection of the body is not to be excluded. In chap. viii. 11, the apostle represents the quickening of our mortal bodies as a necessary consequence of our union with Christ, and the indwelling of his Spirit. If, therefore, we are baptized unto the death of Christ, united and conformed to him in his death, the sure result will be, that we shall be conformed to him in a holy life here, and in a life of glorious immortality of the soul and body hereafter. All this is included in the life which flows to us from Christ.

Verse 6. *Knowing this, that our old man is crucified with him*, &c. What in the preceding verses is represented as the consequence of our union with Christ as a matter of doctrine, is here presented as a matter of experience. We are united to Christ as our head and representative, so as to be partakers of his death and resurrection, as a matter of law or of right. What is thus done, as it were, out of ourselves, is attended by an analogous spiritual experience. *This knowing, i.e.* experiencing this. Our inward experience agrees with this doctrinal statement. *Our old man,* that is, our corrupt nature as opposed to the new man, or holy nature, which is the product of regeneration, and the effect of our union with Christ. In Eph. iv. 22, 24, we are exhorted to put off the old man, and to put on the new man. Col. iii. 8, 9. The Scriptures everywhere assert or assume the fall and native depravity of man. We are born the children of wrath. We are aliens from the commonwealth of Israel, without God, and without hope. This is the inward state and outward condition in which every man comes into the world. Through the redemption that is in Christ, a radical change is effected; old things pass away, all things become new. The old man, the nature which is prior in the order of time, as well as corrupt, is crucified, and a nature new and holy is induced. The word *man* is used, because it is no one disposition, tendency, or faculty that is changed, but the man himself; the radical principle of his being, the self. Hence Paul uses the pronoun *I*—" I am sold under sin ;" " I cannot do the things that I would." It is plain from this whole representation, that regeneration is not merely a change of acts, or of the affections in distinction from the understanding, but a change of the whole man. Another thing is also plain, viz. that such a radical change of nature cannot fail to manifest itself in a holy walk and conversation. This is what Paul here insists upon. To the believer who knows that the old man is crucified with Christ, the objection that gratuitous justification leads to licentiousness, is contradictory and absurd. The old man is said to be *crucified,* not because the destruction of the principle of sin is a slow and painful process, but because Christ's death was by crucifixion, in which death we were associated, and because it is from him, as crucified, the death of sin in us proceeds. " Hunc veterem hominem dicit esse affixum cruci Christi, quia ejus virtute conficitur. Ac nominatim allusit ad crucem, quo expressiùs indicaret non aliunde nos mortificari, quam ex ejus mortis participatione."

That the body of sin might be destroyed. "The body of sin" is only another name for "the old man," or rather for its concrete form. The design of our crucifixion with Christ is the destruction of the old man, or the body of sin ; and the design of the destruction of the inward power or principle of evil, is our spiritual freedom. This latter idea the apostle expresses by saying, *that henceforth we should not serve sin, i.e.* be in bondage to it. The service of sin is a δουλεία, *a slavery,* a state from which we cannot free ourselves ; a power which coerces obedience in despite of the resistance of reason, conscience, and as the apostle teaches, even of the will. It is a bondage from which we can be delivered in no other way than by the death of the inward principle of evil which possesses our nature, and lies back of the will, beyond the reach of our power, and which can be destroyed only by union with Christ in his death, who died for this very purpose, that he might deliver us from the bondage of corruption, and introduce us into the glorious liberty of the sons of God. Compare John viii. 34 ; Heb. ii. 14—16. Although the general sense of this verse is thus plain, there is great diversity of opinion as to the precise meaning of the words σῶμα τῆς ἁμαρτίας, *body of sin.* 1. Some say it means the sinful body, that is, the body which is the seat and source of sin. But it is not the doctrine of the Bible, that sin has its source in matter ; it is spiritual in its nature and origin. The body is not its source, but its instrument and slave. Moreover, the design of Christ's death is never said to be to destroy the body. 2. Others say that σῶμα means the physical body, not as the source, but as the appurtenance of sin, as belonging to it, and ruled by it. But this is subject in part to the same objection. 3. Others say that σῶμα means *mass,* "the mass of sin." "Corpus peccati," says Calvin, "non carnem et ossa, sed massam designat; homo enim naturæ propriæ relictus massa est ex peccato conflata." 4. Others assume that σῶμα has the same sense as σάρξ, *corrupt nature;* so that "body of sin" means our "sinful, carnal nature." This no doubt is the idea, but it is not expressed by the word σῶμα, which is not equivalent to σάρξ. 5. Others take σῶμα, in accordance with the Rabbinical use of the corresponding Hebrew word, to mean *essence* or *substance;* for which, however, there is no authority from the *usus loquendi* of the Scriptures. 6. Perhaps the most satisfactory view is that of those who understand the phrase as figurative. Sin is personified. It is something that has life, is obeyed; that can be put to death. It is represented as *a body,* or organism; as having its members. Compare Col. iii. 5. In Col. ii. 11, the apostle speaks of putting off "the body of the sins of the flesh," by which he means the totality of our corrupt nature. So here, "the body of sin," is sin considered as a body, as something which can be crucified.

VERSE 7. *For he that is dead is free from sin.* The Greek here is, ὁ γὰρ ἀποθανὼν δεδικαίωται ἀπὸ τῆς ἁμαρτίας, *for he who has died is justified from sin.* The particle γάρ, *for,* shows that this verse is a confirmation of what precedes : 'The believer (he who is by faith united to Christ in his death) cannot any longer serve sin, *for* he who has died is justified from sin.' The word ἀποθανών may be taken in a physical, a moral, or a mystical sense. If in a physical sense, then the meaning is, that death frees from sin. This may be understood in two ways : first, on the theory that the body is the source of sin, death, or freedom from the body, involves freedom from sin; or, secondly, death considered as a penalty, is the expiation of sin ; so that he who dies, is judicially free from sin. Some who adopt this interpretation, suppose that the apostle sanctions the unscriptural Jewish doctrine (see Eisenmenger's *Entdeckt. Judenthum,* II., p. 283), that death is the full penalty of sin, and therefore its expiation. Others say he is to be understood as speaking only of sin or guilt in relation to human law : ' He who has died for his crime is free from guilt or further liability.' In either way, the only relation which this verse, when understood of physical death, can have to the apostle's argument, is that of an illustration : 'As the man who has suffered for his crime is freed from it, so he who is crucified with Christ is free from sin. In either case the power of sin is destroyed.' If the moral sense of the word be adopted, then the meaning is either, 'he who is spiritually dead is free from sin,' (which amounts to saying, 'he that is holy is holy;') or, 'he who is spiritually dead is justified from sin.' But this last sense is utterly unsuited to the context, and implies that spiritual death, or holiness, is the ground of justification ; which is contrary to all Scripture, and especially to Paul's doctrine. The mystical sense of the word is the only one consistent with the context. The apostle has not been speaking of natural death, but of death with Christ; of the believer being crucified with him. It is of that he is now speaking. He had just said that the believer cannot continue to serve sin. He here gives the reason : *for* he who has died (with Christ) is justified, and therefore free from sin, free from its dominion. This is the great evangelical truth which underlies the apostle's whole doctrine of sanctification. The natural reason assumes that acceptance with a holy and just God must be founded on character, that men must be holy in order to be justified. The gospel reverses this, and teaches that God accepts the ungodly; that we must be justified in order to become holy. This is what Paul here assumes as known to his readers. As justification is the necessary means, and antecedent to holiness, he that is justified becomes holy; he cannot live in sin. And he who is dead, *i.e.* with Christ, (for it is only his death that secures justification,) is justified from sin. *To be justified from sin* means to be delivered from sin by justification. And that deliverance is twofold; judicial deliverance from its penalty, and subjective deliverance from its power. Both are secured by justification; the former directly, the other consequentially, as a necessary sequence. Compare Gal. ii. 19, 20; vi. 14; Col. ii. 13; iii. 3; 1 Pet. iv. 1, and other passages in which the sanctification of believers is represented as secured by the death of Christ.

VERSES 8—11. These verses contain the application of the truth taught in the preceding passage : ' If we are dead with Christ, we shall share in his life. If he lives, we shall live also. As his life is perpetual, it secures the continued supplies of life to all his members. Death has no more any dominion over him. Having died unto, or on account of, sin once, he now ever lives to, and with God. His people, therefore, must be conformed to him ; dead indeed unto sin, but alive unto God.' This passage does not contain a mere comparison between the literal death and resurrection of Christ, and the spiritual death and resurrection of believers, but it exhibits the connection between the death and life of the Redeemer and the sanctification of his people.

VERSE 8. *Now, if we be dead with Christ,* &c. If the truth stated in the preceding verses be admitted, viz. that our union with Christ is such that his death secures our deliverance from the penalty and power of sin, *we believe we shall also live with him.* That is, we are sure that the consequences of his death are not merely negative, *i. e.*, not simply deliverance from evil, moral and physical, but also a participation in his life. *We believe, i. e.,* we have a confidence, founded on the promise and revealed purpose of God. It is not a conclusion of reason ; it is not simply a hope, a peradventure ; it is a faith, an assured conviction that God, after having justified us through the blood of Christ, will not leave us spiritually defiled. *We shall live,* συζήσομεν, the future, referring not to what is to happen hereafter, but to what is the certain consequence of our union with Christ. If we are united mystically with Christ in his death, we shall certainly live with him, *i. e.*, we shall certainly partake of his life. As, however, this life is a permanent and eternal life, as it pertains to the body as well as to the soul, a participation of his life now involves a participation of it, with all its glorious consequences, for ever. *To live with Christ,* therefore, includes two ideas ; association with him, and similarity to him. We partake of his life, and consequently our life is like his. In like manner, since we die *with* him, we die *as* he died. So, too, when we are said *to reign with him, to be glorified together,* both these ideas are included; see chap. viii. 17, and many similar passages. The life here spoken of is that "eternal life" which believers are said to possess even in this world ; see John iii. 36, v. 24 ; and which is manifested here by devotion to God, and hereafter in the purity and blessedness of heaven. It includes, therefore, all the consequences of redemption. We are not to consider the apostle as merely running a parallel between the natural death and resurrection of Christ, and the spiritual death and resurrection of his people, as has already been remarked, but as showing that, in consequence of union to him in his death, we must die *as* he died, and live *as* he lives.   That is, that the effect of his death is to destroy the power of sin ; and.the result of his living is the communication and preservation of Divine life to all who are connected with him.   This being the case, the objection stated in ver. 1 of this chapter, is seen to be entirely unfounded. This life of Christ, to which we are conformed, is described in the following verses, first as perpetual, and secondly, as devoted unto God.

VERSE 9.   *Knowing that Christ, being raised from the dead, dieth no more.   Knowing* εἰδότες is either equal to καὶ οἴδαμεν, *and we know*, thus introducing a new idea, or it is causal, *because* we know.   The latter is to be preferred.   We are sure we shall be partakers of the life of Christ, because we know that he lives.   Were he not a living Saviour, if his life were not perpetual, he could not be the source of life to his people in all ages.   The perpetuity of Christ's life, therefore, is presented, 1. As the ground of assurance of the perpetuity of the life of believers.   We shall partake of the life of Christ, *i. e*., of the spiritual and eternal blessings of redemption, because he ever lives to make intercession for us, and to grant us those supplies of grace which we need ; see chap. v. 10 : John xiv. 19 ; 1 Cor. xv. 22, &c.   As death has no more dominion over him, there is no ground of apprehension that our supplies of life will be cut off.   This verse, therefore, is introduced as the ground of the declaration, " we shall live with him," at the close of ver. 8.   2. The perpetuity of the life of Christ is one of the points in which our life is to be conformed to his. Christ *dieth no more*, death *hath no more dominion over him*.   This repetition is for the sake of emphasis.   Christ's subjection to death was voluntary.   It was not from a necessity of nature, nor from any obligation to justice.   He laid down his life of himself.   He voluntarily submitted to death for our sakes, and was the master of death even in dying ; and therefore he is, so to speak, in no danger of ever being subject to its power. The object of his voluntary submission to death having been accomplished, he lives for evermore.   This is more fully expressed in the following verse.

VERSE 10.   *For in that he died, he died unto sin once*, &c.   He can never die again, *for* in dying he died once for all.   By the one offering of himself, he has for ever perfected them that are sanctified.   The apostle, in the Epistle to the Hebrews, while arguing to show the necessity of the death of Christ as a sacrifice for sin, argues also to show that such was the efficacy of that sacrifice, it need not, and cannot be repeated.   Heb. vii. 27, ix. 12, x. 10 ; 1 Pet. iii. 18.

In that he died, ὁ ἀπέθανε ; ὁ may be taken absolutely *quod attinet ad id, quod, as to that* he died, so far as concerns his dying ; compare Gal. ii. 20 ; or the relative may be taken as the object, *the death he died*.   See *Winer*, III., § 24. 4. 3.   *He died unto sin*, τῇ ἁμαρτίᾳ ἀπέθανεν, so far as the words are concerned, admits of different interpretations.   It may mean, he died *for the destruction of sin ;* or, he died for its expiation, *i. e*., on account of sin ; or, in accordance with the force of the same words in ver. 2, and the analogous expression, νεκροὺς τῇ ἁμαρτίᾳ, *dead to sin*, ver. 11, he died as to sin, was by death freed from sin.   In this last sense, although the words are the same, the idea is very different in the two cases.   The believer dies to sin in one sense, Christ in another.   In both cases the idea of separation is expressed ; but in the case of the believer, it is separation from personal, indwelling sin ; in that of Christ, it is separation from the burden of his people's sin, which he bore upon the cross. The context and the argument favour this last interpretation. Death has no more dominion over Christ, for he died to sin ; by the one sacrifice of himself, he freed himself from the burden of sin which he had voluntarily assumed. The law is perfectly satisfied ; it has no further penalty to inflict. Of course the same truth or doctrine is expressed, if the other expositions of the phrase be preferred. It is only a question as to the form in which the same general truth is presented. Christ's death was for the destruction of sin, for its expiation; and it was a deliverance from it, *i. e.*, from the burden of its imputed guilt. He came the first time with sin ; he is to come the second time *without sin* (without that burden), unto salvation. *In that he liveth, he liveth unto God.* This is said in contrast to what precedes. He died unto sin, he lives unto God. So must the believer. Death must be followed by life ; the one is in order to the other. It is of course not implied that our Lord's life on earth was not a living unto God, *i. e.*, a living having God for its end and object. The antithetical expression is used simply to indicate the analogy between Christ and his people. They must be freed from sin, and be devoted to God, because their Lord and Saviour, in whose death and life they share, died unto sin, and lives unto God. Many of the Fathers, and some later interpreters, take τῷ Θεῷ as equivalent to τῇ δυνάμει τοῦ Θεοῦ, *by the power of God.* But this is unsuited to the connection. It is not the source of Christ's life, but the nature of it, as perpetual and holy, that the apostle would bring into view. Olshausen says τῷ Θεῷ means *for God, i. e., for righteousness,* as opposed to sin, in the first clause : " He died for the destruction of sin, he lives for the promotion of righteousness." But this is unnecessary, and inconsistent with the context.

VERSE 11. *Likewise reckon ye also yourselves to be dead indeed unto sin, but alive unto God,* &c. What is true in itself, should be true in their convictions and consciousness. If in point of fact believers are partakers of the death and life of Christ ; if they die with him, and live with him, then they should so regard themselves. They should receive this truth, with all its consoling and sanctifying power, into their hearts, and manifest it in their lives. *So also ye,* οὕτω καὶ ὑμεῖς, a point may be placed after ὑμεῖς ; so that the sense is, *so also are ye,* as is done by Griesbach and others. The simpler and more common method is to read the words continuously : *so also regard ye yourselves as dead to sin,* νεκροὺς τῇ ἁμαρτίᾳ ; not reckon yourselves *to be* dead, as the word εἶναι, although found in the common text, is omitted by almost all the critical editors, on the authority of the oldest manuscripts, and the sense is complete without it ; λογίζεσθαι τινά τι, means *to regard one as something.* Believers are to look upon themselves in their true light, viz., *as dead to sin,* freed from its penalty and dominion. This is a freedom which belongs to them as believers, and therefore the apostle adds, ἐν Χριστῷ 'Ιησοῦ, not *through,* but *in* Christ Jesus, that is, in virtue of union with him. These words belong equally to both clauses of this verse. It is in Christ that the believer is dead to sin, and alive to God. The old man is crucified; the new man, the soul as renewed, is imbued with a new life, of which God is the object ; which consists in fellowship with him, and which is manifested by devotion to his service, and by obedience to his will. The words *our Lord,* τῷ Κυρίῳ ἡμῶν, are not found in the best manuscripts.

DOCTRINE.

1. Truth cannot lead to unholiness. If a doctrine encourages sin, it must be false, vers. 1, 2.

2. There can be no greater contradiction and absurdity than for one who lives in sin to claim to be a Christian, ver. 2.

3. Antinomianism is not only an error, it is a falsehood and a slander. It pronounces valid the very objection against the gospel which Paul pronounces a contradiction and absurdity, and which he evidently regards as a fatal objection, were it well founded, vers. 2—4, &c.

4. Baptism includes a profession of the religion taught by him in whose name we are baptised, and an obligation to obey his laws, vers. 3, 4.

5. The grand design of Christianity is the destruction of sin. When sincerely embraced, therefore, it is with a view to this end, ver. 3.

6. The source of the believer's holiness is his union with Christ, by which his reconciliation to God, and his participation of the influences of the Holy Spirit are secured, vers. 4, 6.

7. The fact that Christ lives, renders it certain that his people shall live in holiness here, and in glory hereafter, ver. 8.

8. The only proper evidence that we are partakers of the benefits of the death and life of Christ, is our dying to sin, and living to God, ver. 11.

9. The gospel, which teaches the only true method of justification, is the only system that can secure the sanctification of men. This is not only the doctrine of this section, but it is the leading truth of this and the following chapter.

REMARKS.

1. As the most prominent doctrinal truth of this passage is, that the death of Christ secures the destruction of sin wherever it secures its pardon; so the most obvious practical inference is, that it is vain to hope for the latter benefit, unless we labour for the full attainment of the former, vers. 2—11.

2. For a professing Christian to live in sin, is not only to give positive evidence that he is not a real Christian, but it is to misrepresent and slander the gospel of the grace of God, to the dishonour of religion, and the injury of the souls of men, vers. 2—11.

3. Instead of holiness being in order to pardon, pardon is in order to holiness. This is the mystery of evangelical morals, vers. 4, &c.

4. The only effectual method of gaining the victory over our sins, is to live in communion with Jesus Christ; to regard his death as securing the pardon of sin, as restoring us to the Divine favour, and as procuring for us the influences of the Holy Spirit. It is those who thus look to Christ not only for pardon, but for holiness, that are successful in subduing sin; while the *legalist* remains its slave, vers. 6, 8.

5. It is a consolation to the believer to know, that if he has evidence of being *now* a Christian, he may be sure that he shall live with Christ. As long and as surely as the head lives, so long and so surely must all the members live, ver. 8, &c.

6. To be in Christ is the source of the Christian's life; to be like Christ is the sum of his excellence; to be with Christ is the fulness of his joy, vers. 2—11.

ROMANS VI. 12—23.

ANALYSIS.

PAUL having shown, in the preceding section, that union with Christ secures not only the pardon, but the destruction of sin, exhorts his brethren to live agreeably to the nature and design of the gospel, vers. 12, 13. As an encouragement in their efforts to resist their corruptions, he assures them that sin shall not have dominion over them, because they are not under the law, but under grace, ver. 14. This is another fundamental principle in the doctrine of sanctification. Holiness is not attained, and cannot be attained by those who, being under the law, are still unreconciled to God. It is necessary that we should enjoy his favour, in order to exercise towards him right affections. This doctrine is not justly liable to the objection, that we may sin with impunity if not under the law, ver. 15. The true situation of the Christian is illustrated by a reference to the relation between a servant and his master. Believers, before conversion, were the servants of sin; after it, they are the servants of righteousness. Formerly they were under an influence which secured their obedience to evil; now they are under an influence which secures their obedience to good. The consequence of the former service was death; of the present, life. The knowledge of these consequences tends to secure the continued fidelity of the Christian to his new Master, vers. 16—23.

COMMENTARY.

VERSE 12. *Let not sin therefore reign in your mortal body,* &c. This is a practical inference (οὖν) from what precedes. Since the believer is in fact united to Christ in his death and life, he should live accordingly. The exhortation contained in this and the following verse has a negative and positive form—yield not to sin, but give yourselves up to God—corresponding to the clauses, *dead to sin,* and *alive unto God,* in ver. 11. *To reign* signifies to exercise uncontrolled authority. Sin, although mortified in the believer, is not destroyed. Its power to injure remains after its dominion is overthrown. The exhortation is, that we should not yield to this dethroned adversary of Christ and the soul, but strenuously strive against its efforts to gain ascendency over us, and to bring us again into bondage. Let not sin reign *in your mortal body.* This is a difficult clause. 1. *Mortal body* may be a periphrase for *you* : ' Let not sin reign within you ;' as in the next verse, *your members* may stand for *yourselves.* 2. Others say that θνητός (*mortal*) is to be taken in the figurative sense in which νεκρός, *dead, i. e., corrupt,* is often used. 3. Others take σῶμα in the sense of σάρξ, *corrupt nature,* including everything in man as fallen, which is not due to the indwelling of the Holy Spirit. Thus Calvin says, " Nuper admonui vocem Corporis non pro carne et cute et ossibus accipi, sed pro tota hominis massa, ut ita loquar. Id certius colligere licet ex praesenti loco: quia alterum membrum, quod mox subjiciet de corporis partibus, ad animum quoque extenditur. Sic autem crasse Paulus terrenum hominem significat." He says the word *mortal* is used, " per contemptum, ut doceat totam hominis naturam ad mortem et exitium inclinare." So also Philippi, among the modern commentators says that here, as in Rom.

viii. 10, 13 (where θανατοῦν τὰς πράξεις τοῦ σώματος is opposed to κατὰ σάρκα ζῆν), σῶμα is the antithesis of πνεῦμα, the latter being the soul as pervaded by the Spirit of God, and the former our nature considered as corrupt. This, however, is so contrary to the general usage of Scripture, that the ordinary sense of the words is to be preferred. Paul does not teach that the body is the source of sin, nor its exclusive or principal seat; but it is the organ of its manifestation. It is that through which the dominion of sin is outwardly revealed. The body is under the power of sin, and that power the apostle would have us resist; and on the other hand, the sensual appetites of the body tend to enslave the soul. Body and soul are so united in a common life, that to say, ' Let not sin reign in your mortal body,' and to say, ' Let not sin reign in you,' amount to the same thing. When we speak of sin as dwelling in the soul, we do not deny its relation to the body; so neither does the apostle, when he speaks of sin dwelling in the body, mean to deny its relation to the soul.

That ye should obey it (αὐτῇ, *i.e.*, *sin*,) *in the lusts thereof*, (αὐτοῦ, viz., of the body.) We should not obey sin by yielding to carnal appetites. The common text has here, εἰς τὸ ὑπακούειν αὐτῇ ἐν ταῖς ἐπιθυμίαις αὐτοῦ. Knapp, Lachmann, and other editors, adopt the simpler and better authenticated reading, εἰς τὸ ὑπακούειν ταῖς ἐπιθυμίαις αὐτοῦ, *to obey its lusts, i. e.*, the lusts of the body. "A man," says Olshausen, "must always serve. There is no middle ground between the service of sin and the service of God. We have justification completely, or we have it not at all. Sanctification, as springing from a living faith, and as the fruit of God's love to us, admits of degrees, and may be more or less earnestly cultivated; but this determines, not our salvation, but only the measure of future blessedness. No wisdom or caution," he adds, "can guard this doctrine from misunderstanding, whether such misunderstanding arise unintentionally from the understanding, or designedly from insincerity of heart. It nevertheless is the only way which leads to God, in which the sincere and humble cannot err." "The key to the mystery," he goes on to say, " that the doctrine of redemption, although not demanding good works, produces them, is to be found in the fact that love excites love and the desire for holiness. Hence obedience is no longer slavish. We strive to obey, not in order to be saved or to please God, but because God saves us without works or merit of our own, whom, because he is reconciled in the Beloved, we delight to serve."

VERSE 13. *Neither yield ye your members, &c.* Do not permit sin to reign in you, nor yield your powers as its instruments. *Neither yield*, μηδὲ παριστάνετε. The word means *to place by, to present* (as an offering), Luke ii. 22 ; Rom. xii. 1 ; *to give up to the power or service of*, verses 16, 19, &c. *Your members*, either literally, members of the body, the eye, ear, hand, &c., or figuratively, your powers, whether of mind or body. The choice between the literal and figurative interpretation depends on the view taken of the preceding verse. If there σῶμα (*body*) be understood literally, then *your members* can only mean the members of the body; but if *mortal body* is there a periphrase for *you*, than *your members* must mean *your faculties*. The μέλη (*members*) are the parts of which the σῶμα consists ; and therefore if the σῶμα stands for the whole person, *the members* must include all our powers, mental as well as corporeal. In vii. 5, Paul says that sin " did work in our members;" and in ver. 23, he speaks of " a law in his members." In neither of those cases is the reference exclusively to the body. *As instruments of unrighteousness.* That is, instruments which unrighteousness uses, or which are employed to effect unrighteousness. The word ὅπλα is generic ; it is used in the general sense of instruments, for the tackle of a ship, the tools of an artisan, though most frequently for *weapons.* On occount of this general usage, and of Paul's own use of the word in xiii. 12, "armour of light," (2 Cor. vi. 7, "armour of righteousness," and 2 Cor. x. 4, "the weapons of our warfare,") many prefer the restricted sense in this place. Our members are regarded as weapons which sin uses to regain its dominion, or the predominance of unrighteousness. The context, however, does not favour the assumption of this allusion to a strife ; and therefore the general sense of *instruments,* or *implements,* is more in keeping with the rest of the passage. *But yield yourselves unto God;* ἀλλὰ παραστήσατε, *but, on the contrary,* present yourselves, *i.e.,* give yourselves up to God, not only your several powers, but your very selves, a dedication which of necessity involves that of each separate faculty. In the first clause of the verse the present tense, παριστάνετε, is used ; here it is the first aorist, *present yourselves once for all. As alive from the dead, i.e.,* as those who having been dead, are now alive. Having been quickened by the power of God, raised from the death of sin and all its dreadful consequences, they were bound to live unto God. Who, having been restored to life, would desire to return to the loathsomeness of the grave ? *And, i.e.,* and especially, your members (*i. e.,* παριστάνετε, *present* your members) *as* instruments of righteousness to God. Present all your powers to God, to be employed by him as implements of righteousness ; that is, instruments by which righteousness may be effected.

VERSE 14. *For sin shall not have dominion over you,* &c. The future here is not to be understood as expressing either a command or an exhortation, not only because the third, and not the second person is used, but also because of the connection, as indicated by *for.* We should yield ourselves to God, *for* sin shall not have dominion, &c. It is not a hopeless strnggle in which the believer is engaged, but one in which victory is certain. It is a joyful confidence which the apostle here expresses, that the power of sin has been effectually broken, and the triumph of holiness effectually secured by the work of Christ. The ground of the confidence that sin shall not have dominion, is to be found in the next clause : *For ye are not under the law, but under grace.* By *law* here, is not to be understood the Mosaic law. The sense is not, 'Sin shall not have dominion over you, because the Mosaic law is abrogated.' The word is to be taken in its widest sense. It is the rule of duty, that which binds the conscience as an expression of the will of God. This is plain : 1. From the use of the word through this epistle and other parts of the New Testament. 2. From the whole doctrine of redemption, which teaches that the law from which we are delivered by the death of Christ, is not simply the Mosaic law ; we are not merely delivered from Judaism, but from the obligation of fulfilling the law of God as the condition of salvation. 3. Deliverance from the Mosaic law does not secure holiness. A man may cease to be a Jew, and yet not be a new creature in Christ Jesus. 4. The antithesis between law and grace shows that more than the law of Moses is here intended. If free from the Mosaic law, they may still be under some other law, and as little under grace as the Pharisees. To be under the law is to be under the obligation to fulfil the law of God as a rule of duty, as the condition of salvation. Whosoever is under the law in this sense, is under the curse ; for the law says, "Cursed is every one

who continueth not in all things written in the book of the law to do
them." As no man is free from sin, as no man can perfectly keep the
commandments of God, every man who rests upon his personal conformity
to the law, as the ground of his acceptance with God, must be condemned.
We are not under the law in this sense, but under grace ; that is, under a
system of gratuitous justification. We are justified by grace, without
works. We are not under a legal dispensation, requiring personal conformity to the law, and entire freedom from sin, past and present, as the
condition of our acceptance ; but we are under a gracious dispensation,
according to which God dispenses pardon freely, and accepts the sinner as
a sinner, for Christ's sake, without works or merit of his own. Whoever
is under the law in the sense just explained, is not only under condemnation, but he is of necessity under a legal or slavish spirit. What he
does, he does as a slave, to escape punishment. But he who is under
grace, who is gratuitously accepted of God, and restored to his favour, is
under a filial spirit. The principle of obedience in him is love, and not
fear. Here, as everywhere else in the Bible, it is assumed that the favour
of God is our life. We must be reconciled to him before we can be holy ;
we must feel that he loves us before we can love him. Paul says it was
the love of Christ to him, that constrained him to live for Him who thus
loved him, and gave Himself for him. The only hope therefore of sinners,
is in freedom from the law, freedom from its condemnation, freedom from
the obligation to fulfil it as the condition of acceptance, and freedom from
its spirit. Those who are thus free, who renounce all dependence on their
own merit or strength, who accept the offer of justification as a free gift of
God, and who are assured that God for Christ's sake is reconciled to them,
are so united to Christ that they partake of his life, and their holiness
here and salvation hereafter are rendered perfectly certain.

Verse 15. *What then ? shall we sin, because we are not under the law,
but under grace ? God forbid.* Because works are not the ground of our
justification ; because we are justified freely by his grace, are we at liberty
to sin without fear and without restraint ? Does the doctrine of gratuitous
salvation give a license to the unrestrained indulgence of all evil ? Such
has been the objection to the doctrines of grace in all ages. And the fact
that this objection was made to Paul's teachings, proves that his doctrine
is the same with that against which the same objection is still urged. As
the further consideration of this difficulty is resumed in the following
chapter, the apostle here contents himself with a simple negation, and a
reference to the constraining influence under which the freely pardoned
sinner is brought, which renders it as impossible for him to serve sin, as it
is for the slave of one man to be obedient to another man. The slave *must*
serve his own master.

Verse 16. *Know ye not, that to whom ye yield yourselves servants to
obey, his servants ye are to whom ye obey,* &c. 'Know ye not that those
who obey sin are its slaves ; hurried on from one degrading service to
another, until it works their ruin ; but those who serve holiness are
constrained, though sweetly, to constancy and fidelity, until the glorious
consummation of their course ?' As a servant or slave is under an
influence which secures the continuance of his obedience, and he who
serves holiness is under an influence which effectually secures the constancy of his service. This being the case, it is not possible for the
Christian or servant of holiness to be found engaged in the service

of sin. The language and the construction are here nearly the same as in verse 13. Here, as there, we have παριστάνετε in the sense of giving up to the power and disposal of. Paul says, that those who give themselves up to another as δούλους εἰς ὑπακοήν, *slaves to obedience*, are the δοῦλοι of him whom they thus obey. It enters into the idea of slavery, that the subjection is absolute and continued. The slave does not obey his own will, but his master's. He is subject not for a time, but for life. He is under an influence which secures obedience. This is as true in spiritual as in external relations. He who serves sin is the slave of sin. He is under its power. He cannot free himself from its dominion. He may hate his bondage ; his reason and conscience may protest against it ; his will may resist it ; but he is still constrained to obedience. This is the doctrine of our Lord, as taught in John viii. 34 : " He that committeth sin is the slave of sin." This remains true, although this service is *unto death :* " The wages of sin is death." The death intended is spiritual and eternal. It is the absolute loss of the life of the soul, which consists in the favour and fellowship of God, and conformity to his image. What is true of sin is true of holiness. He who by virtue of union with Christ is made obedient to God, becomes, as Paul says, a δοῦλος ὑπακοῆς, *a slave of obedience.* Obedience (personified) is the master to whom he is now subject. He is not only bound to obey, but he is made to obey in despite of the resistance of his still imperfectly sanctified nature. He cannot but obey. The point of analogy to which reference is here made, is the certainty of the effect, and the constraining influence by which that effect is secured. In the case both of sin and of holiness, obedience is certain ; and it is rendered certain by a power superior to the will of man. The great difference is, that in the one case this subjection is abnormal and destructive, in the other it is normal and beneficent. A wise man is free in being subject to his reason. The more absolute and constant the authority of reason, the more exalted and free is the soul. In like manner, the more completely God reigns in us, the more completely we are subject to his will, so much the more are we free ; that is, so much the more do we act in accordance with the laws of our nature and the end of our being. *Servants of obedience unto right-eousness ;* δικαιοσύνη must here be taken in its subjective sense. It is inward righteousness, or holiness. And in this sense it is eternal life, and therefore antithetical to θάνατος, which is spiritual and eternal death. The service of sin results in death, the service of God results in righteousness ; that is, in our being right, completely conformed to the image of God, in which the life of the soul consists.

VERSE 17. *But God be thanked, that ye were the servants of sin ; but ye have obeyed from the heart,* &c. As it is the apostle's object to show that believers cannot live in sin, inasmuch as they have become the servants of another master, he applies the general truth stated in the preceding verses more directly to his immediate readers, and gives thanks that they, being emancipated from their former bondage, are now bound to a master whose service is perfect liberty. The expression in the first member of this verse is somewhat unusual, although the sense is plain : " God be thanked, that ye *were* the servants of sin ;" that is, that this slavery is past ; or, ' God be thanked, that ye, being the servants of sin, have obeyed,' &c.

Ye have obeyed from the heart ; this obedience is voluntary and sincere. They had not been passively transferred from one master to another ; but the power of sin being broken, they gladly renounced their bondage, and gave themselves unto God. *Ye obeyed*, says the apostle, *the form of doctrine which was delivered to you.* The τύπος διδαχῆς, *the form of doctrine*, may mean the doctrine which is a τύπος, a model or standard to which we should conform—*sentiendi agendique norma et regula.* Calvin says it means " expressam justitiæ imaginem, quam cordibus nostris Christus insculpsit." Another explanation assumes τύπος to be equivalent to *form, contents*, or substance of the doctrine. Compare μόρφωσις τῆς γνώσεως, ii. 20. The former explanation is sustained by a reference to 2 Tim. i. 13, where Paul speaks of a ὑποτύπωσις ὑγιαινόντων λόγων, *a form of sound words;* that is, sound words which are a pattern or standard of faith. Compare Acts xxiii. 25 : ' Having written an epistle containing this type,' *i.e.* form of words. By form of doctrine is to be understood the Gospel, either in its limited sense of the doctrine of gratuitous justification through Christ, of which the apostle had been speaking ; or in its wider sense of the whole doctrine of Christ as a rule both of faith and practice. The former includes the latter. He who receives Christ as priest, receives him as a Lord. He who comes to him for justification, comes also for sanctification ; and therefore obedience to the call to put our trust in Christ as our righteousness, implies obedience to his whole revealed will. The words ὑπηκούσατε εἰς ὃν παρεδόθητε τύπον διδαχῆς, may be resolved thus, ὑπηκούσατε τύπῳ διδαχῆς, εἰς ὃν παρεδόθητε, *ye have obeyed the type of doctrine to which ye have been delivered.* That is, the mould into which, as it were, ye have been cast ; as Beza says, the gospel is regarded "quasi instar typi cujusdam, cui veluti immittamur, ut ejus figuræ conformemur." This last idea is unnatural : εἰς ὃν παρεδόθητε is either equivalent to ὃς παρεδόθη ὑμῖν, *which was delivered unto you*, (see *Winer*, § 24, 2,) or, *to which ye were delivered*, " cui divinitus traditi estis." That is, to which ye were subjected. The intimation is, that faith in the gospel is the gift of God, and obedience is our consequent act. " The passive (παρεδόθητε,)" says Philippi, " indicates the passive relation of men to the work of regeneration, of which his activity (ὑπηκούσατε) is the consequence, according to the familiar dictum : Ita a Spiritu Dei agimur ut ipsi quoque agamus."

Verse 18. *Being made free from sin, ye became the servants of righteousness.* This verse may be regarded as the conclusion from what precedes, δέ being used for οὖν : ' Being freed *then* from sin,' &c. ; or it may be connected immediately with ver. 17, a comma instead of a period intervening : ' Ye have obeyed the form of doctrine, having been freed,' &c. The latter is better. Freed by the grace of God from sin as a despotic master, *ye became the servants*, ἐδουλώθητε, ye were made slaves to righteousness. It was not license, but a change of masters, that they had experienced. This being the case, it is impossible they should serve sin ; they have now another master. A manumitted slave does not continue subject to his former master. "Absurdum est, ut post manumissionem quis in servitutis conditione maneat. Observandum, quomodo nemo possit justitiæ servire nisi Dei potentia et beneficio prius a peccati tyrannide liberatus." *Calvin.* To the same effect our Lord says : " If the Son make you free, ye shall be free indeed." John viii. 36. This subjection to righteousness is perfect liberty. It is the subjection of the soul to God, reason, and conscience, wherein true liberty consists. This being the case, the apostle in the following verse explains the reason why he used a figure apparently so incongruous, in speaking of the relation of the believer to righteousness.

Verse 19. *I speak after the manner of men,* ἀνθρώπινον λέγω; *I say* what is human, *i.e.* common among men. The only difference between this expression and the more common phrase, κατ᾽ ἄνθρωπον λέγω, is, that the former characterizes as human the thing said, and the other the manner of saying it. The idea in this case is the same. The apostle means to say, that he uses an illustration drawn from the common relations of men, to set forth the relation of the believer to God. The slave is bound to serve his master; the obedience of the believer to God is no less certain. The one is slavery, because the obedience is independent of the will, and coerced; the other is perfect freedom, because rendered from the heart, and with full consent of the will. Yet both are a δουλεία, so far as certainty of obedience is concerned. This is the common and natural interpretation of this clause. Others, however, take ἀνθρώπινον in the sense in which it is used in 1 Cor. x. 13. There it is opposed to what is superhuman, beyond the strength of man to bear : 'I demand only what is human. The obedience required is, on account of the weakness of your flesh, only such as you are able to render. *For* as ye served sin, so you can serve righteousness. The one is as easy as the other. The one is the measure of the other.' But this does violence to the connection. The ὥσπερ—οὕτω do not refer to the measure of the obedience, but to the change of masters : 'As ye served sin, so now serve God.' Besides, the principle that the measure of obedience is determined by our ability, is utterly at variance with the word of God and the dictates of conscience. The simple design of the apostle in this passing or parenthetical remark is, to state the reason why he designated our new relation to God a slavery. He used this illustration, he says, *on account of the weakness of their flesh;* not intellectual weakness, but such as arose from the σάρξ, their nature as corrupt. It was their lack of spirituality which rendered such illustrations necessary. The γάρ (*for*) of the next clause refers to ver. 18 : 'Being freed from sin, ye became the servants of righteousness; *for* as ye yielded your members,' &c. *Your members,* yourselves, your various faculties, with special reference to their bodily organs as the outward, visible instruments of evil. Ye yielded your members, δοῦλα, *bound.* This is the only passage in the New Testament in which δοῦλος is used as an adjective. They yielded their members *to uncleanness and to iniquity,* τῇ ἀκαθαρσίᾳ καὶ τῇ ἀνομίᾳ. These two words express the same thing under different aspects. Sin subjectively considered is pollution, a defilement of the soul; relatively to the law of God, it is ἀνομία, what is unlawful, what fails of conformity to the law. In the next clause, *unto iniquity,* the word is used in a wider sense. They gave themselves up to iniquity, that is, to do evil; εἰς τὴν ἀνομίαν being equivalent to εἰς τὸ ποιεῖν ἀνομίαν. Men give themselves up to sin as a master, to do what the law forbids. The same idea is expressed, if εἰς τὴν ἀνομίαν means, *for the manifestation of iniquity. So now yield your members as servants to righteousness.* Having been delivered from bondage to the tyrant sin, ye should act as becomes your new relation, and be obedient to your new master, even to him who hath bought you with his blood. To righteousness, *unto holiness,* εἰς ἁγιασμόν, so as to be pure in heart and life. The proximate result of obedience to God is inward conformity to the Divine image. Compare 1 Thess. iii. 13 ; iv. 7.

Verse 20. *For when ye were the servants of sin, ye were free from righteousness.* This verse introduces a confirmation of what precedes. The foregoing exhortation is enforced by the consideration developed in vers. 21, 22, that the service of sin is death. The particle γάρ, therefore, is used in its common sense, *for,* and not *namely.* Formerly, when the slaves of sin, ye were ἐλεύθεροι τῇ δικαιοσύνῃ, that is, either 'free in the estimation of righteousness,' ("An ille *mihi* liber, cui mulier imperat ?" *Cicero;*) or, what is more natural, *as to righteousness;* so far as righteousness is concerned, ye were free. Righteousness had no power over you ; your service was rendered to another master. This is not to be understood ironically, as though the apostle designed to refer to their former state as one of freedom in their estimation. It is the simple statement of a fact of experience. While the servants of sin, they did not and could not serve righteousness. Here are two services, which is to be preferred ? This is the question which the apostle presents for their consideration.

Verse 21. The sense of this verse depends mainly on the pointing. It may be read thus : ' What fruit had ye then of those things of which ye are now ashamed ? (Answer, *None,*) for the end of those things is death.' Or, ' What fruit had ye then ? (Answer, *Such,*) of which ye are now ashamed, for,' &c. The choice between these interpretations is not very easy, and accordingly commentators are about equally divided between them. The Vulgate, the English version, Calvin, Beza, Bengel, Meyer, Fritzsche, &c., adopt the former. Luther, Melanchthon, Koppe, Tholuck, De Wette, Olshausen, &c., the latter. The decision seems to depend principally on the meaning given to the phrase, *to have fruit.* If this means, *to derive benefit,* then the sense is, ' What benefit did you derive from the things of which you are now ashamed ?' The natural answer is, 'None ; a course of conduct which ends in death can yield no benefit.' This gives a pertinent sense : it is suited to ver. 22, where fruit may also mean *advantage;* and especially it agrees best with the words ἐφ᾽ οἷς, which otherwise must refer to καρπόν, (fruit of which,) which is not natural. In favour of the second interpretation, however, it is urged that *fruit* is never in the New Testament used of reward or emolument, but always of acts. The familiar illustration is that of a tree whose fruit is good or bad according to its nature. According to this view, Paul means to ask, ' What fruit did you then produce ? Such,' he answers, ' of which you are now ashamed.' Besides this general use of the word (fruit), it is urged that in ver. 22, this is the natural sense of the word : " Ye have your fruit unto holiness ;" that is, ' Ye produce fruit which tends to holiness.' " This figure," says Olshausen, " is the more significant, because it is so directly opposed to that Pelagianism which is so congenial with our fallen nature. The natural man, destitute of the knowledge of God, of himself, and of sin, dreams that by his own strength and efforts he can produce a form of virtue which can stand before the bar of God. He does not know that of necessity, and by a law of his nature, he can only produce evil fruit, just as a wild tree can produce only bitter fruit. Even should he succeed in calling into exercise all the good he has in the most perfect form, it is so destitute of love, and so corrupted by conceit, that it merits condemnation, as fully as though the life were openly immoral. The beginning of truth, of which holiness, (which is true liberty,) by a like organic necessity and law of nature, is the fruit, is for man the acknowledgment that death reigns in him, and that he must be imbued with life." All this is true, and all this is really involved in the familiar figure which our Lord uses to illustrate the relation between the state of the heart and of the outward life. But this does not seem to be the idea which the apostle here intends to present. The phrase, καρπὸν ποιεῖν, does indeed always mean to produce fruit, and figuratively, to do good or evil ; but καρπὸν ἔχειν, *to have fruit,* means to have the advantage or profit. Thus, in i. 13, Paul says : " That I might have some fruit among you;" *i. e.* that he might gain something, win some souls for Christ. If this be the true meaning of the phrase here, then the former of the two interpretations is to be preferred. What advantage had you of the service of sin ? None; *for* the end of those things, the τέλος, the final result of the service of sin, is *death ;* not physical death, but the death of the soul, final and hopeless perdition. Such was their former condition ; to this the contrast is given in the next verse.

VERSE 22. *But now, being made free from sin,* ἐλευθερωθέντες ἀπὸ τῆς ἁμαρτίας; having been emancipated from one master. δουλωθέντες δὲ τῷ Θεῷ, *and become slaves to God, i. e.* being subject to his controlling influence by the power of his Spirit, *ye have your fruit unto holiness ;* that is, the benefit or effect derived from the service of God is holiness. Sanctification is the proximate result of this new service. *And the end eternal life.* The final issue of this service is complete salvation ; the restoration of the soul to the favour and enjoyment of God for ever. "Quemadmodum duplicem peccati finem ante proposuit, ita nunc justitiæ. Peccatum in hac vita malæ conscientiæ tormenta affert, deinde aeternam mortem. Justitiæ præsentem fructum colligimus, sanctificationem : in futurum, speramus vitam aeternam."

VERSE 23. *For the wages of sin is death ; but the gift of God is eternal life, through Jesus Christ our Lord.* The reason why death is the result of sin is, that sin deserves death. Death is due to it in justice. There is the same obligation in justice, that sin should be followed by death, as that the labourer should receive his wages. As it would be unjust, and therefore wrong, to defraud the labourer of his stipulated reward, so it would be unjust to allow sin to go unpunished. Those, therefore, who hope for pardon without an atonement, hope that God will in the end prove unjust. The word ὀψώνια is, strictly, the rations of soldiers ; in a wider sense, the same as ἀντιμισθία, or μισθός, anything which is due as a matter of debt. *But the gift of God,* τὸ δὲ χάρισμα τοῦ Θεοῦ, the free, unmerited gift of God, is eternal life. The connection between holiness and life is no less certain than that between sin and death, but on different grounds. Sin deserves death ; holiness is itself the gift of God, and is freely crowned with eternal life. The idea of merit is everywhere and in every way excluded from the gospel method of salvation. It is a system of grace, from the beginning to the consummation. *Through* (rather *in*) *Jesus Christ our Lord.* It is in Christ, as united to him, that we are made partakers of eternal life. Jesus Christ and his gospel, then, instead of being the ministers of sin—as the Jews, and since them, the opponents of the doctrines of grace, confidently asserted—effectually secure what the law never could accomplish, an obedience resulting in holiness here, and in eternal life hereafter.

DOCTRINE.

1. The leading doctrine of this section, and of the whole gospel, in reference to sanctification, is, that grace, instead of leading to the indulgence of sin, is essential to the exercise of holiness. So long as we are under the influence of a self-righteous or legal spirit, the motive and aim of all good works, are wrong or defective. The motive is fear, or some merely natural affection, and the aim, to merit the bestowment of good. But when we accept of the gracious offers of the gospel, and feel that our sins are gratuitously pardoned, a sense of the divine love, shed abroad in the

heart of the Holy Spirit, awakens all holy affections. The motive to obedience is now love, and its aim the glory of God, ver. 14, &c.

2. Paul teaches that it is not only obligatory on Christians to renounce the service of sin, but that, in point of fact, the authority and power of their former master are destroyed, and those of their new master experienced, whenever they embrace the gospel. This is the very nature of the change. The charge, therefore, that the gospel leads to the service of sin, is an absurdity, vers. 15—18.

3. Religion is essentially active. It is the yielding up of ourselves, with all our powers, to God, and the actual employment of them as instruments in doing good. Nothing can be at a greater remove from this, than making religion a mere matter of indolent profession, (a saying, Lord, Lord,) ver. 12, &c.

4. Both from the nature of things, and the appointment of God, the wages of sin is death. It renders intercourse with God, who is the fountain of life, impossible. It consists in the exercise of feelings, in their own nature, inconsistent with happiness ; it constantly increases in malignity, and in power to destroy the peace of the soul. Apart from these essential tendencies, its relation to conscience and the justice of God, renders the connection between sin and misery indissoluble. Salvation in sin is as much a contradiction, as happiness in misery, vers. 21, 23.

5. Eternal life is the GIFT of God. It does not, like eternal death, flow, as a natural consequence, from anything in us. With the holy angels, who have never lost the favour of God, this may be the case. But the tendency of all that belongs to us, is to death ; this must be counteracted ; those excellencies, in which life consists, and from which it flows, must be produced, sustained, and strengthened by the constant, condescending, and long-suffering grace of the Holy Spirit. The life thus graciously produced, and graciously sustained, is at last graciously crowned with eternal glory, vers. 22, 23.

REMARKS.

1. We should cultivate a sense of the Divine favour as a means to holiness. We must cease to be slaves, before we can be children. We must be free from the dominion of fear, before we can be under the government of love. A self-righteous spirit, therefore, is not more inconsistent with reliance on the righteousness of Christ, in order to justification, than it is with the existence and progress of sanctification. Whatever tends to destroy a sense of the Divine favour, must be inimical to holiness. Hence the necessity of keeping a conscience void of offence, and of maintaining uninterrupted our union with Christ as our sacrifice and advocate, ver. 14, &c.

2. Those Christians are under a great mistake, who suppose that despondency is favourable to piety. Happiness is one of the elements of life. Hope and joy are twin daughters of piety, and cannot, without violence and injury, be separated from their parent. To rejoice is as much a duty as it is a privilege, ver. 14, &c.

3. Sinners are slaves. Sin reigns over them ; and all their powers are delivered to this master as instruments of unrighteousness. He secures obedience with infallible certainty ; his bonds become stronger every day, and his wages are death. From his tyranny and recompense there is no deliverance by the law ; our only hope is in Jesus Christ our Lord, vers. 12, 13, 16, &c.

4. Christians are the servants of God. He reigns over them, and all their powers are consecrated to him. He, too, secures fidelity, and his bonds of love and duty become stronger every day. His reward is eternal life, vers. 12, 13, 16, &c.

5. It is of God, that those who were once the servants of sin, become the servants of righteousness. To him, therefore, all the praise and gratitude belong, ver. 17.

6. When a man is the slave of sin, he commonly thinks himself free; and when most degraded, is often the most proud. When truly free, he feels himself most strongly bound to God; and when most elevated, is most humble, vers. 20—22.

7. Self-abasement, or shame in view of his past life, is the necessary result of those views of his duty and destiny, which every Christian obtains when he becomes the servant of God, ver. 21.

CHAPTER VII.

CONTENTS.

THE APOSTLE, HAVING SHOWN IN THE PRECEDING CHAPTER THAT THE DOCTRINES OF GRACE DO NOT GIVE LIBERTY TO SIN, BUT, ON THE CONTRARY, ARE PRODUCTIVE OF HOLINESS, IN THIS CHAPTER FIRST ILLUSTRATES AND CONFIRMS HIS POSITION, THAT WE ARE NOT UNDER THE LAW, BUT UNDER GRACE, AND SHOWS THE CONSEQUENCES OF THIS CHANGE IN OUR RELATION TO GOD. WHILE UNDER THE LAW, WE BROUGHT FORTH FRUIT UNTO SIN; WHEN UNDER GRACE, WE BRING FORTH FRUIT UNTO RIGHTEOUSNESS. THIS OCCUPIES THE FIRST SECTION, VERS. 1—6. THE SECOND, VERS. 7 —25, CONTAINS AN EXHIBITION OF THE OPERATION OF THE LAW, DERIVED FROM THE APOSTLE'S OWN EXPERIENCE, AND DESIGNED TO SHOW ITS INSUFFICIENCY TO PRODUCE SANCTIFICATION, AS HE HAD BEFORE PROVED IT TO BE INSUFFICIENT FOR JUSTIFICATION. THIS SECTION CONSISTS OF TWO PARTS, VERS. 7—13, WHICH EXHIBIT THE OPERATION OF THE LAW IN PRODUCING CONVICTION OF SIN; AND VERS. 14—25, WHICH SHOW THAT IN THE INWARD CONFLICT BETWEEN SIN AND HOLINESS, THE LAW CANNOT AFFORD THE BELIEVER ANY RELIEF. HIS ONLY HOPE OF VICTORY IS IN THE GRACE OF THE LORD JESUS CHRIST.

ROMANS VII. 1—6.

ANALYSIS.

This section is an illustration of the position assumed in ver. 14 of the preceding chapter: we are not under law, but under grace. Paul remarks, as a general fact, that the authority of laws is not perpetual, ver. 1. For example, the law of marriage binds a woman to her husband only so long as he lives. When he is dead, she is free from the obligation which that law imposed, and is at liberty to marry another man, vers. 2, 3. So we, being free from the law, which was our first husband, are at liberty to marry another, even Christ. We are freed from the law by the death of Christ, ver. 4. The fruit of our first marriage was sin, ver. 5. The fruit of the second is holiness, ver. 6.

The apparent confusion in this passage arises from the apostle's not carrying the figure regularly through. As a woman is free from obligation to her husband by *his* death, so we are free from the law by *its* death, is obviously the illustration intended. But the apostle, out of respect probably to the feelings of his readers, avoids saying the law is dead, but expresses the idea that we are free from it, by saying, we are dead to the law by the body of Christ. " Cæterum nequis conturbetur, quod inter se comparata membra non omnino respondent : præmonendi sumus, apostolum data opera voluisse exigua inversione deflectere asperioris verbi invidiam. Debuerat dicere, ut ordine similitudinem contexeret : Mulier post mortem viri soluta est a conjugii vinculo, Lex, quæ locum habet mariti erga nos, mortua est nobis : ergo sumus ab ejus potestate liberi. Sed ne offenderet Judæos verbi asperitate, si dixisset legem esse mortuam, deflectione est usus, dicens nos legi esse mortuos." *Calvin.*

COMMENTARY.

VERSE 1. *Know ye not, brethren, (for I speak to them that know the law,) how that the law hath dominion over a man as long as he liveth.* In the English version of the words, ἡ ἀγνοεῖτε, the particle ἤ, *or*, is overlooked. As that particle is almost always used in reference to the immediately preceding context, Meyer and others insist on connecting this verse with vi. 23 : 'The gift of God is eternal life; *or* are ye ignorant.' That is, you must recognize eternal life as a gift, unless ye are ignorant that the law does not bind the dead. But this is evidently forced. The idea which ἤ is used to recall, is that in vi. 14 : " Ye are not under the law, but under grace." This is the main idea in the whole context, and is that which the following passage carries out and enforces. The thing to be proved is, that we are not under the law. The proof is, that the law does not bind the dead. But we are dead, therefore we are free from the law. This idea, that the law binds a man only so long as he lives, is presented as a general principle, and is then illustrated by a specific example. That example is the law of marriage, which ceases to bind the parties when one of them is dead. So the law, as a covenant of works, ceases to bind us when death has loosed its bonds. We are as free as the woman whose husband is dead. "Sit generalis propositio," says Calvin, "legem non in alium finem latam esse hominibus, quam ut præsentem vitam moderetur : apud mortuos nullum ei superesse locum. Cui postea hypothesin subjiciet, nos illi esse mortuos in Christi corpore." *Brethren ;* a mode of address applicable to all believers. He speaks to his spiritual brethren, and not to the Jewish converts alone, his brethren according to the flesh. *For I speak to them that know the law.* That is, I speak to you as to persons who know the law ; not, I speak to those among you who know the law. He does not distinguish one class of his readers from another. That would require the article in the dative, τοῖς γινώσκουσιν, *to the knowers,* as opposed to those among them who did not know. He assumes that all his readers were fully cognizant of the principle, *that the law has dominion over a man so long as he liveth.* What law does the apostle here refer to it ? It may be understood of law without any restriction. Law, all laws, (in the aspect in which they are contemplated,) bind a man only so long as he lives. Or, it may mean specifically the Mosaic law; or, more definitely still, the marriage law. There is no reason for these limitations. The proposition is a general one; though the application is doubtless to the law of which he had been speaking, and specially to the law referred to in vi. 14, from which he says we are now free. That certainly is not the Mosaic law considered as a transient economy, or as a system of religious rites and ceremonies designed for one people, and for a limited period. It is the Mosaic law considered as a revelation of the moral law, which is holy, just, and good, and which says, "Thou shalt not covet." He illustrates the mode of our deliverance from that law, as a covenant of works, by a reference to the admitted fact, that law has no dominion over the dead.

The original leaves it doubtful whether the last clause of the verse is to be rendered "as long as *he* lives," or "as long as *it* lives." The decision of this point depends on the context. In favour of the latter it may be said, 1. That it is better suited to the apostle's design, which is to show that the law is dead or abrogated. 2. That in verse 6 (according to the common reading) the law is spoken of as being dead. 3. And, especially, that in vers. 2, 3, the woman is said to be free from the law, not by her own, but by her husband's death; which would seem to require that, in the other part of the comparison, the husband (*i. e.* the law) should be represented as dying, and not the wife, that is, those bound by the law. But, on the other hand, it must be admitted that *the law lives*, and *the law dies*, are very unusual modes of expression, and perfectly unexampled in Paul's writings, if the doubtful case in ver. 6 be excepted. 2. This interpretation is inconsistent with ver. 2. It is not the law that dies : "The woman is bound to her husband as long as he liveth; but if the husband be dead," &c. 3. Throughout the passage it is said that we are dead to the law (ver. 4,) delivered from the law (ver 6,) and not that the law is dead. The common interpretation, therefore, is to be preferred : 'The law has dominion as long and no longer than the person lives, to whom it has respect. For example, the law of marriage ceases to be binding when one of the parties is dead.' Instead of understanding the words, as long as *he liveth*, of the natural or physical life, as is done by the great body of interpreters, Philippi and others say the meaning is, 'That the law binds a man so long as his natural, corrupt, unregenerated life continues. When the old man is crucified, he is free from the law.' We have here, he says, the same idea as is expressed above, vi. 7, 'He that dieth is justified from sin.' This interpretation is not only unnatural, but it necessitates a forced allegorical interpretation of the following verses.

VERSE 2. *For the woman which hath a husband*, γυνὴ ὕπανδρος, *viro subjecta, married*, answering to תַּחַת אִישָׁהּ, Num. v. 29. *Is bound by the law to her living husband*, τῷ ζῶντι ἀνδρί, *i. e.* to her husband while living. *But if her husband be dead, she is freed from the law of her husband. Is freed from*, κατήργηται ἀπό is an expression which never occurs in common Greek. The same idiom is found in ver. 6 of this chapter, and in Gal. v. 4. Καταργεῖν means to invalidate, to render void. The idea is, that the relation to her husband is broken off, and she is free. *Law of her husband* means law relating to her husband. The phrase is analogous to those often used in the Old Testament—"law of the sacrifice;" "law of leprosy;" "law of defilement." According to the common interpretation of this verse γάρ (*for*) introduces a confirmatory illustration : 'Law is not of perpetual obligation; *for example*, a married woman is free from the law which

bound her to her husband, by his death.' There is of course a slight
incongruity between the illustration and the form in which the principle is
stated in the first verse. There it is said that the law has dominion over a
man so long as *he lives.* The illustration is, that a wife is free (not when
she dies) when her husband dies. For this and other reasons, many interpreters do not regard this verse as presenting an example, but as an allegory.
Those who take this view give different explanations. After Augustin,
Melanchthon, Beza, and others, say : ' The husband is our corrupt nature,
(vis illa nativa, as Beza calls it, ciens in nobis affectiones peccatorum ;) the
wife is the soul, or our members. When, therefore, the corrupt nature (or
old man) dies, the soul is free from that husband, and is at liberty to marry
another.' Others, with much more regard to the context, say that the wife
is the Church, the husband the law ; so Origen, Chrysostom, Olshausen,
Philippi, &c. This is indeed the application which the apostle makes in
the following verses, but it is not what is said in vers. 2, 3. Here we have
only an example, illustrating the truth of the assertion in ver. 1.

VERSE 3 is an amplification and confirmation of what is said in ver. 2 :
That a woman is bound by the law to her husband as long as he lives, is
plain, because she is called an adulteress if she marries another man while
her husband lives. And that she is free from that law when he dies, is
plain, because she is in that case no adulteress, though she be married to
another man. *She shall be called,* χρηματίσει, authoritatively and solemnly
declared to be. Χρηματίζειν (from χρῆμα) is literally *to transact business,*
and specially the business of the state, to give decisions, or decrees ; and
specially in the New Testament, to utter divine responses, *oracula edere,
divinitus admonere;* see Matt. ii. 12, 22 ; Luke ii. 26 ; Acts x. 22 ; Heb.
viii. 5 ; xi. 7. Compare Rom. xi. 4.

VERSE 4. *Wherefore, my brethren, ye also have become dead to the law
by the body of Christ.* As the woman is free from the law by the death
of her husband, so *ye also* (καὶ ὑμεῖς) are freed from the law by the death
of Christ. This is the application made by the apostle of the illustration
contained in vers. 2, 3. The law is our first husband ; we were bound to
satisfy its demands. But the law being dead, (*i.e.,* fulfilled in Christ,) we
are free from the obligation of obedience to it as the condition of justification, and are at liberty to accept the gospel. "Lex velut maritus fuit,"
says Calvin, "sub cujus jugo detinemur, donec mortua est. Post legis
mortem Christus nos assumpsit, id est, a lege solutos adjunxit sibi. Ergo
Christo e mortuis suscitato copulati adhaerere ei soli debemus ; atque ut
aeterna est Christi vita post resurrectionem, ita posthac nullum futurum
est divortium." Instead of saying, The law is dead, as the consistency of
the figure would demand, the apostle expresses the same idea by saying, Ye are dead to the law, or rather, are slain, put to death, ἐθανατώθητε.
This form of expression is probably used because the death of Christ, in
which we died, was an act of violence. He was put to death, and we in
him. To be slain to the law, means to be freed from the law by death.
Death, indeed, not our own, but ours vicariously, as we were crucified in
Christ, who died on the cross in our behalf, and in our stead. It is therefore added, *by the body of Christ, i.e.,* by his body as slain. He redeemed
us from the law by death ; "by being a curse," Gal. iii. 13 ; "by his
blood," Eph. i. 7, ii. 13 ; "by his flesh," Eph. ii. 15 ; "by the cross,"
Eph. ii. 16 ; "by the body of his flesh," Col. i. 22. These are all equivalent expressions. They all teach the same doctrine, that Christ bore
our sins upon the tree ; that his sufferings and death were a satisfaction

to justice, and, being so intended and accepted, they effect our deliverance from the penalty of the law. We are therefore free from it. Although the law continues evermore to bind us as rational creatures, it no longer prescribes the conditions of our salvation. It is no longer necessary that we should atone for our own sins, or work out a righteousness such as the law demands. Christ has done that for us. We are thus freed from the law, *that we should be married to another*, εἰς τὸ γενέσθαι, as expressing the design. The proximate design of our freedom from the law, is our union with Christ ; and the design of our union with Christ is, that we should bring forth fruit unto God, that is, that we should be holy. Here, therefore, as in the preceding chapter, the apostle teaches that the law cannot sanctify ; that it is necessary we should be delivered from its bondage, and be reconciled to God, before we can be holy. He to whom we are thus united, is said to be he who is *raised from the dead*. As Christ is spoken of, or referred to as having died, it was appropriate to refer to him as now living. It is to the living and life-giving Son of God that we are united by faith and the indwelling of the Spirit ; and therefore it is that we are no longer barren or unfruitful, but are made to bring forth fruit unto God. "Sed ultra progreditur apostolus," says Calvin, "nempe solutum fuisse legis vinculum, non ut nostro arbitrio vivamus, sicuti mulier vidua sui juris est, dum in cœlibatu degit; sed alteri marito nos jam esse devinctos : imo de manu (ut aiunt) in manum a·lege ad Christum nos transiisse."

It need hardly be remarked, that the law of which the apostle is here speaking, is not the Mosaic law considered as the Old Testament economy. It is not the doctrine of this or of similar passages, that Christ has merely delivered us from the yoke of Jewish institutions, in order that we may embrace the simpler and more spiritual dispensation of the gospel. The law of which he speaks, is the law which says, "The man that doeth these things shall live by them," x. 5 ; Gal. iii. 12 ; that is, which requires perfect obedience as the condition of acceptance. It is that which says, "Thou shalt not covet," ver. 7 ; without which sin is dead, ver. 8 ; which is holy, just and good, ver. 12 ; which is spiritual, ver. 14, &c. It is that law by whose works the Gentiles cannot be justified, chap. iii. 20 ; from whose curse Christ has redeemed not the Jews only, but also the Gentiles, Gal. iii. 13, 14. It is plain, therefore, that Paul here means by *the law*, the will of God, as a rule of duty, no matter how revealed. From this law, as prescribing the terms of our acceptance with God, Christ has delivered us. It is the legal system, which says, "Do this and live," that Christ has abolished, and introduced another, which says, " He that believes shall be saved." Since, however, as remarked above (chap. vi. 14), the Old Testament economy, including the Mosaic institutions, was the form in which the law, as law, was ever present to the minds of the apostle and his readers ; and since deliverance from the legal system, as such, involved deliverance from that economy, it is not wonderful that reference to that dispensation should often be made ; or that Paul should at times express the idea of deliverance from the law, as such, by terms which would seem to express only deliverance from the particular form in which it was so familiar to his readers. So, too, in the epistle to the Galatians, we find him constantly speaking of a return to Judaism as a renunciation of the method of gratuitous justification, and a recurrence to a reliance on the righteousness of works. The reason of this is obvious. The Old Testament dispensation, apart from its evangelical import, which lay, like a secondary sense, beneath the cover of its institutions, was but a reënactment of the legal system. To make, however, as is often done, the whole meaning of the apostle to be, that we are freed from the Jewish law, is not only inconsistent in this place with the context, and irreconcileable with many express declarations of Scripture, but destructive of the whole evangelical character of the doctrine. How small a part of the redemption of Christ is deliverance from the Mosaic institutions! How slight the consolation to a soul, sensible of its exposure to the wrath of God, to be told that the law of Moses no longer condemns us! How void of truth and meaning the doctrine, that deliverance from the law is necessary to holiness, if the law means the Jewish economy merely.

Verse 5. *For when we were in the flesh, the motions of sin, which were by the law, &c.* The apostle having, in ver. 4, stated that believers are freed from the law by the death of Christ, in this and the following verse, shows the necessity and the consequences of this change : ' We have been thus freed, *because* formerly, when under the law, we brought forth fruit unto death ; but now, being free from the law, we are devoted to the service of God.' The force of *for*, at the beginning of this verse, is therefore obvious. The former legal state of believers is here described by saying, they *were in the flesh.* In the language of Scripture, the word *flesh* expresses, in such connections, one or the other of two ideas, or both conjointly. First, a state of moral corruption, as in chap. viii. 8, " Those that are in the flesh ; " secondly, a carnal state, *i. e.*, a state in which men are subject to external rites, ceremonies, and commands ; or more generally, a legal state, inasmuch as among the Jews, that state was one of subjection to such external rites. Gal. iii. 3, " Having begun in the Spirit, are ye now made perfect by the flesh ? " Compare Gal. iv. 9, where the expression " weak and beggarly elements " is substituted for the phrase " the flesh ; " see Rom. iv. 1. In the present case, both ideas appear to be included. The meaning is, ' when in your unrenewed and legal state.' The opposite condition is described (ver. 6) as a state of freedom from the law ; which, of course, shows that the second of the two ideas mentioned above was prominent in the apostle's mind when he used the words in the flesh." In vi. 14, the apostle says, " Sin shall not have dominion over you, for ye are not under the law ; " and here, in the exposition of that passage, he shows why it is that while under the law sin does have dominion. It is because, while in that state of condemnation and alienation from God, the effect of the law is to produce sin. He says the παθήματα τῶν ἁμαρτιῶν are διὰ τοῦ νόμου. This does not mean that the passions of sin (*i. e.*, which manifest themselves in sinful acts) are simply made known by the law, but they are *by* it, that is, produced by it. The word παθήματα literally means what is suffered, afflictions : here it is used in a secondary sense for *passions*, (*motions*, in the sense of emotions, feelings.) These two meanings of the word are nearly allied, inasmuch as in *passion*, or *feeling*, the soul is rather the subject than the agent. These sinful feelings, aroused by the law, the apostle says ἐνηργεῖτο, *wrought*, (the word is here, as everywhere else in the New Testament, used in an active sense,) *in our members ; i. e.*, in us, not merely in our bodily members, but in all our faculties, whether of soul or body. *To bring forth fruit ; εἰς τὸ καρποφορῆσαι*, as expressing the result, not the design. The effect of the excitement of sinful feeling by the law, was the production of fruit *unto death ; τῷ θανατῷ*, as opposed to *τῷ Θεῷ* of the preceding verse. Death is personified. He is represented as a master, to whom our works are rendered. They belong to him. Death, in other words, is the consequence or end secured by our sins. The wages of sin is death. The consequence of sinning is, that we die. The death here meant is no more mere physical death than in vi. 23. It is that death which the law of God threatens as the punishment of sin.

VERSE 6. *But now,* (νυνὶ δέ, opposed to ὅτε of ver. 5,) *i. e.*, since our conversion, *we were freed from the law;* κατηργήθημεν ἀπὸ τοῦ νόμου, (the same idiom as in ver. 2.) How were we thus freed from the law ? By death. If ἀποθανόντος, found in the common text, is the true reading, (*that having died,*) then it is by the death (*i. e.*, the abrogation or satisfaction) of the law that we are thus freed, even as the woman is freed by the death of her husband. But if, as all modern editors agree, ἀποθανόντες (*we having died*) is the true reading, then it is by our own vicarious death in Christ, our having died with him whose death is a satisfaction to the law, that we are thus delivered. This is in accordance with ver. 4, where it is said *we* died to the law. The apostle says *we died* (τούτῳ) ἐν ῳ κατειχόμεθα, (to that) *by which we were bound.* The law held us under its authority, and, as it were, in bondage ; from which bondage we have been redeemed by death. *So that,* the consequence of this freedom from the law is, *we serve* (God) *in newness of the Spirit, and not* (sin) *in the oldness of the letter.* That is, we serve God in a new and holy state due to the Spirit, which the Spirit has produced, and not sin in, or according to, the old and corrupt state under the law. *Newness of the Spirit* is that new state of mind of which the Holy Ghost is the author. *Oldness of the letter* is that old state of which the law is the source, in so far as it was a state of condemnation and enmity to God. That Πνεῦμα here is the Holy Spirit, and not the human soul as renewed by the Spirit, may be inferred from the general usage of the New Testament, and from such parallel passages as Gal. iii. 3 ; 2 Cor. iii. 6, in both of which πνεῦμα means the Gospel as the revelation and organ of the Spirit. In the latter passage, the apostle says, " the letter killeth, but the Spirit giveth life." There, as here, the *letter,* γράμμα, is *what is written.* The law is so designated because the decalogue, its most important part, was originally written on stone, and because the whole law, as revealed to the Jews, was written in the Scriptures, or writings. It was therefore something external, as opposed to what was inward and spiritual. Luther's version of this passage gives the sense in a few words : "Als dass wir dienen im neuen Wesen des Geistes, und nicht im alten Wesen des Buchstabens." Believers then are free from the law, by the death of Christ. They are no longer under the old covenant, which said, " Do this and live ;" but are introduced into a new and gracious state, in which they are accepted, not for what they do, but for what has been done for them. Instead of having the legal and slavish spirit which arose from their condition under the law, they have the feelings of children.

DOCTRINE.

1. The leading doctrine of this section is that taught in ver. 14 of the preceding chapter, viz., that believers are not under a legal system ; and that the consequences of their freedom is not the indulgence of sin, but the service of God, ver. 4.

2. This deliverance from the law is not effected by setting the law aside, or by disregarding its demands ; but by those demands being satisfied in the person of Christ, ver. 4 ; chap. x. 4.

3. As far as we are concerned, redemption is in order to holiness. We are delivered from the law, that we may be united to Christ; and we are united to Christ, that we may bring forth fruit unto God, verse 4, &c.

4. Legal or self-righteous strivings after holiness can never be successful. The relation in which they place the soul to God is, from its nature, productive of evil, and not of holy feelings, ver 5.

5. Actual freedom from the bondage and penalty of the law is always attended and manifested by a filial temper and obedience, ver. 6.

6. The doctrine concerning marriage, which is here incidentally taught, or rather which is assumed as known to Jews and Christians, is, that the marriage contract can only be dissolved by death. The only exception to this rule is given by Christ, Matt. v. 32; unless indeed Paul, in 1 Cor. vii. 15, recognizes wilful and final desertion as a sufficient ground of divorce, verses 2, 3.

REMARKS.

1. As the only way in which we can obtain deliverance from the law is by the death of Christ, the exercise of faith in him is essential to holiness. When we lose our confidence in Christ, we fall under the power of the law, and relapse into sin. Everything depends, therefore, upon our maintaining our union with Christ. "Without me ye can do nothing," ver. 4.

2. The only evidence of union with Christ is bringing forth fruit unto God, ver. 4.

3. As deliverance from the penalty of the law is in order to holiness, it is vain to expect that deliverance, except with a view to the end for which it is granted, ver. 4.

4. Conversion is a great change; sensible to him that experiences it, and visible to others. It is a change from a legal and slavish state, to one of filial confidence; manifesting itself by the renunciation of the service of sin, and by devotion to the service of God, ver. 6.

5. A contract so lasting as that of marriage, and of which the consequences are so important, should not be entered into lightly, but in the fear of God, verses 2, 3.

6. The practice, common in many Protestant countries of Europe, and in many States of this Union, of granting divorces on the ground of cruel treatment, or 'incompatibility of temper,' is in direct contravention of the doctrines and precepts of the Bible on this subject, verses 2, 3.

ROMANS VII. 7—13.

ANALYSIS.

PAUL, having shown that we must be delivered from the law, in order to our justification (chapters iii., iv.), and that this freedom was no less necessary in order to sanctification (chap. vi.; chap. vii. 1—6), comes now to explain more fully than he had previously done, what are the use and effect of the law. This is the object of the residue of this chapter. The apostle shows, first, verses 7—13, that the law produces conviction of sin, agreeably to his declaration in chap. iii. 20 ; and, secondly, verses 14—25, that it enlightens the believer's conscience, but cannot destroy the dominion of sin. This section, therefore, may be advantageously divided into two parts. Paul introduces the subject, as is usual with him, by means of an idea intimately associated with the preceding discussion. He had been insisting on the necessity of deliverance from the law. Why? Because it is evil? No ; but because it cannot produce holiness. It can produce only the knowledge and the sense of sin ; which are the constituents of genuine conviction. These two effects are attributed to the operation of the law, in verses 7, 8. These ideas are amplified in verses 9—11. The inference is drawn in ver. 12, that the law is good ; and in ver. 13, that the evil which it incidentally produces is to be attributed to sin, the exceeding turpitude of which becomes thus the more apparent.

COMMENTARY.

Verse 7. *What shall we say then ? Is the law sin ? Far from it,* &c. The apostle asks whether it is to be inferred, either from the general doctrine of the preceding section, respecting the necessity of deliverance from the law, or from the special declaration made in ver. 5, respecting the law producing sin, that the law was itself evil? He answers, By no means ; and shows, in the next verse, that the effect ascribed to the law, in ver. 5, is merely incidental. *Is the law sin ?* means either, Is the law evil? or is it the cause of sin? see Micah i. 5, ' Samaria is the sin of Jacob.' The former is best suited to the context, because Paul admits that the law is incidentally productive of sin. The two ideas, however, may be united, as by Calvin, " An peccatum sic generet, ut illi imputari ejus culpa debeat ; " *Does the law so produce sin, as that the fault is to be imputed to the law itself ? God forbid,* μὴ γένοιτο ; let it not be thought that the law is to blame. *On the contrary* (ἀλλά), so far from the law being evil, it is the source, and the only source of the knowledge of sin. *I had not known sin, but by the law.* Where there is no knowledge of the law, there can be no consciousness of sin ; for sin is want of conformity to the law. If, therefore, the standard of right is not known, there can be no apprehension of our want of conformity to it. *By the law* here, is to be understood the moral law, however revealed. It is not the law of Moses, so far as that law was peculiar and national, but only so far as it contained the rule of duty. It is not the experience of men, as determined by their relation to the Mosaic dispensation, but their experience as determined by their relation to the moral law, that is here depicted. But in what sense does Paul here use the pronoun *I ?* That he does not speak for himself only ; that it is not anything in his own individual experience, peculiar to himself, is obvious from the whole context, and is almost universally admitted. But if he speaks representatively, whom does he represent, whose experience under the operation of the law is here detailed ? Grotius says, that he represents the Jewish people, and sets forth their experience before and after the introduction of the law of Moses. This opinion was adopted by Locke, Estius, and recently by Reiche. Others say that he speaks out of the common consciousness of men. " Das ἐγώ, repræsentirte Subject," says Meyer, " ist der Mensch überhaupt, in seiner rein menschlichen und natürlichen Verfassung." The experience detailed is that of the natural or unrenewed man throughout. This view is the one generally adopted by modern commentators. Others again say, that Paul is here speaking as a Christian ; he is giving his own religious experience of the operation of the law, as that experience is common to all true believers. This does not *necessarily* suppose that the preliminary exercises, as detailed in vers. 7—13, are peculiar to the renewed. There is a "law work," a work of conviction which, in its apparent characteristics, is common to the renewed and the unrenewed. Many are truly and deeply convinced of sin ; many experience all that the law in itself can produce, who are never regenerated. Nevertheless, the experience here exhibited is the experience of every renewed man. It sets forth the work of the law first in the work of conviction, vers. 7—13, and afterwards in reference to the holy life of the Christian. This is the Augustinian view of the bearing of this passage adopted by the Lutherans and Reformed, and still held by the great body of evangelical Christians.

I had not *known* sin. There are two kinds of knowledge. The one has for its object mere logical relations, and is a matter of the intellect ; the other has for its object both the logical relations and the qualities, moral or otherwise, of the thing known, and is a matter of the feelings as well as of the intellect. The kind of knowledge of which the apostle speaks is not mere intellectual cognition, but also conviction. It includes the consciousness of guilt and pollution. The law awakened in him the knowledge of his own state and character. He felt himself to be a sinner ; and by a sinner is to be understood not merely a transgressor, but one in whom sin dwells. It was the corruption of his nature which was revealed to the apostle by the operation of the law. This sense of the word ἁμαρτία in this context is almost universally admitted. "Die ἁμαρτία," says Meyer, "ist das *Princip der Sünde im Menschen* (1. v. 8. 9. 11. 13. 14.), dessen wir erst durch das Gesetz uns bewusst werden, und welches ohne das Gesetz unbewusst geblieben wäre." That is, " " The ἁμαρτία is the principle of sin in men, of which we become conscious through the law, and of which we would without the law have remained unconscious." So De Wette, Tholuck, Rückert, Köllner, Olshausen, and Philippi, among the modern commentators, as well as the older doctrinal expositors.

For I had not known lust, except the law had said, Thou shalt not covet. This may be understood as merely an illustration of the preceding declaration : ' I had not known sin but by the law. *For example,* I had not known lust, except the law had said, Thou shalt not covet.' According to this view, there is no difference between *sin* and *lust*, ἁμαρτία and ἐπιθυμία, except that the latter is specific, and the former general. Lust falls under the general category of sin. But according to this interpretation, neither ἁμαρτία nor ἔγνων (*sin* nor *know*) receives the full force which the connection requires. This clause, therefore, is not simply an illustration, but a confirmation of the preceding : ' I had not known sin, but by the law ; *for* I had not known lust, except the law had said, Thou shalt not covet.' That is, ' From the consciousness of desire striving against the law, arose the conviction of the principle of sin within me.' Desire, revealed as evil by the law, itself revealed the evil source whence it springs. The word ἐπιθυμία means simply *earnest desire*, and the verb ἐπιθυμέω is *to desire earnestly.* It depends on the context whether the desire be good or bad, whether it is directed towards what is lawful or what is forbidden. In the tenth commandment, here quoted, the meaning is, Thou shalt not desire to have (*i. e.*, thou shalt not covet) that which belongs to another. The point of the apostle's argument is, that his knowledge of sin is due to

the law, because without the law he would not have known that mere
desire is evil, and because these evil desires revealed the hidden source of
sin in his nature.

VERSE 8. *But sin, taking occasion by the commandment, wrought in me
all manner of concupiscence.* This verse is not logically connected with the
preceding.   It is rather co-ordinate with it, and is a virtual, or rather, an
additional answer to the question, Is the law evil ?   To this question Paul
replies, No ; on the contrary, it leads to the knowledge of sin.   And hence
he adds, It is not evil in itself, although incidentally the cause of sin in
us.   By *sin*, in this case, cannot be understood actual sin.   It must mean
indwelling sin, or corruption of nature ; sin as the principle or source of
action, and not as an act.   "'Αμαρτία non potest esse hoc loco *peccatum
ipsum*," says Koppe, "sed ipsa potius prava et ad peccandum proclivis in-
doles, vitiosa hominis natura, vitiositas ipsa."   To the same effect, Olshausen: "Aus der allgemeinen sündhaften Natur des Menschen geht die
ἐπιθυμία *prava concupiscentia*, als erste Ausserung hervor und dann
folgt erst die That."   That is, from sin immanent in our nature, comes
first desire, and then the act.   Thus Köllner says, "ἐπιθυμίαν, so von
ἁμαρτία verschieden, dass diese das gleichsam im Menschen ruhende
sündliche Princip bezeichnet, ἐπιθυμία aber die im einzelnen Falle wirk-
same böse Lust, ganz eigentlich die Begierde, die dann zunächst zur Sünde
in concreto fürht."   Such is plainly the meaning of the apostle.   There is
a principle of sin, a corruption of nature which lies back of all conscious
voluntary exercises, to which they owe their origin.   Ἐπιθυμία, *feeling*,
the first form in which sin is revealed in the consciousness, springs from
ἁμαρτία.   This is a truth of great importance.   According to the theology
and religious conviction of the apostle, sin can be predicated not only of
acts, but also of inward states.

Sin taking occasion, ἀφορμήν, opportunity or advantage, *by the commandment, i. e.,* the command, "Thou shalt not covet."   A part is taken for
the whole.   This special precept (ἐντολή) stands, by way of illustration, for
the whole law.   The words διὰ τῆς ἐντολῆς, *by the commandment,* may be
taken with the preceding clause, 'taking advantage of the commandment.'
In favour of this construction is the position of the words, and, as is supposed, the διαὐτῆς in ver. 11, which, it is said, corresponds to these words
in this verse.   This is the construction which is adopted by our translators, and by many commentators.   Others prefer connecting the words in
question with what follows :—" by the commandment wrought in me."
In favour of this is the fact, that the main idea of the passage is thus
brought out.   The apostle designs to show how the law, although good in
itself, produced evil : 'Sin wrought by it.'   Besides, the phrase ἀφορμήν
λαμβάνειν ἐκ, or παρά, or ἀπό, is common, but with διά it never occurs : διά
is not the appropriate preposition ; whereas κατεργάζεσθαι διά is perfectly
appropriate.   *Wrought in me all manner of concupiscence,* πάσαν ἐπιθυμίαν,
every (evil) desire.

For without the law sin (was) dead.   This is designed as a confirmation
of the preceding declaration.   This confirmation is drawn either from a
fact of Paul's personal experience, or from an universally admitted truth.
If the former, then we must supply *was :* 'Sin is excited by the law, for
without the law sin *was* dead ;' *i. e.,* I was not aware of its existence.   If
the latter, then, *is* is to be supplied : 'Without the law sin *is* dead."   This
is an undisputed fact : 'Where there is no law there is no sin; and where
is no knowledge of law there is no knowledge of sin.   The latter view

best suits the context. To say that a thing is dead, is to say that it is inactive, unproductive, and unobserved. All this may be said of sin prior to the operation of the law. It is comparatively inoperative and unknown, until aroused and brought to light by the law. There are two effects of the law included in this declaration—the excitement of evil passions, and the discovery of them. Calvin makes the latter much the more prominent: "Ad cognitionem præcipue refero, acsi dictum foret: Detexit in me omnem concupiscentiam; quæ dum lateret, quodammodo nulla esse videbatur." But the context, and the analogous declarations in the succeeding verses, seem to require the former to be considered as the more important. The law then is not evil, but it produces the conviction of sin, by teaching us what sin is, ver. 7, and by making us conscious of the existence and power of this evil in our own hearts, ver. 8. "Ehe dem Menschen ein νόμος entweder von aussen gegeben wird, oder in ihm selbst sich entwickelt, so ist die Sündhaftigkeit zwar in ihm, als Anlage, aber sie ist todt, d. h. sie ist ihm noch nicht zum Bewusstseyn gekommen, weil noch kein Widerstreit zwischen seiner Sündhaftigkeit und einem Gebote in ihm entstehen konnte." *Usteri Lehrbegriff Pauli,* p. 25. Such is certainly the experience of Christians. They live at ease. Conscience is at rest. They think themselves to be as good as can be reasonably required of them. They have no adequate conception of the power or heinousness of the evil within them. Sin lies, as it were, dead, as the torpid serpent, until the operation of the law rouses it from its slumbers, and reveals its character.

Vᴇʀsᴇ 9. *For I was alive without the law once,* &c. The meaning of this clause is necessarily determined by what precedes. If by sin being dead means its lying unnoticed and unknown, then by *being alive,* Paul must mean that state of security and comparative exemption from the turbulence or manifestation of sin in his heart, which he then experienced. He fancied himself in a happy and desirable condition. He had no dread of punishment, no painful consciousness of sin. *But when the commandment came, i.e.* came to his knowledge, was revealed to him in its authority and in the extent and spirituality of its demands, *sin revived; i.e.* it was roused from its torpor. It was revealed in his consciousness by its greater activity; so that the increase of his knowledge of sin was due to an increase in its activity. *And I died.* As by being alive was meant being at ease in a fancied state of security and goodness, being dead must mean just the opposite, viz. a state of misery arising from a sense of danger and the consciousness of guilt. This interpretation is recommended not only by its agreement with the whole context, but also from its accordance with the common experience of Christians. Every believer can adopt the language of the apostle. He can say he was alive without the law; he was secure and free from any painful consciousness of sin; but when the commandment came, when he was brought to see how holy and how broad is the law of God, sin was aroused and revealed, and all his fancied security and goodness disappeared. He was bowed down under the conviction of his desert of death as a penalty, and under the power of spiritual death in his soul. "Mors peccati," says Calvin, "vita est hominis; rursum vita peccati mors hominis."

The questions, however—When was Paul, or those in whose name he speaks, without the law? In what sense was he then alive? What is meant by the commandment coming? In what sense did sin revive? and, What does Paul mean when he says, he died?—are all answered by different commentators in different ways, according to their different views of the context and of the design of the argument. Grotius and others say, that being without the law designates the ante-Mosaic period of the Jewish history, when the people lived in comparative innocence; the law came when it was promulgated from Mount Sinai, and under its discipline they became worse and worse, or at least sin was rendered more and more active among them. Others say, that Paul was without the law in his childhood, when he was in a state of childish innocence; but when he came to years of discretion, and the law was revealed within him, then he died—then he fell under the power of sin. These interpretations give a much lower sense than the one above-mentioned, and are not in keeping with the grand design of the passage.

VERSE 10. *And the commandment which was unto life, I found to be unto death.* The law was designed and adapted to secure life, but became in fact the cause of death. Life and death, as here opposed, are figurative terms. Life includes the ideas of happiness and holiness. The law was designed to make men happy and holy. Death, on the other hand, includes the ideas of misery and sin. The law became, through no fault of its own, the means of rendering the apostle miserable and sinful. How vain therefore is it to expect salvation from the law, since all the law does, in its operation on the unrenewed heart, is to condemn and to awaken opposition! It cannot change the nature of man. By the law is the knowledge of sin, iii. 20; it produces "the motions of sin," ver. 5; it "works all manner of concupiscence," ver. 8; it revives sin, ver. 9; it seduces into sin, ver. 11. How then can it save? How miserable and deluded are those who have only a legal religion!

VERSE 11. *For sin, taking occasion by the commandment, deceived me, and by it slew me.* The law is the cause of death, ver. 10, *for* by it sin deceived and slew me. The two ideas before insisted upon are again here presented—viz. the law, so far from giving life, is the source of death, spiritual and penal; and yet the fault is not in the law, but in sin, *i.e.* in our own corrupt nature. Here, as in ver. 8, two constructions are possible. We may say, 'Sin took occasion by the commandment;' or, 'Sin taking occasion, by the commandment deceived me.' For reasons mentioned above, ver. 8, the latter is to be preferred: Sin *deceived* me, ἐξηπάτησε. The ἐκ is intensive: 'It completely deceived me, or disappointed my expectations.' How? By leading the apostle to expect one thing, while he experienced another. He expected life, and found death. He expected happiness, and found misery; he looked for holiness, and found increased corruption. He fancied that by the law all these desirable ends could be secured, when its operation was discovered to produce the directly opposite effects. Sin therefore deceived by the commandment, and by it slew him, instead of its being to him the source of holiness and blessedness. The reference is not to the promised joys of sin, which always mock the expectation and disappoint the hopes, but rather to the utter failure of the law to do what he expected from it. Such is the experience of every believer, in the ordinary progress of his inward life. He first turns to the law, to his own righteousness and strength, but he soon finds that all the law can do is only to aggravate his guilt and misery.

VERSE 12. *Wherefore the law is holy, and the commandment holy, just, and good.* This is the conclusion from the preceding exhibition. The law is not evil, ver. 5. Sin is the true source of all the evil which incidentally flows from the law. In itself the law is holy, (*i.e.* the whole law,) and *the* commandment, *i.e.* the specific command, "Thou shalt not covet," is holy, just, and good. That is, it is in every aspect what it should be. It is in every way excellent. It is *holy* as the revelation of the holiness of God; it is in its own nature right, and it is good, *i.e.* excellent. In the next verse all these attributes are summed up in one, τὸ ἀγαθόν, goodness. Hence this is probably the generic term of which the others are the species. " Lex ipsa," says Calvin, "et quicquid lege præcipitur, id totum sanctum est, ergo, summa dignitate reverendum; justum, ergo nullius injustitiæ insimulandum; bonum, ergo omni vitio purum ac vacuum."

Verse 13. *Was then that which is good made death unto me? God forbid.* In order to prevent the possibility of misconception, the apostle again vindicates the law. Τὸ οὖν ἀγαθὸν ἐμοὶ γέγονε θάνατος; *Has the good become death to me? God forbid.* Ἀλλά, on the contrary, ἡ ἁμαρτία (ἐμοὶ γέγονε θάνατος) sin (has become death to me.) Not the law, but sin is the cause of death. And it is made so, ἵνα φανῇ ἁμαρτία, διὰ τοῦ ἀγαθοῦ μοι κατεργαζομένη θάνατον, *in order that it may appear sin, working in me death by means of good.* The true character of sin, as sin, is revealed by its making even that which is in itself good, the means of evil. *In order that it might become exceeding sinful by the commandment.* God has so ordered it, that the sinfulness of sin is brought out by the operation of the law. Such is the design of the law, so far as the salvation of sinners is concerned. It does not prescribe the conditions of salvation. We are not obliged to be sinless; in other words, we are not obliged to fulfil the demands of the law, in order to be saved. Neither is the law the means of sanctification. It cannot make us holy. On the contrary, its operation is to excite and exasperate sin; to render its power more dreadful and destructive, so that instead of being the source of life, it is the instrument of death. By it we are slain. The construction of this passage, given above, is that which the words demand, and which almost all modern commentators adopt. Calvin, Luther, the English translators, and many others, make ἁμαρτία the subject of κατεργαζομένη (ἦν) taken as a verb: *Sin wrought death.* The sense thus expressed is good; but this construction does violence to the words, as it converts a participle into a verb.

DOCTRINE.

1. The law, although it cannot secure either the justification or sanctification of men, performs an essential part in the economy of salvation. It enlightens conscience, and secures its verdict against a multitude of evils, which we should not otherwise have recognized as sins. It arouses sin, increasing its power, and making it, both in itself and in our consciousness, exceedingly sinful. It therefore produces that state of mind which is a necessary preparation for the reception of the gospel, vers. 7, 8.

2. Conviction of sin, that is, an adequate knowledge of its nature, and a sense of its power over us, is an indispensable part of evangelical religion. Before the gospel can be embraced as a means of deliverance from sin, we must feel that we are involved in corruption and misery, ver. 9.

3. The law of God is a transcript of his own nature—holy, just, and good. The clearer our views of its extent and excellence, the deeper will be our sense of our own unworthiness, vers. 9, 12.

4. Sin is exceedingly sinful. Its turpitude is manifested by the fact, that the exhibition of holiness rouses it into opposition; and that the holy law itself is made incidentally to increase its virulence and power, ver. 13.

5. Sin is very deadly. It extracts death from the means of life, and cannot exist unattended by misery, vers. 10-13.

REMARKS.

1. How miserable the condition of those whose religion is all law! vers. 7-13.

2. Though the law cannot save us, it must prepare us for salvation. It should, therefore, be carefully and faithfully preached, both in its extent and authority, vers. 7, 8.

3. It must be wrong and productive of evil, so to describe the nature of evangelical religion as to make the impression that it is a mere change in the main object of pursuit—the choice of one source of happiness in preference to another. It is a return to God, through Jesus Christ, for the purpose of being delivered from sin, and devoted to his service. Its first step is the conviction that we are sinners, and, as such, dead, *i.e.*, helpless, corrupt, and miserable, vers. 7, 13.

4. Nothing is more inconsistent with true religion than self-complacency. Because the more holy we are, the clearer our views of God's law ; and the clearer our views of the law, the deeper our sense of sin, and, consequently, the greater must be our humility, vers. 12, 13.

5. If our religious experience does not correspond with that of the people of God, as detailed in the Scriptures, we cannot be true Christians. Unless we have felt as Paul felt, we have not the religion of Paul, and cannot expect to share his reward, vers. 7—13.

ROMANS VII. 14—25.

ANALYSIS.

THE apostle, having exhibited the operation of the law in producing conviction of sin, comes now to show its effect on the mind of the believer. It cannot secure his sanctification. The cause of this inability is not in the evil nature of the law, which is spiritual, ver. 14, but in the power of indwelling sin ; " I am carnal," says the apostle, " sold under sin," ver. 14. As this is not only a strong, but an ambiguous expression, Paul immediately explains his meaning. He does not intend to say that he was given up to the willing service of sin ; but that he was in the condition of a slave, whose acts are not always the evidence of his inclination. His will may be one way, but his master may direct him another. So it is with the believer. He does what he hates, and omits to do what he approves, ver. 15. This is a description of slavery, and a clear explanation of what is intended by the expression, " sold under sin." There are two obvious inferences to be drawn from this fact. The one is, that the believer, while denying the sufficiency of the law, and maintaining the necessity of deliverance from it, bears an inward testimony to its excellence. He feels and admits that the law is good, ver. 16 ; for it is the law which he approves, and the transgression of it he hates, as stated in the preceding verse. The second inference is, that acts thus performed are not the true criterion of character : " Now then, it is no more I that do it, but sin that dwelleth in me," ver. 17. The acts of a slave are indeed his own acts ; but not being performed with the full assent and consent of his soul, they are not fair tests of the real state of his feelings. The propriety and truth of this representation of the state of the believer, and of the influence of the law, is reasserted and confirmed in vers. 18—20. The law presents duty clearly : the heart and conscience of the believer assent to its excellence ; but what

can the law do in destroying the power of our inward corruptions? These
evil principles remain, so far as the law is concerned, in full force. The
authoritative declaration that a thing must not be done, does not destroy
the inclination to do it.

The result, therefore, is, that notwithstanding the assent of the mind to
the excellence of the law, the power of sin remains, so that when we would
do good, evil is present with us, ver. 21. We delight in the law after the
inward man, but this does not destroy the power of sin in our members,
vers. 22, 23. This inward conflict the law can never end. It only makes
us sensible of our helpless and degraded condition, ver. 24; and drives us
to seek victory, whence alone it can be obtained, *i.e.*, as the gift of God
through Jesus Christ our Lord, ver. 25.

COMMENTARY.

Verse 14. *For we know that the law is spiritual; but I am carnal, sold
under sin.* The connection between this verse and the preceding passage
seems to be this: It had been asserted in ver. 5, that the law was incidentally the cause of sin. This result, however, was no reflection on the
law; for it was holy, just, and good, ver. 12. As the fact that the law
excites sin is consistent with its being good, so is also the fact that it cannot destroy the power of sin. The law indeed is spiritual, but we are
carnal. The fault is again in us. The γάρ thus introduces the confirmation of the whole preceding argument. If the connection is with ver. 13,
the sense is substantially the same: ' Sin, and not the law, works death;
for the law is spiritual, but I am carnal.' The apostle says, οἴδαμεν γάρ,
" for *we* know." It is among Christians an acknowledged and obvious
truth, that the law is spiritual. This is probably the reason that in this
case he uses the plural *we* instead of the singular *I*, which occurs everywhere else in this connection. Semler, indeed, and others, to preserve uniformity, proposes to read οἶδα μὲν γάρ, *I know indeed*, instead of *we know*.
But then there would be no δέ corresponding to the μέν. The ἐγὼ δέ is
opposed to νόμος, and not to ἐγώ in οἶδα. The apostle would have said,
'The law *indeed* is spiritual, *but* I am carnal,' and not, 'I *indeed* know,'
&c. The common division of the words is therefore almost universally
adopted.

The law is said to be *spiritual*, not because it pertains to our spirits,
reaching, as Beza says, to the interior man, ("mentem et interiorem
hominem respicit;") much less because it is *reasonable*, or in accordance
with the πνεῦμα as the higher faculty of our nature; nor because it was
given by inspiration of the Spirit; but as expressing its nature. It is
spiritual in the sense of being Divine, or as partaking of the nature of the
Holy Spirit, its divine Author. This epithet includes, therefore, all that
was before expressed, by saying that the law is holy, just, and good. *But
I am carnal.* The word in the common text is σαρκικός. Griesbach,
Lachmann, and Tischendorf, on the authority of the older manuscripts,
and of the Fathers, read σάρκινος. The difference between these words,
(when they are distinguished,) is, that the former expresses the nature, the
latter the substance out of which a thing is made; so that σάρκινος means
made of flesh, fleshy, corpulent. This is agreeable to the analogy of words
in ινος, λίθινος, *made of stone;* ξύλινος, *made of wood.* This, however, is
not an uniform rule, as ἀνθρώπινος means *human.* In 2 Cor. iii. 3, the
word σάρκινος is used in its strict sense, where, ἐν πλαξὶ καρδίας σαρκίναις

(in tables of the heart made of flesh,) it is opposed to ἐν πλαξὶ λιθίναις (tables made of stone.) Even if σάρκινος, in this case, is the true reading, it must have the same sense as the more common word σαρκικός, which, for internal reasons, the majority of commentators prefer. As *spiritual* expresses the nature of the law, so *carnal* must express the nature, and not the material. *I am carnal*, means I am under the power of the flesh. And by *flesh* is meant not the body, not our sensuous nature merely, but our whole nature as fallen and corrupt. It includes all that belongs to men, apart from the Holy Spirit. In the language of the New Testament, the πνευματικοί, *spiritual*, are those who are under the control of the Spirit of God ; and the σαρκικοί are those who are under the control of their own nature. As, however, even in the renewed, this control of the Spirit is never perfect, as the flesh even in them retains much of its original power, they are forced to acknowledge that they too are carnal. There is no believer, however advanced in holiness, who cannot adopt the language here used by the apostle. In 1 Cor. iii. 3, in addressing believers, he says, " Are ye not carnal ? " In the imperfection of human language the same word must be taken in different senses. Sometimes *carnal* means entirely or exclusively under the control of the flesh. It designates those in whom the flesh is the only principle of action. At other times it has a modified sense, and is applicable to those who, although under the dominion of the Spirit, are still polluted and influenced by the flesh. It is the same with all similar words. When we speak of ' saints and sinners' we do not mean that saints, such as they are in this world, are not sinners. And thus when the Scriptures classify men as πνευματικοί and σαρκικοί, *spiritual* and *carnal*, they do not mean to teach that the spiritual are not carnal. It is, therefore, only by giving the words here used their extreme sense, a sense inconsistent with the context, that they can be regarded as inapplicable to the regenerated. The mystical writers, such as Olshausen, in accordance with the theory which so many of them adopt, that man consists of three subjects or substances, body, soul, and spirit, σῶμα, ψυχή and πνεῦμα, say that by σάρξ, in such connections, we are to understand *das ganze seelische Leben*, the entire psychical life, which only, and not the πνεῦμα, (the spirit or higher element of our nature,) is in man the seat of sin. In angels, on the contrary, the πνεῦμα itself is the seat of sin, and they therefore are incapable of redemption. And in man, when sin invades the πνεῦμα, (spirit) then comes the sin against the Holy Ghost, and redemption becomes impossible. This is only a refined or mystical rationalism, as πνεῦμα is only another name for *reason*, and the conflict in man is reduced to the struggle between sense and reason, and redemption consists in giving the higher powers of our nature ascendency over the lower. According to the Scriptures, the whole of our fallen nature is the seat of sin, and our subjective redemption from its power is effected, not by making reason predominant, but by the indwelling of the Holy Ghost. The conflicting elements are not sense and reason, the *anima* and *animus;* but the flesh and spirit, the human and divine, what we derive from Adam and what we obtain through Christ. " That which is born of the flesh is flesh ; that which is born of the Spirit is spirit." John iii. 6.

The sense in which Paul says he was carnal, is explained by saying he was *sold unto sin*, *i. e.*, sold so as to be under the power of sin. This, of course, is an ambiguous expression. To say that a ' man is sold unto sin ' may mean, as in 1 Kings xxi. 20, and 2 Kings xvii. 17, that he is given up to its service. Sin is that which he has deliberately chosen for a master,

and to which he is devoted.   In this sense of the phrase it is equivalent
to what is said of the unrenewed in the preceding chapter, that they are
the δοῦλοι τῆς ἁμαρτίας, *the slaves of sin.*   From this kind of bondage believers are redeemed, vi. 22.   But there is another kind of bondage.   A
man may be subject to a power which, of himself, he cannot effectually
resist ; against which he may and does struggle, and from which he earnestly desires to be free ; but which, notwithstanding all his efforts, still
asserts its authority.   This is precisely the bondage to sin of which every
believer is conscious.   He feels that there is a law in his members bringing him into subjection to the law of sin ; that his distrust of God, his
hardness of heart, his love of the world and of self, his pride, in short his
indwelling sin, is a real power from which he longs to be free, against which
he struggles, but from which he cannot emancipate himself.   This is the
kind of bondage of which the apostle here speaks, as is plain from the
following verses, as well as from the whole context and from the analogy
of Scripture.

VERSE 15.   *For that which I do, I allow not,* &c.   This is an explanation and confirmation of the preceding declaration.   ' I am sold under sin,
for that which I do, I allow not, &c.'   The word γινώσκω, rendered *I allow,*
properly signifies, *I know,* and as it is used in different senses in the
Scriptures, its meaning in this case is a matter of doubt.   Retaining its
ordinary sense, the word may be used here as in the common phrase, 'I
know not what I do,' expressive of the absence of a calm and deliberate
purpose, and of the violence of the impulse under which one acts.   Inscius
et invitus facio, quæ facio.   Or the meaning may be, that what is done, is
done thoughtlessly.   Non cum pleno mentis proposito.   *Morus.*   This
view is a very common one, expressed in different forms.   "The sinful
decision occurs not by rational self-determination, and, therefore, not with
the full consciousness with which we should act."   *De Wette.*   To the
same effect Meyer, ' the act occurs without the consciousness of its moral
character, in a state of bondage of the practical reason, as a slave acts without a consciousness of the nature or design of what he does.'   Or, 'I do
not do it knowingly, because I know it to be right.'   This comes very
near the old interpretation, according to which to know means to approve,
See Ps. i. 6, "The Lord knoweth the way of the righteous."   With regard to moral objects, knowledge is not mere cognition.   It is the apprehension of the moral quality, and involves of necessity approbation or
disapprobation.   Hence the pious are described in Scripture as those
"who know God," or "the knowers of his name."   Ps. ix. 10 ; xxxvi.
10 ; Hosea viii. 2.   What the apostle, therefore, here says, is, 'what I
perform, *i. e.,* what I actually carry out into action, (κατεργάζομαι,) I
approve not, *i. e.,* I do not recognise as right and good.'

For what I would, that do I not ; but what I hate, that do I.   This is a
further description of this state of bondage.   As the expressions *what I
would,* and *what I hate,* are in antithesis, the former must mean what I
love or delight in.   This use of the Greek word (θέλω) is accommodated to
the corresponding Hebrew term, and occurs several times in the New
Testament.   Matt. xxvii. 43, "Let him deliver him, if he will have him
(εἰ θέλει αὐτόν), *i. e.* if he delight in him ;" Matt. ix. 13 ; xii. 7 ; Heb. x.
5, 8 ; and Ps. xxi. 9 ; xxxix. 7, in the Septuagint.   The word *will,* therefore, does not express so much a mere determination of the mind, as a state
of the feelings and judgment.   'What I love and approve, that I omit ;
what I hate and disapprove, that I do.'   This may not be philosophical,

though it is perfectly correct language. It is the language of common life, which, as it proceeds from the common consciousness of men, is often a better indication of what that consciousness teaches, than the language of the schools. Philosophers themselves, however, at times speak in the same simple language of nature. Epictetus, Enchirid. l. ii. c. 26, has a form of expression almost identical with that of the apostle; ὁ ἁμαρτάνων —ὃ μὲν θέλει, οὐ ποιεῖ, καὶ ὃ μὴ θέλει ποιεῖ. The language of the apostle, in this passage, expresses a fact of consciousness, with which every Christian is familiar. Whether the conflict here described is that which, in a greater or less degree, exists in every man, between the natural authoritative sense of right and wrong, and his corrupt inclinations ; or whether it is peculiar to the Christian, must be decided by considerations drawn from the whole description, and from the connection of this passage with the preceding and succeeding portions of the apostle's discourse. It is enough to remark here, that every Christian can adopt the language of this verse. Pride, coldness, slothfulness, and other feelings which he disapproves and hates, are, day by day, reasserting their power over him. He struggles against their influence, groans beneath their bondage, longs to be filled with meekness, humility, and all other fruits of the love of God, but finds he can neither of himself, nor by the aid of the law, effect his freedom from what he hates, or the full performance of what he desires and approves. Every evening witnesses his penitent confession of his degrading bondage, his sense of utter helplessness, and his longing desire for aid from above. He is a slave looking and longing for liberty.

Two consequences flow from this representation of the experience of the Christian. First, the fault is felt and acknowledged to be his own ; the law is not to be blamed, ver. 16. Second, this state of feeling is consistent with his being a Christian, ver. 17.

VERSE 16. *If then I do that which I would not, I consent unto the law that it is good.* Paul here asserts that his acting contrary to the law was no evidence that he thought the law evil; for what he did he disapproved. But to disapprove and condemn what the law forbids, is to assent to the excellence of the law. There is a constant feeling of self-disapprobation, and a sense of the excellence of the law, in the Christian's mind. He is, therefore, never disposed to blame the extent or severity of the law, but admits the fault to be in himself. *I consent to,* σύμφημι, I speak with, I say the same thing which the law says, when it pronounces itself good. There is no conflict between the law and the believer ; it is between the law and what the believer himself condemns.

VERSE 17. *Now then it is no more I that do it, but sin that dwelleth in me.* Now then, νυνὶ δέ, that is, under these circumstances, or, this being the case. Or the meaning may be *but now, i.e.,* since I became a Christian. The former explanation is to be preferred on account of the connection of this verse with ver. 15, from which this passage is an inference. ' If the case be so, that I am sold under sin and am its unwilling slave ; if I do what I disapprove, and fail to accomplish what I love ; it is clear that it is not properly and fully I that do it, my real self ; my better feelings or renovated nature is opposed to what the law forbids.' Ego quidem in utroque, sed magis ego in eo, quod approbabam, quam in eo quod in me improbabam. *Augustine,* Confess. Lib. viii. chap. 5. This is not said as an exculpation, but to exhibit the extent and power of indwelling sin, which it is beyond our own power, and beyond the power of the law, to eradicate or effectually control. This feeling of helplessness is not only consistent with a sense and acknowledgment of accountability, but is always found united with genuine self-condemnation and penitence. There are, in general, few stronger indications of ignorance of the power and evil of sin, than the confident assertion of our ability to resist and subdue it. Paul groaned beneath its bondage, as if held in the loathsome embrace of a " body of death." The apostle's object, therefore, is not to apologise for sin, but to show that the experience detailed in ver. 15 is consistent with his being a Christian. ' If it is true that I really approve and love the law, and desire to be conformed to it, I am no longer the willing slave of sin ; to the depth and power of the original evil is to be attributed the fact that I am not entirely delivered from its influence.' This is obviously connected with the main object of the whole passage. For if sin remains and exerts its power, notwithstanding our disapprobation, and in despite of all our efforts, it is clear that we must look for deliverance to something out of ourselves, and that the mere perceptive power of the law cannot remove the evil.

VERSES 18, 19, 20. These verses contain an amplification and confirmation of the sentiment of the preceding verses. They re-assert the existence, and explain the nature of the inward struggle of which the apostle had been speaking. ' I am unable to come up to the requirements of the law, not because they are unreasonable, but because I am corrupt; there is no good in me. I can approve and delight in the exhibitions of holiness made by the law, but full conformity to its demands is more than I can attain. It is not I, therefore, my real and lasting self, but this intrusive tyrant dwelling within me, that disobeys the law.' This strong and expressive language, though susceptible of a literal interpretation, which would make it teach not only error but nonsense, is still perfectly perspicuous and correct, because accurately descriptive of the common feelings of men. Paul frequently employs similar modes of expression. When speaking of his apostolic labours, he says, " Yet not I, but the grace of God, which was with me," 1 Cor. xv. 10. And in Gal. ii. 20, he says, " I live, yet not I, but Christ liveth in me." As no one supposes that the labours and life here spoken of were not the labours and life of the apostle, or that they did not constitute and express his moral character ; so no Christian supposes that the greatness and power of his sin frees him from its responsibility, even when he expresses his helpless misery by saying, with the apostle, " It is not I, but sin that dwelleth in me." This doctrine of sin as *indwelling* is irreconcilable with the assumption that sin consists exclusively in acts of the will, or. even, in the widest sense of the terms, in voluntary action. An indwelling act is a solecism. Sin, in this, as in so many other places of Scripture, is presented as an abiding state of the mind, a disposition or principle, manifesting itself in acts. It is this that gives sin its power. We have measurably power over our acts, but over our immanent principles we have no direct control. They master us and not we them. Herein consists our bondage to sin. And as the power of an indwelling principle is increased by exercise, so the strength of sin is increased by every voluntary evil act. No act is isolated. " Nothing," says Olshausen, " is more dangerous than the erroneous opinion that an evil act can stand alone, or that a man can commit one sin and then stop. All evil is concatenated, and every sin increases the power of the indwelling corruption in a fearful progression, until, sooner than the sinner dreams of, his head swims, and he is plunged into the abyss."

VERSE 18. *For I know that in me, that is, in my flesh, there dwe no good thing*, &c. The γάρ refers to the preceding clause, " sin dwelleth in me," which what follows confirms. ' Sin dwells in me, *for* in my flesh there dwelleth no good thing;' literally, *good does not dwell*. Paul is here explaining how it is that there is such a contradiction between his better principles and his conduct, as just described. The reason is, that in himself he was entirely depraved, " In me, that is, in my flesh, there dwelleth no good thing." As Paul is here speaking of himself, he limits the declaration that there was no good in him. In its full sense, as he was a renewed man, this could not be true ; he therefore adds, " in my flesh." Agreeably to the explanation given above, ver. 14, these words evidently mean, ' in my nature considered apart from Divine influence,' *i.e.*, ' in me viewed independently of the effects produced by the Spirit of God.' This is Paul's common use of the word *flesh*. As he ascribes all excellence in man to the Holy Spirit, in men, when destitute of that Spirit, there is " no good thing." To be " in the flesh," is to be unrenewed, and under the government of our own depraved nature ; to be " in the Spirit," is to be under the guidance of the Holy Ghost; chap. viii. 8, 9. So, too, in Scripture language, a *natural* man is a depraved man; and a *spiritual* man is one that is renewed; 1 Cor. .ii. 14, 15. It need hardly be remarked that *in the flesh* cannot here mean in the body. Paul does not mean to say that in his body there was no good thing, as though the body were the seat of sin in man, and that exclusively. He frequently uses the phrase, *works of the flesh*, in reference to sins which have no connection with the body, as envy, pride, seditions, heresies, &c., Gal. v. 19, 20.

For to will is present with me, but to perform that which is good, I find not. This again is connected by γάρ with what precedes. ' Good does not dwell in me, *for* though I have the will to do right, I have not the performance.' Τὸ θέλειν παράκειταί μοι, not *will* as a faculty, but (τὸ θέλειν) as an act. The purpose or desire is present, *i.e.*, *I have it; but the performance of the good I find not ;* οὐχ εὑρίσκω is equivalent to οὐ παράκειται *is not present*. I have the one but not the other. Instead of the common text as given above, Griesbach and Lachmann, on the authority of the Alexandrian manuscript, read simply οὐ, omitting εὑρίσκω, (I find.) The sense is the same, for in that case παράκειται must be understood. ' The one is present, the other is not (present).' The common reading is generally preferred, as the omission is easily accounted for.

VERSE 19. *For the good that I would, I do not ; but the evil that I would not, that I do.* A confirmation of what goes before. ' I do not find good present with me, *for* the good I would I do not.' This is a repetition, nearly in the same words, of what is said in ver. 15. Paul reasserts that he was unable to act up to his purposes and desires. For example, he doubtless desired to love God with all his heart, and at all times, but constantly was his love colder and less operative than the law demands. This verse is, therefore, but an amplification of the last clause of ver. 18. *I would* (θέλω) means either *I approve* or *love*, as in ver. 15 ; or, *I purpose*, as in ver. 18. The numerous passages * quoted by commentators in

---

* The following are a few examples of this kind selected from the multitude collected by Grotius and Wetstein.

Quid est hoc, Lucili, quod nos alio tendentes alio trahit, et eo, unde recedere cupimus, repellit? Quid colluctatur cum animo nostro, nec permittit nobis quidquam semel velle ? Fluctuamus inter varia consilia, nihil libere volumus, nihil absolute, nihil semper.—*Seneca*, Ep. 25.

Sed trahit invitam nova vis, aliudque cupido, mens aliud suadet. Video meliora proboque, deteriora sequor.—*Ovid*, Metam. vii. 19.

illustration of this and the preceding verses, though they may serve to throw light upon the language, are expressive of feelings very different from those of the apostle. When an impenitent man says 'he is sorry for his sins, he may express the real state of his feelings ; and 'yet the import of this language is very different from what it is in the mouth of a man truly contrite. The word *sorrow* expresses a multitude of very different feelings. Thus, also, when wicked men say they approve the good while they pursue the wrong, their approbation is something very different from Paul's approbation of the law of God. And when Seneca calls the gods to witness, 'that what he wills, he does not will,' he too expresses something far short of what the language of the apostle conveys. This must be so, if there is any such thing as experimental or evangelical religion ; that is, if there is any difference between the sorrow for sin and desire of good in the mind of a true Christian, and in the unrenewed and willing votaries of sin in whom conscience is not entirely obliterated.

VERSE 20. *Now if I do that I would not, it is no more I that do it, but sin that dwelleth in me.* The same conclusion from the same premises as in ver. 17. "The things which I do, when contrary to the characteristic desires and purposes of my heart, are to be considered as the acts of a slave. They are indeed my own acts, but not being performed with the full and joyful purpose of the heart, are not to be regarded as a fair criterion of character.'

VERSE 21. *I find then a law, that when I would do good, evil is present with me.* This verse has been subjected to a greater variety of interpretations than any other in the chapter, or perhaps in the whole epistle. The construction in the original is doubtful ; and besides this difficulty, there is no little uncertainty as to the sense in which the word *law* is to be here taken. The question is, whether Paul means the law of God, of which he has been speaking throughout the chapter, or whether he uses the word in a new sense, for a rule, course, or law of action. Our translators have assumed the latter. If the former sense of the word be preferred, the passage may be thus interpreted. ' I find, therefore, that to me wishing to do good, evil (the law as the cause of evil) is present with me.' See *Koppe.* This is very unnatural. Or thus, 'I find, therefore, that to me wishing to act according to the law, *i. e.*, to do good, evil is present with me.* Or, as Tholuck explains it, 'I find, therefore, that while I would do the law, (*i. e.* good) evil is present.' Then τὸν νόμον depends on ποιεῖν, (willing *to do the law*) and τὸ καλόν is in apposition with τὸν νόμον. The law is the good which the apostle desired to do. But in the context, the phrase ποιεῖν τὸν νόμον does not occur, and the passage as thus explained is awkward and unnatural. Besides τὸ καλόν would be entirely superfluous, as τὸν νόμον needs no explanation. The considerations in favour of the second explanation of the word *law* appear to be decisive. 1. The other interpretation does not afford a sense suited to the context, as appears

---

Vos testor, omnes coelites, hoc quod volo, me nolle.—*Seneca*, Hippol. v. 604.

Ἐπεὶ γὰρ ὁ ἁμαρτάνων οὐ θέλει ἁμαρτάνειν, ἀλλὰ κατορθῶσαι, δῆλον ὅτι ὁ μὲν θέλει, οὐ ποιεῖ καὶ ὁ μὴ θέλει, ποιεῖ.—*Arrian's* Epict. ii. 26. "Since the sinner does not wish to err, but to act correctly, it is plain that what he wills he does not, and what he wills not he does."

Μανθάνω μὲν, οἷα δρᾶν μέλλω κακά,
Θυμὸς δὲ κρείσσων τῶν ἐμῶν βουλευμάτων.—*Euripides*, Medea, v. 1077.
" I know indeed that what I am about to do is evil ;
But passion is too strong for my purposes."
* Knapp's Prolusio in locum, Rom. vii. 21, in his Scripta Varii Argumenti. The several interpretations of the passage are given and discussed by that writer.

from Paul's own explanation of his meaning in the following verses. 'I find,' he says, 'this law, that while wishing to do good, I do evil,' ver. 21 ; that is, "I find that while I delight in the law of God, after the inward man, there is another law in my members which causes me to sin," vers. 22, 23. Here it is evident, that the apostle means to explain what he intended by saying in ver. 21, that he found or experienced a law which caused him to act contrary to his better judgment and desires. 2. Having used the word *law* by itself for the Divine law throughout the chapter, he, for the first time, in ver. 22, calls it "the law of God," to mark the distinction between the law intended in ver. 21, and that intended in ver. 22. 3. This sense of the word is not unusual ; it occurs repeatedly in the immediately succeeding verses.

But admitting that νομος is taken here in the sense of controlling principle or inward necessity, the construction of the passage is still doubtful. Τῷ θέλοντι ἐμοί may depend on εὑρίσκω, *I find in me.* The construction is then regular : 'I find in myself willing to do good the law, that evil is present with me,' so Meyer ; or, as Winer (§ 61, 4.) proposes, "Invenio hanc legem (normam) volenti mihi honestum facere, ut mihi," &c. And Beza : "Comperio igitur volenti mihi facere bonum hanc legem esse impositum, quod mihi malum adjaceat." Most commentators, however, assume a trajection of the particle ὅτι, placing it before the first, instead of the second clause of the verse : ' I find this law, *that* (ὅτι) to me willing to do good, evil is present with me ;' instead of, 'I find this law to me willing to do good, *that* (ὅτι) evil is present.' The English version assumes this trajection. The sense is the same ; and if it can be elicited without altering the position of the words, no such alteration should be made. Paul's experience had taught him, that while wishing to do good, he was still subject to evil, and from this subjection nothing but the grace of God could deliver him. This experience is common to all believers. "Fideles," says Calvin, "dum ad bonum nituntur, quandam in se tyrannicam legem reperire, quia eorum medullis et ossibus infixa est vitiositas legi Dei adversa et repugnans."

Verse 22. *For I delight in the law of God after the inward man.* This is both an explanation and confirmation of what precedes. The inward conflict referred to in ver. 21, is here stated more fully. Paul had said that although he purposed to do good evil was present with him : ' *For* I delight in the law of God after the inner man ; but I find a law in my members bringing me into captivity to the law of sin.' *I delight in the law,* συνήδομαι γάρ τῷ νόμῳ, *I rejoice with ;* not however with *others,* to whom the context suggests and allows no reference, but *intus, apud animum meum.* As we say, to rejoice with the whole heart. Compare σύνοιδα, *I am conscious,* i.e., I know with myself. As the apostle recognised in the new man two conflicting principles, he speaks as though there were within him two persons, both represented by *I.* The one is I, *i.e.* my flesh ; the other is I, *i.e.* my inner man. By the *inner man* is to be understood the "new man ;" either the renewed principle in itself considered, or the soul considered or viewed as renewed. That this is the true meaning of the phrase is evident: 1. From its origin. It is a term descriptive of excellence. As the soul is better than the body, so the inner man is better than the outward man. When the contrast is simply between the external and internal, then the inner man means the soul ; but when the contrast is, as here, between two conflicting principles within the soul, then by the inward man must be meant the higher or better principle within us. That this higher principle is not any natural faculty, anything belonging to us in our unrenewed state, is plain from what is predicated of this inner man. Everything is said of it that can be said of what is characteristic of the true children of God. 2. This interpretation is confirmed by a comparison with those passages where the same phrase occurs. In 2 Cor. iv. 16, and Eph. iii. 16, by "inward man" is meant the soul as renewed. It is equivalent to the inner, or divine life, which is daily renewed or strengthened by the communications of the Spirit. 3. The analogous phrases, "the new man," as opposed to the "old man," Rom. vi. 6; Eph. iv. 22; Col. iii. 9, and "hidden man of the heart," 1 Pet. iii. 4, serve to illustrate and confirm this interpretation. As "the new man" is the soul as made new, so "the inward man," of which the same things are predicated, means the renewed nature, or nature as renewed. 4. The use of the terms "inward man," "law of the mind," "the Spirit," "the spiritual man," as opposed to "the law in the members," "the old man," "the flesh," "the natural man," shows that the former all indicate the soul as regenerated, or as the seat of the Spirit's influences, and the latter the soul as unrenewed. 5. The decision of the question as to what is here meant by the "inward man," depends on what is elsewhere taught in the Scriptures concerning the natural state of man. If men, since the fall, are only partially depraved; if sin affects only our lower faculties, leaving the reason undisturbed in its original purity, then by the "inward man," we must understand our rational, as opposed to our sensuous nature. But if the Bible teaches that the whole man is defiled by sin, and that the principle of spiritual life is something supernatural, then it follows that the conflict here depicted is not that between sense and reason, but that between the new and old man, the soul as renewed and indwelling sin. "Interior igitur homo," says Calvin, "non anima simpliciter dicitur, sed spiritualis ejus pars, quæ a Deo regenerata est : membrorum vocabulum residuam alteram partem significat. Nam ut anima est pars excellentior hominis, corpus inferior; ita spiritus superior est carne. Hac ergo ratione, quia Spiritus locum animæ tenet in homine, caro autem, id est corrupta et vitiata anima, corporis, ille interioris hominis, hæc membrorum nomen obtinet." So also Melancthon says, "Interior homo significat hominem, quatenus renovatus est Spiritu sancto." And Luther's marginal note is, "Inwendiger Mensch heisst hier der Geist aus Gnaden geboren, welcher in den Heiligen streitet wider den äusserlichen, dass ist, Vernunft, Sinn und alles was Natur am Menschen ist." And this conflict between the flesh and Spirit, he says, in his preface to this epistle, "continues in us so long as we live, in some more, and in others less, according as the one or the other principle is the stronger. Yet the whole man is both flesh and Spirit, and contends with himself until he is completely spiritual."

Verse 23. *But I see another law in my members, &c.* *I see,* as though looking into his own soul, and observing the principles there in conflict. Besides "the inward man," or principle of the divine life, there was "another *law*," not merely ἄλλον, another numerically, but ἕτερον, another in kind, one that is heterogeneous, of a different nature. This evil principle is called a *law,* because of its permanency and its controlling power. It is not a transient act or mutable purpose, but a law, something independent of the will which defies and controls it. *In my members, i.e.* in me. It is equivalent to "in my flesh," ver. 18. *Warring against the law of my mind.* It is not only passively antagonistic, but it is a constantly active principle, warring, *i.e.* endeavouring to overcome and destroy *the law of my* mind. Ὁ νόμος τοῦ νοός μου, is not the law of which my mind is the author, but which pertains to my higher nature. As the one law is in the members, or flesh, the other is the mind ; νοῦς, not the reason, nor the affections, but the higher or renewed nature. It is antithetical to σάρξ, and as the latter does not mean the body, nor simply our sensuous nature, but our nature considered as corrupt, so the former does not mean the soul, nor the reason, but our nature as renewed. "The law of the mind" is evidently only another designation for "the inward man." It was not the apostle's mind, his rational nature, which strove against the law in his members ; but it was his mind or rational nature as a Christian, and therefore, as such, the dwelling-place of the Holy Spirit. It is not the reason of the natural man, but the illuminated reason of the spiritual man, of which the apostle here speaks. *Bringing me into captivity to the law of sin which is in my members.* The principle of evil is not only active, but it is conquering. It takes the soul captive. So that it is, in the sense of ver. 14, the slave of sin. Not its willing servant, but its miserable, helpless victim. This does not mean that sin always triumphs in act, but simply that it is a power from which the soul cannot free itself. It remains, and wars, in spite of all that we can do. *The law of sin* is only a descriptive designation of that other law mentioned in the preceding clause. They are not two laws. The law in the members, which wars against the law of the mind, is a *law of sin, i.e.* it is sin considered as a law, or controlling power. It is the same as "indwelling sin," ἡ οἰκοῦσα ἐν ἐμοὶ ἁμαρτία. *In my members, i.e.* in me, as what is here expressed by ἐν τοῖς μέλεσί μου, is before expressed by ἐν ἐμοί. It is only a modification of the old anti-Augustinian interpretation, when Olshausen represents, according to his anthropology, man as composed of three parts, the πνεῦμα, ψυχή, and σῶμα, or νοῦς, ψυχή, and σάρξ. The ψυχή he makes the real centre of ou personality. By the νοῦς we are in communion with the spiritual world, by the σάρξ with the material world. The ψυχή, therefore, is the battle-field of the νοῦς and σάρξ. By itself the ψυχή cannot free itself from the dominion or power of the σάρξ, and therefore needs redemption, the effect of which is to give the higher principle of our nature the ascendency. The conflict is, from first to last, a natural one. It is only a struggle between the good principle in man which has survived the fall, with the disorder introduced into his nature by the apostacy.

VERSE 24. *O wretched man that I am ! who shall deliver me from the body of this death ?* The burden of indwelling sin was a load which the apostle could neither cast off nor bear. He could only groan under its pressure, and long for deliverance by a power greater than his. Ταλαίπωρος, (nearly allied to ταλαπείριος, from τλάω and πεῖρα, *much tried,*) *wretched,* Rev. iii. 17, where it is connected with ἐλεεινός, compare James v. 1; iv. 9. *Who shall deliver me ?* this is the expression, not of despair, but of earnest desire of help from without and above himself. "Non quærit," says Calvin, "a quo sit liberandus, quasi dubitans ut increduli, qui non tenent unicum esse liberatorem : sed vox est anhelantis et prope fatiscentis, quia non satis præsentem opem videat." That from which the apostle desired to be delivered is the *body of this death,* τίς με ῥύσεται ἐκ τοῦ σώματος τοῦ θανάτου τούτου. The demonstrative τούτου may be referred either to σώματος, *this* body of death, or to θανάτου, body of *this* death. It is not unusual, especially in Hebrew, for the demonstrative and possessive pronouns to be connected with the noun governed, when they really qualify the governing noun; as "idols of his silver," for his silver idols; "mountains of my holiness," for my holy mountains. If this explanation be here adopted, then the meaning is, this body which is subject to death, *i.e.*, this mortal body. Then what the apostle longed for was death. He longed to have the strife over, which he knew was to last so long as he continued in the body. But this is inconsistent, both with what precedes and with what follows. It was the "law in his members," "the law of sin," which pressed on him as a grievous burden. And the victory for which he gives thanks is not freedom from the body, but deliverance from sin. To avoid these difficulties, *death* may be taken in the sense of spiritual death, and therefore including the idea of sin. "This body of death," would then mean, this body which is the seat of death, in which spiritual death, *i.e.* reigns. It is, however, more natural to take the words as they stand, and connect τούτου with Θανάτου, *this death*. Then *the body of this death* may mean the natural or material body, which belongs or pertains to the death of which he had been speaking. This agrees nearly with the interpretation last mentioned. This supposes that the body is the seat of sin—'who shall deliver me from this death which reigns in the body?' It is not, however, Paul's doctrine that the body is evil, or that it is the seat or source of sin. It is the soul which is depraved, and which contaminates the body, and perverts it to unholy use. It is, therefore, better to take σῶμα (body) in a figurative sense. Sin is spoken of figuratively in the context as a man, as "the old man," as having members, and, in vi. 6, as a body, "the body of sin." The meaning, therefore, is, 'Who will deliver me from the burden of this death?' or, 'this deadly weight.' Calvin explains it thus: "Corpus mortis vocat massam peccati vel congeriem, ex qua totus homo conflatus est." The body under which the apostle groaned was *mortifera peccati massa*. This exclamation is evidently from a burdened heart. It is spoken out of the writer's own consciousness, and shows that although the apostle represents a class, he himself belonged to that class. It is his own experience as a Christian to which he gives utterance.

Verse 25. The burden of sin being the great evil under which the apostle and all other believers labour, from which no efficacy of the law, and no efforts of their own can deliver them, their case would be entirely hopeless but for help from on high. "Sin shall not have dominion over you," is the language of the grace of God in the gospel. The conflict which the believer sustains is not to result in the victory of sin, but in the triumph of grace. In view of this certain and glorious result, Paul exclaims, *I thank God through Jesus Christ our Lord*. This is evidently the expression of a strong and sudden emotion of gratitude. As, however, his object is to illustrate the operation of the law, it would be foreign to his purpose to expatiate on a deliverance effected by a different power; he, therefore, does not follow up the idea suggested by this exclamation, but immediately returns to the point in hand. Instead of the common text εὐχαριστῶ τῷ Θεῷ, *I thank God*, many editors prefer the reading χάρις τῷ Θεῷ, *thanks be to God*. Some manuscripts have ἡ χάρις τοῦ Θεοῦ. Then this verse would be an answer to the preceding. 'Who shall deliver me from this burden of sin?' *Ans.* 'The grace of God.' For this reading, however, there is little authority, external or internal. *Through Jesus Christ our Lord*. Paul does not only render thanks to God through the mediation of Christ, but the great blessing of deliverance for which he gives thanks, is received through the Lord Jesus Christ. He does for us what neither the law nor our own powers could effect. He is the only Redeemer from sin.

So then, ἄρα ουν, *wherefore*. The inference is not from the immediately preceding expression of thanks. 'Jesus Christ is my deliverer, *wherefore* I myself,' &c. But this is an unnatural combination. The main idea of the whole passage, the subject which the apostle laboured to have understood, is the impotence of the law—the impossibility of obtaining deliverance from sin through its influence or agency. The inference is, therefore, from the whole preceding discussion, especially from what is said from ver. 14, onward. The conclusion to which the apostle had arrived is here briefly summed up. He remained, and so far as the law is concerned, must remain under the power of sin. 'With the mind I serve the law of God, but with the flesh the law of sin.' Deliverance from the power of sin the law cannot accomplish. *I myself*, αὐτὸς ἐγώ. The αὐτὸς here is either antithetical, placing the ἐγώ in opposition to some expressed or implied, or it is explanatory. If the former, the opposition is to διά Ιησοῦ Χριστοῦ, *I alone, without the aid of Christ*. So Meyer and others. But the idea thus expressed is not in accordance with the context. Paul had not been teaching what his unrenewed, unaided nature could accomplish, but what was the operation of the law, even on the renewed man. The αὐτός is simply explanatory, *I myself*, and *no other*, *i.e.* the same *Ego* of which he had spoken all along. It is very plain, from the use of this expression, that the preceding paragraph is an exhibition of his own experience. All that is there said, is summarily here said emphatically in his own person. 'I myself, I, Paul, with my mind serve the law of God, but with the flesh the law of sin.' The antithesis is between νοῖ and σαρκί ; the one explains the other. As σάρξ is not the body, nor the sensuous nature, but indwelling sin, ver. 18, so νοῦς is not the mind as opposed to the body, nor reason as opposed to the sensual passions, but the higher, renewed principle, as opposed to the law in the members, or indwelling corruption. This interpretation is sustained by the use of the word in the preceding verses. Paul served the law of God, in so far as he assented to the law that it is good, as he delighted in it, and strove to be conformed to it. He served the *law of sin*, that is, sin considered as a law or inward power, so far as, in despite of all his efforts, he was still under its influence, and was thereby hindered from living in that constant fellowship with God, and conformity to his will, that he earnestly desired.

Having gone through the exposition of this passage, it is time to pause, and ask, Of whom has Paul been speaking, of a renewed or unrenewed man? Few questions of this kind have been more frequently canvassed, or more intimately associated with the doctrinal views of different classes of theologians. The history of the interpretation of the latter part of this chapter, is one of the most interesting sections of the doctrinal history of the Church. A brief outline of this history may be found in the Dissertation of Knapp, before referred to, and somewhat more extended in the Commentary of Tholuck. It appears that during the first three centuries, the Fathers were generally agreed in considering the passage as descriptive of the experience of one yet under the law. Even Augustine at first concurred in the correctness of this view. But as a deeper insight into his own heart, and a more thorough investigation of the Scriptures, led to the modification of his opinions on so many other points, they produced a change on this subject also. This general alteration of his doctrinal views cannot be attributed to his controversy with Pelagius, because it took place long before that controversy commenced. It is to be ascribed to his religious experience, and his study of the word of God.

The writers of the middle ages, in general, agreed with the later views of Augustine on this, as on other subjects. At the time of the Reformation, the original diversity of opinion on this point, and on all others connected with it, soon became manifested. Erasmus, Socinus, and others, revived the opinion of the Greek Fathers; while Luther, Calvin, Melanchthon, Beza, &c., adhered to the opposite interpretation. At a later period, when the controversy with the Remonstrants occurred, it commenced with a discussion of the interpretation of this chapter. The first writings of Arminius, in which he broached his peculiar opinions, were lectures on this passage. All his associates and successors, as Grotius, Episcopius, Limborch, &c., adopted the same view of the subject. As a general rule, Arminian writers have been found on one side of this question, and Calvinistic authors on the other. This is indeed the natural result of their different views of the scriptural doctrine of the natural state of man. Most of the former class, going much farther than Arminius himself ever went—either denying that the corruption consequent on the fall is such as to destroy the power of men to conform themselves to the law of God, or maintaining that this power, if lost, is restored by those operations of the Holy Spirit which are common to all—found no difficulty in considering the expressions, "I consent to" and "delight in the law of God after the inward man," as the language of a person yet in his natural state. On the other hand, those who held the doctrine of total depravity, and of the consequent inability of sinners, and who rejected the doctrine of "common grace," could not reconcile with these opinions the strong language here used by the apostle.

Although this has been the general course of opinion on this subject, some of the most evangelical men, especially on the continent of Europe, have agreed with Erasmus in his view of this passage. This was the case with Francke, Bengel, &c., of a previous age; and with Knapp, Flatt, Tholuck, &c., of our own day; not to mention the distinguished writers of England and our own country, who have adopted the same view. There is nothing, therefore in this opinion, which implies the denial or disregard of any of the fundamental principles of evangelical religion. Still, that the view of the passage which so long prevailed in the Church, and which has been generally adopted by evangelical men, is the correct one, seems evident from the following considerations.

1. The *onus probandi* is certainly on the other side. When the apostle uses not only the first person, but the present tense, and says, "I consent to the law that it is good," "I delight in the law of God," "I see another law in my members warring against the law of my mind," &c., those who deny that he means himself, even though he says *I myself,* or refuse to acknowledge that this language expresses his feelings while writing, are surely bound to let the contrary very clearly be seen. Appearances are certainly against them. It should be remembered that Paul uses this language, not once or twice, but uniformly through the whole passage, and that too with an ardour of feeling indicative of language coming directly from the heart, and expressing its most joyful or painful experience. This is a consideration which cannot be argumentatively exhibited, but it must impress every attentive and susceptible reader. To suppose that the apostle is personating another, either, as Grotius* supposes, the Jew first

* *Ego,* id est, genus Israeliticum cum vixit ante legem—in Aegypto scilicet. See his comment on ver. 9.

before the giving of the law, and then after it ; or as Erasmus thinks, a
Gentile without the law, as opposed to a Jew under it ; or as is more
commonly supposed, an ordinary individual under the influence of a knowledge of the law, is to suppose him to do what he does nowhere else in
any of his writings, and what is entirely foreign to his whole spirit and
manner.   Instead of thus sinking himself in another, he can hardly prevent his own individual feelings from mingling with, and moulding the
very statement of objections to his own reasoning ; see chap. iii. 3—8.
One great difficulty in explaining his epistles, arises from this very source.
It is hard to tell at times what is his language, and what that of an objector.   If any one will examine the passages in which Paul is supposed
to mean another, when he uses the first person, he will see how far short
they come of affording any parallel to the case supposed in this chapter.*
In many of them he undoubtedly means himself, as in 1 Cor. iii. 6 ; iv. 3,
&c.; in others the language is, in one sense, expressive of the apostle's
real sentiments, and is only perverted by the objector, as in 1 Cor.
vi. 12 ; while in others the personation of another is only for a single
sentence.   Nothing analogous to this passage is to be found in all his
writings, if indeed he is not here pouring out the feelings of his own
heart.

II. There is no necessity for denying that Paul here speaks of himself
and describes the exercises of a renewed man.   There is not an expression, from beginning to the end of this section, which the holiest man may
not and must not adopt.   This has been shown in the commentary.   The
strongest declarations, as, for example, " I am carnal, and sold under sin,"
admit, indeed, by themselves, of an interpretation inconsistent with even
ordinary morality ; but, as explained by the apostle, and limited by the
context, they express nothing more than every believer experiences. What
Christian does not feel that he is carnal ?   Alas, how different is he from
the spirits of the just made perfect !   How cheerfully does he recognise
his obligation to love God with all the heart, and yet how constantly does
the tendency to self and the world, the law in his members, war against
the purer and better law of his mind, and bring him into subjection to sin !
If, indeed, it were true, as has been asserted, that the person here described
" *succumbs to sin* IN EVERY INSTANCE *of contest*,"† the description would be
inapplicable not to the Christian only, but to any other than the most immoral of men.   It is rare, indeed, even in the natural conflict between
reason and passion, or conscience and corrupt inclination, that the better
principle does not succeed, not once merely, but often.   There is, however,
nothing even approaching to the implication of such a sentiment in the
whole passage.   Paul merely asserts that the believer is, and ever remains
in this life, imperfectly sanctified ; that sin continues to dwell within
him ; that he never comes up to the full requisitions of the law, however
anxiously he may desire it.   Often as he subdues one spiritual foe, another
rises in a different form ; so that he cannot do the things that he would ;
that is, cannot be perfectly conformed in heart and life to the image of
God.

It must have been in a moment of forgetfulness, that such a man as
Tholuck could quote with approbation the assertion of Dr. A. Clarke :
" This opinion has most pitifully and shamefully, not only lowered the

---

* The passages referred to by Knapp are 1 Cor. iii. 6 ; iv. 3, &c.; vi. 12 ; x. 29, 30; xiii.
11, 12 ; xiv. 14, 15 ; Gal. ii. 18—21.
† Professor Stuart, p. 558.

standard of Christianity, but destroyed its influence and disgraced its character." What lamentable blindness to notorious facts does such language evince ! From the days of Job and David to the present hour, the holiest men have been the most ready to acknowledge and deplore the existence and power of indwelling sin. Without appealing to individual illustrations of the truth of this remark, look at masses of men, at Augustinians and Pelagians, Calvinists and Remonstrants : in all ages the strictest doctrines and the sternest morals have been found united. It is not those who have most exalted human ability, that have most advantageously exhibited the fruits of its power. It has been rather those who, with the lowest views of themselves, and the highest apprehensions of the efficacy of the grace of God, have been able to adopt the language of Paul, "What I would, that do I not ;" and who, looking away from themselves to him through whom they can do all things, have shown the Divine strength manifested in their weakness.

III. While there is nothing in the sentiments of this passage which a true Christian may not adopt, there is much which cannot be asserted by any unrenewed man. As far as this point is concerned, the decision depends, of course, on the correct interpretation of the several expressions employed by the apostle. 1. What is the true meaning of the phrases "inward man" and "law of the mind," when opposed to "the flesh" and "the law in the members ?" The sense of these expressions is to be determined by their use in other passages ; or if they do not elsewhere occur, by the meaning attached to those which are obviously substituted for them. As from the similarity of the passages, it can hardly be questioned, that what Paul here calls "the inward man" and "law of the mind," he, in Gal. v. 17, and elsewhere, calls "the Spirit ;" it is plain that he intends, by these terms, to designate the soul considered as renewed, in opposition to the "flesh," or the soul considered as destitute of Divine influence. 2. It is not in accordance with the scriptural representation of the wicked, to describe them as consenting to the law of God ; as hating sin, and struggling against it ; groaning under it as a tyrant's yoke ; as delighting in the law of God, *i.e.*, in holiness : doing all this, not as men, but as men viewed in a particular aspect as to the inward or new man. This is not the scriptural representation of the natural man, who does not receive the things of the Spirit of God, and cannot know them, 1 Cor. ii. 14. On the contrary, the carnal mind is enmity against God and his law. They therefore who are in the flesh, that is, who have this carnal mind, hate and oppose the law, Rom. viii. 7, 8. The expressions here used by the apostle, are such as, throughout the Scriptures, are used to describe the exercises of the pious, "whose delight is in the law of the Lord," Ps. i. 2. 3. Not only do these particular expressions show that the writer is a true Christian, but the whole conflict here described is such as is peculiar to the sincere believer. There is, indeed, in the natural man, something very analogous to this, when his conscience is enlightened, and his better feelings come into collision with the strong inclination to evil which dwells in his mind. But this struggle is very far below that which the apostle here describes. The true nature of this conflict seems to be ascertained beyond dispute, by the parallel passage in Gal. v. 17, already referred to. It cannot be denied, that to possess the Spirit is, in scriptural language, a characteristic mark of a true Christian. " But ye are not in the flesh, but in the spirit, if so be that the Spirit of God dwell in you. Now if any man have not the Spirit of Christ, he is none of his." Rom. viii. 9. Those, therefore, who have that Spirit, are Christians. This being the case, it will not be doubted that the passage in Galatians, in which the spirit is represented as warring against the flesh, and the flesh against the spirit, is descriptive of the experience of the true believer. But the conflict there described is identical with that of which the same apostle speaks in this chapter. This is evident, not merely from the fact that one of the antagonist principles is, in both cases, called *flesh*, but because the description is nearly in the same words. In consequence of the opposition of the flesh and spirit, Paul tells the Galatians they cannot do the things that they would; and he says here of himself, that in consequence of the opposition between the flesh and the law of his mind, what he would he did not. The same conflict and the same bondage are described in each case; and if the one be descriptive of the exercises of a true Christian, the other must be so also.

IV. The context, or the connection of this passage with the preceding and succeeding chapters, is in favour of the common interpretation. The contrary is, indeed, strongly asserted by those who take the opposite view of the passage. Tholuck seems to admit that, were it not for the context, the whole of the latter part of the chapter might well be understood of the believer : see his remarks on ver. 14. And Professor Stuart says, " I repeat the remark, that the question is not, whether what is here said *might* be applied to Christians; but whether, from the tenor of the context, it appears to have been the intention of the writer that it *should be* so applied. This principle cannot fail to settle the question concerning such an application." P. 558. It may be proper to pause and remark, that such statements involve a renunciation of the arguments derived from the inapplicability to the real Christian, of what is here said. Everything is here admitted to be in itself applicable to him, did but the context allow it to be so applied. Yet every one is aware that no argument is more frequently and strongly urged against the common interpretation, than that the description here given is, in its very nature, unsuitable to Christian experience. On the same page which contains the passage just quoted, Professor Stuart says, " As, however, there is no denying the truth of these and the like declarations,* and no receding from them, nor explaining them away as meaning less than *habitual victory* over sin; so it follows, that when verses 14—25 are applied to Christian experience, they are wrongly applied. The person represented in these verses, *succumbs to sin* IN EVERY INSTANCE of contest." This is certainly an argument against applying the passage in question to the Christian, founded on the assumption that it is, from its nature, entirely inapplicable. And the argument is perfectly conclusive, if the meaning of the passage be what is here stated. But it is believed that this is very far from being its true meaning, as shown above. This argument, however, it appears, is not insisted upon : everything is made to depend upon the context.

Many distinguished commentators, as Alfonso Turrettin, Knapp, Tholuck, Flatt, and Stuart, consider this chapter, from ver. 7 to the end, as a commentary upon ver. 5, in which verse the state of those who are in " the flesh " is spoken of; and the first part of the next chapter as a commentary on ver. 6, which speaks of those who are no longer under the law. Accordingly, verses 7—25 are descriptive of the exercises of a man yet under the law; and viii. 1—17, of those of a man under the gospel, or of a believer. It is said that the two passages are in direct antithesis; the

---

* ' He who loveth Christ, keepeth his commandments,' &c.

one describes the state of a captive to sin, vii. 23 ; and the other the state
of one who is delivered from sin, viii. 2.   This is certainly ingenious and
plausible, but is founded on a twofold misapprehension ; first, as to the
nature of this captivity to sin, or the real meaning of the former passage,
vii. 14—25 ; and, secondly, as to the correct interpretation of the latter
passage, or viii. 1—17.   If vii. 14—25 really describes such a captivity
as these authors suppose, in which the individual spoken of " succumbs to
sin in every instance," there is, of course, an end of this question, and that
too without any appeal to the context for support.   But, on the other
hand, if it describes no such state, but, as Tholuck and Professor Stuart
admit, contains nothing which *might not be* said of the Christian, the
whole force of the argument is gone ; verses 7—25 are no longer necessarily a comment on ver. 5, nor viii. 1—17 on ver. 6.   The antithesis of
course ceases, if the interpretation, to which it owes its existence, be
abandoned.   The matter, after all, therefore, is made to depend on the
correct exposition of the passage (verses 14-25) itself.   A particular interpretation cannot first be assumed, in order to make out the antithesis ; and
then the antithesis be assumed, to justify the interpretation.   This would
be reasoning in a circle.   In the second place, this view of the context is
founded, as is believed, on an erroneous exegesis of viii. 1—17.   The first
part of that chapter is not so intimately connected with the latter part of
this ; nor is it designed to show that the Christian is delivered from " the
law of sin and death" *in his members.*   For the grounds of this statement,
the reader is referred to the commentary on the passage in question.
Even if the reverse were the fact, still, unless it can be previously shown
that verses 14—25 of this chapter describe the state of a man under the
law, there is no ground for the assumption of such an antithesis between
the two passages as is supposed in the view of the context stated above.
Both passages might describe the same individual under different aspects ;
the one exhibiting the operation of the law, and the other that of the gospel on the renewed mind.   But if the exposition given below of viii. 1—
17, is correct, there is not a shadow of foundation for the argument derived
from the context against the common interpretation of vii. 14—25.

The whole tenor of the apostle's argument, from the beginning of the
epistle to the close of this chapter, is not only consistent with the common
interpretation, but seems absolutely to demand it.   His great object in the
first eight chapters, is to show that the whole work of the sinner's salvation,
his justification and sanctification, are not of the law, but of grace ; that
legal obedience can never secure the one, nor legal efforts the other.
Accordingly, in the first five chapters, he shows that we are justified by
faith, without the works of the law ; in the sixth, that this doctrine of
gratuitous justification, instead of leading to licentiousness, presents the
only certain and effectual means of sanctification.   In the beginning of
the seventh chapter, he shows that the believer is really thus free from the
law, and is now under grace ; and that while under the law he brought
forth fruit unto sin, but being under grace, he now brings forth fruit unto
God.   The question here arises, Why is the holy, just, and good law thus
impotent ?   Is it because it is evil?   Far from it; the reason lies in our own
corruption.   Then, to show how this is, and why the objective and authoritative exhibition of truth cannot sanctify, the apostle proceeds to show
how it actually operates on the depraved mind.   In the first place, it enlightens conscience, and in the second, it rouses the opposition of the
corrupt heart.   These are the two elements of conviction of sin ; a know-

ledge of its nature, and a sense of its power over ourselves. Hence the feeling of self-condemnation, of helplessness and misery. Thus the law slays. This is one portion of its effect, but not the whole ; for, even after the heart is renewed, as it is but imperfectly sanctified, the law is still unable to promote holiness. The reason here again is not that the law is evil, but that we are carnal, ver. 14. Indwelling sin, as the apostle calls it, is the cause why the law cannot effect the sanctification even of the believer. It presents, indeed, the form of beauty, and the soul delights in it after the inward man ; but the corrupt affections, which turn to self and the world, are still there : these the law cannot destroy. But though the law cannot do this, it shall eventually be done. Thanks to God, through Jesus Christ, our case is not hopeless.

The apostle's object would have been but half attained, had he not thus exhibited the effect of the law upon the believer's mind. and demonstrated that a sense of legal bondage was not necessary to the Christian, and could not secure his sanctification. Having done this, his object is accomplished. The eighth chapter, therefore, is not so intimately connected with the seventh. It does not commence with an inference from the discussion in vers. 7—25, but from the whole preceding exhibition. "There is, there-fore, now no condemnation to them that are in Christ Jesus." Why ? Because they are sanctified ? No ; but because they are not under the law. This is the main point from first to last. They are delivered from that law, which, however good in itself, can only produce sin and death, ver. 2. In view of this insufficiency of the law, God, having sent his Son as a sacrifice for sin, has delivered them from it, by condemning sin in him, and has thus secured the justification of believers. Through him they satisfy the demands of the law, and their salvation is rendered certain. This, however, implies that they do not live after the flesh, but after the Spirit agreeably to the doctrine of the sixth chapter ; for salvation in sin is a contradiction in terms.

There is, therefore, no such antithesis between the seventh and eighth chapters, as the opposite interpretation supposes. It is not the design of the latter to show that men are delivered from indwelling sin ; or that the conflict between the "law in the members" and "the law of the mind," between the flesh and Spirit, ceases when men embrace the gospel. But it shows that this consummation is secured to all who are in Christ, to all who do not deliberately and of choice walk after the flesh, and make it their guide and master. In virtue of deliverance from the law, and intro-duction into a state of grace, the believer has not only his acceptance with God, but his final deliverance from sin secured. Sin shall not triumph in those who have the Spirit of Christ, and who, by that Spirit, mortify the deeds of the body.

If, then, the context is altogether favourable to the ordinary interpreta-tion ; if the passage is accurately descriptive of Christian experience and analogous to other inspired accounts of the exercises of the renewed heart ; if not merely particular expressions, but the whole tenor of the discourse, is inconsistent with the scriptural account of the natural man ; and if Paul, in the use of the first person and the present tense, cannot, without violence, be considered otherwise than as expressing his own feelings while writing, we have abundant reason to rest satisfied with the obvious sense of the passage.

DOCTRINE.

1. No man is perfectly sanctified in this life. At least, Paul was not, according to his own confession, when he wrote this passage, vers. 14—25.

2. The law is spiritual, that is, perfect, deriving its character from its author, the Spirit of God. It is, therefore, the unerring standard of duty, and the source of moral light or knowledge. It should, therefore, be everywhere known and studied, and faithfully applied as the rule of judgment for our own conduct and that of others. Evangelical doctrines, therefore, which teach the necessity of freedom from the law as a covenant of works, *i. e.* as prescribing the terms of our justification before God, derogate neither from its excellence nor its authority. It is left to do its proper work in the economy of redemption ; to convince of sin, and be a guide to duty, ver. 14, &c.

3. The mere presentation of truth, apart from the influences of the Spirit, can neither renew nor sanctify the heart, ver. 14, &c.

4. Inability is consistent with responsibility. "To perform that which is good I find not," that is, I cannot, ver. 18 ; Gal. v. 17. As the Scriptures constantly recognise the truth of these two things, so are they constantly united in Christian experience. Every one feels that he cannot do the things that he would, yet is sensible that he is to blame for not doing them. Let any man test his power by the requisition to love God perfectly at all times. Alas! how entire our inability ; yet how deep our self-loathing and self-condemnation.

5. The emotions and affections do not obey a determination of the will, vers. 16, 18, 19, 21. A change of purpose, therefore, is not a change of heart.

6. The Christian's victory over sin cannot be achieved by the strength of his resolutions, nor by the plainness and force of moral motives, nor by any resources within himself. He looks to Jesus Christ, and conquers in his strength. In other words, the victory is not obtained in the way of nature, but of grace, vers. 14—25.

REMARKS.

1. As the believer's life is a constant conflict, those who do not struggle against sin, and endeavour to subdue it, are not true Christians, vers. 14—25.

2. The person here described hates sin, ver. 15 ; acknowledges and delights in the spirituality of the divine law, vers. 16, 22 ; he considers his corruption a dreadful burden, from which he earnestly desires to be delivered, ver. 24. These are exercises of genuine piety, and should be applied as tests of character.

3. It is an evidence of an unrenewed heart to express or feel opposition to the law of God, as though it were too strict ; or to be disposed to throw off the blame of our want of conformity to the divine will from ourselves upon the law, as unreasonable. The renewed man condemns himself, and justifies God, even while he confesses and mourns his inability to conform to the divine requisitions, vers. 14—25.

4. The strength and extent of the corruption of our nature are seen from its influence over the best of men, and from its retaining more or less of its power, under all circumstances, to the end of life, ver. 25.

5. This corruption, although its power is acknowledged, so far from being regarded as an excuse or palliation for our individual offences, is recognized as the greatest aggravation of our guilt. To say, with the feelings of the apostle, "I am carnal," is to utter the strongest language of self-condemnation and self-abhorrence, vers. 14—25.

6. Although the believer is never perfectly sanctified in this life, his aim and efforts are ever onward; and the experience of the power of indwelling sin teaches him the value of heaven, and prepares him for the enjoyment of it, vers. 14—25.

CHAPTER VIII.

CONTENTS.

PAUL HAD NOW FINISHED HIS EXHIBITION OF THE PLAN OF SALVATION. HE HAD SHOWN THAT WE ARE JUSTIFIED GRATUITOUSLY, THAT IS, BY FAITH IN JESUS CHRIST, WITHOUT THE WORKS OF THE LAW. HE HAD PROVED THAT, SO FAR FROM THIS FREEDOM FROM THE LAW LEADING TO THE INDULGENCE OF SIN, IT IS NECESSARY TO OUR SANCTIFICATION, BECAUSE THE LAW IS AS INADEQUATE TO THE PRODUCTION OF HOLINESS IN THE SINNER, AS IT IS TO SECURE PARDON OR ACCEPTANCE WITH GOD. THAT SUCH IS THE INSUFFICIENCY OF THE LAW, HE PROVED BY EXHIBITING ITS OPERATION BOTH ON THE RENEWED AND UNRENEWED MIND. HAVING ACCOMPLISHED ALL THIS, HE LEAVES, IN THE CHAPTER BEFORE US, THE FIELD OF LOGICAL ARGUMENT, AND ENTERS ON THE NEW AND MORE ELEVATED SPHERE OF JOYOUS EXULTATION. AS, HOWEVER, THERE IS ALWAYS WARMTH OF FEELING IN THE APOSTLE'S ARGUMENT, SO ALSO IS THERE GENERALLY LOGICAL ARRANGEMENT IN HIS HIGHEST TRIUMPHS.

HIS THEME HERE IS THE SECURITY OF BELIEVERS. THE SALVATION OF THOSE WHO HAVE RENOUNCED THE LAW, AND ACCEPTED THE GRACIOUS OFFERS OF THE GOSPEL, IS SHOWN TO BE ABSOLUTELY CERTAIN. THE WHOLE CHAPTER IS A SERIES OF ARGUMENTS, MOST BEAUTIFULLY ARRANGED, IN SUPPORT OF THIS ONE POINT. THEY ARE ALL TRACED BACK TO THE GREAT SOURCE OF HOPE AND SECURITY, THE UNMERITED AND UNCHANGING LOVE OF GOD IN CHRIST JESUS. THE PROPOSITION IS CONTAINED IN THE FIRST VERSE. THERE IS NO CONDEMNATION TO THOSE WHO ARE IN CHRIST JESUS: THEY SHALL NEVER BE CONDEMNED OR PERISH.

1. BECAUSE THEY ARE DELIVERED FROM THE LAW; ALL ITS DEMANDS BEING FULFILLED IN THEM BY THE MISSION AND SACRIFICE OF CHRIST, VERS. 1—4. 2. BECAUSE THEIR SALVATION IS ACTUALLY BEGUN IN THE REGENERATION AND SANCTIFICATION OF THEIR HEARTS BY THE HOLY SPIRIT. THOSE WHO HAVE THE SPIRIT OF CHRIST HAVE THE SPIRIT OF LIFE, VERSES 5—11. 3. NOT ONLY IS THEIR SALVATION BEGUN, BUT THEY ARE THE CHILDREN OF GOD, AND IF CHILDREN, THEY ARE HEIRS, VERSES 12—17. 4. THE AFFLICTIONS WHICH THEY MAY BE CALLED TO ENDURE, ARE NOT INCONSISTENT WITH THIS FILIAL RELATION TO GOD, BECAUSE THEY ARE UTTERLY INSIGNIFICANT IN COMPARISON WITH THE GLORY THAT SHALL BE REVEALED IN THEM; AND UNDER THESE AFFLICTIONS THEY ARE SUSTAINED BOTH BY HOPE AND THE INTERCESSIONS OF THE HOLY SPIRIT, VERSES 18—28. 5. BECAUSE THEY ARE PREDESTINATED

TO THE ATTAINMENT OF ETERNAL LIFE; OF WHICH PREDESTINATION THEIR
PRESENT SANCTIFICATION OR EFFECTUAL CALLING IS THE RESULT, AND
THEREFORE THE EVIDENCE, VERSES 28—30. 6. BECAUSE GOD HAS GIVEN
HIS SON TO DIE FOR THEM, AND THEREBY TO SECURE THEIR JUSTIFICATION
AND SALVATION, VERSES 31—34. 7. BECAUSE THE LOVE OF GOD IS IN-
FINITE AND UNCHANGEABLE; FROM WHICH NOTHING CAN SEPARATE US,
VERSES 35—39. THUS, FROM THE PROXIMATE CAUSE OF SALVATION, OR
THE INDWELLING OF THE SPIRIT, DOES THE APOSTLE RISE WITH EVER-
INCREASING CONFIDENCE, TO THE GREAT SOURCE AND FOUNTAIN OF ALL,
IN THE LOVE OF GOD.*

Although, according to this view of the chapter, it is one whole, it may,
for the sake of convenience, be divided into three sections.

ROMANS VIII. 1—11.

ANALYSIS.

THIS section contains the development of the first two of the apostle's
arguments in favour of the position, that those who are in Christ Jesus
shall never be condemned. The immediate reason is assigned in the
second verse—they are delivered from the law. For, in view of the insufficiency of the law, God sent forth his Son as a sacrifice for sin, ver. 3 ;
and thus secured the justification of all believers, ver. 4. Being thus delivered from the law, they walk not after the flesh, but after the Spirit,
and this possession of the Spirit is incipient salvation ; because the carnal
mind, which, of course, all who are in the flesh possess, is death ; whereas
a mind under the government of the Spirit is life and peace. Such is the
very nature of the case. Holiness is salvation, verses 5—7. The reason
that death is the necessary consequence of being carnally minded, is the
essential opposition between such a state of mind and God. Hence, those
who have this state of mind are the objects of the Divine displeasure, vers.
7, 8. As, however, believers are not under the government of the flesh,
but of the Spirit, their salvation is secured, even to the resurrection of the
body. For if the Spirit of Him who raised up Jesus from the dead, dwell
in them, he shall also quicken their mortal bodies, vers. 9—11.

COMMENTARY.

VERSE 1. *There is, therefore, now no condemnation to them which are
in Christ Jesus.* It is a matter of considerable importance to the understanding of this chapter, to decide what is its precise relation to the preceding part of the epistle. The word *therefore* indicates that what follows
is an inference ; but from what ? From the conclusion of the seventh
chapter, or from the whole previous discussion ? The latter seems to be
the only correct view of the context ; because the fact that there is no
condemnation to believers, is no fair inference from what is said at the close
of the preceding chapter. Paul does not mean to say, as Luther and
others explain ver. 1, that there is nothing worthy of condemnation in the
Christian, because with his mind he serves the law of God. Nor does he

---

* The same general view of the design of this chapter, and of the course of the apostle's
argument, is given in the analysis of this epistle, by Stephen de Brais.

mean, at least in the first few verses, to argue that believers shall not be condemned, because they are freed from the dominion of sin. But the inference, in the first verse, is the legitimate conclusion of all that Paul had previously established. Believers shall be saved, because they are not under the law, but under grace, which is the main point in all that Paul has yet said. There is, therefore, *now*, *i. e.*, under these circumstances, viz., the circumstances set forth in the previous part of the epistle. The decision of the question as to the connection depends on the view taken of the apostle's argument. If he argues that believers are not liable to condemnation, because with the mind they serve the law of God, then the connection is with what immediately precedes. But if his argument is, that those in Christ are not exposed to condemnation, notwithstanding their imperfect sanctification, because Christ has died as a sacrifice for their sins, then the connection is with the main argument of the epistle. Since men, being sinners, cannot be justified by works; since by the obedience of one man, Jesus Christ, the many are made righteous; and since through him, and not through the law, deliverance from the subjective power of sin is effected, therefore it follows that there is no condemnation to those who are in him.

There is no condemnation, οὐδὲν κατάκριμα, does not mean *nihil damnatione dignum* (nothing worthy of condemnation,) as Erasmus and many others render it, but *there is no condemnation.* Those who are in Christ are not exposed to condemnation. And this again is not to be understood as descriptive of their present state merely, but of their permanent position. They are placed beyond the reach of condemnation. They shall never be condemned. The meaning of a proposition is often best understood by the arguments by which it is sustained. It is so in this case. The whole chapter is a proof of the safety of believers, of their security not only from present condemnation, but from future perdition. Nothing shall ever separate them from the love of God, is the triumphant conclusion to which the apostle arrives. Those to whom there is and never can be any condemnation, are described, first as to their relation to Christ, and secondly as to their character. The first assigns the reason of their security, the second enables us to determine to whom that security belongs. First, *they are in Christ.* In what sense? This must be determined, not so much from the force of the words, as from the teachings of Scripture. 1. They are in him federally, as all men were in Adam, 1 Cor. xv. 22 ; Rom. v. 12—21. 2. They are in him vitally, as the branch is in the vine, John xv. 1—7 ; or, as the head and members of the body are in vital union, 1 Cor. xii. 27 ; Eph. i. 23. This union arises from the indwelling of the Holy Ghost, 1 Cor. xii. 13 ; vi. 15, 19. 3. They are in him by faith, Eph. iii. 17 ; Gal. iii. 26, 27. It is not in virtue of any one of these bonds of union exclusively, but in virtue of them all (so far as adults are concerned,) that there is no condemnation to those who are in Christ Jesus. It follows from the nature of this union, that it must transform the character of those who are its subjects. If, therefore, any man is in Christ Jesus, he is a new creature, 2 Cor. v. 17 ; John xv. 4 ; Phil. iii. 20 ; Col. ii. 6 ; 1 John ii. 5 ; iii. 6. As the union includes the bodies of believers, as well as their souls, 1 Cor. vi. 15—19, so this transforming power will ultimately extend to the former as well as to the latter, Rom. viii. 10, 11. In this verse, (according to the common text,) the transforming power of this union with Christ is expressed by saying, that those who are in him, *walk not after the flesh, but after the Spirit. To walk* means to regulate the inward and outward life. It includes, therefore, the determination of the judgments, the feelings, the purposes, as well as the external conduct. The controlling principle in believers is not the *flesh*, *i.e.* the corrupt nature, but the Holy Spirit who dwells in them, as the source of knowledge, of holiness, of strength, of peace and love. They are not σαρχιχοί governed by the σάρξ, but πνευματιχοί governed by the Spirit. The only evidence therefore to ourselves, or to others, of our being in Christ, is this subjection of the whole life to the control of his Spirit, so that we discern and believe the truth, 1 Cor. ii. 14—16, and are governed by it. When the word πνεῦμα is not only without the article, but opposed to σάρξ, it may be understood of the Spirit as the principle of life in the believer, and in that view be equivalent to the *new man*, or the renewed principle. This is the view adopted by many as the meaning of the word in this passage. This clause, however, is of doubtful authority. It occurs in ver. 4, and may by a transcriber have been transferred to this place. The whole clause is omitted in the majority of the uncial MSS., and by the great body of modern critics. The latter clause only is omitted in the MSS. A. D. in the Vulgate, and by Chrysostom, which reading is adopted by Bengel.

Verse 2. *For the law of the Spirit of life in Christ Jesus, &c.* This verse assigns the reason why there is no condemnation to those who are in Christ, as is evident from the use of *for*, with which the verse commences.

The law of the Spirit is here opposed to *the law of sin and death*, mentioned in the other clause of the verse. The interpretation of the one phrase, therefore, must decide that of the other. There are three different views which may be taken of the verse. 1. The word *law* may be used here, as it is in the vers. 21, 23, of chap. vii., for *a directing power*; and *Spirit*, by metonymy, for that which the Spirit produces, *i.e.* sanctified affections; and the words *of life* may mean, producing life. The sense would then be, ' The power of the renewed principle which tends to life, has delivered me from the power of sin which tends to death.' In other words, ' The law of the mind has delivered me from the law of sin which is in the members.' So Beza and many others. 2. The word *law* is taken in nearly the same sense; but *Spirit of life* is understood to mean the Holy Spirit, considered as the author of life. The sense then is, ' The power of the life-giving Spirit has delivered me from the dominion of the law of sin and death in my members.' So Calvin, and others : " Legem Spiritus improprie vocat Dei Spiritum, qui animas nostras Christi sanguine aspergit, non tantum ut a peccati labe emundet quoad reatum ; sed in veram puritatem sanctificet." The objection to this interpretation, that it seems to refer our freedom from condemnation to our regeneration, he proposes to meet by saying that Paul does not state the cause, but the method of our deliverance from guilt : " Negat Paulus externa legis doctrina id nos consequi, sed dum Spiritu Dei renovamur, simul etiam justificari gratuita venia, ne peccati maledictio in nos amplius recumbat. Perinde ergo valet haec sententia acsi dixisset Paulus, regenerationis gratiam ab imputatione justitiæ nunquam disjungi." 3. According to the third view, *the law of the Spirit of life* is the gospel, *i.e.* the law of which the life-giving Spirit is the author. Of course, the other member of the verse, instead of describing the corrupt principle in men, means the law of God, which, as Paul had taught in chap. vii., is incidentally the cause of sin and death. The sense of the passage then is, ' The gospel has delivered me from the law.' So Witsius, &c.

This last seems decidedly to be preferred, for the following reasons : 1. Although the two former interpretations are consistent with Paul's use of the word *law*, neither of them so well suits the context, because neither assigns the reason why believers are not exposed to condemnation. Paul asserts that those who are in Christ are restored to the divine favour. Why ? Because they are sanctified ? No ; but because they have been freed from the law and its demands, and introduced into a state of grace. 2. It is not true that believers are delivered from the law of sin in their members. If the terms *law of the Spirit*, and *law of sin*, are to be understood of the good and evil principle in the Christian, how can it be said that by the former he is, in this life, delivered from the latter ? This would be in direct contradiction to chap. vii. and to experience. 3. The terms here used may naturally be so understood, because the word *law*, in its general sense, as *rule*, is applicable and is applied to the gospel, Rom. iii. 27, especially when standing in antithesis to the law of works. The gospel is called the law of the Spirit, because he is its author : see the phrase "ministration of the Spirit," 2 Cor. iii. 8. In the other member of the verse the law is called *the law of sin and death*, because productive of sin and death. This is no more than what Paul had said expressly of the law in the preceding chapter, vers. 5, 13, &c. And in 2 Cor. iii. 6, the law is said to kill : it is called the διακονία τοῦ θανάτου, (the ministration of death,) and the διακονία τῆς κατακρίσεως, (ministration of condemnation.) There the same contrast between the διακονία τοῦ θανάτου and the διακονία τοῦ πνεύματος is presented, as here between the νόμος τοῦ θανάτου and the νόμος τοῦ πνεύματος. 4. This interpretation alone assigns an adequate ground for the declaration of the preceding verse. That declaration, the result of all that Paul had yet proved, is that believers, and believers only, are perfectly safe ; and the reason assigned is the sum of all the argument from the commencement of the epistle. They are not under the law, but under grace ; the law of the Spirit has freed them from the old law of works. 5. The next verse favours, if it does not absolutely demand, this interpretation. It gives the reason why believers are thus freed from the law, viz. it was insufficient for their salvation, "it was weak through the flesh." 6. The use of the aorist ἠλευθέρωσε, which shows that the freedom spoken of is an accomplished fact, confirms this interpretation. Deliverance from the law of sin in the members is a gradual process ; deliverance from the law is effected once for all ; and with regard to the believer, it is a fact accomplished.

The words ἐν Χριστῷ, *in Christ*, may be connected with the immediately preceding words τῆς ζωῆς, *the life which-is in Christ ;* or with ὁ νόμος κ.τ.λ., *the law of the Spirit which is in Christ*. As, however, the connecting article (τῆς or ὁ), which is necessary at least definitely to indicate either of those constructions, is wanting, the words in question are generally connected with the following verb, ἠλευθέρωσε, *in Christ freed me ;* that is, it was in him, and therefore through him, that this deliverance was effected. The meaning of this verse, therefore, in connection with the preceding, is, ' There is no condemnation to those who are in Christ, because they have been freed in him by the gospel of the life-giving Spirit, from that law which, although good in itself, is, through our corruption, the source of sin and death.' Being thus free from the curse of the law, and from the obligation to fulfil its demands, as the condition of life, and consequently freed from a legal spirit, their sins are gratuitously pardoned for Christ's sake ; they are made partakers of the Spirit of God, are transformed more and more into his image, and God is pledged to preserve them unto eternal life.

Verse 3. This verse is connected with the preceding by the particle γάρ, *for.* ' We are delivered from the law, *for* the law could not effect our salvation.' The words τὸ ἀδύνατον τοῦ νόμου may be rendered either, *the impotency of the law,* or *what is impossible to the law.* The choice between these renderings depends on the grammatical structure of the passage. First, τὸ ἀδύνατον may be taken as the accusative, and the preposition διά be supplied, *on account of the impotency of the law;* or, secondly, it may be taken as the accusative absolute, *as to the impotency of the law, i.e.* in view of its impotency ; or, thirdly, it may be taken as the nominative, and in apposition with the following clause. The sense would then be, ' The impossibility of the law—God condemned sin :' *i.e.* the condemnation of sin is what is impossible to the law. This is the view commonly adopted, especially by those who understand the apostle to be speaking of sanctification, and who therefore take *condemned sin* to mean *destroyed* sin. As, however, that clause does not mean to destroy sin, but judicially to condemn it, the first clause cannot strictly be in apposition with it. The law could condemn sin. What it cannot do is to free us either from its guilt or power. It can neither justify nor sanctify. On this account, the second exposition of the first clause of the verse just mentioned, is to be preferred : ' In view of the impotency of the law, God sent his Son,' &c. This insufficiency of the law, as the apostle had taught in the preceding chapters, is not due to any imperfection of the law itself. It is holy, just, and good. It requires nothing more than is right. If men could comply with its righteous demands, the law would pronounce them just. If they were free from the infection of sin, "the form of truth and knowledge in the law," the perfect exhibition which it makes of the will of God, would avail to maintain and advance them in holiness. But as they are already under sin, under its guilt and power, the law is entirely impotent to their justification or sanctification. The apostle therefore says, that the law is impotent, ἐν ᾧ, *because that* (see Heb. ii. 18) *it is weak through the flesh,* διὰ τῆς σαρκός, *i.e.* through our corruption. It is our being depraved that renders the law weak, or impotent to save. *God sending* (or having sent πέμψας) *his own Son,* τὸν ἑαυτοῦ υἱόν. The term Son here evidently designates the eternal personal Son. He was from eternity, and in virtue of his Divine nature, and not in virtue either of his miraculous birth, or his exaltation, the Son of God. The greatness of the work to be accomplished, and the greatness of the love of God impelling him to our redemption, are strongly exhibited in these words. It was not a creature, even the most exalted, whom God sent on this mission, but his own Son, one with him in essence and glory.

Two things are further stated concerning this mission of the Son of God. First, the form under which he appeared in the world ; and, secondly, the object for which he was sent. As to the form in which he appeared, it was *in the likeness of sinful flesh.* It was not simply ἐν σαρκί (*in the flesh*), clothed in our nature ; for that might have been said, had he appeared in the glorious, impassive nature of Adam before the fall. Much less was it in ἐν σαρκὶ ἁμαρτίας (*in sinful flesh*), for that would imply that his human nature was defiled, contrary to Heb. iv. 15, and to all Scripture ; but it was ἐν ὁμοιώματι σαρκὸς ἁμαρτίας (*in the likeness of sinful flesh*), that is, in a nature like to our sinful nature, but not itself sinful. Christ took our physically dilapidated nature, subject to the infirmities which sin had brought into it. He was therefore susceptible of pain, and weariness, and sorrow. He could be touched with a sense of our infirmities. He was tempted in all points as we are. He is therefore a merciful and trustworthy High Priest. The object for which God sent his Son, clothed in this feeble, suffering nature of ours, is expressed by καὶ περὶ ἁμαρτίας (*and for sin*). This may mean either *on account of sin*, whether for its expiation or its removal, being undetermined; or it may be understood in a sacrificial sense. Christ was sent for the expiation of sin, or as a sacrifice for sin. 1. In favour of this is the *usus loquendi*, as περὶ ἁμαρτίας is so often used in this sense : see Num. viii. 8 ; Ps. xl. 7 (in the LXX. 396,) Lev. vi. 25, 30 ; Heb. x. 6, 8, 18 ; xiii. 11. Thus also in Gal. i. 4, Christ is said to have given himself περὶ ἁμαρτιῶν ἡμῶν, *for, i.e.* as a sacrifice for, *our sins.* 2. The analogy of Scripture, as it is so abundantly taught in the word of God, is that Christ was sent to make expiation for sin, to wash away sin, to offer himself unto God as a sacrifice for sin. When, therefore, it is said that he was sent *for* sin, or gave himself for our sins, the implication is almost unavoidable that the meaning is, he was sent as a sacrifice for sin. 3. The immediate context demands this interpretation ; for the effect ascribed to this sending Christ for sin, is that which is due to a sacrifice or expiation. What the law could not do, was to reconcile us unto God. It was in view of the impotency of the law to effect the salvation of sinners, that God sent his Son to make expiation for their offences, and thus bring them back to himself. *He thus condemned sin in the flesh;* that is, he condemned it in the flesh, or nature, which his Son had assumed. Christ took upon himself our nature, in order to expiate the guilt of that nature. The expiation must be made in the nature which had sinned. As Christ, the apostle tells us, Heb. ii. 14—18, did not undertake the redemption of angels, he did not assume their nature, but took part in flesh and blood. That the words κατέκρινε τὴν ἁμαρτίαν (*he condemned sin*), does not mean that he destroyed sin, but that he punished it, visited it with the penalty of the law, is evident. 1. Because κατάκρινω never means to destroy, but always means to condemn. It is perfectly arbitrary, therefore, to depart from the ordinary meaning of the word in this particular place. 2. The sacrifice of Christ was the condemnation of sin. That is, he bore our sins. He was made a curse, in the sense that he endured the curse due to sin. His sufferings were penal, as they were judicially inflicted in satisfaction of justice. The proximate design and effect of a sacrifice is expiation, and not reformation or inward purification. When therefore the apostle speaks, as he here does, of what God did by sending his Son as a sacrifice for sin, he must be understood to speak of the sacrificial effect of his death. 3. The context requires this interpretation. The argument of the apostle is, that there is no κατάριμα (*condemnation*) to us, because God κατέρινε (*condemned*) sin in Christ. The other interpretation supposes him to say, that there is no condemnation to us, because sin is destroyed in us. That is, we are justified on the ground of our own inherent goodness or freedom from sin. But this is contrary to the Scriptures, and to the faith of the Church. " Clare affirmat Paulus," says Calvin, " ideo expiata fuisse peccata Christi morte, quia Legi impossibile erat, justitiam nobis conferre." The apostle, he adds, teaches, " Legem nihil prorsus habere momenti ad conferendam justitiam. Vides ergo, nos penitus excludi ab operum justitia : ideoque ad Christi justitiam nos confugere, quia in nobis nulla esse potest. Quod scitu in primis necessarium est ; quia Christi justitia nonquam vestiemur, nisi prius certo noverimus, propriæ justitiæ nihil nos habere." In saying, however, that the proximate object and effect of a sacrifice is to expiate sin, and therefore that sin is thereby condemned and not destroyed, it is not forgotten that propitiation is the end of expiation ; that our sins are atoned for by the blood of Christ, in order to our being restored to his image and favour. Justification is not on account of, or on the ground of sanctification, but it is in order to it ; and therefore the two are inseparable. The justified are always sanctified. And therefore, so far as the meaning is concerned, there is no objection to saying, that the condemnation of sin of which the apostle here speaks, includes the idea of its extirpation or destruction as a necessary consequence. But it is nevertheless important, not only to a due understanding of his argument, but also to the integrity of scriptural doctrine, to remember that the condemnation of sin in the person of Christ, expresses its expiation by his blood, and not the destruction of its power in us. It is Christ as the substitute of sinners, bearing the curse for them, that is here presented to our view. This even Olshausen admits, who says, " The conclusion of this verse expresses in the most decisive terms the vicarious (stellvertretenden) atoning death of the Saviour."

Verse 4. *That the righteousness of the law might be fulfilled in us,* &c. This verse expresses the design of God in sending his Son, and in condemning sin in the flesh. He did thus condemn it, *ἵνα, in order that* the righteousness of the law might be fulfilled. The meaning, therefore, of this passage is determined by the view taken of ver. 3. If that verse means, that God, by sending his Son, destroyed sin in us, then of course this verse must mean, ' He destroyed sin, in order that we should fulfil the law ;" *i.e.,* that we should be holy. But if ver. 3 is understood of the sacrificial death of Christ, and of the condemnation of sin in him as the substitute of sinners, then this verse must be understood of justification, and not of sanctification. He condemned sin, in order that the demands of the law might be satisfied. This is the view of the passage given even by the majority of the early Fathers, and by almost all evangelical interpreters, including the Reformers. " Qui intelligunt Spiritu Christi renovatos legem implere, commentum a sensu Pauli penitus alienum afferunt ; neque enim eo usque proficiunt fideles, quamdia peregrinantur in mundo, ut justificatio legis in illis plena sit, vel integra. Ergo hoc ad veniam referre necesse est ; quia, dum nobis accepta fertur Christi obedientia, legi satisfactum est, ut pro justis censeamur." That this is the true meaning of the passage appears not only from the connection and the course of the argument, but also from the following considerations : 1. It is consistent with the strict and natural meaning of the words. The word δικαίωμα, here used, means, first, something righteous, and then, second, something declared to be righteous and obligatory, an ordinance or precept ; and, third, a righteous decision, a just judgment, as when in Rom. i. 29, the heathen are said to know the δικαίωμα, *the righteous judgment* of God ; and, fourth, the act of declaring righteous, justification. In this sense δικαίωμα is antithetical to κατάκριμα. The δικαίωμα τοῦ νόμου, therefore, may mean, the righteous requirement of the law, that which satisfies its demands. In strict accordance therefore with the sense of the words, we may explain the passage to mean, ' that the demands of the law might be satisfied in us.' That is, that we might be justified. Christ was condemned, that to us there might be no condemnation. He was made sin, that we might be made righteousness, 2 Cor. v. 21. Or, if we take δικαίωμα in the sense of (Rechtfertigungsurtheil) a declaration of righteousness, an act of justification, the same idea is expressed : 'Sin was condemned in Christ, in order that the sentence of justification might be fulfilled, or carried into effect in us.' This is the explanation which Eckermann, Köllner, Philippi, and other modern interpreters adopt.   2. The analogy of Scripture.   To make this passage teach the doctrine of subjective justification, that we are freed from condemnation or delivered from the law by our inward sanctification, is to contradict the plain teaching of the Bible, and the whole drift and argument of this epistle.   3. The concluding clause of the verse, (who walk not after the flesh, &c.) demands the interpretation given above.   In the other view of the passage, the latter clause is altogether unnecessary.   Why should Paul say, that Christ died in order that they should be holy who are holy, *i.e.*, those who walk not after the flesh ?   On the other hand, the second clause of the verse is specially pertinent, if the first treats of justification.   The benefits of Christ's death are experienced only by those who walk not after the flesh.   The gospel is not antinomian.   Those only are justified who are also sanctified.   Holiness is the fruit and evidence of reconciliation with God.   There is no condemnation to those who walk after the Spirit ; and the righteousness of the law is fulfilled by those who walk after the Spirit.   In both cases, the latter clause is designed to describe the class of persons who are entitled to appropriate to themselves the promise of justification in Christ.   4. Finally, as intimated in the above quotation from Calvin, it is not true that the righteousness of the law, in the sense of complete obedience, is fulfilled in believers.   The interpretation which makes the apostle say, that we are delivered from the law by the work of Christ, in order that the complete obedience which the law demands might be rendered by us, supposes what all Scripture and experience contradicts.   For an exposition of the last clause of the verse, see ver. 1.

VERSE 5.   *For they that are after the flesh do mind the things of the flesh.*   The immediate object of this and the following verse is to justify the necessity of limiting the blessings of Christ's death, to those who walk not after the flesh, but after the Spirit.   The *for*, therefore, connects this verse, not with the main idea, but with the last clause of the preceding. Men must be holy, because sin is death, whereas holiness is life and peace. The necessity of *spirituality*, therefore, lies in the very nature of things.

They who are after the flesh, those who are in the flesh, the carnal, are expressions of like import, and describe those who are governed by the flesh, or by their nature considered as corrupt.   The corresponding series, *they who are after the Spirit, who are in the Spirit, the spiritual,* describe those who are under the government of the Holy Ghost.   Of the former class it is said they mind the *things of the flesh,* of the latter, *they mind the things of the Spirit.*   The word φρονεῖν is derived from φρήν, which is used for the seat of all mental affections and faculties, and therefore φρονέω has a wide meaning.   It expresses any form of mental activity, any exercise of the intellect, will, or affections.   *They mind* (φρονοῦσιν,) therefore, means, they make the object of attention, desire, and pursuit.   *The things of the flesh,* are the objects on which their hearts are set, and to which their lives are devoted.   Things of the flesh are not merely sensual things, but all things which do not belong to the category of the things of the Spirit.   Compare Matt. xvi. 23, οὐ φρονεῖς τὰ τοῦ Θεοῦ, *thou savourest not the things of God.*   Phil. iii. 19, οἱ τὰ ἐπίγεια φρονοῦντες. Col. iii. 2, &c.   The English word *mind* is used with much the same latitude. The idea evidently is, that the objects of attention, desire, and pursuit, to the carnal, are corrupt and worldly; while to the spiritual, they are the things which the Spirit proposes and approves.

Verse 6. *For to be carnally minded is death.* The γάρ here is by many taken as a mere particle of transition, equivalent to *but.* ' But to be carnally minded is death.' The utter incompatibility between the indulgence of sin and a state of salvation is thus clearly expressed. It is impossible that justification should be disconnected with sanctification, because a sinful and carnal state of mind is death. It is better, however, to take γάρ in its usual sense of *for.* The connection may then be with ver. 4, so that verses 5 and 6 are coördinate, ver. 6 presenting an additional reason why believers do not walk after the flesh. They do not thus walk, *for* to do so is death. Or, the connection is with ver. 5. Justification is limited to the holy, for to live after the flesh is death. The phrase φρόνημα τῆς σαρκός is substantially of the same import with φρονεῖν τὰ τῆς σαρκός, the minding the things of the flesh. It is thus active in its signification. It is, however, more in accordance with the proper signification of the word to understand it as expressing a state of the mind. This is implied in the English version, *to be carnally minded.* The idea is not merely that the actual seeking the things of the flesh leads to death ; but that a carnal state of mind, which reveals itself in the desire and pursuit of carnal objects, is death. And by death is of course meant spiritual death, the absence and the opposite of spiritual life. It includes alienation from God, unholiness, and misery. On the other hand, the φρόνημα τοῦ πνεύματος is that state of mind which is produced by the Spirit, and which reveals itself in the desire and pursuit of the things of the Spirit. This state of mind is life and peace. Therein consists the true life and blessedness of the soul. This being the case, there can be no such thing as salvation in sin; no possibility of justification without sanctification. If partakers of the benefits of Christ's death, we are partakers of his life. If we died with him, we live with him. This is pertinent to the apostle's main object in this chapter, which is to show that believers never can be condemned. They are not only delivered from the law, and justified by the blood of Christ, but they are partakers of his life. They have the φρόνημα τοῦ πνεύματος, which is life and peace.

Verse 7. *Because the carnal mind is enmity against God.* This is the reason why the φρόνημα τῆς σαρκός is death. It is in its nature opposed to God, who is the life of the soul. His favour is life, and therefore opposition to him is death. The carnal mind is enmity to God, *for* it is not subject to the law of God. The law of God, however, is the revelation of his nature, and therefore opposition to the law, is opposition to God. This opposition on the part of the carnal mind is not casual, occasional, or in virtue of a mere purpose. It arises out of its very nature. It is not only not subject to the law of God, but *it cannot be.* It has no ability to change itself. Otherwise it would not be death. It is precisely because of this utter impotency of the carnal mind, or unrenewed heart, to change its own nature, that it involves the hopelessness which the word *death* implies. Compare 1 Cor. ii. 14, where the same truth is asserted : " The natural man receiveth not the things of the Spirit of God—neither can he know them." " *Nec enim potest.* En," says Calvin, " liberi arbitrii facultas, quam satis evehere sophistæ nequent. Certe Paulus disertis verbis hic affirmat quod ipsi pleno ore detestantur, nobis esse impossibile subjicere legis obedientiæ. . . . Procul igitur sit a Christiano pectore illa de arbitrii libertate gentilis philosophia. Servum peccati se quisque, ut re vera est, agnoscat, quo per Christi gratiam manumissus liberetur; alia libertate prosus stultum est gloriari." To the same effect the modern German commentators, whether mystic, rationalistic, or evangelical. "No man," says Olshausen, "can free himself from himself:" "Von sich selbst kann sich keiner selbst losmachen, es muss eine hohere Liebe kommen, die ihn mehr anzieht, als sein Ich." "The will itself is fallen away from God," says Baumgarten-Crusius. And the evangelical Philippi says: "This verse is a strong argument against the doctrine of the so-called *liberum arbitrium* of the natural man. For this carnal state of mind, which cannot subject itself to the will of God, is not produced by any act of man's will, nor can it be removed by any such act; it constitutes, according to the apostle's doctrine, the original nature of man in its present or fallen state."

Verse 8. The necessary consequence of this opposition of a mind governed by the flesh, towards God, is that those who are in this state are the objects of the divine displeasure. *So then they that are in the flesh cannot please God.* To be *in the flesh,* as before remarked, is to be under the government of the *flesh,* or corrupt nature, to be destitute of the grace of God. It is an expression applied to all unrenewed persons, as those who are not *in the flesh* are *in the Spirit.*

Cannot please God. Ἀρέσκειν τινί generally means to be pleasing, or acceptable to any one; Matt. xiv. 6; 1 Cor. vii. 32; Gal. i. 10; 1 Thess. ii. 15. Not to be pleasing to God, is to be the objects of his displeasure. Enmity towards God (ἔχθρα εἰς Θεόν) has its necessary consequence, subjection to the enmity of God, (ἔχθρα Θεοῦ.) The apostle's immediate purpose is to show, that to be carnally minded is death. It must be so, for it is enmity towards God. But those who hate God are the objects of his displeasure; and to be the objects of the wrath of God, is perdition. Surely, then, to be carnally minded is death. In vers. 9—11, the apostle applies to his readers what he had just said, and shows how it is that (φρόνημα τοῦ πνεύματος,) to be spiritually minded, is life and peace.

Verse 9. *But ye are not in the flesh, but in the Spirit, i.e.,* ye are not carnal, but spiritual. The Spirit, so to speak, is the element in which you live. Such the Roman Christians were by profession and by repute, for their faith was spoken of throughout the world. Their real character, however, was not determined either by their professions or their reputation. The apostle therefore adds, *if so be the Spirit of God dwell in you.* This is the only decisive test. Every other bond of union with Christ is of no avail without this. We may be members of his Church, and united to him by being included in the number of his people, yet unless we are partakers of that vital union which arises from the indwelling of the Holy Ghost, we are his only in name. Our version gives εἴπερ (*if so be*) its ordinary and proper sense. "Εἴπερ," says Hermann ad Viger, § 310, "usurpatur de re, quæ esse sumitur, sed in incerto relinquitur, utrum jure an injuria sumatur; εἴγε autem de re, quæ jure sumta creditur." Sometimes, however, εἴπερ has the same force as εἴγε (*since*); as, 2 Thess. i. 6, "*seeing* it is a righteous thing with God." The ordinary sense of the particle, however, is better suited to this passage. The Spirit of God is everywhere; yet he is said to dwell wherever he specially and permanently manifests his presence. Thus he is said to dwell in heaven: he dwelt of old in the temple; he now dwells in the Church, which is a habitation of God through the Spirit, Eph. ii. 22; and he dwells in each

individual believer whose body is a temple of the Holy Ghost, 1 Cor. vi.
19. Compare John xiv. 17 ; 1 Cor. iii. 16 ; 2 Cor. vi. 16 : 2 Tim. i. 14,
&c. *Now if any man have not the Spirit of Christ.* It is obvious that
the Spirit of Christ is identical with the Spirit of God. The one expression is interchanged with the other : ' If the Spirit of God dwell in you,
you are true Christians ; for if the Spirit of Christ be not in you, you are
none of his.' This is the reasoning of the apostle. " Spirit of Christ,"
therefore, can no more mean the temper or disposition of Christ, than
" Spirit of God " can mean the disposition of God. Both expressions
designate the Holy Ghost, the third person in the adorable Trinity. The
Holy Spirit is elsewhere called the Spirit of Christ, Gal. iv. 6 ; Phil. i.
19 ; 1 Pet. i. 11. Whatever the genitive expresses in the one case, it does
in the other. He is of the Spirit of Christ in the same sense in which he
is the Spirit of God. In other words, the Spirit stands in the same relation to the second, that he does to the first person of the Trinity. This
was one of the points of controversy between the Greek and Latin
Churches; the latter insisting on inserting in that clause of the Creed
which speaks of the procession of the Holy Ghost, the words " filioque,"
(*and from the Son.*) For this the gratitude of all Christians is due to the
Latin Church, as it vindicates the full equality of the Son with the
Father. No clearer assertion, and no higher exhibition of the Godhead of
the Son can be conceived, than that which presents him as the source and
the possessor of the Holy Ghost. The Spirit proceeds from, and belongs
to him, and by him is given to whomsoever he wills. John i. 33, xv. 26,
xvi. 7 ; Luke xxiv. 49, &c.

VERSE 10. *And if,* or rather, *but if,* (εἰδέ) *Christ be in you.* 'If a man
have not the Spirit of Christ, he is none of his ; *but if* Christ be in him,
he is partaker of his life.' From this interchange of expression it is plain
that to say that the Spirit of Christ dwells in us, and to say that Christ
dwells in us, is the same thing. And as the former phrase is interchanged
with Spirit of God, and that again elsewhere with God, it follows, that to
say, God dwells in us, the Spirit of God dwells in us, Christ dwells in us,
and the Spirit of Christ dwells in us, are only different ways of expressing
the same thing. " Qui Spiritum habet, Christum habet; qui Christum
habet, Deum habet." *Bengel.* This scriptural usage finds its explanation
in the doctrine of the Trinity. While there is one only, the living and
true God ; yet as there are three persons in the Godhead, and as these
three are the same in substance, it follows, that where the Father is, there
the Son is, and where the Son is, there is the Spirit. Hence our Lord
says, " If any man love me, he will keep my words, and my Father will
love him, and we will come unto him, and make our abode with him."
John xiv. 23. And the apostle John says, " Whosoever shall confess that
Jesus is the Son of God, God dwelleth in him, and he in God," 1 John
iv. 15. " I and my Father," says Christ, " are one." He therefore who
hath the Son, hath the Father also. There is another familiar scriptural
usage illustrated in this verse. Christ is properly an official designation
of the Theanthropos, as the anointed Prophet, Priest, and King of his
people. It is however used as a personal designation, and is applied to
our Lord, as well in reference to his human as to his divine nature. Hence
the Bible says indifferently, Christ died, and 'that he created all things.
In this and other passages, therefore, when Christ is said to dwell in us,
it is not Christ as man, nor Christ as the Theanthropos, but Christ as
God. Compare 2 Cor. xiii. 5, " Know ye not that Jesus Christ is in

you." His indwelling in his people is as much a function of his divine nature, as his creating and upholding all things by the word of his power.

And if Christ (be) in you, the body is dead because of sin, &c. As this verse is antithetical to the preceding, δέ should be rendered *but:* "If any man have not the Spirit of Christ, he is none of his ; *but* if Christ be in you, although the body must die on account of sin, the spirit shall live because of righteousness." The Spirit is the source of life, and wherever he dwells, there is life.

The body indeed is dead, τὸ μὲν σῶμα νεκρόν. That σῶμα here is to be taken in its literal sense is plain, because such is the proper meaning of the word. It is rarely, if at all, used in the figurative sense in which σάρξ (*flesh*) so often occurs. This interpretation also is required by the antithesis between body and spirit, in this verse. The context also demands this view of the passage, both because of the reference to the resurrection of Christ, which was of course literal, and because in the next verse we have the phrase "mortal bodies," which does not admit of a figurative interpretation. The sense also afforded by the literal meaning of the word is so natural, and so suited to the context, as to preclude the necessity of seeking for any other. In this view the majority of commentators concur. Others, however, understand by σῶμα, the corrupt nature, or the whole nature of man, his soul and body, as distinguished from the Spirit as the principle of divine life. The word νεκρόν is made to mean νενεκρωμένον, *put to death, mortified ;* and δι ἁμαρτίαν, *on account of sin,* is made equivalent to τῇ ἁμαρτίᾳ, *as to sin.* This evidently does unnecessary violence to the literal meaning of the words. The body is *dead* in the sense that it is not only obnoxious to death, but as it is already the seat of death. It includes in it the principle of decay. This necessity of dying is *on account of sin.* It is not inconsistent with the perfection of the redemption of Christ, that its benefits are not received in their fulness the moment we believe. We remain subject to the pains, the sorrows, the trials of life, and the necessity of dying, although partakers of the life of which he is the author. That life which is imparted in regeneration, is gradually developed until it has its full consummation at the resurrection.

The spirit is life because of righteousness. By *spirit* here, is not to be understood the Holy Spirit, but the human spirit, because it stands opposed to *body* in the former clause. The *body* is dead, but the *spirit* is life. It should not therefore be printed with a capital S, as in the ordinary copies of the English version. The sense in which the spirit is life, is antithetical to that in which the body is dead. As the body is infected with a principle of decay which renders its dissolution inevitable, so the soul, in which the Holy Spirit dwells, is possessed of a principle of life which secures its immortal and blessed existence. *Because of righteousness ;* δικαιοσύνη, as opposed to ἁμαρτία, must be taken in its subjective sense. It is inward righteousness or holiness, of which the apostle here speaks, and not our justifying righteousness. It is because the Holy Ghost, as dwelling in believers, is the source of holiness, that he is the source of life. The life of which he is the author, is the life of God in the soul, and is at once the necessary condition and the effect of the enjoyment of his fellowship and favour. We shall continue in the enjoyment of the life just spoken of, because the principles of this new and immortal existence are implanted within us. Regeneration is the commencement of eternal life. The present possession of the Spirit is an earnest of the unsearchable riches of Christ, Eph. i. 14. In this view the verse is directly connected with the main object of the chapter, viz. the security of all who are in Christ Jesus.   To such there is no condemnation, because they have been freed from the law which condemned them to death ; and because the work of salvation is already begun in them.   They *have* eternal life, John vi. 47.

Verse 11.   *But if the Spirit of him that raised up Jesus from the dead dwell in you.*   Such periphrases for *God* as that which this verse contains, are very common with the apostle, (see Rom. iv. 24, &c.,) and are peculiarly appropriate when the force of the argument in some measure rests on the fact to which the descriptive phrase refers.   Because God had raised up Christ, there was ground of confidence that he would raise his people up also.   Two ideas may be included in this part of the verse : first, that the very possession of that Spirit, which is the source of life, is a pledge and security that our bodies shall rise again ; because it would be unseemly that anything thus honoured by the Spirit, should remain under the dominion of death ; and, secondly, that the resurrection of Christ secures the resurrection of those that are his, according to Paul's doctrine in 1 Cor. xv. 23.   The argument of the apostle is, that the same Spirit which was in Christ, and raised him from the dead dwells in us, even in our bodies (1 Cor. vi. 19), and will assuredly raise us up.

He that raised up Christ from the dead shall also quicken your mortal bodies.   This clause cannot, with any regard to usage or the context, be understood of a moral resurrection, or deliverance from sin, as it is explained by Calvin and many others.   See the analogous passage, 2 Cor. iv. 14.   The apostle designs to show that the life which we derive from Christ, shall ultimately effect a complete triumph over death.   It is true that our present bodies must die, but they are not to continue under the power of death.   The same Spirit which raised Christ's body from the grave, shall also quicken our mortal bodies.   The word is not ἐγειρεῖ, but ζωοποιήσει, which imports more than a mere restoration of life.   It is used only of believers.   It expresses the idea of the communication of that life of which Christ is the author and the source.   And this life, so far as the body is concerned, secures its conformity to the glorious body of the risen Son of God.

By his Spirit that dwelleth in you, or, as it must be rendered according to another reading, " *On account of his Spirit that dwelleth in you.*"   For the reading διὰ τὸ ἐνοικοῦν αὐτοῦ πνεῦμα, Wetstein quotes the MSS. D. E. F. G. and many of the more modern MSS., together with the Syriac and Latin versions, and several of the Fathers.   This reading is adopted by Erasmus, Stephens, Mill, Bengel, Griesbach, and Knapp.   For the reading διὰ τοῦ ἐνοικοῦντος, κ.τ.λ., are quoted the MSS. A. 10. 22. 34. 38. 39., the editions of Colinæus, Beza, the Complutensian, and many of the Fathers.   Lachmann and Tischendorf retain the common text.   This passage is of interest, as the reading ἐνοικοῦντος was strenuously insisted on in the Macedonian controversy respecting the personality of the Holy Ghost.   The orthodox Fathers contended, that as the genitive was found in the most ancient copies of the Scriptures then extant, it should be retained.   If the dead are raised by the Holy Ghost, then the Holy Ghost is of the same essence with the Father and the Son, to whom, elsewhere, the resurrection of the dead is referred.   This argument is valid, and, other things being equal, is a good reason for retaining the common text.   The sense, however, is in either case substantially the same.   According to the former, the meaning is, that the resurrection of believers will be effected by the power of the Spirit of God ; and according to the latter, that the indwelling of the Spirit is the ground or reason why the bodies of believers should not be left in the grave. The internal evidence is decidedly in favour of the former reading : 1. Because Paul uses precisely these words elsewhere, " By the Holy Spirit," &c., 2 Tim. i. 14, &c. 2. Because throughout the Scriptures in the Old and New Testaments, what God does in nature or grace, he is said to do by his Spirit. Passages are too numerous and too familiar to be cited. 3. Because the Jews seem to have referred the resurrection of the body specially to the Holy Ghost.* As the external authorities are nearly equally divided, the case must be considered doubtful. If the latter reading be adopted, this clause would then answer to the phrase, *on account of righteousness*, in the preceding verse. ' On account of the indwelling of the Spirit,' expressing the same general idea under another form. Our souls shall live in happiness and glory, because they are renewed : and our bodies too shall be raised up in glory, because they are the temples of the Holy Ghost. In the widest sense then it is true, that to be in the Spirit, is to be secure of life and peace.

It will be remarked, that in this verse, and elsewhere, God is said to have raised up Christ from the dead, whereas, in John x. 17, 18, the Saviour claims for himself the power of resuming his life. So here (according to the common reading) we are said to be raised up by the Holy Spirit ; in John vi. 40, Christ says of the believer, " *I* will raise him up at the last day ; " and in 2 Cor. iv. 14, and in many other places, the resurrection of believers is ascribed to God. These passages belong to that numerous class of texts, in which the same work is attributed to the Father, the Son, and the Holy Spirit, and which, in connection with other sources of proof, show conclusively that " these three are one ; " and that the persons of the Adorable Trinity concur in all works *ad extra*.

DOCTRINE.

1. As the former part of this chapter is an inference from the previous discussion, and presents a summary of the great truths already taught, we find here united the leading doctrines of the first portion of the epistle. For example, justification is by faith, ver. 1 ; believers are not under the law, ver. 2 ; the law is insufficient for our justification ; God has accomplished that object by the sacrifice of his Son, verses 3, 4 ; and this blessing is never disconnected with a holy life, ver. 4.

2. The final salvation of those who are really united to Christ, and who show the reality of their union by good works, is secure. This is the doctrine of the whole chapter. This section contains two of the apostle's arguments in its support. 1. They are free from the law which condemned them to death, verses 2—4. 2. They are partakers of that Spirit which is the author and earnest of eternal life, verses 5—11.

3. Jesus Christ is truly divine. He is " God's own Son," *i.e.*, partaker of his nature. The Holy Ghost is his Spirit, and he dwells in all believers, vers. 3, 11.

4. Jesus Christ is truly a man. He came in the likeness of men, ver. 3.

5. Christ was a sacrifice for sin, and his sufferings were penal, *i. e.*,

---

* Wetstein quotes such passages as the following, from the Jewish writers : " Tempore futuro Spiritus meus vivificabit vos." " Spiritus Sanctus est causa resurrectionis mortuorum," &c.

they were judicially inflicted in support of the law. 'God punished sin in him,' ver. 3.

6. The justification of believers involves a fulfilling of the law; its demands are not set aside, ver. 4.

7. Everything in the Bible is opposed to antinomianism. Paul teaches that justification and sanctification cannot be disjoined. No one is or can be in the favour of God, who lives after the flesh, verses 5—11.

8. The necessity of holiness arises out of the very nature of things. Sin is death, whereas holiness is life and peace. God has made the connection between sin and misery, holiness and happiness, necessary and immutable, ver. 6. The fact that holy men suffer, and that even the perfect Saviour was a man of sorrows, is not inconsistent with this doctrine. Such sufferings never proceed from holiness. On the contrary, the Divine Spirit was, and is a wellspring within of joy and peace, to all who are sanctified. In itself considered, therefore, moral purity is essentially connected with happiness, as cause and effect.

9. All unrenewed men, that is, all "who are in the flesh," are at once the enemies of God, and the objects of his displeasure. Their habitual and characteristic state of mind, that state which every man has who is not "in the Spirit," is enmity to God, and consequently is the object of his disapprobation, verses 6, 8.

10. The Holy Ghost is the source of all good in man. Those who are destitute of his influences, are not subject to the law of God, neither indeed can be; for no man can call Jesus Lord, that is, can really recognise his authority, but by the Holy Ghost, verses 5—8.

11. Death and the other evils to which believers are exposed, are on account of sin, ver. 10. They are no longer, however, the evidences of God's displeasure, but of his paternal love, Heb. xii. 6.

12. The redemption of Christ extends to the bodies as well as the souls of his people, ver. 11.

REMARKS.

1. There can be no safety, no holiness, and no happiness to those who are out of Christ. No safety, because all such are under the condemnation of the law, verses 1—3; no holiness, because only such as are united to Christ have the Spirit of Christ, ver. 9; and no happiness, because "to be carnally minded is death," ver. 6. Hence those who are in Christ, should be very humble, seeing they are nothing, and he is everything; very grateful, and very holy. And those who are out of Christ, should at once go to him, that they may attain safety, holiness, and happiness.

2. The liberty wherewith Christ has made his people free, is a liberty from the law and from sin, verses 2, 5. A legal spirit, and an unholy life, are alike inconsistent with the Christian character.

3. Believers should be joyful and confident, for the law is fulfilled; its demands are satisfied as respects them. Who then can condemn, if God has justified? ver. 4.

4. There can be no rational or scriptural hope without holiness, and every tendency to separate the evidence of the divine favour from the evidence of true piety, is anti-Christian and destructive, verses 4—8.

5. The bent of the thoughts, affections, and pursuits, is the only decisive

test of character. "They who are after the flesh do mind the things of the flesh," &c., ver. 5.

6. It is therefore a sure mark of hypocrisy, if a man who professes to be a Christian, still minds earthly things, that is, has his affections and efforts supremely directed towards worldly objects.

7. We may as well attempt to wring pleasure out of pain, as to unite the indulgence of sin with the enjoyment of happiness, verses 6, 7.

8. How blinded must those be, who, although at enmity with God, and the objects of his displeasure, are sensible neither of their guilt nor danger ! verses 7, 8.

9. The great distinction of a true Christian, is the indwelling of the Holy Spirit. Hence his dignity, holiness, and happiness, verses 9—11.

10. If the Spirit of God dwells in the Christian, how careful should he be, lest anything in his thoughts or feelings would be offensive to this divine guest !

11. Christians are bound to reverence their bodies, and preserve them from all defilement, because they are the members of Christ, and the temples of the Holy Ghost, ver. 11.

ROMANS VIII. 12—28.

ANALYSIS.

This section* contains two additional arguments in support of the great theme of the chapter—the safety of all who are in Christ. The first is derived from their adoption, verses 12—17, and the second from the fact that they are sustained by hope, and aided by the Spirit, under all their trials ; so that everything eventually works together for their good, verses 18—28.

Paul had just shown that believers were distinguished by the indwelling of the Spirit. Hence he infers the obligation to live according to the Spirit, and to mortify the deeds of the body, ver. 12. If they did this, they should live, ver. 13. Not only because, as previously argued, the Spirit is the source of life, but also because all who are led by the Spirit are the children of God. This is a new ground of security, ver. 14. The reality of their adoption is proved, first, by their own filial feelings; as God's relations and feelings towards us are always the counterpart of ours towards him, ver. 15. Secondly, by the testimony of the Spirit itself with our spirits, ver. 16. If children, the inference is plain that believers shall be saved, for they are heirs. Salvation follows adoption, as, among men, heirship does sonship. They are joint heirs with Jesus Christ, ver. 17.

It is nowise inconsistent with their filial relation to God, nor with their safety, that believers are allowed to suffer in this world : 1. Because these sufferings are comparatively insignificant, vers. 18—23. 2. Because they are sustained by hope. 3. Because the Spirit itself intercedes for them.

---

* It was remarked above, that the division of this chapter into sections is merely arbitrary. For, although there are several very distinct topics introduced, yet the whole is intimately interwoven and made to bear on one point. In passing, too, from one argument to another, the apostle does it so naturally, that there is no abruptness of transition. The connection, therefore, between the last verse of the preceding section and the first verse of this and between the last of this and the first of the following, is exceedingly intimate. It is only for the sake of convenient resting places for review, that the division is made.

In amplifying the first of those considerations, the comparative insignificancy of the sufferings of this present state, the apostle presents in contrast the unspeakable blessedness and glory which are in reserve for believers, ver. 18. To elevate our conceptions of this glory, he represents; 1. The whole creation as looking and longing for its full manifestation, ver. 19, &c. 2. All those who have now a foretaste of this blessedness, or the first fruits of the Spirit, as joining in this sense of present wretchedness, and earnest desire of the future good, ver. 23.

These afflictions, then, are not only thus comparatively light in themselves, but they are made still more tolerable by the constant and elevating anticipation of the future inheritance of the saints, vers. 24, 25. And not only so, but the Spirit also sustains us by his intercessions, thus securing for us all the good we need, vers. 26—28. The salvation, then, of believers, is secure, notwithstanding their sufferings, inasmuch as they are children, and are sustained and aided by the Holy Spirit.

COMMENTARY.

VERSE 12. *Therefore, brethren, we are debtors, not to the flesh, to live after the flesh.* We have here an example of what the rhetoricians call *meiosis*, where less is said than intended. So far from being debtors to the flesh, the very reverse is the case. This passage is an inference from the exhibition of the nature and tendency of the *flesh*, or the carnal mind, as hostile to God, and destructive to ourselves, vers. 5, 8. As this is its nature, and believers are no longer in the flesh, but in the Spirit, they are under the strongest obligations not to live after the one, but after the other. *We are debtors;* ὀφειλέται ἐσμέν. We are the debtors, not of the flesh, but, as the implication is, of the Spirit. Of the two controlling principles, the flesh and the Spirit, our obligation is not to the former, but to the latter. *To live after the flesh;* τοῦ κατὰ σάρκα ζῆν. The genitive is, here, either the genitive of design, 'in order that we should live after the flesh;' or it depends on ὀφειλέται, agreeably to the formula, ὀφειλέτης εἰμί τινί τινος, *I am debtor to some one for something.* The sense would then be, 'We do not owe the flesh a carnal life.' The former explanation is the simpler and more natural.

VERSE 13. The necessity of thus living is enforced by a repetition of the sentiment of ver. 6. To live after the flesh is death; to live after the Spirit is life. *For if ye live after the flesh, ye shall die; but if ye through the Spirit,* &c. The necessity of holiness, therefore, is absolute. No matter what professions we may make, or what hopes we may indulge, justification, or the manifestation of the divine favour, is never separated from sanctification. *Ye shall die;* μέλλετε ἀποθνήσκειν, ye are about to die; death to you is inevitable. Compare chap. iv. 24; 1 Thess. iii. 4; James ii. 12. The death here spoken of, as appears from the whole context, and from the nature of the life with which it is contrasted, cannot be the death of the body, either solely or mainly. It is spiritual death, in the comprehensive scriptural sense of that term, which includes all the penal consequences of sin here and hereafter, chap. vi. 21, viii. 6: Gal. vi. 8. *But if ye through the Spirit do mortify the deeds of the body, ye shall live.* The use of the word *mortify*, to put to death or destroy, seems to have been suggested by the context. 'Ye shall die, unless ye put to death the deeds of the body ;' see Col. iii. 5. The destruction of sin is a slow and painful process.

*Deeds of the body.** It is commonly said that *body* is here equivalent to *flesh*, and therefore signifies *corruption*. But it is very much to be doubted whether the word ever has this sense in the New Testament. The passages commonly quoted in its behalf, Rom. vi. 6, vii. 24, viii. 10, 13, are very far from being decisive. If the common reading, therefore, is to be retained, (see note,) it is better to take the word in its literal and usual sense. *The deeds of the body* is then a metonymical expression for sinful deeds in general ; a part being put for the whole. Deeds performed by the body, being the deeds which the body, as the organ of sin, performs.

The destruction of sin is to be effected *through the Spirit*, which does not mean the renewed feelings of the heart, but, as uniformly throughout the passage, the Holy Spirit which dwells in believers : see ver. 14, where this Spirit is called "Spirit of God." *Ye shall live*, that is, enjoy the life of which the Spirit is the author ; including therefore holiness, happiness, and eternal glory.

Verse 14. *For as many as are led by the Spirit of God, they are the sons of God.* This is the reason why all such shall live ; that is, a new argument is thus introduced in support of the leading doctrine of the chapter. Believers shall enjoy eternal life, not because they have the Spirit of life, but because they are the sons of God. *To be led by the Spirit*, and *to walk after the Spirit*, present the same idea, viz., to be under the government of the Spirit, under two different aspects, Gal. v. 18 : 2 Pet. i. 21. The former phrase refers to the constant and effectual influence of the Holy Ghost in regulating the thoughts, feelings, and conduct of believers. *Are the sons of God.* The term *son*, in such connections, expresses mainly one or the other of three ideas, and sometimes all of them united. 1. Similarity of disposition, character, or nature ; Matt. v. 9, 45, "That ye may be the children (Gr. sons) of your Father which is in heaven." So, too, "sons of Abraham" are those who are like Abraham ; and "children of the devil" are those who are like the devil. 2. Objects of peculiar affection. Rom. ix. 26. Those who were not my people, "shall be called the sons of the living God ;" 2 Cor. vi. 18, "Ye shall be my sons and daughters, saith the Lord Almighty." So frequently elsewhere. 3. Those who have a title to some peculiar dignity or advantage. Thus the "sons of Abraham" are those who are heirs with Abraham of the same promise, Gal. iii. 8, seq. ; John i. 12 ; 1 John iii. 2, "Beloved, now are we the sons of God, and it doth not yet appear what we shall be," &c. The term may indeed express any one of the various relations in which children stand to their parents, as derived from them, dependent on them, &c. The above, however, are the most common of its meanings. In this passage, the first and third ideas appear specially intended : ' Believers shall live, because they are the peculiar objects of the divine affection, and are heirs of his kingdom,' vers. 15, 16. That those who are led by the Spirit are really the sons of God, appears from their own filial feelings, and from the testimony of the Spirit. The indwelling of the Spirit of God raises those in whom he dwells, into the state of sons of God. By regeneration, or new birth, they are born into a higher life ; are

---

* Instead of σώματος, D. E. F. G., the Vulgate and many of the early writers have σαρκός, which Bengel and Griesbach approve. Although this reading looks like a gloss, it has much in its favour from the weight of these MSS., and the usual mode of speaking of this apostle.

made partakers, as the apostle Peter says, of the divine nature ; and are thus, through and in Christ, the source of their new life, the objects of the divine love, and the heirs of his kingdom.

Verse 15. *For ye have not received the spirit of bondage again to fear, but ye have received the Spirit of adoption,* &c. That is, 'The Holy Spirit, which you have received, does not produce a slavish and anxious state of mind, such as those experience who are under the law ; but it produces the filial feelings of affection, reverence, and confidence, and enables us, out of the fulness of our hearts, to call God our Father.'

The phrase, the *spirit of bondage,* may mean a feeling or sense of bondage, as " spirit of meekness," 1 Cor. iv. 21, may mean meekness itself ; and " spirit of fear," 2 Tim. i. 7, fear itself. This use of the word *spirit* is not uncommon. Or it may mean the Holy Spirit as the author of bondage : ' Believers have not received a spirit which produces slavish feelings, but the reverse.' The context is decidedly in favour of this view : because Paul has been speaking of the Holy Spirit as dwelling in Christians. This Spirit is that which they have received, and is the author of their characteristic feelings. In the words *again to fear,* there is an evident allusion to the state of believers prior to the reception of the Spirit. It was a state of bondage in which they feared, *i.e.,* were governed by a slavish and anxious apprehension of punishment. In this state are all unconverted men, whether Jews or Gentiles, because they are all under the law, or the bondage of a legal system.

Spirit of adoption ; the Spirit that produces the feelings which children have. The Spirit is so called because he adopts. It is by him we are made the sons of God, and his indwelling, as it produces the character of sons, so it is the pledge or assurance of sonship, and of final salvation, Eph. i. 14. The contrast here presented between the πνεῦμα δουλείας and the πνεῦμα υἱοθεσίας, is parallel to that between δοῦλοι and υἱοί, in Gal. iii. 23—26, iv. 1—8. Those who are unrenewed, and under the law, are δοῦλοι, *slaves ;* they are under the dominion of servile fear, and they have no right to the inheritance. Those who are in Christ by faith and the indwelling of his Spirit, are sons, both in their inward state and feelings, and in their title to everlasting life. The interpretation followed by Luther, who renders πνεῦμα υἱοθεσίας, " ein kindlicher Geist," makes *spirit,* here mean disposition, feeling, and the genitive (υἱοθεσίας) the genitive of the source ; " the disposition which flows from adoption or sonship." But this is not only inconsistent with the context, but with such passages as Gal. iv. 6, where what is here called the Spirit of adoption, is said to be the Spirit of the Son of God, which God sends forth into our hearts. *By which we cry, Abba, Father, i.e.,* which enables us to address God as our Father. " Clamor," says Bengel, " sermo vehemens, cum desederio, fiducia, fide, constantia." *Abba* is the Syriac and Chaldee form of the Hebrew word for *father,* and therefore was to the apostle the most familiar term. As such it would, doubtless, more naturally and fully express his filial feeling towards God, than the foreign Greek word. It is rare, indeed, that any other than our mother tongue becomes so interwoven with our thoughts and feelings, as to come up spontaneously when our hearts are overflowing. Hence, expressions of tenderness are the last words of their native language which foreigners give up ; and in times of excitement, and even delirium, they are sure to come back. Paul, therefore, chose to call God his Father, in his own familiar tongue. Having used the one word, however, the Greek of course became necessary for those to whom he was writing. The repetition of two synonymes may, however, be employed to to give fuller utterance to his feeling. This is Grotius's idea: "Imitatur puerorum patribus blandientium voces. Mos est blandientium repetere voces easdem." It is a very common opinion that Paul used both words, to intimate that all distinction between different nations was now done away. "Significat enim Paulus, ita nunc per totum mundum publicatam esse Dei misericordiam, ut promiscue linguis omnibus invocetur: quemadmodum Augustinus observat. Ergo inter omnes gentes consensum exprimere voluit." *Calvin.* The former explanation seems more natural and satisfactory.

VERSE 16. *The Spirit itself beareth witness with our spirit, that we are the children of God.* 'Not only do our own filial feelings towards God prove that we are his children, but the Holy Spirit itself conveys to our souls the assurance of this delightful fact.'

The Spirit itself (αὐτὸ τὸ πνεῦμα, and not τὸ αὐτὸ πνεῦμα, which would mean, *the same spirit*) is, of course, the Holy Spirit. 1. Because of the obvious distinction between it and *our spirit.* 2. Because of the use of the word throughout the passage. 3. Because of the analogy to other texts, which cannot be otherwise explained. Gal. iv. 6, God hath sent forth the Spirit of His Son into your hearts, crying, Abba, Father;" Rom. v. 5, "The love of God is shed abroad in our hearts by the Holy Ghost given unto us," &c.

Beareth witness with our spirit, συμμαρτυρεῖ τῷ πνεύματι ἡμῶν; that is, 'beareth witness, together with our own filial feelings, to our spirit.' Although it is very common for compound verbs to have the same force with the simple ones, yet, in this case, the context requires the force of the preposition to be retained, as two distinct sources of confidence are here mentioned, one in ver. 15, the other in this verse. *Beareth witness to,* means *confirms* or *assures.* "The Spirit of God produces in our spirit the assurance that we are the children of God.' How this is done we cannot fully understand, any more than we can understand the mode in which he produces any other effect in our mind. The fact is clearly asserted here, as well as in other passages. See Rom. v. 5, where the conviction that we are the objects of the love of God, is said to be produced " by the Holy Ghost which is given unto us." See 2 Cor. i. 22, v. 5 ; Eph. i. 13, iv. 30; and in 1 Cor. ii. 4, 5 ; 1 John ii. 20, 27, and other passages, the conviction of the truth of the gospel is, in like manner, attributed to the Holy Spirit. From this passage it is clear that there is a scriptural foundation for the assurance of salvation. Those who have filial feelings towards God, who love him, and believe that he loves them, and to whom the Spirit witnesses that they are the children of God, cannot doubt that they are indeed his children. And if children, they know they are heirs, as the apostle teaches in the following verse.

VERSE 17. *And if children, then heirs; heirs of God, and joint heirs with Christ,* &c. This is the inference from our adoption, in favour of the great theme of the chapter, the safety of believers. If the children of God, they shall become partakers of the inheritance of the saints in light. The words *to inherit, heirs,* and *inheritance,* are all of them used in a general sense in the Scriptures, in reference to the secure possession of any good, without regard to the mode in which that possession is obtained. They are favourite terms with the sacred writers, because possession by inheritance was much more secure than that obtained by purchase, or by any other method. There are three ideas included in these words, accessory to that which constitutes their prominent meaning—the right, the certainty, and the unalienable character of the possession. Hence, when the apostle says, believers are the heirs of God, he means to recognise their title, in and through the Redeemer, to the promised good, as well as the certainty and security of the possession. " And if ye be Christ's, then are ye Abraham's seed, and heirs according to the promise," Gal. iii. 29. In Gal. iv. 7, we have the same argument as in the passage before us, " Wherefore thou art no more a servant, but a son ; and if a son, then an heir of God through Christ ; " see Col. iii. 24 ; Heb. ix. 15 ; Eph. i. 14, &c. *Joint heirs with Christ.* These words are intended to designate the inheritance which believers are to receive. It is not any possession in this world, but it is that good of which Christ himself is the recipient ; we are to be partakers of his inheritance. This idea is frequently presented in the Scriptures. " Enter thou into the joy of thy Lord," Matt. xxv, 21; " That ye may eat and drink at my table in my kingdom," Luke xxii. 30 ; " To him that overcometh will I grant to sit with me in my throne," &c., Rev. iii. 21, and in many other places.

If so be that we suffer with him, that we may be also glorified together. Those suffer with Christ who suffer as he did, and for his sake. They are thus partakers of the sufferings of Christ. We suffer as Christ suffered, not only when we are subject to the contradiction of sinners, but in the ordinary sorrows of life in which he, the man of sorrows, so largely shared. We are said to suffer with Christ, ἵνα, *in order that* we may be glorified together. That is, the design of God in the affliction of his people, is not to satisfy the demands of justice, but to prepare them to participate in his glory. To creatures in a state of sin, suffering is the necessary condition of exaltation. It is the refining process through which they must pass, 1 Pet. i. 6, 7. The union of believers with Christ, in suffering as well as in glory, is what he and his apostles taught them to expect. " If any man will come after me, let him deny himself, and take up his cross and *follow me*," Matt. xvi. 24 ; " If we be dead with *him*, we shall also live with *him.* If we suffer, we shall also reign with *him*," 2 Tim. ii. 11, 12. The blessedness of the future state is always represented as exalted; it is a glory, something that will elevate us in the rank of beings ; enlarging, purifying, and ennobling all our faculties. To this state we are to attain " through much tribulation," *i. e.* attain it as Christ did. And this is what the apostle here intends to say, and not that the participation of Christ's glory is a reward for our having suffered with him.

Verse 18. *For I reckon that the sufferings of this present time are not worthy to be compared*," &c. ' If children, then heirs ; *for* I do not think our present sufferings inconsistent with our being either the children or the heirs of God : 1. Because they are comparatively insignificant, vers. 18—23; and, 2. Because we are sustained under them, vers. 24—28.' Without much altering the sense, the *for* may be considered as referring to the last clause of the preceding verse : ' We shall be glorified with Christ, *for* these present afflictions are not worthy of thought.' In 2 Cor. iv. 17, Paul speaks much in the same manner of the lightness of the afflictions of this life in comparison with *the glory that shall be revealed in us.* We are not only the recipients of a great favour, but the subjects in which a great display of the divine glory is to be made to others, Eph. iii. 10. It is a revelation of glory in us; see Col. iii. 4 ; 1 John iii. 2. *Not worthy*, οὐκ ἄξια, not of light weight. Ἄξιόν τινος, what outweighs anything. Here, instead of the genitive, πρός is used—Not weighty in reference to, or in comparison with. As the glory so outweighs the suffering, the idea of merit, whether of condignity or of congruity, is of necessity excluded. It is altogether foreign to the context.   For it is not the ground on which eternal life is bestowed, but the greatness of the glory that the saints are to inherit, which the apostle designs to illustrate.   " Neque enim," says Calvin, " dignitatem utriusque confert apostolus, sed gravitatem crucis tantum elevat comparatione magnitudinis gloriæ, idque ad confirmandos patientia fidelium animos."

The apostle, fired with the thought of the future glory of the saints, pours forth the splendid passage which follows, (vers. 19—23,) in which he represents the whole creation groaning under its present degradation, and looking and longing for the revelation of this glory, as the end and consummation of its existence.

VERSE 19.   *For the earnest expectation of the creature,* &c.   This verse is evidently designed to confirm the assertion contained in the preceding verse. As, however, it is there asserted that the glory to be revealed in us is great, that it is certain, and that it is future, which of these points does the apostle here, and in what follows, design to establish ?   Some say, that in the preceding clause, τὴν μέλλουσαν δόξαν ἀποκαλυφθῆναι, μέλλουσαν is the emphatic word. The glory is future, for it is an object of expectation.   We are saved only in hope. Others again say, that the main idea is that this glory is about to be, *i. e.,* certainly shall be revealed, agreeably to the special force of the word μέλλειν. But the main idea of ver. 18 obviously is, that this future glory transcends immeasurably the suffering of this present state. All that follows tends to illustrate and enforce that idea. *The earnest expectation,* ἀποκαραδοκία, from καραδοκεῖν, *erecto capite prospicere,* to look for with the head erect. The ἄπο is intensive ; so that ἀποκαραδοκία is earnest or persistent expectation. It is an expectation that waits the time out, that never fails until the object is attained. The object of this earnest expectation is, *the manifestation of the sons of God.* That is, the time when they shall be manifested in their true character and glory as his sons. "Beloved, now are we the sons of God ; and it doth not yet appear what we shall be : but we know that when he shall appear, we shall be like him." 1 John iii. 2.   The subject of this expectation is the κτίσις, *the creation.* As this word signifies, first, the act of creating, and then, any individual created thing, or all creatures collectively, its meaning in any particular place must be determined by the context. In this passage it has been made to mean : 1. The whole rational and irrational creation, including angels, and all things else, animate and inanimate. 2. The whole world, excluding angels, but inclusive of the irrational animals. 3. The whole material creation, in a popular sense, as we say, all nature. 4. The whole human race.   5. The heathen world, as distinguished from believers. 6. The body of believers. The choice between these several interpretations must be determined by what is predicated of the κτίσις in this immediate connection, and by the analogy of Scripture. Unless the Bible elsewhere speaks of angels as the subjects of redemption, they cannot be here included, especially as they, as a class, are not subject to corruption. How far irrational animals are included, is more doubtful. The prophetic representations of the Messianic period set forth not only inanimate nature, the deserts, mountains, and forests, as rejoicing in the new order of things, but also the beasts of the field ; and therefore there is scriptural ground for including them under the comprehensive words of the apostle. That κτίσις here, is to be taken, not as meaning the whole human family, nor the heathen world, nor all rational creatures, but the whole creation with which we are immediately connected—the earth, and all its tribes of beings, man excepted—is the opinion of the great majority of commentators of all ages. It is supported by the following considerations : 1. In the first place, the words πᾶσα ἡ κτίσις, *the whole creation,* are so comprehensive, that nothing should be excluded which the nature of the subject and the context do not show cannot be embraced within their scope. It has already been remarked, that as Paul is speaking of the benefits of redemption, no class of creatures not included in some way in that redemption, can be here intended. While the good angels are, according to the Scriptures, not only deeply interested in this great work, 1 Peter i. 12, but receive through it the clearest manifestation of the manifold wisdom of God, Eph. iii. 10, yet they are not in such a sense partakers of the redemption of Christ as this passage supposes. They are not burdened with the consequences of man's apostacy, nor can they be represented as longing for deliverance from that burden. Angels, therefore, must be excluded from " the whole creation " here intended. 2. In the second place, as the apostle clearly distinguishes between the κτίσις and believers, the latter cannot be included in the former. ' Not only,' he says, ' the κτίσις, but we believers groan within ourselves,' &c. 3. Neither can "the creature " mean the race of mankind as distinguished from Christians. Hammond, Locke, Semler, Ammon, and others, may be quoted in favour of this interpretation. Wetstein expresses the same view briefly and plausibly thus : " Genus humanum dividitur in eos, qui jam Christo nomen dederunt, quique primitiæ vocantur hic et Jac. i. 18, et reliquos, qui nondum Christo nomen dederunt, qui vocantur *creatura vid.* Marc. xvi. 15. Et Judæi sentiunt onus legis suæ : gentes reliquæ tenebras suas palpant, prædicatione evangelii tanquam e somno excitatæ ; ubique magna rerum convertio expectatur." To this, however, it may be objected :

(*a*) It cannot be said of the world of mankind, that they have an earnest expectation and desire for the manifestation of the sons of God. The common longing after immortality, to which reference is made in defence of the application of this verse to men in general, is very far from coming up to the force of the passage. "The manifestation of the sons of God " is a definite scriptural event, just as much as the second advent of Christ. It can, therefore, no more be said that the world longs for the one event than for the other. Yet had the apostle said the whole creation was longing for the second advent of the Son of God, can any one imagine he meant they were merely sighing after immortality? He evidently intends, that the creature is looking forward, with earnest expectation, to that great scriptural event which, from the beginning, has been held up as the great object of hope, viz., the consummation of the Redeemer's kingdom.

(*b*) It cannot be said, in its full and proper force, that mankind were brought into their present state, not by their own act, or " willingly," but by the act and power of God. The obvious meaning of verse 20 seems to be, that the fact that the creature was subjected to its present state, not by itself, but by God, is the reason, at once, why it longs for deliverance, and may hope to obtain it. Such exculpatory declarations respecting men, are not in keeping with the scriptural mode of speaking either of the conduct or condition of the world.

(*c*) A still greater difficulty is found in reconciling this interpretation with ver. 21. How can it be said of mankind, as a whole, that they are to be delivered from the bondage of corruption, and made partakers of the glorious liberty of the children of God ? And, especially, how can this be said to occur at the time of the manifestation of the sons of God, *i. e.*, at the time of the second advent, the resurrection day, when the consummation of the Redeemer's kingdom is to take place ? According to the description here given, the whole creation is to groan under its bondage until the day of redemption, and then it also is to be delivered. This description can, in no satisfactory sense, be applied to mankind, as distinguished from the people of God.

(*d*) This interpretation does not suit the spirit of the context or drift of the passage. The apostle is represented as saying, in substance, "The very nature and condition of the human race point to a future state : they declare that this is an imperfect, frail, dying, unhappy state ; that man does not and cannot attain the end of his being here ; and even Christians, supported as they are by the earnest of future glory, still find themselves obliged to sympathize with others in these sufferings, sorrows, and deferred hopes."* But how feeble and attenuated is all this, compared to the glowing sentiments of the apostle ! His object is not to show that this state is one of frailty and sorrow, and that Christians must feel this as well as others. On the contrary, he wishes to show that the sufferings of this state are utterly insignificant in comparison with the future glory of the sons of God. And then to prove how great this glory is, he says, the whole creation, with outstretched neck, has been longing for its manifestation from the beginning of the world ; groaning not so much under present evil as from the desire for future good.

As therefore the angels, the human race, and believers as a class, must be excluded, what remains but the creation, in the popular sense of that word—the earth, with all it contains, animate and inanimate, man excepted ? With believers, the whole creation, in this sense, is represented as being burdened, and longing for deliverance. The refutation of the other interpretations shuts us up to the adoption of this. It is, moreover, consistent with the context and the analogy of Scripture. As the object of the apostle is to impress upon believers the greatness of the glory of which they are to be the subjects, he represents the whole creation as longing for its manifestation. There is nothing in this unnatural, unusual, or unscriptural. On the contrary, it is in the highest degree beautiful and effective, and at the same time in strict accordance with the manner of the sacred writers. How common is it to represent the whole creation as a sentient being, rejoicing in God's favour, trembling at his anger, speaking aloud his praise, &c. How often too is it represented as sympathizing in the joy of the people of God ! "The mountains and hills shall break forth before you into singing, and all the trees of the fields shall clap their hands." Isa. lv. 12. It may be objected, that such passages are poetical ; but so is this. It is not written in metre, but it is poetical in the highest degree. There is, therefore, nothing in the strong figurative language of ver. 19, either inappropriate to the apostle's object, or inconsistent with the manner of the sacred writers.

It may also with the strictest propriety be said, that the irrational creation was subjected to vanity, not willingly, but by the authority of God. It shared in the penalty of the fall—"Cursed is the earth for thy sake." Gen. iii. 17. And it is said still to suffer for the sins of its inhabitants: "Therefore hath the curse devoured the earth," Isa. xxiv. 6; "How long

---

* Professor Stuart's Commentary on Romans, p. 340.

shall the land mourn, and the herbs of every field wither, for the wickedness of them that dwell therein ?"   Jer. xii. 4.   This is a common mode of representation in the Scriptures.   How far the face of nature was affected, or the spontaneous fruitfulness of the earth changed by the curse, it is vain to ask.   It is sufficient that the irrational creation was made subject to a frail, dying, miserable state, by the act of God (not by its own,) in punishment of the sins of men.   This is the representation of the Scriptures, and this is the declaration of Paul.   While this is true of the irrational creature, it is not true of mankind.

The principal point in the description of the apostle is, that the subjection of the creature to the bondage of corruption is not final or hopeless, but the whole creation is to share in the glorious liberty of the children of God.   This also is in perfect accordance with the scriptural mode of representation on this subject.   Nothing is more familiar to the readers of the Old Testament, than the idea that the whole face of the world is to be clothed in new beauty when the Messiah appears : " The wilderness and the solitary place shall be glad for them; and the desert shall rejoice and blossom as the rose,"· &c.   Isa. xxxv. 1, xxix. 17, xxxii. 15, 16.   " The wolf also shall dwell with the lamb, and the leopard shall lie down with the kid, and the calf, and the young lion, and the fatling together; and a little child shall lead them."   Isa. xi. 6.   Such passages are too numerous to be cited.   The apostle Peter, speaking of the second advent, says the present state of things shall be changed, the heavens shall be dissolved, and the elements shall melt with fervent heat : " Nevertheless we, according to his promise, look for new heavens and a new earth, wherein dwelleth righteousness," 2 Pet. iii. 7—13.   " And I saw a new heaven and a new earth ; for the first heavens and the first earth were passed away," Rev. xxi. 1 ; see Heb. xii. 26, 27.   It is common, therefore, to describe the advent of the Messiah as attended with a great and glorious change of the external world.   Whether this is intended merely as an exornation, as is doubtless the case with many of the prophetic passages of the Old Testament; or whether it is really didactic, and teaches the doctrine of the restoration of the earth to more than its pristine beauty, which seems to be the meaning of some of the New Testament passages, is perfectly immaterial to our present purpose.   It is enough that the sacred writers describe the consummation of the Redeemer's kingdom as attended with the *palingenesia* of the whole creation.   This ·is all Paul does ; whether poetically or didactically, is too broad a question to be here entered upon.

In further confirmation of this interpretation it may be remarked, that this doctrine of the renewal of the external world, derived from the language of the prophets, was a common doctrine among the Jews.   Abundant evidence of this fact may be seen in Eisenmenger's *Entdecktes Judenthum* (Judaism Revealed,) particularly in chapter fifteenth of the second part.   The following passages are a specimen of the manner in which the Jewish writers speak on this subject : " Hereafter, when the sin of men is removed, the earth, which God cursed on account of that sin, will return to its former state and blessedness, as it was before the sin of men," p. 828.   " At this time the whole creation shall be changed for the better, and return to the perfection and purity which it had in the time of the first man, before sin was."   See this latter quotation, and others of a similar import, in Tholuck.   In the early Christian Church, this opinion was prevalent, and was the germ whence the extravagances of the Millenarians arose.   Almost all such errors contain a portion of truth, to which they are indebted for their origin and extension. The vagaries, therefore, of the early heretics, and the still grosser follies of the Talmudical writers on this subject, furnish presumptive and confirmatory evidence that the sacred writers did teach a doctrine, or at least employed a mode of speaking of the future condition of the external world, which easily accounts for these errors.

The objections to this view of the passage are inconclusive. 1. It is objected that it would require us to understand all such passages as speak of a latter day of glory, literally, and believe that the house of God is to stand on the top of the mountains, &c. But this is a mistake. When it is said, "The heavens declare the glory of God," we do not understand the words literally, although we understand them as speaking of the visible heavens. 2. Neither are the prophetic descriptions of the state of the world at the time of the second advent, explained literally, even when understood didactically, that is, as teaching that there is to be a great and glorious change in the condition of the world. But even this, as remarked above, is not necessary to make good the common interpretation. It is sufficient that Paul, after the manner of the other sacred writers, describes the external world as sympathising with the righteous, and participating in the glories of the Messiah's reign. If this be a poetic exaggeration in the one case, it may be in the other. Again, it is objected that the common interpretation is not suited to the design of the passage. But this objection is founded on a misapprehension of that design. The apostle does not intend to confirm our assurance of the truth of future glory, but to exalt our conceptions of its greatness. Finally, it is said to be very unnatural, that Paul should represent the external world as longing for a better state, and Christians doing the same, and the world of mankind be left unnoticed. But this is not unnatural if the apostle's design be as just stated.

There appears, therefore, to be no valid objection against supposing the apostle, in this beautiful passage, to bring into strong contrast with our present light and momentary afflictions, the permanent and glorious blessedness of our future state ; and, in order to exalt our conceptions of its greatness, to represent the whole creation, now groaning beneath the consequences of the fall, as anxiously waiting for the long expected day of redemption.

Verse 20. *For the creature was made subject to vanity,* &c. In this verse there are three reasons expressed or implied why the creature thus waits for the manifestation of the sons of God. The first is, that it is now subject to vanity. 2. That this subjection was not voluntary, but imposed by God. 3. That it was never designed to be final. *The* creature *was subjected,* (ὑπετάγη, historical aorist : the fact referred to occurred at the fall, when the curse fell on the earth.) *To vanity,* ματαιότητι. This word expresses either physical frailty or worthlessness, or moral corruption. Here it is the former; in Eph. iv. 17 ; 2 Pet. ii. 18, it is the latter. The two ideas, however, are in the Scriptures nearly related. The idea here expressed is antithetical to that expressed by the word *glory.* It includes, therefore, all that distinguishes the present condition of the creature from its original state, and from the glorious future in reserve for it. What is expressed by ματαιότης, is in ver. 21 expressed by φθορᾶς, *corruption.* What the apostle here says of the creature, was familiar to his Jewish readers. Their Rabbis taught that : Quamvis creatæ fuerint res perfectæ, cum primus homo peccaret, corruptæ tamen sunt, et non redibunt ad congruum statum suum, donec veniat Pharez," *i. e.* Messias. See *Eisenmenger.*

This subjection of the creature, the apostle says, was not ἑκοῦσα, *not will-ingly*, not of its own choice. It was neither by the voluntary act of the creature, nor in accordance with its own inclination. The inanimate creature was a passive sufferer, sharing in the curse which fell on man for his apostacy. *But by reason of him who hath subjected*, ἀλλ.ά (on the contrary) διὰ τὸν ὑποτάξαντα, *on account, i. e.* in accordance with the will of Him who rendered it subject. It was the will of God, not of the creature, which caused the creature to be subject to vanity. While this can be said with the strictest propriety, of the material and irrational creation, it cannot properly be said of sinners. Their subjection to the bondage of corruption was by their own voluntary act, or by the voluntary act of their divinely constituted head and representative. The subjection of the creature to vanity, however, was not final and hopeless; it was ἐπ' ἐλπίδι. These words may be connected either with ὑπετάγη or with ὑποτάξαντα : ' the creature was subjected in hope ;' or, 'on account of him subjecting it in hope.' In either case the sense is the same. The subjection was not a hopeless one. By giving ὑπετάγη a middle sense, and connecting ἐπ' ἐλπίδι therewith, we have the beautiful idea, that the creature submitted to the yoke of bondage in hope of ultimate deliverance. "Subjecit se jugo, hac tamen spe, ut et ipsa liberetur tandem ab eo." *Koppe.* "Obedientiæ exemplum," says Calvin, "in creaturis omnibus proponit, et eam addit ex spe nasci, quia hinc soli et lunæ, stellisque omnibus ad assiduum cursum alacritas ; hinc terræ ad fructus gignendos sedulitas obsequii, hinc aeris indefessa agitatio, hinc aquis ad fluxum promptus vigor, quia Deus suas quibusque partes injunxit ; nec tantum praeciso imperio quid fieri vellet, sed spem renovationis intus simul indidit."

Verse 21. *Because the creature itself also shall be delivered from the bondage of corruption*, &c. This verse, according to our version, assigns the reason why the subjection of the creature was not hopeless. This reason is, that the creature was to share in the glorious redemption. The particle ὅτι, however, rendered *because*, may be rendered *that*, and the verse then indicates the object of the hope just spoken of. The subjection was with the hope *that* the creature should be delivered. In either way the sense is nearly the same. *The creature itself also*, is another of the forms of expression which show that Paul speaks of the creation in a sense which does not embrace the children of God. *Bondage of corruption, i.e.* bondage to corruption—the state of frailty and degradation spoken of above.

Delivered, or liberated into the liberty, is an elliptical form of expression for 'delivered and introduced into the liberty.' *Liberty of glory*, as the words literally mean, or *glorious liberty*, refer to that liberty which consists in, or is connected with the glory which is the end and consummation of the work of redemption. This word is often used for the whole of the results of the work of Christ, as far as his people are concerned; (see ver. 18.) The creature then is to be partaker in some way, according to its nature, of the glories in reserve for the sons of God. "Porro non intelligit, consortes ejusdem gloriæ fore creaturas cum filiis Dei, sed suo modo melioris status fore socias : quia Deus simul cum humano genere orbem nunc collapsum in integrum restituet. Qualis vero futura sit integritas illa tam in pecudibus quam in plantis et metallis, curiosius inquirere neque expedit, neque fas est. Quia praecipua pars corruptionis est interitus : Quaerunt arguti, sed parum sobrii homines, an immortale futurum sit omne animalium genus : his speculationibus si frenum laxetur, quorsum tandem nos abripient ? Hac ergo simplici doctrina contenti simus, tale fore temperamentum, et tam concinnum ordinem, ut nihil vel deforme vel fluxum appareat." *Calvin.*

VERSE 22. *For we know that the whole creation groaneth and travaileth in pain together until now.* This verse is a repetition and confirmation of the preceding sentiment : ' The creature is subject to vanity, and longs for deliverance ; for we see, from universal and long continued experience, the whole creation groaning and travailing in pain.' It is, however, as Calvin remarks, the pains of birth, and not of death. After sorrow comes the joy of a new existence. The word *together* may have reference to the *whole creation* which groans together, all its parts uniting and sympathizing ; or it may refer to the sons of God, ' For the whole creation groans together with the sons of God.' On account of the following verse, in which Christians are specially introduced as joining with the whole creation in this sense of present misery and desire of future good, the former method of understanding the passage seems preferable. *Until now*, from the beginning until the present time. The creature has always been looking forward to the day of redemption. " Particula Hactenus, vel ad hunc usque diem, ad levandum diuturni languoris taedium pertinet. Nam si tot sæculis durarunt in suo gemitu creaturæ, quam inexcusabilis erit nostra mollities vel ignavia, si in brevi umbratilis vitæ curriculo deficimus ?" *Calvin.*

VERSE 23. *And not only so, but ourselves also, who have the first fruits of the Spirit,* &c. ' Not only does the whole creation thus groan, but we ourselves, we Christians, who have a foretaste of heavenly bliss, the first fruits of the glorious inheritance, we groan within ourselves, and long for the consummation of glory.' The *first fruits* was that portion of the productions of the earth which was offered to God. From the nature of the case, they contained the evidence and assurance of the whole harvest being secured. The idea, therefore, of an earnest or pledge is included in the phrase, as well as that of priority. This is the general if not constant use of the word in the New Testament. Thus Christ is called " the first fruits of them that slept," 1 Cor. xv. 20, not merely because he rose first, but also because his resurrection was a pledge of the resurrection of his people. See Rom. xi. 16 ; xvi. 5 ; 1 Cor. xvi. 15 ; James i. 18. In all these places, both ideas may be, and probably ought to be retained. In the passages before us, what is here called the first fruits of the Spirit, is elsewhere called the earnest of the Spirit, Eph. i. 14, &c. The phrases, *the Spirit which is the first fruits*, and *the Spirit which is an earnest*, are therefore synonymous. The Spirit is the first fruits of the full inheritance of the saints in light. The expression in the text, therefore, is descriptive of all Christians, and not of any particular class of them ; that is, it is not to be confined to those who first received the influences of the Spirit, or were first converted.

The interpretation given above, of this clause, is the one most commonly received, and the most natural. There is, however, great diversity in the MSS. as to the text, although the sense is substantially the same, whichever of the various readings be adopted. The common text is : οὐ μόνον δέ, ἀλλὰ καὶ αὐτοὶ τὴν ἀπαρχὴν τοῦ πνεύματος ἔχοντες, καὶ ἡμεῖς αὐτοὶ ἐν ἑαυτοῖς στενάζομεν. This may mean, ' Not only (the κτίσις,) but they having the first fruits of the Spirit, and we ourselves groan,' &c. A distinction is thus made between those who have the first fruits of the Spirit, and those meant by *we ourselves*. Those who adopt this interpretation suppose that Paul intended by *we*, either himself individually, or himself and the other apostles. This view of the passage, however, is not the natural one, even assuming the correctness of the common text; and is impossible, if the true reading be ἡμεῖς αὐτοί, as found in the MSS. D. F. G., and adopted by many critics. The αὐτοί in the first clause, and the ἡμεῖς αὐτοί, refer to the same class of persons, and indicate the subject of the verb στενάζομεν. It is more doubtful what force should be given to the participle ἔχοντες. As the article is omitted, most commentators render it, 'although having.' 'Even we groan, although having the present influences and support of the Spirit.' In our version, and by Calvin, Beza, and Bengel, it is rendered as though the article was used, οἱ ἔχοντες, *even we who have, i.e. the possessors of.* This is more pertinent, as the apostle's object is to designate the class intended by *we.* The article in such cases is not always used, (see ver. 1,) according to the common text. In the phrase ἀπαρχὴ τοῦ πνεύματος, the genitive may be taken as the *genitivus partivus.* In favour of this is the signification of the word, and its ordinary use. In such expressions as "first fruits of the corn and of the wine," "of the dead," and others of a like kind, the genitive indicates that of which the first fruits are a part. This gives a good sense here. Believers now possess and now enjoy, in the indwelling of the Spirit, a prelibation of what they are to receive hereafter—a part of the full measure of divine influence in reserve for them. Still the analogy of Scripture is in favour of taking the genitive as the genitive of apposition. The Holy Spirit is the ἀπαρχή; or as it is said in Eph. i. 14; 2 Cor. i. 22; v. 5, ἀρραβών, the earnest of the Spirit. The inheritance of the saints in light, is that of which the Spirit is the first fruits and the earnest.

Even we ourselves groan within ourselves, ἐν ἑαυτοῖς, as expressing the internal load by which the believer is now oppressed. *Waiting for the adoption,* υἱοθεσίαν without the article; 'waiting for adoption.' There is a sense in which believers are now the sons of God and partakers of adoption. But the full enjoyment of their blessedness as the children of God, the time when they shall be recognised as υἱοί, and enter upon their inheritance as such, is still future. Here Christians are in the condition of νήπιοι, minor children; their introduction into the state of υἱοί, in the sense of adult sons entitled to their inheritance, is their υἱοθεσία, for which they now wait, (ἀπεκδεχόμενοι,) with patient, but earnest desire. What, therefore, in the foregoing verse is expressed by "the manifestation of the sons of God," is here expressed by the single word "adoption." *Even the redemption of the body.* The redemption of the body is not so in apposition with *the adoption,* that the two phrases are equivalent. The adoption includes far more than the redemption of the body. But the latter event is to be coincident with the former, and is included in it, as one of its most prominent parts. Both expressions, therefore, designate the same period: 'We wait for the time when we shall be fully recognised as the children of God, *i.e.* for the time when our vile bodies shall be fashioned like unto the glorious body of the Son of God.' How much stress Paul laid upon the redemption of the body, is evident not only from this passage, and that in Philip. iii. 21, just quoted, but also from the whole of 1 Cor. xv., especially the latter part of the chapter. The time of the resurrection of the body, or the manifestation of the sons of God, is the time of the second advent of Jesus Christ. See 1 Cor. xv. 23, "Christ the first fruits; afterwards they that are Christ's, at his coming." 1 Thess. iv. 16, "For the Lord himself shall descend from heaven with a shout; and the dead in Christ shall rise first. Then we which are alive," &c. This is the period towards which all eyes and all hearts have been directed, among those who have had the first fruits of the Spirit, since the fall of Adam ; and for which the whole creation groaneth and is in travail even until now.

Verses 24, 25.   The apostle, intending to show that the present afflictions of believers are not inconsistent with their being the children of God, and are therefore no ground of discouragement, refers not only to their comparative insignificance, but also to the necessity which there is, from the nature of the case, for these sufferings : ' Salvation, in its fulness, is not a present good, but a matter of hope, and of course future ; and if future, it follows that we must wait for it in patient and joyful expectation.'   While, therefore, *waiting* for salvation is necessary, from the nature of the case, the nature of the blessing waited for, converts expectation into desire, and enables us patiently to endure all present evils.

For we are saved by hope, τῇ γὰρ ἐλπίδι ἐσώθημεν.   At the close of the preceding verse, Paul had spoken of believers as *waiting for the adoption.* They thus wait, because salvation is not a present good, but a future one. We are saved *in* hope, *i. e.,* in prospect.   The dative (ἐλπίδι) does not in this case express the means by which anything is done, but the condition or circumstances in which it is, or the way and manner in which it occurs. It is therefore analogous to our forms of expression, *we have a thing in expectation or prospect.*   Salvation is a blessing we have in hope, not in possession : if it be the one, it cannot be the other, *since hope that is seen is not hope.*   It lies in the nature of hope, that its object must be future. The word *hope* is here used objectively for *the thing hoped for,* as in Col. i. 5, "The hope that is laid up for you in heaven ; " Heb. vi. 18 ; Eph. i. 18, &c.   The latter clause of the verse, *for what a man seeth, why doth he yet hope for,* is only a confirmation of the previous declaration, that it lies in the nature of hope to have reference to the future.   "This passage," says Olshausen, "is specially important for determining the true nature of hope.   It stands opposed to βλέπειν, *seeing*—which supposes the object to be externally present.   It is, however, no less opposed to the entire absence of its object.   It is on the contrary, the inward possession of the things hoped for, so far as they are spiritual.   A man can believe, and hope for eternal things, only so far as they are inwardly present to him. Therefore it is that Christian hope is something so exalted.   It is the daughter of experience (Rom. v. 4), and maketh not ashamed.   It is the sister of faith and love.   Good wishes, desires, and longings, are not hope, because they do not involve the real possession of the things longed for."

Verse 25.   *But if we hope for that we see not,* &c.   That is, ' If hope has reference to the unseen and the future, then, as salvation is a matter of hope, it is a matter to be waited for.'   It results, therefore, from the nature of the plan of redemption, that the full fruition of its blessing should not be obtained at once, but that through much tribulation believers should enter into the kingdom ; consequently, their being called upon to suffer is not at all inconsistent with their being sons and heirs. *Then do we with patience wait for it ;* δι᾽ ὑπομονῆς, with constancy, or firmness, which includes the idea of patience, as its consequence.   There is something more implied in these words than that salvation, because unseen, must be waited for.   This, no doubt, from the connection, is the main idea ; but we not only wait, but we wait *with patience,* or *constancy.*   There is something in the very expectation of future good, and especially of such good, the glory that shall be revealed in us, to produce not only patient but even joyful endurance of all present suffering. " Spes ista," says Grotius, " non infructuosa est in nobis, egregiam virtutem operatur, malorum fortem tolerationem."

VERSE 26. Not only does hope thus cheer and support the suffering believer, but *likewise the Spirit also helpeth our infirmities. Likewise,* literally, *in the same way.* As hope sustains, so, in the same manner, the Spirit does also. Not that the mode of assistance is the same, but simply as the one does, so also does the other. In this case at least, therefore, the word thus rendered is equivalent to *moreover.* The translation *likewise* suits the context exactly. *Helpeth,* the word συναντιλαμβάνεται, means *to take hold of any thing with another,* to take part in his burden or work, and thus to aid. Compare Luke x. 40. It is, therefore, peculiarly expressive and appropriate. It represents the condescending Spirit as taking upon himself, as it were, a portion of our sorrows to relieve us of their pressure. " Magna est vis Graeci verbi συναντιλαμβάνεται, quod scilicet partes oneris quo nostra infirmitas gravatur, ad se recipiens Spiritus non modo auxiliatur nobis et succurrit, sed perinde nos sublevat acsi ipse nobiscum, onus subiret." *Calvin. Our infirmities** is the appropriate rendering of the original, which expresses the idea both of weakness and suffering. Heb. iv. 15, "We have not an high priest which cannot be touched with a feeling of our infirmities ;" 2 Cor. xii. 5, " I will not glory, but in mine infirmities."

For we know not what we should pray for as we ought ; but the Spirit, &c. What we know not is : τὸ τί προσευξώμεθα καθὸ δεῖ. The article τὸ belongs to the whole clause, as in Luke ix. 46 ; Acts iv. 21, and after. —*Winer,* 18. 3. This is said as an illustration and confirmation of the previous general declaration ; it is an example of the way in which the Spirit aids us. ' He helpeth our infirmities, for he teaches us how to pray, dictating to us our supplications,' &c. The necessity for this aid arises from our ignorance ; we know not what to pray for. We cannot tell what is really best for us. Heathen philosophers gave this as a reason why men ought not to pray !† How miserable their condition when compared to ours ! Instead of our ignorance putting a seal upon our lips, and leaving our hearts to break, the Spirit gives our desires a language heard and understood of God. As we know not how to pray, the Spirit teacheth us. This idea the apostle expresses by saying, *the Spirit itself maketh intercession for us.* The simple verb (ἐντυγχάνω), rendered *he maketh intercession,* properly means *to meet,* then *to approach any one to make supplication,* Acts xxv. 24. This supplication may be against any one, Rom. xi. 2, or for him, ver. 34; Heb. vii. 25. Hence, *to intercede for,* is to act the part of advocate in behalf of any one. This Christ is said to do for us in the last two passages cited, as well as in Heb. ix. 24 ; 1 John ii. 1 ; and John xiv. 16, for Christ calls the Holy Spirit " *another* advocate," *i. e.,* another than himself. This office is ascribed to the Spirit in the last passage quoted, in John xiv. 26 ; xv. 26 ; and xvi. 7, as well as in the passage before us. As the Spirit is thus said, in the general, to do for us what an advocate did for his client, so he does also what it was the special duty of the advocate to perform, *i. e.,* to dictate to his clients what they ought to

---

* For ταῖς ἀσθενείαις, the singular τῇ ἀσθενείᾳ is read by MSS. A. C. D. 10, 23, 31, 37, 47, and the Syriac and Latin versions. Lachmann has the singular.

† Diogenes, L. VIII. 9. Pythagoras οὐκ ἐᾶ εὔχεσθαι ὑπὲρ ἑαυτῶν· διὰ τὸ μὴ εἰδέναι τὸ συμφέρον.—*Wetstein.*

say, how they should present their cause.* In this sense the present passage is to be understood. We do not know how to pray, but the Spirit teaches us. All true prayer is due to the influence of the Spirit, who not only guides us in the selection of the objects for which to pray, but also gives us the appropriate desires, and works within us that faith without which our prayers are of no avail. We are not to suppose that the Spirit itself prays, or utters the inarticulate groans of which the apostle here speaks. He is said to do what he causes us to do. " Interpellare autem dicitur Spiritus Dei," says Calvin ; " non quod ipse re vera suppliciter se ad precandum vel gemendum demittat, sed quod in animis nostris excitet ea vota, quibus nos sollicitari convenit ; deinde corda nostra sic afficiat ut suo ardore in coelum penetrent." Nevertheless, far more is meant than that the Spirit teaches us to pray, as one man may teach another. And more is meant than that, by a mere *ab extra* influence, certain desires and feelings are awakened in our hearts. The Spirit dwells in the believer as a principle of life. In our consciousness there is no difference between our own actings and those of the Spirit. There is, however, a *concursus*, a joint agency of the divine and human in all holy exercises, and more especially in those emotions, desires, and aspirations which we are unable to clothe in words. The στεναγμοῖς ἀλαλήτοις may mean with *unutterable* or *unuttered groanings*. The former is not only more forcible, but it is more in accordance with the experience and language of men. It is common to speak of emotions too big for utterance, and we all know what that means. The analogy of Scripture is also in favour of this view. The Bible speaks of God's unspeakable gift, 2 Cor. xii. 4, of ἄρρητα ῥήματα, 'words which cannot be uttered ;' and of ' a joy that is unspeakable,' χαρὰ ἀνεκλάλητος.

Verse 27. Although these desires are not, and cannot be uttered, the eye of Him who searches the heart can read and understand them. *And* (rather, *but*) *he who searcheth the hearts.* To search the heart is the prerogative of God, as it implies omniscience. As no man knoweth the things of a man, but the spirit of man that is in him, to read the unexpressed emotions of the soul must be the work of Him to whose eyes all things are naked. " I the Lord, search the heart, I try the reins." Jer. xvii. 10 ; Ps. cxxxix. ; vii. 9 ; Rev. ii. 23. *Knoweth the mind of the Spirit.* By φρόνημα τοῦ πνεύματος is meant the meaning, intention of the Spirit, what he means by these unutterable groanings. By Spirit must be here understood, as the context requires, the Holy Spirit. It is that Spirit who intercedes for the saints and in them, and who is expressly distinguished from the soul in which he dwells. God is said to *know* the mind of the Spirit. As the word *to know* is so often used with the implication of the idea of approval, this may mean, God recognises or approves of the mind of the Spirit. " Hic verbi *nosse*," says Calvin, " adnotanda est proprietas ; significat enim, Deum non novos et insolentes illos Spiritus affectus non animadvertere, vel tanquam absurdos rejicere; sed agnoscere, et simul benigne excipere ut agnitos sibi et probatos." If this be the meaning of the word, then the following ὅτι is causal, and introduces the reason why God thus approves of the mind of the Spirit. It is because the Spirit maketh intercession for the saints κατὰ Θεόν *according to God, i.e.,* agreeably to his will. The desires produced by the Spirit of God himself are, of course, agreeable to the will of God, and secure of being approved and

---

* See Knapp's Dissertation De Spiritu Sancto et Christo Paracletis, p. 114, of his Scripta Varii Argumenti. Or the translation of that Dissertation in the Biblical Repertory, Vol. 1., p. 234.

answered. This is the great consolation and support of believers. They know not either what is best for themselves or agreeable to the will of God; but the Holy Spirit dictates those petitions and excites those desires which are consistent with the divine purposes, and which are directed towards the blessings best suited to our wants. Such prayers are always answered. " And this is the confidence that we have in him, that if we ask any thing according to his will, he heareth us," 1 John v. 14. But if οἶδε is to be taken in its ordinary sense, then ὅτι is explicative. 'God knows *that* the Spirit,' &c. Those who adopt this view generally render κατὰ Θεόν *towards God, i.e.,* before God. 'The Spirit intercedes before God for the saints.' In favour of this interpretation of the passage, it is urged that this is the proper place of the word οἶδε; and as to the clause κατὰ Θεόν, it is said, God's knowing the mind of the Spirit, does not depend on its being according to his will. He would *know* it whether in accordance with his will or not. This difficulty, however, does not exist if οἶδε means ' he recognises and approves.' It is making the verse say comparatively little, if it is made to mean simply ' that the Searcher of hearts knows that the Spirit intercedes in his presence (or toward him) for the saints.' The interpretation adopted by our translators, therefore, is to be preferred. It is more to the apostle's purpose if he assigns the reason why God receives the unutterable desires and longings of the heart as true prayer. This indeed is a consolation to believers.

VERSE 28. *And we know all things work together for good to them that love God,* &c. This may be regarded as virtually, though not formally, an inference from what Paul had taught concerning afflictions. As they are comparatively insignificant, as they call forth the exercises of hope, and give occasion for the kind interposition of the Holy Spirit, far from being inconsistent with our salvation, they contribute to our good. It seems, however, more natural to consider the apostle as presenting the consideration contained in this verse, as an additional reason why the afflictions of this life are not inconsistent with our being the sons of God. These afflictions are real blessings. *All things,* as is usually the case with such general expressions, is to be limited to the things spoken of in the context, *i.e.,* the sufferings of the present time. See 1 Cor. ii. 15, where the spiritual man is said to understand " all things;" Col. i. 20, where Christ is said to reconcile " all things unto God;" and Eph. i. 10, with many other similar passages. Of course it is not intended that other events, besides afflictions, do not work together for the good of Christians, but merely that the apostle is here speaking of the sufferings of believers. " Tenendum est Paulum non nisi de rebus adversis loqui: acsi dixisset Divinitus sic temperari quaecunque sanctis accidunt, ut, quod mundus noxium esse putat, exitus utile esse demonstret. Nam tametsi verum est, quod ait Augustinus, peccata quoque sua, ordinante Dei providentia, sanctis adeo non nocere, ut potius eorum saluti inserviant; ad hunc tamen locum non pertinet, ubi de cruce agitur." *Calvin.*

Those to whom afflictions are a real blessing are described, first, as *those who love God;* and secondly, as those *who are called according to his purpose.* The former of these clauses describes the character of the persons intended, *they love God,* which is a comprehensive expression for all the exercises of genuine religion. The latter clause declares a fact, with regard to all such, which has a most important bearing on the apostle's great object in this chapter, *they are called according to his purpose.* The word *called,* as remarked above, (i. 7,) is never, in the epistles of the New Testament, applied to those who are the recipients of the mere external invitation of the gospel. It always means *effectually called, i.e.*, it is always applied to those who are really brought to accept of the blessings to which they are invited. 1 Cor. i. 24, " But to those who are called," *i.e.*, to true Christians. Jude 1, " To those who are sanctified by God the Father, and are preserved in Jesus Christ, and called," 1 Cor. i. 2, &c. The word is, therefore, often equivalent with *chosen*, as in the phrase " called an apostle," 1 Cor. i. 1 ; Rom. i. 1; and " called of Jesus Christ," Rom. i. 6. And thus in the Old Testament, " Hearken unto me, O Jacob, and Israel my called," Isa. xlviii. 12 ; see Isa. xlii. 6, xlix. 1, li. 2. Those who love God, therefore, are those whom he hath chosen and called by his grace to a participation of the Redeemer's kingdom. This call is not according to the merits of men, but according to the divine *purpose.* " Who hath saved us, and called *us* with a holy calling, not according to our works, but according to his own purpose and grace, which was given us in Christ Jesus before the world began." 2 Tim. i. 9 ; Eph. i. 11; Rom. ix. 11. The design of the apostle, in the introduction of this clause, seems to have been twofold. First, to show, according to his usual manner, that the fact that some men love God is to be attributed to his sovereign grace, and not to themselves ; and, secondly, that if men are called, according to the eternal purpose of God, their salvation is secure. By this latter idea, this clause is associated with the passage that follows, and with the general object of the chapter. That the *calling* of men does secure their salvation, is proved in verses 29, 30.

DOCTRINE.

1. True Christians are the sons of God, objects of his affection, partakers of his moral nature, and heirs of his kingdom, ver. 14.

2. The relation of God to us is necessarily the counterpart of ours to him. If we feel as friends to him, he feels as a friend towards us ; if our sentiments are filial, his are parental, ver. 15.

3. God, who is everywhere present and active, manifests his presence, and communicates with his creatures in a manner accordant with their nature, although in a way that is inscrutable, ver. 16.

4. Assurance of salvation has a twofold foundation, the experience of those affections which are the evidences of true piety, and the witness of the Holy Spirit. The latter can never be separated from the former ; for the Spirit can never testify to what is not the truth. He can never assure an enemy that he is a child of God, ver. 16.

5. Union with Christ is the source of all our blessings of justification and sanctification, as taught in the previous chapters, and of salvation, as taught in this, ver. 17.

6. Afflictions are not inconsistent with the divine favour, nor with our being the sons of God, vers. 18—25.

7. The future glory of the saints must be inconceivably great, if the whole creation, from the beginning of the world, groans and longs for its manifestation, vers. 19—23.

8. The curse consequent on the fall has affected the state of the external world. The consummation of the work of redemption may be attended with its regeneration, vers. 20—22.

9. The present influences of the Spirit are first fruits of the inheritance

of the saints; the same in kind with the blessings of the future state, though less in degree. They are a pledge of future blessedness, and always produce an earnest longing for the fruition of the full inheritance, ver. 23.

10. As, for wise reasons, salvation is not immediately consequent on regeneration, hope, which is the joyful expectation of future good, becomes the duty, solace, and support of the Christian, vers. 24, 25.

11. The Holy Spirit is our Paraclete (John xiv. 16) or advocate, we are his *clients*, we know not how to plead our own cause, but he dictates to us what we ought to say. This office of the Spirit ought to be recognized, and gratefully acknowledged, ver. 26.

12. Prayer, to be acceptable, must be according to the will of God, and it always is so when it is dictated or excited by the Holy Spirit, ver. 27.

13. All events are under the control of God; and even the greatest afflictions are productive of good to those who love him, ver. 28.

14. The calling or conversion of men, involving so many of their free acts, is a matter of divine purpose, and it occurs in consequence of its being so, ver. 28.

REMARKS.

1. If God, by his Spirit, condescends to dwell in us, it is our highest duty to allow ourselves to be governed or led by him, vers. 12, 13.

2. It is a contradiction in terms to profess to be the sons of God, if destitute of the filial feelings of confidence, affection, and reverence, ver. 15.

3. A spirit of fear, so far from being an evidence of piety, is an evidence of the contrary. The filial spirit is the genuine spirit of religion, ver. 15.

4. Assurance of hope is not fanatical, but is an attainment which every Christian should make. If the witness of men is received, the witness of God is greater. As the manifestation of God's love to us is made in exciting our love towards him, so the testimony of his Spirit with ours, that we are the sons of God, is made when our filial feelings are in lively exercise, ver. 16.

5. Christians ought neither to expect nor wish to escape suffering with Christ, if they are to be partakers of his glory. The former is a preparation for the latter, ver. 17.

6. The afflictions of this life, though in themselves not joyous but grievous, are worthy of little regard in comparison with the glory that shall be revealed in us. To bear these trials properly, we should regard them as part of the heritage of the sons of God, ver. 18.

7. As the present state of things is one of bondage to corruption, as there is a dreadful pressure of sin and misery on the whole creation, we should not regard the world as our home, but desire deliverance from this bondage, and introduction into the liberty of the children of God, vers. 19-22.

8. It is characteristic of genuine piety to have exalted conceptions of future blessedness, and earnest longings after it. Those, therefore, who are contented with the world and indifferent about heaven, can hardly possess the first fruits of the Spirit, ver. 23.

9. Hope and patience are always united. If we have a well-founded

hope of heaven, then do we with patience and fortitude wait for it. This believing resignation and joyful expectation of the promises, are peculiarly pleasing in the sight of God and honourable to religion, vers. 24, 25.

10. How wonderful the condescension of the Holy Spirit! How great his kindness in teaching us, as a parent his children, how to pray and what to pray for! How abundant the consolation thus afforded to the pious in the assurance that their prayers shall be heard, vers. 26, 27.

11. Those who are in Christ, who love God, may repose in perfect security beneath the shadow of his wings. All things shall work together for their good, because all things are under the control of him who has called them to the possession of eternal life according to his own purpose, ver. 28.

ROMANS VIII. 29—39.

ANALYSIS.

This section contains the exhibition of two additional arguments in favour of the safety of believers. The first of these is founded on the decree or purpose of God, vers. 29, 30 ; and the second on his infinite and unchanging love, vers. 31—39. In his description of those with regard to whom all things shall work together for good, Paul had just said that they are such who are called or converted in execution of a previous purpose of God, ver. 28. If this is the case, the salvation of believers is secure, because the plan on which God acts is connected in all its parts ; whom he foreknows, he predestinates, calls, justifies, and glorifies. Those, therefore, who are called, shall certainly be saved, vers. 29, 30. Secondly, if God is for us, who can be against us ? If God so loved us as to give his Son for us, he will certainly save us, vers. 31, 32. This love has already secured our justification, and has made abundant provision for the supply of all our wants, vers. 33, 34.

The triumphant conclusion from all these arguments, that nothing shall separate us from the love of Christ, but that we shall be more than conquerors over all enemies and difficulties, is given in vers. 35—39.

COMMENTARY.

Verse 29. *For whom he did foreknow, he also did predestinate,* &c. The connection of this verse with the preceding, and the force of *for*, appears from what has already been said. Believers are called in accordance with a settled plan and purpose of God, *for* whom he calls he had previously predestinated : and as all the several steps or stages of our salvation are included in this plan of the unchanging God, if we are predestinated and called, we shall be justified and glorified. Or the connecting idea is this : All things must work together for good to those who love God, *for* the plan of God cannot fail ; those whom he has called into this state of reconciliation, whom he has made to love him, he will assuredly bring to the glory prepared for his people.

Whom he did foreknow. As the words *to know* and *foreknow* are used in three different senses, applicable to the present passage, there is considerable diversity of opinion which should be preferred. The word may express *prescience* simply, according to its literal meaning ; or, as *to know* is often *to approve* and *love*, it may express the idea of peculiar affection in this case; or it may mean *to select* or *determine upon.* Among those who adopt one or the other of these general views, there is still a great diversity as to the manner in which they understand the passage. These opinions are too numerous to be here recited.

As the literal meaning of the word *to foreknow* gives no adequate sense, inasmuch as all men are the objects of the divine prescience, whereas the apostle evidently designed to express by the word something that could be asserted only of a particular class; those who adopt this meaning here supply something to make the sense complete. *Who he foreknew would repent and believe,* or *who would not resist his divine influence,* or some such idea. There are two objections to this manner of explaining the passage. 1. The addition of this clause is entirely gratuitous; and, if unnecessary, it is, of course, improper. There is no such thing said, and, therefore, it should not be assumed, without necessity, to be implied. 2. It is in direct contradiction to the apostle's doctrine. It makes the ground of our calling and election to be something in us, our works; whereas Paul says that such is not the ground of our being chosen. " Who hath called us not according to our works, but according to his own purpose and grace, &c.," 2 Tim. i. 9, and Rom. ix. 11, where the contrary doctrine is not only asserted, but proved and defended. To say that faith as distinguished from works is what is foreseen, and constitutes the ground of election, does not help the matter. For faith is a work or act, and it is the gift of God, the result or effect of election, and therefore not its ground.

The second and third interpretations do not essentially differ. The one is but a modification of the other; for whom God peculiarly loves, he does thereby distinguish from others, which is in itself a selecting or choosing of them from among others. The usage of the word is favourable to either modification of this general idea *of preferring.* " The people which he foreknew," *i. e.,* loved or selected, Rom. xi. 2; " Who verily was foreordained (Gr. *foreknown*), *i. e., fixed upon, chosen* before the foundation of the world," 1 Peter i. 20; 2 Tim. ii. 19; John x. 14, 15; see also Acts ii. 23; 1 Peter i. 2. The idea, therefore, obviously is, that those whom God peculiarly loved, and by thus loving, distinguished or selected from the rest of mankind; or to express both ideas in one word, those whom *he* elected he predestined, &c.

It is evident, on the one hand, that πρόγνωσις expresses something more than the prescience of which all men and all events are the objects, and, on the other, something different from the προορισμός (predestination) expressed by the following word: " Whom he foreknew, them he also predestinated." The predestination follows, and is grounded on the foreknowledge. The foreknowledge therefore expresses the act of cognition or recognition, the fixing, so to speak, the mind upon, which involves the idea of selection. If we look over a number of objects with the view of selecting some of them for a definite purpose, the first act is to fix the mind on some to the neglect of the others, and the second is to destine them to the proposed end. So God is represented as looking on the fallen mass of men, and fixing on some whom he predestines to salvation. This is the πρόγνωσις, the foreknowledge, of which the apostle here speaks. It is the knowing, fixing upon, or selecting those who are to be predestinated to be conformed to the image of the Son of God. Even De Wette says, Der Begriff der unbedingten Gnadenwahl liegt hier klar vor, (the idea of sovereign election is here clearly presented.)

He also did predestinate to be conformed to the image of his Son. To predestinate is to destine or appoint beforehand, as the original word is used in Acts iv. 28, "To do whatsoever thy hand and counsel determined before to be done;" "Having predestinated us unto the adoption of children," Eph. i. 5; "Being predestinated according to the purpose of Him who worketh all things after the counsel of his own will," Eph. i. 11. In all the cases in which this predestination is spoken of, the idea is distinctly recognised, that the ground of the choice which it implies is not in us. We are chosen in Christ, or according to the free purpose of God, &c. This is a *fore*-ordination, a determination which existed in the divine mind long prior to the occurrence of the event, even before the foundation of the world, Eph. i. 4; so that the occurrences in time are the manifestations of the eternal purpose of God, and the execution of the plan of which they form a part.

The end to which those whom God has chosen are predestined, is conformity *to the image of his Son, i.e.,* that they might be like his Son in character and destiny. He hath chosen us "that we should be holy and without blame before him," Eph. i. 4; iv. 24. "He hath predestined us to the adoption," *i.e.,* to the state of sons, Eph. i. 5. "As we have borne the image of the earthy, we shall also bear the image of the heavenly," 1 Cor. xv. 49; see Phil. iii. 21; 1 John iii. 2. The words συμμόρφους τῆς εἰκόνος τοῦ υἱοῦ αὐτοῦ, express not only the general idea that believers are to be like Christ, but more definitely, that what Christ is we are to be; as He is υἱός we are υἱοί; as He was ἐν μορφῇ Θεοῦ we are to be σύμμορφοι; as He assumed our nature, and thereby purified and exalted it, we are to partake of that purity and glory. We are to have the same μορφή (form) as the εἰκών of Christ has—resemble him as the image answers to the original. As Paul, in verse 17, had spoken of our suffering with Christ, and in the subsequent passage was principally employed in showing that though in this respect we must be like Christ, it was not inconsistent with our being sons and heirs, so here, when we are said to be conformed to the image of Christ, the idea of our bearing the same cross is not to be excluded. We are to be like our Saviour in moral character, in our present sufferings and future glory. As this conformity to Christ includes our moral likeness to him, and as this embraces all that is good in us, it is clear that no supposed excellence originating from our own resources, can be the ground of our being chosen as God's people, since this excellence is included in the end to which we are predestined. "I remark here in passing," says Olshausen, "that according to Paul's doctrine, there is a *praedestinatio sanctorum* in the strict sense of the word; that is, that God does not foreknow those who by their own decision will become holy, but he himself creates that decision in them. In προγινώσκειν the divine knowledge, and in προορίζειν the divine will, (both of which are included in the πρόθεσις,) are expressed."

That he might be the first-born among many brethren. This clause may express the design, or merely the result of what had just been said. 'God predestinated us to be sons, *in order that* Christ might be,' &c., or 'He made us his sons, hence Christ is,' &c. The former is on every account to be preferred. It is not merely an unintended result, but the great end contemplated in the predestination of God's people. That end is the glory and exaltation of Christ. The purpose of God in the salvation of men, was not mainly that men should be holy and happy, but that through their holiness and happiness his glory, in the person of the Son, should be displayed, in the ages to come, to principalities and powers. Christ, therefore, is the central point in the history of the universe. His glory, as the glory of God in the highest form of its manifestation, is the great end of creation and redemption. And this end, the apostle teaches, is accomplished by making him the *first-born among many brethren,* that is, by causing him to stand as the first-born, the head and chief, among and over that countless multitude who through him are made the sons of God. " Igitur," says Calvin, " sicut primogenitus familiae nomen sustinet; ita Christus in sublimi gradu locatur, non modo ut honore emineat inter fideles, sed etiam ut communi fraternitatis nota sub se omnes contineat."

VERSE 30. *Moreover, whom he did predestinate, them he also called.* Those whom he had thus foreordained to be conformed to the image of his Son in moral character, in suffering, and in future glory, he effectually calls, *i.e.,* leads by the external invitation of the gospel, and by the efficacious operation of his grace, to the end to which they are destined. That the *calling* here spoken of is not the mere external call of the gospel, is evident both from the usage of the word, and from the necessity of the case ; see 1 Cor. i. 9, " God is faithful by whom ye were called to the fellowship of his Son," *i.e.,* effectually brought into union with him. In the same chapter, ver. 24, " To those which are called, Christ the power of God," &c. The called are here expressly distinguished from the rejecters of the external invitation. 1 Cor. vii. 15, 18, in which chapter *calling* is repeatedly put for effectual conversion, " Is any man *called,* being circumcised," &c. Heb. ix. 15, " That they which are called may receive the promise of eternal inheritance." Rom. ix. 12 ; Eph. iv. 4 ; 1 Thess. ii. 12, and many similar passages. This use of the word, thus common in the New Testament, is obviously necessary here, because the apostle is speaking of a call which is peculiar to those who are finally saved. Whom he *calls* he justifies and glorifies ; see verse 28.

Whom he called, them he also justified ; and whom he justified, them he also glorified. The aorist here used may express the idea *of frequency.* Whom he calls, he is wont to justify ; and whom he is wont to justify, is he accustomed to glorify. So that the meaning is the same as though the present tense had been used, ' Whom he calls, he justifies,' &c. ; see James i. 11 ; 1 Peter i. 24, where the same tense is rendered as the present, " The grass withereth, and the flower thereof falleth away." Or, as this use of the aorist is doubtful, or at least unusual, that tense is employed, because Paul is speaking of that God, who sees the end from the beginning, and in whose decree and purpose all future events are comprehended and fixed ; so that in predestinating us, he at the same time, in effect, called, justified, and glorified us, as all these were included in his purpose.

The justification here spoken of, is doubtless that of which the apostle has been speaking throughout the epistle, the regarding and treating sinners as just, for the sake of the righteousness of Christ. The blessings of grace are never separated from each other. Election, calling, justification, and salvation are indissolubly united ; and, therefore, he who has clear evidence of his being called, has the same evidence of his election and final salvation. This is the very idea the apostle means to present for the consolation and encouragement of believers. They have no cause for despondency if the children of God, and called according to his purpose, because nothing can prevent their final salvation.

VERSE 31. *What shall we say to these things ?* That is, what is the inference from what has hitherto been said ? *If God be for us,* if he has delivered us from the law of sin and death, if he has renewed us by his Spirit which dwells within us, if he recognises us as his children and his heirs, and has predestinated us to holiness and glory, *who can be against us?* If God's love has led to all the good just specified, what have we to fear for the future? He who spared not his own Son, will freely give us all things. This verse shows clearly what has been the apostle's object from the beginning of the chapter. He wished to demonstrate that to those who accede to the plan of salvation which he taught, *i.e.*, to those who are in Christ Jesus, there is no ground of apprehension; their final salvation is fully secured. The conclusion of the chapter is a recapitulation of all his former arguments, or rather the reduction of them to one, which comprehends them all in their fullest force; God IS FOR US. He, as our Judge, is satisfied; as our Father, he loves us; as the supreme and almighty Controller of events, who works all things after the counsel of his own will, he has determined to save us; and as that Being, whose love is as unchanging as it is infinite, he allows nothing to separate his children from himself.

It has been objected, that if Paul had intended to teach these doctrines, he would have said that apostacy and sin cannot interfere with the salvation of believers. But what is salvation, but deliverance from the guilt and power of sin? It is, therefore, included in the very purpose and promise of salvation, that its objects shall be preserved from apostacy and deadly sins. This is the end and essence of salvation. And, therefore, to make Paul argue that God will save us if we do not apostatize, is to make him say, those shall be saved who are not lost. According to the apostle's doctrine, holiness is so essential and prominent a part of salvation, that it is not so much a means to an end as the very end itself. It is that to which we are predestinated and called, and therefore if the promise of salvation does not include the promise of holiness, it includes nothing. Hence, to ask whether, if one of the called should apostatise and live in sin, he would still be saved, is to ask, whether he will be saved if he is not saved. Nor can these doctrines be perverted to licentiousness without a complete denial of their nature. For they not only represent sin and salvation as two things which ought not to be united, but as utterly irreconcilable and contradictory.

VERSE 32. *He that spared not his own Son, &c.* That ground of confidence and security which includes all others, is the love of God; and that exhibition of divine love which surpasses and secures all others, is the gift of HIS OWN SON. Paul having spoken of Christians as being God's sons by adoption, was led to designate Christ as his own peculiar Son, in a sense in which neither angels (Heb. i. 5) nor men can be so called. That this is the meaning of the phrase is evident, 1. Because this is its proper force; *own* Son being opposed to *adopted* sons. An antithesis, expressed or implied, is always involved in the use of the word ἴδιος, see Acts ii. 6; Rom. xi. 24, xiv. 4; Tit. i. 12. The Jews, we are told, took up stones to stone our Lord, because πατέρα ἴδιον ἔλεγε τὸν Θεόν, thus making himself equal with God. Christ is in such a sense the Son of God, that he is of one nature with him, the same in substance, equal in power and glory. 2. Because the context requires it, as Paul had spoken of those who were sons in a different sense just before. 3. Because this apostle, and the other sacred writers, designate Christ as Son of God in the highest sense, as partaker of the divine nature; see Rom. i. 4.

But delivered him up for us all. He was delivered up to death; see

Gal. i. 4 ; Rom. iv. 25 ; Isa. liii. 6, xxxviii. 13 (in the LXX.,) and Matt.
x. 21. *For us all ;* not merely for our benefit, but in our place. This
idea, however, is not expressed by the peculiar force of the preposition ὑπέρ, but is implied from the nature of the case. The benefit secured
by a sacrifice is secured by substitution. It is offered for the benefit of
the offender because it is offered in his place. There is no restriction or
limitation to be put on the word *all* in this verse, other than that which
the context and the analogy of Scripture imposes. God, says Paul, gave up
his Son for *us* all ; whether he means all rational creatures, or all men, or
all those whom he determined thereby to redeem, and whom he had foreknown and predestinated to eternal life, depends on what the Scripture
elsewhere teaches on the subject.

How shall he not also (καί) *with him freely give us all things.* If God
has done the greater, he will not leave the less undone. The gift of Christ
includes all other gifts. If God so loved us as to give his Son for us, he
will certainly give the Holy Spirit to render that gift effectual. This is presented as a ground of confidence. The believer is assured of salvation, not
because he is assured of his own constancy, but simply because he is assured
of the immutability of the divine love, and he is assured of its immutability because he is assured of its greatness. Infinite love cannot change.
A love which spared not the eternal Son of God, but freely gave him up,
cannot fail of its object. " Christus non nudus aut inanis ad nos missus
est ; sed cœlestibus omnibus thesauris refertus, ne quid eum possidentibus
ad plenam felicitatem desit." *Calvin.*

Verse 33. *Who shall lay any thing to the charge of God's elect ?* This
and the following verse show how fully the security of believers is provided
'for by the plan of redemption. What is it they have to fear under the government of a just and powerful God ? There is nothing to be dreaded but sin ;
if that be pardoned and removed, there is nothing left to fear. In the strongest manner possible, the apostle declares that the sins of believers are pardoned, and shows the ground on which that pardon rests. To them, therefore, there can be neither a disquieting accusation nor condemnation. *Who
can lay any thing ?* τίς ἐγκαλέσει; the word ἐγκαλεῖν means *in jus vocare,*
to summon before the bar of justice. The question is in the form of a
challenge, and implies the strongest confidence that no accuser against God's
elect can appear. If the law of God be satisfied, " the strength of sin," its
condemning power, is destroyed. Even conscience, though it upbraids,
does not terrify. It produces the ingenuous sorrow of children, and not
the despairing anguish of the convict, because it sees that all the ends of
punishment are fully answered in the death of Christ, who bore our sins
in his own body on the tree.

God's elect, i.e., those whom God has chosen; see ver. 29. The word
elect is sometimes used in a secondary sense for *beloved,* which idea is implied in its literal sense, as those chosen are those who are peculiarly
beloved. This sense may be given to it in 1 Peter ii. 4, " elect and precious" may be *beloved* and precious. And so in a multitude of cases it
were optional with a writer to say chosen or beloved, as the one implies
the other. But this does not prove that *chosen* means *beloved,* or that the
idea of choice is to be excluded from the idea of the word. *The elect* are
those whom God has chosen out of the world to be the members of his
family or kingdom ; just as under the Old Testament the Hebrews, whom
he had chosen to be his peculiar people, were his elect. Men may dispute
as to what the elect are chosen to, and why some are chosen and not others.

But there seems to be no ground for dispute whether " the elect" mean the chosen. This passage, however, proves that those who are elect, and whose election has become recognised, are in a state in which they are free from condemnation. No one can lay any thing to their charge. The demands of justice as regards them have been satisfied. This is not true of those who are chosen merely to church privileges. There is an election, therefore, unto grace and salvation. The elect are safe. This is the grand theme of this jubilant chapter.

It is God who justifieth, Θεὸς ὁ δικαιῶν. Editors and commentators are about equally divided on the question whether this and the following clauses should be taken interrogatively or affirmatively. If the former, the idea is, that as God is the being against whom we have sinned, and who alone has the administration of justice in his hands, if he does not accuse there can be no accuser. Who shall lay any thing against the elect of God? Shall God, who justifies them? In favour of this view is the fact, that the questions in ver. 32, and also in ver. 35, are answered by questions, and hence the questions in vers. 33, 34, are most naturally so answered. Nevertheless, the impossibility of any accusation being sustained against the elect of God, is better expressed by the affirmation. It is God who is their justifier. If he justifies, who can condemn? Besides, according to the current representation of Scripture, God is the judge, not the accuser. To justify, is to declare the claims of justice satisfied. If God, the supreme judge, makes this declaration, it must be true, and it must stop every mouth. No rational creature, no enlightened conscience, can call for the punishment of those whom God justifies. If justice is not satisfied, there can be no justification, no peace of conscience, no security either for salvation or for the moral government of God. The Bible knows nothing of mere pardon. There can be no pardon except on the ground of satisfaction of justice. It is by declaring a man just, (that is, that justice in relation to him is satisfied,) that he is freed from the penalty of the law, and restored to the favour of God.

Verse 34. *Who is he that condemneth ?* i. e., no one can condemn. In support of this assertion there are, in this verse, four conclusive reasons presented ; the death of Christ, his resurrection, his exaltation, and his intercession. *It is Christ that died.* By his death, as an atonement for our sins, all ground of condemnation is removed. The death of Christ could not be a proof that the believer cannot be condemned, unless his death removed the ground of condemnation ; and it could not remove the ground of condemnation, unless it satisfied the demands of justice. His death, therefore, was a satisfaction, and not merely an exhibition of love, or a didactic symbol meant to impress some moral truth. *Yea, rather, that is risen again.* The resurrection of Christ, as the evidence of the sacrifice of his death being accepted, and of the validity of all his claims, is a much more decisive proof of the security of all who trust in him, than his death could be. See on chap. i. 4 : iv. 25 : Acts xvii. 31 ; 1 Cor. xv. 17, &c.

Who is even at the right hand of God, i.e., is associated with God in his universal dominion. Psalm cx. 1, " Sit thou on my right hand," i. e., share my throne ; Eph. i. 20 ; Rev. iii. 21. " As I also overcame and am set down with my Father in his throne." Heb. i. 3, " Who sat down at the right hand of the Majesty on high." From these and other passages in their connection, it is evident that Christ is exalted to universal dominion, all power in heaven and earth is given into his hands. If this is the case, how great the security it affords the believer! He who is engaged to effect his salvation is the Director of all events, and of all worlds.

Who also maketh intercession for us, i.e., who acts as our advocate, pleads our cause before God, presents those considerations which secure for us pardon and the continued supply of the divine grace ; see on ver. 26 ; Heb. vii. 25 ; ix. 24 ; 1 John ii. 1.   Christ, as seated at the right hand of God, and invested with universal dominion, is able to save : his interceding for us is the evidence that he is willing to save—willing not only in the sense of being disposed to, but in the sense of purposing.   He intends to save those who put their trust in him, and therefore in their behalf he presents before God the merit of his mediatorial work, and urges their salvation as the reward promised him in the covenant of redemption.   He is our patron, in the Roman sense of the word, one who undertakes our case ; an advocate, whom the Father heareth always.   How complete, then, the security of those for whom he pleads !* Of course this language is figurative ; the meaning is, that Christ continues since his resurrection and exaltation to secure for his people the benefits of his death, every thing comes from God through him, and for his sake.

Verse 35. *Who shall separate us from the love of Christ ?*   This is the last step in the climax of the apostle's argument ; the very summit of the mount of confidence, whence he looks down on his enemies as powerless, and forward and upward with full assurance of a final and abundant triumph.   No one can accuse, no one can condemn, no one can separate us from the love of Christ.   This last assurance gives permanency to the value of the other two.

The love of Christ is clearly Christ's love towards us, and not ours towards him.   Paul is speaking of the great love of God towards us as manifested in the gift of his Son, and of the love of Christ as exhibited in his dying, rising, and interceding for us.   This love, which is so great, he says is unchangeable.   Besides, the apostle's object in the whole chapter is to console and confirm the confidence of believers.   The interpretation just mentioned is not in accordance with this object.   It is no ground of confidence to assert, or even to feel, that we will never forsake Christ, but it is the strongest ground of assurance to be convinced that his love will never change.   And, moreover, verse 39 requires this interpretation ; for there Paul expresses the same sentiment in language which cannot be misunderstood.   "No creature," he says, "shall be able to separate us from the love of God, which is in Christ Jesus."   This is evidently God's love towards us.   The great difficulty with many Christians is that they cannot persuade themselves that Christ (or God) loves them ; and the reason why they cannot feel confident of the love of God, is, that they know they do not deserve his love, on the contrary, that they are in the highest degree unlovely.   How can the infinitely pure God love those who are defiled with sin, who are proud, selfish, discontented, ungrateful, disobedient ?   This, indeed, is hard to believe.   But it is the very thing we are required to believe, not only as the condition of peace and hope, but as the condition of salvation.   If our hope of God's mercy and love is founded

---

* "Porro hanc intercessionem carnali sensu ne metriamur: Non enim cogitandus est supplex, flexis genibus, manibus expansis Patrem deprecari : sed quia apparet ipse assidue cum morte et resurrectione sua, quae vice sunt aeternae intercessionis, et vivae orationis efficaciam habent, ut Patrem nobis concilient, atque exorabilem reddant, merito dicitur intercedere."—*Calvin.*

on our own goodness or attractiveness, it is a false hope. We must believe that his love is gratuitous, mysterious, without any known or conceivable cause, certainly without the cause of loveliness in its object; that it is, in short, what it is so often declared to be in the Bible, analogous to the love of a parent for his child. A father's or mother's love is independent of the attractiveness of its object, and often in spite of its deformity.

Shall tribulation, or distress, or persecution, &c. This is merely an amplification of the preceding idea. Nothing shall separate us from the love of Christ, neither tribulation, nor distress, nor persecution, &c. That is, whatever we may be called upon to suffer in this life, nothing can deprive us of the love of him who died for us, and who now lives to plead our cause in heaven; and, therefore, these afflictions, and all other difficulties, are enemies we may despise. "Sicut enim nebulae quamvis liquidum solis conspectum obscurent, non tamen ejus fulgore in totum nos privant: sic Deus in rebus adversis per caliginem emittit gratiae suae radios, nequa tentatio desperatione nos obruat: imo fides nostra promissionibus Dei tanquam alis fulta sursum in coelos per media obstacula penetrare debet."—*Calvin.*

VERSE 36. *As it is written, for thy sake we are killed all the day long,* &c. A quotation from Psalm xliv. 22, agreeably to the Septuagint translation. The previous verse of course implied that believers should be exposed to many afflictions, to famine, nakedness, and the sword; this, Paul would say, is in accordance with the experience of ·the pious in all ages. We suffer, as it is recorded of the Old Testament saints, that they suffered.

VERSE 37. *Nay, in all these things we are more than conquerors,* &c. This verse is connected with the 35th. 'So far from these afflictions separating us from the love of Christ, they are more than conquered.' That is, they are not only deprived of all power to do us harm, they minister to our good, they swell the glory of our victory. *Through him that loved us.* The triumph which the apostle looked for was not to be effected by his own strength or perseverance, but by the grace and power of the Redeemer. 1 Cor. xv. 10; Gal. ii. 20; Philip. iv. 13, "I can do all things through Christ which strengtheneth me."

VERSES 38, 39. In these verses the confidence of the apostle is expressed in the strongest language. He heaps words together in the effort to set forth fully the absolute inability of all created things, separately or united, to frustrate the purpose of God, or to turn away his love from those whom he has determined to save.

For I am persuaded, that neither death, nor life, &c. It is somewhat doubtful how far the apostle intended to express distinct ideas by the several words here used. The enumeration is by some considered as expressing the general idea that nothing in the universe can injure believers, the detail being designed merely as amplification. This, however, is not very probable. The former view is to be preferred. *Neither death.* That is, though cut off in this world, their connection with Christ is not thereby destroyed. "They shall never perish, neither shall any pluck them out of my hand," John x. 28. *Nor life,* neither its blandishments nor its trials. "Whether we live, we live unto the Lord, or whether we die, we die unto the Lord. So that living or dying we are the Lord's." Rom. xiv. 8.

Nor angels, nor principalities, nor powers. Principalities and powers are by many understood here to refer to the authorities of this world as distinguished from angels. But to this it may be objected, that Paul frequently uses these terms in connection to designate the different orders of spiritual beings, Eph. i. 21 ; Col. i. 16 ; and secondly, that corresponding terms were in common use among the Jews in this sense. It is probable, from the nature of the passage, that this clause is to be taken generally, without any specific reference to either good or bad angels as such. 'No superhuman power, no angel, however mighty, shall ever be able to separate us from the love of God.' *Neither things present, nor things to come.* Nothing in this life, nor in the future ; no present or future event, &c.

Verse 39. *Nor height, nor depth.* These words have been very variously explained. That interpretation which seems, on the whole, most consistent with scriptural usage and the context, is that which makes the terms equivalent to *heaven* and *earth.* 'Nothing in heaven or earth ;' see Eph. iv. 8, Isa. vii. 11, "Ask it either in the depth or the height above," &c., &c. *Nor any other creature.* Although the preceding enumeration had been so minute, the apostle, as if to prevent despondency having the possibility of a foothold, adds this all-comprehending specification, *no created thing* shall be able to separate us from the love of God. This love of God, which is declared to be thus unchangeable, is extended towards us only on account of our connection with Christ, and therefore the apostle adds, *which is in Christ Jesus our Lord ;* see Eph. i. 6, 2 Tim. i. 9.

DOCTRINE.

1. God chooses certain individuals and predestinates them to eternal life. The ground of this choice is his own sovereign pleasure ; the end to which the elect are predestinated, is conformity to Jesus Christ, both in character and destiny, ver. 29.

2. Those who are thus chosen shall certainly be saved, ver. 30.

3. The only evidence of election is effectual calling, that is, the production of holiness. And the only evidence of the genuineness of this call and the certainty of our perseverance, is a patient continuance in welldoing, vers. 29, 30.

4. The love of God, and not human merit or power, is the proper ground of confidence. This love is infinitely great, as is manifested by the gift of God's own Son; and it is unchangeable, as the apostle strongly asserts, verses 31—39.

5. The gift of Christ is not the result of the mere general love of God to the human family, but also of special love to his own people, ver. 32.

6. Hope of pardon and eternal life should rest on the death, the resurrection, universal dominion, and intercession of the Son of God, ver. 34.

7. Trials and afflictions of every kind have been the portion of the people of God in all ages ; as they cannot destroy the love of Christ towards us, they ought not to shake our love towards him, ver. 35.

8. The whole universe, with all that it contains, as far as it is good, is the friend and ally of the Christian ; as far as it is evil, it is a more than conquered foe, vers. 35—39.

9. The love of God, infinite and unchangeable as it is, is manifested to sinners only through Jesus Christ our Lord, ver. 39.

REMARKS.

1. The plan of redemption, while it leaves no room for despondency, affords no pretence for presumption. Those whom God loves he loves un-

changeably; but it is not on the ground of their peculiar excellence, nor can this love be extended towards those who live in sin, vers. 29—39.

2. As there is a beautiful harmony and necessary connection between the several doctrines of grace, between election, predestination, calling, justification, and glorification, so must there be a like harmony in the character of the Christian. He cannot experience the joy and confidence flowing from his election, without the humility which the consideration of its being gratuitous must produce; nor can he have the peace of one who is justified, without the holiness of one who is called, vers. 29, 30.

3. As Christ is the first born or head among many brethren, all true Christians must love him supremely, and each other as members of the same family. Unless we have this love, we do not belong to this sacred brotherhood, ver. 29.

4. If the love of God is so great and constant, it is a great sin to distrust or doubt it, vers. 30—39.

5. Believers need not be concerned if they are condemned by the world, since God justifies them, vers. 33, 34.

6. If God spared not his own Son, in order to effect our salvation, what sacrifice on our part can be considered great, as a return for such love, or as a means of securing the salvation of others, ver. 32.

7. The true method to drive away despondency, is believing apprehensions of the scriptural grounds of hope, viz., the love of God, the death of Christ, his resurrection, his universal dominion, and his intercession, ver. 34.

8. Though the whole universe were encamped against the solitary Christian, he would still come off more than conqueror, vers. 35—39.

9. Afflictions and trials are not to be fled from or avoided, but overcome, ver. 37.

10. All strength to endure and to conquer comes to us through him that loved us. Without him we can do nothing, ver. 37.

11. How wonderful, how glorious, how secure is the gospel! Those who are in Christ Jesus are as secure as the love of God, the merit, power, and intercession of Christ can make them. They are hedged around with mercy. They are enclosed in the arms of everlasting love. "Now unto Him that is able to keep us from falling, and to present us faultless before the presence of his glory with exceeding joy; to the only wise God our Saviour, be glory and majesty, dominion and power, both now and for ever. Amen!"

CHAPTER IX.

With the eighth chapter, the discussion of the plan of salvation, and of its immediate consequences, was brought to a close. The consideration of the calling of the Gentiles, and the rejection of the Jews, commences with the ninth, and extends to the end of the eleventh. Paul, in the first place, shows that God may consistently reject the Jews, and extend the blessings of the Messiah's reign to the Gentiles, ix. 1—24; and in the second place, that he has already declared that such was his purpose, vers. 25—29.

Agreeably to these prophetic declarations, the apostle announces that the Jews were cast off and the Gentiles called; the former having refused submission to the righteousness of faith, and the latter having been obedient, vers. 30—33. In the tenth chapter, Paul shows the necessity of this rejection of the ancient people of God, and vindicates the propriety of extending the invitation of the gospel to the heathen, in accordance with the predictions of the prophets. In the eleventh, he teaches that this rejection of the Jews was neither total nor final. It was not total, inasmuch as many of the Jews of that generation believed; and it was not final, as the period approached when the great body of that nation should acknowledge Jesus as the Messiah, and be reingrafted into their own olive tree. So that we have in this and the following chapters, 1st. Paul's lamentation over the rejection of the Jews, ix. 1—5. 2d. The proof that God had the right to deal thus with his ancient people, ix. 6—29. 3d. The proof that the guilt of this rejection was on the Jews themselves, ix. 30—33, and x. 1—21. 4th. The consolation which the promises and revealed purposes of God afford in view of this sad event.

CONTENTS.

In entering on the discussion of the question of the rejection of the Jews, and the calling of the Gentiles, the apostle assures his brethren of his love for them, and of his respect for their national privileges, vers. 1—5. That his doctrine on this subject was true, he argues, 1. because it was not inconsistent with the promises of God, who is perfectly sovereign in the distribution of his favours, vers. 6—24. And secondly, because it was distinctly predicted in their own scriptures, vers. 25—29. The conclusion from this reasoning is stated in vers. 20—33. The Jews are rejected for their unbelief, and the Gentiles admitted to the Messiah's kingdom.

ROMANS IX. 1—5.

ANALYSIS.

As the subject about to be discussed was of all others the most painful and offensive to his Jewish brethren, the apostle approaches it with the greatest caution. He solemnly assures them that he was grieved at heart on their account; and that his love for them was ardent and disinterested, verses 1—3. Their peculiar privileges he acknowledged and respected. They were highly distinguished by all the advantages connected with the Old Testament dispensation, and, above all, by the fact that the Messiah was, according to the flesh, a Jew, verses 4, 5.

COMMENTARY.

Verse 1. *I say the truth in Christ, I lie not,* &c. There are three ways in which the words *in Christ,* or *by Christ,* may here be understood. 1. They may be considered as part of the formula of an oath, *I* (swear) *by Christ, I speak the truth.* But in oaths the preposition πρός, and not ἐν, is used. In a few cases, indeed, where a verb of swearing is used, the latter preposition occurs, but not otherwise. In addition to this objection, it may be urged that no instance occurs of Paul's appealing to Christ in the form of an oath. The case which looks most like such an appeal is 1 Tim. v. 21, " I charge thee before God, and the Lord Jesus Christ, and the elect angels," &c. But it is evident from the mention of the angels, that this is not of the nature of an oath. Paul merely wishes to urge Timothy to act as in the presence of God, Christ, and angels. This interpretation, therefore, is not to be approved. 2. The words _in Christ_ may be connected with the pronoun _I._ ' _I in Christ,_' _i.e._, as a Christian, or, ' In the consciousness of my union with Christ, I declare,' &c. So the words are used in a multitude of cases, " You in Christ," " I in Christ," " We in Christ," being equivalent to _you_, _I_, or _we_, _as Christians_, _i.e._, considered as united to Christ. See 1 Cor. i. 30, " Of him are ye in Christ," _i.e._, ' By him ye are Christians, or united to Christ ;' Rom. xvi. 3, 7, 9 ; 1 Cor. iii. 1, and frequently elsewhere. 3. The words may be used adverbially, and be translated _after a Christian manner._ This also is a frequent use of this and analogous phrases. See 1 Cor. vii. 39, " Only in the Lord," _i.e._, only after a religious manner, _in the Lord_ being equivalent with _in a manner becoming_, or _suited to the Lord._ Rom. xvi. 22, " I salute you in the Lord." Philip. ii. 29, " Receive him, therefore, in the Lord ;" Eph. vi. 1 ; Col. iii. 18. The sense of the passage is much the same, whether we adopt the one or the other of the last two modes of explanation. Paul means to say that he speaks in a solemn and religious manner, as a Christian, conscious of his intimate relation to Christ.

I say the truth, and lie not. This mode of assertion, first affirmatively, and then negatively, is common in the Scriptures. " Thou shalt die, and not live," Isaiah xxxviii. 1. " He confessed, and denied not," John i. 20. There is generally something emphatic in this mode of speaking. It was a solemn and formal assertion of his integrity which Paul here designed to make. _My conscience also bearing me witness ;_ συμμαρτυρούσης, my conscience bearing witness with my words. _In the Holy Ghost._ These words are not to be taken as an oath, nor are they to be connected with the subject of οὐ ψεύδομαι, ' _I_, instructed, or influenced by the Holy Ghost, lie not ;" but rather with συμμαρτυρούσης, his conscience bore this testimony guided by the Holy Spirit, _Spiritu Sancto duce et moderatore_, as Beza expresses it.

VERSE 2. _That I have great heaviness_, &c. This it is which Paul so solemnly asserts. He was not an indifferent spectator of the sorrow, temporal and spiritual, which was about to come on his countrymen. All their peculiar national advantages, and the blessings of the Messiah's kingdom which they had wickedly rejected, were to be taken away ; they were, therefore, left without hope, either for this world or the next. The consideration of their condition filled the apostle with great and constant heaviness. The sincerity and strength of this sorrow for them he asserts in the strongest terms in the next verse.

VERSE 3. _For I could wish that myself were accursed from Christ for my brethren_, &c. The word _anathema_ (Attic ἀνάθημα, Hellenistic ἀνάθεμα,) means any thing consecrated to God, τὸ ἀνατιθέμενον τῷ Θεῷ, as Suidas explains it. The Attic form of the word occurs in the New Testament only in Luke xxi. 5. In the Old Testament, the Hebrew word to which it answers occurs very frequently, and probably the root originally meant _to cut off_, _to separate._ Hence, the substantive derived from it, meant _something separated or consecrated._ In usage, however, it was applied only to such things as could not be redeemed,* and which, when possessed of life, were to be put to death. It is evident from the passages quoted in the margin, that the word usually designates a person or thing set apart to destruction on religious grounds; something accursed.

In the New Testament the use of the Greek word is very nearly the same. The only passages in which it occurs, besides the one before us, are the following; Acts xxiii. 14, "We have bound ourselves under a great curse, (we have placed ourselves under an anathema,) that we will eat nothing until we have slain Paul." The meaning of this passage evidently is, 'We have imprecated on ourselves the curse of God, or we have called upon him to consider us as anathema.' 1 Cor. xii. 3, "No man speaking by the Spirit of God calleth Jesus accursed (anathema);" 1 Cor. xvi. 22, "Let him be anathema maranatha;" Gal. i. 8, 9, "Let him be accursed (anathema)." In all these cases it is clear that the word is applied to those who were regarded as deservedly exposed, or devoted to the curse of God. In this sense it was used by the early Christian writers, and from them passed into the use of the church. "Let him be anathema," being the constant formula of pronouncing any one, in the judgment of the church, exposed to the divine malediction.

Among the later Jews, this word, or the corresponding Hebrew term, was used in reference to the second of the three degrees into which they divided excommunication (see Buxtorf's Rabbinical Lexicon.) But no analogous use of the word occurs in the Bible. Such being the meaning of this word in the Scriptures, its application in this case by the apostle admits of various explanations. The most common interpretations of the passage are the following.

As those men or animals pronounced anathema in the Old Testament were to be put to death, many consider the apostle as having that idea in his mind, and meaning nothing more than 'I could wish to die for my brethren,' &c. But the objections to this interpretation are serious. Even in the Old Testament the word expresses something more than the idea of devotion to death. An anathema was a person devoted to death as *accursed;* see the passages quoted above. And in the New Testament this latter idea is always the prominent one.

The connection is also unfavourable to this interpretation. The phrase is, "accursed *from Christ.*" How are the words *from Christ* to be explained? Some say they should be rendered *by Christ.* 'I could wish myself devoted to death by Christ.' But this is an unusual use of the

---

* Levit. xxvii. 28, 29, "No devoted thing that a man shall devote unto the Lord of all that he hath, both of man and beast, and of the field of his possession, shall be sold or redeemed: every devoted thing (חֵרֶם ἀνάθεμα) is most holy unto the Lord. None devoted, which shall be devoted from among men, shall be redeemed, but shall surely be put to death."

Deut. vii. 26, "Neither shalt thou bring an abomination into thy house, lest thou be *a cursed thing* (ἀνάθεμα) like it, but thou shalt utterly detest it, and utterly abhor it; for it is a cursed thing." The sacred writer is here speaking of the images, &c., of the heathen, which were devoted to destruction.

Joshua vi. 17, "And the city shall be (ἀνάθεμα) accursed, even it and all that is therein, to the Lord," &c. Verse 18, "And ye, in any wise keep yourselves from *the accursed thing,* lest ye make yourselves accursed, when ye take of the *accursed thing,* and make the camp of Israel *a curse,* and trouble it."

1 Sam. xv. 21, "And the people took of the spoil, sheep and oxen, the chief *of the things which should have been utterly destroyed,*" &c. In Hebrew, simply הַחֵרֶם, of which the words in italics are a paraphrase.

preposition (ἀπό) which our version correctly renders *from;* and the whole expression is, besides, unusual and unnatural.   Others, therefore, say that the passage should be rendered thus : ' I could wish from Christ, that I might be devoted to death.'   But this, too, is an unusual and forced construction.

Others think that Paul has reference here to the Jewish use of the word, and means only that he would be willing to be cut off from the church, or excommunicated.   In this view the word *Christ* is commonly taken for the *body of Christ,* or the church.   But, in the first place, this is not a scriptural use of the word anathema, and is clearly inapplicable to the other cases in which it is used by the apostle ; and, in the second place, it gives a very inadequate sense.   Excommunication from the church would not be a great evil in the eyes of the Jews.

Others render the verb which, in our version, is translated, ' I could wish,' *I did wish.*   The sense would then be, ' I have great sorrow on account of my brethren, because I can sympathize in their feelings, for I myself once wished to be accursed from Christ on their account.'   But, in the first place, had Paul intended to express this idea, he would have used the aorist, the common tense of narration, and not the imperfect.*   2. It is no objection to the common translation, that the imperfect indicative, instead of some form of the optative, is here used, and that, too, without an optative particle, see Acts xxv. 22.   3. This interpretation does not give a sense pertinent to the apostle's object.   He is not expressing what was his state of mind formerly, but what it was when writing.   It was no proof of his love for his brethren that he once felt as they then did, but the highest imaginable, if the ordinary interpretation be adopted.   4. The language will hardly admit of this interpretation.   No Jew would express his hatred of Christ, and his indifference to the favours which he offered, by saying he wished himself accursed of Christ.   Paul never so wished himself before his conversion, for this supposes that he recognised the power of Christ to inflict on him the imprecated curse, and that his displeasure was regarded as a great evil.

The common interpretation, and that which seems most natural, is, ' I am grieved at heart for my brethren, for I could wish myself accursed from Christ, that is, I could be willing to be regarded and treated as anathema, a thing accursed, for their sakes.†   That this interpretation suits the force and meaning of the words, and is agreeable to the context, must, on all hands, be admitted.   The only objection to it is of a theological kind.   It is said to be inconsistent with the apostle's character to wish that he should be accursed from Christ.   But to this it may be answered, 1. Paul does not say that he did deliberately and actually entertain such a wish.   The expression is evidently hypothetical and conditional, ' I could wish, were the thing allowable, possible, or proper.'   So far from saying he actually desired to be thus separated from Christ, he impliedly says the very reverse. ' I could wish it, were it not wrong ; or, did it not involve my being unholy as well as miserable, but as such is the case, the desire cannot be entertained.'   This is the proper force of the imperfect indicative when thus used ; it implies the presence of a condition which is known to be impossible.   Speaking of the use of the imperfect ἐβουλόμην in Acts xxv. 22, Dr. Alexander says : " Most interpreters, and especially the most exact

---

* That is, ηὐξάμην ποτε instead of ηὐχόμην.—*Noesselt.*

† Sensus est : optabam Judaeorum miseriam in meum caput conferre, et illorum loco esse.   Judaei, fidem repudiantes, erant anathema a Christo.—*Bengel.*

philologists of modern times, explain the Greek verb, like the similar imperfect used by Paul in Rom. ix. 3, as the indirect expression of a present wish, correctly rendered in the English version. The nice distinction in Greek usage, as explained by these authorities, is that the present tense would have represented the result as dependent on the speaker's will (as in Rom. i. 13, 16, 19; 1 Cor. xvi. 7; 1 Tim. ii. 8); the imperfect with the qualifying particle ἄν would have meant, *I could wish* (but I do not); whereas this precise form is expressive of an actual and present wish, but subject to the will of others, ' I could wish, if it were proper, or if you have no objection.'* 2. Even if the words expressed more than they actually do, and the apostle were to be understood as saying that he wished to be cut off from Christ, yet, from the nature of the passage, it could fairly be understood as meaning nothing more than that he was willing to suffer the utmost misery for the sake of his brethren. The difficulty arises from pressing the words too far, making them express definite ideas, instead of strong and indistinct emotions. The general idea is, that he considered himself as nothing, and his happiness as a matter of no moment compared with the salvation of his brethren.† *Brethren according to the flesh.* Paul had two classes of brethren; those who were with him the children of God in Christ; these he calls *brethren in the Lord,* Philip. i. 14, holy brethren, &c. The others were those who belonged to the family of Abraham. These he calls brethren after the flesh, that is, in virtue of natural descent from the same parent. Philemon he addresses as his brother καὶ ἐν σαρκὶ καὶ ἐν Κυρίῳ, *both in the flesh and in the Lord.* The Bible recognises the validity and rightness of all the constitutional principles and impulses of our nature. It therefore approves of parental and filial affection, and, as is plain from this and other passages, of peculiar love for the people of our own race and country.

Verse 4. The object of the apostle in the introduction to this chapter, contained in the first five verses, is to assure the Jews of his love and of his respect for their peculiar privileges. The declaration of his love he had just made; his respect for their advantages is expressed in the enumeration of them contained in this verse. *Who are Israelites, i. e.,* the peculiar people of God. This includes all the privileges which are afterwards mentioned. The word *Israel* means *one who contends with God,* or *a prince with God.* Hosea xii. 3, " He took his brother by the heel in the womb, and by his strength he had power with God." As it was given to Jacob as an expression of God's peculiar favour, Gen. xxxii. 28, its application to his descendants implied that they too were the favourites of God. *To whom pertaineth the adoption.* As Paul is speaking here of the external or natural Israel, the *adoption* or *sonship* which pertained to them, as such, must be external also, and is very different from that which he had spoken of in the preceding chapter. They were the sons of God, *i. e.,* the objects of his peculiar favour, selected from the nations of the earth to be the re-

---

* Buttmann's Larger Grammar, by Professor Robinson, p. 187. Matthiae, sect. 508, 509. And Winer's Grammar, 41, 2, *a,* who thus translates the passage before us: "Vellem ego (si fieri posset): ich wünschte (wenn es nur nicht unmöglich wäre)." Tholuck says: " The indicative of the imperfect expresses exactly the impossibility of that for which one wishes, on which account it is not, properly speaking, really wished at all. The optative admits the possibility of the thing wished for, and the present supposes the certainty of it."

† Utrum privationem duntaxat omnis boni, et destructionem vel annihilationem sui, an etiam perpessionem omnis mali, eamque et in corpore et in anima, et sempiternam, optaret, aut in ipso voti illus paroxysmo intellectui suo observantem habuerit, quis scit, an Paulus ipse interrogatus definiret? Certe illud ego penitus apud illum in pausa erat : tantum alios honoris divini causa, spectabat.—*Bengel.*

cipients of peculiar blessings, and to stand in a peculiar relation to God. Exod. iv. 22, "Thou shalt say unto Pharaoh, Israel is my son, even my first-born;" Deut. xiv. 1, "Ye are the children of the Lord your God;" Jer. xxxi. 9, "I am a father to Israel, and Ephraim is my first-born." As the whole Old Testament economy was a type and shadow of the blessings of the New, so the sonship of the Israelites was an adumbration of the sonship of believers. That of the former was in itself, and as common to all the Jews, only the peculiar relation which they sustained to God as partakers of the blessings of the theocracy. The latter, common to all the true children of God under any dispensation, is that relation in which we stand to God in virtue of regeneration, the indwelling of the Holy Spirit, and adoption into the household of God.

And the glory. These words are variously explained. They may be connected with the preceding, as explanatory of the adoption, or as qualifying it, and the two words be equivalent to *glorious adoption.* But as every other specification in this verse is to be taken separately, so should this be. Others understand it, of the dignity and distinction of the theocratical people. It was their glory to be the people of God. In the Old Testament, however, that symbolical manifestation of the divine presence which filled the tabernacle and rested over the ark, is called *the glory of the Lord.* Exod. xl. 34, "A cloud covered the tent of the congregation; and the glory of the Lord filled the tabernacle;" Exod. xxix. 43, "There will I meet with the children of Israel, and *the tabernacle* shall be sanctified by my glory;" Lev. xvi. 2, "I will appear in the cloud upon the mercy-seat;" 1 Kings viii. 11, "The glory of the Lord had filled the house of the Lord;" 2 Chron. v. 14; Haggai ii. 7; Rev. xv. 8. By the Jews this symbol was called the *Shekinah, i. e.,* the presence of God. Besides this, the manifestation of God's presence in general is called his glory; Isa. vi. 3, "The whole earth is full of his glory," &c. It is probable, therefore, that Paul intended by this word to refer to the fact that God dwelt in a peculiar manner among the Jews, and in various ways manifested his presence, as one of their peculiar privileges.

The covenants. The plural is used because God at various times entered into covenant with the Jews and their forefathers; by which he secured to them innumerable blessings and privileges; see Gal. iii. 16, 17; Eph. ii. 12. *The giving of the law,* (ἡ νομοθεσία) *the legislation.* The word is sometimes used for the *law itself* (see the Lexicons); it may here be taken strictly, *that giving of the law, i. e.,* the solemn and glorious annunciation of the divine will from Mount Sinai. The former is the most probable; because the possession of the law was the grand distinction of the Jews, and one on which they peculiarly relied; see chap. ii. 17. *The service* means the whole ritual, the pompous and impressive religious service of the tabernacle and temple. *The promises* relate, no doubt, specially to the promises of Christ and his kingdom. This was the great inheritance of the nation. This was the constant subject of gratulation and object of hope. See Gal. iii. 16, "Now to Abraham and his seed were the promises made;" ver. 21, "Is the law against the promises of God?" So in other places the word *promises* is used specially for the predictions in reference to the great redemption, Acts xxvi. 6.

VERSE 5. *Whose are the fathers, and of whom, as concerning the flesh, Christ came,* &c. The descent of the Jews from men so highly favoured of God as Abraham, Isaac, and Jacob, was justly regarded as a great distinction. *And of whom.* The *and* here shows that *whom* refers, not to the fathers, but to the Israelites, to whom pertained the adoption, the law, the service, and of whom Christ came. This was the great honour of the Jewish race. For this they were separated as a peculiar people, and preserved amidst all their afflictions. As it was true, however, only in one sense, that Christ was descended from the Israelites, and as there was another view of his person, according to which he was infinitely exalted above them and all other men, the apostle qualifies his declaration by saying *as concerning the flesh.* The word *flesh* is used so often for human nature in its present state, or for *men*, that the phrase *as to the flesh*, in such connections, evidently means *in as far as he was a man*, or *as to his human nature*, chap. i. 3. In like manner, when it is said Christ was manifested or came in the flesh, it means, he came in our nature, 1 Tim. iii. 16 ; 1 John iv. 2, &c.

Who is over all, God blessed for ever. Amen. There is but one interpretation of this important passage which can, with the least regard to the rules of construction, be maintained. The words ὁ ὤν are equivalent here to ὅς ἐστι, as in John i. 18 ; xii. 17 ; 2 Cor. xi. 31. *Over all, i. e.*, over all things, not over all persons. The πάντων is neuter, and not masculine ; see Acts x. 36, 1 Cor. xv. 28. It is supremacy over the universe which is here expressed, and therefore this language precludes the possibility of Θεός being taken in any subordinate sense. In the Greek fathers, ὁ ἐπὶ πάντων Θεός is the constantly recurring designation of the supreme God. So exalted is its import, that some of them used it only in reference to the Father, who, being the first Person in the Trinity, was, they say, alone *as a person*, God over all. It is not the relation of the persons of the Trinity, however, which is here brought into view, but simply the true and supreme divinity of our Lord. Paul evidently declares that Christ, who, he had just said, was, as to his human nature, or as a man, descended from the Israelites, is, in another respect, the supreme God, or God over all, and blessed for ever. That this is the meaning of the passage, is evident from the following arguments : 1. The relative *who* must agree with the nearest antecedent. There is no other subject in the context sufficiently prominent to make a departure from this ordinary rule, in this case, even plausible. "Of whom Christ came, who is," &c. Who is ? Certainly Christ, for he alone is spoken of. 2. The context requires this interpretation, because, as Paul was speaking of Christ, it would be very unnatural thus suddenly to change the subject, and break out into a doxology to God. Frequently as the pious feelings of the apostle led him to use such exclamations of praise, he never does it except when God is the immediate subject of discourse. See chap. i. 25, " Who worship and serve the creature more than the Creator, who is blessed for evermore ;" Gal. i. 5 ; 2 Cor. xi. 31. Besides, it was the very object of the apostle to set forth the great honour to the Jews of having Christ born among them, and this, of course, would lead to his presenting the dignity of the Redeemer in the strongest light. For the greater he was, the greater the honour to those of whose race he came. 3. The antithesis, which is evidently implied between the two clauses of the verse, is in favour of this interpretation. Christ, according to the flesh, was an Israelite, but, according to his higher nature, the supreme God. On any other interpretation there is nothing to answer to the τὸ κατὰ σάρκα. These words are used in distinct reference, and for the sake of the clause *who is over all.* Why not simply say, " of whom Christ came ?" This would have expressed everything, had not the apostle designed to bring into view the divine nature. Having, however, the purpose to exalt Christ, in order to present in the highest form the honour conferred on the Jewish race in giving the Messiah to the world, he limits the first clause. It was only *as to the flesh* that Christ was descended from the patriarchs ; as to his higher nature, he was the supreme God. See the strikingly analogous passage in chap. i. 3, 4, where Christ is said, according to one nature, to be the Son of David, according to the other, the Son of God. 4. No other interpretation is at all consistent with the grammatical construction, or the relative position of the words. One proposed by Erasmus is to place a full stop after the words *Christ came,* and make all the rest of the verse refer to God. The passage would then read thus :—" Of whom, as concerning the flesh, Christ came. God blessed for ever. Amen." But this is not only opposed by the reasons already urged, that such doxologies suppose God to be the immediate subject of discourse, or are preceded by some particle which breaks the connection, and shows plainly what the reference is, &c. ; but, apart from these objections, no such doxology occurs in all the Bible. That is, the uniform expression is, " blessed be God," and never " God be blessed."* The word *blessed* always stands first, and the word *God* after it with the article. Often as such cases occur in the Greek and Hebrew Scriptures, there is, it is believed, no case of the contrary arrangement. In Psalm lxviii. 19 (Septuagint lxvii. 19), the only apparent exception, the first clause is probably not a doxology, but a simple affirmation, as in the old Latin version, *Dominus Deus benedictus est.* In the Hebrew it is, as in all other cases, *Blessed be the Lord,* and so in our version of that Psalm. See also Ps. xxxi. 21 ; lxxii. 18, 19 ; xli. 13 ; lxviii. 35 ; lxxxix. 52 ; Gen. ix. 26, Exod. xviii. 10, and a multitude of other examples. In all these and similar passages, the expression is *blessed be God,* or *blessed be the Lord,* and never *God blessed,* or *Lord blessed.* This being the case, it is altogether incredible that Paul, whose ear must have been perfectly familiar with this constantly recurring formula of praise, should, in this solitary instance, have departed from the established usage. This passage, therefore, cannot be considered as a doxology, or an ascription of praise to God, and rendered *God be blessed,* but must be taken as a declaration, *who is blessed ;* see chap. i. 25, " The Creator, who is blessed for ever." 2 Cor. xi. 31, " The God and Father of our Lord Jesus Christ, who is blessed for evermore." See Matt. xxi. 9 ; Luke i. 68 ; 2 Cor. i. 3 ; Eph. i. 3 ; 1 Pet. i. 3 ; in these and all other cases, where, as here, the copula is omitted, it is εὐλογητὸς ὁ Θεός. Where the relative and verb are used, then it is not an exclamation but an affirmation, as Rom. i. 25 : τὸν κτίσαντα, ὅς ἐστιν εὐλογητὸς εἰς τοὺς αἰῶνας. Ἀμήν. 2 Cor. xi. 31: ὁ Θεὸς καὶ πατήρ—ὁ ὢν εὐλογητὸς εἰς τοὺς αἰῶνας ; and here, Χριστὸς, ὁ ὢν ἐπὶ πάντων Θεὸς, εὐλογητὸς εἰς τοὺς αἰῶνας. Ἀμήν. To separate this passage from the class to which it obviously belongs, and to make it a solitary exception, is to do violence to the text. A second method of pointing the verse, also proposed by Erasmus, and followed by many others, is to place the pause after the word *all.* The verse would then read, " Of whom, as concerning the flesh, Christ came, who is over all. God be blessed for ever." This avoids some of the difficulties specified above, but it is subject to all the others. It breaks unnaturally the connection, and makes a doxology out of a form of expres-

---

* In the Greek version of the Old Testament, the constant form of the doxology is εὐλογητὸς ὁ Θεός, or εὐλογητὸς κύριος ὁ Θεός, never the reverse. And so in Hebrew, always בָּרוּךְ יְהֹוָה

sion which, in the Scriptures, as just stated, is never so used. 5. There is
no reason for thus torturing the text to make it speak a different language
from that commonly ascribed to it; because the sense afforded, according
to the common interpretation, is scriptural, and in perfect accordance with
other declarations of this apostle. Titus i. 3, "According to the commandment of God our Saviour." "Looking for that blessed hope, and the glorious appearing of the great God and (even) our Saviour Jesus Christ,"
Titus ii. 13 ; see Phil. ii. 6 ; Col. ii. 9, &c., &c.

Over all is equivalent to *most high, supreme.* The same words occur in
Eph. iv. 6, "One God, who is above all." This passage, therefore, shows
that Christ is God in the highest sense of the word. *Amen* is a Hebrew
word signifying *true.* It is used as in the New Testament often adverbially
and is rendered *verily ;* or, at the close of a sentence, as expressing desire,
let it be, or merely approbation. It does not, therefore, necessarily imply
that the clause to which it is attached contains a wish. It is used here,
as in Rom. i. 25, for giving a solemn assent to what has been said. "God
who is blessed for ever, Amen." 'To this declaration we say, Amen. It
is true.'

DOCTRINE.

1. The Holy Ghost is ever present with the souls of the people of God.
He enlightens the judgment and guides the conscience, so that the true and
humble Christian often has an assurance of his sincerity, and of the correctness of what he says or does, above what the powers of nature can
bestow, ver. 1.

2. There is no limit to the sacrifice which one man may make
for the benefit of others, except that which his duty to God imposes,
ver. 3.

3. Paul does not teach that we should be willing to be damned for the
glory of God. 1. His very language implies that such a wish would be
improper. For in the ardour of his disinterested affection, he does not
himself entertain or express the wish, but merely says, in effect, that were
it proper or possible, he would be willing to perish for the sake of his
brethren. 2. If it is wrong to *do* evil that good may come, how can it be
right to wish to *be* evil that good may come ? 3. There seems to be a
contradiction involved in the very terms of the wish. Can one love God
so much as to wish to hate him ? Can he be so good as to desire to be
bad ? We must be willing to give up houses and lands, parents and
brethren, and our life also, for Christ and his kingdom, but we are never
required to give up holiness for his sake, for this would be a contradiction.

4. It is, in itself, a great blessing to belong to the external people
of God, and to enjoy all the privileges consequent on this relation,
ver. 4.

5. Jesus Christ is at once man and God over all, blessed for ever.
Paul asserts this doctrine in language too plain to be misunderstood,
ver. 5.

REMARKS.

1. Whatever we say or do, should be said or done as in Christ, *i. e.*, in a Christian manner, ver. 1.

2. If we can view, unmoved, the perishing condition of our fellow-men, or are unwilling to make sacrifices for their benefit, we are very different from Paul, and from Him who wept over Jerusalem, and died for our good upon Mount Calvary, verses 2, 3.

3. Though we may belong to the true Church, and enjoy all its privileges, we may still be cast away. Our external relation to the people of God cannot secure our salvation, ver. 4.

4. A pious parentage is a great distinction and blessing, and should be felt and acknowledged as such, ver. 5.

5. If Jesus Christ has come in the flesh, if he has a nature like our own, how intimate the union between him and his people; how tender the relation; how unspeakable the honour done to human nature in having it thus exalted! If Jesus Christ is God over all, and blessed for ever, how profound should be our reverence, how unreserved our obedience, and how entire and joyful our confidence! ver. 5.

6. These five verses, the introduction to the three following chapters, teach us a lesson which we have before had occasion to notice. Fidelity does not require that we should make the truth as offensive as possible. On the contrary, we are bound to endeavour, as Paul did, to allay all opposing or inimical feelings in the minds of those whom we address, and to allow the truth, unimpeded by the exhibition of any thing offensive on our part, to do its work upon the heart and conscience.

ROMANS IX. 6—24.

ANALYSIS.

The apostle now approaches the subject which he had in view, the rejection of the Jews, and the calling of the Gentiles. That God had determined to cast off his ancient covenant people, as such, and to extend the call of the gospel indiscriminately to all men, is the point which the apostle is about to establish. He does this by showing, in the first place, that God is perfectly free thus to act, vers. 6—24, and in the second, that he had declared in the prophets that such was his intention, verses 25—33.

That God was at liberty to reject the Jews and to call the Gentiles, Paul argues, 1. By showing that the promises which he had made, and by which he had graciously bound himself, were not made to the natural descendants of Abraham as such, but to his spiritual seed. This is plain from the case of Ishmael and Isaac; both were the children of Abraham, yet one was taken and the other left. And also from the case of Esau and Jacob. Though children of the same parents, and born at one birth, yet " Jacob have I loved and Esau have I hated," is the language of God respecting them, vers. 6—13. 2. By showing that God is perfectly sovereign in the distribution of his favours; that he is determined neither by the external relations, nor by the personal character of men, in the selec-

tion of the objects of his mercy. This is proved by the examples just referred to ; by the choice of Isaac instead of Ishmael, and especially by that
of Jacob instead of Esau. In this case the choice was made and announced
before the birth of the children, that it might be seen that it was not
according to works, but according to the sovereign purpose of God, verses
6—13.

Against this doctrine of the divine sovereignty, there are two obvious
objections, which have been urged in every age of the world, and which
the apostle here explicitly states and answers. The first is, that it is unjust
in God thus to choose one, and reject another, at his mere good pleasure,
ver. 14. To this Paul gives two answers : 1. God claims the prerogative
of *sovereign* mercy ; saying, " I will have mercy on whom I will have
mercy," verses 15, 16. 2. He exercises this right, as is evident from the
case of Pharaoh, with regard to whom he says, "For this same purpose
have I raised thee up," verses 17, 18. The second objection is, that
if this doctrine be true, it destroys the responsibility of men, ver. 19.
To this also Paul gives a twofold answer : 1. The very urging of an
objection against a prerogative which God claims in his word, and
exercises in his providence, is an irreverent contending with our
Maker, especially as the right in question necessarily arises out of the relation between men and God as creatures and Creator, verses 20, 21. 2.
There is nothing in the exercise of this sovereignty inconsistent with
either justice or mercy. God only punishes the wicked for their sins,
while he extends undeserved mercy to the objects of his grace. There is no
injustice done to one wicked man in the pardon of another, especially as
there are the highest objects to be accomplished both in the punishment
of the vessels of wrath, and the pardon of the vessels of mercy. God
does nothing more than exercise a right inherent in sovereignty, viz., that
of dispensing pardon at his pleasure, verses 22—24.

COMMENTARY.

Verse 6. It has already been remarked (chap. iii. 3), that it was a
common opinion among the Jews, that the promises of God being made to
Abraham and to his seed, all his natural descendants, sealed, as such, by
the rite of circumcision, would certainly inherit the blessings of the
Messiah's reign. It was enough for them, therefore, to be able to say,
" We have Abraham to our father." This being the case, it was obvious
that it would at once be presented as a fatal objection to the apostle's
doctrine of the rejection of the Jews, that it was inconsistent with the
promises of God. Paul, therefore, without even distinctly announcing
the position which he intended to maintain, removes this preliminary objection. It is indeed peculiarly worthy of remark, as characteristic of the
apostle's tenderness and caution, that he does not at all formally declare
the truth which he labours in this chapter to establish. He does not tell
the Jews at once they were to be cast off; but begins by professing his
affection for them, and his sorrow for their destiny ; thus simply, by implication, informing them that they were not to be admitted to the
Messiah's kingdom. When he has shown that this rejection involved no
failure on the part of God in keeping his promises, and was consistent with
his justice and mercy, he more distinctly announces that, agreeably to the
predictions of their own prophets, they were no longer the peculiar people

of God. The remark, therefore, which Calvin makes on ver. 2, is applicable to the whole introductory part of the chapter. Non caret artificio, quod orationem ita abscidit, nondum exprimens qua de re loquatur ; nondum enim opportunum erat, interitum gentis Judaicae aperte exprimere. In verses 2, 3, in which he professed his sorrow for his brethren, and his readiness to suffer for them, it was, of course, inplied that they were no longer to be the peculiar people of God, heirs of the promises, &c., &c. This, Paul shows, involves no failure on the part of the divine promises. *Not as though the word of God hath taken none effect,* &c. That is, 'I say nothing which implies that the word of God has failed.' The simplest explanation of the words οὐχ οἶον δὲ ὅτι, is, *not as that,* i. e., I say no such thing as that. It is thus an elliptical phrase for οὐ τοῖον δὲ λέγω οἶον ὅτι, *non tale (dico,) quale (hoc est) excidisse etc,* Winer, § 64. 6. Others give οὐχ οἶον δὲ followed by ὅτι, the force of οὐχ οἶον τε followed by an infinitive, viz., *it is not possible.* This, however, is not only contrary to usage, but to the context. Paul does not intend to say that it is impossible the promise should fail, but simply that his doctrine did not conflict with the promise. God had not bound himself never to cast off the Jews ; and therefore what the apostle taught concerning their rejection did not involve the failure of the word of God. Meyer, who generally defends the apostle from the charge of violating Greek usage, assumes that he here confounds two forms of expression, οὐχ οἶον ἐκπέπτωκεν and οὐχ ὅτι ἐκπέπτωκεν. He agrees, however, with the explanation quoted above from Winer. The *word of God* means anything which God has spoken, and here, from the connection, the promise made to Abraham, including the promise of salvation through Jesus Christ. *Hath taken none effect,* literally, *hath fallen,* i. e., failed. "It is easier for heaven and earth to pass, than one tittle of the law to fail," literally, *to fall,* Luke xvi. 17. So this word is used frequently. The reason why the rejection of the Jews involved no failure on the part of the divine promise, is, that the promise was not addressed to the mere natural descendants of Abraham. *For they are not all Israel which are of Israel,* i. e., all the natural descendants of the patriarch are not the true people of God, to whom alone the promises properly belong. The word *Israel* may refer either to Jacob or to the people. 'All descended from the patriarch Jacob called Israel, are not the true people of God ;' or, 'all belonging to the external Israel are not the true Israel ;' *i.e.,* all who are in the (visible) Church do not belong to the true Church. The sense is the same, (but the former explanation is the more natural. In the following verse the apostle distinguishes between the natural and spiritual seed of Abraham, as here he distinguishes between the two classes of the descendants of Israel.

VERSE 7. *Neither because they are the seed of Abraham are they all children.* In this and the following verses the sentiment is confirmed, that natural descent from Abraham does not secure a portion in the promised inheritance. The language of this verse is, from the context, perfectly intelligible. The seed, or natural descendants of Abraham, are not all his children in the true sense of the term ; *i. e.,* like him in faith, and heirs of his promise. So in Gal. iii. 7, Paul says, "They which are of faith, the same are the children of Abraham." This verse is part of the sentence begun in the preceding verse. It presents the same idea in a different form. 'All the descendants of Israel are not the true Israel, neither are all the seed of Abraham his (true, or spiritual) children.' *Children,* viz., of Abraham. Others supply τοῦ Θεοῦ, "the seed of Abraham are not all children of God." This is true, but it is not what the apostle here says. His object is to show that the promises made to the children of Abraham were not made to his natural descendants as such.

But in Isaac shall thy seed be called. As the word rendered *called* sometimes means *to choose*, Isa. xlviii. 12, xlix. 1, the meaning of the phrase may be ' In Isaac shall thy seed be chosen.' 'I will select him as the recipient of the blessings promised to you.' 2. *To be called* is often equivalent to *to be, to be regarded*, as Isa. lxii. 4, "Thou shalt not be called desolate," *i. e.*, thou shalt not be desolate. Hence, in this case, the text may mean, ' In Isaac shall thy seed be,' *i. e.*, he shall be thy seed. Or, **3.** ' *After Isaac* shall thy seed be called,' they shall derive their name from him.' *Shall be named, i. e.*, shall be so regarded and recognised. ' Not all the children of Abraham were made the heirs of his blessings, but Isaac was selected by the sovereign will of God to be the recipient of the promise.' This is the general meaning of the passage ; but here, as before, it may be understood either of the individual Isaac, or of his descendants. ' Isaac shall be to thee for a seed ; " or, ' Through Isaac shall a seed be to thee.' The former is the more consistent with the context, because Paul's immediate object is to show that natural descent from Abraham did not make a man one of his true seed. Ishmael was a son of Abraham as well as Isaac, but the latter only was, in the spiritual sense of the term, his seed. The Greek here answers exactly to the original Hebrew, ' In Isaac a seed shall be called to thee, or for thee.' That is, ' Isaac (not Ishmael) shall be to thee a son and heir.' God therefore is sovereign in the distribution of his favours. As he rejected Ishmael notwithstanding his natural descent from Abraham, so he may reject the Jews, although they also had Abraham as a father.

Verse 8. *That is, they which are the children of the flesh, these are not the children of God.* The simplest view of this verse would seem to be, to regard it as an explanation of the historical argument contained in the preceding verse. 'The Scriptures declare that Isaac, in preference to Ishmael, was selected to be the true seed and heir of Abraham, *that is*, or *this proves*, that it is not the children of the flesh that are regarded as the children of God, &c.' This suits the immediate object of the apostle, which is to show that God, according to his good pleasure, chooses one and rejects another, and that he is not bound to make the children of Abraham, as such, the heirs of his promise. It is very common, however, to consider this passage as analogous to that in Gal. iv. 22—31; and to regard the apostle as unfolding the analogy between the history of Isaac and Ishmael, and that of the spiritual and natural children of Abraham ; Isaac being the symbol of the former, and Ishmael of the latter. As Ishmael, " who was born after the flesh, (Gal. iv. 23,) *i. e.*, according to the ordinary course of nature, was rejected, so also are the children of the flesh ; and as Isaac, who was born " by promise," *i. e.*, in virtue of the promised interference of God, was made the heir, so also are they heirs, who in like manner are the children of the promise, that is, who are the children of God, not by their natural birth, but by his special and effectual grace. The point of comparison, then, between Isaac and believers is, that both are born, or become the children of God, not in virtue of ordinary birth, but in virtue of the special interposition of God. In favour of this view is certainly the strikingly analogous passage referred to in Galatians, and also the purport of the next verse. Besides this, if Paul meant to say nothing more in this and the following verse, than that it appears from the choice

of Isaac that God is free to select one from among the descendants of
Abraham and to reject another, these verses would differ too little from
what he had already said in vers. 6, 7. It is best, therefore, to consider
this passage as designed to point out an instructive analogy between the
case of Isaac and the true children of God ; he was born in virtue of a
special divine interposition, so now, those who are the real children of God,
are born not after the flesh, but by his special grace.

The children of the promise. This expression admits of various explanations. 1. Many take it as meaning merely *the promised children*, as
child of promise is equivalent to *child which is promised*. But this evidently does not suit the application of the phrase to believers as made here,
and in Gal. iv. 28. 2. It may mean, according to a common force of the
genitive, *children in virtue of a promise*. This suits the context exactly.
It assigns to the genitive ἐπαγγελίας in this clause the same force that
σαρκός has in the preceding. Isaac was not born after the ordinary course
of nature, but in virtue of a divine promise. See Gal. iv. 23, where the
expressions *born after the flesh*, and *born by promise*, are opposed to each
other. It is, of course, implied in the phrase *children in virtue of a promise*, that it is by a special interposition that they become children, and
this is the sense in which Paul applies the expression to believers generally. In Gal. iv. 28, he says, " We, as Isaac was, are the children of promise." Believers, therefore, are children of the promise in the same sense
as Isaac. The birth of Isaac was κατὰ πνεῦμα *supernatural ;* believers also
are the children of God in virtue of a spiritual or supernatural birth. This
is the main idea, although not the full meaning. The children of promise
are those to whom the promise belongs. This is what the apostle has specially in view in the passage in Galatians. He there desires to show that
believers are the true children of Abraham, and heirs of the promise made
to the father of the faithful. This idea, therefore, is not to be excluded
even here. Isaac was not only born in virtue of a promise, but was, on
that account, heir of the promised blessing. The former, however, as just
stated, is the prominent idea, as appears from the following verse. Comp.
John i. 13. " Who are born not of blood, nor of the will of the flesh, nor
of the will of man, but of God." This idea seems to be included in the
apostle's use of the expression. Gal. iv. 28, " Now we, brethren, as Isaac
was, are the children of promise," and iii. 29, " Ye are Abraham's seed, and
heirs according to the promise ; " see, too, Gal. iii. 18, 22 ; Rom. iv. 16,
" To the end the promise might be sure to all the seed." Though this
idea seems to have been in the apostle's mind, the second explanation is
most in accordance with the context. *Are counted for the seed, i. e.,* are
regarded and treated as such. " Not the natural descendants of Abraham
are the children of God, but those who are born again by his special interposition, are regarded and treated as his true children." See the same form
of expression in Gen. xxxi. 15.

VERSE 9. *For this is the word of promise, at this time will I come, and
Sarah shall have a son.* Literally, (the word of) *the promise is this word.*
This verse is evidently designed to show the propriety, and to explain the
force of the phrase, *children of the promise.* Isaac was so called because
God said *at this time I will come*, &c. This is not only a prediction and
promise that Isaac should be born, but also a declaration that it should be
in consequence of God's coming, *i.e.*, of the special manifestation of his
power ; as, in scriptural language, God is said to come, wherever he specially manifests his presence or power, John xiv. 23 ; Luke i. 68, &c. The

apostle does not follow exactly the Hebrew or the Septuagint. He gives the substance of Gen. xviii. 10 ; and xviii. 14. The words כָּעֵת חַיָּה *at the*

living time, either *tempore vivente, i.e., redeunte,* or, the time being, *i.e.,* the current time, are rendered by the LXX. and the apostle, κατὰ τὸν καιρὸν τοῦτον, *at this season.* That is, when this season of the year returns again.

VERSE 10. *And not only* (this); *but when Rebecca had conceived by one,* (even) *by our father Isaac.* Not only does the case of Isaac and Ishmael prove that the choice of God does not depend on natural descent, but on the sovereign will of God, but that of Rebecca evinces the same truth still more clearly. In the former case, it might be supposed that Isaac was chosen because he was the son of Sarah, a free woman, and the legitimate wife of Abraham, whereas Ishmael was the son of a maid-servant. In the choice between Jacob and Esau, there is no room for any such supposition. They had the same father, the same mother, and were born at one birth. Here, assuredly, the choice was sovereign. The original is here elliptical, something must be supplied to complete the sense. On the principle that an ellipsis should, if possible, be supplied from the immediate context, Winer, Meyer, and others, supply the ellipsis thus : ' Not only did Sarah receive a promise of a son, but Rebecca also.' In this view the construction of the passage is regular ; otherwise, an irregularity, or change of grammatical construction, must be assumed in ver. 12. ' Not only Rebecca—it was said to her.' To this however, it is objected, first, that the promise was not made to Sarah, but to Abraham ; and secondly, that no promise was made to Rebecca. Others, therefore, prefer supplying simply, *did this happen.* That is, not only was Isaac chosen instead of Ishmael, although both were the sons of Abraham, but also Rebecca. Then we must either assume a grammatical irregularity, or the nominative (Rebecca) must be taken absolutely ; or we can supply some such phrase as, Rebecca also *proves this, i.e.,* the sovereignty of God in election. These questions do not affect the sense of the passage. The apostle proceeds with his historical proof that God, according to his own good pleasure, does choose one and reject another. He has therefore the right to cast off the Jews.

VERSE 11. *For the* children *being not yet born, neither having done any good or evil,* &c. The force of *for* is clear by a reference to the preceding verse, and the object of the apostle. ' Not only does the case of Isaac and Ishmael evince the sovereignty of God, but that of Rebecca and her children does the same, in a still more striking manner, *for* the decision between her children was made previously to their birth, for the very purpose of showing that it was not made on the ground of works, but of the sovereign pleasure of God.' This is an example which cannot be evaded. With regard to Ishmael, it might be supposed that either the circumstances of his birth, or his personal character, was the ground of his rejection ; but with regard to Esau neither of these suppositions can be made. The circumstances of his birth were identical with those of his favoured brother, and the choice was made before either had done any thing good or evil. The case of Ishmael was, indeed, sufficient to prove that having Abraham for a father was not enough to secure the inheritance of the promise, but it could not prove the entire sovereignty of the act of election on the part of God, as is so fully done by that of Jacob and Esau. This passage shows clearly that the design of the apostle is not simply to show that natural descent from Abraham was a title to Messianic blessings, but that works also were excluded ; that the choice of God was sovereign.

Neither having done good or evil. The design of the introduction of these words is expressly stated in the next clause. It was to show that the ground of choice was not in them, but in God ; and this is the main point in regard to the doctrine of election, whether the choice be to the privileges of the external theocracy, or to the spiritual and eternal blessings of the kingdom of Christ.

That the purpose of God, according to election, might stand. This is the reason why the choice was made prior to birth. The original here admits of various interpretations, which, however, do not materially alter the sense. The word rendered *purpose,* is that which was used in the previous chapter, ver. 28, and means here, as there, *a determination of the will,* and of itself expresses the idea of its being sovereign, *i.e.,* of having its ground in the divine mind and not in its objects. Hence, in 2 Tim. i. 9, it is said, " Who hath called us not according to our works, but according to his own purpose, &c., see Eph. i. 11 ; iii. 11. The words (κατ' ἐκλογήν) *according to election,* are designed to fix more definitely the nature of this purpose. The word *election* often means the act of choice itself, as 1 Thess. i. 4, " Knowing, brethren beloved, your election of God." In this sense, the clause means, ' the purpose of God in reference to election, or in relation to this choice.' This view of the passage is perfectly consistent with the context. The choice was made prior to birth, in order that the true nature of the purpose of God in reference to it might appear. It is objected to this interpretation that the ἐκλογή (election) follows the πρόθεσις (the purpose) and not the reverse. This does not amount to much. It relates merely to the order of conception. We can conceive of God's electing some to eternal life, and then purposing to save them, as well as his purposing to save them and then electing them. The real meaning is expressed by giving κατ' ἐκλογήν an adjective force, *the electing purpose,* electivum Dei propositum, as Bengel renders it. Others give ἐκλογή here the sense of free choice, or free will. ' The purpose according to free choice,' for, ' free or sovereign purpose.' Many commentators adopt this view of the passage. This is, perhaps the most common interpretation. But as the word does not occur in this sense in the New Testament, the former mode of explanation is perhaps to be preferred. *Should stand, i.e.,* should be established and recognised in its true character, that is, that it might be seen it was *not of works, but of him that calleth.* This purpose of God, in reference to election, or the choice itself, is *not of works, i.e.,* does not depend on works, but on *him that calleth.* It is not to be traced to works as its source. That is, as plainly as language can express the idea, the ground of the choice is not in those chosen, but in God who chooses. In the same sense our justification is said to be " not of works," Gal. ii. 16, and often ; *i.e.,* is not on the ground of works ; see Rom. xi. 6 ; 2 Tim. i. 9. The language of the apostle in this verse, and the nature of his argument, are so perfectly plain, that there is little diversity of opinion as to his general meaning. It is almost uniformly admitted that he here teaches that the election spoken of is perfectly sovereign, that the ground on which the choice is made is not in men, but in God. Commentators of every class unite in admitting that the apostle does here teach the sovereignty of God in election. Unde sensus totius loci sic constituitur ; ut appareret, quicquid Deus decernit, libere eum decernere non propter hominis meritum, sed pro sua decernentis voluntate.—*Koppe.* Ut benevola Dei voluntas

maneret, ut quae non a meritis cujus quam pendeat, sed benefactore ipso.—
Noesselt. Das der Rathschluss Gottes fest stehe, als ein solcher, der nicht
abhange von menschlichen Verdiensten, sondern von dem gnädigen oder
freien Willen Gottes. 'That the decree of God might stand firm, as one
which depended not on human merit, but the gracious or free will of God.'—
Flatt. And even Tholuck makes Paul argue thus, " Dass wie Gott, ohne
Anrechte anzuerkennen, die äussere Theokratie und mancherlei Vortheile
übertrug wem er wollte, er so auch jetzt die innere dem überträgt, oder
den darein eingehen lässt welchen er will." 'That as God, without recog-
nising any claims, committed the external theocracy and manifold advantages to whom he pleased, so also now he commits the internal to whom
he will, or allows whom he will to enter it.' To the same effect Meyer
says, " Er wollte nämlich dadurch für immer festsetzen, dass sein zufolge
einer Auswahl unter den Menschen eintretender Beschluss, mit den Mes-
sianischen Heile zu beglücken, unabhängig sei von menschlichen Leistun-
gen, und nur von seinem, des zum Messiasheil Berufenden, eigenen Willen
dependire." *His design was to establish, once for all,* (the principle) *that
his purpose in reference to the choice of those who were to enter the Messiah's kingdom, was independent of human conduct, and was determined by
the will of him who calls.*

The opposers of the doctrine of personal election endeavour to escape
the force of this passage, by saying that the choice of which the apostle
speaks, is not to eternal life, but to the external advantages of the theocracy ; and that it was not so much individuals as nations or communities
which were chosen or rejected. With regard to this latter objection, it
may be answered, 1. That the language quoted by the apostle from the Old
Testament is there applied to the individuals, Jacob and Esau ; and that
Jacob, as an individual, was chosen in preference to his brother ; and that
Paul's whole argument turns on this very point. 2. That the choice of
nations involves and consists in the choice of individuals; and that the
same objections obviously lie against the choice in the one case as in the
other. With regard to the former objection, that the choice here spoken
of is to the external theocracy and not to eternal life, it may be answered,
1. Admitting this to be the case, how is the difficulty relieved ? Is there
any more objection to God's choosing men to a great than to a small blessing, on the ground of his own good pleasure ? The foundation of the
objection is not the character of the blessings we are chosen to inherit, but
the sovereign nature of the choice. Of course it is not met by making
these blessings either greater or less. 2. A choice to the blessings of the
theocracy, *i. e.*, of a knowledge and worship of the true God, involved, in
a multitude of cases at least, a choice to eternal life ; as a choice to the
means is a choice to the end. And it is only so far as these advantages
were a means to this end, that their value was worth consideration. 3. The
whole design and argument of the apostle show that the objection is destitute of force. The object of the whole epistle is to exhibit the method
of obtaining access to the Messiah's kingdom. The design here is to show
that God is at liberty to choose whom he pleases to be the recipients of the
blessings of this kingdom, and that he was not confined in his choice to
the descendants of Abraham. His argument is derived from the historical
facts recorded in the Old Testament. As God chose Isaac in preference to
Ishmael, and Jacob in preference to Esau, not on the ground of their works,
but of his own good pleasure, so now he chooses whom he will to a participation of the blessings of the kingdom of Christ : these blessings are

pardon, purity, and eternal life," &c., &c.   That such is the apostle's argument and doctrine, becomes, if possible, still more plain, from his refutation of the objections urged against it, which are precisely the objections which have ever been urged against the doctrine of election.

Verse 12.   *It was said to her, the elder shall serve the younger.*   These words are to be connected with the 10th verse, according to our version, in this manner, " Not only *this*, but Rebecca also, when she had conceived, &c., it was said to her, &c."   According to this view, although the construction is irregular, the sense is sufficiently obvious.   As it was said to Rebecca that the elder of her sons should serve the younger, prior to the birth of either, it is evident that the choice between them was not on account of their works.   It has been said that this declaration relates not to Jacob and Esau personally, but to their posterity, 1. Because in Gen. xxv. 23, whence the quotation is made, it is said, " Two nations are within thy womb, and *the one* people shall be stronger than *the other* people ; and the elder shall serve the younger."   2. Because Esau did not personally serve Jacob, although the descendants of the one were subjected to those of the other.   It is no doubt true that the prediction contained in this passage has reference not only to the relative standing of Jacob and Esau as individuals, but also to that of their descendants.   It may even be allowed that the latter was principally intended in the annunciation to Rebecca. But it is too clear to be denied, 1. that this distinction between the two races presupposed and included a distinction between the individuals. Jacob was made the special heir to his father Isaac, obtained as an individual the birth-right and the blessing, and Esau as an individual was cast off.   The one, therefore, was personally preferred to the other.   2. In Paul's application of this event to his argument, the distinction between the two as individuals, was the very thing referred to.   This is plain from the 11th verse, in which he says, " The *children* being not yet born, neither having done any good or evil," &c.   It is, therefore, the nature of the choice between the children that is the point designed to be presented.   As to the objection that Esau never personally served Jacob, it is founded on the mere literal sense of the words.   Esau did acknowledge his inferiority to Jacob, and was in fact postponed to him on various occasions.   The main idea, however, is that Esau forfeited his birthright.   Jacob was preferred to his elder brother, and constituted head of the theocracy.   In a spiritual or religious sense, and therefore in the highest sense, or in reference to the highest interests, Esau was placed below Jacob, as much as Ishmael was below Isaac.   This is the real spirit of the passage.   This prophecy, as is the case with all similar predictions, had various stages of fulfilment.   The relation between the two brothers during life ; the loss of the birthright blessing and promises on the part of Esau; the temporary subjugation of his descendants to the Israelites under David, their final and complete subjection under the Maccabees; and especially their exclusion from the peculiar privileges of the people of God, through all the early periods of their history, are all included.   Compare the prediction of the subjection of Ham to his brethren ; and of Japheth's dwelling in the tents of Shem, Gen. ix. 25—27.

Verse 13.   *As it is written, Jacob have I loved, but Esau have I hated.* These words are quoted from Malachi i. 2, 3, where the prophet is reproving the Jews for their ingratitude.   As a proof of his peculiar favour, God refers to his preference for them from the first, " Was not Esau Jacob's brother, saith the Lord ; yet I loved Jacob, and I hated Esau, &c."   This passage, as well as the one quoted in ver. 12, and just referred to, relates to the descendants of Jacob and Esau, and to the individuals themselves; the favour shown to the posterity of the one, and withheld from that of the other, being founded on the distinction originally made between the two brothers. The meaning therefore is, that God preferred one to the other, or chose one instead of the other. As this is the idea meant to be expressed, it is evident that in this case the word *hate* means *to love less, to regard and treat with less favour.* Thus in Gen. xxix. 33, Leah says, she was hated by her husband; while in a preceding verse, the same idea is expressed by saying, " Jacob loved Rachel more than Leah," Matt. vi. 24; Luke xiv. 26; " If a man come to me and hate not his father and mother," &c." John xii. 25. The quotation from the prophet may be considered either as designed in confirmation of the declaration that the elder should serve the younger; or it may be connected in sense with the close of the 11th, ' God is sovereign in the distribution of his favours, as it is written, Jacob have I loved, and Esau have I hated;' the distinction made between these two individuals being cited as an illustration and confirmation of the apostle's doctrine.

The doctrine of the preceding verses is, that God is perfectly sovereign in the distribution of his favours, that the ground of his selecting one and rejecting another is not their work, but his own good pleasure. To this doctrine there are two plausible objections; first, it is not consistent with the divine justice, ver. 14; second, it is incompatible with human responsibility, ver. 19. To the former the apostle answers, first, God claims distinctly in his word this prerogative, ver. 15 : and secondly, he obviously exercises it, as is seen in the dispensations of his providence, ver. 17. Here again the sense is so plain that commentators of all classes agree in their interpretations. Thus Meyer says, " God does not act unjustly in his sovereign choice; since he claims for himself in the Scriptures the liberty to favour or to harden, whom he will."

Verse 14. *What shall we say then, is there unrighteousness with God ? God forbid.* The apostle, according to his usual manner, proposes the objection to his own doctrine in the form of a question, denies its validity, and immediately subjoins his reason; see Rom. iii. 5; Gal. iii. 21. The obvious objection here presented is, that it is unjust in God, thus, according to his own purpose, to choose one and reject another. This Paul denies, and supports his denial by an appeal, in the first place, to Scripture, and the second, to experience. It will be remarked that these arguments of the apostle are founded on two assumptions. The first is, that the Scriptures are the word of God; and the second, that what God actually does cannot be unrighteous. Consequently any objection which can be shown to militate against either an express declaration of Scripture, or an obvious fact in providence, is fairly answered. And if, as is almost always the case, when it militates against the one, it can be shown to militate against the other, the answer is doubly ratified.

Verse 15. *For God saith to Moses, I will have mercy on whom I will have mercy, and I will have compassion on whom I will have compassion.* The connection and argument are obvious. ' It is not unjust in God to exercise his sovereignty in the distribution of his mercies, *for* he expressly claims the right.' The passage quoted is from the account of the solemn interview of Moses with God. In answer to the prayer of the prophet for his people and for himself, God answered, " I will proclaim my name before thee, and will be gracious to whom I will be gracious, &c." Exodus xxxiii. 19. It is, therefore, a formal declaration of a divine prerogative. The form of expression *I will do what I will*, or *I do what I do*, is here, as in Exod. xvi. 23; 2 Sam. xv. 20, designed to convey the idea that it rests entirely with the agent to act or not, at his pleasure. The ground of decision is in himself. In the connection of this verse with the former, therefore, it is obvious that Paul quotes this declaration to prove that God claims the sovereignty which he had attributed to him. In order to avoid the force of this passage, many deny that it expresses the sentiment of the apostle. They consider this and the following verses as the objections of a Jewish fatalist, a mode of interpretation so obviously inconsistent with the context, and even the proper force of the words, that it is mentioned only to show how hard it is to close the eyes against the doctrine which the apostle so clearly teaches. Gottes Erbarmen und Huld sei lediglich von seinem eigenen unumschränkten Willen abhängig; auf wen einmal sein Erbarmen gerichtet sei, dem werde er's erweisen.—*Meyer.* *God's mercy and favour depend solely on his own sovereign will, he will manifest that mercy towards him to whom it has been once directed.* Tittmann, in his *Synon. in N. T.*, says that the difference between οἰκτείρειν and ἐλεεῖν is, that the former denotes the feeling experienced in view of the sufferings of others, and the latter the desire to relieve them. The difference is very much the same as that between our words *compassion* and *mercy*.

Verse 16. *So, then, it is not of him that willeth, nor of him that runneth,* &c. If the ground of the decision or choice of the objects of mercy be in God, as asserted in ver. 15, then that it is not in man, is a conclusion which flows of course from the previous declarations. The word *it* refers to the result contemplated in the context, viz., the attainment of the divine favour, or more definitely, admission into the Messiah's kingdom. This result, when attained, is to be attributed not to the wishes or efforts of man, but to the mercy of God. That one, therefore, is taken, and another left, that one is introduced into this kingdom and another not, is to be referred to the fact asserted in the preceding verse, that " God will have mercy on whom he will have mercy." This seems plainly to have been the apostle's meaning. It is said, however, that the efforts here declared to be vain are those of the self-righteous ; that Paul intends to say that the Jews, by the works of the law, could not attain the favour of God, &c. But no such sentiment is expressed by the apostle ; it is all supplied by the commentator. The sentiment, moreover, is not only not expressed, but it is in direct contradiction to the language and design of the apostle. He says the ground of choice, or of admission into the kingdom of Christ, is not in us ; this interpretation says it is in us. Paul says it is in God; this interpretation says, it is not in God. It is neither the will nor the efforts of men which determines their admission into Christ's kingdom. It depends on the sovereign will of God. Neque in voluntate nostra, neque in conatu esse situm, ut inter electos censeamur : sed totum id divinae bonitatis, quae nec volentes, nec conantes, ac ne cogitantes quidem ultro assumit.—*Calvin.* This is not an interpretation peculiar to Augustinians. It is, as has been shown, the view of the passage adopted by commentators of every shade of doctrine. Also ist's (nämlich Gottes Erbarmen und Huld zu empfangen) nicht von dem Wollenden noch von dem Laufenden abhängig, sondern von dem barmherzig scienden Gotte.—*Meyer.*

Verse 17. *For the Scripture saith unto Pharaoh,* &c. The connection of this verse is with the 14th, rather than with the one immediately preceding. Paul is still engaged in answering the objection proposed in the

14th verse. There is no injustice with God, because he saith to Moses, 'I will have mercy,' &c. ver. 15, and because the Scripture saith to Pharaoh, for this purpose, &c. ver. 17. His second answer to the objection is, that God, in point of fact, does exercise this sovereignty, as is evident from the case of Pharaoh. Pharaoh was no worse than many other men who have obtained mercy ; yet God, for wise and benevolent reasons, withheld from him the saving influences of his grace, and gave him up to his own wicked heart, so that he became more and more hardened, until he was finally destroyed. God did nothing to Pharaoh beyond his strict deserts. He did not make him wicked; he only forbore to make him good, by the exertion of special and altogether unmerited grace. The reason, therefore, of Pharaoh's being left to perish, while others were saved, was not that he was worse than others, but because God has mercy on whom he will have mercy ; it was because, among the criminals at his bar, he pardons one and not another, as seems good in his sight. He, therefore, who is pardoned, cannot say it was because I was better than others ; while he who is condemned must acknowledge that he receives nothing more than the just recompense of his sins. In order to establish his doctrine of the divine sovereignty, Paul had cited from Scripture the declaration that God shows mercy to whom he will ; he now cites an example to show that he punishes whom he will.

Even for this same purpose have I raised thee up. This is what God said to Pharaoh, as recorded in Exod. ix. 16. The meaning of the declaration may be variously explained. In the Old Testament, the Hebrew word used in the passage quoted, means literally, *I have caused thee to stand.* This is understood by some as meaning, *I have called thee into existence.* 2. By others, *I have preserved thee.* 3. By others, *I have raised thee up as king.* 4. By others, *I have placed* and *continued thee in thy post.* Either of these interpretations admits of being defended on philological grounds more or less satisfactory. The first is sufficiently suitable to the word used by the apostle, but does not agree so well with the original. The Hebrew word עָמַד, in Hiphil, is used not only in the literal sense, *to cause to stand,* but also in the sense, *to continue, to preserve,* as in 1 Kings xv. 4, and also *to appoint* (to office). The LXX. (changing the person) have, in Exod. ix. 16, διετηρήθης, equivalent to vivus servatus es, *thou hast been kept alive.* Paul renders the Hebrew ἐξήγειρά σε, which answers to the use of the word in Nehem. vi. 7, "Thou hast appointed (caused to appear) prophets ; and Dan. xi. 11, " The king of the south shall set forth a great multitude." In no case, however, is the Hebrew word used for calling into existence in the sense of creating. For the second, it may be urged that verbs in the form (Hiphil) used in the passage quoted, signify frequently the continuance of a thing in the state which the simple form of the verb expresses. Thus the verb meaning *to live,* in this form, signifies *to preserve alive,* Gen. vi. 19, 20, xix. 19, &c. Besides, the particular word used in Exod. ix. 16, signifies *to preserve, to cause to continue,* in 1 Kings xv. 4; 2 Chron. ix. 8 ; Prov. xxix. 4, &c. The third interpretation is too definite, and supplies an idea not in the text. The fourth, which is only a modification of the second, is perhaps the nearest to the apostle's intention. 'For this purpose have I raised thee up, and placed thee where thou art; and instead of cutting thee off at once, have so long endured thy obstinacy and wickedness.' It is not the design of Pharaoh's creation that is here asserted ; but the end for which God determined his appearance and position in the history of the world.   Nor does the apostle refer Pharaoh's wickedness to God as its author, but his appearance at that period, the form in which the evil of his heart developed itself, and the circumstances attending its manifestation, were all determined by the providence of God, and ordered for the promotion of his infinitely wise and benevolent purposes.

That I might show my power in thee, and that my name might be declared in all the earth.   This is the reason why God dealt with Pharaoh in the manner described.   It was not that he was worse than others, but that God might be glorified.   This is precisely the principle on which all punishment is inflicted.   It is that the true character of the divine lawgiver should be known.   This is of all objects, when God is concerned, the highest and most important ; in itself the most worthy, and in its results the most beneficent.   The ground, therefore, on which Pharaoh was made an object of the divine justice, or the reason why the law was in his case allowed to take its course, is not to be sought in any peculiarity of his character or conduct in comparison with those of others, but in the sovereign pleasure of God.   This result of the argument Paul formally states in the next verse.

Verse 18.   *Therefore hath he mercy on whom he will have mercy, and whom he will he hardeneth.*   This is the conclusion, not merely from the preceding verse, but from the whole passage, vers. 14—17.   This perfect sovereignty in the selection of the objects of his mercy and of his judgment, Paul had attributed to God in ver. 11, and, in the subsequent verses, had proved that he claims and exercises it, both in reference to the recipients of his favour, ver. 15, and the objects of his wrath, ver. 15.   The doctrine, therefore, is fully established.

The latter clause of this verse, *whom he will he hardeneth*, admits of various explanations.   The word may be taken either in its ordinary meaning, or it may be understood in its secondary sense.   According to the latter view, it means *to treat harshly, to punish.*   This interpretation, it must be admitted, is peculiarly suited to the context, ' He hath mercy on whom he will, and he punishes whom he will.'   Nor is it entirely destitute of philological support.   In Job xxxix. 16, it is said of the ostrich, " she treateth hardly her young."   But, on the other hand, it is liable to serious objections.   1. It is certain that it is a very unusual sense of the word, and opposed to the meaning in which it frequently occurs.   There should be very strong reasons for departing from the usual meaning of an expression so common in the Scriptures.   2. It is inconsistent with those passages in the Old Testament which speak of the hardening of Pharaoh's heart.   3. It removes no difficulty ; for what, according to the usual sense of the word, is here said, is frequently said elsewhere.

1. The common sense of the word is, therefore, doubtless, to be preferred, *whom he will he hardens.*   This is by many understood to express a direct and positive influence of God on the soul in rendering it obdurate,   But, in the first place, this interpretation is by no means necessary, as will presently be shown ; and, in the second, it can hardly be reconciled with our ideas of the divine character.

2. Others think that this phrase is to be explained by a reference to that scriptural usage, according to which God is said to do whatever indirectly and incidentally results from his agency ; on the same principle that a father is said to ruin his children, or a master his servants, or that Christ is said to produce wars and divisions.   Thus, Isa. vi. 10, the prophet is commanded to make the heart of the people fat, and their ears heavy,

and shut their eyes, &c., as though to him were to be ascribed the incidental effects of his preaching. In the same way the gospel is the cause of death (not of misery only, but of insensibility also,) to those who hear and disregard it.

3. Nearly allied to this mode of explanation is that which rests on the assumption that God is said to do what he permits to be done. Reference is made to such passages as the following. 2 Sam. xii. 11, " I will give thy wives unto thy neighbour," *i. e.*, I will permit him to take them. 2 Sam. xvi. 10, " The Lord hath said unto him, curse David." Isa. lxiii. 17, " O Lord, why hast thou caused us to err from thy ways, and hardened our heart from thy fear." Deut. ii. 30, " For the Lord thy God hardened his spirit (Sihon's,) that he might deliver him into thy hand." 1 Kings xi. 23, " The Lord stirred up another adversary." Ps. cv. 25, " He turned their heart to hate his people." In 2 Sam. xxiv. 1, God is said to have moved David to number the people ; but in 1 Chron. xxi. 1, Satan is said to have provoked David to number Israel. From these and similar passages, it is evident that it is a familiar scriptural usage, to ascribe to God effects which he allows in his wisdom to come to pass. Hence, almost everything is, at times, spoken of as if it was produced by divine agency, although, in a multitude of other places, these same results are referred, as in some of the examples cited above, to their immediate authors. According to this mode of representation, God is understood as merely permitting Pharaoh to harden his own heart, as the result is often expressly referred to Pharaoh himself, Exod. viii. 15, 32, &c.

4. But there seems to be more expressed by the language of the text than mere permission, because it is evidently a punitive act that is here intended, and because this view does not suit the other passages in which God is said to give sinners up to the evil of their own hearts, Rom. i. 24, 28. It is probable, therefore, that the judicial abandonment of men " to a reprobate mind," a punitive withdrawing of the influences of his Holy Spirit, and the giving them up to the uncounteracted operation of the hardening or perverting influences by which they are surrounded, are all expressed by the language of the apostle. In this God does no more than what he constantly threatens to do, or which the Scriptures declare he actually does, in the case of those who forsake him ; and nothing more than every righteous parent does in reference to a reprobate son. This, in connection with the principle referred to above, (in No. 2,) seems as much as can fairly be considered as included in the expressions. De Wette here wisely says, that we are to exclude, on the one hand, the idea that God merely permits evil, and on the other, that he is its author, and to hold fast the doctrine, that evil is from man, and that God orders and directs it, and that to punishment. It is to be remembered that the hardening of the sinner's heart is itself punitive. It supposes evil, and is its punishment. As a ruined constitution is at once the inevitable consequence and the punishment of intemperance, so insensibility, obduracy of conscience, and blindness of mind, are the penal consequences of a course of sin, and become themselves the just ground of further punishment, because they are in their own nature evil. This we instinctively recognise as true in our moral judgments of men. A man whom a long course of crime has rendered perfectly callous, is, on account of his callousness, justly the object of execration and abhorrence. It is therefore not only a doctrine of Scripture (Rom. i. 24) that sin is the punishment of sin, but a fact of experience. Satis est, says Augustine, (Ad Sixtum Ep.,) interim Chris-

tiano ex fide adhuc viventi, et nondum cernenti quod perfectum est, sed ex parte scienti, nosse vel credere quod neminem Deus liberet nisi gratuita misericordia per Dominum nostrum Jesus Christum, et neminem damnet nisi aequissima veritate per eundem Dominum nostrum Jesum Christum. Cur autem illum potius quam illum liberet aut non liberet, scrutetur qui potest judiciorum ejus tam magnum profundum—verumtamen caveat præcipitium.   The Lutheran Church, after the days of Luther, endeavoured to find a middle ground between the Augustinian and the semi-Pelagian doctrine.   In the Form of Concord it is taught that the choice of the vessels of mercy is to be referred to the good pleasure of God, but the passing by of the non-elect is to be referred to their voluntary resistance of his offered grace.   Election is founded, according to this view, on the sovereignty of God, but preterition on the foresight of impenitence.   This, however, seems to involve a contradiction ; for if faith be the gift of God, the purpose to give it only to some, involves the purpose not to give it to others.   Besides, it is the very object of the apostle in the whole context to teach the sovereignty of God in dealing with the vessels of wrath.   This Olshausen admits.   " This reference," he says, " to the foreknowledge of God, although not unfounded so far as evil is concerned, tends rather to pervert than to elucidate the passage, inasmuch as the precise object of the apostle is to render prominent the sovereignty of the divine will."

Verse 19.   *Thou wilt then say unto me, why doth he yet find fault ? for who hath resisted his will ?*   This is the second leading objection to the apostle's doctrine.   If it be true, as he had just taught, that the destiny of men is in the hands of God, if it is not of him who willeth, or of him that runneth, but of God that showeth mercy, what can we do ?   If the fact that one believes and is saved, and another remains impenitent and is lost, depends on God, how can we be blamed ?   Can we resist his will ? It will at once be perceived that this plausible and formidable objection to the apostle's doctrine is precisely the one which is commonly and confidently urged against the doctrine of election.   There would be no room either for this objection, or for that contained in the 14th verse, if Paul had merely said that God chooses those whom he foresees would repent and believe ; or that the ground of distinction was in the different conduct of men.   It is very evident, therefore, that he taught no such doctrine. How easy and obvious an answer to the charge of injustice would it have been to say, God chooses one and rejects another according to their works. But teaching as he does the sovereignty of God in the selection of the subjects of his grace and of the objects of his wrath, declaring as he does so plainly, that the destiny of men is determined by his sovereign pleasure, the objection (how can he yet find fault ?) is plausible and natural.   To this objection the apostle gives two answers ; 1. That it springs from ignorance of the true relation between God and men as Creator and creatures, and of the nature and extent of the divine authority over us, vers. 20, 21 ; 2. That there is nothing in his doctrine inconsistent with the divine perfections ; since he does not make men wicked, but from the mass of wicked men, he pardons one and punishes another, for the wisest and most benevolent reasons, vers. 22, 23.

Why doth he yet find fault ?   If God hardens us, why does he blame us for being hard.   Gross as is this perversion of the apostle's doctrine on the part of the objector, Paul at first rebukes the spirit in which it is made, before he shows it to be unfounded.   It is not the doctrine of the Bible, that God first makes men wicked, and then punishes them for their wickedness. The Scriptures only assert, what we see and know to be true, that God permits men, in the exercise of their own free agency, to sin, and then punishes them for their sins, and in proportion to their guilt. He acts towards them as a perfectly righteous judge, so that no one can justly complain of his dealings. This strictness in the administration of justice, is, however, perfectly consistent with the sovereignty of God in determining whom he will save, and whom he will permit to suffer the just recompense of their deeds. *Who hath resisted*, rather, *who resists, i.e.*, who can resist. The perfect ἀνθέστηκε (as ἕστηκεν) is present ; see xiii. 2. *His will, i.e.*, his purpose, βούλημα.

VERSE 20. *Nay, but, O man, who art thou that repliest against God ? Shall the thing formed*, &c. In these words we have both a reproof and an answer. The reproof is directed against the irreverent spirit, whence such cavils always arise. After the clear proof given in the preceding verses, that God claims this sovereignty in his word, and exercises it in his providence, it argues great want of reverence for God, to assert that this claim involves the grossest injustice. It is very common with the sacred writers, and with Christ himself, when questions or cavils are presented, to direct their answers more to the feeling which the question indicated, than to the question itself. Tholuck refers, in illustration of this remark, to John iii. 3 ; Matt. viii. 19, 20, 22 ; xix. 16 ; xxii. 29. But in this case, besides this reproof of presumption in attempting to call our Maker to account, instead of considering that the mere fact that God claims any thing as his right, is evidence enough that it is just, there is a direct answer to the difficulty. The objection is founded on ignorance or misapprehension of the true relation between God and his sinful creatures. It supposes that he is under obligation to extend his grace to all. Whereas he is under obligation to none. All are sinners, and have forfeited every claim to his mercy ; it is, therefore, the prerogative of God to spare one and not another ; to make one vessel to honour, and another to dishonour. He, as their sovereign Creator, has the same right over them that a potter has over the clay. It is to be borne in mind, that Paul does not here speak of the right of God over his creatures as creatures, but as sinful creatures, as he himself clearly intimates in the next verses. It is the cavil of a sinful creature against his Creator, that he is answering ; and he does it by showing that God is under no obligation to give his grace to any, but is as sovereign as the potter in fashioning the clay. *Nay, but, O man*, μενοῦνγε. This particle is often used in replies, and is partly concessive and partly corrective, as in Luke xi. 28, where it is rendered, *yea, rather*, in Rom. x. 18, *yes, verily*. It may here, as elsewhere, have an ironical force. Sometimes it is strongly affirmative, as in Phil. iii. 8, and at others, introduces, as here, a strong negation or repudiation of what had been said.

Shall the thing formed say to him that formed it, Why hast thou made me thus ? See Isaiah xlv. 9. In this clause Paul presents mainly the idea of God's right, and in the subsequent verses he shows that nothing unjust is included in the right here claimed. We are at his mercy ; and it is the height of irreverence and folly for us to call him to account for the manner in which he may see fit to dispose of us.

VERSE 21. *Hath not the potter power over the clay, out of the same lump to make one vessel*, &c., &c. The word ἐξουσία rendered *power*, means also *authority* and *right*. In this case it means, *the lawful power* or *right;* he not only can do it, but he has a perfect right to do it ; see the use of the Greek word in Matt. xxi. 23 ; 1 Cor. viii. 9, and frequently elsewhere.

This verse is merely an illustration of the idea contained in the last clause of the preceding. The Creator has a perfect right to dispose of his creatures as he sees fit. From the very idea of a creature, it can have no claim on the Creator; whether it exists at all, or how, or where, from the nature of the case, must depend on him, and be at his sovereign disposal. The illustration of this truth which follows, is peculiarly appropriate. When the potter takes a piece of clay into his hands, and approaches the wheel, how entirely does it rest with himself to determine the form that clay shall take, and the use to which it shall be destined? Can any thing be more unreasonable, than that the clay, supposing it endued with intelligence, should complain that the form given it was not so comely, or the use to which it was destined not so honourable, as those which fell to the lot of a different portion of the same mass? Are not these points on which the potter has a most perfect right to decide for himself, and regarding which the thing formed can have no right to complain or question? And so it is with God; the mass of fallen men are in his hands, and it is his right to dispose of them at pleasure; to make all vessels unto honour, or all unto dishonour, or some to one and some to the other. These are points on which, from the nature of the relation, we have no right to question or complain. The illustration here employed occurs elsewhere in Scripture, as in Isa. lxiv. 8, "But now, O Lord, thou art our Father; we are the clay, and thou art our Potter; and we all are the work of thy hands." See also Isa. xxix. 16, and Jer. xviii. 3—6, "Then I went down to the potter's house, and, behold, he wrought a work on the wheels. And the vessel which he made of clay was marred in the hands of the potter; so he made it again another vessel, as seemed good to the potter to make it. O house of Israel, cannot I do with you as this potter? saith the Lord. Behold, as clay is in the potter's hand, so are ye in my hand, O house of Israel." In the sovereignty here asserted, it is God as moral governor, and not God as creator, who is brought to view. It is not the right of God to create sinful beings in order to punish them, but his right to deal with sinful beings according to his good pleasure, that is here, and elsewhere asserted. He pardons or punishes as he sees fit.

Verse 22, 23. *But what if God, willing to show his wrath, and to make his power known, endured with much long-suffering the vessels of wrath fitted to destruction; and that he might make known the riches of his glory on the vessels of mercy, which he had afore prepared unto glory, even us,* &c.? These verses contain Paul's second answer to the difficulty presented in the 19th verse. He had shown in vers. 20, 21, that in virtue of his relation to men as his sinful creatures, God is at perfect liberty to dispose of them at his pleasure, pardoning one and punishing another, as seemeth good in his sight. He now shows that in the exercise of this right there is nothing unreasonable or unjust, nothing of which his creatures have the least right to complain. The punishment of the wicked is not an arbitrary act, having no object but to make them miserable; it is designed to manifest the displeasure of God against sin, and to make known his true character. On the other hand, the salvation of the righteous is designed to display the riches of his grace. Both in the punishment of the one class and the salvation of the other, most important and benevolent ends are to be answered. And since for these ends it was necessary that some should be punished, while others might be pardoned, as all are equally undeserving, it results from the nature of the case that the decision between the vessels of wrath and the vessels of mercy must be left to God.

The apostle would, moreover, have it remarked, that even in the necessary punishment of the wicked, God does not proceed with any undue severity, but, on the contrary, deals with them with the greatest long-suffering and tenderness. Such seems to be the general purport and object of these difficult verses.

The attentive reader will perceive, that even with the insertion of the word *what*, which has nothing to answer to it in the original, and with a sign of interrogation at the end of ver. 24, the construction of the passage in our version remains ungrammatical and the sense incomplete. As the difficulty exists in the Greek text, and not merely in our translation, the explanations which have been proposed are very numerous. Many of these are presented and canvassed by Tholuck and Wolf, particularly the latter. There are three views taken of the connection, which are the most plausible. 1. The two verses are considered as both referring to the rejection of the wicked, for which ver. 22 assigns one reason, and ver. 23 another. 'What if God, willing to show his wrath, endured with much long-suffering the vessels of wrath, so that also he might make known the riches of his glory on the vessels of mercy,' &c. The treatment of the wicked was not only to display the divine displeasure against sin, but also, by contrast, his mercy towards his people.* But, in order to make the two verses cohere in this way, it is necessary to transpose the words at the beginning of the 23rd verse, and read *that also*, instead of *and that*, which alters the sense materially, while for such a transposition there is no authority. Besides this, it makes ver. 23 too subordinate to ver. 22; that is, it makes God's dealings towards the vessels of mercy merely an incidental topic, instead of having equal prominence with his treatment of the vessels of wrath. From the context we are led to expect a vindication of his course, not only in the destruction of the latter, but in the salvation of the former.

2. A second explanation is to make the second clause of ver. 22 and the beginning of ver. 23 depend on the first words of ver. 22. 'God willing to show his wrath and make his power known, and (willing) that the riches of his glory should be known,' &c. This gives a good sense, though the construction is suddenly, and rather violently, changed at the beginning of ver. 23, "that he might make known," being substituted for the infinitive, "to make known."

3. Tholuck makes ver. 24 parallel with ver. 23, and explains the passage thus, 'God, willing to manifest his wrath, bore with the vessels of wrath ; and that he might make known his mercy, called us,' &c. This gives a very good sense, but assumes the construction to be irregular to a very unusual degree. Though the second method be somewhat irregular, it seems, on the whole, the least objectionable, and gives a sense obviously consistent with the context. The meaning of the apostle is sufficiently plain. He asks a question εἰ δέ, *but if.* 'What can be said if God, to manifest his justice, bears with the vessels of wrath, and to manifest his

* So, among others, Calvin, who translates verse 23 thus, Ut notas quoque faceret divitias gloriae suae in vasa misericordiae, quae praeparavit in gloriam. And in his comment he remarks, Est autem secunda ratio quae gloriam Dei in reproborum interitu manifestat; quod ex eo luculentius divinae bonitatis erga electos amplitudo confirmatur.

Much in the same way Winer explains the passage, connecting the καὶ ἵνα of ver 23, immediately with the verb ἤνεγκεν of ver 22, "Wenn Gott beschliessend mit aller Langmuth die Gefässe seines Zornes trug * * auch in der Absicht, den Reichthum * * zuerkennen zu begen." "If God willing * * * bore with all long-suffering the vessels of wrath * * * also with the view to make known the riches," &c. Gram. p. 443. (6th edition, p. 503).

grace prepares the vessels of mercy?' There is nothing in this inconsistent with the character of God, or the rights of his creatures.

The two objects which Paul here specifies as designed to be answered by the punishment of the wicked, are the manifestation of the *wrath of God*, and the exhibition of his power. The word *wrath* is used here as in chap. i. 18, for the divine displeasure against sin, the calm and holy disapprobation of evil, joined with the determination to punish those who commit it.* The power of God is conspicuously displayed in the destruction of the wicked, no matter how mighty or numerous they may be. Though the inherent ill-desert of sin must ever be regarded as the primary ground of the infliction of punishment, a ground which would remain in full force, were no beneficial results anticipated from the misery of the wicked, yet God has so ordered his government that the evils which sinners incur shall result in the manifestation of his character, and the consequent promotion of the holiness and happiness of his intelligent creatures throughout eternity.

God treats the wicked, not as a severe judge, but with much long-suffering. The expression *vessels of wrath*, no doubt suggests itself from the illustration of the potter used in the preceding verse; though the term *vessel* is used not unfrequently in reference to men, Acts ix. 15; 1 Peter iii. 7. *Vessels of wrath, i.e.*, vessels to receive wrath, or which are destined to be the objects of wrath. This is a modification of the expression in ver. 21, σκεῦος εἰς ἀτιμίαν, *vessel unto dishonour.*

Fitted to destruction, κατηρτισμένα εἰς ἀπώλειαν. This phrase admits of two interpretations. The passive participle may be taken as a verbal adjective, *fit* for destruction. This leaves undetermined the agency by which this fitness was effected. Comp. 2 Cor. x. 10; 1 Peter i. 8. In favour of this view is the change of expression adopted in ver. 23. Of the vessels of wrath, it is simply said that they are fit for destruction; but of the vessels of mercy, that God prepares them for glory. Why this change, if the apostle did not intend to intimate that the agency of God is very different in the one case from what it is in the other? Besides, as it is the object of the writer to vindicate the justice of God in these dispensations, it is specially pertinent to represent the vessels of wrath as fit for destruction in the sense of deserving it. The other interpretation assumes that the reference is to God, and that κατηρτισμένα has its full participial force; *prepared* (by God) *for destruction*. This is adopted not only by the majority of Augustinians, but also by many Lutherans and Neologists. This sense they say is demanded by the context. God is compared to a potter, who prepares one vessel to honour, and another to dishonour. So God prepares some for wrath and some for mercy. This, however, is not to be understood in a supralapsarian sense. God does not create men in order to destroy them. The preparation intended is that illustrated in the case of Pharaoh. God did not make him wicked and obdurate; but as a punishment for his sin, he so dealt with him that the evil of his nature revealed itself in a form, and under circumstances, which made him a fit object of the punitive justice of God. The dealings of God as a sovereign are often, by the Jewish writers, spoken of in the same terms as those here used; see *Moed Katon*, fol. 9, 1. Exiit filia vocis, dixitque eis; vos omnes ordinati estis ad vitam seculi futuri. *Megilla*, fol. 12, 2.

---

* Ira Dei non, perturbatio animi ejus est, sed judicium quo irrogatur poena peccato. August. De Civit. Dei, 1, 15. c. 35.

Memuchan, Esther i. 14, *i.e.*, Haman. Cur vocatur nomen ejus Memucan ? quia ordinatas est ad poenas. *R. Bechai* in Pentateuch, fol. 132. Gentes ordinatae ad gehennam : Israel vero ad vitam. Fol. 220, 4, Duas istas gentes vocat Salomo duas filias, dicitque ad gehennam ordinatas esse. *Bechoroth*, fol. 8, 2. R. Joseph docuit, hi sunt Persae, qui preparati sunt in gehennam. Wetstein on Acts xiii. 48.

VERSE 23. *And that he might make known the riches of his glory*, &c. The grammatical construction of this clause, as before remarked, is doubtful. The ἵνα γνωρίσῃ may depend on ἤνεγκεν, he bore with the vessels of wrath *in order that* he might make known the riches of his glory on the vessels of mercy ; or, they may be connected with κατηρτισμένα, vessels prepared for destruction, *in order that* he might make known, &c. Or, we must assume that ἵνα γνωρίσῃ is used for the infinitive, and that this clause is coördinate with the preceding. 'What if God, to manifest his wrath, bears with the wicked, and *to make* known his mercy, prepares others for glory.' *The vessels of mercy, i.e.*, those destined to mercy. The riches of, *i. e.*, the abundance or greatness of *his glory*. The glory refers to the divine majesty or excellence which is glorious, that is, the proper object of admiration. It may be used of the divine perfections in general, or for any of the divine attributes in particular, for his power, as Rom. vi. 4, or his mercy, in Eph. iii. 16. Here it should be taken in its comprehensive sense, although from its opposition to the word *wrath*, the reference is specially to the mercy of God. That is the attribute most conspicuously displayed in the salvation of sinners.

Which he had afore prepared, προητοίμασεν. This word is used both in the sense of preparing beforehand, and of predestinating. Many prefer the latter sense here ; *whom* he had predestined to glory. Comp. Eph. ii. 10. But the context is in favour of the ordinary meaning of the word. God, as the potter, prepares or fashions the vessels of mercy *unto glory*. The word *glory* here evidently refers to the glorious state of existence for which God is preparing his people, and in hope of which they now rejoice, v. 2.

VERSE 24. *Even us whom he hath called, not of the Jews only, but also of the Gentiles.* We are the vessels of his mercy, even we whom he hath called, *i. e.*, effectually introduced by his Spirit into the kingdom of Christ ; see chap. viii. 28, 30. The use of the masculine relative οὕς, although the antecedent σκεύη ἐλέους is neuter, may be explained as a constructio ad sensum, or better as a case of attraction ; οὕς taking the gender of the following ἡμᾶς. *Winer*, § 63, 1. How naturally does the apostle here return to the main subject of discussion ! How skilfully is the conclusion brought out at which he has continually aimed ! God chose Isaac in preference to Ishmael, Jacob in preference to Esau ; it is a prerogative which he claims and exercises, of selecting from among the guilty family of men, whom he pleases as the objects of his mercy, and leaving whom he pleases to perish in their sins, unrestricted in his choice by the descent or previous conduct of the individuals. He has mercy upon whom he will have mercy. He calls men, therefore, from among the Gentiles and from among the Jews indiscriminately. This is the conclusion at which the apostle aimed. The Gentiles are admitted into the Messiah's kingdom, vers. 25, 26 ; and the great body of the Jews are excluded, ver. 27. This conclusion he confirms by explicit declarations of Scripture. Ex disputatione, quam hactenus de libertate divinæ electionis habuit, duo consequebantur : nempe Dei gratiam non ita inclusam esse in populo Judaico, ut non ad alias quoque

nationes emanare, et in orbem universum effundere se posset : deinde ne
sic quidem alligatam esse Judaeis, ut ad omnes Abrahae filios secundum
carnem sine exceptione perveniat.—*Calvin.*

DOCTRINE.

1. No external circumstance, no descent from pious parents, no connection with the true church, can secure admission for men into the kingdom
of Christ, vers. 6—12.

2. Paul teaches clearly the doctrine of the personal election of men to
eternal life, an election founded not on works, but on the good pleasure of
God.   The choice is *to eternal life*, and not to external privileges merely.
1. Because the very point to be illustrated and established through this
and the two following chapters, is the free admission of men into the
Messiah's kingdom, and its spiritual and eternal blessings.   2. Because
the language of the apostle seems of itself to preclude the other idea, in
vers. 15, 16, and especially in ver. 18, " Therefore he hath mercy on whom
he will, and whom he will he hardeneth."   This is not applicable to the
reception of men to a state of peculiar external privileges or their rejection
from it.   3. The case of Pharaoh is not an illustration of the refusal to
admit some men to peculiar privileges.   4. The choice is between the vessels of mercy and vessels of wrath ; vessels of mercy chosen *unto glory,*
not unto church privileges, and vessels of wrath who were to be made the
examples of God's displeasure against sin.   5. The character of the objections to the apostle's doctrine shows that such was the nature of the choice.
If this election is to eternal life, it is, of course, *a choice of individuals,*
and not of communities, because communities, as such, do not inherit eternal life.   This is still further proved by the cases of Isaac and Ishmael, and
Jacob and Esau, between whom, as individuals, the choice was made.
From the illustration derived from the case of Pharaoh.   From the objections presented in vers. 14, 19.   From the answer to these objections in
vers. 15, 16, 20, 23, especially from the passage just referred to, which
speaks of the vessels of mercy prepared unto glory; which cannot be
applied to nations or communities.   *This election is sovereign, i. e.,* is
founded on the good pleasure of God, and not on any thing in its objects.
1. Because this is expressly asserted.   The choice betwen Jacob and Esau
was made prior to birth, that it might be seen that it was not founded on
works, but on the good pleasure of God, ver. 11.   The same is clearly
stated in ver. 16, " It is not of him that willeth or of him that runneth,
but of God that showeth mercy ;" and also in ver. 18, " Therefore he hath
mercy on whom he will, &c."   The decision rests with God.   2. Because
otherwise there would be no shadow of objection to the doctrine.   How
could men say it was unjust if God chose one and rejected another according to their works ?   And how could any one object, as in ver. 19, ' that
as the will of God could not be resisted, men were not to be blamed,' if
the decision in question did not depend on the sovereign will of God ?
How easy for the apostle to have answered the objector, ' You are mis-
taken, the choice is not of God ; he does not choose whom he will, but
those who he sees will choose him.   It is not his will, but man's that de-
cides the point.'   Paul does not thus answer.   He vindicates the doctrine
of the divine sovereignty.   The fact, therefore, that Paul had to answer
the same objections which are now constantly urged against the doctrine

of election, goes far to show that that doctrine was his. 3. That the election is sovereign, is taught elsewhere in Scripture. In 2 Tim. i. 9, it is said to be " not according to our works, but according to his own purpose and grace." Eph. i. 5, it is said to be "according to the good pleasure of his will," *i. e.*, his sovereign pleasure. 4. This view alone harmonises with the doctrine, that all good thoughts and right purposes and feelings proceed from God, which is clearly taught in the Scriptures. For if the purpose not to resist ' common grace,' is a right purpose, it is of God, and, of course, it is of him that one man forms it, and another does not. 5. This doctrine is alone consistent with Christian experience. "Why was I made to hear thy voice ?" No Christian answers this question by saying, because I was better than others.

3. The two leading objections against the doctrine of election, viz., that it is inconsistent with the divine character, and incompatible with human responsibility, are answered by the apostle. It cannot be unjust, because God claims and exercises the right of sovereign choice. It is not inconsistent with human responsibility, because God does not make men wicked. Though, as their Sovereign, he has a right to dispose of wicked men as he pleases. He can, of the same corrupt mass, choose one to honour, and the other to dishonour, vers. 14—23.

4. Scripture must ever be consistent with itself. The rejection of the Jews could not be inconsistent with any of God's promises, ver. 6.

5. The true children of God become such in virtue of a divine promise, or by the special exercise of his grace. They are born not of the will of the flesh, but of God, ver. 8.

6. Though children prior to birth do neither good nor evil, yet they may be naturally depraved. They neither hunger nor thirst, yet hunger and thirst are natural appetites. They exercise neither love nor anger, yet these are natural passions. They know probably neither joy nor sorrow, yet are these natural emotions, ver. 11.

7. The manifestation of the divine perfections is the last and highest end of all things, vers. 17, 22, 23.

8. The fact that the destiny of men is in the hands of God (that it is not of him that willeth, or him that runneth,) is not inconsistent with the necessity of the use of means. The fact that the character of the harvest depends on the sovereign pleasure of God, does not render the labour of the husbandman of no account. The same God who says, "I will have mercy on whom I will," says also, " Work out your salvation with fear and trembling." The sovereignty of God and the necessity of human efforts are both clearly taught in the Scriptures. At times the former, as in this chapter, at times the latter doctrine is most insisted upon. Neither should be forgotten or neglected, as both combine to produce the right impression on the mind, and to lead us to God in the way of his own appointment, ver. 16.

9. Men, considered as the objects of election, are regarded as fallen. It is from the corrupt mass that God chooses one vessel to honour and one to dishonour, vers. 22, 23.

10. The judicial abandonment of men to their own ways, the giving them up to work out their own destruction, is a righteous though dreadful doom, vers. 18, 22, also chap. i. 24, 26.

REMARKS.

1. If descent from Abraham, participation in all the privileges of the theocracy, the true and only church, failed to secure for the Jews the favour of God, how foolish the expectation of those who rely on outward ordinances and church-relations as the ground of their acceptance, vers. 6—13.

2. The doctrine of the sovereignty of God in the choice of the objects of his mercy should produce, 1. The most profound humility in those who are called according to his purpose. They are constrained to say, "Not unto us, not unto us, but unto thy name be all the glory." 2. The liveliest gratitude, that we, though so unworthy, should from eternity have been selected as the objects in which God displays "the riches of his glory." 3. Confidence and peace, under all circumstances, because the purpose of God does not change ; whom he has predestinated, them he also calls, justifies, and glorifies. 4. Diligence in the discharge of all duty, to make our calling and election sure. That is, to make it evident to ourselves and others, that we are the called and chosen of God. We should ever remember that election is to holiness, and consequently to live in sin, is to invalidate every claim to be considered as one of "God's elect."

3. As God is the immutable standard of right and truth, the proper method to answer objections against the doctrines we profess, is to appeal to what God says, and to what he does. Any objection that can be shown to be inconsistent with any declaration of Scripture, or with any fact in providence, is sufficiently answered, vers. 15, 17.

4. It should, therefore, be assumed as a first principle, that God cannot do wrong. If he does a thing, it must be right. And it is much safer for us, corrupt and blinded mortals, thus to argue, than to pursue the opposite course, and maintain that God does not and cannot do so and so, because in our judgment it would be wrong, vers. 15—19.

5. All cavilling against God is wicked. It is inconsistent with our relation to him as our Creator. It is a manifestation of self-ignorance, and of irreverence toward God, ver. 20.

6. What proof of piety is there in believing our own eyes, or in receiving the deductions of our own reasoning ? But to confide in God, when clouds and darkness are round about him ; to be sure that what he does is right, and that what he says is true, when we cannot see how either the one or the other can be, this is acceptable in his sight. And to this trial he subjects all his people, ver. 20—24.

7. If the manifestation of the divine glory is the highest end of God in creation, providence, and redemption, it is the end for which we should live and be willing to die. To substitute any other end, as our own glory and advantage, is folly, sin, and self-destruction, vers. 17, 22, 23.

8. The fact that God says to some men, "Let them alone ;" that "he gives them up to a reprobate mind ;" that he withholds from them, in punishment of their sins, the influences of his Spirit, should fill all the impenitent with alarm. It should lead them to obey at once his voice, lest he swear in his wrath that they shall never enter into his rest, vers. 17, 18.

9. We and all things else are in the hands of God. He worketh all things after the counsel of his own will. The Lord reigns, let the earth rejoice, vers. 14—24.

ROMANS IX. 25—33.

ANALYSIS.

The conclusion at which the apostle had arrived in the preceding section, was, that God is at liberty to select the objects of his mercy, indiscriminately, from among the Gentiles and Jews. This conclusion he now confirms by the declarations of the Old Testament, according to which it is clear, 1. That those were to be included in the kingdom of God, who originally were considered as aliens, vers. 25, 26 ; and 2. That, as to the Israelites, only a small portion should attain to the blessings of the Messiah's reign, and of course, the mere being a Jew by birth was no security of salvation, vers. 27—29. The inference from all this is, that the Gentiles are called, and the Jews, as Jews, are rejected, vers. 30, 31. The reason of this rejection is that they would not submit to the terms of salvation presented in the gospel, ver. 32. As it had been long before predicted, they rejected their Messiah, taking offence at him, seeing in him no form or comeliness that they should desire him, ver. 33.

COMMENTARY.

VERSE 25. The first part of the general conclusion, contained in the 24th verse, is, that the Gentiles are eligible to the blessings of Christ's kingdom. This the apostle confirms by two passages from the prophecies of Hosea, which express the general sentiment, that those who, under the old economy, were not regarded as the people of God, should hereafter (*i.e.*, under the Messiah) become his people. The first passage cited is from Hosea ii. 23, which in our version is, " I will have mercy on her that had not obtained mercy ; and I will say to *them which were* not my people, Thou art my people." The Hebrew, however, admits of the rendering given by the apostle, as the word translated *to have mercy* may signify *to love.* The difficulty with regard to this passage is, that in Hosea it evidently has reference not to the heathen, but to the ten tribes. Whereas, Paul refers it to the Gentiles, as is also done by Peter, 1 Peter ii. 10. This difficulty is sometimes gotten over by giving a different view of the apostle's object in the citation, and making it refer to the restoration of the Jews. But this interpretation is obviously at variance with the context. It is more satisfactory to say, that the ten tribes were in a heathenish state, relapsed into idolatry, and, therefore, what was said of them, is of course applicable to others in like circumstances, or of like character. What amounts to much the same thing, the sentiment of the prophet is to be taken generally, ' those who were excluded from the theocracy, who were regarded and treated as aliens, were hereafter to be treated as the people of God.' In this view, it is perfectly applicable to the apostle's object, which was to convince the Jews, that the blessings of Christ's kingdom were not to be confined within the pale of the Old Testament economy, or limited to those who, in their external relations, were considered the people of God ; on the contrary, those who, according to the rules of that economy, were not the people of God, should hereafter become such. This method of interpreting and applying Scripture is both common and correct. A general truth, stated in reference to a particular class of persons, is to be considered as intended to apply to all those whose character and circumstances are the same, though the form or words of the original enunciation may not be applicable to all embraced within the scope of the general sentiment. Thus what is said of one class of heathen, as such, is applicable to all others, and what is said of one portion of aliens from the Old Testament covenant, may properly be referred to others.

Verse 26. *And it shall come to pass, that in the place where it was said to them, Ye are not my people, &c.* This quotation is more strictly conformed to the Hebrew than the preceding. It is from Hosea i. 10. The sentiment is the same as before. The combination of two or more disconnected passages in one quotation, is not unusual in the New Testament, and was a common practice with the Jewish Rabbins, who, as Surenhusius says, Interdum plura loca sacrae Scripturae in unum contrahi solent ad efficaciorem rei demonstrationem. *In the place where,* ἐν τῷ τόπῳ οὗ, is by many understood of Palestine. The prophet predicts the ten tribes should be restored, and that they should be again recognised as part of the people of God in the very place where they had been regarded as apostates and outcasts. Others think that the apostle refers to the church, *in coetu* Christianorum, ubi diu dubitatum est, an recte Gentiles reciperentur, ibi appellabantur filii Dei.—*Fritzsche.* Much the most common and natural explanation is, that the reference is indefinitely to the heathen world. Wherever, in every place, where the people had been regarded as aliens, they should be called the children of God. That is, those formerly not his people, should become his people.

Verses 27, 28. The second part of the apostle's conclusion, ver. 24, is, that the Jews, as such, were not to be included in the kingdom of Christ, which, of course, is implied in all those predictions which speak of them as in general cut off and rejected. Two such passages Paul quotes from Isaiah. The first is from Isaiah x. 22, 23. *Though the number of the children of Israel be as the sand of the sea, a remnant shall be saved, for he will finish the work and cut it short in righteousness: because a short work will the Lord make upon the earth.* This passage is nearer the LXX. translation than to the Hebrew. The general sense is the same in both, and also in the apostle's version, ' However numerous the children of Israel might be, only a small portion of them should escape the judgments of God.' This being the case, it is evident that the mere being a Jew was never considered sufficient to secure the divine favour. The portion of the prophecy contained in ver. 27 is the principal point, ' Only a few of the Jews were to be saved.' What is contained in ver. 28 is an amplification, or states the converse of the preceding proposition. ' Most of the Jews should be cut off.' The passage in Isaiah, therefore, is strictly applicable to the apostle's object.*

Our version of ver. 28 is consistent with the original.† But it may also be rendered, "He will execute and determine on the judgment with righteousness, for a judgment determined on, will the Lord execute in the

---

* Sed quia id de suo tempore vaticinatus est propheta; videndum, quomodo ad institutum suum Paulus rite accommodet. Sic autem debet: Quum Dominus vellet e captivitate Babylonica populum suum liberare, ex immensa illa multitudine ad paucissimos modo liberationis suae beneficium pervenire voluit; qui excidii reliquiae merito dici possent prae numeroso illo populo quem in exilio perire sinebat. Jam restitutio illa carnalis veram ecclesiae Dei instaurationem figuravit, quae in Christo peragitur, imo ejus duntaxat fuit exordium. Quod ergo tunc accidit, multo certius nunc adimpleri convenit in ipso liberationis progressu et complemento.—*Calvin.*

† Calvin translates it much in the same way, Sermonem enim consummans et abbrevians, quoniam sermonem abbreviatum faciet Dominus in terra.

earth." The word (λόγον) rendered *work* in our version, means properly *a word, something spoken,* and may refer to *a promise,* or *threatening,* according to the context. Here of course a threatening is intended ; the judgment threatened by the prophet in the context. The word (συντελῶν) rendered *he will finish,* means *bringing to an end,* and here perhaps, *executing at once, bringing to an end speedily.* And the term (συντέμνων) translated *cutting short,* may mean *deciding upon.* See Dan. ix. 24, " Seventy weeks *are determined* (συνετμήθησαν) upon my people." But the ordinary sense of the word is in favour of our version, and so is the context.* If it were allowable to take the same word in different senses in the same passage, the verse might be rendered thus, ' For he will execute the judgment, and accomplish it speedily, for the judgment determined upon will the Lord execute in the earth.' The same word is used in one of these senses, Dan. ix. 24, and in the other in ver. 26 of the same chapter. See, too, an analogous example in 1 Cor. iii. 17, "If any man (φθείρει) defile the temple of God, him will God (φθερεῖ) destroy." Here the same word is rendered correctly, first *defile,* and then *destroy.* We may, therefore, render the last clause of the verse either as in our version, or as given above.

Verse 29. The second passage quoted by the apostle is from Isa. i. 9, *Except the Lord of hosts had left us a seed, we had been as Sodom, been made like unto Gomorrah.* The object of this quotation is the same as that of the preceding, viz., to show that being Israelites was not enough to secure either exemption from divine judgments or the enjoyment of God's favour. The passage is perfectly in point, for although the prophet is speaking of the national judgments which the people had brought upon themselves by their sins, and by which they were well nigh cut off entirely, yet it was necessarily involved in the destruction of the people for their idolatry and other crimes, that they perished from the kingdom of God. Of course the passage strictly proves what Paul designed to establish, viz., that the Jews, as Jews, were as much exposed to God's judgments as others, and consequently could lay no special claim to admission into the kingdom of heaven.

Paul here again follows the Septuagint. The only difference, however, is, that the Greek version has (σπέρμα) *a seed,* instead of *a remnant,* as it is in the Hebrew. The sense is precisely the same. The Hebrew word means *that which remains;* and *seed,* as used in this passage, means the seed reserved for sowing. The figure, therefore, is striking and beautiful. *Lord of Hosts* is a frequent designation for the Supreme God in the Old Testament. As the word *host* is used in reference to any multitude arranged in order, as of men in an army, of angels, of the stars, or of all the heavenly bodies, including the sun and moon, so the expression *Lord of hosts,* may mean, Lord of armies, Lord of angels, or Lord of heaven, or of the universe as a marshalled host ; see 1 Kings xxii. 19, " I saw the Lord sitting on his throne, and all the host of heaven standing by him ;" 2 Chron. xviii. 18, Ps. ciii. 21, Ps. cxlviii. 2, "Praise ye him, all his angels, praise ye him, all his hosts." In other passages, the reference is, with equal distinctness, to the stars, Jer. xxxiii. 22, Deut. iv. 19, and frequently. It is most probable, therefore, that God is called Lord of hosts in reference to his Lordship over the whole heavens, and all that they contain, Lord of hosts being equivalent to Lord of the universe.

---

* See Koppe and Wetstein for a satisfactory exhibition of the *usus loquendi* as to this word.

Verse 30. Having proved that God was free to call the Gentiles as well as the Jews into his kingdom, and that it had been predicted that the great body of the Jews were to be rejected, he comes now to state the immediate ground of this rejection. *What shall we say then ?* This may mean either, ' What is the inference from the preceding discussion ?' and the answer follows, ' The conclusion is, the Gentiles are called and the Jews rejected ;' or, ' What shall we say, or object to the fact that the Gentiles are accepted,' &c. &c. So Flatt and others. But the former explanation is better suited to the context, especially to ver. 32, and to the apostle's common use of this expression ; see ver. 14, chap. vii. 7 ; viii. 31.

That the Gentiles which followed not after righteousness, have attained, &c. The inference is, that what to all human probability was the most unlikely to occur, has actually taken place. The Gentiles, sunk in carelessness and sin, have attained the favour of God, while the Jews, to whom religion was a business, have utterly failed. Why is this ? The reason is given in ver. 32 ; it was because the Jews would not submit to be saved on the terms which God proposed, but insisted on reaching heaven in their own way. *To follow after righteousness,* is to press forward towards it as towards the prize in a race, Phil. iii. 14. *Righteousness,* δικαιοσύνη uniformly in Paul's writings, means either an attribute, as when we ascribe righteousness to God ; or, what constitutes righteousness, *i.e.*, that which satisfies the demands of justice or of the law, as when God is said to impute righteousness. That is, he ascribes to men, or sets to their account, that which constitutes them righteous in the sight of the law. Sometimes, however, the word includes by implication, the consequences of possessing this righteousness. This is the case in this passage. Those who sought after righteousness, sought to be regarded and treated as righteous in the sight of God ; that is, they sought after justification. This, however, does not imply that δικαιοσύνη signifies justification. It means *righteousness,* the possession of which secures justification. Justification is a declarative act of God ; righteousness is the ground on which that declaration is made.

Even the righteousness which is of faith, i. e., even that righteousness which is attained by faith. Throughout this verse, the word *righteousness,* as expressing the sum of the divine requisitions, that which fulfils the law retains its meaning. ' The Gentiles did not seek this righteousness, yet they attained it ; not that righteousness which is of the law, but that which is through the faith of Christ, the righteousness of God by faith,' Phil. iii. 9. They obtained that which satisfied the demands of the law, and was acceptable in the sight of God.

Verse 31. What the Gentiles thus attained, the Jews failed to secure. The former he had described as "not following after righteousness ;" the latter he characterizes as those who *follow after the law of righteousness.* The expression *law of righteousness* may be variously explained. *Law* may be taken in its general sense of *rule,* as in chap. iii. 27, and elsewhere. The meaning would then be, ' They followed after, *i. e.,* they attended diligently to, the rule which they thought would lead to their attaining righteousness or being justified, but they did not attain unto that rule which actually leads to such results.' *Law of righteousness* is, then, norma juxta quam Deus justificat. This is the interpretation of Calvin, Calovius, Bengel, and many others. Or, 2. The word *law* may be redundant, and Paul may mean to say nothing more than that ' The Jews sought righteousness or justification, but did not attain it.' This, no doubt, is the substance, though it may not be the precise form of the thought. 3. *Law of righteousness* is often understood here as equivalent to *righteousness which is of the law.* This, however, is rather forced, and not very consistent with the latter clause of the verse, " Have not attained to the law of righteousness," which can hardly be so interpreted. Meyer, Tholuck, and others, take the phrase *law of righteousness* in both parts of the verse in what they call an ideal sense. The Jews strove to realize the justifying law, *i. e*, to attain that standard which secured their justification. It is more common to take the words as referring to the Mosaic and moral law, as revealed in the Scriptures, in the former part of the verse, and in the latter, the law of faith. 'The Jews made the Mosaic law, (the law of works,) the object of their zeal, as the means of attaining righteousness, and therefore did not attain to that law (the law of faith, Rom. iii. 27,) which really secures righteousness.' They were zealous to attain righteousness, but failed. Why? The answer is given in the next verse.

VERSE 32. *Because they sought it not by faith, but, as it were, by the works of the law.* In other words, they would not submit to the method of justification proposed by God, which was alone suitable for sinners, and persisted in trusting to their own imperfect works. The reason why one man believes and is saved, rather than another, is to be sought in the sovereign grace of God, according to Paul's doctrine in the preceding part of this chapter, and chapter viii. 28, 2 Tim. i. 9, &c. ; but the ground of the rejection and condemnation of men is always in themselves. The vessels of wrath which are destroyed, are destroyed on account of their sins. No man, therefore, can throw the blame of his perdition on any other than himself. This verse, consequently, is very far from being inconsistent with the doctrine of the divine sovereignty as taught above. The force of the word rendered *as it were*, may be explained by paraphrasing the clause thus, ' as though they supposed it could be obtained by the works of the law.' (See 2 Cor. iii. 5, xiii. 7,) ' They sought it as (*being*) of the works of the law.' *For they stumbled at that stumbling-stone.* That is, they did as it had been predicted they would do, they took offence at the Messiah and at the plan of salvation which he came to reveal.

VERSE 33. What it was they stumbled at, the apostle declares in this verse, and shews that the rejection of the Messiah by the Jews was predicted in the Old Testament. *As it is written, Behold, I lay in Zion a stumbling-stone, and a rock of offence; and whosoever believeth on him shall not be ashamed.* This passage is apparently made up of two, one occurring in Isa. xxviii. 16, the other in Isa. viii. 14. In both of these passages mention is made of a stone, but the predicates of this stone, as given in the latter passage, are transferred to the other, and those there mentioned omitted. This method of quoting Scripture is common among all writers, especially where the several passages quoted and merged into each other refer to the same subject. It is obvious that the writers of the New Testament are very free in their mode of quoting from the Old, giving the sense, as they, being inspired by the same Spirit, could do authoritatively, without binding themselves strictly to the words. The former of the two passages here referred to stands thus in our version, " Behold, I lay in Zion for a foundation a stone, a tried stone, a precious corner stone, a sure foundation ; he that believeth shall not make haste," which is according to the Hebrew. The other passage, Isa. viii. 14, is, " And he shall be for a sanctuary ; but for a stone of stumbling and a rock of offence to both houses of Israel."

Isaiah xxviii. is a prophecy against those who had various false grounds of confidence, and who desired a league with Egypt as a defence against the attacks of the Assyrians. God says, he has laid a much more secure foundation for his church than any such confederacy, even a precious, tried corner-stone ; those who confided to it should never be confounded. The prophets, constantly filled with the expectation of the Messiah, and, in general, ignorant of the time of his advent, were accustomed, on every threatened danger, to comfort the people by the assurance that the efforts of their enemies could not prevail, because the Messiah was to come. Until his advent, they could not, as a people, be destroyed, and when he came, there should be a glorious restoration of all things ; see Isa. vii. 14—16, and elsewhere. There is, therefore, no force in the objection, that the advent of Christ was an event too remote to be available to the consolation of the people, when threatened with the immediate invasion of their enemies. This passage is properly quoted by the apostle, because it was intended originally to apply to Christ. The sacred writers of the New Testament so understood and explain it ; see 1 Peter ii. 6, Matt. xxi. 42, Acts iv. 11 ; compare also Ps. cxviii. 22, 1 Cor. iii. 11, Eph. ii. 20, and other passages, in which Christ is spoken of as the foundation or corner stone of his Church. The same interpretation of the passage was given by the ancient Jews.*

The other passage, Isa. viii. 14, is of much the same character. God exhorts the people not to be afraid of the combination between Syria and Ephraim. The Lord of hosts was to be feared and trusted, he would be a refuge to those who confided in him, but a stone of stumbling and a rock of offence to all others. This passage, too, as appears from a comparison of the one previously cited with Ps. cxviii. 22, and the quotation and application of them by the New Testament writers refers to Christ. What is said in the Old Testament of Jehovah, the inspired penmen of the New do not hesitate to refer to the Saviour ; compare John xii. 41 ; Isa. vi. 1 ; Heb. i. 10, 11 ; Ps. cii. 25 ; 1 Cor. x. 9 ; Exod. xvii. 2, 7. When God, therefore, declared that he should be a sanctuary to one class of the people, and a rock of offence to another, he meant that he, in the person of his Son, as the Immanuel, would thus be confided in by some, but rejected and despised by others. The whole spirit, opinions, and expectations of the Jews were adverse to the person, character, and doctrines of the Redeemer. He was, therefore, to them a stumbling-block, as he was to others foolishness. They could not recognise him as their fondly anticipated Messiah, nor consent to enter the kingdom of heaven on the terms which he prescribed. In them, therefore, were fulfilled the ancient prophecies, which spoke of their rejection of Christ, and consequent excision from the people of God.

DOCTRINE.

1. Exclusion from the pale of any visible church does not of itself imply that men are without the reach of divine mercy, vers. 25, 26.

2. As the world has hitherto existed, only a small portion of the nominal members of the Church, or of the professors of the true religion, has been the real people of God, vers. 27, 28, 29.

3. Error is often a greater obstacle to the salvation of men than carelessness or vice. Christ said that publicans and harlots would enter the king-

---

* Martini Pugio Fidei, Lib. II. cap. 5. p. 342, and the passages quoted by Rosenmüller and Gesenius on Isa. xxviii. 16.

dom of God before the Pharisees. In like manner the thoughtless and sensual Gentiles were more susceptible of impression from the Gospel, and were more frequently converted to Christ, than the Jews, who were wedded to erroneous views of the plan of salvation, vers. 30, 31.

4. Agreeably to the declarations of the previous portion of this chapter, and the uniform tenor of Scripture, the ground of the distinction between the saved and the lost, is to be found not in men, but in God. He has mercy on whom he will have mercy. But the ground of the condemnation of men is always in themselves. That God gave his saving grace to more Gentiles than Jews, in the early ages of the Church, must be referred to his sovereign pleasure ; but that the Jews were cut off and perished, is to be referred to their own unbelief. In like manner, every sinner must look into his own heart and conduct for the ground of his condemnation, and never to any secret purpose of God, vers. 32.

5. Christ crucified has ever been either foolishness or an offence to unrenewed men. Hence, right views of the Saviour's character, and cordial approbation of the plan of salvation through him, are characteristic of those " who are called ;" *i.e.*, they are evidences of a renewed heart, vers. 33.

REMARKS.

1. The consideration that God has extended to us, who were not his people, all the privileges and blessings of his children, should be a constant subject of gratitude, vers. 25, 26.

2. If only a remnant of the Jewish Church, God's own people, were saved, how careful and solicitous should all professors of religion be, that their faith and hope be well founded, vers. 27—29.

3. Let no man think error in doctrine a slight practical evil. No road to perdition has ever been more thronged than that of false doctrine. Error is a shield over the conscience, and a bandage over the eyes, vers. 30, 31.

4. No form of error is more destructive than that which leads to self-dependence; either reliance on our own powers, or on our own merit, ver. 32.

5. To criminate God, and excuse ourselves, is always an evidence of ignorance and depravity, ver. 32.

6. Christ declared those blessed who were not offended at him. If our hearts are right in the sight of God, Jesus Christ is to us at once the object of supreme affection, and the sole ground of confidence, ver. 33.

7. The gospel produced at first the same effects as those we now witness. It had the same obstacles to surmount ; and it was received or rejected by the same classes of men then as now. Its history, therefore, is replete with practical instruction.

CHAPTER X.

CONTENTS.

THE OBJECT OF THIS CHAPTER, AS OF THE PRECEDING AND OF THE ONE WHICH FOLLOWS, IS TO SET FORTH THE TRUTH IN REFERENCE TO THE REJECTION OF THE JEWS AS THE PECULIAR PEOPLE OF GOD, AND THE EXTENSION TO ALL NATIONS OF THE OFFERS OF SALVATION. THE FIRST VERSES ARE AGAIN, AS THOSE AT THE BEGINNING OF CHAP. IX., INTRODUCTORY AND CONCILIATORY, SETTING FORTH THE GROUND OF THE REJECTION OF THE JEWS, VERS. 1—4. THE NEXT SECTION CONTAINS AN EXHIBITION OF THE TERMS OF SALVATION, DESIGNED TO SHOW THAT THEY WERE AS ACCESSIBLE TO THE GENTILES AS THE JEWS, VERS. 5—10. THE PLAN OF SALVATION BEING ADAPTED TO ALL, AND GOD BEING THE GOD OF ALL, THE GOSPEL SHOULD BE PREACHED TO ALL, VERS. 11—17. THE TRUTH HERE TAUGHT (THE CALLING OF THE GENTILES, &C.,) WAS PREDICTED CLEARLY IN THE OLD TESTAMENT, VERS. 18—21.

ROMANS X. 1—10.

ANALYSIS.

WITH his usual tenderness, the apostle assures his brethren of his solicitude for their welfare, and of his proper appreciation of their character, vers. 1, 2. The difficulty was, that they would not submit to the plan of salvation proposed in the gospel, and, therefore, they rejected the Saviour. This was the true ground of their excision from the people of God, vers. 3, 4. The method of justification, on which the Jews insisted, was legal, and from its nature must be confined to themselves, or to those who would consent to become Jews. Its terms, when properly understood, were perfectly impracticable, ver. 5. But the gospel method of salvation prescribes no such severe terms, it simply requires cordial faith and open profession, vers. 6—10. This, he shows, in the next verses, is the doctrine of the Scriptures, and from it he infers the applicability of this plan to all men, Gentiles as well as Jews.

COMMENTARY.

VERSE 1. *Brethren, my heart's desire and prayer to God for Israel is, that they might be saved.** As the truth which Paul was to reiterate in the ears of the Jew was, of all others, to them the most offensive, he endeavours to allay their enmity, first, by assuring them of his affection, and secondly, by avoiding all exaggeration in the statement of their case. The word εὐδοκία means either *good pleasure*, sovereign *purpose*, Matt. xi. 26 ; Luke ii. 14 ; 2 Thess. i. 11; Eph. i. 5, 9, or *benevolence*, kind feeling, or desire, as in Phil. i. 15. The latter sense best suits this passage. Paul meant to assure his brethren according to the flesh, that all his feelings towards them were kind, and that he earnestly desired their salvation. He

---

* Hinc videmus, quanta sollicitudine sanctus vir offensionibus obviaret. Adhuc enim, ut temperet quicquid erat accerbitatis in exponenda Judæorum rejectione, suam, ut prius, erga eos benevolentiam testatur, et eam ab effectu comprobat, quod sibi eorum salus curae esset coram Domino.—*Calvin.*

had no pleasure in contemplating the evils which impended over them, his earnest desire and prayer was (εἰς σωτηρίαν) *that they might be saved;* literally *to salvation,* as expressing the end or object towards which his wishes or prayers tend ; see chap. vi. 22 ; Gal. iii. 17, and frequent examples elsewhere of this use of the preposition εἰς.

Verse 2. *For I bear them record that they have a zeal of God.* So far from desiring to exaggerate the evil of their conduct, the apostle, as was his uniform manner, endeavoured to bring every thing commendable and exculpatory fully into view. The word *for,* has here its appropriate force, as it introduces the ground or reason of the preceding declaration. ' I desire their salvation, *for* they themselves are far from being unconcerned as to divine things.' *Zeal of God* may mean very great zeal, as *cedars of God* mean great cedars, according to a common Hebrew idiom ; or *zeal of which God is the object;* the latter explanation is to be preferred. John ii. 17, " The zeal of thy house hath eaten me up." Acts xxi. 20, " Zealous of the law." Acts xxii. 3, " Zealous of God." Gal. i. 14, &c., &c. The Jews had great zeal about God, but it was wrong as to its object, and of consequence wrong in its moral qualities. Zeal, when rightly directed, however ardent, is humble and amiable. When its object is evil, it is proud, censorious, and cruel. Hence, the importance of its being properly guided, not merely to prevent the waste of feeling and effort, but principally to prevent its evil effects on ourselves and others. *But not according to knowledge.* Commentators notice that Paul uses the word ἐπίγνωσις. The Jews had γνῶσις (knowledge), what they lacked was ἐπίγνωσις, correct knowledge and appreciation. Their knowledge was neither enlightened nor wise ; neither right as to its objects, nor correct in its character. The former idea is here principally intended. The Jews were zealous about their law, the traditions of their fathers, and the establishment of their own merit. How naturally would a zeal for such objects make men place religion in the observance of external rites ; and be connected with pride, censoriousness, and a persecuting spirit. In so far, however, as this zeal was a zeal about God, it was preferable to indifference, and is, therefore, mentioned by the apostle with qualified commendation.

Verse 3. *For they being ignorant of God's righteousness, and going about to establish their own righteousness, have not,* &c. The grand mistake of the Jews was about the method of justification. Ignorance on this point implied ignorance of the character of God, of the requirements of the law, and of themselves. It was, therefore, and is, and must ever continue to be a vital point. Those who err essentially here, err fatally; and those who are right here, cannot be wrong as to other necessary truths. *Their own righteousness,* τὴν ἰδίαν δικαιοσύνην, which Theophylact correctly interprets, τὴν ἐξ ἔργων ἰδίων καὶ πόνων κατορθουμένην. The phrase *righteousness of God,* admits here, as in other parts of the epistle, of various interpretations. 1. It may mean *the divine holiness* or general moral perfection of God. In this way the passage would mean, ' Being ignorant of the perfections or holiness of God, and, of course, of the extent of his demands, and going about to establish their own excellence, &c.' This gives a good sense, but it is not consistent with the use of the expression *righteousness of God,* in other similar passages, as chap. i. 17, iii. 21, &c. And, secondly, it requires the phrase to be taken in two different senses in the same verse ; for the last clause, ' Have not submitted themselves to the righteousness of God,' cannot mean, ' They have not submitted to the divine holiness.' 2. The term may mean *that righteousness of which God is the author,* that

which he approves and accepts. This interpretation is, in this case, peculiarly appropriate, from the opposition of the two expressions, *righteousness
of God* and *their own righteousness.* ' Being ignorant of that righteousness which God has provided, and which he bestows, and endeavouring to
establish their own, they refused to accept of his.' The sense here is perfectly good, and the interpretation may be carried through the verse, being
applicable to the last clause as well as to the others. A comparison of this
passage with Phil. iii. 9, "Not having my own righteousness, but the
righteousness which is of God," is also in favour of this interpretation.
For there the phrase *the righteousness which is of God,* can only mean that
which he gives, and with this phrase the expression *the righteousness of
God,* in this verse, seems to be synonymous.* 3. Thirdly, Some interpreters take *righteousness* in the sense of *justification,* "justification of
God" being taken as equivalent to ' *God's method of justification.'* Being
ignorant of God's method of justification, and going about to establish their
own, they have not submitted themselves to the method which he has proposed.' The cause of the rejection of the Jews was the rejection of the
method of salvation through a crucified Redeemer, and their persisting in
confiding in their own merits and advantages as the ground of their
acceptance with God. Although this is the meaning of the passage, it is
not the sense of the words. *Righteousness* does not signify justification.
It is that on which the sentence of justification is founded. Those who
have righteousness, either personal and inherent, or imputed, are justified.
As we have no righteousness of our own, nothing that we have done or
experienced, nothing personal or subjective, that can answer the demands
of the law, we can be justified only through the righteousness of God, imputed to us and received by faith.

Verse 4. *For Christ is the end of the law for righteousness to every one
that believeth.* The precise connection of this verse with the preceding,
depends on the view taken of its meaning. The general import of the
passage is sufficiently obvious, but its exact sense is not so easy to determine,
on account of the ambiguity of the word (τέλος) translated *end.* The word
may signify, 1. *The object to which any thing leads.* Christ is, in this
sense, the end of the law, inasmuch as the law was a schoolmaster to lead
us to him, Gal. iii. 24 ; and as all its types and prophecies pointed to him,
"They were a shadow of things to come, but the body is of Christ," Col. ii.
17, Heb. ix. 9. The meaning and connection of the passage would then be,
' The Jews erred in seeking justification from the law, *for* the law was designed, not to afford justification, but to lead them to Christ, in order that
they might be justified.' To Christ all its portions tended, he was the
object of its types and the subject of its predictions, and its precepts and
penalty urge the soul to him as the only refuge. So Calvin, Bengel, and
the majority of commentators.†

---

* Judaei habuere et habent zelum sine scientia, nos contra, proh dolor, scientiam sine
zelo.—*Flacius,* quoted by *Bengel.* Melius est vel claudicare in via, quam extra viam strenue
currere, ut ait Augustinus. Si religiosi esse volumus, meminerimus verum esse, quod Lac-
tantius docet, eam demum veram esse religionem quae conjuncta est cum Dei verbo.—
Calvin.

† Indicat legis praeposterum interpretem esse, qui per ejus opera justificari quaerit, quoniam in hoc lex data est, quo nos ad aliam justitiam manu duceret. Imo quicquid doceat
lex, quicquid praecipiat, quicquid promittat semper Christum habet pro scopo ; ergo in ipsum dirigendae sunt omnes partes —*Calvin.*

Lex hominem urget, donec is ad Christum confugit. Tum ipsa dicit: *asylum es nactus,
desino te persequi, sapis, salvus es* —*Bengel.*

2. The word may be taken in the sense of *ccmpletion* or *fulfilmt.*
Then Christ is the end of the law, because he fulfils all its requisitions, all
its types and ceremonies, and satisfies its preceptive and penal demands. See
Mat. v. 17, "Think not that I am come to destroy the law or the prophets,
I am not come to destroy, but to fulfil;" and Rom. viii. 4. The philological ground for this interpretation is slight. 1 Tim. i. 5, is compared
with Rom. xiii. 10, in order to prove that the word (τέλος) here translated
end, is equivalent to the word (πλήρωμα) which is there (Rom. xiii. 10)
rendered *fulfilling.* The sense, according to this interpretation, is scriptural, but is not consistent with the meaning of the word.

3. We may take the word in its more ordinary sense of *end* or *termina-
tion*, and understand it metonymically for *he who terminates or puts an
end to.* The meaning and connection would then be, 'The Jews mistake
the true method of justification, because they seek it from the law, whereas
Christ has abolished the law, in order that all who believe may be justified.'
Compare Eph. ii. 15, "Having abolished in his flesh the enmity, even the
law of commandments;" Col. ii. 14, "Blotting out the handwriting of ordinances that was against us, &c," Gal. iii. 10, 12, Rom. vi. 14, vii. 4, 6, and
the general drift of the former part of the epistle. In sense, this interpretation amounts to the same with the preceding, though it differs from it in
form. Christ has abolished the law, not by destroying, but by fulfilling it.
He has abolished the law as a rule of justification, or covenant of works,
and the whole Mosaic economy having met its completion in him, has by
him been brought to an end. In Luke xvi. 16, it is said, "The law and
the prophets were until John;" then, in one sense, they ceased, or came
to an end. When Christ came, the old legal system was abolished, and a
new era commenced. The same idea is presented in Gal. iii. 23, "Before
faith came we were kept under the law," but when Christ appeared, declaring, "Believe and thou shalt be saved," we were no longer under that
bondage. The doctrine is clearly taught in Scripture, that those who are
out of Christ are under the law, subject to its demands and exposed to its
penalty. His coming and work have put an end to its authority, we are
no longer under the law, but under grace, Rom. vi. 14 ; we are no longer
under the system which says, Do this, and live ; but under that which
says, Believe, and thou shalt be saved. This abrogation of the law, however, is not by setting it aside, but by fulfilling its demands. It is because
Christ is the fulfiller of the law, that he is the end of it. It is the latter
truth which the apostle here asserts. The word *law* is obviously here
used in its prevalent sense throughout this epistle, for the whole rule of
duty prescribed to man, including for the Jews the whole of the Mosaic
institutions. That *law* is intended which has been fulfilled, satisfied, or
abrogated by Jesus Christ. *For righteousness to every one that believeth.*
The general meaning of this clause, in this connection, is, 'So that, or, in
order that, every believer may be justified ;' Christ has abolished the law,
ἵνα δικαιωθῇ πᾶς ὁ πιστεύων ἐπ' αὐτῷ, in order that every believer may attain
righteousness, which is unattainable by the law. The law is abolished by
Christ, not as a rule of life, but as a covenant prescribing the condition of
life. The way in which this idea is arrived at, however, may be variously
explained. 1. The preposition (εἰς) rendered *for*, may be rendered *as to,
as it relates to.* 'Christ is the end of the law, as it relates to righteousness.'
2. It may be understood of the *effect*, or *result*, and be resolved into the
verbal construction with *that* or *so that;* 'Christ is the end, &c., *that*
righteousness is to every believer ; or *so that* every believer is justified.'

It may point out the *end* or *object.* 'Christ has abolished the law in order that every one that believes, &c.' The last is the correct explanation. The Jews, then, did not submit to the righteousness of God, that is, to the righteousness which he had provided, for they did not submit to Christ, who is the end of the law. He has abolished the law, in order that every one that believes may be justified.

VERSE 5. *For Moses describeth the righteousness which is of the law.* That is, concerning the righteousness which is of the law, Moses thus writes. In the last clause of the preceding verse it was clearly intimated that faith was the condition of salvation under the gospel. 'To every one, without distinction, that believeth, is justification secured.' On this the apostle connects his description and contrast of the two methods of justification, the one by works and the other by faith, with the design of showing that the former is in its nature impracticable, while the other is reasonable and easy, and adapted to all classes of men, Jews and Gentiles, and should therefore be offered to all.

The righteousness which is of the law. The word *righteousness* has here its common and proper meaning. It is that which constitutes a man righteous, which meets the demands of the law, or satisfies the claims of justice. The man who is righteous, or who possesses righteousness, cannot be condemned. The apostle in his whole argument proceeds on the assumption that God is just; that he does and must demand righteousness in those whom he justifies. There are but two possible ways in which this righteousness can be obtained—by works, or by faith. We must either have a righteousness of our own, or receive and trust in a righteousness which is not our own, but which has been wrought out for us, and presented to us, as the ground of our acceptance with God. The quotation is from Lev. xviii. 5, "The man that doeth those things shall live by them." *Those things* are the things prescribed in the law. It is the clear doctrine of the Scriptures, that obedience to the law, to secure justification, must be perfect. For it is said, "Cursed is every one who continueth not in all things written in the book of the law to do them;" and, he that offendeth in one point, is guilty of all. It is not necessary that a man who commits murder should also steal, in order to bring him under the penalty of the law. The legal system, then, which demanded obedience, required perfect obedience. Those, and those only, who were thus free from sin, should *live, i.e.*, shall enjoy that life which belongs to him as a rational and immortal being. It is a life which includes the whole man, soul and body, and the whole course of his existence, in this world and in that which is to come. Ζήσεται ex mente Judaeorum interpretatur de vita aeterna, ut *Targum*, Levit. xviii. 4. The Jewish writers also well remark, that Moses says, Qui fecerit ea homo; non dicitur, Sacerdos, Levita, Israelita, sed homo; ut discas, etiam gentilem, si proselytus fiat, et det legi operam, intelligi. See *Wetstein.*

VERSES 6, 7. *But the righteousness which is of faith speaketh on this wise, Say not, &c.* Moses says one thing; the righteousness of faith says another thing. The same kind of personification occurs in Gal. iii. 23, 25. The phrase *righteousness of faith*, or as it is here, *which is of faith*, admits of different interpretations, if we limit ourselves to the mere force of the words. *Righteousness of faith*, may mean that righteousness which consists in faith; or, which flows from faith, (*i. e.*, that inward excellence which faith produces); or, the righteousness which is received by faith. This last is the only interpretation consistent with the context, or with the analogy of Scripture. The righteousness which consists in faith, or which flows from faith, is our own righteousness. It is as true and properly our own as any righteousness of works on which Pharisees relied. Besides, it is the whole doctrine of the apostle and of the gospel, that it is Christ's righteousness, his obedience, blood, or death, which is the ground of our acceptance with God, and which it receives and rests upon.

It is clearly implied in that verse that the attainment of justification, by a method which prescribed perfect obedience, is for sinful men impossible. It is the object of this and the succeeding verses, to declare that the gospel requires no such impossibilities; it neither requires us to scale the heavens, nor to fathom the great abyss; it demands only cordial faith and open profession. In expressing these ideas the apostle skilfully avails himself of the language of Moses, Deut. xxx. 10—14. It is clear that the expressions used by the ancient lawgiver were a familiar mode of saying that a thing could not be done. The passage referred to is the following, "For this commandment which I command thee this day, it is not hidden from thee, neither is it far off. It is not in heaven, that thou shouldest say, Who shall go up for us to heaven, and bring it unto us, that we may hear it, and do it? Neither is it beyond the sea, that thou shouldest say, Who shall go over the sea for us, and bring it unto us, that we may hear it and do it? But the word is very nigh unto thee, in thy mouth and in thy heart, that thou mayest do it." The obvious import of this passage is, that the knowledge of the will of God had been made perfectly accessible, no one was required to do what was impossible; neither to ascend to heaven, nor to pass the *boundless* sea, in order to attain it; it was neither hidden, nor afar off, but obvious and at hand. Without directly citing this passage, Paul uses nearly the same language to express the same idea. The expressions here used seem to have become proverbial among the Jews. To be "high," or "afar off," was to be unattainable; Ps. cxxxix. 6 ; Prov. xxiv. 7. "To ascend to heaven," or "to go down to hell," was to do what was impossible, Amos ix. 2; Ps. cxxxix. 8, 9. As the sea was to the ancients impassable, it is easy to understand how the question, 'Who can pass over the sea?' was tantamount to 'Who can ascend up into heaven?' Among the later Jews the same mode of expressions not unfrequently occur. *Bava Mezia*, f. 94, 1. Si quis dixerit mulieri, si adscenderis in firmamentum, aut descenderis in abyssum, eris mihi desonsata, haec conditio frustranea est.—*Wetstein.*

Instead of using the expression, 'Who shall go over the sea for us?' *P*aul uses the equivalent phrase, 'Who shall descend into the deep?' as more pertinent to his object. The word (ἄβυσσον) rendered *deep*, is the same which elsewhere is rendered *abyss*, and properly means, *without bottom, bottomless,* and therefore, is often applied to the sea as fathomless, Gen. i. 2, vii. 11 (in the Septuagint), and also to the great cavern beneath the earth, which, in the figurative language of the Scriptures, is spoken of as the abode of the dead, and which is often opposed to heaven. Job xxviii. 14, "The abyss says it is not in me;" compare the enumeration of things in heaven, things in earth, and things under the earth, in Phil. ii. 10, and elsewhere; see also Gen. xlix. 25, God "shall bless thee with the blessings of heaven above, blessings of the abyss which lieth under." In the New Testament, with the exception of this passage, it is always used for the abode of fallen spirits and lost souls, Luke viii. 31 ; Rev. xvii. 8 ; xx. 1, and frequently in that book, where it is appropriately rendered *the bottomless pit.* The expression is, therefore, equivalent to that which is commonly rendered *hell* in our version. Psalm cxxxix. 8, "If I make my bed in hell." Amos ix. 2, "Though they dig into hell," &c., and was no doubt chosen by the apostle, as more suitable to the reference to the resurrection of Christ, with which he meant to connect it, than the expression used by Moses in the same general sense, "Who shall pass over the sea?"

Paul connects each of the questions, virtually borrowed from the Old Testament, with a comment designed to apply them more directly to the point which he had in view. *Say not, Who shall ascend into heaven ? that is, to bring Christ down,* &c. The precise intent of these comments, however, may be differently understood. 1. The words *that is,* may be taken as equivalent to *namely,* or *to wit,* and the apostle's comment be connected, as an explanatory substitute, with the questions, 'Say not who shall ascend into heaven ? to wit, to bring Christ down ; or who shall descend into the deep ? to bring him up again from the dead.' The sense would then be, 'The plan of salvation by faith does not require us to do what cannot be done, and which is now unnecessary ; it does not require us to provide a Saviour, to bring him from heaven, or to raise him from the dead ; a Saviour has been provided, and we are now only required to believe,' &c. 2. The words *that is,* may be taken as equivalent to the fuller expression, *that is to say,* 'To ask who shall ascend into heaven ?' is as much as to ask, Who shall bring Christ down from above ? And to ask, 'Who shall descend into the deep ? is as much as to ask, who shall bring Christ again from the dead ?' The comments of the apostle may, therefore, be regarded as a reproof of the want of faith implied in such questions, and the passage may be thus understood, Do not reject the gospel. Say not in thy heart that no one can ascend to heaven, as the gospel says Christ has done : and no man can descend into the abyss and thence return, as is said of Christ. The incarnation of the Son of God, and his ascension to heaven, are not impossibilities, which would justify unbelief. The doctrines of the gospel are plain and simple.

Instead of regarding the apostle as intending to state generally the nature of the method of justification by faith, many suppose that it is his object to encourage and support a desponding and anxious inquirer. 'Do not despairingly inquire who shall point out the way of life ? No one, either from heaven or from the deep, will come to teach me the way. Speak not thus, for Christ has come from heaven, and arisen from the dead for your salvation, and no other Saviour is required.'* But this view does not seem to harmonize with the spirit of the context.

It has been questioned whether Paul meant, in this passage, merely to allude to the language of Moses in Deut. xxx. 10—14, or whether he is to be understood as quoting it in such a manner as to imply that the ancient prophet was describing the method of justification by faith. This latter view is taken by Calvin, De Brais, and many others. They suppose that in the passage quoted in the 5th verse from Levit. xviii. 5, Moses describes the legal method of justification, but that here he has reference to salvation by faith. This is, no doubt, possible. For in Deut. xxx. 10, &c., the context shows that the passage may be understood of the whole system of instruction given by Moses ; a system which included in it, under its various types and prophecies, an exhibition of the true method of salvation. Moses, therefore, might say with regard to his own law, that it set before

* See Knapp's Diatribe in Locum, Rom. x. 4—11, &c., p. 543 of his *Scripta Varii Argumenti.*

the people the way of eternal life, that they had now no need to inquire who should procure this knowledge for them from a distance, for it was near them, even in their hearts and in their mouths. But, on the other hand, it is very clear that this interpretation is by no means necessary. Paul does not say, 'Moses describes the righteousness which is of faith in this wise,' as immediately above he had said of the righteousness which is of the law. There is nothing in the language of the apostle to require us to understand him as quoting Moses in proof of his own doctrine. It is, indeed, more in accordance with the spirit of the passage, to consider him as merely expressing his own ideas in scriptural language, as in ver. 19 of this chapter, and frequently elsewhere. 'Moses teaches us that the legal method of justification requires perfect obedience ; but the righteousness which is by faith, requires no such impossibility, it demands only cordial faith and open profession.' The modern interpreters who understand the apostle as quoting the language of Moses to prove the true nature of the gospel, differ among themselves. Meyer and most other advocates of this view of the context, assume that Paul departs entirely from the historical meaning of the original text, and gives it a sense foreign to the intention of the sacred writer. Others, as Olshausen, suppose him to give its true spiritual sense. The passage in Deuteronomy is, in this view, strictly Messianic. It describes, in contrast with the inexorable demand of obedience made by the law, the spiritual power of the future dispensation. All this, however, requires unnecessary violence done both to the passage in Deuteronomy and to the language of the apostle. In this very chapter, ver. 18, we have another clear example of Paul's mode of expressing his own ideas in the language of the Scriptures. This is done without hesitation by every preacher of the gospel. The apostle, therefore, is not to be understood as saying, Moses describes the righteousness of the law in one way, and the righteousness of faith in another way ; but he contrasts what Moses says of the law with what the gospel says.

According to the interpretation given above, it is assumed the design of this passage is to present the simplicity and suitableness of the gospel method of salvation, which requires only faith and confession, in opposition to the strict demands of the law, which it is as impossible for us to satisfy as it is to scale the heavens. According to the other view, mentioned above, the design of the apostle was to rebuke the unbelief of the Jews. They were not to regard the resurrection and ascension of Christ as impossible. But the whole context shows that the purpose of the apostle is to contrast the legal and the gospel method of salvation—to show that the one is impracticable, the other easy. By works of the law no flesh living can be justified ; whereas, whosoever simply calls on the name of the Lord shall be saved.

VERSE 8. *But what saith it ? The word is nigh thee, even in thy mouth and in thy heart, that is, the word of faith which we preach.* As the expressions *to be hidden, to be far off,* imply that the thing to which they refer is inaccessible or difficult, so *to be near, to be in the mouth* and *in the heart,* mean to be accessible, easy and familiar. They are frequently thus used ; see Joshua i. 8, "This law shall not depart out of thy mouth," *i.e.,* it shall be constantly familiar to thee ; Exod. xiii. 9, "That the law may be in thy mouth ;" Ps. xxxvii. 31 ; xl. 8. The meaning of this passage then is, 'The gospel, instead of directing us to ascend into heaven, or to go down to the abyss, tells us the thing required is simple and easy. Believe with thy heart and thou shalt be saved.' *The word is nigh thee, i.e.,* the doctrine or truth contemplated, and by implication, what that doctrine demands. Paul, therefore, represents the gospel as speaking of itself. The method of justification by faith says, 'The word is near thee, in thy mouth, *i. e.*, the word or doctrine of faith is thus easy and familiar.' This is Paul's own explanation. The expression, *word of faith,* may mean *the word or doctrine concerning faith,* or *the word to which faith is due,* which should be believed. In either case, it is the gospel, or doctrine of justification, which is here intended.

VERSE 9. *That if thou shalt confess with thy mouth the Lord Jesus,* &c. The connection of this verse with the preceding may be explained by making the last clause of ver. 8 a parenthesis, and connecting this immediately with the first clause. 'It says, the word is nigh thee; it says, that if thou shalt confess and believe, thou shalt be saved.' According to this view, this verse is still a part of what the gospel is represented as saying. Perhaps, however, it is better to consider this verse as Paul's own language, and an explanation of the "word of faith" just spoken of. 'The thing is near and easy, to wit, the word of faith which we preach, that if thou wilt confess,' &c. The two requisites for salvation mentioned in this verse are confession and faith. They are mentioned in their natural order; as confession is the fruit and external evidence of faith. So in 2 Peter i. 10, calling is placed before election, because the former is the evidence of the latter. The thing to be confessed is that Jesus Christ is Lord. That is, we must openly recognize his authority to the full extent in which he is Lord; acknowledge that he is exalted above all principality and powers, that angels are made subject to him, that all power in heaven and earth is committed unto him, and of course that he is our Lord. This confession, therefore, includes in it an acknowledgment of Christ's universal sovereignty, and a sincere recognition of his authority over us. To confess Christ as Lord, is to acknowledge him as the Messiah, recognized as such of God, and invested with all the power and prerogatives of the Mediatorial throne. This acknowledgment is consequently often put for a recognition of Christ in all his offices. 1 Cor. xii. 3, "No man can say that Jesus is the Lord, but by the Holy Ghost." Phil. ii. 11, "Every tongue shall confess that Jesus Christ is Lord." 'To preach the Lord Jesus,' or 'that Jesus is the Lord,' Acts xi. 20, is to preach him as the Saviour in all his fulness. Rom. xiv. 9, "For to this end Christ both died, and rose, and revived, that he might be Lord both of the dead and of the living." The necessity of a public confession of Christ unto salvation is frequently asserted in the Scriptures. Matt. x. 32, "Whosoever, therefore, shall confess me before men, him will I confess also before my Father which is in heaven." Luke xii. 8; 1 John iv. 15, "Whosoever shall confess that Jesus is the Son of God, God dwelleth in him, and he in God."

The second requisite is faith. The truth to be believed is that God hath raised Christ from the dead. That is, we must believe that by the resurrection of Christ, God has publicly acknowledged him to be all that he claimed to be, and has publicly accepted of all that he came to perform. He has recognised him as his Son and the Saviour of the world, and has accepted of his blood as a sacrifice for sin. See Rom. iv. 25, i. 4; Acts xiii. 32, 33; 1 Peter i. 3—5; 1 Cor. xv. 14, *et seq.* ; Acts xvii. 31, "Whereof he hath given assurance unto all men, in that he hath raised him from the dead." To believe, therefore, that God has raised Christ from the dead, involves the belief that Christ is all that he claimed to be, and that he has accomplished all that he came to perform. *In thy heart.* Faith is very far from being a merely speculative exercise. When moral or religious truth is its object, it is always attended by the exercise of the affections. The word *heart*, however, is not to be taken in its limited sense, for the seat of the affections. It means the whole soul, or inner man. Confession is an outward act, faith is an act of the mind in the wide sense of that word. It includes the understanding and the affections. Saving faith is not mere intellectual assent, but a cordial receiving and resting on Christ alone for salvation.

VERSE 10. *For with the heart man believeth unto righteousness, and with the mouth confession is made unto salvation.* This is the reason why faith and confession are alone necessary unto salvation ; because he who believes with the heart is justified, and he who openly confesses Christ shall be saved. That is, such is the doctrine of Scripture, as the apostle proves in the subsequent verse. Here, as in the passages referred to above, in which confession is connected with salvation, it is not a mere saying, Lord, Lord, but a cordial acknowledgment of him, before men, as our Lord and Redeemer. *Unto righteousness, i. e.,* so that we may become righteous. The word *righteousness* has two senses, answering to the two aspects of sin, guilt and moral depravity. According to the former sense, it is that which satisfies justice ; in the latter, it is conformity to the precepts of the law. A man, therefore, may be righteous and yet unholy. Were this not so, there could be no salvation for sinners. If God cannot justify, or pronounce righteous the ungodly, how could we be justified ? Here, as generally, where the subject of justification is discussed in the Bible, righteousness has its forensic, as distinguished from its moral sense. And when Paul says, " With the heart man believeth unto righteousness," he expresses the relation of faith, not to our sanctification, but to justification. *Unto salvation* is equivalent to saying ' that we may be saved.' The preposition rendered *unto*, expressing here the *effect* or *result.* Acts x. 4 ; Heb. vi. 8. By faith we secure an interest in the righteousness of Christ, and by confessing him before men, we secure the performance of his promise that he will confess us before the angels of God. Caeterum viderint quid respondeant Paulo, qui nobis hodie imaginariam quandam fidem fastuose jactant, quae secreto cordis contenta, confessione oris, veluti re supervacanea et inani, supersedeat. Nimis enim nugatorium est, asserere ignem esse, ubi nihil sit flammae neque caloris.—*Calvin.*

DOCTRINE.

1. Zeal, to be either acceptable to God or useful to men, must not only be right as to its ultimate, but also as to its immediate objects. It must not only be about God, but about the things which are well pleasing in his sight. The Pharisees, and other early Jewish persecutors of Christians, really thought they were doing God service when they were so exceedingly zealous for the traditions of their fathers. The moral character of their zeal and its effects were determined by the immediate objects towards which it was directed, ver. 2.

2. The doctrine of justification, or method of securing the pardon of sin and acceptance with God, is the cardinal doctrine in the religion of sinners. The main point is, whether the ground of pardon and acceptance be in ourselves or in another, whether the righteousness on which we depend be of ourselves or of God, ver. 3.

3. Ignorance of the divine character and requirements is at the founda-

tion of all ill-directed efforts for the attainment of salvation, and of all false hopes of heaven, ver. 3.

4. The first and immediate duty of the sinner is to submit to the righteousness of God ; to renounce all dependence on his own merit, and cordially to embrace the offers of reconciliation proposed in the gospel, ver. 3.

5. Unbelief, or the refusal to submit to God's plan of salvation, is the immediate ground of the condemnation or rejection of those who perish under the sound of the gospel, ver. 3.

6. Christ is every thing in the religion of the true believer. He fulfils, and by fulfilling abolishes the law, by whose demands the sinner was weighed down in despair ; and his merit secures the justification of every one that confides in him, ver. 4.

7. Christ is the end of the law, whether moral or ceremonial. To him, both, as a schoolmaster, lead. In him all their demands are satisfied, and all their types and shadows are answered, ver. 4.

8. The legal method of justification is, for sinners, as impracticable as climbing up into heaven or going down into the abyss, vers. 5—7.

9. The demands of the gospel are both simple and intelligible. The sincere acceptance of the proffered righteousness of God, and the open acknowledgment of Jesus Christ as Lord, vers. 6—9.

10. The public profession of religion or confession of Christ is an indispensable duty. That is, in order to salvation, we must not only secretly believe, but also openly acknowledge that Jesus is our prophet, priest, and king. Though faith and confession are both necessary, they are not necessary on the same grounds, nor to the same degree. The former is necessary as a means to an end, as without faith we can have no part in the justifying righteousness of Christ ; the latter as a duty, the performance of which circumstances may render impracticable. In like manner Christ declares baptism, as the appointed means of confession, to be necessary, Mark xvi. 16 ; not, however, as a *sine qua non*, but as a command, the obligation of which providential dispensations may remove, as in the case of the thief on the cross, ver. 9.

11. Faith is not the mere assent of the mind to the truth of certain propositions. It is a cordial persuasion of the truth, founded on the experience of its power or the spiritual perception of its nature, and on the divine testimony. Faith is, therefore, a moral exercise. Men believe with the heart, in the ordinary scriptural meaning of that word. And no faith, which does not proceed from the heart, is connected with justification, ver. 10.

REMARKS.

1. If we really desire the salvation of men, we shall pray for it, ver. 1.

2. No practical mistake is more common or more dangerous than to suppose that all zeal about God and religion is necessarily a godly zeal. Some of the very worst forms of human character have been exhibited by men zealous for God and his service ; as, for example, the persecutors both in the Jewish and Christian churches. Zeal should be according to knowledge, *i. e.*, directed towards proper objects. Its true character is easily ascertained by noticing its effects, whether it produces self-righteousness or humility, censoriousness or charity ; whether it leads to self-denial or self-gratulation and praise ; and whether it manifests itself in prayer and effort, or in loud talking and boasting, ver. 2.

3. We should be very careful what doctrines we hold and teach on the subject of justification. He who is wrong here, ruins his own soul ; and

if he teaches any other than the scriptural method of justification, he ruins the souls of others, ver. 3.

4. A sinner is never safe, do what else he may, until he has submitted to God's method of justification.

5. As every thing in the Bible leads us to Christ, we should suspect every doctrine, system, or theory which has a contrary tendency. That view of religion cannot be correct which does not make Christ the most prominent object, ver. 4.

6. How obvious and infatuated is the folly of the multitude in every age, country, and church, who, in one form or another, are endeavouring to work out a righteousness of their own, instead of submitting to the righteousness of God. They are endeavouring to climb up to heaven, or to descend into the abyss, vers. 5—7.

7. The conduct of unbelievers is perfectly inexcusable, who reject the simple, easy, and gracious offers of the gospel, which requires only faith and confession, vers. 8—9.

8. Those who are ashamed or afraid to acknowledge Christ before men, cannot expect to be saved. The want of courage to confess, is decisive evidence of the want of heart to believe, vers. 9, 10.

ROMANS X. 11—21.

ANALYSIS.

The object of the apostle in the preceding comparison and contrast of the two methods of justification, was to show that the gospel method was, from its nature, adapted to all men : and that if suited to all it should be preached to all. In ver. 11 the quotation from the Old Testament proves two points. 1. That faith is the condition of acceptance ; and 2. That it matters not whether the individual be a Jew or Gentile, if he only believes. For there is really no difference, as to this point, between the two classes ; God is equally gracious to both, as is proved by the express declarations of Scripture, vers. 12, 13. If, then, the method of salvation be thus adapted to all, and God is equally the God of the Gentiles and of the Jews, then, to accomplish his purpose, the gospel must be preached to all men, because faith cometh by hearing, ver. 14—17. Both the fact of the extension of the gospel to the Gentiles, and the disobedience of the great part of the Jews, were clearly predicted in the writings of the Old Testament, vers. 18—21.

COMMENTARY.

Verse 11. *For the Scripture saith, Whosoever believeth on him shall not be ashamed.* This passage is cited in support of the doctrine just taught, that faith alone is necessary to salvation. There are clearly two points established by the quotation ; the first is, the universal applicability of this method of salvation ; whosoever, whether Jew or Gentile, believes, &c. ; and the second is, that it is faith which is the means of securing the divine favour ; whosoever believes on him shall not be ashamed. The passage, therefore, is peculiarly adapted to the apostle's object ; which was not merely to exhibit the true nature of the plan of redemption, but mainly to show the propriety of its extension to the Gentiles. The passage quoted is Isa. xxviii. 16, referred to at the close of the preceding chapter. We must not only believe Christ, but believe upon him. The language of Paul is, πᾶς ὁ πιστεύων ἐπ᾽ αὐτῷ, Πιστεύειν ἐπί τινι, to trust upon any one. That is, it expresses confiding reliance on its object. It is all important to know what the Bible teaches, both as to the object and nature of saving faith. That object is Christ, and saving faith is trust. He is so complete a Saviour as to be able to save all who come unto God by him; and therefore *whosoever* believeth on him shall not be ashamed. Hoc monosyllabon, says Bengel, πᾶς (omnis), toto mundo pretiosus, propositum, ver. 11, ita repetitur, ver. 12 et 13, et ita confirmatur ulterius, vers. 14, 15, ut non modo significet, quicumque invocaret, salvum fore; sed, Deum velle, se invocari ab omnibus salutariter.

Verse 12. *For there is no difference between the Jew and the Greek,* &c. This verse is evidently connected logically with the *whosoever* of ver. 12, ‘ *Whosoever* believes shall be saved, for there is no difference between the Jew and Gentile.’ That is, there is no difference in their relation to the law or to God. They are alike sinners, and are to be judged by precisely the same principles, (see chap. iii. 22); and consequently, if saved at all, are to be saved in precisely the same way. *For the same Lord over all, is rich unto all who call upon him.* This is the reason why there is no difference between the two classes. Their relation to God is the same. They are equally his creatures, and his mercy towards them is the same. It is doubtful whether this clause is to be understood of Christ or of God. If the latter, the general meaning is what has just been stated. If the former, then the design is to declare that the same Saviour is ready and able to save all. In favour of this latter, which is perhaps the most common view of the passage, it may be urged that Christ is the person referred to in the preceding verse; and secondly, that he is so commonly called Lord in the New Testament. But, on the other hand, *the Lord* in the next verse refers to God; and secondly, we have the same sentiment, in the same general connection, in chap. iii. 29, 30, “ Is he the God of the Jews only? &c. It is the same God which shall justify the circumcision by faith, and the uncircumcision through faith.” *The same Lord over all,* in this connection, means ‘ one and the same Lord is over all.’ All are equally under his dominion, and may, therefore, equally hope in his mercy. As good reasons may be assigned for both interpretations, commentators are nearly equally divided on the question whether the immediate reference be to Christ or to God. Doctrinally, it matters little which view be preferred. Faith in God is faith in Christ, for Christ is God. This is the great truth to be acknowledged. The condition of salvation, under the gospel, is the invocation of Christ as God. The analogy of Scripture, therefore, as well as the context, is in favour of the immediate reference of κύριος to Christ. The words *is rich,* may be either a concise expression for *is rich in mercy,* or they may mean *is abundant in resources.* He is sufficiently rich to supply the wants of all; whosoever, therefore, believes in him shall be saved.

Unto all who call upon him, i. e., who invoke him, or worship him, agreeably to the frequent use of the phrase in the Old and New Testament, Gen. iv. 26, xii. 8; Isa. lxiv. 7; Acts ii. 21, ix. 14, xxii. 16; 1 Cor. i. 2; 2 Tim. ii. 22. This religious invocation of God implied, of course, the exercise of faith in him; and, therefore, it amounts to the same thing whether it is said, ‘ Whosoever believes,’ or, ‘ Whosoever calls on the name of the Lord shall be saved.’ This being the case, the passage quoted from

Joel, in the next verse, is equivalent to that cited from Isaiah, in verse 11. The meaning, then, of this verse is, ' That God has proposed the same terms of salvation to all men, Jews and Gentiles, because he is equally the God of both, and his mercy is free and sufficient for all.'

Verse.13. *For whosoever shall call upon the name of the Lord shall be saved.* As this verse is not introduced by the usual form of quotation from the Old Testament, *as it is written,* or *as the Scripture,* or *the prophet saith,* it is not absolutely necessary to consider it as a direct citation, intended as an argument from Scripture, (compare ver. 11.) Yet, as the passage is in itself so pertinent, it is probable that the apostle intended to confirm his declaration, that the mercy of God should be extended to every one who called upon him, by showing that the ancient prophets had held the same language. The prophet Joel, after predicting the dreadful calamities which were about to come upon the people, foretold, in the usual manner of the ancient messengers of God, that subsequent to those judgments should come a time of great and general blessedness. This happy period was ever characterized as one in which true religion should prevail, and the stream of divine truth and love, no longer confined to the narrow channel of the Jewish people, should overflow all nations. Thus Joel says, " It shall come to pass afterward, that I will pour out my Spirit upon all flesh, &c., and whosoever shall call upon the name of the Lord shall be delivered," Joel ii. 28, 32. Whosoever, therefore, betakes himself to God as his refuge, and calls upon him, in the exercise of faith, as his God, shall be saved, whether Gentile or Jew, (see 1 Cor. i. 2.) The prophecy in Joel has direct reference to the Messianic period, and therefore the Lord, who was to be invoked, who was to be looked to, and be called upon for salvation, is the Messiah. All, whosoever, without any limitation as to family or nation, who call on him, shall be saved. This is Paul's doctrine, and the doctrine, with one accord, of all the holy men who spake of old, as the Spirit gave them utterance. This being the case, how utterly preposterous and wicked the attempt to confine the offers of salvation to the Jewish people, or to question the necessity of the extension of the gospel through the whole world. Thus naturally and beautifully does the apostle pass from the nature of the plan of mercy, and its suitableness to all men, to the subject principally in view, the calling of the Gentiles, or the duty of preaching the gospel to all people.

Verses 14, 15. *How then shall they call on him in whom they have not believed ? and how shall they believe in him of whom they have not heard ?* &c., &c. Paul considered it as involved in what he had already said, and especially in the predictions of the ancient prophets, that it was the will of God that all men should call upon him. This being the case, he argues to prove that it was his will that the gospel should be preached to all. As invocation implies faith, as faith implies knowledge, knowledge instruction, and instruction an instructor, so it is plain that if God would have all men to call upon him, he designed preachers to be sent to all, whose proclamation of mercy being heard, might be believed, and being believed, might lead men to call on him and be saved. This is agreeable to the prediction of Isaiah, who foretold that the advent of the preachers of the gospel should be hailed with great and universal joy. According to this, which is the common and most natural view of the passage, it is an argument founded on the principle, that if God wills the end, he wills also the means; if he would have the Gentiles saved, according to the predictions of his prophets, he would have the gospel preached to them. " Qui vult finem, vult etiam media. Deus vult ut homines invocent ipsum salutariter. Ergo vult ut credant. Ergo vult ut audiant. Ergo vult ut habeant praedicatores. Itaque praedicatores misit."—*Bengel.* Calvin's view of the object of the passage is the same, but his idea of the nature of the argument is very different. He supposes the apostle to reason thus. The Gentiles actually call upon God; but invocation implies faith, faith hearing, hearing preaching, and preaching a divine mission. If therefore, the Gentiles have actually received and obeyed the gospel, it is proof enough that God designed it to be sent to them. This interpretation is ingenious, and affords a good sense; but it is founded on an assumption which the Jew would be slow to admit, that the Gentile was an acceptable worshipper of God. If he admitted this, he admitted every thing and the argument becomes unnecessary. According to De Wette, Meyer, and others, the design of the apostle is to show the necessity of divine messengers in order to ground thereon a reproof of disobedience to that message. The whole context, however, shows, that he is not here assigning the reasons for the rejection of the Jews, but vindicating the propriety of preaching to the Gentiles. God had predicted that the Gentiles should be saved; he had provided a method of salvation adapted to all men; he had declared that whosoever called upon the name of the Lord should be saved; from which it follows, that it is his will that they should hear of him whom they were required to invoke.

Verse 15. *As it is written, How beautiful are the feet of them that preach the gospel of peace, and bring glad tidings of good things.* The word here rendered *preach the gospel,* is the same as that immediately afterwards translated, *bring glad tidings.* The word *gospel,* therefore, must be taken in its original meaning, *good news, the good news of peace.* The passage in Isa. lii. 7, which the apostle faithfully, as to the meaning, follows, has reference to the Messiah's kingdom. It is one of those numerous prophetic declarations, which announce in general terms the coming deliverance of the Church, a deliverance which embraced, at the first stage of its accomplishment, the restoration from the Babylonish captivity. This, however, so far from being the blessing principally intended, derived all its value from being introductory to that more glorious deliverance to be effected by the Redeemer. *How beautiful the feet,* of course means, how delightful the approach. The bearing of this passage on the object of the apostle is sufficiently obvious. He had proved that the gospel should be preached to all men, and refers to the declaration of the ancient prophet, which spoke of the joy with which the advent of the messengers of mercy should be hailed.

Verse 16. *But they have not all obeyed the gospel, for Isaiah saith, Lord, who hath believed our report?* This verse may be viewed as an objection to the apostle's doctrine, confirmed by the quotation of a passage from Isaiah. 'You say the gospel ought to be preached to all men, but if God had intended that it should be preached to them, they would obey it; which they have not done.' This view of the passage would have some plausibility if Calvin's representation of Paul's argument were correct. Did the apostle reason from the fact that the Gentiles believed that it was God's intention they should have the gospel preached to them, it would be very natural to object, that as only a few have obeyed, it was evidently not designed for them. But even on the supposition of the correctness of this view of the argument, this interpretation of ver. 16 is barely possible, for the quotation from Isaiah cannot be understood otherwise than as the language of the apostle, or as intended to confirm what he himself had said. There is no necessity for the assumption that this verse is the language of an objection. Paul had said that the preaching of the gospel to all men, whether Jews or Gentiles, was according to the will of God. This is true *although* (ἀλλά) all have not obeyed. This disobedience was foreseen and predicted, *for* Isaiah saith, Lord, who hath believed our report? The complaint of the prophet was not confined to the men of his generation. It had reference mainly to the general rejection of the gospel, especially by the theocratical people. Christ came to his own and his own received him not. And this was predicted of old. *Our report*, or message. The word is ἀκοή, literally the faculty or act of hearing ; then metonymically, what is heard, *i.e.*, a message, preaching, or teaching. The message of the prophet concerning the servant of the Lord, and what he was to do and suffer for his people, as recorded in Isaiah liii., it was predicted would be believed by the great majority of those to whom it was addressed.

VERSE 17. *So then faith* (cometh) *by hearing, and hearing by the word of God.* The passage in Isaiah speaks of an ἀκοή, a message, something addressed to the ear. The design of that message was that men should believe. They were required to receive and rest upon it as true. Without it there could be no ground of faith ; nothing on which faith could rest. Therefore faith is from hearing. It is receiving the message as true. But this message is by the word or command of God. It is therefore a sure foundation of faith. And as all men are required to believe, the message should be sent to all, and the divine command on which it rests, must include an injunction to make the proclamation universal. Thus the two ideas presented in the context, viz., the necessity of knowledge to faith, and the purpose of God to extend that knowledge to the Gentiles, are both confirmed in this verse. The above is the common interpretation of this passage. It assumes that ῥῆμα Θεοῦ is to be taken in the sense of command of God, whereas it commonly means the word or message of God. If this sense be retained here, then ἀκοή must mean the act of hearing. 'Faith cometh by hearing, and hearing supposes something to be heard, a ῥῆμα, or word of God.' In Luke v. 5; Heb. xi. 3, (compare Heb. i. 3), ῥῆμα Θεοῦ means God's (or the Lord's) command. There is no necessity, therefore, for giving ἀκοή a different sense here from that which it must have in the preceding verse.

VERSE 18. *But I say, Have they not heard? Yes, verily, their sound went into all the earth*, &c. The concise and abrupt manner of argument and expression in this and the verses which precede and follow, renders the apostle's meaning somewhat doubtful. This verse is frequently considered as referring to the Jews, and designed to show that their want of faith could not be excused on the ground of want of knowledge. The sense of the passage would then be, 'As faith cometh by hearing, have not the Jews heard? Have they not had the opportunity of believing? Yes, indeed, for the Gospel has been proclaimed far and wide.' So Koppe, Flatt, Tholuck, Meyer, Philippi, &c. But there are several objections to this view of the passage. In the first place it is not in harmony with the context. Paul is not speaking now of the rejection of the Jews, or the grounds of it, but of the calling of the Gentiles. 2. If the 16th verse refers to the Gentiles, "They have not all obeyed the gospel," and therefore this verse, "Have they not heard?" cannot, without any intimation of change, be naturally referred to a different subject. 3. In the following verse, where the Jews are really intended, they are distinctly mentioned, "Did not Israel know?"

Paul's object in the whole context is to vindicate the propriety of extending the gospel call to all nations. This he had beautifully done in vers. 14, 15, by showing that preaching was a necessary means of accomplishing the clearly revealed will of God, that men of all nations should participate in his grace. 'True, indeed, as had been foretold, the merciful offers of the gospel were not universally accepted, ver. 16, but still faith cometh by hearing, and therefore the gospel should be widely preached, ver. 17. Well, has not this been done? has not the angel of mercy broke loose from his long confinement within the pale of the Jewish Church, and flown through the heavens with the proclamation of love?' ver. 18. This verse, therefore, is to be considered as a strong declaration that what Paul had proved ought to be done, had in fact been accomplished. The middle wall of partition had been broken down, the gospel of salvation, the religion of God, was free from its trammels, the offers of mercy were as wide and general as the proclamation of the heavens. This idea the apostle beautifully and appositely expresses in the sublime language of Psalm xix., "The heavens declare the glory of God, day unto day uttereth speech, there is no speech nor language where their voice is not heard, their line is gone through all the earth, and their words to the end of the world." The last verse contains the words used by the apostle. His object in using the words of the Psalmist was, no doubt, to convey more clearly and affectingly to the minds of his hearers the idea that the proclamation of the gospel was now as free from all national or ecclesiastical restrictions, as the instructions shed down upon all people by the heavens under which they dwell. Paul, of course, is not to be understood as quoting the Psalmist as though the ancient prophet was speaking of the gospel. He simply uses scriptural language to express his own ideas, as is done involuntarily almost by every preacher in every sermon.* It is, however, nevertheless true, as Hengstenberg remarks in his Christology, that "The universal revelation of God in nature, was a providential prediction of the universal proclamation of the gospel. If the former was not fortuitous, but founded in the nature of God, so must the latter be. The manifestation of God in nature, is, for all his creatures to whom it is made, a pledge of their participation in the clearer and higher revelations."

It will be perceived that the apostle says, "Their *sound* has gone, &c.," whereas in the 19th Psalm it is, "Their *line* is gone." Paul follows the Septuagint, which, instead of giving the literal sense of the Hebrew word, gives correctly its figurative meaning. The word signifies *a line*, then *a musical chord*, and then, metonymically, *sound*.

VERSE 19. *But I say, Did not Israel know? First Moses saith, I will provoke you to jealousy,* &c. Another passage difficult from its conciseness. The difficulty is to ascertain what the question refers to. Did not Israel know what? The gospel? or, The calling of the Gentiles and their own rejection? The latter seems, for two reasons, the decidedly preferable interpretation. 1. The question is most naturally understood as referring to the main subject under discussion, which is, as frequently remarked, the calling of the Gentiles and rejection of the Jews. 2. The question is ex-

---

* Calvin's view of this passage is peculiar—Quaerit, an Deus nunquam ante gentes vocem suam direxit, et doctoris officio functus sit erga totum mundum.—Accipio igitur ejus citationem in proprio et germano prophetae sensu, ut tale sit argumentum: Deus jam ab initio mundi suam gentibus divinitatem manifestaret, et si non hominum praedicatione, creaturarum tamen suarum testimonio.—Apparet ergo, Dominum etiam pro eo tempore, quo foederis sui gratiam in Israele continebat, non tamen ita sui notitiam gentibus subduxisse, quin aliquam semper illis scintillam accenderet.

plained by the quotations which follow. 'Does not Israel know what Moses and Isaiah so plainly teach?' viz., that a people who were no people, should be preferred to Israel; while the latter were to be regarded as disobedient and gainsaying. According to the other interpretation, the meaning of the apostle is, 'Does not Israel know the gospel? Have not the people of God been instructed? If, therefore, as was predicted, they are superseded by the heathen, it must be their own fault.' Calvin thinks there is an evident contrast between this and the preceding verse. 'If even the heathen have had some knowledge of God, how is it with Israel, the favoured people of God? &c.' But this whole interpretation, as intimated above, is inconsistent with the drift of the context, and the spirit of the passages quoted from the Old Testament.

First Moses says, I will provoke you to jealousy by them that are *no people,* &c. The word *first* seems evidently to be used in reference to Isaiah, who is quoted afterward, and should not be connected, as it is by many, with Israel. 'Did not Israel first learn the gospel, &c.' So Storr, Flatt, &c. Better in the ordinary way, 'First Moses, and then Isaiah, say, &c.' The passage quoted from Moses is Deut. xxxii. 21. In that chapter the sacred writer recounts the mercies of God, and the ingratitude and rebellion of the people. In ver. 21 he warns them, that as they had provoked him to jealousy by that which is not God, he would provoke them to jealousy by them that are no people. That is, as they forsook him and made choice of another god, so he would reject them and make choice of another people. The passage, therefore, plainly enough intimates that the Jews were in no such sense the people of God, as to interfere with their being cast off and others called.

VERSES 20, 21. *But Esaias is very bold, and saith,* &c. That is, according to a very common Hebrew construction, in which one verb qualifies another adverbially, *saith very plainly* or *openly.* Plain as the passage in Deuteronomy is, it is not so clear and pointed as that now referred to, Isaiah lxv. 1, 2.

Paul follows the Septuagint version of the passage, merely transposing the clauses. The sense is accurately expressed. 'I am sought of *them that* asked not *for me,* I am found of them that sought me not,' is the literal version of the Hebrew, as given in our translation. The apostle quotes and applies the passage in the sense in which it is to be interpreted in the ancient prophet. In the first verse of that chapter Isaiah says, that God will manifest himself to those "who were not called by his name;" and in the second, he gives the immediate reason of this turning unto the Gentiles, "I have stretched out my hand all the day to a rebellious people." This quotation, therefore, confirms both the great doctrines taught in this chapter; the Jews were no longer the exclusive or peculiar people of God, and the blessings of the Messiah's kingdom were thrown wide open to all mankind. With regard to Israel, the language of God is peculiarly strong and tender. *All day long I have stretched forth my hands. The stretching forth the hands* is the gesture of invitation, and even supplication. God has extended wide his arms, and urged men frequently and long to return to his love; and it is only those who refuse, that he finally rejects.

DOCTRINE.

1. Christianity is, from its nature, adapted to be an universal religion. There is nothing, as was the case with Judaism, which binds it to a particular location, or confines it to a particular people. All its duties may be performed, and all its blessings enjoyed, in every part of the world, and by every nation under heaven, vers. 11—13.

2. The relation of men to God, and his to them, is not determined by any national or ecclesiastical connection. He deals with all, on the same general principles, and is ready to save all who call upon him, ver. 12.

3. WHOSOEVER will, may take of the water of life. The essential conditions of salvation have in every age been the same. Even under the Old Testament dispensation, God accepted all who sincerely invoked his name, ver. 13.

4. The preaching of the gospel is the great means of salvation, and it is the will of God that it should be extended to all people, vers. 14, 15.

5. As invocation implies faith, and faith requires knowledge, and knowledge instruction, and instruction teachers, and teachers a mission, it is evident not only that God wills that teachers should be sent to all those whom he is willing to save, when they call upon him, but that all parts of this divinely connected chain of causes and effects are necessary to the end proposed, viz., the salvation of men. It is, therefore, as incumbent on those who have the power, to send the gospel abroad, as it is on those to whom it is sent, to receive it, vers. 14, 15.

6. As the rudiments of the tree are in the seed, so all the elements of the New Testament doctrines are in the Old. The Christian dispensation is the explanation, fulfilment, and development of the Jewish, vers. 11, 13, 15.

REMARKS.

1. Christians should breathe the spirit of an universal religion : a religion which regards all men as brethren, which looks on God, not as the God of this nation, or of that church, but as the God and Father of all, which proposes to all the same conditions of acceptance, and which opens equally to all the same boundless and unsearchable blessings, vers. 11—13.

2. It must be very offensive to God, who looks on all men with equal favour, (except as moral conduct makes a difference,) to observe how one class of mortals looks down upon another, on account of some merely adventitious difference of rank, colour, external circumstances, or social or ecclesiastical connection, ver 12.

3. How will the remembrance of the simplicity and reasonableness of the plan of salvation, and the readiness of God to accept of all who call upon him, overwhelm those who perish from beneath the sound of the gospel ! ver. 13.

4. It is the first and most pressing duty of the church to cause all men to hear the gospel. The solemn question implied in the language of the apostle, How CAN THEY BELIEVE WITHOUT A PREACHER ? should sound day and night in the ears of the churches, vers. 14, 15.

5. "How can they preach except they be sent ?" The failure of the whole must result from the failure of any one of the parts of the system of means. How long, alas ! has the failure been in the very first step.

Preachers have not been sent, and if not sent, how could men hear, believe, or call upon God ? vers. 14, 15.

6. If "faith comes by hearing," how great is the value of a stated ministry ! How obvious the duty to establish, sustain, and attend upon it ! ver. 17.

7. The gospel's want of success, or the fact that few believe our report, is only a reason for its wider extension. The more who hear, the more will be saved, even should it be but a small proportion of the whole, ver. 16.

8. How delightful will be the time when literally the sound of the gospel shall be as extensively diffused as the declaration which the heavens, in their circuit, make of the glory of God ! ver. 18.

9. The blessings of a covenant relation to God are the unalienable right of no people and of no church, but can be preserved only by fidelity on the part of men to the covenant itself, ver. 19.

10. God is often found by those who apparently are the farthest from him, while he remains undiscovered by those who think themselves always in his presence, ver. 20.

11. God's dealings, even with reprobate sinners, are full of tenderness and compassion. All the day long he extends the arms of his mercy, even to the disobedient and the gainsaying. This will be felt and acknowledged at last by all who perish, to the glory of God's forbearance, and to their own confusion and self-condemnation, ver. 21.

12. Communities and individuals should beware how they slight the mercies of God, and especially how they turn a deaf ear to the invitations of the gospel. For when the blessings of a church relation have once been withdrawn from a people, they are long in being restored. Witness the Jewish and the fallen Christian churches. And when God ceases to urge on the disobedient sinner the offers of mercy, his destiny is sealed, ver. 21.

CHAPTER XI.

CONTENTS.

This chapter consists of two parts, verses 1—10, and 11—36. in the former the apostle teaches that the rejection of the jews was not total. there was a remnant, and perhaps a much larger remnant than many might suppose, excepted, although the mass of the nation, agreeably to the predictions of the prophets, was cast off, verses 1—10. in the latter, he shows that this rejection is not final. in the first place, the restoration of the jews is a desirable and probable event, verses 11—24. in the second, it is one which god has determined to bring to pass, verses 25—32. the chapter closes with a sublime declaration of the unsearchable wisdom of god, manifested in all his dealings with men, verses 33—36. in the consideration of the great doctrinal truths taught in this chapter, paul intersperses many practical remarks, designed to give these truths their proper influence both on the jews and gentiles, especially the latter.

ROMANS XI. 1—10.

ANALYSIS.

The rejection of the Jews is not total, as is sufficiently manifest from the example of the apostle himself, to say nothing of others, ver. 1. God had reserved a remnant faithful to himself as was the case in the times of Elias, vers. 2—4. That this remnant is saved, is a matter entirely of grace, vers. 5, 6. The real truth of the case is, that Israel, as a nation, is excluded from the kingdom of Christ, but the chosen ones are admitted to its blessings, ver. 7. This rejection of the greater part of the Jews, their own Scriptures had predicted, vers. 8—10.

COMMENTARY.

Verse 1. *1 say, then,* λέγω οὖν, *I ask, then, i.e.,* Is it to be inferred from what I have said, that God hath rejected his people? When we consider how many promises are made to the Jewish nation, as God's peculiar people; and how often it is said, as in Psalm xciv. 14, "The Lord will not cast off his people," it is not surprising that the doctrine of the rejection of the Jews, as taught in the preceding chapters, was regarded as inconsistent with the word of God. Paul removes this difficulty, first by showing that the rejection of the Jews was neither total nor final; and secondly, by proving that the promises in question had reference, not to the Jewish nation as such, but to the elect, or, the spiritual Israel. The word ἀπώσατο stands at the beginning of the sentence, to show that it is emphatic. Has God utterly, (*i.e.,* totally and finally) rejected his people? This Paul denies. He had not asserted any thing of the kind. The rejection of the Jews as a nation, was consistent with all that God had promised to their fathers. Those promises did not secure the salvation of all Jews, or of the Jews as a nation. And the doctrine which he had inculcated did not involve the rejection of all Jews. In proof, he adds, *For I also am an Israelite.* Paul had not taught his own rejection. The fact that he claimed for himself, and for all who with him believed on Christ, a part in the Messiah's kingdom, made it clear that he did not teach the rejection of all Israel. De Wette, and Meyer, in opposition to almost common consent, give a different view of the apostle's language. They understand him as repudiating the idea of the universal rejection of the Jews, as inconsistent with his patriotic feeling. For I also am an Israelite. How can a Jew believe that God has cast off his people? But the context is clearly in favour of the common interpretation. The apostle goes on to show that a general apostacy did not involve an entire rejection. The nation, as a nation, had before turned to idols, and yet a remnant had remained faithful. And so it was now. *Of the seed of Abraham,* and *of the tribe of Benjamin,* see Phil. iii. 5. Paul was a Jew by descent from Abraham, and not merely a proselyte; and he was of one of the most favoured tribes. Judah and Benjamin, especially after the exile, were the chief representatives of the theocratical people.

Verse 2. *God hath not cast away his people which he foreknew.* This verse admits of two interpretations. The words *his people* may be understood, as in the preceding verse, as meaning *the Jewish nation,* and the clause *which he foreknew,* as, by implication, assigning the reason for the declaration that God had not cast them off. The clause, according to this view, is little more than a repetition of the sentiment of the preceding verse. ' It is not to be inferred from what I have said of the rejection of the Jews, that God has cast away all his chosen people. Multitudes are excepted now, as in the days of Elias.' The second interpretation requires more stress to be laid upon the words *which he foreknew*, as qualifying and distinguishing the preceding phrase, *his people*. ' God has indeed rejected his external people, the Jewish nation as such, but he has not cast away his people whom he foreknew.' According to this view, *his people* means the elect, his spiritual people, or the true Israel. This interpretation seems decidedly preferable, 1. Because it is precisely the distinction which Paul had made, and made for the same purpose, in chap. ix. 6—8, ' The rejection of the external Israel does not invalidate the promises of God, because those promises did not contemplate the natural seed as such, but the spiritual Israel. So, now, when I say that the external Israel is rejected, it does not imply that the true chosen Israel, to whom the promises pertained, is cast away.' 2. Because this is apparently Paul's own explanation in the sequel. The mass of the nation were cast away, but " a remnant, according to the election of grace," were reserved, ver. 5. Israel, as such, Paul says in ver. 7, failed of admission to the Messiah's kingdom, " but the election hath obtained it." It is, therefore, evident that the *people which God foreknew*, and which were not cast off, is " the remnant" spoken of in ver. 5, and " the election" mentioned in ver. 7. 3. Because the illustration borrowed from the Old Testament best suits this interpretation. In the days of Elias, God rejected the great body of the people ; but reserved to himself a remnant, chosen in sovereign grace. The distinction, therefore, in both cases, is between the external and the chosen people.

Which he foreknew. On the different senses of the word rendered *he foreknew*, see chap. viii. 29. Compare Rom. vii. 15 ; 2 Tim. ii. 19 ; 1 Cor. viii. 3 ; Gal. iv. 9 ; Prov. xii. 10 ; Ps. ci. 4 ; 1 Thes. v. 12 ; Matt. vii. 23. In foreknowledge, as thus used, is involved something more than simple prescience, of which all persons and all events are the objects. The people whom God foreknew, were a people distinguished by that foreknowledge from all other people. All are not Israel who are of Israel. God knows those who are his, and in the midst of general apostasy, preserves and saves those whom he thus foreknows as his own. Even Luther gives this view of the passage. " Es ist nicht alles Gottes-Volk, was Gottes Volk heisset ; darum wird nicht alles verstossen, ob der mehere Theil auch verstossen wird." And Olshausen says, " Vom *sichtbaren* geht er aber weiter, auf den unsichtbaren Kern des Volkes Gottes über . . . Offenbar kann Paulus hier nicht von bloss die zur Kirche übergetretenen Juden meinen, die waren kenntlich, sondern die jedem menschlichen Auge unbekannten, die den verborgenen Schatz der Treue und Aufrichtigkeit ihnen selbst unbewusst im Herzen trugen. Diese verhalten sich zur Masse des Volks, wie im Individuum die Reste des göttlichen. Ebenbildes zum alten Menschen ; oder wie im wiedergebornen der unentwickelte, oft von der Sünde zurückgedrängte neue Mensch zu dem ihm umgebenden sündlichen Menschen. Wie dieser sterben muss, damit jener herrsche, so muss auch das λεῖμμα frei gemacht werden von der fremden Schale, in der er wohnt, um sich ausbreiten zu können. Immer ist es das eigentliche Volk (9, 6 ff.) auf das alle Verheissungen gehen, wie der unscheinbare neue Mensch in dem ungeschlachtigen alten Menschen allein der wahre Mensch ist."

Wot ye not what the Scripture saith of Elias? ἐν Ἠλίᾳ, *in* Elias, *i. e.*, in the section which treats of Elias, or which is designated by his name. Another example of this method of referring to Scripture is found in Mark xii. 26, " In the bush God spake unto him ;" *i.e.*, in the section which treats of the burning bush. This method of quotation is common with the Rabbins, *Surenh.* p. 493, and occurs in the classic writers. *How he maketh intercession to God against Israel;* ἐντυγχάνειν means to approach or draw near to any one, either ὑπέρ, *in behalf of,* or κατά, *against.* The latter form occurs here and in 1 Macc. x. 60.

VERSE 3. *Lord, they have killed thy prophets, and digged down thine altars, and I am left alone,* &c. 1 Kings xix. 10. Paul gives the sense, and nearly the words of the original. The event referred to was the great defection from the true religion, and the murder of the prophets of God, under the reign of Ahab. The point of the analogy to which the apostle refers, is that although then, as now, the defection was apparently entire, yet many unknown of men remained faithful, and escaped the doom visited on the nation as such. As the law allowed only one altar, and that at Jerusalem, it has been asked, How the prophet could speak of digging down the *altars* of God, as though there were many ? To this it is commonly answered, that the probability is, that after the defection of the ten tribes, many altars to the true God were erected in secret places, by those who adhered to the religion of their fathers, and which, as access to Jerusalem was impossible, were then tolerated by the prophets, and the destruction of which, out of hatred to the true religion, was evidence of apostacy from God.

VERSE 4. *But what saith the answer of God unto him ? I have reserved to myself seven thousand men,* &c. 1 Kings xix. 18. Here again the apostle gives the sense of the original, with slight variations both from the Hebrew and Greek. In the LXX., the future καταλείψω is used where Paul has the aorist κατέλιπον. Paul also inserts the pronoun (ἐμαυτῷ), which is neither in the Greek nor Hebrew. " I have reserved for myself ;" *i.e.*, as my own peculiar people. In Kings, God threatens the general destruction of the people, but promises to reserve seven thousand, who had not gone after false gods. No special stress is to be laid on the number *seven*, as the whole design of the apostle is to show that national destruction does not involve the destruction of the true people of God. He always has an invisible church within the visible ; and the destruction or dispersion of the latter does not affect the former. *Answer of God,* χρηματισμός, *divine response,* or *oracle.* The verb χρηματίζω occurs in Heb. xii. 25, xi. 7 ; Matt. ii. 12 ; Luke ii. 26 ; Acts x. 22. Those who remained faithful in the time of Elias, were those who had not bowed the knee to Baal. *Baal* signifies lord, ruler, and is used as the designation of a Phœnician deity. Among the Chaldeans he was called Bel, or Belus. He was regarded as the generative, controlling principle, of which the sun or the planet of Jupiter was the symbol, and to the people the direct object of worship. With him was associated a female deity, *Ashtaroth,* the Greek Astarte, called queen of heaven, the moon. But as Baal was also associated with the planet Jupiter, so was Ashtaroth with Venus. In this passage the feminine article is used before Baal, τῇ Βάαλ. This is explained by our interpreters, by supposing that εἰκών, *image,* is omitted. But this is unsatisfactory, not only because if such ellipsis occurred, the expression would properly be, τῇ τοῦ Βάαλ ; but also because in the LXX. and the Apocrypha, Baal has repeatedly the feminine article. Zeph. i. 4 ;

Hos. ii. 8; 1 Sam. vii. 4. Some say this is done in the way of contempt, as with the Rabbins the feminine form is sometimes thus used. There is, however, no special indication of any such purpose in those cases where the feminine article occurs. It is more satisfactory to assume that, at least with the later Hebrews, both the active generative principle in nature, and the passive, or birth-giving principle, was expressed by the same word; so that Baal was really androgyne, both male and female.

Verse. 5. *Even so then at this present time also there is a remnant according to the election of grace.* As in the days of Elias, there was a number which, although small in comparison with the whole nation, was still much greater than appeared to human eyes, who remained faithful, so at the present time, amidst the general defection of the Jews, and their consequent rejection as a people, there is a remnant, (λεῖμμα, *what is left,* answering to κατέλιπον in ver. 4,) *according to the election of grace;* that is, graciously chosen. The election was *gracious,* not merely in the sense of *kind,* but *gratuitous, sovereign,* not founded on the merits of the persons chosen, but the good pleasure of God. This explanation of the term is given by the apostle himself in the next verse. *Remnant according to the gracious election* is equivalent to *remnant gratuitously chosen;* see chap. ix. 11, and vers. 21, 24 of this chapter. Paul, therefore, designs to teach that the rejection of the Jews was not total, because there was a number whom God had chosen, who remained faithful, and constituted the true Israel or elected people, to whom the promises were made. As in the days of Elias, the number of those who had not bowed the knee to Baal was far greater than the prophet believed it to be, so the number of those who acknowledged Christ as the Messiah, in the times of the apostle, was much larger probably than is generally supposed. The apostle James speaks of *many myriads* (πόσαι μυριάδες), Acts xxi. 20, of believing Jews.

Verse 6. *And if by grace, then it is no more of works; otherwise grace is no more grace.* This verse is an exegetical comment on the last clause of the preceding one. If the election spoken of be of grace, it is not founded on works, for the two things are incompatible. It evidently was, in the apostle's view, a matter of importance that the entire freeness of the election of men to the enjoyment of the blessings of the Messiah's kingdom, should be steadily kept in view. He would not otherwise have stopped in the midst of his discourse to insist so much on this idea. This verse serves to illustrate several declarations of the apostle in the preceding chapter. For example, ver. 11, in which, as here, men are said to be chosen in a sovereign manner, and not according to their works. It is obvious that *foreseen* works are as much excluded as any other. For a choice founded upon the foresight of good works, is as really made on account of works as any choice can be, and, consequently, is not of grace, in the sense asserted by the apostle. In the second place, the choice which is here declared to be so entirely gratuitous, is a choice to the kingdom of Christ. This is evident from the whole context, and especially from ver. 7. It was from this kingdom and all its spiritual and eternal blessings that the Jews, as a body, were rejected, and to which "the remnant according to the election of grace" was admitted. The election, therefore, spoken of in the ninth chapter, is not to external privileges merely.

The latter part of this verse is simply the converse of the former. *But if of works, then it is no more grace; otherwise work is no more work.* If founded on any thing in us, it is not founded on the mere good pleasure of God. If the one be affirmed, the other is denied. This clause is omitted in the uncial MSS. A. C. D. E. F. G., and in several of the ancient versions, and by all the Latin fathers. On these grounds it is rejected as a gloss by Erasmus, Grotius, Wetstein, Griesbach, and the later editors. It is found, however, in the MS. B., and in the Syriac version, both of which are important authorities, and is retained by Beza and Bengel, and defended by Fritzsche, Tholuck, and others. The internal evidence, and a comparison with similar passages, as Rom. iv. 4; Eph. ii. 8, 9, are in its favour.

Verse 7. *What then? Israel hath not obtained that which he seeketh for: but the election hath obtained it, &c.* Seeketh, ἐπιζητεῖ expresses earnest seeking, and the use of the present tense indicates the persistency of the search. The Jews zealously and perseveringly sought after righteousness. They failed, however, as the apostle says, because they sought it by works. This verse is by many pointed differently, and read thus, " What then? Hath not Israel obtained that which he seeketh for? *nay*, but the election have," &c. The sense is not materially different. The apostle evidently designs to state the result of all he had just been saying. Israel, as a body, have not attained the blessing which they sought, but the chosen portion of them have. The rejection, therefore, is not total, and the promises of God made of old to Israel, which contemplated his spiritual people, have not been broken. It is clear, from the whole discourse, that the blessing sought by the Jews was justification, acceptance with God, and admission into his kingdom; see chap. x. 3, ix. 30, 31. This it is which they failed to attain, and to which the election were admitted. It was not, therefore, external advantages merely which the apostle had in view. The *election* means *those elected;* as *the circumcision* means *those who are circumcised. The election, i. e.,* reliquiae ejus populi, quas per gratiam suam Deus eligit.

And the rest were blinded. The verb (ἐπωρώθησαν) rendered *were blinded,* properly means, in its ground form, *to harden, to render insensible,* and is so translated in our version, Mark vi. 52, viii. 17; John xii. 40. In 2 Cor. iii. 14, the only other place in which it occurs in the New Testament, it is rendered as it is here. It is used in reference to the eyes in the Septuagint, Job xvii. 7, " My eyes are dim by reason of sorrow." Either rendering, therefore, is admissible, though the former is preferable, as more in accordance with the usual meaning of the word, and with Paul's language in the previous chapters. *And the rest were hardened,* that is, were insensible to the truth and excellence of the gospel, and, therefore, disregarded its offers and its claims. This πώρωσις affected the understanding as well as the heart. It was both blindness and obduracy. The passive form here used, may express simply the idea that they became hard, or the reference may be to the judicial act of God, see ix. 18. They were hardened by God, *i. e.,* abandoned by him to the hardness of their own hearts.

Verse 8. *According as it is written, God hath given them the spirit of slumber, eyes that they should not see, ears that they should not hear.* This passage, as is the case with ix. 33, is composed of several passages found in the Old Testament. In Isa. vi. 9, it is said, " Hear ye indeed, but understand not; see ye indeed, but perceive not;" ver. 10, " Lest they see with their eyes, and hear with their ears." Deut. xxix. 4, " Yet the Lord hath not given you an heart to perceive, and eyes to see, and ears to hear, unto this day." Isa. xxix. 10, " For the Lord hath poured upon you the spirit of deep sleep, and hath closed your eyes." The spirit, and to some extent, the language of these passages, Paul cites in support of his argument. They are in part descriptive of what had occurred in the times of the prophets, and in part prophetic of what should hereafter occur, and are therefore applicable to the character and conduct of the Jews during the apostolic age. See Matt. xiii. 14. The design of such citations frequently is to show that what was fulfilled partially in former times, was more perfectly accomplished at a subsequent period. The Jews had often before been hardened, but at no former period were the people so blinded, hardened, and reprobate, as when they rejected the Son of God, and put him to an open shame. It had often been predicted that such should be their state when the Messiah came. The punitive character of the evils here threatened, cannot escape the reader's notice. This blindness and hardness were not mere calamities, nor were they simply the natural effects of the sins of the people. They were punitive inflictions. They are so denounced. God says, I will give you eyes that see not. It is a dreadful thing to fall into the hands of the living God. The strokes of his justice blind, bewilder, and harden the soul. The words *even unto this day*, may, as by our translators, be connected with the last words of the preceding verse, 'The rest were blinded even unto this day.' Or they may be considered as a part of the quotation, as they occur in Deut. xxix. 4.

VERSES 9, 10. *And David saith, Let their table be made a snare, and a trap*, &c. This Psalm (lxix.) is referred to David in the heading prefixed to it, and the propriety of the reference to him as its author is confirmed both by external and internal evidence. See *Hengstenberg's Commentary on the Psalms.* No portion of the Old Testament Scriptures is more frequently referred to, as descriptive of our Lord's sufferings, than the Psalms lxix. and xxii. There is nothing in this Psalm which forbids its being considered as a prophetic lamentation of the Messiah over his afflictions, and a denunciation of God's judgments upon his enemies. Verse 9, " The zeal of thy house hath eaten me up," and ver. 21, " They gave me vinegar to drink," are elsewhere quoted and applied to Christ. Viewed in this light, the Psalm is directly applicable to the apostle's object, as it contains a prediction of the judgments which should befall the enemies of Christ. *Let their table be*, is only another and a more forcible way of saying, *their table shall be.* Isa. xlvii. 5, " Sit thou silent, and get thee into darkness, O daughter of the Chaldeans," for 'Thou shalt sit, &c.' And so in a multude of cases in the prophetic writings. In the Psalm, indeed, the future form in the Hebrew is used, though it is correctly rendered by the Septuagint and in our version as the imperative, in these passages. The judgments here denounced are expressed in figurative language. The sense is, their blessings shall become a curse; blindness and weakness, hardness of heart and misery shall come upon them. This last idea is forcibly expressed by a reference to the dimness of vision, and decrepitude of old age; as the vigour and activity of youth are the common figure for expressing the results of God's favour.

Even if the Psalm here quoted be considered as referring to the sorrows and the enemies of the sacred writer himself, and not to those of Christ, it would still be pertinent to the apostle's object. The enemies of the Psalmist were the enemies of God; the evils imprecated upon them were imprecated on them as such, and not as enemies of the writer. These denunciations are not the expression of the desire of private revenge, but of the just and certain judgments of God. And as the Psalmist declared how the enemies of God should be treated, how dim their eyes should become, and how their strength should be broken, so, Paul says, it actually occurs.   David said, let them be so treated, and we find them, says the apostle, suffering these very judgments.   Paul, therefore, in teaching that the great body of the Jews, the rejecters and crucifiers of the Son of God, were blinded and cast away, taught nothing more than had already been experienced in various portions of their history, and predicted in their prophets.

DOCTRINE.

1. The gifts and calling of God are without repentance.   The people whom God had chosen for himself, he preserved amidst the general defection of their countrymen, vers. 1, 2.

2. The apparent apostacy of a church or community from God, is not a certain test of the character of all the individuals of which it may be composed.   In the midst of idolatrous Israel, there were many who had not bowed the knee unto Baal.   Denunciations, therefore, should not be made too general, vers. 2—4.

3. The fidelity of men in times of general declension is not to be ascribed to themselves, but to the grace of God.   Every remnant of faithful men, is a remnant according to the election of grace.   That is, they are faithful, because graciously elected, ver. 5.

4. Election is not founded on works, nor on any thing in its objects, but on the sovereign pleasure of God ; and it is not to church privileges merely, but to all the blessings of Christ's kingdom, vers. 6, 7.

5. It is not of him that willeth nor of him that runneth.   Israel, with all their zeal for the attainment of salvation, were not successful, while those whom God had chosen attained the blessing, ver. 7.

6. Those who forsake God, are forsaken by God.   In leaving him, they leave the source of light, feeling, and happiness, ver. 7.

7. When men are forsaken of God all their powers are useless, and all their blessings become curses.   Having eyes, they see not, and their table is a snare, vers. 8—10.

REMARKS.

1. As in the times of the greatest defection, there are some who remain faithful, and as in the midst of apparently apostate communities, there are some who retain their integrity, we should never despair of the church, nor be too ready to make intercession against Israel.   The foundation of God standeth sure, having this seal, The Lord knoweth them that are his, vers. 1—4.

2. Those only are safe whom the Lord keeps.   Those who do not bow the knee to Baal, are a remnant according to the election of grace, and not according to the firmness of their own purposes, vers. 5, 6.

3. All seeking after salvation is worse than useless, unless properly directed.   Those who are endeavouring to work out a righteousness of their own, or to secure the favour of God in any way by their own doings, are beating the air.   Success is to be attained only by submission to the righteousness of God, ver. 7.

4. As the fact that any attain the blessing of God is to be attributed to their election, there is no room for self-complacency or pride ; and where

these feelings exist and are cherished in reference to this subject, they are evidence that we are not of the number of God's chosen, ver. 7.

5. Men should feel and acknowledge that they are in the hands of God; that, as sinners, they have forfeited all claim to his favour, and lost the power to obtain it. To act perseveringly as though either of these truths were not so, is to set ourselves in opposition to God and his plan of mercy, and is the very course to provoke him to send on us the spirit of slumber. This is precisely what the Jews did, vers. 7, 8.

6. Men are commonly ruined by things in which they put their trust or take most delight. The whole Mosaic system, with its rites and ceremonies, was the ground of confidence and boasting to the Jews, and it was the cause of their destruction. So, in our day, those who take refuge in some ecclesiastical organization instead of Christ, will find what they expected would prove their salvation, to be their ruin. So, too, all misimproved or perverted blessings are made the severest curses, vers. 9, 10.

ROMANS XI. 11—36.

ANALYSIS.

As the rejection of the Jews was not total, so neither is it final. They have not so fallen as to be hopelessly prostrated. First, God did not design to cast away his people entirely, but, by their rejection, in the first place, to facilitate the progress of the gospel among the Gentiles, and ultimately to make the conversion of the Gentiles the means of converting the Jews, ver. 11. The latter event is in itself desirable and probable. 1. Because if the rejection of the Jews has been a source of blessing, much more will their restoration be the means of good, vers. 12, 15. (The verses 13, 14, are a passing remark on the motive which influenced the apostle in preaching to the Gentiles.) 2. Because it was included and contemplated in the original election of the Jewish nation. If the root be holy, so are the branches, ver. 16.

The breaking off and rejection of some of the original branches, and the introduction of others of a different origin, is not inconsistent with this doctrine; and should lead the Gentiles to exercise humility and fear, and not boasting or exultation, vers. 17—22. As the rejection of the Jews was a punishment of their unbelief, and not the expression of God's ultimate purpose respecting them, it is, as intimated in ver. 16, more probable that God should restore the Jews, than that he should have called the Gentiles, vers. 23, 24.

This event, thus desirable and probable, God has determined to accomplish, vers. 25, 26. The restoration of the Jews to the privileges of God's people is included in the ancient predictions and promises made respecting them, vers. 26, 27. Though now, therefore, they are treated as enemies, they shall hereafter be treated as friends, ver. 28. For the purposes of God do not alter; as his covenant contemplated the restoration of his ancient people, that event cannot fail to come to pass, ver. 29. The plan of God, therefore, contemplated the calling of the Gentiles, the temporary rejection and final restoration of the Jews, vers. 30—32.

How adorable the wisdom of God manifested in the plan and conduct of the work of redemption! Of him, through him, and to him, are all things; to whom be glory for ever. Amen. Vers. 33—36.

COMMENTARY.

Verse 11. *I say then, Have they stumbled that they should fall ?　God forbid, &c.* This verse begins with the same formula as the first verse of the chapter, and for the same reason. As there the apostle wished to have it understood that the rejection of God's ancient people was not entire, so here he teaches that this rejection is not final. That this is the meaning of the verse seems evident, 1. From the comparative force of the words *stumble* and *fall.* As the latter is a much stronger term than the former, it seems plain that Paul designed it should here be taken emphatically, as expressing *irrevocable ruin,* in opposition to that which is *temporary.* The Jews have stumbled, but they are not prostrated. 2. From the context ; all that follows being designed to prove that the fall of the Jews was not final. This is indeed intimated in this very verse, in which it is implied that the conversion of the Gentiles would lead to the ultimate conversion of the Jews. The word (πέσωσιν) rendered *should fall,* is used here as elsewhere to mean, *should perish, become miserable,* Heb. iv. 11. The particle ἵνα, *that,* here as usually, expresses design. Have the Jews stumbled, in order that they should fall ? There are two views, however, as to the meaning of the passage. The first is that just mentioned, Was it the design of God, in permitting the stumbling of the Jews, that they should finally perish ? In other words, Was their rejection designed to be a permanent casting them out of the kingdom of Christ ? This view is sustained by the whole subsequent discussion, in which the apostle proves that the Jews, as a nation, are to be converted. The other interpretation assumes that the apostle means to say, that the design of God in the rejection of the Jews, was not so much their punishment, as to facilitate the calling of the Gentiles. ' Has God caused or allowed them to stumble, for the sake of punishing them, or simply that they should fall ? By no means, but,' &c. This interpretation, although it is suited to the verse, considered separately, is not so agreeable to the context, and the design of the apostle. It is not his object in what follows, to prove that God had not cast off his people for the simple purpose of causing them to suffer, but to show that their rejection was not final.

But through their fall salvation has come unto the Gentiles. The stumbling of the Jews was not attended with the result of their utter and final ruin, but was the occasion of facilitating the progress of the Gospel among the Gentiles. It was, therefore, not designed to lead to the former but to the latter result. From this very design it is probable that they shall be finally restored, because the natural effect of the conversion of the Gentiles is to provoke the emulation of the Jews. That the rejection of the gospel on the part of the Jews was the means of its wider and more rapid spread among the Gentiles, seems to be clearly intimated in several passages of the New Testament. " It was necessary," Paul says to the Jews, " that the word of God should first have been spoken to you ; but seeing ye put it from you, and judge yourselves unworthy of eternal life, lo, we turn to the Gentiles." Acts xiii. 46. And in Acts xxviii. 28, after saying that the prophecy of Isaiah was fulfilled in their unbelief, he adds, " Be it known therefore unto you, that the salvation of God is sent unto the Gentiles." Compare Isa. xlix. 4—6. The Jews, even those who were professors of Christianity, were, in the first place, very slow to allow the gospel to be preached to the Gentiles ; and in the second, they appear almost uniformly to have desired to clog the gospel with the ceremonial observances of the law. This was one of the greatest hindrances to the progress of the cause of Christ during the apostolic age, and would, in all human probability, have been a thousand-fold greater, had the Jews, as a nation, embraced the Christian faith. On both these accounts, the rejection of the Jews was incidentally a means of facilitating the progress of the gospel. Besides this, the punishment which befell them on account of their unbelief, involving the destruction of their nation and power, of course prevented their being able to forbid the general preaching of the gospel, which they earnestly desired to do. 1 Thess. ii. 15, 16, "They please not God, and are contrary to all men; forbidding us to speak to the Gentiles, that they might be saved."

For to provoke them to jealousy. As the result and design of the rejection of the Jews was the salvation of the Gentiles, so the conversion of the latter was designed to bring about the restoration of the former. The Gentiles are saved in order to provoke the Jews to jealousy. That is, this is one of the many benevolent purposes which God designed to accomplish by that event. This last clause serves to explain the meaning of the apostle in the former part of the verse. He shows that the rejection of the Jews was not intended to result in their being finally cast away, but to secure the more rapid progress of the gospel among the heathen, in order that their conversion might react upon the Jews, and be the means of bringing all, at last, within the fold of the Redeemer. To provoke to jealousy, παραζηλῶσαι, to excite emulation; *i. e.*, to stimulate to follow. The word is not to be taken in a bad sense, notwithstanding the παρά. All the apostle intended to say was, that he hoped the conversion of the Gentiles would be the means of exciting the Jews to seek salvation in the gospel.

Verse 12. *Now, if the fall of them be the riches of the world, and the diminishing of them the riches of the Gentiles, how much more their fulness?* Although there is considerable difficulty in fixing the precise sense of the several clauses of this verse, its general meaning seems sufficiently obvious. 'If the rejection of the Jews has been the occasion of so much good to the world, how much more may be expected from their restoration?' In this view it bears directly upon the apostle's object, which, in the first place, is to show that the restoration of the Jews is a probable and desirable event. There is in the verse a twofold annunciation of the same idea. In the first, the sentence is incomplete. 'If the fall of them be the riches of the world, *how much more their recovery?* if their diminishing, how much more their fulness?' The principal difficulty in this passage results from the ambiguity of the words (ἥττημα and πλήρωμα) rendered *diminishing* and *fulness.* The former may mean *fewness* or *inferiority, a condition worse than that of others,* or *worse than a former one.* Those who adopt the former of these senses, understand the verse thus: 'If the few Jews, who have been converted, have been such an advantage to the Gentiles, how much more will the great multitude of them, when brought to Christ, be a source of blessing.' But to this interpretation it may be objected, 1. The word has rarely, if ever, the meaning here assigned to it. Passow gives it no such signification in his Lexicon. The cognate verb signifies, *I am inferior in strength or condition to any one.* 2 Peter ii. 19; 2 Cor. xii. 13. The adjective means *inferior, worse:* 1 Cor. xi. 17, "Ye come together not for the better, but for the worse." The only place in which the word here used occurs elsewhere in the New Testament, is 1 Cor. vi.

7, "There is utterly a fault among you," or as it might be rendered, 'It is an injury to you.' Such too is the meaning of the word in the Old Testament: Isa. xxxi. 8, "His young men shall be discomfited," which expresses the sense of the original; and so does the Septuagint, which employs the word used by the apostle, 'His young men shall be brought into an inferior condition,' *i.e.*, shall be conquered. 2. This interpretation does not suit the context. Paul does not say that the conversion of the few Jews who had become Christians, had been the occasion of good to the Gentiles, but the rejection of the great body of the nation. 3. It does not at all suit the first clause of the verse. *The fall of them*, answers to and explains *the diminishing of them*. As the former clause cannot receive the interpretation objected to, neither can the latter. Tholuck and others take ἥττημα in a moral sense; *their fault*, so as to correspond with παράπτωμα. But this would make the two clauses of the verse tautological, and destroy the antithesis between ἥττημα and πλήρωμα, as the latter cannot mean, their goodness. The sense is clear and good if we give ἥττημα its natural meaning; their *worse estate*, or *loss*. The Jews lost their peculiar privileges and blessings, and their loss was the *riches* of the Gentiles. It enriched them by being the means of transferring to them the treasures of the gospel.

The word πλήρωμα has various senses in the New Testament. It properly means *that with which anything is filled*, as in the frequent phrase, *the fulness of the earth*, or *of the sea*, &c. So *fulness of the Godhead*, all that is in God, *the plenitude of Deity*. John i. 16, "Of his fulness have all we received;" Eph. iii. 19, "That ye might be filled with all the fulness of God." It also means *the complement* or *supplement of anything, the remaining part;* see Matt. ix. 16. So in Eph. i. 23, the church may be called *the fulness* of Christ, because he is the head, the church, the residue, or complement, by which the mystical body is completed. Of these several meanings, Storr selects the last, and explains the verse thus: 'If the ruin of the unbelieving Jews has been a source of blessing to the Gentiles, how much more shall the remaining portion of the nation, *i. e.*, those converted to Christianity, be the means of good.' But, 1. This interpretation destroys the obvious antithesis of the sentence; "the remaining part" does not answer to the word rendered *ruin*, as it obviously should do. 2. It is not in accordance with the context, which is not designed so much to set forth the usefulness of the Jews then converted, as to declare the blessings likely to be consequent on the final conversion of the whole nation. 3. A comparison of this, with the 15th verse, is unfavourable to this interpretation. These verses evidently express the same idea, and therefore illustrate each other. 'If the casting away of them be the occasion of reconciling the world, what will the receiving of them be?' &c. Ver. 15. Retaining the sense, *complement*, the passage admits of a different interpretation from that given by Storr. The Jewish nation are the πλήρωμα, *the complement*, that which completes the whole number of the people of God. A rent, or loss had occurred by their rejection; they were, however, *the complement* by which that loss was to be made good. This is evidently forced.

The common interpretation, therefore, is to be preferred: 'If the injury or ruin of the Jews has been the occasion of good to the Gentiles, how much more shall their full restoration or blessedness be?' 1. This agrees with the antithesis, 'If the fall, then the recovery; if the ruin, then the blessedness,' &c. 2. It suits the context and the design of the apostle.

3. It is in strict accordance with the obviously parallel passage in the 15th verse, just quoted. The remark of Thomas Aquinas is of great weight : " Bonum est potentius ad utilitatem inferendam, quam malum, sed malum Judæorum gentilibus magnam utilitatem contulit, ergo multo majorem confert mundo eorum bonum." The πλήρωμα of the Gentiles is, therefore, that which fills them, and renders their blessedness full. The word is thus retained in its ordinary sense.

Verse 13. *For I speak to you Gentiles, inasmuch as I am the apostle to the Gentiles.* This and the following verse contain a transient remark relating to the apostle's own feelings and mode of acting in reference to the subject in hand. His readers were not to suppose, that because he was the apostle to the Gentiles, his labours had no reference to the Jews, or that he was unconcerned about their salvation. This passage is therefore connected with the last clause of the preceding verse, in which Paul had said that the conversion of the Gentiles was adapted and designed to bring about the restoration of the Jews. These two events, instead of being at all inconsistent, were intimately related, so that both ought to be kept constantly in view, and all efforts to promote the former had a bearing on the accomplishment of the latter. This being the case, the Gentiles ought to consider the restoration of the Jews as in no respect inimical to their interests, but as on every account most desirable. Paul therefore says, that what he had just stated in reference to the effect on the Jews, of the conversion of the Gentiles, he designed specially for the latter. He wished them to consider that fact, as it would prevent any unkind feelings towards the Jews. He had the better right thus to speak, as to him, especially, " the gospel of the uncircumcision had been committed." He himself, in all he did to secure the salvation of the Gentiles, or to render his office successful, had an eye to the conversion of the Jews. The word (δοξάζω) rendered *I magnify*, means, first, *to praise, to estimate, and speak highly of a thing ;* secondly, *to render glorious,* as chap. viii. 30, " Whom he justifies, them he also glorifies ;" and so in a multitude of cases. Either sense of the word suits this passage. The latter, however, is much better adapted to the following verse, and therefore is to be preferred : ' I endeavour to render my office glorious by bringing as many Gentiles as possible into the Redeemer's kingdom ; if so be it may provoke and arouse my countrymen.' His magnifying his office consisted in the faithful discharge of its duties ; and in thus labouring assiduously for the salvation of the Gentiles, he aimed also at the salvation of the Jews. " Sic gentes alloquitur : Quum sim vobis peculiariter destinatus apostolus ideoque salutem vestram mihi commissam singulari quodam studio debeam procurare, et quasi rebus omnibus omissis unum illud agere : officio tamen meo fideliter fungar, si quos e mea gente Christo lucrifecero : idque erit in gloriam ministerii mei, atque adeo in vestrum bonum." *Calvin.* The object of the apostle, therefore, in these verses, is to declare that he always acted under the influence of the truth announced at the close of the 12th verse. He endeavoured to make the conversion of the Gentiles a means of good to the Jews.

Verse 14. *If by any means I may provoke to emulation them* which are *my flesh, and might save some of them.* This is the reason (of course one among many) why Paul desired the conversion of the Gentiles. If the two events, the salvation of both classes, were intimately related, there was no ground of ill feeling on either part. The Gentiles need not fear that the restoration of the Jews would be injurious to them, as though the happiness of one class were incompatible with that of the other.

Verse 15. *For if the casting away of them be the reconciling of the world, what* shall *the receiving* of them be *but life from the dead ?* Although Paul here returns to the sentiment of the 12th verse, this passage is logically connected with the preceding. The apostle had said, that even in labouring for the Gentiles, he had in view the salvation of the Jews ; for if their rejection had occasioned so much good, how desirable must be their restoration. *If the casting away of them be the reconciling of the world.* The reconciliation here spoken of is that which Paul so fully describes in Eph. ii. 11—22. A reconciliation by which those who were aliens and strangers have been brought nigh ; reconciled at once to the church, the commonwealth of Israel, and to God himself, " by the blood of Christ." This event has been facilitated, as remarked above, by the rejection of the Jews ; what will the restoration of the Jews then be, *but life from the dead ?* That is, it will be a most glorious event ; as though a new world had risen, not only glorious in itself, but in the highest degree beneficial to the Gentiles. De Brais and many others suppose that the apostle refers to the future declension of the Gentile church, from which the restoration of the Jews shall be the means of arousing them. Of such an allusion, however, there is no intimation in the text. The most common and natural interpretation is that which considers the latter clause as merely a figurative expression of a joyful and desirable event. The conversion of the Jews will be attended with the most glorious consequences for the whole world.

Not only in the Scriptures, but also in profane literature, the transition from a state of depression and misery to one of prosperity, is expressed by the natural figure of passing from death to life. The Old Testament prophets represented the glorious condition of the theocracy, consequent on the coming of Christ, in contrast with its previous condition, as a rising from the dead. This interpretation of the passage before us, is adopted by many of the best commentators, ancient and modern. There are, however, two other views presented. According to some, the life here spoken of is strictly spiritual life, and the dead from which it springs are the spiritually dead. The meaning would then be, that the conversion of the Jews would be the occasion, or the means, of awakening many of the Gentiles to spiritual life. This idea, however, is included in the former interpretation, because the *summa felicitas,* the state of great prosperity which the church is to enjoy when the Jews are restored, is a religious prosperity. It supposes the conversion of great multitudes of men, and the general spread and power of the gospel. But this does not justify us in confining the words to this spiritual sense. The latter clause, according to this view, expresses no more than the former clause. *The reconciliation of the world,* implies, of course, the conversion of multitudes of men, and the prevalence of true religion. *The life from the dead* is more than this. It is not only a greater measure of the former blessing, but a glorious and happy condition therewith connected, and consequent thereon. The other view of the passage is that given by Chrysostom, and adopted by many of the best modern commentators, as Tholuck (in his second edition), De Wette, Meyer, and others. It assumes that ζωὴ ἐκ νεκρῶν (*life from the dead*), refers to the resurrection of the dead. The idea is, that the conversion of the Jews is the condition precedent of that great event. When the Jews are converted, then comes the resurrection and the consummation of Christ's kingdom. But nowhere else in Scripture is the literal resurrection expressed by the words ζωὴ ἐκ νεκρῶν. Had Paul intended a reference to the resurrection, no reason can be assigned why he did not employ the established and familiar words ἀνάστασις ἐκ νεκρῶν. If he meant the resurrection, why did he not say so ? Why use a general phrase, which is elsewhere used to express another idea? Besides this, it is not according to the analogy of Scripture that the resurrection of the dead, and the change in those who shall be then alive (1 Cor. xv. 51 ; 1 Thess. iv. 14—18), are to be immediate, consequent on the conversion of the Jews. The resurrection is not to occur until " the end." A new state of things, a new mode of existence, is to be then introduced. Flesh and blood, *i. e.,* our bodies as now organized (the σῶμα ψυχικόν,) cannot inherit the kingdom of God. They are not suited for the state of being which is to follow the resurrection. If, therefore, the world is to continue after the conversion of the Jews, that event will not inaugurate the resurrection.

VERSE 16. *For if the first-fruits be holy, the lump is also holy; and if the root be holy, so also are the branches.* Under two striking and appropriate figures, the apostle expresses the general idea, ' If one portion of the Jewish people is holy, so also is the other.' With regard to this interesting passage, the first point to be settled is the allusion in the figurative expression in the first clause. The Jews were commanded to offer a certain portion of all the productions of the earth to God, as an expression of gratitude and acknowledgment of dependence. This offering, called the first-fruits, was to be made first, from the productions in their natural state (Exod. xxiii. 19) ; and, secondly, from the meal, wine, oil, and dough, as prepared for use. Num. xv. 21, " Of the first of your dough ye shall give unto the Lord a heave-offering in all your generations ;" Neh. x. 37 ; Deut. xviii. 4. If the allusion of the apostle is to the former of these offerings, then the *first-fruits* must refer to a portion of the harvest or vintage presented to God, and the *lump* to the residue of the grain or grapes. If the allusion be to the second, then the *first-fruits* mean the portion of dough offered to God, and the *lump* the residue of the mass. The latter is undoubtedly most consistent with the meaning of the word (φύραμα) used by the apostle, which can hardly be understood as referring to heaps of grain, or other productions of the earth. In either case, however, the purport of the illustration is the same.

A second question is, Who are intended by the first-fruits and the root, and by the lump and the branches, in these two figures? With respect to this question, the following are the most common and plausible answers : 1. The first-fruits are understood to mean the Jews first converted to the Christian faith, who became, as it were, the root of the Christian church. According to this view of the passage, the apostle designs to say, ' Since the first converts to the gospel were Jews, it is evident that the nation, as such, is not cast off by God ; as a portion of them is holy (or have been accepted of God), so may the residue be.' 2. By the first-fruits and the root, may be understood the patriarchs, the forefathers of the Jews ; and by the lump and the branches, the residue of the nation, or the Jews as a people. That this latter is the true meaning of the passage seems very evident : 1. Because this interpretation alone preserves the propriety of the figure. How can the unconverted Jews or the Jewish nation be called the branches of the portion that became followers of Christ ? The Gentile Christians might be so called, but not the Jewish people, as such. On the other hand, nothing is more natural than to call the ancestors the root, and their descendants the branches.　2. This interpretation best suits the design of the apostle.　He wishes to show that the conversion of the Jews, which he had declared to be so desirable for the Gentiles, was a probable event.　He proves this by referring to the relation of their ancestors to God.　If they were the peculiar people of God, their descendants may be regarded as his also, since the covenant was not with Abraham only, but also with his seed.　3. This is the apostle's own explanation in ver. 28, where the unconverted Jews, or Hebrew nation, as such, are said to be " beloved for the fathers' sake."　4. This interpretation alone can be consistently carried through the following verses.　The Gentile Christians are not said (ver. 17) to be grafted into the stock of the converted Jews, but as branches with them they are united to a common stock.　And the stock into which the branches, now broken off, are to be again grafted, is not the Jewish part of the Christian church, but the original family or household of God.

The word (ἅγιος) rendered *holy*, which properly means *clean*, is used in two general senses in the Scriptures : 1. *Consecrated ;* 2. *Pure.*　In the former of these, it is applied, times without number, in the Old Testament, to persons, places, and things considered as peculiarly devoted to the service of God.　So the whole people, without reference to their moral character, are called a holy people.　So, too, the temple, tabernacle, and all their contents, were called holy, &c.　The use of the word in this sense, in reference to places and things, is not unfrequent in the New Testament. Matt. iv. 5, where Jerusalem is called the " holy city;" see Matt. vii. 6 ; xxiv. 15 ; xxvii. 53, and often.　It is, however, rarely so used in relation to persons.　In the vast majority of instances, when thus applied, it means *morally pure ;* yet, in some cases, it signifies *devoted to God.*　Luke ii. 23, " Every male that openeth the womb shall be called holy unto the Lord." Perhaps, too, in the expressions, " the holy prophets," Luke i. 70, and "holy apostles," Eph. iii. 5, the reference is rather to their relation to God, as persons devoted to his service, than to their moral character.　In 1 Cor. vii. 14, the children of professing Christians are called " holy," not in reference to their moral condition, but their relation to the church.　In like manner, in this passage, the Jews, as a people, are called holy, because peculiarly consecrated to God, separated from the rest of the world for his service.*

The connection of this verse with the preceding, its import and bearing on the apostle's object are therefore clear.　The restoration of the Jews, which will be attended with such beneficial results for the whole world, is to be expected, because of their peculiar relation to God as his chosen people.　God, in selecting the Hebrew patriarchs, and setting them apart for his service, had reference to their descendants, as well as to themselves ; and designed that the Jews, as a people, should, to the latest generations, be specially devoted to himself.　They stand now, therefore, and ever have stood, in a relation to God which no other nation ever has sustained ; and, in consequence of this relation, their restoration to the divine favour is an event in itself probable, and one, which Paul afterwards teaches (ver. 25), God has determined to accomplish.

Verses 17—24.　The object of these verses is to make such an applica-

---

* Non est mirum, si in patre suo Judæi sanctificati sint.　Nihil hic erit difficultatis, si sanctitatem intelligas nihil esse aliud, quam spiritualem generis nobilitatem, et eam quidem non propriam naturæ, sed quae ex fœdere manabat. . . . Electi populi dignitas, proprie loquendo, supernaturale privilegium est.—*Calvin.*

tion of the truths which Paul had just taught as should prevent any feeling of exultation or triumph of the Gentile Christians over the Jews. It is true that the Jews have been partially rejected from the church of God ; that the Gentiles have been introduced into it ; and that the Jews are ultimately to be restored. These things, however, afford no ground of boasting to the Gentiles, but rather cause of thankfulness and caution. Paul illustrates these truths by a very appropriate figure.

Verse 17. *And if some of the branches be broken off, and thou, being a wild olive tree wert grafted in among them,* &c. The words ἐν αὐτοῖς may refer to the branches in general, and be rendered as in our version, *among them ;* or they may refer to the rejected branches, and be rendered, *in their place.* 'Some of the branches have been broken off, and you have been inserted in their place.' The purport of the passage is plain. Some of the Jews were broken off and rejected ; the Gentiles, though apparently little susceptible of such a blessing, were introduced into the church, and made to partake of all its peculiar and precious privileges. The Jewish church is compared to the olive tree, one of the most durable, productive, and valuable of the productions of the earth, because it was highly favoured, and therefore valued in the sight of God. The Gentiles are compared to the wild olive, one of the most worthless of trees, to express the degradation of their state, considered as estranged from God. As it is customary to engraft good scions on inferior stocks, the nature of the product being determined by the graft, and not the root, it has been thought that the illustration of the apostle is not very apposite. But the difficulty may result from pressing the comparison too far. The idea may be simply this, ' As the scion of one tree is engrafted into another, and has no independent life, but derives all its vigour from the root, so the Gentiles are introduced among the people of God, not to confer but to receive good.' It is however said, on the authority of ancient writers and modern travellers, to have been not unusual to graft the wild on the cultivated olive.* Even if this were so, it would not be pertinent to the apostle's object. He does not mean to say, that the *graft* imparts life and vigour to the root, but the very reverse. There is no necessity for departing from the common view. The Gentiles are saved by their introduction into that church of which the patriarchs were the root.

It is plain from this verse, that *the root* in this passage cannot be the early converts from among the Jews, but the ancient covenant people of God. The ancient theocracy was merged in the kingdom of Christ. The latter is but an enlargement and elevation of the former. There has, therefore, never been other than one family of God on earth, existing under different institutions, and enjoying different degrees of light and favour. This family was composed, of old, of Abraham, Isaac, and Jacob, and their descendants. At the advent, its name and circumstances were changed ; many of its old members were cast out, and others introduced, but it is the same family still. Or, to return to the apostle's illustration, it is the same tree, some of the branches only being changed.

Verse 18. *Boast not thyself against the branches ;* κατακαυχάομαι means, *to boast against,* in the sense of glorying over any one. *But if thou boast, thou bearest not the root, but the root thee.* A concise expres-

---

* Columella *de Re rustica,* V. 9. Solent terebrari oleæ laetæ, in foramen talea viridis oleastri demittitur, et sic velut inita arbor fœcundo semine fertilior exstat.

Palladius *de Re rustica,* XIV. 53. Fœcundat sterilis pinguis oleaster olivas, et quae non novit munera ferre docet.

sion, for, *If thou boast* (*i. e.*, art disposed to do it), *consider that* thou bearest not the root, &c. The Gentiles had been brought into fellowship with the patriarchs, not the patriarchs with them. Salvation was from the Jews. The truth that the Jews were the channel of blessings to the Gentiles, and not the reverse, was adapted to prevent all ungenerous and self-confident exultation of the latter over the former.

VERSE 19. *You will say then, The branches were broken off, that I might be grafted in.* The apostle guards against a further ground of self-complacency on the part of the Gentile. Although forced to admit that the root bore him, and not he the root, yet he might pride himself on the fact that the branches were broken off, and he put in their place. To this it is answered, that the Gentiles are not authorized to infer, from the fact that the Jews were rejected, and they chosen, that this occurred on the ground of their being in themselves better than the Jews. The true reason of this dispensation is assigned in the next verse.

VERSE 20. *Well, because of unbelief they were broken off,* &c. The fact that they were broken off is admitted, but the inference drawn by the Gentiles is denied. It was not for any personal considerations that the one was rejected and the other chosen. The Jews were rejected because they rejected the Saviour, and the only tenure by which the advantages of a covenant relation to God can be retained is faith. The Gentiles will not be secure, because Gentiles, any more than the Jews were safe, because Jews. Instead, therefore, of being high-minded, they should fear.

VERSE 21. *If God spared not the natural branches, take heed lest he also spare not thee.* The clause, μήπως οὐδὲ σοῦ φείσηται, must depend on something understood. Our translators supply βλέπετε, *take heed;* others φοβοῦμαι, *I fear.* The Gentile has even more reason to fear than the Jew had. It was in itself far more probable that God would spare a people so long connected with him in the most peculiar manner, than that he should spare those who had no such claims on his mercy. The idea intended to be expressed by this verse probably is, that the Jews, from their relation to God, were more likely to be spared than the Gentiles, inasmuch as God is accustomed to bear long with the recipients of his mercy, before he casts them off; even as a father bears long with a son, before he discards him and adopts another.

VERSE 22. *Behold, therefore, the goodness and severity of God: on them which fell, severity; but on thee, goodness.* Instead of the accusatives ἀποτομίαν and χρηστότητα, Lachmann and Tischendorf read ἀποτομία and χρηστότης. If this reading be adopted, ἐστίν must be supplied. 'Towards the one class there is severity, towards the other kindness.' The effect which the consideration of these dispensations of God should produce, is gratitude and fear. Gratitude, in view of the favour which we Gentiles have received, and fear lest we should be cut off; for our security does not depend upon our now enjoying the blessings of the church of God, but is dependent on our *continuing in the divine goodness or favour*, (Rom. ii. 4; Titus iii. 4,) that is, on our doing nothing to forfeit that favour; its continuance being suspended on the condition of our fidelity. *If thou continue in (his) goodness*, ἐὰν ἐπιμείνῃς τῇ χρηστότητι, is sometimes explained to mean, *if thou continue in goodness*, *i.e.*, in being good, according to the analogy of the following clause, μὴ ἐπιμείνωσι τῇ ἀπιστίᾳ, *if they continue not in unbelief.* But this is inconsistent with the context. The χρηστότης spoken of, is the goodness or love of God. Compare Acts xiii. 43, προσμένειν τῇ χάριτι τοῦ Θεοῦ, *to remain in the grace of God.* "Otherwise thou also shalt be cut off," ἐπεὶ καὶ σὺ ἐκκοπήσῃ, *since,* in that case, (*i.e.,* if thou continuest not in his goodness,) thou also shalt be cut off ; ἐκκοπήσῃ, second future indicative passive.   There is nothing in this language inconsistent with the doctrine of the final perseverance of believers, even supposing the passage to refer to individuals ; for it is very common to speak thus hypothetically, and say that an event cannot or will not come to pass, unless the requisite means are employed, when the occurrence of the event had been rendered certain by the previous purpose and promise of God ; see Acts. xxvii. 31.   The foundation of all such statements is the simple truth, that He who purposes the end, purposes also the means ; and he brings about the end by securing the use of the means.   And when rational agents are concerned, he secures the use of the means by rational considerations presented to their minds, and rendered effectual by his grace, when the end contemplated is good.   This passage, however, has no legitimate bearing on this subject.   Paul is not speaking of the connection of individual believers with Christ, which he had abundantly taught in chap. viii. and elsewhere, to be indissoluble, but of the relation of communities to the church and its various privileges.   There is no promise or covenant on the part of God, securing to the Gentiles the enjoyment of these blessings through all generations, any more than there was any such promise to protect the Jews from the consequences of their unbelief.   The continuance of these favours depends on the conduct of each successive generation.   Paul therefore says to the Gentile, that he must continue in the divine favour, " otherwise thou also shalt be cut off."

Verse 23.   *And they also, if they abide not in unbelief, shall be graffed in,* &c.   The principle which the apostle had just stated as applicable to the Gentiles, is applicable also to the Jews.   Neither one nor the other, simply because Jew or Gentile, is either retained in the church or excluded from it.   As the one continues in this relation to God, only on condition of faith, so the other is excluded by his unbelief alone.   Nothing but unbelief prevents the Jews being brought back, " for God is able to graff them in again."*   That is, not merely has God the power to accomplish this result, but the difficulty or impediment is not in him, but solely in themselves. There is no inexorable purpose in the divine mind, nor any insuperable obstacle in the circumstances of the case, which forbids their restoration ; on the contrary, the event is, in itself considered, far more probable than the calling of the Gentiles.

Verse 24.   *For if thou wert cut out of the olive-tree which is wild by nature, and wert graffed contrary to nature into a good olive-tree ; how much more,* &c.   The connection indicated by γάρ (*for,*) is not with the preceding clause, *God is able to graff them in again,* because what follows does not prove the power of God to restore the Jews to their ancient privileges, but that their restoration is a probable event.   The connection, therefore, is with the main idea in the context, as expressed in ver. 23, " They shall *be graffed in.*"   This may be expected, he says, *for,* &c.   The Gentiles were of the wild olive, having no natural connection with the tree into which they were graffed.   The Jews were its natural branches. In itself considered, therefore, their reunion with their native stalk was more probable than the graffing in of the Gentiles.   The opposition, however, between κατὰ φύσιν and παρὰ φύσιν, does not refer to any natural fit-

---

* Frigidum apud homines profanos argumentum hoc foret. . . . At quia fideles quoties Dei potentiam nominari audiunt, quasi præsens opus intuentur, hanc rationem satis putavit valere, ad percellendas eorum mentes.—*Calvin.*

ness of the Jews, as a race, for the true religion, in opposition to the unsuitableness of the Gentiles. According to the Scriptures, there is no difference, so far as their relation to God is concerned, between the different races of men, since all have sinned. They are all alike unfit for the service and enjoyment of God, and alike unable to save themselves. And, on the other hand, they are alike susceptible of the salvation of the gospel, which is adapted to all classes of men. The words in question are used only to preserve the figure of a tree and its branches. The simple meaning, therefore, of this verse is, that the future restoration of the Jews is, in itself, a more probable event than the introduction of the Gentiles into the church of God. This, of course, supposes that God regarded the Jews, on account of their relation to him, with peculiar favour, and that there is still something in their relation to the ancient servants of God, and his covenant with them, which causes them to be regarded with special interest. As men look upon the children of their early friends with kinder feelings than on the children of strangers, God refers to this fact to make us sensible that he still retains purposes of peculiar mercy towards his ancient people. The restoration of this people, therefore, to the blessings of the church of God, is far from being an improbable event.

Verse 25. *For I would not, brethren, have you ignorant of this mystery, lest ye should be wise in your own conceits, that blindness in part has happened unto Israel, until the fulness of the Gentiles be come in.* Although the interpretations given of this and the following verses are very numerous, they are all modifications of one or the other of the two following general views of the passage. 1. Many understand the apostle as not predicting any remarkable future conversion of the Jewish nation, but merely declaring that the hardening or blinding of the nation, was not such as to prevent many Jews entering the Christian church, as long as the Gentiles continued to come in. Thus all the true Israel, embracing Jews as well as Gentiles, should ultimately be saved. 2. The second general view supposes the apostle, on the contrary, to predict a great and general conversion of the Jewish people, which should take place when the fulness of the Gentiles had been brought in, and that then, and not till then, those prophecies should be fully accomplished which speak of the salvation of Israel. The former of these views was presented, in different forms, by the great body of the authors who lived about the time of the Reformation; who were led by the extravagancies of the Millennarians, who built much on this passage, to explain away its prophetic character almost entirely.* Olshausen, in order to show the hostile feeling entertained by the Reformers towards the Jews, quotes a passage from Luther, which does not admit of translation : "Ein jüdisch Herz ist so stoch-stein-eisen-teufelhart, das mit keiner Weise zu bewegen ist ;—es sind junge Teufel zur Hölle verdammt, diese Teufelskinder zu bekehren ist unmöglich, wie etliche solchen Wahn schöpfen aus der Epistel an die Römer."

The second view has been the one generally received in every age of the church, with the exception of the period just referred to. That it is the correct interpretation, appears evident for the following reasons : 1. The whole context and drift of the apostle's discourse is in its favour. In the

---

* Wolfius, in his Curæ, gives an account of the authors who discuss the meaning of this and the following verses, as Calovius in Bibliis Illustratis ; Buddeus in Institutio Theol. Dog., p. 672. Wolfius himself says, "Contextus suadet credere, Paulum id hic tantum agere, ut conversi e Gentilibus non existiment, Judæis omnem spem ad Christum in posterum perveniendi præcisam esse, sed ita potius statuant, ipsis non minus ceteris Gentilibus. nondum conversis, viam patere, qua ad Christum perducantur."

preceding part of the chapter, Paul, in the plainest terms, had taught that
the conversion of the Jews was a probable event, and that it would be in
the highest degree beneficial and glorious for the whole world.   This idea
is presented in various forms ; and practical lessons are deduced from it
in such a way as to show that he contemplated something more than merely
the silent addition of a few Israelites to the church during successive ages.
2. It is evident that Paul meant to say, that the Jews were to be restored
in the sense in which they were then rejected.   They were then rejected
not merely as individuals, but as a community, and therefore are to be
restored as a community ; see vers. 11, 15.   How can the latter passage
(ver. 15,) especially, be understood of the conversion of the small number
of Jews which, from age to age, have joined the Christian Church ?   This
surely has not been as " life from the dead," for the whole world.   3. It
is plain from this and other parts of the discourse, that Paul refers to a
great event ; something which should attract universal attention.   4. In
accordance with this idea, is the manner of introducing this verse, *I would
not have you ignorant, brethren ;* see 1 Cor. x. 1 ; xii. 1, and elsewhere.
Paul uses this form of address when he wishes to rouse the attention of
his readers to something specially important.   5. The gradual conversion
of a few Jews is no *mystery*, in the scriptural sense of the word.   The
word *μυστήριον, secret*, is not generally used, in the New Testament, in the
sense of the word *mystery*.   It means simply, what is hidden, or unknown;
whether because it is an unrevealed purpose of God ; or because it is
future ; or because it is covered up in parables or symbols, (as the *mystery*
of the seven candlesticks, Rev. i. 20 ;) or because it lies beyond the
reach of the human mind, Eph. v. 32.   It is only in the last mentioned case that *μυστήριον* answers to our word mystery.   Whatever
needs an *ἀποκάλυψις* to become an object of knowledge, is a *μυστήριον*.   It
is therefore used in reference to all the doctrines of the gospel which are
not the truths of reason, but matters of divine revelation ; Rom. xvi. 25 ;
1 Cor. ii. 7 ; iv. 1 ; Eph. vi. 19, &c.   Hence ministers are called stewards
of the mysteries (*i.e.*, of the revelations) of God.   It is also used of some
one doctrine, considered as previously unknown and undiscoverable by
human reason, however simple and intelligible in its own nature.   Thus,
the fact that the Gentiles should be admitted into the church of God, Paul
calls a *mystery*, Eph. i. 9 ; iii. 4.   Any future event, therefore, which
could be known only by divine revelation, is a mystery.   The fact that all
should not die, though all should be changed, was a mystery, 1 Cor. xv.
51.   In like manner, here, when Paul says, " I would not, brethren, have
you ignorant of this mystery," he means to say, that the event to which he
referred, was one which, depending on no secondary cause, but on the
divine purpose, could be known only by divine revelation.   This description is certainly far more suitable to the annunciation of a prophecy, than
to the statement of a fact which might have been confidently inferred
from what God had already revealed.   6. The words, *all Israel*, in the
next verse, cannot, as the first interpretation mentioned above would require, be understood of the *spiritual* Israel ; because the word is just
before used in a different sense, " blindness in part has happened unto
Israel."   This blindness is to continue until a certain time, when it is to
be removed, and then all Israel is to be saved.   It is plain, that *Israel* in
these cases must be understood as referring to the same class of persons.
This is also clear from the opposition between the terms Israel and Gentile.
7. The words (*ἄχρις οὗ,*) correctly rendered in our version, *until*, cannot,
so consistently with usage, be translated, *as long as*, or *so that*, followed as

they are here by the aorist subjunctive; see Rev. xv. 8; xvii. 17; com-pare Heb. iii. 13. 8. The following verses seem to require this interpre-tation. The result contemplated is one which shall be a full accomplish-ment of those prophecies which predicted the salvation of the Jews. The reason given in vers. 28, 29, for the event to which Paul refers, is the unchangeableness of God's purposes and covenant. Having once taken the Jews into special connection with himself, he never intended to cast them off for ever. The apostle sums up his discourse by saying, ' As the Gentiles were formerly unbelieving, and yet obtained mercy, so the Jews who now disbelieve, shall hereafter be brought in; and thus God will have mercy on all, both Jews and Gentiles.' From all these considerations, it seems obvious that Paul intended here to predict that the time would come when the Jews, as a body, should be converted unto the Lord; compare 2 Cor. iii. 16. The prediction contained in this verse is to be explained by the context. The rejection of the Jews at the time of Christ, did not involve the perdition of every individual of that nation. Thousands, and even myriads, believed and were saved. So the restoration here foretold is not to be understood as including every individual of the Jewish people, but simply that there is to be a national restoration.

Lest ye should be wise in your own conceits. This is given as the reason why the apostle wished the Gentiles to know and consider the event which he was about to announce. This clause may mean either, ' Lest ye proudly imagine that your own ideas of the destiny of the Jews are correct;' or, ' Lest ye be proud and elated, as though you were better and more highly favoured than the Jews.' The former is perhaps most in accordance with the literal meaning of the words (ἐν ἑαυτοῖς φρόνιμοι ;) see Prov. iii. 7.

Blindness in part, i. e., partial blindness; *partial* as to its extent and continuance. Because not all the Jews were thus blinded, nor was the nation to remain blind for ever. The words ἀπὸ μέρους are not to be con-nected with πώρωσις, nor with τῷ Ἰσραήλ; but with γέγονεν. 'Blindness has partially happened to Israel.' The reference, however, is not to the degree, but to the continuance of this blindness. It is not final and hope-less; it is only for a time. The word (πώρωσις) rendered *blindness,* is more correctly rendered, in Mark iii. 5, *hardness;* compare Eph. iv. 18; see ver. 7, and chap. ix. 18.

Until the fulness of the Gentiles be come in. Until ἄχρις οὐ, marks the terminus *ad quem.* This blindness of Israel is to continue until something else happened. There were to be, and have been numerous conversions to Christianity from among the Jews, in every age since the advent; but their national conversion is not to occur until the heathen are converted. What, however, is definitely meant by the πλήρωμα τῶν ἐθνῶν, it is not easy to determine. The question is not to be decided by the mere signifi-cation of the words. In whatever way they may be explained, the general idea is the same. The πλήρωμα of the Gentiles may mean, that which makes the Gentiles, as to number, full. Or, according to others, the Gen-tiles themselves are the πλήρωμα, i.e., the complement; they make full the vacancy left by the rejection of the Jews. Or, as is commonly assumed, πλήρωμα is to be taken in a secondary sense, for *multitude.* Compare Gen. xlviii. 19 : " Multitude (literally fulness) of nations ;" and Isa. xxxi. 4, " Multitude (fulness) of shepherds." This does not mean the totality of the Gentiles. It is not Paul's doctrine, that all Gentiles who ever lived are to be introduced into the kingdom of Christ. Nor does it mean, that all the Gentiles who may be alive when the Jews are converted, shall be true

Christians. All that can be safely inferred from this language is, that the Gentiles, as a body, the mass of the Gentile world, will be converted before the restoration of the Jews, as a nation. Much will remain to be accomplished after that event; and in the accomplishment of what shall then remain to be done, the Jews are to have a prominent agency. Their conversion will be as life from the dead to the church. We must remember that Paul is here speaking as a prophet, ἐν ἀποκαλύψει, 1 Cor. xiv. 6, and therefore his language must be interpreted by the rules of prophetic interpretation. Prophecy is not proleptic history. It is not designed to give us the knowledge of the future which history gives us of the past. Great events are foretold; but the mode of their occurrence, their details, and their consequences, can only be learned by the event. It is in the retrospect that the foreshadowing of the future is seen to be miraculous and divine.

Verse 26. *And so all Israel shall be saved, as it is written.* Israel, here, from the context, must mean the Jewish people, and *all Israel*, the whole nation. The Jews, as a people, are now rejected; as a people, they are to be restored. As their rejection, although national, did not include the rejection of every individual; so their restoration, although in like manner national, need not be assumed to include the salvation of every individual Jew. Πᾶς Ἰσραήλ is not therefore to be here understood to mean, all the true people of God, as Augustin, Calvin, and many others explain it; nor all the elect Jews, *i.e.*, all that part of the nation which constitute "the remnant according to the election of grace;" but the whole nation, as a nation.

In support of what he had said, the apostle appeals to the Old Testament prophecies. It is probable that here, as elsewhere, he does not intend to refer exclusively to any one prediction, but to give the general sense of many specific declarations of the ancient prophets. Isa. lix. 20, 21; xxvii. 9; Jer. xxxi. 31—34; Ps. xiv. 7, are the passages which seem to have been immediately before the apostle's mind, and to have given colour to his language. In Isa. lix. 20, it is said, "The Redeemer shall come to Zion, and unto them that turn from transgression in Jacob." Instead of ἐκ Σιών, *out of Zion,* the LXX. have ἕνεκεν Σιών, *for the sake of Zion,* the English version, *to Zion.* In Ps. xiv. 7, it is *out of Zion.* The latter part of the verse, as given by Paul, does not agree with the Hebrew, which is correctly rendered in our version, "To such as turn from transgression (literally, *to the converts of transgression*) in Jacob." Paul follows the LXX., καὶ ἀποστρέψει ἀσεβείας ἀπὸ Ἰακώβ, *and shall turn iniquity from Jacob.* In Isa. xxvii. 9, the phrase is, "the iniquity of Jacob shall be purged." The general idea expressed in these passages is, "The God, the deliverer, shall come for the salvation of Jacob," *i. e.*, of the Jews. And this is all that Paul desired to establish by these ancient prophecies. The apostle teaches, that the deliverance promised of old, and to which the prophet Isaiah referred in the passage above cited, included much more than the conversion of the comparatively few Jews who believed in Christ at the advent. The full accomplishment of the promise, that he should turn away ungodliness from Jacob, contemplated the conversion of the whole nation, as such, to the Lord. We are, of course, bound to receive the apostle's interpretation as correct; and there is the less difficulty in this, as there is nothing in the original passage at all incompatible with it, and as it accords with the nature of God's covenant with his ancient people.

VERSE 27. *For this is my covenant unto them;* αὕτη αὐτοῖς ἡ παρ
ἐμοῦ διαθήκη, *this for them is the covenant which proceeds from me.* In
the Hebrew it is simply, *my covenant;* so that παρ ἐμοῦ is for the genitive. See, however, Winer, iii. § 30. The pronoun αὕτη, *this,* is to be
referred to what follows ; this is my covenant (ὅταν, *when*), *that* I will take
away their sins. The demonstrative pronoun may be followed, and its
reference determined, by ἵνα, John xvii. 3 ; ἐάν, 1 John ii. 3 ; and as in
this case, and in 1 John v. 2, by ὅταν. The quotation in this verse, as
that in ver. 26, is not from any one place. The words, *This is my covenant with them,* occur in Isa. lix. 21 ; the clause, *When I shall take away
their sins,* is from Isa. xxvii. 9, as rendered by the LXX., who give the
sense of the Hebrew, "Their iniquity shall be purged ;" or, literally, *to
take away his sin.* All the apostle intended to prove, is proved by the
language of the prophets. The covenant of God with his ancient people
secured, after their apostacy and consequent banishment in Babylon, and
their dispersion over the earth, and their rejection of Christ, the ultimate
purging away of their sin, and their restoration, as a nation, to the
Messiah's kingdom. This national conversion is also predicted in Zech.
xii. 10, and in many other passages of the Old Testament.

VERSE 28. *As concerning the gospel, they are enemies for your sakes;
but as touching the election, they are beloved for the fathers' sakes.* In
this and the few following verses, the apostle sums up what he had previously taught. The Jews, he says, were now, as far as the gospel was
concerned, regarded and treated as enemies, for the benefit of the Gentiles ;
but, in reference to the election, they were still regarded as the peculiar
people of God, on account of their connection with the patriarchs. *They
are enemies,* whether of the gospel, of the apostle, or of God, is not expressed, and therefore depends on the context. Each view of the clause
has its advocates. The last is the correct one, because they are *enemies* to
him, by whom, on one account, they are *beloved.* The word ἐχθροί may
be taken actively or passively ; see v. 10. They are inimical to God, or
they are regarded and treated as enemies by him. The latter best suits
the context. They are now aliens from their own covenant of promise.

As concerning the gospel, κατὰ τὸ εὐαγγέλιον, that is, the gospel is the
occasion of their being regarded as enemies. This is explained by a reference to vers. 11, 15. By their punishment the progress of the gospel has
been facilitated among the Gentiles ; and therefore the apostle says, it is
for your sakes they are thus treated. On the other hand, κατὰ δὲ τὴν
ἐκλογήν, as it regards *the election,* or the covenant of God, they are still regarded with peculiar favour, because descended from those patriarchs to
whom and to whose seed the promises were made. This is but expressing
in a different form the idea which the apostle had previously presented, viz.,
that the covenant made with Abraham was inconsistent with the final rejection of the Jews, as a people. God foresaw and predicted their temporary defection and rejection from his kingdom, but never contemplated
their being for ever excluded ; see vers. 16, 25—27. "Paulus autem docet,
ita (Judæos) fuisse ad tempus Dei providentia excæcatos, ut via evangelio
ad gentes sterneretur : cæterum non esse in perpetuum a Dei gratia exclu-
sos. Fatetur ergo—Deum non esse immemorem fœderis, quod cum patribus eorum pepigit, et quo testatus est, se æterno consilio gentem illam
dilectione complexam esse." *Calvin.*

VERSE 29. *For the gifts and calling of God are without repentance;* τὰ
χαρίσματα καὶ ἡ κλῆσις, the gifts of God in general, and specially the call-

ing of God. Compare Mark xvi. 7. God is not a man, that he should chnage. Having chosen the Jews as his people, the purpose which he had in view in that choice can never be altered; and as it was his purpose that they should ever remain his people, their future restoration to his favour and kingdom is certain. Having previously explained the nature of God's covenant with his ancient people, Paul infers from the divine character, that it will be fully accomplished. *Calling* is equivalent to *election*, as appears from the context, the one word being substituted for the other, and also from the use of the cognate terms, (see chap. viii. 28, i. 7, &c., &c.) The general proposition of the apostle, therefore, is, that the purposes of God are unchangeable; and, consequently, those whom God has chosen for any special benefit cannot fail to attain it. The persons whom he hath chosen to eternal life shall certainly be saved; and the people whom he chooses to be his peculiar people, as the Jews were chosen in Abraham, must for ever remain his people. The purpose once formed, and the promise once given, never can be changed. As in the whole context Paul is speaking, not of individuals, but of the rejection and restoration of the Jews as a body, it is evident that the calling and election which he here has in view, are such as pertain to the Jews as a nation, and not such as contemplate the salvation of individuals.

Verses 30, 31. *For as ye in times past have not believed God, yet have now obtained mercy through their unbelief; even so,* &c. These verses contain a repetition and confirmation of the previous sentiment. The cases of the Gentiles and Jews are very nearly parallel. Formerly the Gentiles were disbelieving, yet the unbelief of the Jews became the occasion of their obtaining mercy; so now, though the Jews are disobedient, the mercy shown to the Gentiles is to be the means of their obtaining mercy. As the gospel came from the Jews to the Gentiles, so it is to return from the Gentiles to the Jews. Paul had before stated how the unbelief of the Israelites was instrumental in promoting the salvation of other nations, and how the conversion of the Gentiles was to react upon the Jews.

It is in confirmation of what had just been said, that the apostle introduces what follows by γάρ, *for*. *For as ye in time past have not believed.* *Ye*, of course referring to the Gentiles. *In times past, i. e.,* before the coming of Christ. *Have not believed God*, ἠπειθήσατε τῷ Θεῷ, *disobeyed God.* According to the Scriptures, however, faith is an act of obedience, and unbelief is disobedience. Hence the *to obey* often means to believe or confide in. That is, the same act may be expressed by either word. Thus in Heb. v. 9, Christ is said to be the author of salvation to all those who obey Him. In the New Testament ἀπειθεῖν and ἀπείθεια are always used to express disobedience to the truth; that is, the act of rejecting the truth. It is not, therefore, moral disobedience in general that is here referred to, but unbelief. *Have obtained mercy through their unbelief*, τῇ τούτων ἀπειθείᾳ. The dative has here a causal force. The unbelief of the Jews was, as an historical fact, the occasion of the gospel's being extended to the Gentiles. *So have these also not believed, that through your mercy they may also obtain mercy* οὕτω καὶ οὗτοι, νῦν ἠπείθησαν τῷ ὑμετέρῳ ἐλέει ἵνα καὶ αὐτοὶ ἐλεηθῶσι. The translation given of this clause in the English version, supposes that ἵνα is out of its proper place, and should stand before τῷ ὑμετέρῳ ἐλέει, *that* through your mercy they may obtain mercy. In the Greek these words are connected with ἠπείθησαν; and accordingly in the Vulgate they are rendered, "ita et isti nunc non crediderunt in vestram misericordiam." And Luther translates, "And these now have not chosen to believe the mercy which you have accepted or experienced." Calvin : "Si nunc increduli facti sunt, eo quod adepti estis misericordiam," (*because* ye have obtained mercy.) Lachmann, in his edition of the Greek Testament, adopts the same construction, putting a comma after ἐλέει. The parallelism of the verse, and the obvious antithesis between ἐλέει and ἀπειθείᾳ, (*your mercy* and *their unbelief,*) demand the other mode of explanation. This trajection of the particle ἵνα is not unusual. For the sake of emphasis, some clause or word is placed before, when its logical position would be after the particle. See 2 Cor. ii. 4, τὴν ἀγάπην ἵνα γνῶτε.

VERSE 32. *For God hath concluded all in unbelief;* συγκλείω εἰς, in a literal or local sense, means, *to shut up together in a place ;* and metaphorically, to deliver over to the power of. Here the idea is, that God, in the dispensation of his providence and grace, has so ordered things, that all Gentiles and Jews, first the one, and then the other, should reveal their true character as sinners, and stand out in history confessed as unbelievers. For examples of a similar form of expression, see Ps. xxxi. 8, " Thou hast shut me up (συνέκλεισας) into the hands of the enemy;" Ps. lxxviii. 50, " He gave their life over (συνέκλεισεν) to the pestilence." Compare Gal. iii. 22. In none of these cases is the word used simply declaratively, " God declared them to be unbelievers." Nor is mere permission all that is expressed. God's efficiency or control is directly asserted. God gave the Psalmist into the hands of his enemy, and he gave up first the Gentiles and then the Jews, unto unbelief. The agency of God in giving men up to sin is punitive ; it is consistent with their liberty and responsibility, and with his own holiness. He does not cause their sin, but he so orders his dispensations, that their sinfulness is revealed, and the mode of its manifestations determined. It seems also to enter into the design of the apostle to show that God had dealt alike with Gentile and Jew. They stood on the same ground. Both were dependent on sovereign mercy. Both had sunk into a state from which the grace of God alone could save them. As all were equally miserable and helpless, God determined to have mercy upon all, and to bring all, Jews as well as Gentiles, into the fold of Christ.

VERSES 33—36. The apostle having finished his exhibition of the plan of redemption, having presented clearly the doctrine of justification, sanctification, the certainty of salvation to all believers, election, the calling of the Gentiles, the present rejection and final restoration of the Jews, in view of all the wonders and all the glories of the divine dealings with men, pours forth this sublime and affecting tribute to the wisdom, goodness, and sovereignty of God. Few passages, even in the Scriptures, are to be compared with this, in the force with which it presents the idea that God is all, and man is nothing. It is supposed by many that these verses have reference to the doctrines taught in the immediate context ; and that it is the wisdom of God, as displayed in the calling of men, Gentiles and Jews, which Paul here contemplates. Others restrict them still further to the display of the mercy of God, of which the apostle had just been speaking. But the passage should be applied to that to which it is most naturally applicable. The question is, what called forth these admiring views of the dispensations of God ? The truth that he would ultimately restore his ancient people ? or the whole exhibition of the economy of redemption ? As the passage occurs at the close of this exhibition, as it expresses precisely the feelings which it might be expected to produce, and as there is nothing to restrict it to the immediate context, it is most natural to consider it as referring to all that the apostle had hitherto taught.

The principal ideas presented in this passage are—1. The incomprehensible character and infinite excellence of the divine nature and dispensations, ver. 33. 2. God's entire independence of man, vers. 34, 35. 3. His comprehending all things within himself; being the source, the means, and the end of all, ver. 35.

Verse 33. *O the depth of the riches both of the wisdom and knowledge of God! How unsearchable are his judgments, and his ways past finding out.* There are two methods of interpreting these words. First, the three genitives, πλούτου, σοφίας, γνώσεως, may stand in the same relation to βάϑος. O the depth of the riches, and of the wisdom, and of the knowledge of God. Or πλούτου may qualify βάϑος, O the depth of the riches (the inexhaustible, or inconceivable, depth) both of the wisdom and knowledge of God. So far as commentators are concerned, they are about equally divided as to these explanations. If the former method be adopted, *riches* may be understood to refer specially to the mercy or goodness of God, ii. 4; x. 12; or, to his resources in general. 'How inconceivable are the resources of God,' *i.e.*, his plenitude of perfections and of means. If the latter, then it refers simply to the inconceivableness of God's wisdom and knowledge. As, however, the grace of God is not only prominently presented throughout the epistle, but is specially referred to as an object of admiration in these verses, the former explanation is on the whole to be preferred. Although it is not probable that, in such a passage, every word was designed to be taken in a very precise and definite sense, yet it is likely that Paul meant to express different ideas by the terms *wisdom* and *knowledge*, because both are so wonderfully displayed in the work of redemption, of which he had been speaking. All-comprehending knowledge, which surveyed all the subjects of this work, all the necessities and circumstances of their being, all the means requisite for the accomplishment of the divine purpose, and all the results of those means from the beginning to the end. Infinite wisdom, in selecting and adapting the means to the object in view, in the ordering of the whole scheme of creation, providence, and redemption, so that the glory of God, and the happiness of his creatures are, and are to be, so wonderfully promoted. *His judgments,* τὰ κρίματα αὐτοῦ, may be understood in the wide sense, his decisions, *i. e.*, his purposes, or decrees; or in the more restricted and proper sense, his judicial decisions, his judgments concerning men; or it may refer to his providential judgments or dispensations, and be perfectly parallel with αἱ ὁδοὶ αὐτοῦ, *his ways.* As of old, the ruler was also the judge—to judge often means to rule—and the same word is used for the decisions of the judge and the decrees or ordinances of the ruler. In this case, however, as Paul distinguishes between wisdom and knowledge, so it is better to retain the shade of distinction between *judgments* and *ways.* The former are ἀνεξερεύνητα, incapable of being investigated as to their grounds or reasons; the latter are ἀνεξιχνίαστοι, impossible to trace (from ἴχνος, *footprint.*) We can only wonder and adore. We can never understand. And it is well that it is so. What can be understood must be limited. What is fully comprehended no longer exercises, excites, or enlarges. It is because God is infinite in his being, and incomprehensible in his judgments and in his ways, that he is an inexhaustible source of knowledge and blessedness.

Verse 34. *For who hath known the mind of the Lord? or, who hath been his counsellor?* This verse is designed to confirm what is said in ver. 33. These clauses may be taken as synonymous, or the first may refer to God's judgments, and the second, to his ways. Who hath known what

God designed to do, and the reasons of his decrees? and, Who hath counselled him as to the mode of their execution? In his purposes and his dispensations he is equally and perfectly independent, infinitely exalted above the supervision or direction of his creatures.

VERSE 35. *Or who hath first given to him, and it shall be recompensed to him again?* This is not to be confined to giving counsel or knowledge to God, but expresses the general idea that the creature can do nothing to place God under obligation. It will be at once perceived how appropriate is this thought, in reference to the doctrines which Paul had been teaching. Men are justified, not on the ground of their own merit, but of the merit of Christ; they are sanctified, not by the power of their own good purposes, and the strength of their own will, but by the Spirit of God; they are chosen and called to eternal life, not on the ground of anything in them, but according to the purpose of him who worketh all things after the counsel of his own will. God, therefore, is the Alpha and the Omega of salvation. The creature has neither merit nor power. His hopes must rest on sovereign mercy alone. There is a correspondence between the several clauses in these verses. 'Who hath given to God,' refers to the plenitude and sovereignty of his grace (βάθος πλούτου); 'Who hath known the mind of the Lord?' to his unsearchable knowledge; and 'who hath been his counsellor?' to his infinite wisdom. This was remarked long ago. Thus Theodoret says: τὰ τρία ταῦτα πρὸς τὰ τρία τέθεικε, τὸν πλοῦτον καὶ τὴν σοφίαν καὶ τὴν γνῶσιν· τὸ μὲν τίς ἔγνω νοῦν κυρίου πρὸς τὴν γνῶσιν, τὸ δὲ τίς σύμβουλος αὐτοῦ ἐγένετο πρὸς τὴν σοφίαν, τὸ δὲ τίς προέδωκεν αὐτῷ καὶ ἀνταποδοθήσεται πρὸς τὸν πλοῦτον.

VERSE 36. *For of him, and through him, and to him, are all things: to whom be glory for ever. Amen.* The reason why man can lay God under no obligation is, that God is himself all and in all; the source, the means, and the end. By him all things are; through his power, wisdom, and goodness, all things are directed and governed; and to him, as their last end, all things tend. The prepositions ἐκ, διά, εἰς, here used, indicate that God is the source, the constantly working cause, and end of all things. Among the fathers, it was a common opinion that the apostle had reference to the Trinity, and intended in these words to indicate the relation of all things to the several persons of the Godhead. All things are *of* the Father, *through* the Son, and *to* the Spirit. So Tholuck and Olshausen. To this, however, it is objected, that such reference is not demanded by the context, and that the Spirit's relation to what is out of himself is expressed by ἐν, not by εἰς. Compare Eph iv. 6. It is God as God, the Godhead, and not the persons of the Trinity in their distinct relations, that is here brought into view. When Paul asks, Who hath first given to God? the answer is, No one, *for* of him, through him, and to him, are all things. It is for the display of his character everything exists, and is directed, as the highest and noblest of all possible objects. Creatures are as nothing, less than vanity and nothing in comparison with God. Human knowledge, power, and virtue, are mere glimmering reflections from the brightness of the divine glory. That system of religion, therefore, is best in accordance with the character of God, the nature of man, and the end of the universe, in which all things are of, through, and to God; and which most effectually leads men to say, NOT UNTO US, BUT UNTO THY NAME BE ALL THE GLORY!

Such is the appropriate conclusion of the doctrinal portion of this wonderful epistle; in which more fully and clearly than in any other portion of the word of God, the plan of salvation is presented and defended. Here are the doctrines of grace ; doctrines on which the pious in all ages and nations have rested their hopes of heaven, though they may have had comparatively obscure intimations of their nature. The leading principle of all is, that God is the source of all good ; that in fallen man there is neither merit nor ability ; that salvation, consequently, is all of grace, as well sanctification as pardon, as well election as eternal glory. For of him, and through him, and to him, are all things ; to whom be glory for ever. Amen.

DOCTRINE.

1. There is to be a general conversion of the Jews, concerning which the apostle teaches us—1. That it is to be in some way consequent on the conversion of the Gentiles, vers. 11—31. 2. That it will be attended with the most important and desirable results for the rest of the world, vers. 12, 15. 3. That it is to take place after the fulness of the Gentiles is brought in ; that is, after the conversion of multitudes of the Gentiles, (how many, who can tell?) ver. 25. Nothing is said of this restoration being sudden, or effected by a miracle, or consequent on the second advent, or as attended by a restoration of the Jews to their own land. These particulars have all been added by some commentators, either from their own imagination, or from their views of other portions of the Scriptures. They are not taught by the apostle. On the contrary, it is *through the mercy shown to the Gentiles,* according to Paul, that the Jews are to be brought in, which implies that the former are to be instrumental in the restoration of the latter. And he everywhere teaches, that within the church the distinction between Jew and Gentile ceases. In Christ there is neither Jew nor Greek, Barbarian nor Scythian, bond nor free, Col. iii. 11 ; all classes are merged in one, as was the case under the direction of the apostles in the first ages of the church.

2. The church of God is the same in all ages and under all dispensations. It is the society of the true people of God, together with their children. To this society the ancient patriarchs and their posterity belonged ; into this society, at the time of Christ, other nations were admitted, and the great body of the Jews were cast out, and into this same community the ancient people of God are to be again received. In every stage of its progress, the church is the same. The olive-tree is one, though the branches are numerous, and sometimes changed, vers. 17—24.

3. The web of Providence is wonderfully woven. Good and evil are made with equal certainty, under the government of infinite wisdom and benevolence, to result in the promotion of God's gracious and glorious designs. The wicked unbelief and consequent rejection of the Jews, are made the means of facilitating the conversion of the Gentiles ; the holy faith and obedience of the Gentiles, are to be the means of the restoration of the Jews, vers. 11, 31.

4. All organised communities, civil and ecclesiastical, have a common responsibility, a moral personality in the sight of God, and are dealt with accordingly, rewarded or punished according to their conduct, as such. As their organized existence is confined to this world, so must the retributive dispensations of God respecting them be. Witness the rejection, dispersion, and sufferings of the Jews, as a national punishment for their national rejection of the Messiah. Witness the state of all the Eastern churches

broken off from the olive-tree for the unbelief of former generations. Their fathers sinned, and their children's children, to the third and fourth generation, suffer the penalty, as they share in the guilt, vers. 11—24.

5. The security of every individual Christian is suspended on his continuing in faith and holy obedience; which is indeed rendered certain by the purpose and promise of God. In like manner, the security of every civil and ecclesiastical society, in the enjoyment of its peculiar advantages, is suspended on its fidelity as such, for which fidelity there is no special promise with regard to any country or any church, vers. 20—24.

6. God does sometimes enter into covenant with communities, as such. Thus he has covenanted with the whole human race that the world shall not be again destroyed by a deluge, and that the seasons shall continue to succeed each other, in regular order, until the end of time. Thus he covenanted with the Jews to be a God to them and to their seed for ever, and that they should be to him a people. This, it seems, is a perpetual covenant, which continues in force until the present day, and which renders certain the restoration of the Jews to the privileges of the church of God, vers. 16, 28, 29.

7. It is the radical principle of the Bible, and consequently of all true religion, that God is all and in all; that of him, and through him, and to him, are all things. It is the tendency of all truth to exalt God, and to humble the creature; and it is characteristic of true piety to feel that all good comes from God, and to desire that all glory should be given to God, vers. 33—36.

REMARKS.

1. The mutual relation between the Christian church and the Jews should produce in the minds of all the followers of Christ,—1. A deep sense of our obligations to the Jews as the people through whom the true religion has been preserved, and the blessings of divine truth extended to all nations, vers. 17, 18. 2. Sincere compassion for them, because their rejection and misery have been the means of reconciling the world to God, *i.e.*, of extending the gospel of reconciliation among men, vers. 11, 12, 15. 3. The banishment of all feelings of contempt towards them, or exultation over them, vers. 18, 20. 4. An earnest desire, prompting to prayer and effort, for their restoration, as an event fraught with blessings to them and to all the world, and one which God has determined to bring to pass, vers. 12, 15, 25, &c.

2. The dealings of God with his ancient people should, moreover, teach us—1. That we have no security for the continuance of our privileges but constant fidelity, ver. 20. 2. That, consequently, instead of being proud and self-confident, we should be humble and cautious, vers. 20, 21. 3. That God will probably not bear with us as long as he bore with the Jews, ver. 21. 4. That if for our unbelief we are cast out of the church, our punishment will probably be more severe. There is no special covenant securing the restoration of any apostate branch of the Christian church, vers. 21, 24, with 16, 27—29.

3. It is a great blessing to be connected with those who are in covenant with God. The promise is "to thee and thy seed after thee." "The Lord thy God, he is God, the faithful God, which keepeth covenant and mercy with them that love him and keep his commandments, to a thousand generations," Deut. vii. 9. The blessing of Abraham reaches, in some of

its precious consequences, to the Jews of this and every coming age, vers. 16, 27—29.

4. The destiny of our children and our children's children is suspended, in a great measure, on our fidelity. "God is a jealous God, visiting the iniquities of the fathers upon the children unto the third and fourth generation of them that hate him." What words of woe for unborn thousands, were those, "His blood be on us and on our children!" As the Jews of the present age are suffering the consequences of the unbelief of their fathers, and the nominal Christians of the Eastern churches suffer for the apostacy of previous generations, so will our children perish, if we, for our unbelief as a church and nation, are cast off from God, vers. 19—24.

5. As the restoration of the Jews is not only a most desirable event, but one which God has determined to accomplish, Christians should keep it constantly in view even in their labours for the conversion of the Gentiles. This Paul did, vers. 13, 14. Every effort to hasten the accession of the fulness of the Gentiles is so much done towards the restoration of Israel, ver. 25.

6. Christians should not feel as though they were isolated beings, as if each one need be concerned for himself alone, having no joint responsibility with the community to which he belongs. God will deal with our church and country as a whole, and visit our sins upon those who are to come after us. We should feel, therefore, that we are one body, members one of another, having common interests and responsibilities. We ought to weep over the sins of the community to which we belong, as being in one sense, and in many of their consequences, our sins, vers. 11—24.

7. As the gifts and calling of God are without repentance, those to whom he has given the Holy Spirit, and has called unto holiness, may rejoice in the certainty of the continuance of these blessings, ver. 29.

8. Does the contemplation of the work of redemption, and the remembrance of our own experience, lead us to sympathize with the apostle in his adoring admiration of the wisdom and goodness of God, and feel that, as it regards our salvation, everything is of him, and through him, and to him? vers. 33—36.

9. As it is the tendency and result of all correct views of Christian doctrine to produce the feelings expressed by the apostle at the close of this chapter, those views cannot be scriptural which have a contrary tendency; or which lead us to ascribe, in any form, our salvation to our own merit or power, vers. 33—36.

CHAPTER XII.

CONTENTS.

This chapter consists of two parts. The first, vers. 1—8, treats of piety towards God, and the proper estimation and use of the various gifts and offices employed or exercised in the church. The second, vers. 9—21, relates to love and its various manifestations towards different classes of men.

ROMANS XII. 1—8.

ANALYSIS.

As the apostle had concluded the doctrinal portion of the epistle with the preceding chapter, in accordance with his almost uniform practice, he deduces from his doctrines important practical lessons. The first deduction from the exhibition which he had made of the mercy of God in the redemption of men, is that they should devote themselves to him as a living sacrifice, and be conformed to his will and not to the manners of the world, vers. 1, 2. The second is, that they should be humble, and not allow the diversity of their gifts to destroy the sense of their unity as one body in Christ, vers. 3—5. These various gifts were to be exercised, not for selfish purposes, but in a manner consistent with their nature and design; diligently, disinterestedly, and kindly, vers. 6—8.

COMMENTARY.

Verse 1. *I beseech you, therefore, brethren, by the mercies of God,* &c. As the sum of all that Paul had said of the justification, sanctification, and salvation of men is, that these results are to be attributed not to human merit nor to human efforts, but to the mercy of God, he brings the whole discussion to bear as a motive for devotion to God. Whatever gratitude the soul feels for pardon, purity, and the sure prospect of eternal life, is called forth to secure its consecration to that God who is the author of all these mercies.

That ye present your bodies a living sacrifice, holy, acceptable unto God. All the expressions of this clause seem to have an obvious reference to the services of the Old Testament economy. Under that dispensation, animals free from blemish were presented and devoted to God; under the new dispensation a nobler and more spiritual service is to be rendered; not the oblation of animals, but the consecration of ourselves. The expression, *your bodies,* is perhaps nearly equivalent to *yourselves;* yet Paul probably used it with design, not only because it was appropriate to the figure, but because he wished to render the idea prominent, that the whole man, body as well as soul, was to be devoted to the service of God. "Ye are bought with a price; therefore glorify God in your body, and in your spirit, which are God's," 1 Cor. vi. 20. The apostle carries the figure out; the sacrifice is to be *living, holy,* and *acceptable.* The first of these epithets is generally considered as intended to express the contrast between the sacrifice here intended, and the victims which were placed lifeless upon the altar; thus believers, in 1 Pet. ii. 5, are called "living stones," in opposition to the senseless materials employed in a literal building. We are to present Θυσίαν ζῶσαν, *a sacrifice that lives.* "Abominabile est, cadaver offere."— *Bengel.* The word *living,* however, may mean *perpetual, lasting, never neglected;* as in the phrases, "living bread," John vi. 51, 'bread which never looses its power;' "living hope," 1 Peter i. 3, 'hope which never fails;' "living waters," "a living way," &c.; (see *Wahl's Lexicon,* under the word ζάω.) The sacrifice then which we are to make is not a transient service, like the oblation of a victim, which was in a few moments consumed upon the altar, but it is a living or perpetual sacrifice never to be neglected or recalled. The epithet *holy* has probably direct reference to the frequent use of a nearly corresponding word (תְּמִים) in the Hebrew scriptures, which, when applied to sacrifices, is commonly rendered *without blemish.* The word *holy* is then in this case equivalent to *immaculate, i. e.,* free from those defects which would cause an offering to be rejected. The term *acceptable* is here used in the same sense as the phrase, "for a sweet smelling savour," Eph. v. 2; Phil. iv. 18; Lev. i. 9, *i. e., grateful, well-pleasing;* a sacrifice in which God delights. Τῷ Θεῷ is to be connected with εὐάρεστον and not with παραστῆσαι.

Your reasonable service. There is doubt as to the grammatical construction of this clause. The most natural and simple explanation is to consider it in apposition with the preceding member of the sentence, as has been done by our translators, who supply the words *which is.* This consecration of ourselves to God, which the apostle requires, is a *reasonable service.* The word λατρεία does not mean an offering, but *worship.* It is not the thing offered that is said to be *reasonable* in the sense of, endowed with reason, but the nature of the service. It is rendered by the mind. The word (λογικήν) rendered *reasonable,* is indeed variously explained. The simplest interpretation is that which takes the word in its natural sense, viz., *pertaining to the mind;* it is a mental or spiritual service, in opposition to ceremonial and external observations. Compare the phrase (λογικὸν γάλα), 'milk suited, or pertaining to the mind,' 1 Peter ii. 2. Others understand these words as expressing the difference between the sacrifices under the Christian dispensation and those under the Old. Formerly animals destitute of reason (ἄλογα ζῶα) were offered unto God, but now men possessed of a rational soul. But this interpretation is neither so well suited to the meaning of the word, nor does it give a sense so consistent with the context; compare 1 Peter ii. 5.

VERSE 2. *And be not conformed to this world, but be ye transformed by the renewing of your mind,* &c. Not only is God to be worshipped in spirit and in truth, as required in the preceding verse, but there must be a corresponding holiness of life. This idea is expressed in the manner most common with the sacred writers. Regarding men universally as corrupted and devoted to sin, *the world* is with them equivalent to *the wicked;* to be conformed to the world, therefore, is to be like unrenewed men in temper and in life. The word accurately rendered *conformed,* expresses strongly the idea of similarity in character and manners; and that rendered *transformed* expresses with equal strength the opposite idea. *This world.* The origin of this term, as used in the New Testament, is no doubt to be sought in the mode of expression so common among the Jews, who were accustomed to distinguish between the times before, and the times under the Messiah, by calling the former period *this world*, or *this age*, (עוֹלָם הַזֶּה) and the latter, *the world*, or *age to come* (עוֹלָם הַבָּא). The former phrase thus naturally came to designate those who were without, and the latter those who were within the kingdom of Christ; they are equivalent to the expressions *the world* and *the church ;* the mass of mankind and the people of God ; compare 1 Cor. ii. 8 ; Eph. ii. 2 ; 2 Cor. iv. 4 ; Luke xx. 35 ; Heb. ii. 5 ; vi. 5.   There is, therefore, no necessity for supposing, as is done by many commentators, that the apostle has any special reference, in the use of this word, to the Jewish dispensation; as though his meaning were, 'Be not conformed to the Jewish opinions and forms of worship, but be transformed and accommodated to the new spiritual economy under which ye are placed.' The word (αἰών) here used, and the equivalent term (κόσμος) commonly translated *world*, are so frequently used for the mass of mankind, considered in opposition to the people of God, that there can be no good reason for departing from the common interpretation, especially as the sense which it affords is so good in itself, and so well suited to the context.

By the renewing of your mind. This phrase is intended to be explanatory of the preceding. The transformation to which Christians are exhorted, is not a mere external change, but one which results from a change of heart, an entire alteration of the state of the mind. The word νοῦς, *mind*, is used as it is here, frequently in the New Testament, Rom. i. 28 ; Eph. iv. 17, 23 ; Col. ii. 18, &c. In all these and in similar cases, it does not differ from the word *heart, i.e.,* in its wide sense for the whole soul.

That ye may be able to prove what is that good and acceptable and perfect will of God. The logical relation of this clause to the preceding is doubtful, as the original (εἰς τὸ δοκιμάζειν) admits of its being regarded as expressing either the design or the result of the change just spoken of. Our translators have adopted the former view, 'Ye are renewed, in order that ye may be able to prove, &c.' The other, however, gives an equally good sense, 'Ye are renewed so that ye prove, &c ;' such is the effect of the change in question. The word rendered *to prove*, signifies also *to approve ;* the sense of this passage, therefore, may be either, 'that ye may try or prove what is acceptable to God,' *i.e.,* decide upon or ascertain what is right ; or, 'that ye may approve what is good, &c.' The words *good, acceptable,* and *perfect*, are by many considered as predicates of the word *will*. As, however, the expression 'acceptable will of God' is unnatural and unusual, the majority of modern commentators, after Erasmus, take them as substantives ; 'that ye may approve what is good, acceptable, and perfect, viz., the will of God.' The last phrase is then in apposition with the others. The design and result then of that great change of which Paul speaks, is, that Christians should know, delight in, and practise, whatever is good and acceptable to God ; compare Eph. v. 10, 17 ; Phil. iv. 8.

VERSE 3.   *For I say, through the grace given unto me, to every man that is among you, not to think of himself more highly than he ought to think,* &c. The apostle connects with the general exhortation contained in the preceding verses, and founds upon it, an exhortation to special Christian virtues. The first virtue which he enjoins upon believers is modesty or humility. This has reference specially to the officers of the church, or at least to the recipients of spiritual gifts. It is very evident from 1 Cor. xii. and xiv., that these gifts were coveted and exercised by many of the early Christians for the purpose of self-exaltation. They, therefore, desired not those which were most useful, but those which were most attractive ; and some were puffed up, while others were envious and discontented. This evil the apostle forcibly and beautifully reproved in the chapters referred to, in the same manner that he does here, and much more at length. He showed his readers that these gifts were all gratuitous, and were, therefore, occasions of gratitude, but not grounds of boasting. He reminds his readers that the design for which these gifts were bestowed, was the edification of the church, and not the exaltation of the receiver ; that, however diversified in their nature, they were all manifestations of one and the same Spirit, and were as necessary to a perfect whole as the several members of the body, with their various offices, to a perfect man. Having one Spirit, and constituting one body, any exaltation of one over the other was as unnatural as the eye or ear disregarding and despising the hand or the foot. As this tendency to abuse their official and spiritual distinctions was not confined to the Corinthian Christians, we find the apostle, in this passage, giving substantially the same instructions to the Romans.

Through the grace given unto me. The word *grace* in this clause is by many understood to mean the apostolic office, which Paul elsewhere speaks of as a great favour. "Tantundem valent ejus verba acsi dixisset : Non loquor a me ipso, sed legatus Dei, quae mihi mandata ille injunxit, ad vos perfero. Gratiam (ut prius) vocat apostolatum, quo Dei bonitatem in eo commendet, ac simul innuat, se non irrupisse propria temeritate, sed Dei vocatione assumptum."—*Calvin.* Compare chap i. 5 ; xv. 15 ; Eph. iii. 2, 8. But this is too limited ; the word probably includes all the *favour* of God towards him, not merely in conferring on him the office of an apostle, but in bestowing all the gifts of the Spirit, ordinary and extraordinary, which qualified him for his duties, and gave authority to his instructions. *Through* διά, *i.e.*, on account of, or out of regard to.

Not to think of himself more highly than he ought to think. The word *to think* is an inadequate translation of the Greek, (φρονεῖν,) inasmuch as the latter includes the idea of the exercise of the affections as well as of the intellect ; see chap. viii. 5 ; Col. iii. 2 ; Phil. iii. 19. *To think of oneself too highly,* is to be puffed up with an idea of our own importance and superiority.

But to think soberly, according as God hath dealt to every man the measure of faith. There is in the first member of this clause a beautiful paranomasia in the original (φρονεῖν εἰς τὸ σωφρονεῖν) which is lost in a translation. The word rendered *soberly* properly means *to be of a sane mind ;* and then *to be moderate* or *temperate.* Paul speaks of one who over-estimates or praises himself as being beside himself ; and of him who is modest and humble as being of a sane mind, *i.e.*, as making a proper estimate of himself. " For whether we be beside ourselves, it is to God ; or whether we be sober, it is for your cause," 2 Cor. v. 13, *i.e.*, 'If we commend ourselves, it is that God may be honoured ; and if we act modestly and abstain from self-commendation, it is that you may be benefited.' *To think soberly,* therefore, is to form and manifest a right estimate of ourselves, and of our gifts. A right estimate can never be other than a very humble one, since whatever there is of good in us is not of ourselves, but of God.

The expression *measure* or *proportion of faith,* is variously explained. Faith may be taken in its usual sense, and the meaning of the clause be, ' Let every one think of himself according to the degree of faith or confidence in God which has been imparted to him, and not as though he had more than he really possesses.' Or *faith* may be taken for what is believed, or for knowledge of divine truth, and the sense be, 'according to the degree of knowledge which he has attained.' Or it may be taken for *that which is confided* to any, and be equivalent to *gift.* The sense then is, 'Let every one think of himself according to the nature or character of the gifts which he has received.' This is perhaps the most generally received interpretation, although it is arrived at in different ways; many considering the word *faith* here as used metonymically for its effects, viz., for the various (χαρίσματα) *graces,* ordinary and extraordinary, of which it is the cause. This general sense is well suited to the context, as the following verses, containing a specification of the gifts of prophesying, teaching, ruling, &c., appear to be an amplification of this clause. The first mentioned interpretation is, however, most in accordance with the usual meaning of πίστις.

VERSES 4, 5.   *For as we have many members in one body, and all members have not the same office; so we,* &c. In these verses we have the same comparison that occurs more at length in 1 Cor. xii., and for the same purpose. The object of the apostle is in both cases the same. He designs to show that the diversity of offices and gifts among Christians, so far from being inconsistent with their union as one body in Christ, is necessary to the perfection and usefulness of that body. It would be as unreasonable for all Christians to have the same gifts, as for all the members of the human frame to have the same office. This comparison is peculiarly beautiful and appropriate; because it not only clearly illustrates the particular point intended, but at the same time brings into view the important truth that the real union of Christians results from the indwelling of the Holy Spirit, as the union of the several members of the body is the result of their being all animated and actuated by one soul. Nothing can present in a clearer light the duty of Christian fellowship, or the sinfulness of divisions and envyings among the members of Christ's body, than the apostle's comparison. 'Believers, though many, are one body in Christ, and every one members one of another.' Οἱ πολλοὶ ἓν σῶμά ἐσμεν. *We, the many, are one body.* In one respect we are many, in another we are one. Just as the body is many as to its members, and one in their organic connection. Believers are one body, *i.e.,* a living organic whole, not in virtue of any external organization, but *in Christ, i.e.,* in virtue of their common union with him. And as this union with Christ is not merely external, or by profession, or by unity of opinion and sentiment only, but vital, arising from the indwelling of the Holy Ghost, the Spirit of Christ, so, the apostle adds, the union of believers one with another, is also a vital union. They are ὁ καθ᾽ εἷς ἀλλήλων μέλη, *every one members one of another.* The relation of believers to each other is far more intimate than that between the members of any external organization, whether civil or ecclesiastical. It is analogous to the mutual relation of the members of the same body, animated by one soul. ὁ καθ᾽ εἷς for ὁ καθ᾽ ἕνα, in the sense of εἷς ἕκαστος, is a solecism occurring only in the later Greek.

VERSE 6.   *Having therefore gifts differing according to the grace given unto us,* &c. In this and the following verses we have the application of the preceding comparison to the special object in view. 'If Christians are all members of the same body, having different offices and gifts, instead of being puffed up one above another, and instead of envying and opposing each other, they should severally discharge their respective duties diligently and humbly for the good of the whole, and not for their own advantage.'

It is a common opinion that the apostle, in specifying the various gifts to which he refers, meant to arrange them under the two heads of *prophesying* and *administering;* or that he specifies the duties of two classes of officers, the prophets and deacons (διάκονοι). To the former would then belong prophesying, teaching, exhortation; to the latter, ministering, giving, ruling, showing mercy. This view of the passage, which is adopted by De Brais, Koppe, and others, requires that the terms prophet and deacon should be taken in their widest sense. Both are indeed frequently used with great latitude; the former being applied to any one who speaks as the mouth of God, or the explainer of his will; and the latter to any ministerial officer in the church, 1 Cor. iii. 5; Eph. iii. 7; Col. i. 7, 23, &c. Although this interpretation is consistent with the usage of the words, and in some measure simplifies the passage, yet it is by no means necessary. There is no appearance of such a systematic arrangement; on the contrary, Paul seems to refer without any order to the various duties which the officers and even private members of the church were called upon to perform. The construction in the original is not entirely regular, and, therefore, has been variously explained. There is no interpretation more natural than that adopted by our translators, who, considering the passage as elliptical, have supplied in the several specifications the phrases which in each case the sense requires. Instead of beginning a new sentence with ver. 6, many commentators connect ἔχοντες with ἐσμέν in ver. 5, and make the following accusatives depend on it. The whole passage is then regarded as declarative, and not exhortative. 'We are one body having gifts, prophecy according to the proportion of faith; or the gift of ministering, in the ministry, he that teacheth, in teaching,' &c. It is plain, however, that this requires a very forced interpretation to be given to the several terms here used. Διακονία does not in the same clause mean first the gift, and then the exercise of the gift; much less can ἐν τῇ παρακλήσει, ἐν ἁπλότητι, &c., indicate the sphere within which the gifts mentioned are exercised. Others retaining the exhortatory character of the passage, still connect ἔχοντες with ver. 5. 'We are having gifts, whether prophecy or ministry, *let us use them aright.*' On the whole, the simplest method is to begin a new sentence with ἔχοντες, and supply the necessary verb in the several clauses, as is done in our version, and by Olshausen, Fritzsche, Phillipi. Compare 1 Peter iv. 11, εἴ τις λαλεῖ, ὡς λόγια Θεοῦ (sc. λαλείτω), &c.

Having therefore gifts differing according to the grace given unto us, i.e., as there are in the one body various offices and gifts, let every one act in a manner consistent with the nature and design of the particular gift which he has received. *Whether prophecy,* let us prophesy *according to the proportion of faith.* The first gift specified is that of *prophecy,* with regard to the precise nature of which there is no little diversity of opinion. The original and proper meaning of the Hebrew word rendered *prophet* in the Old Testament, is *interpreter,* one who explains or delivers the will of another. And to this idea the Greek term also answers. It matters little whether the will or purpose of God which the prophets were called upon to deliver, had reference to present duty or to future events. They derived their Hebrew name not from predicting what was to come to pass, which was but a small part of their duty, but from being the interpreters of God, men who spoke in his name. We accordingly find the term *prophet* applied to all classes of religious teachers under the old dispensation. Of Abraham it is said, "He is a prophet, and he shall pray for thee and thou shalt live," Gen. xx. 7. The name is often applied to Moses as the great interpreter of the will of God to the Hebrews, Deut. xviii. 18; and the writers of the historical books are also constantly so called. The passage in Exod. vii. 1, is peculiarly interesting, as it clearly exhibits the proper meaning of this word. "And the Lord said unto Moses, See, I have made thee a god to Pharaoh; and Aaron thy brother shall be thy prophet," *i.e.*, he shall be thy interpreter. In chap. iv. 16, it is said, "He shall be a mouth to thee;" and of Jeremiah, God says, "Thou shalt be as my mouth," Jer. xv. 19; compare Deut. xviii. 18. Any one, therefore, who acted as the mouth of God, no matter what was the nature of the communication, was a prophet. And this is also the sense of the word in the New Testament;* it is applied to any one employed to deliver a divine message, Matt. x. 41; xiii. 57; Luke iv. 24; vii. 26-29, "What went ye out to see? A prophet? yea, I say unto you, and much more than a prophet. This is he of whom it is written, Behold I send my messenger, &c." John iv. 19, "Sir, I perceive that thou art a prophet," *i.e.*, an inspired man. Acts xv. 32, "And Judas and Silas, being prophets also themselves, exhorted the brethren and confirmed them." 1 Cor. xii. 28, "God hath set in the church, first, apostles; secondarily, prophets; thirdly, teachers; &c." 1 Cor. xiv. 29-32, "Let the prophets speak two or three, and let the other judge. If *anything* be revealed to another that sitteth by, let the first hold his peace. For ye may all prophesy one by one, that all may learn and all may be comforted. And the spirits of the prophets are subject to the prophets." "If any man think himself to be a prophet or spiritual (inspired), let him acknowledge, &c." From these and numerous similar passages, it appears that the prophets in the Christian church were men who spoke under the immediate influence of the Spirit of God, and delivered some divine communication relating to doctrinal truths, to present duty, to future events, &c., as the case might be.† The point of distinction between them and the apostles, considered as religious teachers, appears to have been that the inspiration of the apostles was abiding, they were the infallible and authoritative messengers of Christ; whereas the inspiration of the prophets was occasional and transient. The latter differed from the teachers (διδάσκαλοι), inasmuch as these were not necessarily inspired, but taught to others what they themselves had learned from the Scriptures, or from inspired men.

Agreeably to this view of the office of the prophets, we find the sacred writers speaking of the gift of prophecy as consisting in the communication of divine truth by the Spirit of God, intended for instruction, exhortation,

---

* In common Greek, also, this is the meaning of the word. The μάντις was the immediate receiver of the divine influence, and declarer of the oracles, and the προφήτης was the interpreter. Hence μουσῶν προφῆται *the interpreters of the Muses.* These two words, however, μάντις and προφήτης, are frequently used indiscriminately, the latter being applied to any person who spoke under a divine influence. As poets were supposed to speak under a certain kind of inspiration, they too were called prophets. Paul used the word in this sense when he wrote to Titus, Tit. i. 12, "A prophet of their own said, the Cretians are always liars," &c.

† Προφήτης, vates *i. e.*, vir divinus, qui afflatu divino gaudet et cui numen retegit, quae antea incognita erant, maxime ad religionem pertinentia.—*Wahl.*

Sunt qui *prophetiam* intelligunt divinandi facultatem, quae circa evangelii primordia in ecclesia vigebat. . . . Ego vero eos sequi malo, qui latius extendunt hoc nomen ad peculiare revelationis donum, ut quis dextre ac perite in voluntate Dei enarranda munus interpretis obeat.—*Calvin.*

On the nature of the office of prophet, see Koppe's Excursus III., appended to his Commentary on the Epistle to the Ephesians; and Winer's Realwörterbuch, under the word *Propheten.* Both these treatises are rationalistic, yet both contain the materials for a fair examination of the subject. See also Neander on the Planting of the Christian Church, Vol. I.

or consolation. " Though I have *the gift* of prophecy, and understand all mysteries and all knowledge," 1 Cor. xiii. 2 ; " He that prophesieth speaketh unto men *to* edification, and exhortation, and comfort," 1 Cor. xiv. 3 ; " If all prophesy, and there come in one that believeth not, or *one* unlearned, he is convinced of all, he is judged of all, &c.," ver. 24.

The gift of which Paul here speaks, is not, therefore, the faculty of predicting future events, but that of immediate occasional inspiration, leading the recipient to deliver, as the mouth of God, the particular communication which he had received, whether designed for instruction, exhortation, or comfort. The apostle required that those who enjoyed this gift should exercise it *according to the proportion of faith.* This clause admits of different interpretations. The word (ἀναλογία) rendered *proportion,* may mean either *proportion,* or *measure, rule, standard.* Classic usage is rather in favour of the former of these meanings. The latter, however, is necessarily included in the former ; and the word is defined by Hesychius, *measure, canon,* or *rule.* The choice between the two meanings of the word must depend on the sense given to the word *faith,* and on the context. *Faith* may here mean inward confidence or belief ; or it may mean the gift received, *i.e., that which is confided* (τὸ πεπιστευμένον) ; or, finally, that which is believed, truths divinely revealed. If the first of these three senses be adopted, the passage means, 'Let him prophesy according to his internal convictions ; that is, he must not exceed in his communication what he honestly believes to have been divinely communicated, or allow himself to be carried away by enthusiasm, to deliver, as from God, what is really nothing but his own thoughts.' If the second sense (of πίστις) be preferred, the clause then means, ' Let him prophesy according to the proportion of the gifts which he has received ; *i.e.,* let every one speak according to the degree and nature of the divine influence, or the particular revelation imparted to him.' If, however, *faith* here means, as it does in so many other places, the *object of faith,* or *the truths to be believed,* (see Gal. i. 23 ; iii. 25 ; vi. 10 ; Eph. iv. 5 ; 1 Thess. iii. 5, &c.,) then *according to the proportion* signifies, *agreeably to the rule or standard ;* and the apostle's direction to the prophets is, that in all their communications they are to conform to the rule of faith, and not contradict those doctrines which had been delivered by men whose inspiration had been established by indubitable evidence. In favour of this view of the passage is the frequent use of the word *faith* in the sense thus assigned to it. The ordinary subjective sense of the word does not suit the passage. The amount or strength of faith does not determine either the extent to which the gift of prophecy is enjoyed, or the manner in which it is exercised. There were prophets who had no saving faith at all ; just as many performed miracles who were not the true disciples of Christ. " In that day," says our Lord, " many shall say unto me, Lord, Lord, have we not prophesied in thy name, and in thy name cast out devils ? and in thy name done many wonderful works ?" to whom he will say, " I never knew you." The second sense given to πίστις, that *which is confided to any one,* *i.e., a gift,* is without any authority. The objective sense of the word, although denied by many of the strict philological interpreters, is nevertheless well established by such expressions, " obedience to the faith," " doer of faith," " faith once delivered to the saints," and is perfectly familiar in ecclesiastical usage. 2. The fact that similar directions respecting those who consider themselves prophets or inspired persons, occur in other passages. Thus Paul says, " If any man think himself to be a prophet, or spiritual, let him acknowledge that the things that I write unto you are the commandments of the Lord," 1 Cor. xiv. 37. This was the standard ; and no man had a right to consider himself inspired, or to require others so to regard him, who did not conform himself to the instructions of men whose inspiration was beyond doubt. Thus, too, the apostle John commands Christians, " Believe not every spirit, but try the spirits whether they are of God ; because many false prophets are gone out into the world," 1 John iv. 1. And the standard by which these prophets were to be tried, he gives in verse 6 : "We are of God : he that knoweth God, heareth us ; he that is not of God, heareth not us. Hereby we know the spirit of truth and the spirit of error." It was obviously necessary that Christians, in the age of immediate inspiration, should have some means of discriminating between those who were really under the influence of the Spirit of God, and those who were either enthusiasts or deceivers. And the test to which the apostles directed them was rational, and easily applied. There were inspired men to whose divine mission and authority God had borne abundant testimony by " signs and wonders, and divers miracles, and gifts of the Holy Spirit." As God cannot contradict himself, it follows that anything inconsistent with the teachings of these men, though proceeding from one claiming to be a prophet, must be false, and the pretension of its author to inspiration unfounded. Accordingly, the apostle directed that while one prophet spoke, the others were to judge, *i.e.*, decide whether he spoke according to the analogy of faith ; and whether his inspiration was real, imaginary, or feigned. 3. This interpretation is also perfectly suitable to the context. Paul, after giving the general direction contained in the preceding verses, as to the light in which the gifts of the Spirit were to be viewed, and the manner in which they were to be used, in this and the following verses, gives special directions with respect to particular gifts. Those who thought themselves prophets should be careful to speak nothing but truth, to conform to the standard ; those who ministered should devote themselves to their appropriate duties, &c.

Verse 7. *Or ministry, let us wait on our ministering; or he that teacheth, on teaching.* The terms *minister* and *ministry* (διάκονος and διακονία, *deacon* and *deaconship*) are used in the New Testament both in a general and a restricted sense. In the former, they are employed in reference to all classes of ecclesiastical officers, even the apostles ; see 1 Cor. iii. 5 ; 2 Cor. vi. 4 ; Eph. iii. 7 ; vi. 21 ; Col. i. 7, 23 ; 1 Tim. iv. 6 ; Acts i. 17, 25 ; xx. 24 ; Rom. xi. 13 ; 1 Cor. xii. 5 ; 2 Cor. iv. 1, &c. In the latter, they are used in reference to a particular class of officers, to whom were committed the management of the external affairs of the church, the care of the poor, attention to the sick, &c. ; see Acts vi. 1—3 ; Phil. i. 1 ; 1 Tim. iii. 8—13, &c. It is doubtful in which of these senses the latter of the above-mentioned words is here used by the apostle, most probably in the restricted sense. The apostle exhorts different classes of officers to attend to their own peculiar vocation, and to exercise their own gifts, without intruding into the sphere of others, or envying their superior endowments. The deacons, therefore, were to attend to the poor and the sick, and not attempt to exercise the office of teachers. Luther, and many others, give the words their wide sense. " Hat jemand ein Amt, so warte er des Amtes :" *If a man has an office, let him attend to it.* But this would render unnecessary the specifications which follow. The apostle, in this context, refers to definite ecclesiastical offices in connection

with ordinary Christian duties.   That is, he exhorts both church officers
and private Christians.

He that teacheth, on teaching.   Teachers are elsewhere expressly distinguished from *prophets,* 1 Cor. xii. 28, 29 : " God hath set some in the
church : first, apostles ; secondarily, prophets ; thirdly, teachers.   Are all
apostles ? are all prophets ? are all teachers ? are all workers of miracles ?"
And in this passage they are not to be confounded, nor is teaching to be
regarded, in this place, as one part of prophesying.   As remarked above
on verse 6, the teachers were distinguished from prophets, inasmuch as
the former were not necessarily inspired, and were a regular and permanent
class of officers.   Those who had the gift of prophecy were to exercise it
aright ; those who were called to the office of deacons, were to devote
themselves to their appropriate duties ; and those who had the gift of
teaching were to teach.

Verse 8.   *He that exhorteth, on exhortation.*   The word (παρακαλέω)
here used, means *to invite, exhort,* and *to comfort.*   Our translators have
probably selected the most appropriate sense.   Teaching is addressed to
the understanding ; exhortation, to the conscience and feelings.   There
was probably no distinct class of officers called exhorters, as distinguished
from teachers ; but as the apostle is speaking of gifts as well as officers,
(both are included in the word χαρίσματα,) his direction is, that he who
had the gift of teaching, should teach ; and that he who had a gift for
exhortation, should be content to exhort.

He that giveth, let him do it *with simplicity ; he that ruleth, with diligence ; he that showeth mercy, with cheerfulness.*   These directions have
reference to the manner in which the duties of church officers and of
private Christians ought to be performed.   In this connection, the former
no doubt are principally, though not exclusively intended.   It is a common
opinion, that giving, ruling, showing mercy, (ὁ μεταδιδούς, ὁ προϊστάμενος, ὁ
ἐλεῶν,) refer to different functions of the deaconate.   But not only the use
of μεταδιδούς instead of διαδιδούς—the former properly meaning *giving,*
(what is one's own,) and the latter, *distributing*—is opposed to this view,
but the whole exhortation, which refers with equal, or greater propriety,
to the state of mind and the manner in which the private duties of Christian fellowship are to be performed.   There seems to be no good reason for
the restriction of the directions here given to either class, officers or private
members, exclusively.   *He that giveth, with simplicity,* ἁπλότητι, *singleness of mind.*   This direction, considered in reference to the deacons,
whom, no doubt, Paul included in his exhortation, contemplates their duty
of *imparting* or *distributing* to the necessity of the saints.   This duty, by
whomsoever performed, is to be done with *simplicity, i.e.,* with purity
of motive, free from all improper designs.   This same word is rendered
singleness of heart in Eph. vi. 5 ; Col. iii. 22, and occurs in the same
sense, in the phrase, " simplicity and godly sincerity," 2 Cor. i. 12.   Considered in reference to private Christians, this clause may be rendered, *he
that giveth, with liberality ;* see 2 Cor. viii. 2 ; ix. 11, 13.

He that ruleth, with diligence.   Here again the right discharge of eccle-
siasticial duties is principally intended ; 1 Thess. v. 12, " We beseech you,
brethren, to know (esteem, love) them that are over you in the Lord ;"
1 Tim. v. 17, " The elders that rule well."   There is considerable diversity
of opinion as to the explanation to be here given to ὁ προϊστάμενος.   The
word properly means, *one who is placed over,* who presides, or rules.   It
is, however, used in a more restricted sense, for a *patron,* one who befriends

others, and especially strangers.   Hence in xvi. 2, Phœbe is called a *προστάτις, a patroness,* one who befriended strangers.   As what precedes and what follows, giving and showing mercy, relate to acts of kindness, the one to the poor, the other to the sick, so this word, it is urged, should be understood of showing kindness to strangers.   There is certainly force in this consideration.   But as there is very slight foundation for the ascription of this meaning to the word in the New Testament, and as it is elsewhere used in its ordinary sense, (see 1 Thess. v. 12, comp. 1 Tim. v. 17,) it is commonly understood of *rulers.*   Some take it in reference to rulers in general, civil or ecclesiastical ; others, of church-rulers or elders ; others, specifically of the *forestaer,** or pastor, or bishop of the congregation. The objection against this restricted reference to the presiding officer of a church, is the introduction of the term in the enumeration of ordinary Christian duties.   He that gives, he that acts as pastor, he that shows mercy, is rather an incongruous association.   It is more common, there-fore, to understand *προϊστάμενος,* of any one who exercises authority in the church.   Those who were called to exercise the office of ruler, were re-quired to do it (*ἐν σπουδῇ*) with *diligence, i.e.,* with attention and zeal. This is opposed to inertness and carelessness.   The government of the church, in correcting abuses, preventing disorders, and in the administra-tion of discipline, calls for constant vigilance and fidelity.   " Προϊσταμένους tametsi proprie nuncupat eos, quibus mandata erat ecclesiæ gubernatio (erant autem illi seniores, qui aliis præibant ac moderabantur, vitæque censuram exercebant,) quod autem de illis dicit extendi in universum ad præfecturas omne genus potest.   Neque enim aut parva ab iis solicitudo requiritur, qui omnium securitati consulere, aut parva sedulitas ab iis, qui pro salute omnium noctes diesque excubare debent."—*Calvin.*

He that showeth mercy, with cheerfulness, (*ἱλαρότης, hilarity.*)   As the former direction (he that giveth, with simplicity) had reference to the care of the poor, this relates to the care of the sick and afflicted.   These were the two great departments of the deacons' duties.   The former was to be discharged with honesty, this with cheerfulness ; not as a matter of con-straint, but with alacrity and kindness.   On this, the value of any service rendered to the children of sorrow mainly depends.

DOCTRINE.

1. The great principle, that truth is in order to holiness, which is so frequently taught in the Scriptures, is plainly implied in this passage.   All the doctrines of justification, grace, election, and final salvation, taught in the preceding part of the epistle, are made the foundation for the practical duties enjoined in this, ver. 1.

2. The first great duty of redeemed sinners is the dedication of them-selves to God.   This consecration must be entire, of the body as well as the soul ; it must be constant, and according to his will, ver. 1.

3. Regeneration is a renewing of the mind, evincing itself in a trans-formation of the whole character, and leading to the knowledge and appro-bation of whatever is acceptable to God, ver. 2.

4. God is the giver of all good, of honours and offices as well as of talents and graces ; and in the distribution of his favours he renders to every man according to his own will, vers. 3—6.

5. Christians are one body in Christ.   This unity is not only consistent

* Vorsteher ?—*Ed.*

with great diversity of gifts, but necessarily implies it ; as the body is one from the union of various members, designed for the performance of various functions, vers. 4, 5.

6. The different offices of the church are of divine appointment, and are designed for the benefit of the whole body, and not for the advantage of those who hold them, vers. 6—8.

REMARKS.

1. The effect produced upon us by the mercies of God, in redemption, and in his providence, affords an excellent criterion of character. If they lead us to devote ourselves to his service, they produce the effect for which they were designed, and we may conclude that we are of the number of his children. But if they produce indifference to duty, and cherish the idea that we are the special favourites of heaven, or that we may sin with impunity, it is an evidence that our hearts are not right in the sight of God, ver. 1.

2. While Christians should remember that the service which they are called upon to render is a rational service, pertaining to the soul, they should not suppose that it consists merely in the secret exercises of the heart. The whole man and the whole life must be actively and constantly devoted to God, ver. 1.

3. Those professors of religion who are conformed to the world, cannot have experienced that renewing of the mind which produces a transformation of character, ver. 2.

4. Self-conceit and ambition are the besetting sins of men entrusted with power, or highly gifted in any respect, as discontent and envy are those to which persons of inferior station or gifts are most exposed. These evil feelings, so offensive to God, would be subdued, if men would properly lay to heart, that peculiar advantages are bestowed according to the divine pleasure ; that they are designed to advance the glory of God, and the good of his church, and not the honour or emolument of those who receive them ; and that very frequently those which are least attractive in the sight of men, are the most important in the sight of God. It is here as in the human frame ; not the most comely parts are the most valuable, but those which are the least so. The vital parts of our system never attract the praise of men, and are never the source of vanity or pride, ver. 3.

5. As Christians are one body in Christ, they should feel their mutual dependence and their common interest in their Head, from whom life, intelligence, enjoyment, and every good comes. They should sympathize in each other's joys and sorrows ; the hand should not envy the eye, nor the eye despise the foot. How can they, who are destitute of this common feeling with their fellow-Christians, be partakers of that Spirit by which true believers are constituted really and not merely nominally one ? vers. 4, 5.

6. Real honour consists in doing well what God calls us to do, and not in the possession of high offices or great talents, vers. 6—8.

7. No man's usefulness is increased by going out of his sphere. It is a great mistake to suppose because one possession or employment may, in itself considered, afford better opportunity of doing good than another, that therefore any or every man would be more useful in the one than in the other. The highest improvement of the individual, and the greatest good

of the whole, are best secured by each being and doing what God sees fit to determine. If all were the same member, where were the body? 'God is not the author of confusion, but of order, in all the churches of the saints,' vers. 6—8.

8. No amount of learning, no superiority of talent, nor even the pretension to inspiration, can justify a departure from the analogy of faith, *i.e.*, from the truths taught by men to whose inspiration God has borne witness. All teachers must be brought to this standard; and even if an angel from heaven should teach anything contrary to the Scriptures, he should be regarded as anathema, Gal. i. 8. It is a matter of constant gratitude that we have such a standard whereby to try the spirits whether they be of God. Ministers of Christ should see to it, that they do not incur the curse which Paul denounces on those who preach another gospel, ver. 6.

9. Private Christians, and especially ecclesiastical officers, are required to discharge their respective duties with singleness of heart, and in the exercise of those virtues which the peculiar nature of their vocation may demand, vers. 6—8.

ROMANS XII. 9—21.

ANALYSIS.

HAVING treated of those duties which belong more especially to the officers of the church, the apostle exhorts his readers generally to the exercise of various Christian virtues. There is no logical arrangement observed in this part of the chapter, except that the general exhortation to love precedes the precepts which relate to those exercises which are, for the most part, but different manifestations of this primary grace. The love of the Christian must be sincere, and lead to the avoiding of evil, and the pursuit of good, ver. 9. It must produce brotherly affection and humility, ver. 10; diligence and devotion, ver. 11; resignation, patience, and prayer, ver. 12; charity and hospitality, ver. 13; forgiveness of injuries, ver. 14; sympathy with the joys and sorrows of others, ver. 15; concord and lowliness of mind, ver. 16; and a constant endeavour to return good for evil, vers. 17—21.

COMMENTARY.

VERSE 9. *Let love be without dissimulation*, or, Love *is* without hypocrisy, *i.e.*, sincere, not hypocritical, and not consisting in words merely. The love intended in this verse, is probably love to all men, and not to Christians exclusively, as in ver. 10, *brotherly affection* is particularly specified. Much less is love to God the idea meant to be expressed.

Abhor that which is evil; cleave to that which is good. There is a number of participles following this verse, to which our translators supply the imperative of the substantive verb; 'be abhorring,' 'be kindly affectioned,' &c. Others connect them all with εὐλογεῖτε in ver. 14; 'abhorring evil,' 'being kindly affectioned,' 'bless those,' &c. But these participles do not express what should qualify, or characterize, the act of blessing our persecutors; 'hating,' 'loving the brethren,' '*bless* your enemies,' &c. It is more natural to assume that the apostle departs slightly from the regular construction, and writes as though, in ver. 9, he had said, ἀγαπᾶτε ἀνυποκρίτως, ἀποστυγοῦντες, κ.τ.λ. Compare 2 Cor. i. 7. and Heb. xiii. 5, ἀφιλάργυρος ὁ τρόπος, (for, ἀφιλάργυροι περιπατεῖτε,) ἀρκούμενοι τοῖς παροῦσιν. This is the explanation given by Philippi and others. The words rendered *to abhor* (ἀποστυγέω) and *to cleave to* (κολλάομαι) are peculiarly forcible, and express the highest degree of hatred on the one hand, and of persevering devotion on the other. The latter word, in the active form, properly means, *to glue,* and in the middle, *to attach one's self to any person or thing.* The words *evil* and *good,* in this passage, may be understood of moral good and evil; and the exhortation be considered as a general direction to hate the one and love the other. But the great majority of commentators, out of regard to the context, take the terms in a restricted sense, making the former mean *injurious,* and the latter *kind.* The sense of the whole verse would then be, ' Let love be sincere ; strive to avoid what is injurious to others, and earnestly endeavour to do whatever is kind and useful.' As the words themselves admit of either of these interpretations, the choice between them depends upon the context. The latter is, on this ground, perhaps to be preferred.

VERSE 10. *Be kindly affectioned one to another with brotherly love, in honour preferring one another.* ' As to brotherly love, be kindly affectioned one towards another.' This exhortation seems to have special reference to Christians. The word (φιλόστοργος) used by the apostle, expresses properly the strong natural affection between parents and children (στοργή), but is applied also to tender affection of any kind. Here, no doubt, the idea is, that Christians should love each other with the same sincerity and tenderness as if they were the nearest relatives.

In honour preferring one another. This passage, thus translated, cannot be understood otherwise than an exhortation to humility ; and such is the interpretation generally given to it. But the word (προηγεῖσθαι) rendered *to prefer,* never occurs in that sense elsewhere. It means properly *to go before, to lead ;* and then, figuratively, *to set an example.* And the word translated *honour,* may mean *deference, respect,* and even *kindness,* (*observantia et omnia humanitatis officia quae aliis debemus.* Schleusner.) The sense of the clause may then be, 'as to respect and kindness (τιμῇ) going before each other, or setting an example one to another.' This interpretation, which is given by most of the recent commentators, is not only better suited to the meaning of the words, but also to the context. The Vulgate translates, " Honore invicem prævenientes," and Luther, " Einer komme dem Andern mit Ehrerbietung zu vor." It is not only an injunction of politeness, but that in all acts of respect and kindness we should take the lead. Instead of waiting for others to honour us, we should be beforehand with them in the manifestation of respect.

VERSE 11. *Not slothful in business; fervent in spirit; serving the Lord.* The love to which the apostle exhorts his readers is not inactive or cold ; on the contrary, it manifests itself in diligence, zeal, and devotion to God. The word rendered *business* (σπουδή) properly means *haste, activity.* It is the effect or outward manifestation of zeal. The exhortation has not the reference which our version would naturally suggest, viz., to the active performance of our several vocations ; it refers rather to religious activity : ' As to activity or diligence, do not grow weary or be indolent ; on the contrary, be fervent in spirit.' The word *spirit* is by many understood of the Holy Spirit ; it most naturally refers to the mind ; compare Acts xviii. 25, where it is said of Apollos, " being fervent in spirit (*i.e.,* zealous) he spake and taught diligently." This clause, 'therefore, stands in opposition to the preceding. Instead of being inactive, we should be zealous.

Serving the Lord, i.e., doing service to the Lord ; influenced in our activity and zeal by a desire to serve Christ. This member of the sentence thus understood, describes the motive from which zeal and diligence should proceed. Compare Eph. vi. 5—8, especially the expressions *as unto Christ, as the servants of Christ, as to the Lord,* &c.; and Col. iii. 22, 23. Instead of *serving the Lord,* there is another reading, according to which the passage must be rendered, *serving the time,* * (tempori servientes. *Calvin,*) *i.e.,* making the most of every opportunity (see Eph. v. 16 ;) or, as others understand it, 'adapting your conduct to circumstances.' Zeal is to be tempered with prudence. The common text is the best authenticated, and is generally adopted. The zeal which the apostle recommends is zeal for Christ, and not for our own advancement or interests.

VERSE 12. *Rejoicing in hope ; patient in tribulation ; continuing instant in prayer.* These exhortations refer to nearly related duties : Christians are to be joyful, patient, and prayerful. However adverse their circumstances, hope, patience, and prayer are not only duties, but the richest sources of consolation and support. 'Rejoicing *on account* of hope, or in the joyful expectation of future good.' This hope of salvation is the most effectual means of producing patience under present afflictions ; for if we feel "that the sufferings of this present time are not worthy to be compared with the glory which shall be revealed in us," it will not be difficult to bear them patiently. Intercourse with God, however, is necessary to the exercise of this and all other virtues, and therefore the apostle immediately adds, *continuing instant in prayer.* The original could hardly be better translated ; as the Greek term (προσκαρτερέω, *intentus sum rei*) expresses the idea of perseverance and ardour in the prosecution of any object. There are no attributes of acceptable prayer more frequently presented in the Scriptures than those here referred to, viz., perseverance and fervour, which, from their nature, imply faith in the ability and willingness of God to grant us needed good, Acts i. 14; vi. 4 ; Eph. vi. 18, &c.

VERSE 13. *Distributing to the necessity of saints ; given to hospitality.* These virtues are the immediate fruits of the love enjoined in vers. 9, 10. The word rendered *to distribute* (κοινωνέω) signifies, intransitively, *to become a partaker with ;* and, transitively, *to cause others to partake with us, to communicate to.* It is commonly followed by a dative of the person to whom the communication is made, Gal. vi. 6. In this case the construction may be the same as in the preceding verses, '*as to the necessity* of the saints, be communicative ;' or, '*give* to the necessity of the saints.' The transitive meaning of κοινωνέω is by many denied, and is, at least, infrequent. It is, therefore, commonly taken here in its ordinary sense : 'Taking part in the necessities of the saints ; regard them as your own.' Believers are κοινωνοί in everything, because they are all members of the body of Christ. The members of the same body have the same interests, feelings, and destiny. The joy or sorrow of one member, is the joy or sorrow of all the others. The necessities of one are, or should be, a common burden. As

---

* Καιρῷ, instead of κυρίῳ, is read only in the MSS. D. F. G. All the other MSS., and the Coptic, Ethiopic, Armenian, Vulgate, and Syriac versions, have κυρίῳ. Mill and Griesbach prefer the former ; but Wetstein, Bengel, Knapp, Lachmann, the latter. This diversity of reading is not surprising, as ΚΩ was a frequent contraction both for κυρίῳ and καιρῷ.

intimately connected with this injunction, the apostle adds, *given to hospitality*, as our translators aptly render the strong expression of the original. The phrase is φιλοξενίαν διώκοντες, *following after hospitality;* sectantes, ut hospites non modo admittatis, sed quaeratis.   The value which the early Christians placed upon the virtue of hospitality is plain, from Paul's enumerating it among the requisite qualifications of a bishop, Titus i. 8. During times of persecution, and before the general institution of houses of entertainment, there was peculiar necessity for Christians to entertain strangers.   As such houses are still rarely to be met with in the East, this duty continues to be there regarded as one of the most sacred character.

Verse 14. *Bless them which persecute you; bless, and curse not.*   The exercise of love, and the discharge of the duties of benevolence, are not to be confined to the *saints,* or people of God ; but the same spirit is to be manifested towards our enemies.   The word (εὐλογέω) rendered *to bless,* signifies both *to pray for good to anyone,* and *to do good.*   Here, from the context, the former meaning is to be preferred, as it is opposed *to cursing,* which signifies *to imprecate evil on anyone.*   The command therefore is, that, so far from wishing or praying that evil may overtake our persecutors and enemies, we must sincerely desire and pray for their good.   It is not sufficient to avoid returning evil for evil, nor even to banish vindictive feelings ; we must be able sincerely to desire their happiness.   How hard this is for corrupt human nature, everyone who is acquainted with his own heart well knows.   Yet this is the standard of Christian temper and character exhibited in the Scriptures, Matt. v. 44.   " Ardua res est, fateor, et naturæ hominis penitus contraria ; sed nihil tam arduum, quod non virtute Dei superetur, quae nobis nunquam deerit, modo ne ipsam invocare negligamus.   Et quanquam vix unum reperias qui tantos in lege Dei progressus fecerit, ut præceptum istud impleat ; nemo tamen filium Dei jactare se potest, aut Christiani nomine gloriari, qui non animum istum ex parte induerit, et cum affectu adverso quotidie pugnet.   Dixi hoc esse difficilius quam remittere vindictam, ubi quis læsus fuerit.   Quidam enim licet manus contineant, neque etiam agentur nocendi libidine, cuperent tamen aliunde hostibus suis accidere cladem vel damnum.   Deus autem verbo suo non tantum manus coercet a maleficiis, sed amarulentos quoque affectus in animis domat ; neque id modo, sed etiam vult de eorum salute esse sollicitos qui nos injuste vexando sibi exitium accersunt."   *Calvin.*

Verse 15. *Rejoice with them that do rejoice, and weep with them that weep.*   Love produces not only the forgiveness of enemies, but a general sympathy in the joys and sorrows of our fellow-men, and especially of our fellow-Christians.   The disposition here enjoined is the very opposite of a selfish indifference to any interests but our own.   The gospel requires that we should feel and act under the impression that all men are brethren ; that we have a common nature, a common Father, and a common destiny. How lovely is genuine sympathy.   How much like Christ is the man who feels the sorrows and joys of others, as though they were his own !

Verse 16. *Be of the same mind one towards another; mind not high things, but condescend to men of low estate.   Be not wise in your own conceits.*   The phrase (τὸ αὐτὸ φρονεῖν) used by the apostle expresses the general idea of *concord, unanimity ;* whether of opinion or feeling depends on the context ; see 2 Cor. xiii. 11 ; Phil. ii. 2 ; Rom. xv. 5.   Here the latter idea is the prominent one.   ' Be of the same mind,' *i.e.,* be united in feeling, interests, and object, let there be no discord or disagreement. This idea is then amplified in the following clauses ; do not be aspiring,

but be humble. Ambition and contempt for lowly persons or pursuits,
are the states of mind most inconsistent with that union of heart by which
all Christians should be united. " Quocirca illud τὸ αυτὸ non intelligo
idem quod alii de nobis sentiunt, sed *idem* quod nos de nobis ipsi sentimus,
vel quod alios de nobis sentire postulamus." *De Brais.* Erasmus and
others understand this clause to mean, 'Think of others as well as you do
of yourselves' (*nemo putet alium se minorem.*) But this gives too restricted
a sense, and is no better suited to the context than the common interpretation given above. The command is, that we should be united ; feeling
towards others as we would have them feel towards us.

Mind not high things, i.e., do not aspire after them, do not desire and
seek them ; see the use of the Greek word here employed in chap. viii. 5 ;
Col. iii. 2 (τὰ ἄνω φρονεῖτε.) *But condescend to men of low estate.* The
general idea expressed by these two clauses is obviously this, ' Be not high-
minded, but humble.' The precise meaning of the latter clause, however,
is a matter of much doubt. The word (συναπάγω) rendered *condescend*
properly means, in the passive or middle voice, *to allow one's self to be
carried along with others, i.e.,* influenced by them, as in Gal. ii. 13,
" Insomuch that Barnabas also was (allowed himself to be) carried away with
their dissimulation." And 2 Peter iii. 17, "Beware lest ye also, being led
away with the error of the wicked, fall from your own steadfastness."
" With the dative of a person, συναπάγεσθαι means to be carried along with
him ; with the dative of a thing, it means to be carried along by it."
Philippi. If ταπεινοῖς be here taken as masculine, one sense is, allow
yourselves to be carried along with the lowly, *i.e.,* to associate with them,
and share their condition. If it be taken as neuter, to correspond with
the τὰ ὑψηλά in the first clause, then the meaning is, allow yourselves
to be carried along together by lowly things : *i.e.,* instead of being
concerned about high things, let lowly things occupy and control you.
So Calvin : "Non arroganter de vobis sentientes sed humilibus vos
accommodantes. Vocem *humilibus* in neutro genere accipio, ut antithesis
ita compleatur. Hic ergo damnatur ambitio, et quae sub magnanimitatis
nomine se insinuat animi elatio : siquidem praecipua fidelium virtus mode-
ratio est, vel potius submissio, quae honorem semper malit aliis ceder quam
praeripere." Most modern commentators concur in this view of the passage.
In either way the general sense is the same. The thing forbidden is
ambition ; the thing enjoined is lowliness of mind.

Be not wise in your own conceit. This precept is intimately connected
with the preceding, since ambition and contempt for lowly persons and pursuits generally arise from overweening self-estimation. No species of pride is
more insidious or more injurious than the pride of intellect, or a fancied
superiority to those around us, which leads to a contempt of their opinions,
and a confident reliance upon ourselves. The temper which the gospel
requires is that of a little child, docile, diffident, and humble ; see chap.
xi. 25 ; Prov. iii. 7 ; Isa. v. 21.

Verse 17. *Recompense to no man evil for evil. Provide things honest
in the sight of all men.* Paul having, in the preceding verses, enjoined the
duties of love, condescension, and kindness towards all men, comes in this
and the following passages, to forbid the indulgence of a contrary disposition, especially of a spirit of retaliation and revenge. The general direction in the first clause is, not to retaliate ; which is but a lower exercise
of the virtue afterward enjoined in the command to " overcome evil with
good."

Provide things honest in the sight of all men. Our translation of this clause is not very happy, as it suggests an idea foreign to the meaning of the original. Paul does not mean to direct us to make provision for our-selves or families in an honest manner, which is probably the sense commonly attached to the passage by the English reader, but to act in such a manner as to command the confidence and good opinion of men. In this view, the connection of this with the preceding member of the verse is ·obvious. ' We must not recompense evil for evil, but act in such a way as to commend ourselves to the consciences of all men.' There should not, therefore, be a period after the word *evil*, since this clause assigns a motive for the discharge of the duty enjoined in the first. The word (προνοεῖσθαι) rendered *to provide*, signifies also *to attend to, to care for.* The sense then is, ' Do not resent injuries, having regard to the good opinion of men,' *i.e.*, let a regard to the honour of religion and your own character prevent the returning of evil for evil. Thus Paul (2 Cor. viii. 20, 21) says of himself that he wished others to be associated with him in the distribution of the alms of the church, "having regard to what was right, (προνοούμενοι καλά,) not only in the sight of the Lord, but also in the sight of men." " Summa est, dandam sedulo esse operam, ut nostra integritate omnes aedificentur. Ut enim necessaria est nobis conscientiae innocentia coram Deo ; ita famae integritas apud homines non est negli-genda. Nam si Deum in bonis nostris operibus glorificari convenit, tan-tundem decedit ejus gloriae, ubi nihil laude dignum in nobis homines con-spiciunt." *Calvin.* In Proverbs iii. 4, we have the same exhortation, nearly in the same words as given in the LXX. : προνοοῦ καλὰ ἐνώπιον κυρίου καὶ ἀνϑρώπων.

VERSE 18. *If it be possible, as much as lieth in you, live peaceably with all men.* The retaliation of injuries necessarily leads to contention and strife, while peace is the natural result of a forgiving disposition. The command in this verse, therefore, is naturally connected with that contained in ver. 17. So far from resenting every offence, we should do all we can to live at peace with all men. As the preservation of peace is not always within our control, Paul limits his command by saying, *if it be possible, so far as lieth in you*, τὸ ἐξ ὑμῶν, *as to what is of you.* The cause of con-flict must not arise from you. Your duty is to preserve peace. From the wickedness of others, this is often impossible ; and Paul's own example shows that he was far from thinking that either truth or principle was to be sacrificed for the preservation of peace. His whole life was an active and ardent contention against error and sin. The precept, however, is plain, and the duty important. As far as it can be done consistently with higher obligations and more important interests, we must endeavour to promote peace, and for this end avoid giving offence and avenging injuries. Grotius well expresses the meaning of this verse : " Omnium amici este, si fieri potest ; si non potest utrimque, certe ex vestra parte amici este."

VERSE 19. *Dearly beloved, avenge not yourselves ; but* rather *give place unto wrath,* &c. This is a repetition and amplification of the previous injunction, not to recompense evil for evil. There are three interpreta-tions of the phrase *give place unto wrath*, which deserve to be mentioned. According to the first, the wrath here intended is that of the injured party, and *to give place to*, is made to signify, to allow to pass, *i.e.*, let it go, do not cherish or indulge it. But this is in direct contradiction to the common and proper meaning of the phrase in question, which signifies, *give free scope to ;* and no example of a contrary usage is adduced. In

Latin, the phrase, *dare spatium irae*, is frequently used in the sense of deferring the indulgence of anger, giving it space or time to cool. But *spatium* in these cases has reference to time, *temporis spatium*, a sense in which the Greek τόπος is not used. The second interpretation refers the *wrath* to the injurer. The meaning then is, 'Do not avenge yourselves, but rather yield (*cedite irae*) or submit to the anger of your enemies.' This is consistent with the literal meaning of the phrase *to give place, i.e.*, to get out of the way; and Schoettgen says that the Jewish writers use the corresponding Hebrew phrase (נָתַ־ מָקוֹם) in the sense of *avoiding;* of this usage, however, there is no example in the Bible. It is certainly contrary to the uniform scriptural usage of the expression, which is never employed to convey this idea, but uniformly means, as just stated, to give room to, to allow free exercise to any person or thing; see Eph. iv. 27, "Neither give place to the devil." The third interpretation, therefore, according to which it is the *wrath of God* that is here intended, is the only one consistent with the meaning of the phrase or with the context. 'Dearly beloved, avenge not yourselves, leave that matter to God.' Stand out of the way. Give scope to the wrath of God. It is his prerogative to punish. The passage, *Vengeance is mine, I will repay, saith the Lord*, is quoted from Deut. xxxii. 35, and is obviously cited to show the propriety of the command to leave vengeance to God, and not attempt to take it into our own hands. This does not imply a desire that the divine vengeance should overtake our enemies, but simply that we should not usurp the prerogative of God as the avenger.

VERSE 20. *Therefore, if thine enemy hunger, feed him; if he thirst, give him drink,* &c. That is, instead of avenging ourselves by returning evil for evil, we must return good for evil. The expressions, *feed him* and *give him drink*, are obviously not to be confined to their literal meaning, nor even to the discharge of the common offices of humanity; they are figurative expressions for all the duties of benevolence. It is not enough, therefore, that we preserve an enemy from perishing; we must treat him with all affection and kindness.

For in so doing thou shalt heap coals of fire upon his head. This whole verse is taken from Prov. xxv. 21, 22, "If thine enemy be hungry, give him bread to eat; and if he be thirsty, give him water to drink: for thou shalt heap coals of fire upon his head, and the Lord shall reward thee." The common and natural meaning of the expression, *to heap coals of fire upon any one*, is to inflict the greatest pain upon him, to punish him most severely; see Ps. cxl. 10, "Let burning coals fall upon them;" Ps. xi. 6, "Upon the wicked he shall rain coals (פֶּחִים for פֶּחָמִים), fire and brimstone, and an horrible tempest;" Ezek. x. 2, 2 Esdr. xvi. 53, "Let not the wicked deny that he has sinned, for coals of fire shall burn upon the head of him who denies that he has sinned against the Lord God." The most probable explanation of this figurative expression is, that the allusion is to the lightning or fire from heaven, which is the symbol of the divine vengeance. To rain fire upon any one, is to visit him with the severest and surest destruction. This explanation is much more natural than to suppose the allusion is to the practice of throwing fire-brands upon the heads of the besiegers of a city, or to the fusing of metals.

There are three leading interpretations of this interesting clause. The first, which is perhaps the oldest, and very generally received, is, that Paul means to say that our enemies will be much more severely punished if we leave them in the hands of God, than if we undertake to avenge ourselves. 'Treat your enemy kindly, for in so doing you secure his being punished by God in the severest manner.' The revolting character of this interpretation, which every one must feel, is mitigated by the remark, that the enemy is not to be thus treated from any wish or intention of drawing down the divine wrath upon him; it is only meant that such will be the consequence. But this remark does not meet the difficulty. This clause is so connected with the preceding, that it must be understood as assigning the motive or reason for the discharge of the duty enjoined: 'Treat thine enemy kindly, *for* in so doing,' &c. The second interpretation is, that by heaping coals of fire on his head, is meant, you will cause him pain, *i.e.*, the pain of remorse and shame. So Tholuck, and many other commentators. The third, which seems much the most simple and natural, is, 'for in so doing, you will take the most effectual method of subduing him.' To heap coals of fire on any one, is a punishment which no one can bear; he must yield to it. Kindness is no less effectual; the most malignant enemy cannot always withstand it. The true and Christian method, therefore, to subdue an enemy is, to "overcome evil with good." This interpretation, which suits so well the whole context, seems to be rendered necessary by the following verse, which is a repetition of the previous injunctions in plainer and more general terms. The sentiment which the verse thus explained expresses, is also more in harmony with the spirit of the gospel. " *Vincere dulce et præclarum* est. Optimam autem vincendi rationem sapientissime docet Salomo (Prov. xxv. 21) jubens nos esurientibus inimicis cibum, sitientibus potum præbere : quia beneficiis eos devincientes fortius superabimus, quam qui hostem a vallo et mœnibus flammis superjectis arcent et repellunt." *De Brais.*

Among the numerous striking classical illustrations of the sentiment of this verse, quoted by Wetstein, are the following: *Justinus*, XI. 12, 8, "Tunc Darius se ratus vere victum, cum post prælia etiam beneficiis ab hoste superaretur. *Cæsar* ap. Cic. ad Atticum, IX. 8, "Haec nova sit ratio vincendi, ut misericordia nos muniamus, id quemadmodum fieri possit, nonnulla mi in mentem veniunt, et multa reperiri possunt." *Seneca* de Beneficiis, VII. 31, "Vincit malos pertinax bonitas, nec quisquam tam duri infestique adversus diligenda animi est, ut etiam vi victus bonos non amet." 32, "Ingratus est—huic ipsi beneficium dabo iterum, et tanquam bonus agricola cura cultuque sterilitatem soli vincam." De Ira, II. 32, "Non enim ut in beneficiis honestum est merita meritis repensare, ita injurias injuriis ; illic vinci turpe est, hic vincere."

Verse 21. *Be not overcome of evil, but overcome evil with good.* It is only by disconnecting this verse from the preceding, and considering it as nearly independent of it, that any plausibility can be given to the first interpretation mentioned above, of ver. 20. That it is not thus independent of it, almost every reader must feel. 'We are not to conquer evil by vil, but to treat our enemies with kindness. Thus we shall most effectually subdue them. Do not therefore allow yourself to be overcome of evil, (*i.e.*, to be provoked to the indulgence of a spirit of retaliation,) but overcome evil with good ; subdue your enemies by kindness, not by injuries.'

DOCTRINE.

1. Love is the fulfilling of the law ; it leads to the avoiding of every thing injurious to our neighbour, and to sedulous attention to everything adapted to promote his welfare, ver. 9.

2. The relation in which Christians stand to each other, is that of members of the same family. As, however, it is not a relation constituted by birth, nor secured by the adoption of a name, there is no evidence of its existence but that which consists in the exercise of that 'brotherly affection' (that spiritual στοργή) which brethren in Christ feel for each other, ver. 10.

3. Religion is the soul of morality, without which it is but a lovely corpse. Our moral duties we must perform as "serving the Lord." The religious affections and emotions do not supersede those of a simply benevolent or social character, but mingle with them, and elevate all social and relative duties into acts of religion and genuine morality, ver. 11.

4. The source of our life is in God; without intercourse with him, therefore, we cannot derive those supplies of grace which are requisite to preserve the spirit of piety in our hearts, and to send a vital influence through the various duties and avocations of life. Hence the absolute necessity of being "instant in prayer," ver. 12.

5. God has made of one blood all men that dwell upon the face of the earth. There is in this fact of a common origin, and the possession of a common nature, a sufficient ground for the inculcation of an universal sympathy with all our fellow-men. As he is no true Christian who is destitute of a genuine sympathy for his fellow-Christians, so he is very far from being a man such as God approves, who does not "rejoice with them that do rejoice, and weep with them that weep," ver. 15.

6. A wrong estimate of ourselves is a fruitful source of evil. Viewed in relation to God, and in our own absolute insignificance, we have little reason to be wise or important in our own conceits. A proper self-knowledge will preserve us from pride, ambition, and contempt of others, ver. 16.

7. Abstaining from evil is but one half of duty. It is not enough to avoid imprecating evil upon our enemies; we must sincerely desire and pray for their welfare. Nor is it sufficient not to recompense evil for evil; we must return good for evil, vers. 17—21.

8. The prerogatives of judgment and vengeance belong to God, we have no right, therefore, to arrogate them to ourselves, except in those cases in which, for his glory and the good of society, he has given us authority. All condemnation of others for self-gratification, and all private revenge is inconsistent with the gospel, vers. 11—21.

REMARKS.

1. Christians should never forget that faith without works is dead. It is not more important to believe what God has revealed, than to do what he has commanded. A faith, therefore, which does not produce love, kindness, sympathy, humility, the forgiveness of injuries, &c., can do us little good, vers. 9—21.

2. It is peculiarly characteristic of the spirit of the gospel that it turns the heart towards others, and away from our own interests. Self is not the Christian's centre; men are loved because they are men, Christians because they are Christians; the former with sincere sympathy and benevolence, the latter with brotherly affection. The happiness and feelings of others, the gospel teaches us to consult in small, as well as in great matters, anticipating each other in all acts of kindness and attention, vers. 9—13.

3. The benevolence of the gospel is active and religious; it leads to constant efforts, and is imbued with the spirit of piety, ver. 11.

4. We must remember that without Christ we can do nothing ; that it is not we that live, but Christ that liveth in us. If, therefore, we attempt to discharge the duties here enjoined apart from him, we shall be as a branch severed from the vine ; and unless we are " instant in prayer," this union with Christ cannot be kept up, ver. 12.

5. Alms-giving and hospitality, in some ages of the church, have been unduly exalted, as though they were the whole of benevolence, and the greater part of piety. While we avoid this extreme, we should remember that we are stewards of God, and that "Whoso hath this world's good, and seeth his brother have need, and shutteth up his bowels *of compassion* from him, hath not the love of God dwelling in him," ver. 13. 1 John iii. 17.

6. One of the most beautiful exhibitions of the character of our Saviour was afforded by his conduct under persecution. " He was led as a lamb to the slaughter ;" " when he was reviled, he reviled not again ; when he suffered, he threatened not." Even martyrs dying for the truth have not always been able to avoid the prediction of evil to their persecutors ; so much easier is it to abstain from recompensing evil for evil, than really to love and pray for the good of our enemies. This, however, is Christian duty ; such is the spirit of the gospel. Just so far, therefore, as we find our hearts indisposed to bless those who curse us, or inclined to indulge even a secret satisfaction when evil comes upon them, are we unchristian in our temper, vers. 19—21.

7. Nothing is so powerful as goodness ; it is the most efficacious means to subdue enemies, and put down opposition. Men whose minds can withstand argument, and whose hearts rebel against threats, are not proof against the persuasive influence of unfeigned love ; there is, therefore, no more important collateral reason for being good, than that it increases our power to do good, vers. 20, 21.

CHAPTER XIII.

CONTENTS.

The chapter treats mainly of our political duties. From ver. 1 to ver. 7 inclusive, the apostle enforces the duties which we owe to civil magistrates. From ver. 8 to ver. 10, he refers to the more general obligations under which Christians are placed, but still with special reference to their civil and social relations. From ver. 11 to the end of the chapter, he enjoins an exemplary and holy deportment.

ROMANS XIII. 1—14.

ANALYSIS.

The duty of obedience to those in authority is enforced, 1. By the consideration that civil government is a divine institution, and, therefore, resistance to magistrates in the exercise of their lawful authority is disobedience to God, vers. 1, 2.   2. From the end or design of their appointment, which is to promote the good of society, to be a terror to evil doers, and a praise to them that do well, vers. 3, 4.   3. Because such subjection is a moral as well as civil duty, ver. 5.   On these grounds the payment of tribute or taxes, and general deference, are to be cheerfully rendered, vers. 6, 7.

Christians are bound not only to be obedient to those in authority, but also to perform all social and relative duties, especially that of love, which includes and secures the observance of all others, vers. 8—10. A pure and exemplary life as members of society is enforced by the consideration that the night is far spent and that the day is at hand, that the time of suffering and trial is nearly over, and that of deliverance approaching, vers. 11—14.

COMMENTARY.

VERSE 1.   *Let every soul be subject to the higher powers.*   The expression *every soul* is often used as equivalent to *every one;* it is at times, however, emphatic, and such is probably the case in this passage.   By *higher powers* are most commonly and naturally understood those in authority, without reference to their grade of office, or their character.   We are to be subject not only to the *supreme* magistrates, but to all who have authority over us.   The abstract word *powers* or *authorities* (ἐξουσίαι) is used for those who are invested with power, Luke xii. 11 ; Eph. i. 21 ; iii. 10, &c. &c.   The word (ὑπερέχων) rendered *higher*, is applied to any one who, in dignity and authority, excels us.   In 1 Peter ii. 13, it is applied to the king as supreme, *i.e.*, superior to all other magistrates.   But here one class of magistrates is not brought into comparison with another, but they are spoken of as *being over* other men who are not in office.   It is a very unnatural interpretation which makes this word refer to the character of the magistrates, as though the sense were, 'Be subject to good magistrates.' This is contrary to the usage of the term, and inconsistent with the context.   Obedience is not enjoined on the ground of the personal merit of those in authority, but on the ground of their official station.

There was peculiar necessity, during the apostolic age, for inculcating the duty of obedience to civil magistrates.   This necessity arose in part from the fact that a large portion of the converts to Christianity had been Jews, and were peculiarly indisposed to submit to the heathen authorities. This indisposition (as far as it was peculiar) arose from the prevailing impression among them, that this subjection was unlawful, or at least highly derogatory to their character as the people of God, who had so long lived under a theocracy.   In Deut. xvii. 15 it is said, "Thou shalt in any wise set *him* king over thee, whom the Lord thy God shall choose ; *one* from among thy brethren shalt thou set king over thee ; thou mayest not set a stranger over thee, which *is* not thy brother."   It was a question, therefore, constantly agitated among them, "Is it lawful to pay tribute unto Cæsar, or not ?"   A question which the great majority were at least secretly inclined to answer in the negative.   Another source of the restlessness of the Jews under a foreign yoke, was the idea which they entertained of the nature of the Messiah's kingdom.   As they expected a temporal Prince, whose kingdom should be of this world, they were ready to rise in rebellion at the call of every one who cried, "I am Christ."   The history of the Jews at this period shows how great was the effect produced by these and similar causes on their feelings towards the Roman government. They were continually breaking out into tumults, which led to their expulsion from Rome,* and, finally, to the utter destruction of Jerusalem. It is therefore not a matter of surprise, that converts from among such a people should need the injunction, " Be subject to the higher powers." Besides the effect of their previous opinions and feelings, there is something in the character of Christianity itself, and in the incidental results of the excitement which it occasions, to account for the repugnance of many of the early Christians to submit to their civil rulers. They wrested, no doubt, the doctrine of Christian liberty, as they did other doctrines, to suit their own inclinations. This result, however, is to be attributed not to religion, but to the improper feelings of those into whose minds the form of truth, without its full power, had been received.

For there is no power but of God ; and the powers that be are ordained of God. Οὐ γάρ ἐστιν ἐξουσία εἰ μὴ ἀπὸ θεοῦ. This is a very comprehensive proposition. All authority is of God. No man has any rightful power over other men, which is not derived from God. All human power is delegated and ministerial. This is true of parents, of magistrates, and of church officers. This, however, is not all the passage means. It not only asserts that all government (ἐξουσία, *authority*) is (ἀπὸ θεοῦ) derived from God, but that every magistrate is of God; that is, his authority is *jure divino*. The word ἐξουσία is evidently, in this connection, used in a concrete sense. This is plain from the use of the word in the other clauses of the verse. " The higher powers," and " the powers that be," are concrete terms, meaning those invested with power. Compare vers. 3, 4, where " rulers" and " ministers" are substituted for the abstract " powers." The doctrine here taught is the ground of the injunction contained in the first clause of the verse. We are to obey magistrates, because they derive their authority from God. Not only is human government a divine institution, but the form in which that government exists, and the persons by whom its functions are exercised, are determined by his providence. All magistrates of whatever grade are to be regarded as acting by divine appointment ; not that God designates the individuals, but it being his will that there should be magistrates, every person, who is in point of fact clothed with authority, is to be regarded as having a claim to obedience, founded on the will of God. In like manner, the authority of parents over their children, of husbands over their wives, of masters over their servants, is of God's ordination. There is no limitation to the injunction in this verse, so far as the objects of obedience are concerned, although there is as to the extent of the obedience itself. That is, we are to obey all that is in actual authority over us, whether their authority be legitimate or usurped, whether they are just or unjust. The actual reigning emperor was to be obeyed by the Roman Christians, whatever they might think as to his title to the sceptre. But if he transcended his authority, and required them to worship idols, they were to obey God rather than man. This is the limitation to all human authority. Whenever obedience to man is inconsistent with obedience to God, then disobedience becomes a duty.

Verse 2. *Whoso, therefore, resisteth the power, resisteth the ordinance of God.* This is an obvious inference from the doctrine of the preceding verse. If it is the will of God that there should be civil government, and

---

* *Suetonius,* Claud. 25, says, " Judæos impulsore Chresto *assidue tumultuantes* (Claudius) Roma expulit;" see Acts xviii. 2.

persons appointed to exercise authority over others, it is plain that to resist such persons in the exercise of their lawful authority is an act of disobedience to God.

And they that resist shall receive to themselves damnation. This also is an obvious conclusion from the preceding. If disobedience is a sin it will be punished. The word (κρίμα) rendered *damnation,* means simply *sentence,* judicial decision; whether favourable or adverse, depends on the context. Here it is plain it means a sentence of condemnation. He shall be condemned, and, by implication, punished. As the word *damnation* is by modern usage restricted to the final and eternal condemnation of the wicked, it is unsuited to this passage and some others in which it occurs in our version; see 1 Cor. xi. 29. Paul does not refer to the punishment which the civil magistrate may inflict; for he is speaking of disobedience to those in authority as a sin against God, which he will punish.

It is clear that this passage (vers. 1, 2) is applicable to men living under every form of government, monarchical, aristocratical, or democratical, in all their various modifications. Those who are in authority are to be obeyed within their sphere, no matter how or by whom appointed. It is the οὖσαι ἐξουσίαι, the powers *that be,* the *de facto* government, that is to be regarded as, for the time being, ordained of God. It was to Paul a matter of little importance whether the Roman emperor was appointed by the senate, the army, or the people; whether the assumption of the imperial authority by Cæsar was just or unjust, or whether his successors had a legitimate claim to the throne or not. It was his object to lay down the simple principle, that magistrates are to be obeyed. The extent of this obedience is to be determined from the nature of the case. They are to be obeyed as magistrates, in the exercise of their lawful authority. When Paul commands wives to obey their husbands, they are required to obey them as husbands, not as masters, nor as kings; children are to obey their parents as parents, not as sovereigns; and so in every other case. This passage, therefore, affords a very slight foundation for the doctrine of passive obedience.

VERSE 3. *For rulers are not a terror to good works, but to evil.* This verse is not to be connected with the second, but with the first, as it assigns an additional reason for the duty there enjoined. Magistrates are to be obeyed, for such is the will of God, and because they are appointed to repress evil and promote good. There is a ground, therefore, in the very nature of their office, why they should not be resisted.

Wilt thou then not be afraid of the power? do that which is good, and thou shall have praise of the same. That is, government is not an evil to be feared, except by evil doers. As the magistrates are appointed for the punishment of evil, the way to avoid suffering from their authority is not to resist it, but to do that which is good. Paul is speaking of the legitimate design of government, not of the abuse of power by wicked men.

VERSE 4. *For he is the minister of God to thee for good,* &c. This whole verse is but an amplification of the preceding. 'Government is a benevolent institution of God, designed for the benefit of men; and, therefore, should be respected and obeyed. As it has, however, the rightful authority to punish, it is to be feared by those that do evil.' *For good,* *i.e.,* to secure or promote your welfare. Magistrates or rulers are not appointed for their own honour or advantage, but for the benefit of society, and, therefore, while those in subjection are on this account to obey them, they themselves are taught, what those in power are so apt to forget, that they are the servants of the people as well as the servants of God, and that the welfare of society is the only legitimate object which they as rulers are at liberty to pursue.

But if thou do that which is evil, be afraid ; for he beareth not the sword in vain : for he is the minister of God, a revenger to execute *wrath* (εἰς ὀργήν, *i.e.,* for the purpose of punishment) *upon him that doeth evil.* As one part of the design of government is to protect the good, so the other is to punish the wicked. The existence of this delegated authority is, therefore, a reason why men should abstain from the commission of evil. *He beareth not the sword in vain, i.e.,* it is not in vain that he is invested with authority to punish. The reference is not to the dagger worn by the Roman emperors as a sign of office, as μάχαιρα in the New Testament always means sword, which of old was the symbol of authority, and specially of the right of life and death. As the common method of inflicting capital punishment was by decapitation with a sword, that instrument is mentioned as the symbol of the right of punishment, and, as many infer from this passage, of the right of capital punishment. "Insignis locus ad jus gladii comprobandum ; nam si Dominus magistratum armando gladii quoque usum illi mandavit, quoties sontes capitali poena vindicat, exercendo Dei ultionem, ejus mandatis obsequitur. Contendunt igitur cum Deo qui sanguinem nocentium hominum effundi nefas esse putant." *Calvin.*

Verse 5. *Wherefore* ye *must needs be subject, not only for wrath, but also for conscience' sake.* That is, subjection to magistrates is not only a civil duty enforced by penal statutes, but also a religious duty, and part of our obedience to God. *For wrath, i.e.,* from fear of punishment. *For conscience' sake, i.e.,* out of regard to God, from conscientious motives. In like manner, Paul enforces all relative and social duties on religious grounds. Children are to obey their parents, because it is right in the sight of God ; and servants are to be obedient to their masters, as unto Christ, doing the will of God from the heart, Eph. vi. 1, 5, 6.

Verse 6. *For, for this cause, pay ye tribute also.* This verse may be connected, by the words (διὰ τοῦτο) rendered *for this cause,* with the preceding, thus, ' Wherefore (*i.e.,* for conscience' sake) ye should pay tribute also.' But it is better to consider this clause as containing an inference from the foregoing exhibition of the nature and design of civil government : ' Since civil government is constituted for the benefit of society, for the punishment of evil doers and for the praise of those that do well, ye should cheerfully pay the contributions requisite for its support.'

For they are the ministers of God, attending continually on this very thing. This clause introduces another reason for the payment of tribute. *They,* not the tax-gatherers, but οἱ ἄρχοντες, the rulers, to whom the tribute is due. Magistrates are not only appointed for the public good, but they are the ministers of God, and consequently it is his will that we should contribute whatever is necessary to enable them to discharge their duty. The word (λειτουργοί) rendered *ministers,* means public servants, men appointed for any public work, civil or religious. Among the Greek democratical states, especially at Athens, those persons were particularly so called, who were required to perform some public service at their own expense. It is used in Scripture in a general sense, for servants or ministers, Rom. xv. 16; Heb. i. 7; viii. 2. The words εἰς αὐτὸ τοῦτο, *to this very thing,* may refer to tax-gathering. The magistrates are divinely commissioned, or authorized to collect tribute. This is necessary to the support of government ; and government being a divine institution, God, in ordaining the end, has thereby ordained the means. It is because magistrates, in the collection of taxes, act as the λειτουργοὶ Θεοῦ, *the executive officers of God*, that we are bound to pay them. Others make the αὐτὸ τοῦτο refer to the λειτουργία, or service of God, which is implied in magistrates being called λειτουργοί. 'They are the ministers of God attending constantly to their ministry.' The former interpretation is the more consistent with the context.

VERSE 7. *Render therefore to all their dues : tribute to whom tribute ; custom to whom custom ; fear to whom fear ; honour to whom honour.* 'Such being the will of God, and such the benevolent design of civil government, render to magistrates (and to all others) what properly belongs to them, whether pecuniary contribution, reverence, or honour.' The word *all* seems, from the context, to have special reference to all in authority, though it is not necessary to confine it to such persons exclusively. The word (φόρος) *tribute* is applied properly to land and capitation tax ; and (τέλος) to the imposts levied on merchandise. The words (φόβος) *fear*, and (τιμή) *honour*, are generally considered in this connection as differing only in degree ; the former expressing the reverence to superiors, the latter the respect to equals.

VERSE 8. *Owe no man any thing, but to love one another*, &c. That is, acquit yourselves of all obligations, except love, which is a debt that must remain ever due. This is the common, and considering the context, which abounds with commands, the most natural interpretation of this passage. Others, however, take the verb (ὀφείλετε) as in the indicative, instead of the imperative mood, and understand the passage thus : ' Ye owe no man any thing but love, (which includes all other duties,) for he that loves another fulfils the law.' This gives a good sense, when this verse is taken by itself ; but viewed in connection with those which precede and follow, the common interpretation is much more natural. Besides, "the indicative would require οὐδενὶ οὐδέν, and not μηδενὶ μηδέν. The use of the subjective negative shows that a command is intended." *Meyer.* The idea which a cursory reader might be disposed to attach to these words, in considering them as a direction not to contract pecuniary debts, is not properly expressed by them ; although the prohibition, in its spirit, includes the incurring of such obligations, when we have not the certain prospect of discharging them. The command, however, is, ' Acquit yourselves of all obligations, tribute, custom, fear, honour, or whatever else you may owe, but remember that the debt of love is still unpaid, and always must remain so ; for love includes all duty, since he that loves another fulfils the law.'* He that loveth another *hath fulfilled* (πεπλήρωκε) the law. It is already done. That is, all the law contemplated, in its specific commands relating to our social duties, is attained when we love our neighbour as ourselves.

VERSE 9. *For this, Thou shalt not commit adultery, Thou shalt not kill, Thou shalt not steal, Thou shalt not bear false witness,† Thou shalt not covet ; and if* there be *any other commandment, it is briefly compre-*

---

* *Amare;* debitum immortale. Si amabitis, nil debitis nam amor implet legem. Amare' libertas est.—*Bengel.* Argute et eleganter dictum : dilectionis debitum et semper solvitur et semper manet.—*Wetstein.*

A grateful mind,
By owing owes not, and still pays, at once
Indebted and discharged.—*Milton's Paradise Lost*, IV. 55.

† The words οὐ ψευδομαρτυρήσεις are omitted in the MSS. A. D. E. F. G., 1, 2, 29, 34, 36, 38, 39, 41, 43, 46, 47, 52, and in the Syriac version. They are rejected in the Complutensian edition, and in those of Mill, Bengel, Griesbach, Knapp, and Lachmann.

hended in this saying, namely, Thou shalt love thy neighbour as thyself.
This verse is evidently a confirmation of the declaration at the close of the
preceding one, that love includes all our social duties. This is further
confirmed in the following verse.

Verse 10. *Love worketh no ill to his neighbour, therefore love is the
fulfilling of the law.* That is, as love delights in the happiness of its
object, it effectually prevents us from injuring those we love, and, consequently, leads us to fulfil all the law requires, because the law requires
nothing which is not conducive to the best interests of our fellow-men.
He, therefore, who loves his neighbour with the same sincerity that he
loves himself, and consequently treats him as he would wish, under
similar circumstances, to be treated by him, will fulfil all that the law
enjoins ; hence the whole law is comprehended in this one command,
Thou shalt love thy neighbour as thyself.

Verse 11. *And that, knowing the time, that now it is high time to
awake out of sleep ; for now is our salvation nearer than when we believed.*
From this verse to the end of the chapter, Paul exhorts his readers to discharge the duties already enjoined, and urges on them to live a holy and
exemplary life. The consideration by which this exhortation is enforced,
is, that the night is far spent, and that the day is at hand, the time of
deliverance is fast approaching. The words (και τοῦτο) rendered *and that,*
are by many considered as elliptical, and the word (ποιεῖτε) *do* is supplied ;
'And this *do.*' The demonstrative pronoun, however, is frequently used
to mark the importance of the connection between two circumstances for
the case in hand, (Passow, Vol. II., p. 319,)* and is, therefore, often equivalent to the phrases, *and indeed, the more,* &c. So in this case, 'We
must discharge our various duties, *and that* knowing,' &c., *i.e.,* 'the rather,
because we know,' &c.; compare Heb. xi. 12; 1 Cor. vi. 6; Eph. ii. 8.
Knowing the time, i.e., considering the nature and character of the period
in which we now live. The original word (καιρός) does not mean *time* in
the general sense, but a portion of time considered as appropriate, as fixed,
as short, &c. Paul immediately explains himself by adding, *that now it
is high time to awake out of sleep ;* it was the proper time to arouse themselves from their slumbers, and, shaking off all slothfulness, to address
themselves earnestly to work. *For now is our salvation nearer than when we
believed.* This is the reason why it is time to be up and active, salvation
is at hand. There are three leading interpretations of this clause. The
first is, that it means that the time of salvation, or special favour to the
Gentiles, and of the destruction of the Jews, was fast approaching. So
Hammond, Whitby, and many others. But for this there is no foundation
in the simple meaning of the words, nor in the context. Paul evidently
refers to something of more general and permanent interest than the over-
throw of the Jewish nation, and the consequent freedom of the Gentile
converts from their persecutions. The night that was far spent, was not
the night of sorrow arising from Jewish bigotry ; and the day that was at
hand was something brighter and better than deliverance from its power.
A second interpretation very generally received of late is, that the reference
is to the second advent of Christ. It is assumed that the early Christians,
and even the inspired apostles, were under the constant impression that
Christ was to appear in person for the establishment of his kingdom,
before that generation passed away. This assumption is founded on
such passages as the following : Phil. iv. 5, "The Lord is at hand ;"

* Edition of Palm and Rost, p. 598.

1 Thess. iv. 17, "We that are alive and remain shall be caught up together with them to meet the Lord in the air;" 1 Cor. xv. 51, "We shall not all sleep, but we shall all be changed," &c. With regard to this point, we may remark—1. That neither the early Christians nor the apostles knew when the second advent of Christ was to take place. "But of that day and hour knoweth no man, no, nor the angels of heaven, but my Father only. But as the days of Noe *were*, so shall the coming of the Son of man be," Matt. xxiv. 36, 37. "They (the apostles) asked of him, saying, Lord, wilt thou at this time restore the kingdom to Israel? And he said unto them, It is not for you to know the times or the seasons which the Father hath put in his own power," Acts i. 6, 7. "But of the times and seasons, brethren, ye have no need that I write unto you; for ye yourselves know perfectly that the day of the Lord so cometh as a thief in the night," 1 Thess. v. 1, 2. 2. Though they knew not when it was to be, they knew that it was not to happen immediately, nor until a great apostasy had occurred. "Now we beseech you, brethren, by (or concerning) the coming of the Lord Jesus, and our gathering together to him, that ye be not soon shaken in mind . . . as that the day of Christ is at hand. Let no man deceive you by any means : for *that day shall not come*, except there come a falling away first, and that man of sin be revealed," &c., 2 Thess. ii. 1—3 ; and ver. 5, " Remember ye not, that when I was yet with you, I told you these things ?" Besides this distinct assertion, that the second advent of Christ was not to occur before the revelation of the man of sin, there are several other predictions in the writings of Paul, which necessarily imply his knowledge of the fact, that the day of judgment was not immediately at hand, 1 Tim. iv. 1—3 ; Rom. xi. 25. The numerous prophecies of the Old Testament relating to the future conversion of the Jews, and various other events, were known to the apostles, and precluded the possibility of their believing that the world was to come to an end before those prophecies were fulfilled. 3. We are not to understand the expressions, *day of the Lord, the appearing of Christ, the coming of the Son of man*, in all cases in the same way. The *day of the Lord* is a very familiar expression in the Scriptures to designate any time of the special manifestation of the divine presence, either for judgment or mercy ; see Ezek. xiii. 5 ; Joel i. 15 ; Isa. ii. 12 ; xiii. 6, 9. So also God or Christ is said to come to any person or place, when he makes any remarkable exhibition of his power or grace. Hence the Son of man was to come for the destruction of Jerusalem, before the people of that generation all perished ; and the summons of death is sometimes represented as the coming of Christ to judge the soul. What is the meaning of such expressions must be determined by the context, in each particular case. 4. It cannot, therefore, be inferred from such declarations as "the day of the Lord is at hand;" "the coming of the Lord draweth nigh;" "the judge is at the door," &c., that those who made them supposed that the second advent and final judgment were to take place immediately. They expressly assert the contrary, as has just been shown. 5. The situation of the early Christians was, in this respect, similar to ours. They believed that Christ was to appear the second time without sin unto salvation ; but when this advent was to take place, they did not know. They looked and longed for the appearing of the great God their Saviour, as we do now ; and the prospect of this event operated upon them as it should do upon us, as a constant motive to watchfulness and diligence, that we may be found of him in peace. There is nothing, therefore, in the Scriptures, nor in

this immediate context, which requires us to suppose that Paul intended to say that the time of the second advent was at hand, when he tells his readers that their salvation was nearer than when they believed.

The third and most common, as well as the most natural interpretation of this passage is, that Paul meant simply to remind them that the time of deliverance was near; that the difficulties and sins with which they had to contend, would soon be dispersed as the shades and mists of night before the rising day. The *salvation*, therefore, here intended, is the consummation of the work of Christ in their deliverance from this present evil world, and introduction into the purity and blessedness of heaven. Eternity is just at hand, is the solemn consideration that Paul urges on his readers as a motive for devotion and diligence.

Verse 12. *The night is far spent, the day is at hand: let us therefore cast off the works of darkness, and let us put on the armour of light.* The general sentiment of this verse is very obvious. Night or darkness is the common emblem of sin and sorrow; day or light, that of knowledge, purity, and happiness. The meaning of the first clause therefore is, that the time of sin and sorrow is nearly over, that of holiness and happiness is at hand. The particular form and application of this general sentiment depends, however, on the interpretation given to the preceding verse. If that verse refers to the destruction of Jerusalem, then Paul means to say, that the night of persecution was nearly gone, and the day of peace and prosperity to the Gentile churches was at hand. But if ver. 11 refers to final salvation, then this verse means, that the sins and sorrows of this life will soon be over, and the day of eternal blessedness is about to dawn. The latter view is to be preferred.

Paul continues this beautiful figure through the verse. *Therefore let us cast off the works of darkness, and let us put on the armour of light.* That is, let us renounce those things which need to be concealed, and clothe ourselves with those which are suited to the light. *The works of darkness* are those works which men are accustomed to commit in the dark, or which suit the dark; and *armour of light* means those virtues and good deeds which men are not ashamed of, because they will bear to be seen. Paul probably used the word (ὅπλα) *armour*, instead of *works*, because these virtues constitute the offensive and defensive weapons with which we are here to contend against sin and evil; see Eph. vi. 11. The words ἀποτίθεσθαι and ἐνδύεσθαι suggest the idea of clothing. We are to cast off one set of garments and to put on another. The clothes which belong to the night are to be cast aside, and we are to array ourselves in those suited to the day.

Verse 13. *Let us walk honestly as in the day: not in rioting and drunkenness; not in chambering and wantonness; not in strife and envying.* This verse is an amplification of the preceding, stating some of those works of darkness which we are to put off; as ver. 14 states what is the armour of light which we are to put on. The word (εὐσχημόνως) rendered *honestly*, means *becomingly, properly.* There are three classes of sins specified in this verse, to each of which two words are appropriated, viz., intemperance, impurity, and discord. *Rioting and drunkenness* belong to the first. The word (κῶμος) appropriately rendered *rioting*, is used both in reference to the disorderly religious festivals kept in honour of Bacchus, and to the common boisterous carousing of intemperate young men, (see Passow, Vol. I., p. 924.)* The words *chambering and wantonness*, include all kinds of

* Edition of Palm and Rost, p. 1878.

uncleanness ; and *strife and envying,* all kinds of unholy emulation and discord.

Verse 14. *But put ye on the Lord Jesus Christ, i.e.,* be as he was. *To put on Christ,* signifies to be intimately united to him, so that he, and not we, may appear, Gal. iii. 27 : ' Let not your own evil deeds be seen, (*i.e.,* do not commit such,) but let what Christ was appear in all your conduct, as effectually as if clothed with the garment of his virtues.'

And make no provision for the flesh, to fulfil *the lusts* thereof. That is, let it not be your care to gratify the flesh. By *flesh,* in this passage, is perhaps generally understood the *body;* so that the prohibition is confined to the vicious indulgence of the sensual appetites. But there seems to be no sufficient reason for this restriction. As the word is constantly used by Paul for whatever is corrupt, and in the preceding verse the sins of envy and contention are specially mentioned, it may be understood more generally, ' Do not indulge the desires of your corrupt nature.'

DOCTRINE.

1. Civil government is a divine institution, *i.e.,* it is the will of God that it should exist, and be respected and obeyed, ver. 2.

2. While 'government is of God, the form is of men.' God has never enjoined any one form obligatory on all communities ; but has simply laid down certain principles, applicable to rulers and subjects, under every form in which governments exist, vers. 1—7.

3. The obedience which the Scriptures command us to render to our rulers is not unlimited ; there are cases in which disobedience is a duty. This is evident, first, from the very nature of the case. The command to obey magistrates is, from its nature, a command to obey them as magistrates in the exercise of their rightful authority. They are not to be obeyed as priests or as parents, but as civil rulers. No one doubts that the precept, "Children, obey your parents in all things," is a command to obey them in the exercise of their rightful parental authority, and imposes no obligation to implicit and passive obedience. A parent who should claim the power of a sovereign over his children, would have no right to their obedience. The case is still plainer with regard to the command, " Wives, submit to your own husbands." Secondly, from the fact that the same inspired men who enjoin, in such general terms, obedience to rulers, themselves uniformly and openly disobeyed them whenever their commands were inconsistent with other and higher obligations. " We ought to obey God rather than men," was the principle which the early Christians avowed, and on which they acted. They disobeyed the Jewish and heathen authorities, whenever they required them to do anything contrary to the will of God. There are cases, therefore, in which disobedience is a duty. How far the rightful authority of rulers extends, the precise point at which the obligation to obedience ceases, must often be a difficult question ; and each case must be decided on its own merits. The same difficulty exists in fixing the limits of the authority of parents over their children, husbands over their wives, masters over their servants. This, however, is a theoretical rather than a practical difficulty. The general principles on which the question in regard to any given case is to be decided are sufficiently plain. No command to do anything morally wrong can be binding ; nor can any which transcends the rightful authority of the power whence it

emanates. What that rightful authority is, must be determined by the institutions and laws of the land, or from prescription and usage, or from the nature and design of the office with which the magistrate is invested. The right of deciding on all these points, and determining where the obligation to obedience ceases, and the duty of resistance begins, must, from the nature of the case, rest with the subject, and not with the ruler. The apostles and early Christians decided this point for themselves, and did not leave the decision with the Jewish or Roman authorities. Like all other questions of duty, it is to be decided on our responsibility to God and our fellow-men, vers. 1—7.

4. The design of civil government is not to promote the advantage of rulers, but of the ruled. They are ordained and invested with authority, to be a terror to evil doers, and a praise to them that do well. They are the ministers of God for this end, and are appointed for "this very thing." On this ground our obligation to obedience rests, and the obligation ceases when this design is systematically, constantly, and notoriously disregarded. Where unfaithfulness on the part of the government exists, or where the form of it is incompatible with the design of its institution, the governed must have a right to remedy the evil. But they cannot have the moral right to remedy one evil, by the production of a greater. And, therefore, as there are few greater evils than instability and uncertainty in governments, the cases in which revolutions are justifiable must be exceedingly rare, vers. 3—7.

5. The proper sphere of civil government is the civil and social relations of men, and their temporal welfare ; conscience, and of course religion, are beyond its jurisdiction, except so far as the best interests of civil society are necessarily connected with them. What extent of ground this exception covers, ever has been, and probably will ever remain a matter of dispute. Still it is to be remembered, that it is an exception ; religion and morality, as such, are not within the legitimate sphere of the civil authority. To justify the interference of the civil government, therefore, in any given case, with these important subjects, an exception must be made out. It must be shown that an opinion or a religion is not only false, but that its prevalence is incompatible with the rights of those members of the community who are not embraced within its communion, before the civil authority can be authorized to interfere for its suppression. It is then to be suppressed, not as a religion, but as a public nuisance. God has ordained civil government for the promotion of the welfare of men as members of the same civil society ; and parental government, and the instruction and discipline of the church, for their moral and religious improvement. And the less interference there is between these two great institutions, in the promotion of their respective objects, the better. We do not find in the New Testament any commands addressed to magistrates with regard to the suppression of heresies or the support of the truth ; nor, on the other hand, do we meet with any directions to the church to interfere with matters pertaining to the civil government, vers. 3—6.

6. The discharge of all the social and civil duties of life is to the Christian a matter of religious obligation, vers. 5—7.

REMARKS.

1. The Christian religion is adapted to all states of society and all forms of civil government. As the Spirit of God, when it enters any human

heart, leaves unmolested what is peculiar to its individual character, as far as it is innocent, and effects the reformation of what is evil, not by violence, but by a sweetly constraining influence; so the religion of Christ, when it enters any community of men, does not assail their form of government, whether despotic or free; and if there is anything in their institutions inconsistent with its spirit, it is changed by its silent operation on the heart and conscience, rather than by direct denunciation. It has thus, without rebellion or violent convulsions, curbed the exercise of despotic power, and wrought the abolition of slavery throughout the greater part of Christendom, vers. 1—14.

2. The gospel is equally hostile to tyranny and anarchy. It teaches rulers that they are ministers of God for the public good; and it teaches subjects to be obedient to magistrates, not only for fear, but also for conscience' sake, ver. 5.

3. God is to be recognised as ordering the affairs of civil society : " He removeth kings, and he setteth up kings ;" by him "kings reign, and princes decree justice." It is enough, therefore, to secure the obedience of the Christian, that, in the providence of God, he finds the power of government lodged in certain hands. The early Christians would have been in constant perplexity, had it been incumbent on them, amidst the frequent poisonings and assassinations of the imperial palace, the tumults of the pretorian guards, and the proclamation by contending armies of rival candidates, to decide on the individual who had *de jure* the power of the sword, before they could conscientiously obey, vers. 1—5.

4. When rulers become a terror to the good, and a praise to them that do evil, they may still be tolerated and obeyed, not however, of right, but because the remedy may be worse than the disease, vers. 3, 4.

5. Did genuine Christian love prevail, it would secure the right discharge, not only of the duties of rulers towards their subjects, and of subjects towards their rulers, but of all the relative social duties of life; for he that loveth another fulfilleth the law, vers. 7, 8.

6. The nearness of eternity should operate on all Christians as a motive to purity and devotedness to God. The night is far spent, the day is at hand; now is our salvation nearer than when we believed, vers. 13, 14.

7. All Christian duty is included in putting on the Lord Jesus ; in being like him, having that similarity of temper and conduct which results from being intimately united to him by the Holy Spirit, ver. 14.

CHAPTER XIV.

CONTENTS.

As in chapter XII., Paul had insisted principally upon moral and religious duties, and in chapter XIII., on those of a political character, he here treats particularly of the duties of church members towards each other, in relation to matters not binding on the conscience. There are two points specially presented : the first is the manner in which scrupulous Christians, who make conscience of matters of indifference, are to be treated, vers. 1—12 ; and the second, the manner in which those who are strong in faith should use their Christian liberty, vers. 13—23.

ROMANS XIV. 1—23.

ANALYSIS.

Scrupulous Christians, whose consciences are weak, are to be kindly received, and not harshly condemned, ver. 1. This direction the apostle enforces in reference to those who were scrupulous as to eating particular kinds of food, and the propriety of neglecting the sacred days appointed in the law of Moses. Such persons are not to be condemned—1. Because this weakness is not inconsistent with piety ; notwithstanding their doubts on these points, God has received them, ver. 3. 2. Because one Christian has no right to judge another, (except where Christ has expressly authorized it, and given him the rule of judgment;) to his own master he stands or falls, ver. 4. 3. Because such harsh treatment is unnecessary ; God can and will preserve such persons, notwithstanding their feebleness, ver. 4. 4. Because they act religiously, or out of regard to God, in this matter ; and, therefore, live according to the great Christian principle, that no man liveth to himself, and no man dieth to himself, but whether he lives or dies, belongs to God, vers. 6—9. On these grounds we should abstain from condemning or treating contemptuously our weaker brethren, remembering that we are all to stand before the judgment-seat of Christ, vers. 10—13.

As to the use of Christian liberty, the apostle teaches that it is not to be given up or denied ; that is, we are not to make things sinful which are in themselves indifferent, ver. 14. But it does not follow, that because a thing is not wrong in itself, it is right for us to indulge in it. Our liberty is to be asserted ; but it is to be exercised in such a way as not to injure others. We must not put a stumbling-block in our brother's way, ver. 12. This consideration of others, in the use of our liberty, is enforced—1. From the great law of love. It is inconsistent with Christian charity, for our own gratification, to injure a brother for whom Christ died, ver. 15. 2. From a regard to the honour of religion. We must not cause that which is good to be evil spoken of, ver. 16. 3. From the consideration that religion does not consist in such things, vers. 17, 18. 4. Because we are bound to promote the peace and edification of the church, ver. 19. 5. Though the things in question may be in themselves indifferent, it is morally wrong to indulge in them to the injury of others, vers. 20, 21.   6. The course enjoined by the apostle requires no concession of principle, or adoption of error. We can retain our full belief of the indifference of things which God has not pronounced sinful ; but those who have not our faith, cannot act upon it, and therefore should not be encouraged so to do, vers. 22, 23.

COMMENTARY.

VERSE 1. *Him that is weak in faith receive, but not to doubtful disputations.* This verse contains the general direction that weak and scrupulous brethren are to be kindly received, and not harshly condemned. Who these weak brethren were, and what was the nature of their scruples, is matter of doubt. Some say they were Jewish converts, who held to the continued obligation of the ceremonial law. But to this it is objected, that they abstained from all flesh (ver. 2,) and refused to drink wine (ver. 21;) things not prohibited in the law of Moses. Others think they were persons who scrupled about the use of such flesh only as had been offered in sacrifice to idols, and of the wine employed in libation to false gods. But for this limitation there is no ground in the context. Eichhorn, Einleitung III. p. 222, supposes that they were the advocates, of Gentile birth, of the ascetic school of the new Pythagorean philosophy, which had begun to prevail among the heathen, and probably to a certain extent among the Jews. But it is plain that they held to the continued authority of the Jewish law, which converts from among the heathen would not be likely to do. The most probable opinion is, that they were a scrupulous class of Jewish Christians ; perhaps of the school of the Essenes, who were more strict and abstemious than the Mosaic ceremonial required. Asceticism, as a form of self-righteousness and will-worship, was one of the earliest, most extensive and persistent heresies in the church. But there is nothing inconsistent with the assumption that the weak brethren here spoken of were scrupulous Jewish Christians. Josephus says, that some of the Jews at Rome lived on fruits exclusively, from fear of eating something unclean. *Weak in faith i.e.*, weak as to faith (πίστει.) *Faith* here means, persuasion of the truth ; a man may have a strong persuasion as to certain truths, and a very weak one as to others. Some of the early Christians were, no doubt, fully convinced that Jesus was the Messiah, and yet felt great doubts whether the distinction between clean and unclean meats was entirely done away. This was certainly a great defect of Christian character, and arose from the want of an intelligent and firm conviction of the gratuitous nature of justification, and of the spirituality of the gospel. Since, however, this weakness was not inconsistent with sincere devotion to Christ, such persons were to be *received.* The word (προσλαμβάνομαι) rendered *receive,* has the general signification, *to take to one-self ;* and this is its meaning here : ' Him that is weak in faith, take to yourselves as a Christian brother, treat him kindly ;' see Acts xxviii. 2 ; Rom. xv. 7 ; Philemon vers. 15, 17.

There is much more doubt as to the meaning of the words (μὴ εἰς διαχρίσεις διαλογισμῶν) translated *not to doubtful disputations.* The former of the two important words of this clause means, *the faculty of discrimination,* 1 Cor. xii. 10 ; *the act of discerning,* Heb. v. 14, and then, *dijudication, judgment.* It is said also to signify *doubt* or *inward conflict ;* see the use of the verb in chap. iv. 20. It is taken in this sense in our version, *not to the doubtfulness of disputes,* not for the purpose of doubtful disputation. That is, not so as to give rise to disputes on doubtful matters. Luther (und verwirret die Gewissen nicht,) and many others take διαχρίσεις in the sense of *doubt*, and refer the διαλογισμοί to the weak brethren: 'Not so as to awaken doubts of thought, *i.e.*, scruples.' Although the verb διαχρίνω, in the passive, often means to hesitate or doubt, the noun διαχρίσις is not used in that sense, either in the classics or in the New Testament. It is therefore better to take the word in its ordinary sense, which gives a meaning to the passage suited to the context, not to the *judging of thoughts; i.e.*, not presuming to sit in judgment on the opinions of your brethren. *Grotius:* "Non sumentes vobis dijudicandas ipsorum cogitationes." This is the injunction which is enforced in the following verses.

Verse 2. *For one believeth he may eat all things: another, who is weak, eateth herbs*—ὃς μὲν πιστεύει φαγεῖν πάντα does not mean, *one believeth he may eat all things*; much less, *he that believeth eats all things*, but, *one has confidence to eat all things*. Instead of ὃς μέν being followed by ὃς δέ, *one eats all things, another* eats herbs, Paul says, ὁ δὲ ἀσθενῶν, he who is weak eateth herbs. This is an illustration of the weakness of faith to which the apostle refers in ver. 1. It was a scrupulousness about the use of things considered as unclean, and with regard to sacred days, ver. 5. There were two sources whence the early Christian church was disturbed by the question about meats. The first, and by far the most important, was the natural prejudices of the Jewish converts. It is not a matter of surprise that, educated as they had been in a strict regard for the Mosaic law, they found it difficult to enter at once into the full liberty of the gospel, and disencumber their consciences of all their early opinions. Even the apostles were slow in shaking them off; and the church in Jerusalem seems to have long continued in the observance of a great part of the ceremonial law. These scruples were not confined to the use of meats pronounced unclean in the Old Testament, but, as appears from the Epistles to the Corinthians, extended to partaking of anything which had been offered to an idol; and, in these latter scruples, some even of the Gentile converts may have joined. The second source of trouble on this subject was less prevalent and less excusable. It was the influence of the mystic ascetic philosophy of the East, which had developed itself among the Jews, in the peculiar opinions of the Essenes, and which, among the Christian churches, particularly those of Asia Minor, produced the evils which Paul describes in his Epistles to the Colossians (chap. ii. 10—23,) and to Timothy (1 Tim. iv. 1—8,) and which subsequently gave rise to all the errors of Gnosticism. There is no satisfactory evidence that the persons to whom Paul refers in this passage were under the influence of this philosophy. The fact that they abstained from all meat, as seems to be intimated in this verse, may have arisen from the constant apprehension of eating meat which, after having been presented in sacrifice, was sold in the market-place, or which had in some other way been rendered unclean. Every thing in the context is consistent with the supposition that Jewish scruples were the source of the difficulty; and as these were by far the most common cause, no other need be here assumed.

Verse 3. *Let not him that eateth despise him that eateth not; and let not him which eateth not judge him that eateth: for God hath received him.* There is mutual forbearance to be exercised in relation to this subject. The strong are not to despise the weak as superstitious and imbecile; nor the weak to condemn those who disregard their scruples. Points of indifference are not to be allowed to disturb the harmony of Christian

fellowship. *For God hath received him, i.e.,* God has recognised him as
a Christian, and received him into his kingdom. This reason is not designed to enforce merely the latter of the two duties here enjoined, but is
applied to both. As God does not make eating or not eating certain kinds
of food a condition of acceptance, Christians ought not to allow it to interfere with their communion as brethren. The Jewish converts were perhaps quite as much disposed to condemn the Gentile Christians, as the
latter were to despise the Christian Jews ; Paul therefore frames his admonition so as to reach both classes. It appears, however, from the first
verse, and from the whole context, that the Gentiles were principally intended.

VERSE 4. *Who art thou that judgest another man's servant ? to his own
master he standeth or falleth.* If God has not made the point in question
a term of communion, we have no right to make it a ground of condemnation. We have no right to exercise the office of judge over the servant of
another. This is the second reason for mutual forbearance with regard to
such matters as divided the Jewish and Gentile converts. It cannot fail
to be remarked how differently the apostle speaks of the same things under
different circumstances. He who circumcised Timothy, who conformed in
many things to the law of Moses, and to the Jews became a Jew, and who
here exhorts Christians to regard their external observances as matters of
indifference, resisted to the uttermost, as soon as these things were urged
as matters of importance, or were insisted upon as necessary to acceptance
with God. He would not allow Titus to be circumcised, nor give place
even for an hour to false brethren, who had come in privily to act as spies,
Gal. ii. 3, 5. He warned the Galatians, that if they were circumcised,
Christ would profit them nothing ; that they renounced the whole method
of gratuitous justification, and forfeited its blessings, if they sought acceptance on any such terms. How liberal and how faithful was the apostle !
He would concede everything, and become all things to all men, where
principle was not at stake ; but when it was, he would concede nothing
for a moment. What might be safely granted, if asked and given as a
matter of indifference, became a fatal apostasy when demanded as a matter
of necessity or a condition of salvation.

To his own master he standeth or falleth, i.e., it belongs to his own
master to decide his case, to acquit or to condemn. These terms are often
used in this judicial sense, Ps. i. 5, lxxvi. 7 ; Luke xxi. 36 ; Rev. vi. 17.
Yea, he shall be holden up : for God is able to make him stand ; i.e., he
shall stand, or be accepted, for God has the right and the will to make
him stand, that is, to acquit and save him. This clause seems designed
to urge a further reason for forbearance and kindness towards those who
differ from us on matters of indifference. However weak a man's faith
may be, if he is a Christian, he should be recognised and treated as such ;
for his weakness is not inconsistent with his acceptance with God, and
therefore is no ground or necessity for our proceeding against him with
severity. The objects of discipline are the reformation of offenders and
the purification of the church ; but neither of these objects requires the
condemnation of those brethren whom God has received. " God is *able*
to make him stand ;" he has not only the power, but the disposition and
determination. Compare chap. xi. 23, " For God is able to graft them in
again." The interpretation given above, according to which *standing* and
falling are understood judicially, is the one commonly adopted. It is however objected, that justifying, causing to stand in judgment, is not an act

of power but grace. On this ground, standing and falling are taken to refer to continuing or falling away from the Christian life. God is able, notwithstanding their weakness, to cause his feeble children to persevere. But this is against the context. The thing condemned is unrighteous judgments. The brethren are not responsible to each other, or the church, or their scruples. God is the Lord of the conscience. To him they must answer. Before him they stand or fall.

VERSE 5. *One man esteemeth one day above another; another esteemeth every day* alike. Κρίνει ἡμέραν παρ ἡμέραν (εἶναι), *judges one day* (to be) *before another,* (i.e., better,) κρίνει πᾶσαν ἡμέραν (εἶναι ἡμέραν) *to be a day,* and nothing more. He has the same judgment (or estimation) of every day. As the law of Moses not only made a distinction between meats as clean and unclean, but also prescribed the observance of certain days as religious festivals, the Jewish converts were as scrupulous with regard to this latter point as the former. Some Christians, therefore, thought it incumbent on them to observe these days; others were of a contrary opinion. Both were to be tolerated. The veneration of these days was a weakness; but still it was not a vital matter, and therefore should not be allowed to disturb the harmony of Christian intercourse, or the peace of the church. It is obvious from the context, and from such parallel passages as Gal. iv. 10, " Ye observe days, and months, and times, and years," and Col. ii. 16, " Let no man judge you in meat, or in drink, or in respect of a holy day, or of the new moon, or of Sabbath-days," that Paul has reference to the Jewish festivals, and therefore his language cannot properly be applied to the Christian Sabbath. The sentiment of the passage is this, ' One man observes the Jewish festivals, another man does not.' Such we know was the fact in the apostolic church, even among those who agreed in the observance of the first day of the week.

Let every man be fully persuaded in his own mind. The principle which the apostle enforces in reference to this case, is the same as that which he enjoined in relation to the other, viz., that one man should not be forced to act according to another man's conscience, but every one should be satisfied in his own mind, and be careful not to do what he thought wrong.

VERSE 6. *He that regardeth the day, regardeth it unto the Lord ; and he that regardeth not the day, to the Lord he doth not regard it. He that eateth, eateth to the Lord,* &c. That is, both parties are actuated by religious motives in what they do; they regulate their conduct by a regard to the will of God, and therefore, although some, from weakness or ignorance, may err as to the rule of duty, they are not to be despised or cast out as evil. The strong should not contemn the scrupulous, nor the scrupulous be censorious towards the strong. This is a fourth argument in favour of the mutual forbearance enjoined in the first verse. *He that eateth, eateth to the Lord; for he giveth God thanks,* &c. That is, he who disregards the Mosaic distinction between clean and unclean meats, and uses indiscriminately the common articles of food, acts religiously in so doing, as is evident from his giving God thanks. He could not deliberately thank God for what he supposed God had forbidden him to use. In like manner, he that abstains from certain meats, does it religiously, for he also giveth thanks to God; which implies that he regards himself as acting agreeably to the divine will. *The Lord* is he who died and rose again, that he might be Lord both of the living and the dead. It is to him the believer is responsible, as to the Lord of his inner life.

VERSE 7. *For none of us liveth to himself, and no man dieth to himself;*

ἑαυτῷ, *in dependence on himself.* This verse is an amplification and confirmation of the preceding. The principle on which both the classes of persons just referred to acted, is a true Christian principle. No Christian considers himself as his own master, or at liberty to regulate his conduct according to his own will, or for his own ends ; he is the servant of Christ, and therefore endeavours to live according to his will and for his glory. They, therefore, who act on this principle, are to be regarded and treated as true Christians, although they may differ as to what the will of God, in particular cases, requires. *No man dieth to himself, i.e.*, death as well as life must be left in the hands of God, to be directed by his will and for his glory. The sentiment is, 'We are entirely his, having no authority over our life or death.'

VERSE 8. *For whether we live, we live unto the Lord ; or whether we die, we die unto the Lord ; whether we live, therefore, or die, we are the Lord's.* The same sentiment as in the preceding verse, rather more fully and explicitly stated. In ver. 7, Paul had stated, negatively, that the Christian does not live according to his own will, or for his own pleasure ; he here states affirmatively, that he does live according to the will of Christ, and for his glory. This being the case, he is a true Christian ; he belongs to Christ, and should be so recognised and treated. It is very obvious, especially from the following verse, which speaks of death and resurrection, that Christ is intended in the word *Lord*, in this verse. It is for Christ, and in subjection to his will, that every Christian endeavours to regulate his heart, his conscience, and his life. This is the profoundest homage the creature can render to his Creator ; and as it is the service which the Scriptures require us to render to the Redeemer, it of necessity supposes that Christ is God. This is rendered still plainer by the interchange, throughout the passage (vers. 6—9), of the terms Lord and God : ' He that eateth, eateth to the Lord, for he giveth God thanks. We live unto the Lord ; we are the Lord's. For to this end Christ died and rose, that he might be the Lord,' &c. It is clear that, to the apostle's mind, the idea that Christ is God was perfectly familiar. *Whether we live, therefore, or die, we are the Lord's.* We are not our own, but Christ's, 1 Cor. vi. 19. This right of possession, and the consequent duty of devotion and obedience, are not founded on creation, but on redemption. We are Christ's, because he has bought us with a price.

VERSE 9. *For to this end Christ both died, and rose, and revived,** *that he might be the Lord both of the dead and living.* The dominion which Christ, as Mediator or Redeemer, exercises over his people, and which they gladly recognize, is therefore referred to his death and resurrection. By his death he purchased them for his own, and by his resurrection he attained to that exalted station which he now occupies as Lord over all, and received those gifts which enable him to exercise as Mediator this universal dominion. The exaltation and dominion of Christ are frequently represented in the Scriptures, as the reward of his sufferings : " Wherefore

---

* The common text reads καὶ ἀπέθανε καὶ ἀνέστη καὶ ἀνέζησεν ; most corrected editions read καὶ ἀπέθανε καὶ ἔζησεν ; and some omit καὶ before ἀπέθανε. The words καὶ ἀνέστη are omitted in the MSS. A. C., in the Coptic, Ethiopic, Syriac, and Armenian versions, and by many of the Fathers. They are rejected by Erasmus, Bengel, Schmidt, Knapp, Lachmann, and others. The words καὶ ἀνέζησεν are omitted by some few MSS. and Fathers ; καὶ ἔζησεν are read in MSS. A. C. and in forty-four others. They are adopted in the Complutensian edition, and in those of Mill, Bengel, Wetstein, Griesbach, Knapp, Lachmann, &c. These diversities do not materially affect the sense. The words ἀνέστη and ἀνέζησεν have very much the appearance of explanatory glosses.

God also hath highly exalted him, and given him a name which is above every name ; that at the name of Jesus every knee should bow," &c.. Phil. ii. 8, 9. This authority of Christ over his people is not confined to this world, but extends beyond the grave. He is Lord both of the dead and the living.

VERSE 10. *But why dost thou judge thy brother ? or why dost thou set at naught thy brother ? for we shall all stand before the judgment-seat of Christ.** In this and the following verses to the 13th, Paul applies his previous reasoning to the case in hand. If a man is our *brother*, if God has received him, if he acts from a sincere desire to do the divine will, he should not be condemned, though he may think certain things right which we think wrong ; nor should he be despised if he trammels his conscience with unnecessary scruples. The former of these clauses relates to scrupulous Jewish Christians ; the latter to the Gentile converts. The last member of the verse applies to both classes. As we are all to stand before the judgment-seat of Christ, as he is our sole and final judge, we should not usurp his prerogative, or presume to condemn those whom he has received.

VERSE 11. *For it is written, As I live, saith the Lord, every knee shall bow to me, and every tongue shall confess.* This quotation is from Isa. xlv. 23, " I have sworn by myself, the word is gone out of my mouth in righteousness, and shall not return, that unto me every knee shall bow, and every tongue shall swear." The apostle, it will be perceived, does not adhere to the words of the passage which he quotes, but contents himself with giving the sense. *As I live*, being the form of an oath, is a correct exhibition of the meaning of the phrase, *I have sworn by myself.* And since to swear by any being, is to recognise his power and authority over us, the expressions, *every tongue shall swear*, and *every tongue shall confess*, are of similar import. Both indeed are parallel to the clause, *every knee shall bow*, and are but different forms of expressing the general idea that every one shall submit to God, *i. e.*, recognise his authority as God, the supreme ruler and judge. The apostle evidently considers the recognition of the authority of Christ as being tantamount to submission to God, and he applies without hesitation the declarations of the Old Testament in relation to the universal dominion of Jehovah, in proof of the Redeemer's sovereignty. In Paul's estimation, therefore, Jesus Christ was God. This is so obvious, that commentators of all classes recognise the force of the argument hence deduced for the divinity of Christ. Luther says : " So muss Christus rechter Gott sein, weil solches vor seinem Richterstuhl geschehen." Calvin : " Est etiam insignis locus ad stabiliendam fidem nostram de æterna Christi divinitate." Bengel : " Christus est Deus, nam dicitur Dominus et Deus. Ipse est, cui vivimus et morimur. Ipse jurat per se ipsum." Even Koppe says, " Quae Jes. xlv. 23, de Jehova dicuntur, eadem ad Christum transferri ab apostolo, non est mirandum, cum hunc illi artissime conjunctum cogitandum esse, perpetua sit tum Judæorum, quotiescunque de Messia loquuntur, tum imprimis Pauli et Joanis sententia." This verse may be considered as intended to confirm the truth of the declaration at the close of the one preceding : ' We shall all stand before the judgment-seat of Christ ; for it is

---

* Instead of χριστοῦ, at the close of this verse, the MSS. A. D. E. F. G. read ϑεοῦ, which is adopted by Mill, Lachmann, and Tischendorf. The common reading is supported by the great majority of the MSS., most of the ancient versions, and almost all the Fathers. It is therefore retained by most critical editors.

written, To me every knee shall bow.' And this seems the natural relation of the passage. Calvin understands this verse, however, as designed
to enforce humble submission to the judgment of Christ : ' We should not
judge others, since we are to be judged by Christ ; and to his judgment we
must humbly bow the knee.' This is indeed clearly implied ; but it is
rather an accessory idea, than the special design of the passage.

VERSE 12. *So then every one of us shall give account of himself to God.*
' As, therefore, God is the supreme judge, and we are to render our account
to him, we should await his decision, and not presume to act the part of
judge over our brethren.'

VERSE 13. *Let us not therefore judge one another any more ; but judge*
this rather, that no man put a stumbling-block or an occasion to fall in his
brother's way. After drawing the conclusion from the preceding discussion, that we should leave the office of judging in the hands of God, the
apostle introduces the second leading topic of the chapter, viz., the manner
in which Christian liberty is to be exercised. He teaches that it is not
enough that we are persuaded a certain course is, in itself considered, right,
in order to authorize us to pursue it. We must be careful that we do not
injure others in the use of our liberty. The word (κρίνω) rendered *judge,*
means also, *to determine, to make up one's mind.* Paul uses it first in the
one sense, and then in the other : ' Do not judge one another, but determine to avoid giving offence.' The words (πρόσκομμα and σκάνδαλον) rendered a *stumbling-block* and *an occasion to fall,* do not differ in their meaning ; the latter is simply exegetical of the former.

VERSE 14. *I know, and am persuaded by the Lord Jesus, that* there is
nothing unclean of itself ; but to him that esteemeth anything to be un-
clean, to him it is unclean. 'The distinction between clean and unclean
meats is no longer valid. So far the Gentile converts are right. But they
should remember that those who consider the law of the Old Testament
on this subject as still binding, cannot, with a good conscience, disregard
it. The strong should not, therefore, do anything which would be likely
to lead such persons to violate their own sense of duty.' *I know and am*
persuaded by (in) *the Lord Jesus, i.e.,* this knowledge and persuasion I owe
to the Lord Jesus ; it is not an opinion founded on my own reasonings,
but a knowledge derived from divine revelation. *That there is nothing*
unclean of itself. The word (κοινός) rendered *unclean,* has this sense only
in Hellenistic Greek. It means *common,* and as opposed to (ἅγιος) *holy,*
(*i. e.,* separated for some special or sacred use), it signifies *impure* ; see Acts
x. 14, 28 ; Mark vii. 2, &c. *But to him that esteemeth anything to be*
unclean, to him it is unclean ; i. e., though not unclean in itself, it ought not
to be used by those who regard its use as unlawful. *But,* εἰ μή, which seems
here to be used in the sense of ἀλλά ; compare Matt. xii. 4 ; Gal. i. 19.
The ordinary sense of *except* may, however, be retained, by restricting the
reference to a part of the preceding clause : ' Nothing is unclean, *except*
to him who esteems it to be unclean.' The simple principle here taught is,
that it is wrong for any man to violate his own sense of duty. This being
the case, those Jewish converts who believed the distinction between clean
and unclean meats to be still in force, would commit sin in disregarding it ;
and, therefore, should not be induced to act contrary to their consciences.

VERSE 15. *But if thy brother be grieved with* thy *meat, now walkest thou*
not charitably. Destroy not him *with* thy *meat, for whom Christ died.*
Instead of δέ, *but,* which is found in the common text, Griesbach,
Lachmann, and Tischendorf, on the authority of the majority of the

Uncial MSS., read γάρ, *for*. As this verse, however, does not assign a reason for the principle asserted in ver. 14, but does introduce a limitation to the practical application of that principle, the majority of commentators and editors retain the common text. The sense obviously is, ' Though the thing is right in itself, yet if indulgence in it be injurious to our Christian brethren, that indulgence is a violation of the law of love.' This is the first consideration which the apostle urges, to enforce the exhortation not to put a stumbling-block in our brother's way. The word (λυπεῖται,) *is grieved*, may mean *is injured*. Either sense suits the context: ' If thy brother, emboldened by thy example, is led to do what he thinks wrong, and is thus rendered miserable,' &c. Or, ' If thy brother, by thy example, is injured (by being led into sin), thou walkest uncharitably.' This use of the word, however, is foreign to the New Testament. It is a moral grievance of which the apostle speaks, a wounding of the conscience. *Destroy not (μὴ ἀπόλλυε.)* These words have been variously explained. The meaning may be, ' Avoid every thing which has a tendency to lead him to destruction.' So De Brais, Bengel, Tholuck, Stuart, and many others. Or, ' Do not injure him, or render him miserable.' So Elsner, Koppe, Flatt, Wahl, and others. There is no material difference between these two interpretations. The former is more consistent with the common meaning of the original word, from which there is no necessity to depart. Believers (the elect) are constantly spoken of as in danger of perdition. They are saved only, if they continue steadfast unto the end. If they apostatize, they perish. If the Scriptures tell the people of God what is the tendency of their sins, as to themselves, they may tell them what is the tendency of such sins as to others. Saints are preserved, not in despite of apostacy, but from apostacy. ' If thy brother be aggrieved, thou doest wrong ; do not grieve or injure him.' *For whom Christ died.* This consideration has peculiar force. ' If Christ so loved him as to die for him, how base in you not to submit to the smallest self-denial for his welfare.'

VERSE 16. *Let not your good be evil spoken of;* that is, ' Do not so use your liberty, which is good and valuable, as to make it the occasion of evil, and so liable to censure.' Thus Calvin and most other commentators. This supposes that the exhortation here given is addressed to the strong in faith. The ὑμῶν, however, may include both classes, and the exhortation extend to the weak as well as to the good. *Your good*, that special good which belongs to you as Christians, viz., the gospel. This view is taken by Melancthon, and most of the later commentators. "Lædunt utrique evangelium cum rixantur de rebus non necessariis. Ita fit ut imperiti abhorreant ab evangelio cum videtur parere discordias."

VERSE 17. *For the kingdom of God is not meat and drink ; but righteousness, and peace, and joy in the Holy Ghost.* This is a new reason for forbearance. No principle of duty is sacrificed ; nothing essential to religion is disregarded, for religion does not consist in external observances, but in the inward graces of the Spirit. It has already been remarked (ver. 4), that with all his desire of peace, no one was more firm and unyielding, when any dereliction of Christian principle was required of him, than the apostle. But the case under consideration is very different. There is no sin in abstaining from certain meats, and therefore, if the good of others require this abstinence, we are bound to exercise it. The phrase, *kingdom of God*, almost uniformly signifies the *kingdom of the Messiah*, under some one of its aspects, as consisting of all professing Christians, of all his own people, of glorified believers, or as existing in the heart. It is the spiritual theocracy. The theocracy of the Old Testament was ceremonial and ritual ; that of the New is inward and spiritual. Christianity, as we should say, does not consist in things external. *Meat and drink,* or rather, *eating* (βρῶσις) and *drinking* (πόσις.) The distinction between these words and βρῶμα and πόμα, is constantly observed in Paul's epistles. *Righteousness, peace, and joy in the Holy Ghost.* These words are to be taken in their scriptural sense. Paul does not mean to say, that Christianity consists in morality ; that the man who is just, peaceful, and cheerful, is a true Christian. This would be to contradict the whole argument of this epistle. The righteousness, peace, and joy intended, are those of which the Holy Spirit is the author. Righteousness is that which enables us to stand before God, because it satisfies the demands of the law. It is the righteousness of faith, both objective and subjective ; peace is the concord between God and the soul, between reason and conscience, between the heart and our fellow-men. And the joy is the joy of salvation ; that joy which only those who are in the fellowship of the Holy Ghost ever can experience.

VERSE 18. *For he that in these things serveth Christ, is acceptable to God and approved of men.* This verse is a confirmation of the preceding. These spiritual graces constitute the essential part of religion ; for he that experiences and exercises these virtues, is regarded by God as a true Christian, and must commend himself as such to the consciences of his fellow-men. Where these things, therefore, are found, difference of opinion or practice in reference to unessential points, should not be allowed to disturb the harmony of Christian intercourse. It is to be observed, that the exercise of the virtues here spoken of, is represented by the apostle as a service rendered to Christ ; "he that in these things serveth Christ," &c. which implies that Christ has authority over the heart and conscience. Instead of ἐν τούτοις, many of the oldest MSS. read ἐν τούτῳ, referring to πνεύματι : 'He that in the Holy Spirit serveth Christ.' This reading is adopted by Lachmann, Tischendorf, and many others. The external authorities, however, in favour of the common text, are of much weight, and the context seems to demand it.

VERSE 19. *Let us therefore follow after the things which make for peace, and things whereby one may edify another.* That is, let us earnestly endeavour to promote peace and mutual edification. *The things which make for peace,* is equivalent to peace itself (τὰ τῆς εἰρήνης=εἰρήνην ; and *things wherewith one may edify another,* is mutual edification (τὰ τῆς οἰκοδομῆς=οἰκοδομήν. This verse is not an inference from the immediately preceding, as though the meaning were, 'Since peace is so acceptable to God, therefore let us cultivate it ;' but rather from the whole passage : 'Since Christian love, the example of Christ, the comparative insignificance of the matters in dispute, the honour of the truth, the nature of real religion, all conspire to urge us to mutual forbearance, let us endeavour to promote peace and mutual edification.'

VERSE 20. *For meat destroy not the work of God.* This clause is, by De Brais and many other commentators, considered as a repetition of ver. 15. "Destroy not him with thy meat, for whom Christ died." *The work of God* then means a Christian brother ; see Eph. ii. 10. Others refer the passage to the immediately preceding verses, in which the nature of true religion is exhibited. *The work of God,* in that case, is *piety,* and the exhortation is, ' Do not, for the sake of indulgence in certain kinds of food, injure the cause of true religion, *i. e.,* pull not down what God is building up.' The figurative expression used by the apostle μὴ κατάλυε, *pull not down,* carries out the figure involved in the preceding verse. Believers are to be *edified, i. e.,* built up. They are the building of God, which is not to be dilapidated or injured by our want of love, or consideration for the weakness of our brethren.

All things (*i.e.,* all kinds of food) *are pure; but it is evil* (κακόν, not merely *hurtful,* but sin, evil in a moral sense) *for that man that eateth with offence.* This last clause admits of two interpretations. It may mean, It is sinful to eat in such a way as to cause others to offend. The sin intended is that of one strong in faith who so uses his liberty as to injure his weaker brethren. This is the view commonly taken of the passage, and it agrees with the general drift of the context, and especially with the following verse, where causing a brother to stumble is the sin against which we are cautioned. A comparison, however, of this verse with ver. 14, where much the same sentiment is expressed, leads many interpreters to a different view of the passage. In ver. 14 it is said, 'Nothing is common of itself, but to him that esteemeth any thing to be unclean, to him it is unclean;' and here, 'All things are pure, but it is evil to him who eateth with offence.' To eat with offence, and, to eat what we esteem impure, are synonymous expressions. If this is so, then the sin referred to is that which the weak commit, who act against their own conscience. But throughout the whole context, to offend, to cause to stumble, offence, are used, not of a man's causing himself to offend his own conscience, but of one man's so acting as to cause others to stumble. And as this idea is insisted upon in the following verse, the common interpretation is to be preferred.

Verse 21. It is *good neither to eat flesh, nor to drink wine, nor any thing whereby thy brother stumbleth, or is offended, or is made weak.* That is, abstaining from flesh, wine, or any thing else which is injurious to our brethren, is right, *i.e.,* morally obligatory ; (καλόν, *id quod rectum et probum est.*) The words *stumbleth, offended, made weak,* do not, in this connection, differ much from each other. Calvin supposes they differ in force, the first being stronger than the second, and the second than the third. The sense then is, ' We should abstain from every thing whereby our brother is cast down, or even offended, or in the slightest degree injured.' This, however, is urging the terms beyond their natural import. It is very common with the apostle to use several nearly synonymous words for the sake of expressing one idea strongly. The last two words (ἢ σκανδαλίζεται ἢ ἀσθενεῖ) are indeed omitted in some few manuscripts and versions, but in too few seriously to impair their authority. Mill is almost the only editor of standing who rejects them.

There is an ellipsis in the middle clause of this verse which has been variously supplied. ' Nor to drink wine, nor to (drink) any thing ;' others, ' nor to (do) any thing whereby,' &c. According to the first method of supplying the ellipsis, the meaning is, ' We should not drink wine nor any other intoxicating drink, when our doing so is injurious to others.' But the latter method is more natural and forcible, and includes the other, ' We should do nothing which injures others.' The ground on which some of the early Christians thought it incumbent on them to abstain from wine, was not any general ascetic principle, but because they feared they might be led to use wine which had been offered to the gods ; to which they had the same objection as to meat which had been presented in sacrifice. "*Augustinus* de moribus Manichaeorum, II. 14, Eo tempore, quo haec scribebat apostolus, multa immoliticia caro in macello vendebatur. Et quia vino etiam libabatur Diis gentilium, multi fratres infirmiores, qui etiam rebus his venalibus utebantur, penitus a carnibus se et vino cohibere maluerunt, quam vel nescientes incidere in eam, quam putabant, cum idolis communicationem." *Wetstein.*

VERSE 22. *Hast thou faith ? have it to thyself before God. Happy is he that condemneth not himself in that which he alloweth.* Paul presents in this verse, more distinctly than he had before done, the idea that he required no concession of principle or renunciation of truth. He did not wish them to believe a thing to be sinful which was not sinful, or to trammel their own consciences with the scruples of their weaker brethren. He simply required them to use their liberty in a considerate and charitable manner. He, therefore, here says, 'Hast thou faith ? (*i.e.*, a firm persuasion, *e.g.*, of the lawfulness of all kinds of meat) it is well, do not renounce it, but retain it and use it piously, as in the sight of God.' Instead of reading the first clause interrogatively, *Hast thou faith ?* it may be read, *Thou hast faith.* It is then presented in the form of an objection, which a Gentile convert might be disposed to make to the direction of the apostle to accommodate his conduct to the scruples of others. ' Thou hast faith, thou mayest say ; well, have it, I do not call upon thee to renounce it.' By *faith* here seems clearly to be understood *the faith* of which Paul had been speaking in the context ; a faith which some Christians had, and others had not, viz., a firm belief "that there is nothing (no meat) unclean of itself." *Have it to thyself,* (χατὰ σεαυτὸν ἔχε,) keep it to yourself. There are two ideas included in this phrase. The first is, keep it privately, *i.e.*, do not parade it, or make it a point to show that you are above the weak scruples of your brethren ; and the second is, that this faith or firm conviction is not to be renounced, but retained, for it is founded on the truth. *Before God, i.e.*, in the sight of God. As God sees and recognises it, it need not be exhibited before men. It is to be cherished in our hearts, and used in a manner acceptable to God. Being right in itself, it is to be piously, and not ostentatiously or injuriously paraded and employed.

Blessed is he that condemneth not himself in that which he alloweth. That is, blessed is the man that has a good conscience ; who does not allow himself to do what he secretly condemns. The faith, therefore, of which the apostle had spoken, is a great blessing. It is a source of great happiness to be sure that what we do is right, and, therefore, the firm conviction to which some Christians had attained, was not to be undervalued or renounced. Compare chap. i. 28, 1 Cor. xvi. 3, for a similar use of the word (δοχιμάζω) here employed. This interpretation seems better suited to the context, and to the force of the words, than another which is also frequently given, ' Blessed is the man who does not condemn himself, *i.e.*, give occasion to others to censure him for the use which he makes of his liberty.' This gives indeed a good sense, but it does not adhere so closely to the meaning of the text, nor does it so well agree with what follows.

VERSE 23. *But he that doubteth is damned if he eat, because* he eateth *not of faith ; for whatsoever is not of faith is sin.* That is, however sure a man may be that what he does is right, he cannot expect others to act on his faith. If a man thinks a thing to be wrong, to him it is wrong. He, therefore, who is uncertain whether God has commanded him to abstain from certain meats, and who notwithstanding indulges in them, evidently sins ; he brings himself under condemnation. Because whatever is not of faith is sin ; *i.e.*, whatever we do which we are not certain is right, to us is wrong. The sentiment of this verse, therefore, is nearly the same as of ver. 14. " To him that esteemeth any thing to be unclean, to him it is unclean." There is evidently a sinful disregard of the divine authority on the part of a man who does anything which he supposes God has forbidden, or which he is not certain he has allowed. The principle of morals contained in this verse is so obvious, that it occurs frequently in the writings of ancient philosophers. Cicero de Officiis, lib. 1, c. 9. Quodcirca bene praecipiunt, qui vetant quidquam agere, quod dubites aequum sit, an iniquum. Aequitas enim lucet ipsa per se : dubitatio cogitationem significat injuriae. This passage has an obvious bearing on the design of the apostle. He wished to convince the stronger Christians that it was unreasonable in them to expect their weaker brethren to act according to their faith ; and that it was sinful in them so to use their liberty as to induce these scrupulous Christians to violate their own consciences.*

DOCTRINE.

1. The fellowship of the saints is not to be broken for unessential matters ; in other words, we have no right to make any thing a condition of Christian communion which is compatible with piety. Paul evidently argues on the principle that if a man is a true Christian, he should be recognised and treated as such. If God has received him, we should receive him, vers. 1—12.

2. The true criterion of a Christian character is found in the governing purpose of the life. He that lives unto the Lord, *i.e.*, he who makes the will of Christ the rule of his conduct, and the glory of Christ his constant object, is a true Christian, although from weakness or ignorance he may sometimes mistake the rule of duty, and consider certain things obligatory which Christ has never commanded, vers. 6—8.

3. Jesus Christ must be truly God, 1. Because he is the Lord, according to whose will and for whose glory we are to live, vers. 6—8. 2. Because he exercises an universal dominion over the living and the dead, ver. 9. 3. Because he is the final judge of all men, ver. 10. 4. Because passages

---

* The three verses which, in the common text, occur at the close of chapter xvi., are found at the close of this chapter in the MSS. A, and in all those written in small letters on Wetstein's catalogue, from 1 to 55, except 13, 15, 16, 25, 27, 28, 50, 53, (two of these, 27, 53, do not contain this epistle, and 25, 28, are here defective.) To these are to be added many others examined by later editors, making one hundred and seven MSS. in which the passage occurs at the close of this chapter. Of the versions, only the later Syriac, Sclavonic, and Arabic, assign it this position ; with which, however, most of the Greek fathers coincide. Beza, (in his 1st and 2d editions,) Grotius, Mill, Hammond, Wetstein, Griesbach, consider the passage to belong to this chapter.

On the other hand, the MSS. C, D, E, and several of the *codd. minusc.*, the early Syriac, Coptic, Ethiopic, and Vulgate versions, and the Latin fathers, place the contested verses at the close of chapter xvi. This location is adopted in the Complutensian edition, by Erasmus, Stephens, Beza, (in his 3d, 4th, and 5th editions,) Bengel, Koppe, Knapp, Lachmann, and others.

These verses are left out in both places in the MSS. F, G, 57, 67, 68, 69, 70. And are found in both places in A 17, and in the Armenian version. The weight due to the early versions in deciding such a question, is obviously very great; and as these versions all coincide with the received text and some of the oldest MSS. in placing the passage at the close of the epistle, that is most probably its proper place. The doxology which those verses contain, so evidently breaks the connection between the close of the 14th chapter and the beginning of the 15th, that it is only by assuming with Semler that the epistle properly terminates here, or with Tholuck and others that Paul, after having closed with a doxology, begins anew on the same topic, that the presence of the passage in this place can be accounted for. But both these assumptions are unauthorised, and that of Semler destitute of the least plausibility.—See Koppe's Excursus II. to this epistle.

of the Old Testament which are spoken of Jehovah, are by the apostle applied to Christ, ver. 11.   5. Because, throughout this passage, Paul speaks of God and Christ indiscriminately, in a manner which shows that he regarded Christ as God.   To live unto Christ is to live unto God ; to stand before the judgment-seat of Christ is to give an account unto-God; to submit to Christ is to bow the knee to Jehovah.

4. The gospel does not make religion to consist in external observances. "Meat commendeth us not to God ; for neither if we eat are we the better ; neither if we eat not are we the worse," vers. 6, 7.

5. Though a thing may be lawful, it is not always expedient.   The use of the liberty which every Christian enjoys under the gospel, is to be regulated by the law of love ; hence it is often morally wrong to do what, in itself considered, may be innocent, vers. 15, 20, 21.

6. It is a great error in morals, and a great practical evil, to make that sinful which is in fact innocent.   Christian love never requires this or any other sacrifice of truth.   Paul would not consent, for the sake of avoiding offence, that eating all kinds of food, even what had been offered to idols, or disregarding sacred festivals of human appointment, should be made a sin ; he strenuously and openly maintained the reverse.   He represents those who thought differently, as weak in faith, as being under an error, from which more knowledge and more piety would free them.   Concession to their weakness he enjoins on a principle perfectly consistent with the assertion of the truth, and with the preservation of Christian liberty, vers. 13—23.

7. Whatsoever is not of faith is sin.   It is wrong to do anything which we think to be wrong.   The converse of this proposition, however, is not true.   It is not always right to do what we think to be right.   Paul, before his conversion, thought it right to persecute Christians; the Jews thought they did God service when they cast the disciples of the Saviour out of the synagogue.   The cases, therefore, are not parallel.   When we do what we think God has forbidden, we are evidently guilty of disobedience or contempt of the divine authority.   But when we do what we think he has required, we may act under a culpable mistake ; or, although we may have the judgment that the act in itself is right, our motives for doing it may be very wicked.   The state of mind under which Paul and other Jews persecuted the early Christians, was evil, though the persecution itself they regarded as a duty.   It is impossible that a man should have right motives for doing a wrong action ; for the very mistake as to what is right, vitiates the motives.   The mistake implies a wrong state of mind ; and, on the other hand, the misapprehension of truth produces a wrong state of mind.   There may, therefore, be a very sinful zeal for God and religion (see Rom. x. 2); and no man will be able to plead at the bar of judgment, his good intention as an excuse for evil conduct, ver. 23.

REMARKS.

1. Christians should not allow anything to alienate them from their brethren, who afford credible evidence that they are the servants of God. Owing to ignorance, early prejudice, weakness of faith, and other causes, there may and must exist a diversity of opinion and practice on minor points of duty.   But this diversity is no sufficient reason for rejecting from Christian fellowship any member of the family of Christ.   It is, however, one thing to recognise a man as a Christian, and another to recognise him

as a suitable minister of a church, organized on a particular form of government and system of doctrines, vers. 1—12.

2. A denunciatory or censorious spirit is hostile to the spirit of the gospel. It is an encroachment on the prerogatives of the only Judge of the heart and conscience : it blinds the mind to moral distinctions, and prevents the discernment between matters unessential and those vitally important ; and it leads us to forget our own accountableness, and to overlook our own faults, in our zeal to denounce those of others, vers. 4—10.

3. It is sinful to indulge contempt for those whom we suppose to be our inferiors, vers. 3, 10.

4. Christians should remember that, living or dying, they are the Lord's. This imposes the obligation to observe his will and to seek his glory ; and it affords the assurance that the Lord will provide for all their wants. This peculiar propriety in his own people, Christ has obtained by his death and resurrection, vers. 8, 9.

5. We should stand fast in the liberty wherewith Christ has made us free, and not allow our consciences to be brought under the yoke of bondage to human opinions. There is a strong tendency in men to treat, as matters of conscience, things which God has never enjoined. Wherever this disposition has been indulged or submitted to, it has resulted in bringing one class of men under the most degrading bondage to another; and in the still more serious evil of leading them to disregard the authority of God. Multitudes who would be shocked at the thought of eating meat on Friday, commit the greatest moral offences without the slightest compunction. It is, therefore, of great importance to keep the conscience free ; under no subjection but to truth and God. This is necessary, not only on account of its influence on our own moral feelings, but also because nothing but truth can really do good. To advocate even a good cause with bad arguments does great harm, by exciting unnecessary opposition ; by making good men, who oppose the arguments, appear to oppose the truth ; by introducing a false standard of duty ; by failing to enlist the support of an enlightened conscience, and by the necessary forfeiture of the confidence of the intelligent and well informed. The cause of benevolence, therefore, instead of being promoted, is injured by all exaggerations, erroneous statements, and false principles, on the part of its advocates, vers. 14, 22.

6. It is obviously incumbent on every man to endeavour to obtain and promote right views of duty, not only for his own sake, but for the sake of others. It is often necessary to assert our Christian liberty at the expense of incurring censure, and offending even good men, in order that right principles of duty may be preserved. Our Saviour consented to be regarded as a Sabbath-breaker, and even a "wine-bibber and friend of publicans and sinners ;" but wisdom was justified of her children. Christ did not in these cases see fit to accommodate his conduct to the rule of duty set up, and conscientiously regarded as correct by those around him. He saw that more good would arise from a practical disregard of the false opinions of the Jews, as to the manner in which the Sabbath was to be kept, and as to the degree of intercourse which was allowed with wicked men, than from concession to their prejudices. Enlightened benevolence often requires a similar course of conduct, and a similar exercise of self-denial on the part of his disciples.

7. While Christian liberty is to be maintained, and right principles of duty inculcated, every concession consistent with truth and good morals

should be made for the sake of peace and the welfare of others. It is important, however, that the duty of making such concessions should be placed on the right ground, and be urged in a right spirit, not as a thing to be demanded, but as that which the law of love requires. In this way success is more certain and more extensive, and the concomitant results are all good. It may at times be a difficult practical question, whether most good would result from compliance with the prejudices of others, or from disregarding them. But where there is a sincere desire to do right, and a willingness to sacrifice our own inclinations for the good of others, connected with prayer for divine direction, there can be little danger of serious mistake. Evil is much more likely to arise from a disregard of the opinions and the welfare of our brethren, and from a reliance on our own judgment, than from any course requiring self-denial, vers. 13, 15, 20, 21.

8. Conscience, or a sense of duty, is not the only, and perhaps not the most important principle to be appealed to in support of benevolent enterprises. It comes in aid, and gives its sanction to all other right motives, but we find the sacred writers appealing most frequently to the benevolent and pious feelings ; to the example of Christ ; to a sense of our obligations to him ; to the mutual relation of Christians, and their common connection with the Redeemer, &c., as motives to self-denial and devotedness, vers. 15, 21.

9. As the religion of the gospel consists in the inward graces of the Holy Spirit, all who have these graces should be recognised as genuine Christians ; being acceptable to God, they should be loved and cherished by his people, notwithstanding their weakness or errors, vers. 17, 18.

10. The peace and edification of the church are to be sought at all sacrifices except those of truth and duty ; and the work of God is not to be destroyed or injured for the sake of any personal or party interests, vers. 19, 20.

11. An enlightened conscience is a great blessing ; it secures the liberty of the soul from bondage to the opinions of men, and from the self-inflicted pains of a scrupulous and morbid state of moral feeling ; it promotes the right exercise of all the virtuous affections, and the right discharge of all relative duties, ver. 22.

CHAPTER XV.

CONTENTS.

This chapter consists of two parts. In the former, vers. 1—13, the apostle enforces the duty urged in the preceding chapter, by considerations derived principally from the example of Christ. In the latter part, vers. 14—33, we have the conclusion of the whole discussion, in which he speaks of his confidence in the Roman Christians, of his motives in writing to them, of his apostolical office and labours, and of his purpose to visit Rome after fulfilling his ministry for the saints at Jerusalem.

ROMANS XV. 1—13.

ANALYSIS.

The first verse of this chapter is a conclusion from the whole of the pre
ceding. On the grounds there presented, Paul repeats the command that
the strong should bear with the infirmities of the weak, and that instead
of selfishly regarding their own interests merely, they should endeavour to
promote the welfare of their brethren, vers. 1, 2. This duty he enforces
by the conduct of Christ, who has set us an example of perfect disinterestedness, as what he suffered was not for himself, ver. 3. This and
similar facts and sentiments recorded in the Scripture are intended for our
admonition, and should be applied for that purpose, ver. 4. The apostle
prays that God would bestow on them that harmony and unanimity which
he had urged them to cultivate, vers. 5, 6. He repeats the exhortation
that they should receive one another, even as Christ had received them,
ver. 7. He shows how Christ had received them, and united Jews and
Gentiles in one body, vers. 8—13.

COMMENTARY.

Verse 1. *We then that are strong ought to bear the infirmities of the*
weak, and not to please ourselves. The separation of this passage from the
preceding chapter is obviously unhappy, as there is no change in the subject. 'As the points of difference are not essential, as the law of love, the
example of Christ, and the honour of religion require concession, we that
are fully persuaded of the indifference of those things about which our
weaker brethren are so scrupulous, ought to accommodate ourselves to their
opinions, and not act with a view to our own gratification merely.' *We*
that are strong, (δυνατοί) *strong* in reference to the subject of discourse, *i.e.,*
faith, especially faith in the Christian doctrine of the lawfulness of all
kinds of food, and the abrogation of the Mosaic law. *Ought to bear i. e.,*
ought to tolerate, (βαστάζειν.) The *infirmities, τὰ ασθενήματα,* that is, the
prejudices, errors, and faults which arise from weakness of faith. Compare
1 Cor. ix. 20—22, where the apostle illustrates this command by stating
how he himself acted in relation to this subject. *And not to please our-*
selves ; we are not to do every thing which we may have a right to do, and
make our own gratification the rule by which we exercise our Christian
liberty. "Significat non oportere studium suum dirigere ad satisfactionem
sibi, quemadmodum solent, qui proprio judicio contenti alios secure negli-
gunt." *Calvin.*

Verse 2. *Let each one of us please* his *neighbour, for* his *good for edi-*
fication. The principle which is stated negatively at the close of the preceding verse, is here stated affirmatively. We are not to please ourselves,
but others ; the law of love is to regulate our conduct ; we are not simply
to ask what is right in itself, or what is agreeable, but also what is
benevolent and pleasing to our brethren. The object which we should
have in view in accommodating ourselves to others, however, is their good.
For good to edification most probably means with a view to his good
so that he may be edified. The latter words, *to edification,* are, therefore, explanatory of the former ; the good we should contemplate is their
religious improvement; which is the sense in which Paul frequently
uses the word (οἰκοδομή) *edification ;* chap. xiv. 19 ; 2 Cor. x. 8 ; Eph.
iv. 12, 29. It is not therefore, a weak compliance with the wishes

of others, to which Paul exhorts us, but to the exercise of an enlightened benevolence; to such compliances as have the design and tendency to promote the spiritual welfare of our neighbour.

VERSE. 3. *For even Christ pleased not himself, but as it is written, The reproaches of them that reproached thee fell on me.* 'For even Christ, so infinitely exalted above all Christians, was perfectly disinterested and condescending.' The example of Christ is constantly held up, not merely as a model, but a motive. The disinterestedness of Christ is here illustrated by a reference to the fact that he suffered not for himself, but for the glory of God. The sorrow which he felt was not on account of his own privations and injuries, but zeal for God's service consumed him, and it was the dishonour which was cast on God that broke his heart. The simple point to be illustrated is the disinterestedness of Christ, the fact that he did not please himself. And this is most affectingly done by saying, in the language of the Psalmist (Ps. lxix. 9), "The zeal of thy house hath eaten me up; and the reproaches of them that reproached thee are fallen upon me;" that is, such was my zeal for thee, that the reproaches cast on thee I felt as if directed against myself. This Psalm is so frequently quoted and applied to Christ in the New Testament, that it must be considered as directly prophetical. Compare John ii. 17; xv. 25; xix. 28; Acts i. 20.*

VERSE 4. *For whatsoever things were written aforetime were written for our learning, that we, through patience and comfort of the Scriptures might have hope.* The object of this verse is not so much to show the propriety of applying the passage quoted from the Psalms to Christ, as to show that the facts recorded in the Scriptures are designed for our instruction. The character of Christ is there portrayed that we may follow his example and imbibe his spirit. The προ in προεγράφη has its proper temporal sense; before us, before our time. The reference is to the whole of the Old Testament Scriptures, and assumes, as the New Testament writers always assume or assert, that the Scriptures are the word of God, holy men of old writing as they were moved by the Holy Ghost. God had an immediate design in the Scriptures being just what they are; and that design was the sanctification and salvation of men. The words, *through patience and consolation of the Scriptures,* may be taken together, and mean, 'through that patience and consolation which the Scriptures produce;' or the words *through patience* may be disconnected from the word *Scriptures,* and the sense be, 'that we through patience, and *through* the consolation of the Scriptures,' &c. The former method is the most commonly adopted, and is the most natural.* *Might have hope.* This may mean, that the design of the divine instructions is to prevent all despondency, to sustain us under our present trials; or the sense is, that they are intended to secure the attainment of the great object of our hopes, the blessedness of heaven.

---

* Quod si regnet in nobis Christus, ut in fidelibus suis regnare eum necesse est, hic quoque sensus in animis nostris vigebit, ut quicquid derogat Dei gloriæ non aliter nos excruciet, quam si in nobis resideret. Eant nunc, quibus summa votorum est, maximos honores apud eos adipisci qui probris omnibus Dei nomen afficiunt, Christum pedibus conculcant, evangelium ipsius et contumeliose lacerant, et gladio flammaque persequuntur. Non est sane tutum ab iis tantopere honorari, a quibus non modo contemnitur Christus, sed contumeliose etiam tractatur.—*Calvin.*

* The MSS. A. C. 1, 29, 30, 34, 36, 38, 39, 41, 43, 47, read διά before τῆς παρακλήσεως which would render the second mode of explaining the passage stated in the text the more probable. The Complutensian edition, Bengel, and Lachmann, adopt this reading, though the preponderance of evidence is greatly against it.

Either interpretation of the word *hope* is consistent with usage, and gives a good sense. The former is more natural.

Verse 5. *Now the God of patience and consolation grant you to be like minded one towards another, according to Jesus Christ.* 'May God, who is the author of patience and consolation, grant,' &c. Here the *graces*, which in the preceding verse are ascribed to the Scriptures, are attributed to God as their author, because he produces them by his Spirit, through the instrumentality of the truth. *The patience,* ὑπομονή, of which the apostle speaks, is the calm and steadfast endurance of suffering, of which the *consolation,* παράκλησις, afforded by the Scriptures, is the source. This resignation of the Christian is very different from stoicism, as Calvin beautifully remarks : — "Patientia fidelium non est illa durities, quam præcipiunt philosophi : sed ea mansuetudo, qua nos libenter Deo subjicimus, dum gustus bonitatis ejus paternique amoris dulcia omnia nobis reddit. Ea spem in nobis alit ac sustinet, ne deficiat." Luther says :— "Scriptura quidem docet, sed gratia donat, quod illa docet." External teaching is not enough ; we need the inward teaching of the Holy Spirit to enable us to receive and conform to the truths and precepts of the word. Hence Paul prays that God would give his readers the patience, consolation, and hope which they are bound to exercise and enjoy. Paul prays that God would grant them that concord and unanimity which he had so strongly exhorted them to cherish. The expression (τὸ αὐτὸ φρονεῖν), *to be like minded,* does not here refer to unanimity of opinion, but to harmony of feeling ; see chap. viii. 5 ; xii. 3. *According to Jesus Christ, i.e.,* agreeably to the example and command of Christ ; in a Christian manner. It is, therefore, to a Christian union that he exhorts them.

Verse 6. *That ye may with one mind and with one mouth glorify God, even the Father of our Lord Jesus Christ.* This harmony and fellowship among Christians is necessary, in order that they may glorify God aright. To honour God effectually and properly, there must be no unnecessary dissensions among his people. *God, even the Father of our Lord Jesus Christ,* means either that God who is the Father of the Lord Jesus, or the God and Father of Christ. This expression occurs frequently in the New Testament ; see 2 Cor. i. 3 ; xi. 31 ; Eph. i. 3 ; 1 Pet. i. 3. Most commonly the genitive τοῦ κυρίου is assumed to belong equally to the two preceding nouns, God and Father. Many of the later commentators restrict it to the latter, and explain καί as exegetical : 'God, who is the Father of the Lord Jesus Christ.' In favour of this explanation, reference is made to such passages as 1 Cor. xv. 24 ; Eph. v. 20, and others, in which ὁ θεὸς καὶ πατήρ occurs without the genitive τοῦ κυρίου κ.τ.λ.

Verse 7. *Wherefore receive ye one another, as Christ also received us,* to the glory of God. Wherefore, i.e.,* in order that with one heart they may glorify God. This cannot be done, unless they are united in the bonds of Christian fellowship. The word (προσλαμβάνεσθε *receive,* has the same sense here that it has in chap. xiv. 1 : 'Take one another to yourselves, treat one another kindly, even as Christ has kindly taken us to himself ;' προσελάβετο, *sibi sociavit.* The words, *to the glory of God,* may be connected with the first or second clause, or with both : 'Receive ye one another, that God may be glorified ;' or, 'as Christ has received us in order that God might be glorified ;' or, if referred to both clauses, the idea is, 'as

---

* For ἡμᾶς, ὑμᾶς is read in the MSS. A. C. D. (ex emendatione), E. F. G. 1, 21, 23, 29, 30, 37, 38, 39, 43, 52, 61, in both the Syriac, in the Coptic, Gothic, Latin, and Armenian versions, and in several of the Fathers. It is adopted in the Complutensian edition, and in those of Griesbach, Mill, Knapp, Lachmann, and Tischendorf.

the glory of God was illustrated and promoted by Christ's reception of us, so also will it be exhibited by our kind treatment of each other.' The first method seems most consistent with the context, as the object of the apostle is to enforce the duty of mutual forbearance among Christians, for which he suggests two motives, the kindness of Christ towards us, and the promotion of the divine glory. If instead of " received *us*," the true reading is, " received *you*," the sense and point of the passage is materially altered. Paul must then be considered as exhorting the Gentile converts to forbearance towards their Jewish brethren, on the ground that Christ had received them, though aliens, into the commonwealth of Israel.

VERSE 8. *Now I say that Jesus Christ was a minister of the circumcision for the truth of God, to confirm the promises* made *unto the fathers.* This verse follows as a confirmation or illustration of the preceding. *Now I say, i.e.,* this I mean. The apostle intends to show how it was that Christ had *received* those to whom he wrote. He had come to minister to the Jews, ver. 8, and also to cause the Gentiles to glorify God, ver. 9. The expression, *minister* or *servant, of the circumcision,* means *a minister sent to the Jews,* as 'apostle of the Gentiles,' means ' an apostle sent to the Gentiles.' *For the truth of God, i.e.,* to maintain the truth of God in the accomplishment of the promises made to the fathers, as is immediately added. The truth of God is his veracity or fidelity. Christ had exhibited the greatest condescension and kindness in coming, not as a Lord or ruler, but as an humble minister to the Jews, to accomplish the gracious promises of God. As this kindness was not confined to them, but as the Gentiles also were received into his kingdom, and united with the Jews on equal terms, this example of Christ furnishes the strongest motives for the cultivation of mutual affection and unanimity.

VERSE 9. *And that the Gentiles might glorify God for his mercy.* Might glorify, δοξάσαι, *have glorified.* The effect is considered as accomplished. The apostle's language is, as usual, concise. There are two consequences of the work of Christ which he here presents ; the one, that the truth of God has been vindicated by the fulfilment of the promises made to the Jews ; and the other, that the Gentiles have been led to praise God for his mercy. The grammatical connection of this sentence with the preceding is not very clear. The most probable explanation is that which makes (δοξάσαι) *glorify* depend upon (λέγω) *I say,* in ver. 8 : ' I say that Jesus Christ became a minister to the Jews, *and I say* the Gentiles have glorified God ;' it was thus he *received* both. Calvin supplies δεῖν, and translates, " The Gentiles *ought* to glorify God for his mercy ; " which is not necessary, and does not so well suit the context. The *mercy* for which the Gentiles were to praise God, is obviously the great mercy of being received into the kingdom of Christ, and made partakers of all its blessings.

As it is written, I will confess to thee among the Gentiles, and sing unto thy name, Ps. xviii. 49. In this and the following quotations from the Old Testament, the idea is more or less distinctly expressed, that true religion was to be extended to the Gentiles ; and they therefore all include the promise of the extension of the Redeemer's kingdom to them, as well as to the Jews. In Psalm xviii. 49, David is the speaker. It is he that says : " I will praise thee among the Gentiles." He is contemplated as surrounded by Gentiles giving thanks unto God, which implies that they were the worshippers of God. Our version renders ἐξομολογήσομαι, *I will confess,* make acknowledgment to thee. The word in itself may mean, to acknowledge the truth, or sin, or God's mercies ; and therefore it is pro-

perly rendered, at times, to give thanks, or to praise, which is an acknowledgment of God's goodness.

Verse 10. *And again, Rejoice ye Gentiles with his people.* This passage
is commonly considered as quoted from Deut. xxxii. 43, where it is found
in the Septuagint precisely as it stands here. The Hebrew admits of three
interpretations, without altering the text. It may mean, ' Praise his people,
ye Gentiles ;' or, ' Rejoice, ye tribes, his people ;' or, ' Rejoice ye Gentiles,
(rejoice,) his people.' Hengstenberg on Ps. xviii. 49, adopts the last
mentioned explanation of the passage in Deuteronomy. The English version brings the Hebrew into coincidence with the LXX. by supplying *with* :
' Rejoice, ye Gentiles, *with* his people.' And this is probably the true
sense. As the sacred writer (in Deut. xxxii) is not speaking of the blessing of the Jews being extended to the Gentiles, but seems rather in the
whole context, to be denouncing vengeance on them as the enemies of
God's people, Calvin and others refer this citation to Ps. lxvii. 3, 5, where
the sentiment is clearly expressed, though not in precisely the same words.

Verse 11. *And again, Praise the Lord, all ye Gentiles ; and laud him,
all ye people.* This passage is from Ps. cxvii. 1, and strictly to the apostle's purpose.

Verse 12. *And again, Esaias saith, There shall be a root of Jesse, and
he that shall rise to rule over the Gentiles ; in him shall the Gentiles trust,*
Isa. xi. 1, 10. This is an explicit prediction of the dominion of the
Messiah over other nations besides the Jews. Here again the apostle follows the Septuagint, giving, however, the sense of the original Hebrew.
The promise of the prophet is, that from the decayed and fallen house of
David, one should arise, whose dominion should embrace all nations, and
in whom Gentiles as well as Jews should trust. In the fulfilment of this
prophecy Christ came, and preached salvation to those who were near and
to those who were far off. As both classes had been thus kindly received
by the condescending Saviour, and united into one community, they should
recognise and love each other as brethren, laying aside all censoriousness
and contempt, neither judging nor despising one another.

Verse 13. *Now then the God of hope fill you with all joy and peace in
believing, that ye may abound in hope through the power of the Holy
Ghost.* *All joy* means all possible joy. Paul here, as in ver. 5, concludes
by praying that God would grant them the excellencies which it was their
duty to possess. Thus constantly and intimately are the ideas of accountableness and dependence connected in the sacred Scriptures. We are to
work out our own salvation, because it is God that worketh in us both to
will and to do, according to his good pleasure. *The God of hope, i. e.,*
God who is the author of that hope which it was predicted men should
exercise in the root and offspring of Jesse.

Fill you with all joy and peace in believing, i. e., fill you with that joy
and concord among yourselves, as well as peace of conscience and peace
towards God, which are the results of genuine faith. *That ye may abound
in hope.* The consequence of the enjoyment of the blessings, and of the
exercise of the graces just referred to, would be an increase in the strength
and joyfulness of their hope ; *through the power of the Holy Ghost,* through
whom all good is given and all good exercised.

ROMANS XV. 14—33.

ANALYSIS.

The apostle, in the conclusion of his epistle, assures the Romans of his confidence in them, and that his motive for writing was not so much a belief of their peculiar deficiency, as the desire of putting them in mind of those things which they already knew, vers. 14, 15. This he was the rather entitled to do on account of his apostolic office, conferred upon him by divine appointment, and confirmed by the signs and wonders, and abundant success with which God had crowned his ministry, vers. 15, 16. He had sufficient ground of confidence in this respect, in the results of his own labours, without at all encroaching upon what belonged to others; for he had made it a rule not to preach where others had proclaimed the gospel, but to go to places where Christ was previously unknown, vers. 17 —21. His labours had been such as hitherto to prevent the execution of his purpose to visit Rome. Now, however, he hoped to have that pleasure, on his way to Spain, as soon as he had accomplished his mission to Jerusalem, with the contributions of the Christians in Macedonia and Achaia, for the poor saints in Judea, vers. 22—28. Having accomplished this service, he hoped to visit Rome in the fulness of the blessing of the gospel of Christ. In the meantime he begs an interest in their prayers, and commends them to the grace of God, vers. 29—33.

COMMENTARY.

Verse 14. *And I myself also am persuaded of you, my brethren, that ye also are full of goodness, filled with all knowledge, able also to admonish one another.** Paul, with his wonted modesty and mildness, apologises, as it were, for the plainness and ardour of his exhortations. They were given from no want of confidence in the Roman Christians, and they were not an unwarrantable assumption of authority on his part. The former of these ideas he presents in this verse, and the latter in the text. *I also myself,* i.e., I of myself, without the testimony of others. Paul had himself such knowledge of the leading members of the church of Rome, that he did not need to be informed by others of their true character. *That ye also are full of goodness,* i.e., of kind and conciliatory feelings; or, taking αγαθωσύνη in its wider sense, full of virtue, or excellence. *Filled with all knowledge,* i.e., abundantly instructed on these subjects, so as to be able to instruct or admonish each other. It was, therefore, no want of confidence in their disposition or ability to discharge their duties, that led him to write to them; his real motive he states in the next verse. They were able, νουθετεῖν, *to put in mind,* to bring the truth seasonably to bear on the mind and conscience. It does not refer exclusively to the correction of faults, or to reproof for transgression. " Duae monitoris praecipuae sunt dotes, humanitas quae et illius animum ad juvandos consilio suo fratres inclinet, et vultum verbaque comitate temperet : et consilii dexteritas, sive

---

* For ἀλλήλους, *each other,* ἄλλους, *others,* is read in the MSS. 1, 2, 4, 6, 10, 14, 15, 17, 18, 20, 23, 29, 32, 35, 38, 43, 46. 48, 52, 54, 62, 63 ; in the Syriac version, and by many of the Greek Fathers. The Complutensian editors, Beza, Wetstein, and Greisbach, adopt this reading.

prudentia, quae et auctoritatem illi conciliet, ut prodesse queat auditoribus ad quos dirigit sermonem.   Nihil enim magis contrarium fraternis monitionibus, quam malignitas et arrogantia, quae facit ut errantes fastuose contemnamus et ludibrio habere malimus, quam corrigere." *Calvin.*

VERSE 15. *Nevertheless, brethren, I have written the more boldly unto you in some sort, as putting you in mind. because of the grace given to me of God.*   It was rather to remind than to instruct them, that the apostle wrote thus freely.   The words (ἀπὸ μέρους) *in some sort,* are intended to qualify the words *more boldly,* ' I have written somewhat too boldly.' How striking the blandness and humility of the great apostle !   The preceding exhortations and instructions, for which he thus apologises, are full of affection and heavenly wisdom.   What a reproof is this for the arrogant and denunciatory addresses which so often are given by men who think they have Paul for an example !   These words, (*in some sort,*) however, may be connected with *I have written ;* the sense would then be, ' I have written in part (*i.e.,* in some parts of my epistle,) very boldly.'   The former method seems the more natural.   When a man acts the part of a monitor, he should not only perform the duty properly, but he should, on some ground, have a right to assume this office.   Paul therefore says, that he reminded the Romans of their duty, because he was entitled to do so in virtue of his apostolical character ; *because of the grace given to me of God.*   Grace here, as appears from the context, signifies the *apostleship* which Paul represents as a favour ; see chap. i. 5.

VERSE 16. *That I should be the minister of Jesus Christ to the Gentiles ;* λειτουργὸν εἰς τὰ ἔθνα, a minister *for,* or *in reference* to the Gentiles.   This is the explanation of the *grace* given to him of God ; it was the favour of being a minister of Jesus Christ to the Gentiles.   Compare Eph. iii. 8, " Unto me, who am less than the least of all saints, is this grace given, that I should preach among the Gentiles the unsearchable riches of Christ."   The word (λειτουργός) rendered *minister,* means a public officer or servant ; see chap. xiii. 6, where it is applied to the civil magistrate.   It is, however, very frequently used (as is also the corresponding verb) of those who exercised the office of a priest, Deut. x. 8 ; Heb. x. 11.   As the whole of this verse is figurative, Paul no doubt had this force of the word in his mind, when he called himself a *minister,* a sacred officer of Jesus Christ ; not a priest, in the proper sense of the term, for the ministers of the gospel are never so called in the New Testament, but merely in a figurative sense.   The sacrifice which they offer are the people, whom they are instrumental in bringing unto God.

Ministering the gospel of God, that the offering up of the Gentiles might be acceptable, being sanctified by the Holy Ghost.   This is the apostle's explanation of the preceding clause.   ' He was appointed a minister of Christ to administer, or to act the part of a priest in reference to the gospel, that is, to present the Gentiles as a holy sacrifice to God.'   Paul, therefore, no more calls himself a priest in the strict sense of the term, than he calls the Gentiles a sacrifice in the literal meaning of that word.   The expression, ἱερουργοῦντα τὸ εὐαγγέλιον) rendered *ministering the gospel,* is peculiar, and has been variously explained.   Erasmus translates it *sacrificans evangelium,* ' presenting the gospel as a sacrifice ;' Calvin *consecrans evangelium,* which he explains, ' performing the sacred mysteries of the gospel.' The general meaning of the phrase probably is, ' acting the part of a priest in reference to the gospel.'   Compare Macc. iv. 7, 8, ἱερουργεῖν τὸν νόμον.

The sense is the same, if the word (εὐαγγέλιον) *gospel* be made to depend on a word understood, and the whole sentence be resolved thus, 'That I should be a preacher of the gospel (εἰς τὸ εἶναί με κηρύσσοντα τὸ εὐαγγέλιον) to the Gentiles, a ministering priest (*i.e.*, a minister acting the part of a priest,) of Jesus Christ,' *Wahl's Clavis*, p. 740. Paul thus acted the part of a priest that *the offering of the Gentiles might be acceptable.* The word (προσφορά) *offering* sometimes means the act of oblation, sometimes the thing offered. Our translators have taken it here in the former sense ; but this is not so suitable to the figure or the context. It was not Paul's act that was to be acceptable, or which was ' sanctified by the Holy Spirit.' The latter sense of the word, therefore, is to be preferred ; and the meaning is, ' That the Gentiles, as a sacrifice, might be acceptable ;' see chap. xii. 1 ; Phil. ii. 17 ; 2 Tim. iv. 6. *Being sanctified by the Holy Ghost.* As the sacrifices were purified by water and other means, when prepared for the altar, so we are made fit for the service of God, rendered holy or acceptable, by the influences of the Holy Spirit. This is an idea which Paul never omits ; when speaking of the success of his labours, or of the efficacy of the gospel, he is careful that this success should not be ascribed to the instruments, but to the real author. In this beautiful passage we see the nature of the only priesthood which belongs to the Christian ministry. It is not their office to make atonement for sin, or to offer a propitiatory sacrifice to God, but by the preaching of the gospel to bring men, by the influence of the Holy Spirit, to offer themselves as a living sacrifice, holy and acceptable to God. It is well worthy of remark, that amidst the numerous designations of the ministers of the gospel in the New Testament, intended to set forth the nature of their office, they are never officially called priests. This is the only passage in which the term is even figuratively applied to them, and that under circumstances which render its misapprehension impossible. They are not mediators between God and man ; they do not offer propitiatory sacrifices. Their only priesthood, as Theophylact says, is the preaching of the gospel, (αὕτη γάρ μοι ἱερωσύνη τὸ καταγγέλλειν τὸ εὐαγγέλιον,) and their offerings are redeemed and sanctified men, saved by their instrumentality. " Et sane hoc est Christiani pastoris sacerdotium, homines in evangelii obedientiam subigendo veluti Deo immolare; non autem, quod superciliose hactenus Papistae jactarunt, oblatione Christi homines reconciliare Deo. Neque tamen ecclesiasticos pastores simpliciter hic vocat sacerdotes, tanquam perpetuo titulo ; sed quum dignitatem efficaciamque ministerii vellet commendare Paulus, hac metaphora per occasionem usus est." *Calvin.*

VERSE 17. *I have therefore whereof to glory through Jesus Christ in those things which pertain to God.* That is, ' seeing I have received this office of God, and am appointed a minister of the gospel to the Gentiles, I have (καύχησιν) confidence and rejoicing.' As, in the previous verses, Paul had asserted his divine appointment as an apostle, he shows, in this and the following verses, that the assertion was well founded, as God had crowned his labours with success, and sealed his ministry with signs and wonders. He, therefore, was entitled, as a minister of God, to exhort and admonish his brethren with the boldness and authority which he had used in this epistle. This *boasting*, however, he had only *in* or *through Jesus Christ*, all was to be attributed to him ; and it was in *reference to things pertaining to God, i.e.,* the preaching and success of the gospel, not to his personal advantages or worldly distinctions. There is another interpretation of the latter part of this verse, which also gives a good sense. ' I have therefore ground of boasting, (*i.e.,* I have) offerings for God, viz., Gentile converts.'

(The words τὰ πρὸς τὸν Θεόν are understood as synonymous with the word προσφορά of the preceding verse, προσενεχθέντα being supplied.) The common view of the passage, however, is more simple and natural.

Verses 18, 19. In these verses the apostle explains more fully what he had intended by saying he gloried, or exulted. It was that God had borne abundant testimony to his claims as a divinely commissioned preacher of the gospel ; so that he had no need to refer to what others had done ; he was satisfied to rest his claims on the results of his own labours and the testimony of God. *For I will not dare to speak of any of those things which Christ hath not wrought by me.* That is, ' I will not claim the credit due to others, or appeal to results which I have not been instrumental in effecting.' According to another view, the meaning is, ' I will not speak of any thing as the ground of boasting which Christ has not done by me.' The contrast implied, therefore, is not between what he had done and what others had accomplished, but between himself and Christ. He would not glory in the flesh, or in any thing pertaining to himself, but only in Christ, and in what he had accomplished. The conversion of the Gentiles was Christ's work, not Paul's ; and therefore Paul could glory in it without self-exaltation. It is to be remarked that the apostle represents himself as merely an instrument in the hands of Christ for the conversion of men ; the real efficiency he ascribes to the Redeemer. This passage, therefore, exhibits evidence that Paul regarded Christ as still exercising a controlling agency over the souls of men, and rendering effectual the labours of his faithful ministers. Such power the sacred writers never attribute to any being but God. *To make the Gentiles obedient, i.e.,* to the gospel ; compare chap i. 5, where the same form of expression occurs. The obedience of which Paul speaks is the sincere obedience of the heart and life. This result he says Christ effected, through his instrumentality, *by word and deed,* not merely by truth, but also by that operation which Christ employed to render the truth effectual. It was not only by the truth as presented in the word, but also by the effectual inward operation of his power, that Christ converted men to the faith.

Verse 19. *Through mighty signs and wonders, by the power of the Spirit of God, i. e.,* by miracles, and by the influences of the Holy Ghost. The Greek is, ἐν δυνάμει σημείων καὶ τεράτων, ἐν δυνάμει πνεύματος ἁγίου, that is, by the power of (*i. e.,* which comes from) signs and wonders, and, the power which flows from the Holy Spirit. It was thus Christ rendered the labours of Paul successful. He produced conviction, or the obedience of faith in the minds of the Gentiles, partly by miracles, partly and mainly by the inward working of the Holy Ghost. That Christ thus exercises divine power both in the external world, and in the hearts of men, clearly proves that he is a divine person. *Signs and wonders* are the constantly recurring words to designate those external events which are produced, not by the operation of second causes, but by the immediate efficiency of God. They are called *signs* because evidences of the exercise of God's power, and proofs of the truth of His declarations, and *wonders* because of the effect which they produce on the minds of men. This passage is, therefore, analogous to that in 1 Cor. ii. 4, " My speech and preaching was not in the enticing words of man's wisdom, but in demonstration of the Spirit and of power." That is, he relied for success not on his own skill or eloquence, but on the powerful demonstration of the Spirit. This demonstration of the Spirit consisted partly in the miracles which He enabled the first preachers of the gospel to perform, and partly

in the influence with which he attended the truth to the hearts and consciences of those that believed ; see Gal. iii. 2—5 ; Heb. ii. 4.

*So that from Jerusalem, and round about unto Illyricum, I have fully
preached the gospel of Christ. Round about,* καὶ κύκλῳ, *in a circle.*
Jerusalem was the centre around which Paul prosecuted his labours.   He
means to say, that throughout a most extensive region I have successfully
preached the gospel.   God had given his seal to Paul's apostleship, by
making him so abundantly useful.   *I have fully preached,* expresses no
doubt, the sense of the original, (πεπληρωκέναι τὸ εὐαγγέλιον) to bring the
gospel (*i. e.,* the preaching of it) to an end, to accomplish it thoroughly ;
see Col. i. 25.   In this wide circuit had the apostle preached, founding
churches, and advancing the Redeemer's kingdom with such evidence of
the divine coöperation, as to leave no ground of doubt that he was a
divinely appointed minister of Christ.

Verses 20, 21. In further confirmation of this point, Paul states that
he had not acted the part of a pastor merely, but of an apostle, or founder
of the church, disseminating the gospel where it was before unknown, so
that the evidence of his apostleship might be undeniable ; compare 1
Cor. ix. 2 ; " If I be not an apostle unto others, yet doubtless I am to you;
for the seal of my apostleship are ye in the Lord ;" and 2 Cor. iii. 2, 3,
*Yea, so have I strived to preach the gospel, not where Christ was named,
lest I should build on another man's foundation;* that is, ' I have been
desirous of not preaching where Christ was before known, but in such a
way as to accomplish the prediction that those who had not heard should
understand.' Φιλοτιμεῖσθαι, *so to prosecute an object as to place one's
honour in it.* The motive which influenced him in taking this course was
lest he should build upon another man's foundation. This may mean either
lest I should appropriate to myself the result of other men's labours ; or,
lest I should act the part not of an apostle, (to which I was called), but
of a simple pastor.

Verse 21. *But, as it is written, To whom he was not spoken of, they
shall see; and they that have not heard shall understand.* That is, I acted
in the spirit of the prediction, that Christ should be preached where He
had not been known.   It had been foretold in Isa. lii. 15, that Christ
should be preached to the Gentiles, and to those who had never heard of
His name ; it was in accordance with this prediction that Paul acted.
There is, however, no objection to considering this passage as merely an
expression, in borrowed language, of the apostle's own ideas ; the meaning
then is, ' I endeavoured to preach the gospel not where Christ was named,
but to cause those to see to whom he had not been announced, and those
to understand who had not heard.' This is in accordance with the apostle's
manner of using the language of the Old Testament ; see chap. x. 15, 18.
But as, in this case, the passage cited is clearly a prediction, the first
method of explanation should probably be preferred.   A result of this
method of interweaving passages from the Old Testament, is often, as in
this case and ver. 3, a want of grammatical coherence between the different members of the sentence; see 1 Cor. ii. 9.

Verse 22. *For which cause also I have been much hindered from coming
to you.* That is, his desire to make Christ known where he had not been
named, had long prevented his intended journey to Rome, where he knew
the gospel had already been preached. *Much,* τὰπολλά, *plerumque,* in
most cases.   The pressure of the constant calls to preach the gospel where
he then was, was the principal reason why he had deferred so long visit-

ing Rome. *Hindered from coming,* ἐνεκοπτόμην τοῦ ἐλθεῖν, the genitive
following verbs signifying *to hinder.*

VERSE 23. *But now having no more place in these parts, and having a
great desire these many years to come unto you,* &c. *Great desire* ἐπιπο-
θίαν, summum desiderium. The expression, *having no more place* (μηκέτι
τόπον ἔχων,) in this connection, would seem obviously to mean, 'having no
longer a place in these parts where Christ is not known.' This idea is
included in the declaration that he had fully preached the gospel in all
that region. Others take the word (τόπον) rendered *place,* to signify *occasion,
opportunity,* 'Having no longer an opportunity of preaching here;' see
Acts xxv. 16 ; Heb. xii. 17.

VERSE 24. *Whensoever I take my journey into Spain, I will come to
you for I trust to see you in my journey, and to be brought on my way
thitherward by you, if first I be somewhat filled with your* company.
Whensoever (ὡς ἐάν for ὡσ ἄν) *as soon as ;* 'As soon as I take my journey,'
&c. The words in the original, corresponding to *I will come unto you, for*
are omitted in many MSS.* The sense is complete without them : 'As
soon as I take my journey into Spain, I hope to see you on my way.' If
the word *for* be retained, the passage must be differently pointed : 'Having a great desire to see you, as soon as I go to Spain, (for I hope on my
way to see you, &c.) but now I go to Jerusalem.' *Spain,* the common
Greek name for the great Pyrenian Peninsula, was Ἰβηρία, although
Σπανίο was also used. The Romans called it Ἰσπανία. Whether Paul
ever accomplished his purpose of visiting Spain, is a matter of doubt.
There is no historical record of his having done so, either in the New
Testament, or in the early ecclesiastical writers ; though most of those
writers seem to have taken it for granted. His whole plan was probably
deranged by the occurrences at Jerusalem, which led to his long imprisonment at Cesarea, and his being sent in bonds to Rome. *To be brought on
my way.* The original word means, in the active voice, to attend any
one on a journey for some distance, as an expression of kindness and
respect ; and also to make provision for his journey ; see Acts xv. 3 ;
xx. 38 ; 1 Cor. xvi. 6 2 Cor. i. 16.

VERSE 25. *But now I go unto Jerusalem to minister unto the saints, i. e.,*
to supply the wants of the saints, distributing to them the contributions
of the churches ; see Heb. vi. 10 ; compare also Matt. viii. 15 ; Mark i.
31 ; Luke iv. 39. The word διακονέω is used for any kind of service. The
present participle is used to imply that the journey itself was a part of
the service Paul rendered to the saints at Jerusalem.

VERSES 26, 27. *For it hath pleased them of Macedonia and Achaia to
make a contribution for the poor saints which are at Jerusalem. To make
a contribution,* κοινωνίαν τινὰ ποιήσασθαι, to bring about a communion or
participation. That is, to cause the poor in Jerusalem to partake of the
abundance of the brethren in Achaia. In this way the ordinary intran-
sitive sense of the word κοινωνία is retained. Compare, however, 2 Cor.
ix. 13, and Heb. xiii. 16, where the transitive sense of the word is
commonly preferred. Having mentioned this fact, the apostle immediately
seizes the opportunity of showing the reasonableness and duty of making
these contributions. This he does in such a way as not to detract from

---

* The MSS. A. C. D. E. F. G. the Syriac, Coptic, Ethiopic, and Latin versions, some of
the Greek, and most of the Latin Fathers, omit ἐλεύσομαι πρὸς ὑμᾶς, and most of these
authorities omit γάρ. Mill, Griesbach, and Knapp, omit both; Lachmann retains γάρ.

the credit due to the Grecian churches, while he shows that it was but a matter of justice to act as they had done. *It hath pleased them verily; and their debtors they are;* i. e., 'It hath pleased them, *I say* (γάρ, *redordiendæ rationi inservit*) they did it voluntarily, yet it was but reasonable they should do it.' The ground of this statement is immediately added : *For if the Gentiles have been made partakers of their spiritual things, their duty is also to minister to them in carnal things.* ' If the Gentiles have received the greater good from the Jews, they may well be expected to contribute the lesser. The word (λειτουργῆσαι) rendered *to minister,* may have the general sense of *serving;* or it may be used with some allusion to the service being a sacred duty, a kind of offering which is acceptable to God. " Nec dubito, quin significet Paulus sacrificii speciem esse, quum de suo erogant fideles ad egestatem fratrum levandam. Sic enim persolvunt quod debent caritatis officium, ut Deo simul hostiam grati odoris offerant : sed proprie hoc loco ad illud mutuum jus compensationis respexit." *Calvin.* This, however, is not very probable, as the expression is λειτουργῆσαι αὐτοῖς *to minister to them.* The λειτουργία was rendered to the brethren, not to God.

VERSE 28. *When therefore I have done this, and sealed unto them this fruit, I will come by you into Spain.* The word *sealed* appears here to be used figuratively, ' When I have *safely delivered* this fruit to them ;' compare 2 Kings xxii. 4, " Go up to Hilkiah, the high priest, and sum (seal, σφράγισον,) the silver," &c. Commentators compare the use of the Latin words *consignare, consignatio,* and of the English word *consign.*

VERSE 29. *And I am sure that when I come unto you, I shall come in the fulness of the blessing of the gospel* of Christ.* The *fulness of the blessing,* means the abundant blessing. Paul was persuaded that God, who had so richly crowned his labours in other places, would cause his visit to Rome to be attended by those abundant blessings which the gospel of Christ is adapted to produce. He had, in chap. i. 11, expressed his desire to visit the Roman Christians, that he might impart unto them some spiritual gift, to the end that they might be established.

VERSE 30. *Now I beseech you, brethren, for our Lord Jesus Christ's sake, and for the love of the Spirit, that ye strive together with me in your prayers to God for me.* As the apostle was not immediately to see them, and knew that he would, in the meantime, be exposed to many dangers, he earnestly begged them to aid him with their prayers. He enforces this request by the tenderest considerations ; *for our Lord Jesus Christ's sake,* i. e., out of regard to the Lord Jesus ; ' whatever regard you have for him, and whatever desire to see his cause prosper, in which I am engaged, let it induce you to pray for me.' *And for the love of the Spirit, i.e.,* ' for that love of which the Holy Spirit is the author, and by which he binds the hearts of Christians together, I beseech you,' &c. He appeals, therefore, not only to their love of Christ, but to their love for himself as a fellow Christian. *That ye strive together with me* (συναγωνίσασθαί μοι,) *i.e.,* ' that ye aid me in my conflict, by taking part in it.' This they were to do by their prayers.

VERSE 31. *That I may be delivered from them that do not believe in Judea.* There are three objects for which he particularly wished them to

---

* The words τοῦ εὐαγγελίου τοῦ are omitted in the MSS. A. C. D. F. G. 67, in the Coptic and Ethiopic versions, and by some of the Latin Fathers. Mill, Griesbach, Lachmann, Tischendorf, and others, leave them out. The sense remains the same : " I shall come in the fulness of the blessing of Christ."

pray; his safety, the successful issue of his mission, and that he might come to them with joy. How much reason Paul had to dread the violence of the unbelieving Jews is evident from the history given of this visit to Jerusalem, in the Acts of the Apostles. They endeavoured to destroy his life, accused him to the Roman governor, and effected his imprisonment for two years in Cesarea, whence he was sent in chains to Rome. Nor were his apprehensions confined to the unbelieving Jews; he knew that even the Christians there, from their narrow-minded prejudices against him as a preacher to the Gentiles, and as the advocate of the liberty of Christians from the yoke of the Mosaic law, were greatly embittered against him. He, therefore, begs the Roman believers to pray *that the service which* (he had) *for Jerusalem* might be *accepted of the saints.* The words *service which I have, &c.,* (ἡ διακονία μου ἡ εἰς Ἱερουσαλήμ) means *the contribution which I carry to Jerusalem* ; see the use of this word (διακονία) in 2 Cor. viii. 4 ; ix. 1, 13. The ordinary sense of διακονία, *service,* however, may be retained. Paul desired that the work of love on which he was to go to Jerusalem might be favourably received by the Christians of that city. Paul laboured for those whom he knew regarded him with little favour; he calls them *saints,* recognises their Christian character, notwithstanding their unkindness, and urges his brethren to pray that they might be willing to accept of kindness at his hands.

Verse 32. *That I may come unto you with joy by the will of God, and that I may with you be refreshed.* These words may depend upon the former part of the preceding verse, 'Pray that I may come ;' or, upon the latter part, 'Pray that I may be delivered from the Jews, and my contributions be accepted, so that I may come with joy, &c.' *By the will of God, i.e.,* by the permission and favour of God. Instead of Θεοῦ, the MS. B. has Κυρίου Ἰησοῦ; D.* E. F. G. the Italic version, read Χριστοῦ Ἰησοῦ; most editors, however, retain the common text. Paul seemed to look forward to his interview with the Christians at Rome, as a season of relief from conflict and labour. In Jerusalem he was beset by unbelieving Jews, and harrassed by Judaizing Christians; in most other places he was burdened with the care of the churches; but at Rome, which he looked upon as a resting-place, rather than a field of labour, he hoped to gather strength for the prosecution of his apostolic labours in still more distant lands.

Verse 33. *Now the peace of God be with you all.* As he begged them to pray for him, so he prays for them. It is a prayer of one petition; so full of meaning, however, that no other need be added. *The peace of God,* that peace which God gives, includes all the mercies necessary for the perfect blessedness of the soul.

DOCTRINE.

1. The sacred Scriptures are designed for men in all ages of the world, and are the great source of religious knowledge and consolation, ver. 4.

2. The moral excellences which we are justly required to attain, and the consolations which we are commanded to seek in the use of appropriate means, are still the gifts of God. There is, therefore, no inconsistency between the doctrines of free agency and dependence, vers. 5, 13.

3. Those are to be received and treated as Christians whom Christ himself has received. Men have no right to make terms of communion which Christ has not made, ver. 7.

4. There is no distinction, under the gospel, between the Jew and Gen-

tile ; Christ has received both classes upon the same terms and to the same privileges, vers. 8—12.

5. The quotation of the predictions of the Old Testament by the sacred writers of the New, and the application of them in proof of their doctrines, involves an acknowledgment of the divine authority of the ancient prophets. And as these predictions are quoted from the volume which the Jews recognise as their Bible, or the word of God, it is evident that the apostles believed in the inspiration of all the books included in the sacred canon by the Jews, vers. 9—12.

6. Christian ministers are not priests, *i.e.*, they are not appointed to "offer gifts and sacrifices for sins." It is no part of their work to make atonement for the people ; this Christ has done by the one offering up of himself, whereby he has for ever perfected them that are sanctified, ver. 16. A priest, according to the Scriptures, is one appointed for men who have not liberty of access to God, to draw nigh to him in their behalf, and to offer both gifts and sacrifices for sin. In this sense Christ is our only Priest. The priesthood of believers consists in their having (through Christ) liberty of access unto God, and offering themselves and their services as a living sacrifice unto him. In one aspect, the fundamental error of the church of Rome is the doctrine that Christian ministers are priests. This assumes that sinners cannot come to God through Christ, and that it is only through the intervention of the priests men can be made partakers of the benefits of redemption. This is to put the keys of heaven into the hands of priests. It is to turn men from Christ to those who cannot save.

7. The truth of the gospel has been confirmed by God, by signs and wonders, and by the power of the Holy Ghost. Infidelity, therefore, is a disbelief of the testimony of God. When God has given satisfactory evidence of the mission of his servants, the sin of unbelief is not relieved by the denial that the evidence is satisfactory. If the gospel is true, therefore, infidelity will be found not merely to be a mistake, but a crime, ver. 19.

8. The success of a minister in winning souls to Christ may be fairly appealed to as evidence that he preaches the truth. It is, when clearly ascertained, as decisive an evidence as the performance of a miracle ; because it is as really the result of a divine agency. This, however, like all other evidence, to be of any value, must be carefully examined and faithfully applied. The success may be real, and the evidence decisive, but it may be applied improperly. The same man may preach (and doubtless every uninspired man does preach) both truth and error ; God may sanction and bless the truth, and men may appeal to this blessing in support of the error. This is often done. Success therefore is of itself a very difficult test for us to apply, and must ever be held subject to the authority of the Scriptures. Nothing can prove that to be true which the Bible pronounces to be false, vers. 18, 19.

9. Prayer (and even intercessory prayer) has a real and important efficacy ; not merely in its influence on the mind of him who offers it, but also in securing the blessings for which we pray. Paul directed the Roman Christians to pray for the exercise of the divine providence in protecting him from danger, and for the Holy Spirit to influence the minds of the brethren in Jerusalem. This he would not have done, were such petitions of no avail, vers. 30, 31.

REMARKS.

1. The duty of a disinterested and kind regard to others, in the exercise of our Christian liberty, is one of the leading topics of this, as it is of the preceding chapter, vers. 1—13.

2. The desire to please others should be wisely directed, and spring from right motives. We should not please them to their own injury, nor from the wish to secure their favour; but for their good, that they may be edified, ver. 2.

3. The character and conduct of Jesus Christ are at once the most perfect model of excellence and the most persuasive motive to obedience. The dignity of his person, the greatness of his condescension, the severity of his sufferings, the fervour of his love towards us, all combine to render his example effective in humbling us, in view of our own shortcomings, and in exciting us to walk even as he walked, vers. 4—13.

4. We should constantly resort to the Scriptures for instruction and consolation. They were written for this purpose; and we have no right to expect these blessings unless we use the means appointed for their attainment. As God, however, by the power of the Holy Ghost, works all good in us, we should rely neither on the excellence of the means, nor the vigour and diligence of our own exertions, but on his blessing, which is to be sought by prayer, vers. 4, 5, 13.

5. The dissensions of Christians are dishonourable to God. They must be of one mind, *i.e.*, sincerely and affectionately united, if they would glorify their Father in heaven, vers. 5—7.

6. A monitor or instructor should be full of goodness and knowledge. The human heart resists censoriousness, pride, and ill-feeling, in an admonisher; and is thrown into such a state, by the exhibition of these evil dispositions, that the truth is little likely to do it any good. As oil poured on water smooths its surface, and renders it transparent, so does kindness calm the minds of men, and prepare them for the ready entrance of the truth. Besides these qualifications, he who admonishes others should be entitled thus to act. It is not necessary that this title should rest on his official station; but there should be superiority of some kind—of age, excellence or knowledge—to give his admonitions due effect. Paul's peculiar modesty, humility, and mildness, should serve as an example to us, vers. 14, 15.

7. We should be careful not to build improperly on another man's foundation. Pastors and preachers must of course preach Christ where he had before been known; but they should not appropriate to themselves the results of the labours of others, or boast of things which Christ has not wrought by them. The man who reaps the harvest, is not always he who sowed the seed. One plants, and another waters, but God giveth the increase. So then neither is he that planteth anything, neither he that watereth, but God that giveth the increase, vers. 19, 20.

8. It is the duty of those who have the means, to contribute to the necessities of others, and especially to the wants of those from whom they themselves have received good, vers. 26, 27.

9. The fact that men are prejudiced against us, is no reason why we should not do them good. The Jewish Christians were ready to denounce Paul, and cast out his name as evil; yet he collected contributions for them, and was very solicitous that they should accept of his services, ver. 31.

10. Danger is neither to be courted nor fled from ; but encountered with humble trust in God, ver. 31.

11. We should pray for others in such a way as really to enter into their trials and conflicts ; and believe that our prayers, when sincere, are a real and great assistance to them.   It is a great blessing to have an interest in the prayers of the righteous.

CHAPTER XVI.

CONTENTS.

In this concluding chapter, Paul first commends to the church at Rome the deaconess Phebe, vers. 1, 2.   He then sends his salutations to many members of the church, and other Christians who were then at Rome, vers. 3—16.   He earnestly exhorts his brethren to avoid those who cause contentions ; and after commending their obedience, he prays for God's blessing upon them, vers. 17—21.   Salutations from the apostle's companions, vers. 22—24.   The concluding doxology, vers. 25—27.

ROMANS XVI. 1—.27

COMMENTARY.

Verse 1. *I commend unto you Phebe our sister, which is a servant of the church which is at Cenchrea.   Phebe,* from Phœbus (Apollo.)   The early Christians retained their names, although they were derived from the names of false gods, because they had lost all religious significance and reference.   In like manner we retain the use of the names of the days of the week, without ever thinking of their derivation.   Corinth, being situated on a narrow isthmus, had two ports, one towards Europe, and the other towards Asia.   The latter was called Cenchrea, where a church had been organized, of which Phebe was *a servant* (διάκονος) *i. e., deaconess.*   It appears that in the apostolic church, elderly females were selected to attend upon the poor and sick of their own sex.   Many ecclesiastical writers suppose there were two classes of these female officers ; the one (πρεσβύτιδες, corresponding iu some measure in their duties to the elders,) having the oversight of the conduct of the younger female Christians ; and the other, whose duty was to attend to the sick and the poor.   See Suicer's Thesaurus, under the word διάκονος ; Bingham's Ecclesiastical Antiquities, 11, 12; Augusti's Denkwürdigkeiten der christl. Archäologie.

Verse 2. *That ye receive her in the Lord.*   The words *in the Lord,* may be connected either with *receive,* 'receive *her* in a religious manner, and from religious motives ; or with the pronoun, *her in the Lord,* her as a Christian.   The apostle presents two considerations to enforce this exhortation ; first, regard for their Christian character ; and, secondly, the service which Phebe had rendered to others.   *As becometh saints ;* this expression at once describes the manner in which they ought to receive her, and suggests the motive for so doing. The words ἀξίως τῶν ἁγίων may mean, ' as it becomes Christians to receive their brethren,' or, ' sicut sanctos excipi oportet, as saints ought to be received.' In the former case, ἁγίων (saints) are those who received, and in the latter, those who are received. *And that ye assist her in whatsoever business she hath need of you.* They were not only to receive her with courtesy and affection, but to aid her in any way in which she required their assistance. The words (ἐν ᾧ ἂν πράγματι) *in whatsoever business,* are to be taken very generally, *in whatever matter,* or in whatever respect. *For she hath been a succourer of many, and of myself also.* The word (προστάτις) *succourer,* means *a patroness, a benefactor ;* it is a highly honourable title. As she had so frequently aided others, it was but reasonable that she should be assisted.

VERSE 3. *Salute Priscilla* and Aquila, my helpers in Christ Jesus, i.e.,* my fellow labourers in the promotion of the gospel. *Priscilla* is the diminutive form of Prisca ; compare Livia and Livilla, Drusa and Drusilla, Quinta and Quintilla, Secunda and Secundilla. *Grotius.* Aquila and Priscilla are mentioned in Acts xviii. 2, as having left Rome in consequence of the edict of Claudius. After remaining at Ephesus a long time, it seems that they had returned to Rome, and were there when Paul wrote this letter ; Acts xviii. 18, 26 ; 1 Cor. xvi. 19 ; 2 Tim. iv. 19.

VERSE 4. *Who have for my life laid down their own necks, i.e.,* they exposed themselves to imminent peril to save me. On what occasion this was done, is not recorded. *Unto whom not only I give thanks, but also all the churches of the Gentiles.* Their courageous and disinterested conduct must have been generally known, and called forth the grateful acknowledgments of all the churches interested in the preservation of a life so precious as that of the apostle.

VERSE 5. *The church that is in their house.* These words (καὶ τὴν κατ' οἶκον αὐτῶν ἐκκλησίαν) are understood, by many of the Greek and modern commentators, to mean *their Christian family;* so Calvin, Flatt, Koppe, Tholuck, &c. The most common and natural interpretation is, ' the church which is accustomed to assemble in their house ;' see 1 Cor. xvi. 19, where this same expression occurs in reference to Aquila and Priscilla. It is probable that, from his occupation as tent-maker, he had better accommodations for the meetings of the church than most other Christians.

Salute my well beloved Epenetus, who is the first fruits of Achaia†unto Christ. This passage is not irreconcileable with 1 Cor. xvi. 15, " Ye know the household of Stephanas, that it is the first-fruits of Achaia;" for Epenetus may have belonged to this family. So many of the oldest MSS. and versions, however, read *Asia,* instead of *Achaia,* in this verse, that the great majority of editors have adopted that reading. This, of course, removes even the appearance of contradiction.

VERSES 6, 7. *Greet Mary, who bestowed much labour upon us. Salute Andronicus and Junia, my kinsmen and my fellow-prisoners.* Instead of εἰς ἡμᾶς, some of the older MSS. read εἰς ὑμᾶς, and others ἐν ὑμῖν. The common text is, however, retained in the latest editions, and is better suited to the context, as the assiduous service of Mary, rendered to the apostle, is a more natural reason of his salutation, than that she had been

---

* Instead of Πρίσκιλλαν, Πρίσκαν is read in the MSS. A. C. D. E. F. G., and in many *codd. minusc;* and this reading is adopted in the editions of Bengel, Mill, Wetstein, Griesbach, Knapp, Lachmann.

† Ἀσίας is read in MSS. A. C. D. E. F. G. 6, 67; and in the Coptic, Ethiopic, and Latin versions. Mill, Bengel, Griesbach, Knapp, and Lachmann, adopt that reading.

serviceable to the Roman Christians. It is very doubtful whether Junia be the name of a man or of a woman, as the form in which it occurs ('Ιουνίαν) admits of either explanation. If a man's name, it is Junias ; if a woman's, it is Junia. It is commonly taken as a female name, and the person intended is supposed to have been the wife or sister of Andronicus. *My kinsmen, i.e.,* relatives, and not merely of the same nation ; at least there seems no sufficient reason for taking the word in this latter general sense. *Fellow-prisoners.* Paul, in 2 Cor. xi. 23, when enumerating his labours, says, " In stripes above measure, in prisons more frequent, in deaths oft," &c. He was often in bonds, (Clemens Romanus, in his Epistle to the Corinthians, sect. 5, says seven times,) he may, therefore, have had numerous fellow-prisoners. *Who are of note among the apostles ;* ἐπίσημοι ἐν τοῖς ἀποστόλοις. This may mean either they were distinguished apostles, or they were highly respected by the apostles. The latter is most probably the correct interpretation ; because the word *apostle,* unless connected with some other word, as in the phrase, " messengers (apostles) of the churches," is very rarely, if ever, applied in the New Testament to any other than the original messengers of Jesus Christ. It is never used in Paul's writings, except in its strict official sense. The word has a fixed meaning, from which we should not depart without special reason. Besides, the article (ἐν τοῖς ἀποστόλοις,) among *the* apostles, seems to point out the definite well-known class of persons almost exclusively so called. The passage is so understood by Koppe (*magna eorum fama est apud apostolos,*) Flatt, Bloomfield, Meyer, Philippi, and the majority of commentators. *Who also were in Christ before me, i.e.,* who were Christians before me.

VERSES 8—15. *My beloved in the Lord.* The preposition in (ἐν,) here, as frequently elsewhere, points out the relation or respect in which the word, to which it refers is to be understood ; *brother beloved, both in the flesh and in the Lord* (Philemon, ver. 16,) both in reference to our external relations, and our relation to the Lord. And thus in the following, ver. 9, *our helper in Christ, i.e.,* as it regards Christ ; ver. 10, *approved in Christ, i.e.,* in his relation to Christ ; an approved or tried Christian ; ver. 12, *who labour in the Lord ;* and, *which laboured much in the Lord, i.e.,* who, as it regards the Lord, laboured much ; it was a Christian or religious service. The names, *Tryphena, Tryphosa,* and *Persis,* all are feminine. The last is commonly supposed to indicate the native country of the person who bore it, as it was not unusual to name persons from the place of their origin, as *Mysa, Syria, Lydia, Andria,* &c. ; such names, however, soon became common, and were given without any reference to the birth-place of those who received them. *Chosen in the Lord, i.e.,* not one chosen by the Lord ; *chosen, (i.e.,* approved, precious ; see 1 Peter ii. 4,) in his relation to the Lord, as a Christian. It is not merely elect in Christ, that is, chosen to eternal life, for this could be said of every Christian ; but Rufus is here designated as a chosen man, as a distinguished Christian. It is worth noticing, that at Rome, as at Corinth, few of the great or learned seem to have been called. These salutations are all addressed to men not distinguished for their rank or official dignity. Mylius, as quoted by Calov, says : " Notanda hic fidelium istorum conditio : nemo hic nominatur consul, nemo quæstor aut dictator insignitur, minime omnium episcopatuum et cardinalatuum dignitate hic personant : sed operarum, laborum, captivitate titulis plerique notantur. Ita verum etiam in Romana ecclesia fuit olim, quod apostolus scribit, non multi potentis, non multi nobiles, sed stulta mundi electa sunt a Deo. Papatus autem Cæsarei, qualis adjuvante diabolo, in perniciem religionis, posteris saeculis Romæ involuit, ne umbra quidem apostolorum aetate istic fuit : tantum abest, ut ille originem ab apostolis ipsis traxerit."

Verse 16.　*Salute one another with a holy kiss.*　Reference to this custom is made also in 1 Cor. xvi. 20 ; 1 Thess. v. 26 ; 1 Peter v. 14.　It is supposed to have been of oriental origin, and continued for a long time in the early churches ;* after prayer, and especially before the celebration of the Lord's Supper, the brethren saluting in this way the brethren, and the sisters the sisters.　This salutation was expressive of mutual affection and equality before God.

Verse 17.　*Now I beseech you, brethren, mark them which cause divisions and offences contrary to the doctrine which ye have learned, and avoid them.*　While he urges them to the kind reception of all faithful ministers and Christians, he enjoins upon them to have nothing to do with those who cause divisions and offences.　There were probably two evils in the apostle's mind when he wrote this passage ; the divisions occasioned by erroneous doctrines, and the offences or scandals occasioned by the evil conduct of the false teachers.　Almost all the forms of error which distracted the early church, were intimately connected with practical evils of a moral character.　This was the case to a certain extent with the Judaizers ; who not only disturbed the church by insisting on the observance of the Mosaic law, but also pressed some of their doctrines to an immoral extreme; see 1 Cor. v. 1—5.　It was still more obviously the case with those errorists, infected with a false philosophy, who are described in Col. ii. 10—23; 1 Tim. iv. 1—8.　These evils were equally opposed to the doctrines taught by the apostle.　Those who caused these dissensions, Paul commands Christians, first, *to mark* (σχοπεῖν,) *i.e.*, to notice carefully, and not allow them to pursue their corrupting course unheeded; and, secondly, *to avoid, i.e.*, to break off connection with them.

Verse 18.　*For they that are such serve not our Lord Jesus Christ, but their own belly ; and by good words and fair speeches deceive the hearts of the simple.*　These men are to be avoided, because they are wicked and injurious.　The description here given is applicable, in a great degree, to errorists in all ages.　They are not actuated by zeal for the Lord Jesus ; they are selfish, if not sensual ; and they are plausible and deceitful.　Compare Phil. iii. 18, 19 ; 2 Tim. iii. 5, 6.　The words (χρησστολογία and εὐλογία, *blandiloquentia* et *assentatio*) rendered *good words* and *fair speeches*, do not in this connection materially differ.　They express that plausible and flattering address by which false teachers are wont to secure an influence over the *simple.*　The word (ἄκακος) *simple*, signifies not merely *innocent*, but *unwary*, he who is liable to deception.　(Prov. xiv. 15, ἄκακος πιστεύει παντὶ λόγῳ, *the simple believes everything.*)

Verse 19.　*For your obedience is come abroad unto all men,* &c.　This clause admits of two interpretations : the word *obedience* may express either their *obedience to the gospel*, their faith, (see chap. i. 8,) or their *obedient disposition*, their readiness to follow the instructions of their

---

* *Justin* Apol. II., ἀλλήλους φιλήματι ἀσπαζόμεθα παυσάμενοι τῶν εὐχῶν ; 'After prayers we salute one another with a kiss.'　*Tertullian* de Oratione : " Quae oratio cum divortio sancti osculi integra ?　Quem omnino officium facientem impedit pax ?　Quale sacrificium sine pace receditur ?"　By *peace*, is here intended the kiss of peace, for he had before said, " Cum fratribus subtrahant osculum pacis quod est signaculum orationis."　In the Apostolic Constitutions, it is said (L. 2, c. 57,) " Then let the men apart, and the women apart, salute each other with a kiss in the Lord."　*Origen* says, on this verse, " From this passage the custom was delivered to the churches, that after prayers the brethren should salute one another with a kiss."—See Grotius and Whitby.

religious teachers. If the former meaning be adopted, the sense of the passage is this, ' Ye ought to be on your guard against these false teachers, for since your character is so high, your faith being every where spoken of, it would be a great disgrace and evil to be led astray by them.' If the latter meaning be taken, the sense is, ' It is the more necessary that you should be on your guard against these false teachers, because your ready obedience to your divine teachers is so great and generally known. This, in itself, is commendable, but I would that you joined prudence with your docility.' This latter view is, on account of the concluding part of the verse, most probably the correct one ; see 2 Cor. x. 6 ; Phil. ver. 21.

I am glad, therefore, on your behalf; but yet I would have you wise unto that which is good, and simple concerning evil. That is, 'Simplicity (an unsuspecting docility) is indeed good ; but I would have you not only simple, but prudent. You must not only avoid doing evil, but be careful that you do not suffer evil. Grotius' explanation is peculiarly happy, *ita prudentes ut non fallamini ; ita boni ut non fallatis;* 'too good to deceive, too wise to be deceived.' The word (ἀχέραιος from α et χεράω) *simple,* means *unmixed, pure,* and then *harmless.* ' Wise as to (εἰς) good, but simple as to evil ;' or, 'wise so that good may result, and simple so that evil may not be done.' This latter is probably the meaning. Paul would have them wise to know how to take care of themselves ; and yet harmless.

Verse 20. *And the God of peace shall bruise Satan under your feet shortly. The grace of our Lord Jesus Christ be with you. Amen.* As the evils produced by the false teachers were divisions and scandals, the apostle, in giving them the assurance of the effectual aid of God, calls him the *God of peace, i. e.,* God who is the author of peace in the comprehensive scriptural sense of that term. *Shall bruise* is not a prayer, but a consolatory declaration that Satan should be trodden under foot. As Satan is constantly represented as "working in the children of disobedience," the evil done by them is sometimes referred to him as the instigator, and sometimes to the immediate agents who are his willing instruments. *The grace of our Lord Jesus Christ be with you.* This is a prayer for the favour and aid of Christ, and of course is an act of worship, and a recognition of the Saviour's divinity.

Verses 21—24. These verses contain the salutations of the apostle's companions to the Roman Christians, and a repetition of the prayer just mentioned. *I Tertius, who wrote this epistle, salute you in the Lord.* Tertius was Paul's amanuensis. The apostle seldom wrote his epistles with his own hand ; hence he refers to the fact of having himself written the letter to the Galatians as something unusual ; Gal. vi. 11, " Ye see how large a letter I have written unto you with my own hand." In order to authenticate his epistles, he generally wrote himself the salutation or benediction at the close ; 1 Cor. xvi. 21, "The salutation of *me* Paul, with mine own hand ;" 2 Thess. iii. 17, "The salutation of Paul with mine own hand ; which is the token in every epistle : so I write." *Gaius mine host, and of the whole church, i.e.,* Gaius, who not only entertains me, but Christians generally ; or, in whose house the congregation is accustomed to assemble. *Erastus the chamberlain of the city,* (οἰχονόμος) the treasurer of the city, the *quaestor.*

Verses 25, 27. These verses contain the concluding doxology. *Now to him that is of power to establish you according to my gospel and the preaching of Jesus Christ, according to the revelation of the mystery,* &c. As the apostle interweaves with his doxology a description and eulogium of the gospel, he renders the sentence so long and complicated that the regular grammatical construction is broken. There is nothing to govern the words (τῷ δυναμένῳ) *to him that is of power.* The words, *be glory for ever*, (which are repeated at the end in connection with ῷ) are, therefore, most probably to be supplied. *To him that is able to establish you*, *i. e.*, to render you firm and constant, to keep you from falling. *According to my gospel.* The word (κατά) *according to*, may be variously explained. It may be rendered, 'establish you in my gospel;' but this the proper meaning of the words will hardly allow ; or, *agreeably to my gospel*, in such a manner as the gospel requires ; or, *through, i. e.*, by means of my gospel. The second interpretation is perhaps the best. *And the preaching of Jesus Christ.* This may mean either 'Christ's preaching,' or 'the preaching concerning Christ;' either interpretation gives a good sense, the gospel being both a proclamation by Christ, and concerning Christ. The apostle dwells upon this idea, and is led into a description and commendation of the gospel. *According to the revelation of the mystery.* These words may be considered as co-ordinate with the preceding clause ; the sense then is, 'Who is able to establish you agreeably to (or through) my gospel, agreeably to (through) the revelation of the mystery, &c.' It is, however, more common to consider this clause as subordinate and descriptive. 'The gospel is a revelation of the mystery which had been hid for ages.' The word *mystery*, according to the common scriptural sense of the term, does not mean something obscure or incomprehensible, but simply something previously unknown and undiscoverable by human reason, and which, if known at all, must be known by a revelation from God. In this sense the gospel is called a mystery, or "the wisdom of God in a mystery, that is, a hidden wisdom," which the wise of this world could not discover, but which God has revealed by his Spirit, 1 Cor. ii. 7—10 ; iv. 1 ; Eph. vi. 19 ; Col. i. 25—27 ; ii. 2, &c. In the same sense any particular doctrine, as the calling of the Gentiles, Eph. iii. 4—6 ; the restoration of the Jews, Rom. xi. 25 ; the change of the bodies of living believers at the last day, 1 Cor. xv. 51 ; is called a mystery, because a matter of divine revelation. According to this passage, Paul speaks of the gospel as something "which had been kept secret since the world began ;" (χρόνοις αἰωνίοις,) *i.e.*, hidden from eternity in the divine mind. It is not a system of human philosophy, or the result of human investigation, but it is a revelation of the purpose of God. Paul often presents the idea that the plan of redemption was formed from eternity, and is such as no eye could discover, and no heart conceive, 1 Cor. ii. 7—9 ; Col. i. 26.

Verse 26. *But is now made manifest, and by the Scriptures of the prophets ;* that is, 'this gospel or mystery, hidden from eternity, is now revealed ; not now for the first time indeed, since there are so many intimations of it in the prophecies of the Old Testament.' It is evident that the apostle adds the words *and by the Scriptures of the prophets*, to avoid having it supposed that he overlooked the fact that the plan of redemption was taught in the Old Testament ; compare chap. i. 2 ; iii. 21. *According to the command of the everlasting God*, that is, this gospel is now made manifest by command of God. Paul probably uses the expression, *everlasting* (αἰωνίου) *God*, because he had just before said that the gospel was hid from eternity. 'It is now revealed by that eternal Being in whose mind the wonderful plan was formed, and by whom alone it could be revealed.' *Made known to all nations for the obedience of the faith.* 'Made known *among* (εἰς, see Mark xiii. 10 ; Luke xxiv. 47) all nations.' *For the obedience of faith, i.e.*, that they should become obedient to the faith ; see chap i. 5. 'This gospel, so long concealed, or but partially revealed in the ancient prophets, is now, by the command of God, to be made known among all nations.

Verse 27. *To the only wise God be glory through Jesus Christ for ever, Amen.* There is an ambiguity in the original which is not retained in our version. 'To the only wise God, through Jesus Christ, to whom *be* glory for ever.' The construction adopted by our translators is perhaps the one most generally approved. 'To him that is able to establish you, to the only wise God, through Jesus Christ, be glory.' In this case the relative, ᾧ, *to whom*, in verse 27, is pleonastic. Others explain the passage thus, 'To the only wise God, made known through Jesus Christ, to whom (*i.e.*, Christ) be glory for ever.' The simplest construction is, 'To the only wise God, through Jesus Christ, to him, I say, be glory for ever. ' As Paul often calls the gospel the "wisdom of God," in contrast with the wisdom of men, he here, when speaking of the plan of redemption as the product of the divine mind, and intended for all nations, addresses his praises to its author as the ONLY WISE GOD, as that Being whose wisdom is so wonderfully displayed in the gospel and in all his other works, that he alone can be considered truly wise.

REMARKS.

1. It is the duty of Christians to receive kindly their brethren, and to aid them in every way within their power, and to do this from religious motives and in a religious manner, as becometh saints, vers. 1, 2.

2. The social relations in which Christians stand to each other as relatives, countrymen, friends, should not be allowed to give character to their feelings and conduct to the exclusion of the more important relation which they bear to Christ. It is as friends, helpers, fellow-labourers in the Lord, that they are to be recognised ; they are to be received in the Lord ; our common connection with Christ is ever to be borne in mind, and made to modify all our feelings and conduct, vers. 3—12.

3. From the beginning females have taken an active and important part in the promotion of the gospel. They seem, more than others, to have contributed to Christ of their substance. They were his most faithful attendants, "last at the cross, and first at the sepulchre." Phebe was a servant of the church, a succourer of Paul, and of many others ; Tryphena, Tryphosa, and Persis, laboured much in the Lord, vers. 1, 2, 3, 6, 12.

4. It does not follow, because a custom prevailed in the early churches, and received the sanction of the apostles, that we are obliged to follow it. These customs often arose out of local circumstances and previous habits, or were merely conventional modes of expressing certain feelings, and were never intended to be made universally obligatory. As it was common in the East, (and is so, to a great extent, at present, not only there, but on the continent of Europe,) to express affection by 'the kiss of peace,' Paul exhorts the Roman Christians to salute one another with a holy kiss ; *i.e.*, to manifest their Christian love to each other, according to the mode to which they were accustomed. The exercise and manifestation of the feeling but not the mode of its expression, are obligatory on us. This is but one example ; there are many other things connected with the manner of conducting public worship, and with the adminstration of baptism and the Lord's Supper, common in the apostolic churches, which have gone out of use. Christianity is a living principle, and was never intended to be confined to one unvarying set of forms, ver. 16.

5. It is the duty of Christians to be constantly watchful over the peace and purity of the church, and not to allow those who cause divisions and scandals, by departing from the true doctrines, to pursue their course unnoticed. With all such we should break off every connection which either sanctions their opinions and conduct, or gives them facilities for effecting evil, ver. 17.

6. False teachers have ever abounded in the church. All the apostles were called upon earnestly to oppose them. Witness the epistles of Paul, John, Peter, and James. No one of the apostolical epistles is silent on this subject. Good men may indeed hold erroneous doctrines; but the false teachers, the promoters of heresy and divisions, as a class, are characterized by Paul as not influenced by a desire to serve Christ, but as selfish in their aims, and plausible, flattering, and deceitful in their conduct, ver. 18.

7 Christians should unite the harmlessness of the dove with the wisdom of the serpent. They should be careful neither to cause divisions or scandals themselves, nor allow others to deceive and beguile them into evil, ver. 19.

8. However much the church may be distracted and troubled, error, and its advocates cannot finally prevail. Satan is a conquered enemy with a lengthened chain; God will ultimately bruise him under the feet of his people, ver. 20.

9. The stability which the church and every Christian should maintain, is a steadfastness, not in forms or matters of human authority, but in the gospel and the preaching of Jesus Christ. God alone is able thus to make his people stand; and, therefore, we should look to him, and depend upon him for our own preservation and the preservation of the church; and ascribe to him, and not to ourselves, all glory and thanks, vers. 25, 27.

10. The gospel is a mystery, *i.e.*, a system of truth beyond the power of the human mind to discover, which God has revealed for our faith and obedience. It was formed from eternity in the divine mind, revealed by the prophets and apostles, and the preaching of Jesus Christ; and is, by the command of God, to be made known to all nations, vers. 25, 26.

11. God alone is wise. He charges his angels with folly; and the wisdom of men is foolishness with him. To God, therefore, the profoundest reverence and the most implicit submission are due. Men should not presume to call in question what he has revealed, or consider themselves competent to sit in judgment on the truth of his declarations or the wisdom of his plans. To God only wise, be glory, through Jesus Christ, for ever. *Amen.*

The subscriptions to this and the other epistles were not added by the sacred writers, but appended by some later and unknown persons. This is evident, 1. Because it cannot be supposed that the apostles would thus formally state (as in this case) what those to whom their letters were addressed must have already known. The Romans had no need to be informed that this epistle was sent by Phebe, if she actually delivered it to them. 2. They are frequently incorrect, and at times contradict the statements made in the epistles to which they are appended. Thus the subscription to the first Epistle to the Corinthians, states that it was written from Philippi, whereas Paul, chap. xvi. 8, speaks of himself as being in Ephesus when he was writing. 3. They are either left out entirely by the oldest and best manuscripts and versions, or appear in very different forms. In the present case many MSS. have no subscription at all; others simply, "To the Romans;" others, "To the Romans, written from Corinth;" others, "Written to the Romans from Corinth, by Phebe," &c. These subscriptions, therefore, are of no other authority than as evidence of the opinion which prevailed to a certain extent, at an early date, as to the origin of the epistles to which they were attached. Unless confirmed from other sources, they cannot be relied upon.

INDEX.

I.—PRINCIPAL MATTERS.

II.—GREEK WORDS AND PHRASES EXPLAINED.